2B

SIMON FRASER UNIVERSITY
W.A.C. BENNETT LIBRARY

QA 76.758 E544 2005

Engineering and Managing
Software Requirements

Aybüke Aurum · Claes Wohlin (Eds.)

Engineering and Managing Software Requirements

With 54 Figures and 48 Tables

 Springer

Editors

Aybüke Aurum
School of Information Systems, Technology and Management
University of New South Wales
Sydney, NSW 2052, Australia
aybuke@unsw.edu.au

Claes Wohlin
School of Engineering
Blekinge Institute of Technology
Box 520, 372 25 Ronneby, Sweden
Claes.Wohlin@bth.se

Library of Congress Control Number: 2005927220

ACM Computing Classification (1998): D.2.1, D.2.9, K.6.1

ISBN-10 3-540-25043-3 Springer Berlin Heidelberg New York
ISBN-13 978-3-540-25043-2 Springer Berlin Heidelberg New York

Springer is a part of Springer Science+Business Media
springeronline.com

© Springer-Verlag Berlin Heidelberg 2005
Printed in Germany

Cover design: KünkelLopka, Heidelberg
Typesetting: Camera ready by the editors
Production: LE-TeX Jelonek, Schmidt & Vöckler GbR, Leipzig
Printed on acid-free paper   45/3142/YL - 5 4 3 2 1 0

Foreword

The effects of integration and evolution of Information and Communication Technologies (ICT) are having a profound effect on both the way that organizations function and people interact with each other. The increasing reliance of our every day activities on ICT systems demands sustainable service levels from such systems commensurate with our expectations and levels of investment for their implementation. Such investments, however, have been regrettably risky and the mortality rates of ICT systems have been above average in any industry. Whilst the rate of failed projects and cost overruns has decreased in recent years bust still remaining unacceptably high over half of commissioned projects fail to meet their initial objectives. If we have been less than successful in delivering yesterday's systems, what chance is there for developing tomorrow's highly complex and demanding systems?

Using the field of Requirements Engineering as their focal point, Aurum and Wohlin address this question in this book from a multidisciplinary perspective. As a field of intellectual endeavor and industrial practice Requirements Engineering has traditionally been concerned with goals for, functions of and constraints on software intensive systems. This book argues for a broader perspective in order to gain a better understanding of the interdependencies between enterprise stakeholders, processes and information systems that would in turn give rise to more appropriate techniques and higher quality systems.

It is this broader perspective that gives this book its distinct appeal and should be of interest not only to software engineers but also to researchers and practitioners working in other disciplines such as business process engineering, organizational change, enterprise integration, and design theories and across many different business sectors. A common issue of concern across all these different areas is how one should tackle "ill-structured problems" where the problem state is not known at the outset and there is no definitive formulation, and where multiple stakeholders from different divisions and often different organizations need to reach agreement about the intended systems. Decisions taken at this stage have a profound effect on the technical and economic feasibility of the project. It is no longer appropriate for information systems professionals to focus only on functional and non-functional aspects of the intended system and somehow assume that organizational context and needs are outside their scope.

Here in these pages the reader will find a clear exposition of the processes involved in requirements together with a critique of current theories and practice. The book is thoughtfully assembled as a series of articles from leading researchers and practitioners, each article focusing on a specific issue. Whilst each article, presented as a distinct chapter, represents an important contribution in its own right, the confluence and structuring of these articles into this book provide the reader with a unique opportunity to begin a journey of exploration about Requirements Engineering. I commend to you the journey that Aurum and Wohlin have begun for you with this book.

Author Biography

Pericles Loucopoulos holds the chair of Information Systems in the School of Informatics, The University of Manchester. He is the co-editor-in-chief of the *Journal of Requirements Engineering* published by Springer and is on the editorial board of five other international journals. He has served as General Chair and Programme Chair of six international conferences and has been a member of over 100 Programme Committees of international conferences. His research work is concerned with the engineering of information, and the tools, methods and processes used to design, develop and deploy information systems in order to meet organisational goals. He works closely with industrial, commercial and governmental institutions in improving the way that information systems could be deployed to implement change in an effective and efficient manner. He is the co-author of 6 books and the author and co-author of over 150 papers published in academic journals and conference proceedings.

Preface

Aybüke Aurum and Claes Wohlin

This book explores the interdisciplinary nature of Requirements Engineering (RE) and portrays the current status of understanding, analyzing, modeling and managing of RE activities for current as well as future systems, with particular emphasis on innovative ideas, frameworks and empirical studies, and future directions of RE practice.

Introduction

As we enter the third millennium, organizations have to cope with accelerating rates of change in technology and increased levels of competition on a global scale more than ever before. There is incredible pressure on companies to achieve and sustain competitive advantage. In order to stay competitive within this changing business environment, organizations are forced to constantly pursue new strategies to differentiate themselves from their competition, such as offering a stream of new products and services. Organizations in search of competitive advantage become more conscious of how software products have become a strategic asset to their business. Software companies, like many other organizations, are forced to adapt to the strategic challenges and opportunities presented by the new economy where new technology causes dramatic changes in business processes, products and services. Since software products play a vital role in supporting strategic challenges and opportunities in business, it is important that these products function according to customers' or markets' requirements. Hence, an important task in software development is the identification and understanding of key business requirements to ensure that software products will fully support and evolve with the system.

Requirements Engineering (RE) is the process by which the requirements for software products are gathered, analyzed, documented, and managed throughout the SE lifecycle. RE is concerned with interpreting and understanding stakeholders' goals, needs and beliefs. There are many problems associated with RE which may lead to inconsistent and incomplete requirements and cancellation of software projects. As RE is one of the main contributors to the success of software projects, improving the RE process can significantly increase the likelihood of software project success. Software developers realize that a strong requirements management process is essential to the successful completion of software projects. Furthermore, understanding, identifying and articulating the role of business requirements which are elicited from stakeholders from diverse backgrounds with different needs, expectations and goals is a challenge in RE. Quality management in software development starts with an accurate description of business processes and a basic understanding of stakeholder needs. Requirements analysis is a critical task in software development as it involves investigating and learning about the problem domain in order to develop a better understanding of stakeholders' actual goals, needs, and expectations.

This book looks at software requirements from both engineering and management perspectives. We believe that RE is both an "engineering" and "management" activity. It is an engineering activity because it is concerned with identifying appropriate methodologies to develop software solutions and identifying cost effective ways of doing so. In other words, the aim of RE is to introduce engineering principles into the practice of software systems analysis while integrating RE with a quality assurance process of utmost value to practitioners. Requirements change during the software development lifecycle and evolve after the system has become operational. Thus, RE is also a "management" activity as it is concerned with managing RE activities such as monitoring product requirements and managing the project scope, cost and schedule throughout the software development process, while ensuring that all essential business applications are delivered as specified in different requirements documents on different levels, for example, product and project levels.

This book is intended to draw engineering and management perspectives together to discuss the issues that face the RE in the third millennium.

Aims of the Book and Target Audience

Engineering and managing software requirements are key means for systematic software development. This book presents several examples of how this vision is supported by theory, as well as how to apply these solutions to industrial practice. Furthermore, it provides a collection of state-of-the-art RE research as well as information about current industry practices. The intention is that the book should primarily function as a textbook for research students and researchers, although it should also be useful to undergraduate and graduate students as well as requirements engineers operating in industry. The typical reader has most likely taken a basic course, read an introductory book to RE or worked with RE in industry for some time. Although it is recommended that readers have a sound background in software development, this book offers new insights into the software development process for both novice software developers as well as experienced professionals.

Book Overview

This book is organized into three major parts. Each part contains five to seven chapters. In addition, Chap. 1 provides an exploration of some of key issues in requirements engineering. This includes offering an understanding of the different levels of requirements involved in requirements engineering and illustrating the role of different stakeholders in requirements engineering. Chapter 1 also demonstrates how the three parts of this book are interrelated. Although it is preferable to firstly familiarize yourself with the first chapter, the book is designed to permit reading of the parts in any order, depending on readers' interests.

Part 1: State-of-the-Art Surveys of Requirements Engineering Process Research

Part 1 of this book provides a general introduction to the field of RE. It aims to enable readers to understand the motivation behind RE activities. The objective is to illustrate the strengths as well as weaknesses of this discipline and, as such, this part will present surveys of state-of-the art RE process research along with critical assessments of existing models, frameworks and techniques. Part 1 contains a collection of articles and up-to-date survey chapters that address the phases of the RE process, namely, requirements elicitation and capturing, modeling and specification, prioritization, dependencies, impact analysis, negotiation and quality assurance.

Part 2: The Next Practice in Requirements Engineering

Building complex systems is still a challenge for software developers. The technological improvements in the global market are closely related to business environments. New concepts such as enterprise systems, e-business and telecommunications have led to new trends for researchers and practitioners. The growth in strategic importance of IT implies that tools, techniques and processes need to be integrated with software system requirements so that they are aligned with the strategic business objectives and business model of the organizations they support. Part 2 covers articles that address new trends in RE. Topics covered in this part include market-driven requirements, decision support and decision making in RE, RE for agile methods, goal modeling, web-based information systems, requirements ambiguity and use of natural language in RE.

Part 3: Studies and Industrial Experience

Empirical research compares theory to reality, helping us draw conclusions and to evaluate new methods and tools. It is also important to learn more about technologies used in industrial practice. Part 3 concludes the book with articles that present empirical evidence. The studies in this part report on RE solutions and practices. This part focuses on state-of-the-practices that address overall RE issues including industrial experience, non-functional requirements and RE metrics.

Acknowledgements

There are many people whom we would like to thank for their help and support. We wish to thank all the authors for their hard work and effort in creating this book. We are especially grateful to the following colleagues who participated in the external review process and for their valuable comments: Mark Staples, Karl Cox, Cat Kutay, Paul Bannerman, Niazi Mahmoud, Jenny Liu, from National ICT Australia; Ghassan Beydoun and Ken Stevens from University of New South Wales, Australia.

We would also like to thank Kerrie Miller and Max Mail for their assistance in formatting this book and Irem Sevinç for assisting with proofreading. Special thanks go to Ralf Gerstner of Springer Germany for providing professional advice during the publishing process. Finally, a big thank you is due to our families for enduring the lengthy editing process. This book is dedicated to our families.

Contents

List of Contributors

Anneliese K. Amschler Andrews
School of Electrical Engineering and
Computer Science
Washington State University
PO Box 642752
Pullman, WA 99164-2752, USA
Email: aandrews@eecs.wsu.edu

Patrik Berander
Department of Systems and Software
Engineering
School of Engineering
Blekinge Institute of Technology
Box 520
SE-372 25 Ronneby, Sweden
Email: patrik.berander@bth.se

Sjaak Brinkkemper
Institute of Information and
Computing Sciences
Utrecht University
P.O. Box 80.089
3508 TB Utrecht
The Netherlands
Email: S.Brinkkemper@cs.uu.nl

Jacob L. Cybulski
School of Information Systems
Faculty of Business and Law
Deakin University
Burwood, Vic 3125, Australia
Email: jlcybuls@deakin.edu.au

Christian Denger
Fraunhofer Institute for
Experimental Software Engineering
Sauerwiesen 6
D-67661 Kaiserslautern, Germany
Email: denger@iese.fhg.de

Aybüke Aurum
School of Information Systems, Technology
and Management
University of New South Wales
Sydney NSW 2052 Australia
Email: aybuke@unsw.edu.au

Lars Borner
Institute for Computer Science
University of Heidelberg
Im Neuenheimer Feld 326
D-69120 Heidelberg, Germany
Email: lars.borner@informatik.uni-
heidelberg.de

Chad Coulin
Department of Software Engineering
Faculty of Information Technology
University of Technology, Sydney
P O Box 123 Broadway
NSW 2007, Australia
Email: chadc@it.uts.edu.au

Åsa G. Dahlstedt
School of Humanities and Informatics
University of Skövde
Box 408
SE-541 28 Skövde, Sweden
Email: asa.dahlstedt@his.se

Christof Ebert
Alcatel
54 rue La Boetie,
75008 Paris, France
Email: Christof.Ebert@alcatel.com

João M. Fernandes
Dept. Informatica
Universidade do Minho, Campus de
Gualtar
4700-320 Braga, Portugal
Email: jmf@di.uminho.pt

Tony Gorschek
Department of Systems and Software
Engineering
School of Engineering
Blekinge Institute of Technology
Box 520
SE-372 25 Ronneby Sweden
Email: tony.gorschek@bth.se

Paul Grünbacher
Systems Engineering & Automation
Johannes Kepler University Linz
Altenbergerstr. 69
4040 Linz, Austria
Email: pg@sea.uni-linz.ac.at

Erik Kamsties
Institute for Computer Science and
Business Information Systems (ICB)
University of Duisburg-Essen
Schuetzenbahn 70
D-45117 Essen, Germany
Email: kamsties@sse.uni-essen.de

Mikael Lindvall
Fraunhofer USA
University of Maryland
4321 Hartwick rd, suite 500
College Park, MD 20740, USA
Email: mikli@fc-md.umd.edu>

Vincenzo Gervasi
Dipartimento di Informatica
via F. Buonarroti, 2
I-56127 Pisa, Italy
Email: gervasi@di.unipi.it

Shirley Gregor
School of Business and Information
Management
Faculty of Economics and Commerce
Hanna Neumann Building 021
Australian National University
ACT 0200 Australia
Email: shirley.gregor@anu.edu.au_

Per Jönsson
Department of Systems and Software
Engineering
School of Engineering
Blekinge Institute of Technology
Box 520
SE-372 25 Ronneby, Sweden
Email: per.jonsson@bth.se

Tom Koenig
Fraunhofer Institute Experimental Software
Engineering
Sauerwiesen 6
D-67661 Kaiserslautern, Germany
Email: Tom.Koenig@iese.fraunhofer.de

Pericles Loucopoulos
School of Informatics
The University of Manchester
P.O. Box 88
Manchester M60 1QD, UK
Email: p.loucopoulos@manchester.ac.uk

Ricardo J. Machado
Dept. Sistemas de Informacao
Universidade do Minho, Campus de
Azurem
4800-058 Guimaraes, Portugal
Email: rmac@dsi.uminho.pt

Johan Natt och Dag
Dept. of Communication Systems
Lund University
Box 118,
SE-221 00 Lund, Sweden
Email: johan.nattochdag@telecom.
lth.se

Thomas Olsson
Fraunhofer Institute of Experimental
Software Engineering
Sauerwiesen 6
67661 Kaiserslautern, Germany
Email: olsson@iese.fhg.de

Anne Persson
School of Humanities and
Informatics
University of Skövde
Box 408
SE-541 28 Skövde Sweden
Email: anne.persson@his.se

Bjorn Regnell
Dept. of Communication Systems
Lund University
Box 118
SE-221 00 Lund, Sweden
Email: bjorn.regnell@telecom.lth.se

Guenther Ruhe
University of Calgary
2500 University Drive NW
Calgary, Alberta, Canada T2N 1N4
Email: ruhe@ucalgary.ca

Nigel Martin
14 Derham Court
Wanniassa, Canberra
ACT 2903 Australia
Email: Nigel.Martin@defence.gov.au

An Ngo-The
Laboratory of Software Engineering
Decision Support
University of Calgary
2500 University Drive NW
Calgary, Alberta, Canada T2N 1N4
Email: ango@cpsc.ucalgary.ca

Barbara Paech
Institute for Computer Science
University of Heidelberg
Im Neuenheimer Feld 326
D-69120 Heidelberg, Germany
Email: paech@informatik.uni-heidelberg.de

Isabel Ramos
Dept. Sistemas de Informacao
Universidade do Minho, Campus de
Azurem
4800-058 Guimaraes, Portugal
Email: iramos@dsi.uminho.pt

Colette Rolland
Centre de Recherche en Informatique
Université Paris 1 - Panthéon Sorbonne
90, rue de Tolbiac,
F-75013 Paris, France
Email: Colette.Rolland@univ-paris1.fr

Camille Salinesi
Centre de Recherche en Informatique
Université Paris 1 - Panthéon Sorbonne
90, rue de Tolbiac,
F-75013 Paris, France
Email: Camille.Salinesi@univ-paris1.fr

Pradip K. Sarkar
School of Information Systems,
Deakin University,
221 Burwood Highway, Burwood,
Vic 3125, Australia
Email: pks1@deakin.edu.au

Alberto Sillitti
Center for Applied Software
Engineering
Faculty of Computer Science
Free University of Bozen
Piazza Domenicani 3,
I-39100 Bolzano, Italy
Email: Alberto.Sillitti@unibz.it

Mikael Svahnberg
Department of Systems and Software
Engineering
School of Engineering
Blekinge Institute of Technology
Box 520
SE-372 25 Ronneby Sweden
Email: mikael.svahnberg@bth.se

Claes Wohlin
Department of Systems and Software
Engineering
School of Engineering
Blekinge Institute of Technology
Box 520,
SE-372 25 Ronneby, Sweden
E-mail: claes.wohlin@bth.se

Didar Zowghi
Department of Software Engineering
Faculty of Information Technology
University of Technology, Sydney
P O Box 123 Broadway
NSW 2007 Australia
Email: didar@it.uts.edu.au

Norbert Seyff
Systems Engineering & Automation
Johannes Kepler University Linz
Altenbergerstr. 69
4040 Linz, Austria
Email: ns@sea.uni-linz.ac.at

Giancarlo Succi
Center for Applied Software Engineering
Faculty of Computer Science
Free University of Bozen
Piazza Domenicani 3,
I-39100 Bolzano, Italy
Email: Giancarlo.Succi@unibz.it

Roel Wieringa
Dept. of Computer Science,
Faculty of Electrical Eng., Mathematics and
Computer Science,
University of Twente,
PO Box 217, 7500 AE Enschede,
Netherlands;
Email: R.J.Wieringa@ewi.utwente.nl

Nur Yilmaztürk
ABB AB
Corporate Research
SE-721 78 Västerås, Sweden
Email: nur.yilmazturk@se.abb.com

1 Requirements Engineering: Setting the Context

Aybüke Aurum and Claes Wohlin

Abstract: This chapter presents a brief overview of requirements engineering and provides an introduction to some of the critical aspects of this field. This includes offering and understanding of the different levels of requirements involved in requirements engineering, namely organizational, product and project level requirements, and illustrating the role of different stakeholders in requirements engineering. The chapter also aims to demonstrate how the three parts of this book are interrelated.

Keywords: Requirements management, Business requirements, Product requirements, Project requirements, Stakeholders, Requirements taxonomy.

1.1 Introduction

The objective of this chapter is twofold. First, it aims to provide a brief introduction to requirements engineering, and secondly it aims to set a common context for the other chapters of the book. This introductory chapter is provided to set the stage for the remaining chapters and highlight some of the important areas covered by this book. The remaining chapters require a basic understanding of requirements engineering to benefit from the deeper insights provided. These chapters are divided into three parts, each with a different focus, as shown in the table of contents and described briefly in the Preface.

Requirements engineering is accepted as one of the most crucial stages in software design and development as it addresses the critical problem of designing the right software for the customer. Requirements engineering is increasingly becoming a set of processes that operates on different levels, including organizational, product and project levels. Furthermore, it is a continuous process on organizational and product levels and a process limited in time on the project level. However, most requirements engineering research to date is devoted to handling requirements on the project level, making this the main focus of this chapter. The different levels are revisited in Sect. 1.4. Requirements engineering on the project level is the process by which the requirements for a software project are gathered, documented and managed throughout the software development lifecycle.

The development of a software requirements specification is widely recognized as the bases of system functionality. Software requirements are the critical determinants of software quality, given empirical studies showing that errors in requirements are the most numerous in the software life-cycle and also the most expensive and time-consuming to correct. According to the Standish group report in 1995 [10], 52.7% of projects cost (named as challenged projects) 189% of their original budget estimates, and only a disappointing 42% of the original features of challenged projects were implemented. The study demonstrates that only 16.1% of all US software projects are developed on-schedule, on-budget and with all originally planned features, while 31.1% of projects are terminated before completion. It was also observed that the average project is delivered at approximately three times the budget and in three times the scheduled time.

Such poor figures lead to questioning the causes of these deficiencies. Often these problems are a result of inadequate requirements [25]. According to a survey conducted with 350 organizations in the USA (with over 8000 projects), one third of the projects were never completed and one half succeeded only partially. About half of the managers interviewed identified poor requirements as a major source of problems, along with other factors such as low user involvement and unclear objectives. Similarly, according to another survey which was conducted with 3800 organizations from over 17 countries in Europe, most problems are in the area of requirements specifications (50%) and requirements management (50%) [18]. In 1999, the Standish group report [11] revealed that three of the top ten reasons for "challenged" projects and project failure were lack of user involvement, unstable requirements and poor project management. In a 2001 report, while user involvement was no longer a key concern, unstable requirements and poor project management remained amongst the primary reasons for project failure [12].

In a more recent survey of twelve UK companies' requirements problems accounted for 48% of all software problems [20]. In one of the case studies, Tveito and Hasvold [38] observed that there was a huge gap between the day to day operations of a hospital and software developers' domain knowledge of these operations, though every year healthcare organizations spend large amounts of money and resources on IT systems. Tveito and Hasvold argue that this gap is due to insufficient requirements gathering and misunderstanding requirements due to the lack of domain knowledge.

These facts and figures only depict the sad reality of "software depression". Furthermore, the cost of repairing requirements-related problems dramatically increases as the software development process progresses. A study by Boehm and Papaccio [6] revealed that it costs US$1 to locate and fix an error in the requirements definition stage, US$5 in the design phase, US$10 in the coding phase, $20US during unit testing, and up to US$200 after system delivery. It is therefore evident that the RE process has important ramifications for the overall success of a software project. Although the above example dates back just over 15 years, the ratio remains the same today.

Requirements engineering is concerned with the identification of goals for a proposed system, the operation and conversion of these goals into services and constraints, as well as the assignment of responsibilities for the resulting requirements to agents such as humans, devices and software. Requirements engineering has now moved from being the first phase in the software development lifecycle to a key activity that spans across the entire software development lifecycle in many organizations. New products or new releases of products are entering the market or delivered to customers at an increasingly faster pace. In order to improve requirements engineering processes, current practices in the real world need to be examined. Understanding and modeling current requirements engineering processes is an important step towards improving requirements engineering practices and therefore increasing the success of software projects [31].

Researchers agree that the requirements engineering process should consist of structured and repeatable activities where both engineering and management aspects are properly handled [39]. Unfortunately, there is no consensus regarding the appropriate requirements engineering process models to use across different industries, as the selection of available models spans from activity-based process models to decision-oriented paradigms, each with their own subset of model structures.

The objective of this chapter is to provide the context in which the other chapters of this book operate. As briefly mentioned above, this context includes an understanding of the different process levels involved in requirements engineering. Moreover, the different stakeholders and their respective roles in requirements engineering must be understood. The activities involved in the processes are presented at a high level, providing the reader insight into the work being performed as part of requirements engineering. This chapter provides a brief introduction to some fundamental building blocks of requirements engineering to allow the reader reap the full benefit and obtain a clear understanding of the other chapters.

The chapter is outlined as follows. Sect. 1.2 provides an introductory background to the area of requirements engineering. This is followed by a brief discussion of the roles of stakeholders in Sect. 1.3. In Sect. 1.4, different levels of requirements are presented. The management of requirements is discussed in Sect. 1.5 while Sect. 1.6 explores the future of the area. Finally, empirical evidence is touched upon in Sect. 1.7 and some conclusions are presented in Sect. 1.8.

1.2 Background

This objective of this section is to present background information on requirements engineering.

1.2.1 What is a Requirement?

All projects begin with a statement of requirements. Requirements are descriptions of how a software product should perform. A *requirement* typically refers to some aspect of a new or enhanced product or service. The widely cited IEEE 610.12-1990 standard [24] defines a requirement as:

(1) A condition or capability needed by a user to solve a problem or achieve an objective,

(2) A condition or capability that must be met or possessed by a system or system component to satisfy a contract, standard, specification, or other formally imposed documents,

A documented representation of a condition or capability as in (1) or (2).

Therefore, requirements include not only user needs but also those arising from general organizational, government and industry standards. Clearly, a requirement is a collection of needs arising from the user and various other stakeholders (general organization, community, government bodies and industry standards), all of which must be met. Ideally, requirements are independent of design, showing "what" the system should do, rather than "how" it should be done. However, this is not always possible in practice. That is, the meanings of "what" and "how" differ from person to person [15].

Requirements can be classified in many ways, as illustrated in Table 1.1. While the literature draws a distinction between different types of requirements, in practice it is not always easy to identify such differences [4]. For example, a user requirement concerned with security may be classified as a non-functional requirement. However, during implementation other requirements may evolve which are distinguishably functional such as user authorization [37]. More examples of this issue can be found in Chap. 6.

Table 1.1 Types of requirements

Requirements Classification
• *Functional requirements* — what the system will do
• *Non-functional requirements* — constraints on the types of solutions that will meet the functional requirements e.g. accuracy, performance, security and modifiability
• *Goal level requirements* — related to business goals • *Domain level requirements* — related to problem area • *Product level requirements* — related to the product • *Design level requirements* — what to build
• *Primary requirements* — elicited from stakeholders • *Derived requirements* — derived from primary requirements
Others classifications, e.g. • *Business requirements* versus *technical requirements* • *Product requirements* versus *process requirements* —- i.e. business needs versus how people will interact with the system • *Role based requirements,* e.g. customer requirements, user requirements, IT requirements, system requirements, and security requirements

Having understood the basics of what constitutes a requirement, the next step is to elaborate on the process used to manage and engineer requirements.

1.2.2 Requirements Engineering Process

Requirements engineering refers to all life-cycle activities related to requirements. This primarily includes gathering, documenting and managing requirements. With the growing awareness of the significance of requirements in the software process, requirements engineering increasingly becomes an area of focus in software engineering research.

Common requirements engineering activities are elicitation, interpretation and structuring (analysis and documentation), negotiation, verification and validation, change management and requirements tracing. There are several process models available to describe the requirements engineering process. The process itself is often depicted in different forms, including linear, incremental, non-linear and spiral models. Kotonya and Sommerville [25] suggest a conceptual linear requirements engineering process model, which indicates iterations between activities. On the other hand, Macaulay [30] provides a purely linear requirements engineering process model that does not indicate the overlapping or iteration of activities suggested by the Kotonya and Sommerville [25] model. While some researchers tend to portray the requirements engineering process as a linear model, non-linear models have also been suggested. Loucopoulos and Karakostas [27] depict the requirements engineering process as iterative and cyclical in nature. Alternatively, the spiral model represents a sequence of activities being performed in iterations, resulting in gradual progression requirements engineering process [5]. However, it has implications on the requirements engineering process model. A spiral approach would require requirements to be handled in each round. The spiral model is similar to the ideas presented by Kotonya and Sommerville [25]. They provide a second requirements engineering process model, which depicts the same requirements engineering activities as in their linear model, only occurring in a spiral representation. The activities from the linear process model are repeated in iterations, forming a spiral. At the end of each iteration a decision is made as to whether to accept the requirements document or to perform a further iteration.

Results from studies of the requirements engineering processes in practice have indicated that the systematic and incremental requirements engineering models presented in literature may not necessarily reflect the requirements engineering processes in current practice. Martin et al. (2002), who examined the requirements engineering process in a case by case study, found that projects were generally handled by following a linear model, with some iteration of activities. Most of the projects they examined generally followed a linear process until the prototyping phase, which then resulted in an iterative process. Martin et al., [32] indicated that the Loucopoulos and Karakostas [27] model was a good representation of the ad hoc process and the iterative nature of prototyping, but did not show the progression of phases. On the other hand, Nguyen and Swatman [35] found that the requirements engineering process in their case study did not occur in a systematic, smooth and incremental way. Rather, it was opportunistic, with sporadic simplification and restructuring of the requirements model when it reached points of high complexity. Furthermore, Houdek and Pohl [22] performed a case study in the field but could not produce a monolithic requirements engineering process model of requirements engineering activities, as they were too heavily intertwined and not seen as separate tasks by the participants of the study.

Requirements engineering field studies have also gathered conflicting results as to the status of requirements engineering process standards in organizations. This indicates that the area has not fully matured in the sense that there is no universally used and accepted process. Instead, several different requirements engineering processes have been presented. Kotonya and Sommerville [25] put forward that not many organizations have a standard requirements engineering process definition. Consistent with this, Hofmann and Lehner [21] examined, requirements engineering processes of 15 requirements engineering teams in industry and found that most participants saw requirements engineering as ad hoc, with only some projects using an explicitly defined requirements engineering process or customizing a company-wide requirements engineering process standard. Furthermore, studies of requirements engineering in web development projects have further confirmed the ad hoc nature of requirements engineering [28]. In contrast to these findings, El Emam and Madhavji [17] concluded that organizations tend to use standard requirements engineering processes, as they are viewed as best practices. Chatzoglou [13] used a three-phased mail-out survey to examine the requirements engineering process in 64 projects to understand the differences between projects with different characteristics. Particular focus was placed on human resources. The main conclusions were that a standard process methodology should be used but should also be tailored to the specific needs of each project. Furthermore, resources should be put into the initial iteration of the requirements engineering process.

Since requirements engineering processes are fundamental to the success of software projects, it surprisingly not improving the requirements engineering process can subsequently enhance the chances of developing successful software. Prior to devising strategies for software process improvement, research and analysis of present requirements engineering processes must be undertaken to provide a solid grasp of current requirements engineering practices.

1.3 The Role of Stakeholders in Requirements Engineering

In essence, requirements engineering aims to transform potentially incomplete, inconsistent and conflicting stakeholder goals into a complete set of high quality requirements. Information systems researchers define stakeholders "…as those participants in the development process together with any other individuals, groups or organizations whose actions can influence or be influenced by the development and use of the system whether directly or indirectly" [36]. Typical stakeholders are product managers, various types of users and administrators from the client side, and software team members from the software development side. This view is somewhat limiting when considering software development for markets. The traditional view of software development and requirements engineering, is that of bespoke software development. This is the situation when software is developed with a specific customer in mind and when it is often possible to have direct contact with this one user/customer. This situation becomes different when developing software for a market or a set of customers, in particular if all customers are not known at the time of development. This has led to studies of market-driven software development, where one important issue is to identify and handle the dif-

ferent stakeholders under these situations. More information on market-driven requirements can be found in Chap. 13.

As software projects became increasingly complex, software developers face
the challenge of identifying the goals of stakeholders who come from a diverse
range of backgrounds. It may also be very difficult to represent the essential requirements of software in a way which is accessible to all stakeholders, as software is effectively invisible [9]. The importance of stakeholder involvement in requirements engineering activities is widely accepted given that accurate
identification of stakeholder needs largely determines the quality of the software
product.

One of the major problems in requirements engineering is the management of
different types of inconsistencies resulting from requirements elicitation, modeling, specification, and prioritization activities. Inconsistencies become particularly
apparent when there are multiple stakeholders and viewpoints, since different
stakeholders have varying ways of expressing themselves and different opinions
as well as priorities. Although some researchers point out that inconsistencies between requirements models may be desirable, as they allow further elicitation (in
capturing requirements models) and they recommend tolerating some internal inconsistencies during requirements modeling [23, 33], the success of requirements
engineering projects depends on accurate analysis of these perspectives for incompleteness and inconsistencies. Therefore, requirements need to be negotiated
and validated before they are documented and developers commit to implementing
them.

1.4 Different Levels of Requirements

Effective management of the software development process contributes to sustainable competitive advantage for software companies. This implies that managers
need to consider customers' and business requirements, as well as the technological opportunities which may be distinct or overlap. It is important to stay on
budget, reduce life cycle time and achieve product performance goals to ensure
that the software requirements are aligned with business goals. These challenges
are not unique to software development and are in fact typical of complex system
products. In the Internet age there have been significant changes in business environments creating more complex demands on the technologies that support business information systems. Consequently, understanding, analyzing, modeling and
managing requirements have become equally complex task. In order to deliver
high quality software systems on time and on budget, it is essential to have properly structured and controlled requirements specifications that are understandable,
comprehensive and consistent.

The requirements engineering process is one of the main contributors to the
success of software projects. This is particularly true in a global competitive market where time-to-market and meeting stakeholder requirements are key success
factors. Thus, improving the requirements engineering process can significantly

increase the likelihood of software project success. According to Edwards et al., [16] contemporary software design approaches often mix business issues with IT implementation issues to form monolithic systems that are no more responsive to change than their predecessors. IT systems in this industry would therefore need to be dynamic and quickly adaptable to their environments.

Table 1.2 Requirements classification in three levels

	Strategic Management	**Tactical Management**	**Operational Management**
Requirements at organizational level	*Business strategy *Competitiveness *Technology * Marketing *Economic value of the product	* Planned benefits of the product	* Tradeoff between technology-push and market-pull
Requirements at product level	* Packaging requirements for a specific release * Product architectures	* Resource management *Implementation of a specific release	*Change management * Requirements volatility e.g. whether a particular requirement is subject to a syntactic or semantic change
Requirements at project level	*Project planning *Feasibility study *Recruiting people	* Project management * Quality control	*Validation in terms of which requirements will go to the next release

The current expanded perspective of software products in business has various implications for managing software development processes, i.e., software requirements should not be solely handled in software projects. Based on Anthony's [1] three level managerial decision making model, namely strategic, tactical and operational decisions, Aurum and Wohlin [2] illustrate how to conduct an analysis of the requirements engineering process and its underlying decision-making processes using classical decision making frameworks. In this book, we adopt a similar view, i.e. that the management of software requirements is subject to organization-oriented, product-oriented and process-oriented activities and that need to be managed at strategic, tactical and operational levels. Table 1.2 illustrates classification of software requirements in 3*3 matrixes, where each cell provides a few examples of requirements activities or decisions. The three levels can be briefly described as follows:

a) Requirements at the Organizational Level. The senior management team of an organization may have strategic objectives and long-term goals in terms of market share and so forth. The goals and strategies at the organizational level will inevitably influence which products an organization ought to develop. Thus, requirements posed on products must first be evaluated on at organizational level to ensure that they are aligned with the goals and strategies of the organization. One of the main challenges faced when successfully developing software products is that of determining how the end product will support business objectives.

b) Requirements at the Product Level. The requirements of software products must be aligned with the business goals of the software development organization. One of the crucial questions is how to balance customers' concerns with developers' concerns. Goal modeling techniques in requirements engineering serve as a mechanism by which one can link requirements to strategic objectives anchored in the context of the overall business strategy model. The requirements are typically both functional and non-functional requirements. Product management has to ensure that the requirements are aligned with the goals and objectives in terms of the product. This may mean selecting the requirements for the product that are best aligned with the overall goals and strategies of the organization.

c) Requirements at the Project Level. Requirements on the product level must be packaged into parts that go into specific projects or releases of the software. It is important that requirements are prioritized and selected based on their fulfillment of both product and organizational goals and strategies. Requirements may be chosen for implementation based on whether they fulfill the needs of a specific and important customer, or whether they potentially open up a new market segment to the organization. These requirements define the conditions under which the project will be run, including issues related to project planning, risk management, budget and cost.

The growth in strategic importance of IT implies that tools, techniques and processes need to be integrated with software system requirements so they are aligned with the strategic business objectives and business model of the organizations they support. Business change is a part of system development. As systems become more integrated and involve more users from diverse backgrounds, software developers are pressured to understand the implications of their decisions in relation to cost/benefit analysis, particularly during early life cycle activities [8, 19, 26]. System engineering and management literature, in particular risk management literature, stress the importance of project planning effort, schedule planning, cost planning, and risk assessment in product development as being essential to the generation of products that meet customer requirements and align with strategic business goals.

1.5 Requirements Management

The quality of a software product is largely determined by the quality of the development process used to create it. Many projects fail due to mistakes in the elucidation of requirements, while others fail because of the requirements have become outdated by the time the project is delivered [9]. It is also a major challenge developers to determine which requirements changes will cause a major problem in the project or the product itself [9]. Managing requirements engineering phases is crucial to the successful development of software products. In order to deliver high quality software systems on time and on budget it is essential to have properly structured and controlled requirements specifications that are understandable, comprehensive and consistent.

As mentioned above, it is important to have a good understanding of stakeholder goals and ensure their involvement in the requirements engineering process. The management of requirements involves establishing a shared understanding between the stakeholders and the requirements they have specified for inclusion in the software product. The essential practices of requirements managements are:

- **Requirements Elicitation, Specification and Modeling:** This involves understanding the needs of stakeholders, eliciting requirements, modeling and collecting them in a repository. This is an important stage in software development. However, for a variety of reasons, including cognitive, communicative and motivational reasons, the requirements tend to be incomplete and inconsistent. Therefore, there is always room for improvement in these activities.
- **Prioritization:** It is not always easy for developers to decide which requirements are important to customers. This activity assists project managers with resolving conflicts (where customers and developers collaborate on requirements prioritization), plan for staged deliveries, and make necessary trade-off decisions.
- **Requirements Dependencies and Impact Analysis:** It is important to acknowledge that requirements change and that this may significantly impact the software project [14]. Several issues such as recording decisions, understanding the effect of business changes and the use of domain models are yet to be addressed [29].
- **Requirements Negotiation:** Requirements engineering is essentially a complex communication and negotiation process involving customers, designers, project managers and maintainers. The people, or stakeholders, involved in the process are responsible for deciding what to do, when to do it, what information is needed, and what tools need to be used [25]. In many situations conflict is inherent in requirements, thus they need to be negotiated between stakeholders. Some tools, such as Win-Win Groupware, have been developed to support stakeholders throughout the negotiation process [7]. The requirements negotiation activity is one of the most crucial activities in software development as it has a great impact on the final product. In reality, this activity is carried out in parallel with the activities mentioned above and continues until the requirements are implemented. Further information on negotiation can be found in Chap. 7.
- **Quality Assurance:** The objective is to ensure that high quality requirements are recorded in the specification document. The purpose of quality assurance is to establish reasonable and realistic levels of confidence when writing and managing requirements. It is important that both customers and developers are

involved in quality assurance activities in requirements engineering as they influence the success of a project. It is important to stress that quality assurance of requirements is not only an activity in the requirements phase in projects. Quality assurance must be addressed throughout the software lifecycle. Requirements should be traced throughout development and the quality assured, for example, through inspections, reviews and testing.

1.6 New Trends and the Next Practice

The technological improvements in the global market are closely related to business environments. New concepts such as enterprise systems, e-business and telecommunications have led to new trends in research for researchers and practitioners. Furthermore, the complexity of working in a distributed and heterogeneous environment is causing profound changes in the skills needed and the technology used to develop and maintain software applications. In this ever-changing business and technology environment, new trends have started emerging and have caused fundamental shifts in software development. In a similar fashion, requirements engineering has begun to evolve from its traditional role, as a mere front-end in the software development lifecycle, towards becoming a key focus in the software development process; a process that requires a more precise understanding of the field itself. Today, the definition of what the software development lifecycle constitutes is expanding and evolving as new technologies emerge, forcing software developers to scramble to position themselves in a rapidly changing business environment [34].

The requirements engineering process is a decision-rich complex problem solving activity. Decision making and managing the phases of requirements engineering is becoming increasingly crucial to the successful development of software products. The complexity of the activities involved in the requirements engineering process call for the need for organizations to coordinate the decision-making process and increase visibility of the decisions and the roles played with respect to decision-making in requirements engineering more visible. In order to support the requirements engineering process, a better understanding of activities involved in the process itself as well as an appreciation of the decisions made throughout these activities is necessary [2]. In other words, software developers need to have a better understanding of the range of decisions made at the organizational, product and project levels to ensure effective management of the requirements engineering process.

Software developers need a better understanding of what it takes to generate adequate management support and stakeholders' participation in the requirements engineering process. The effective management of the requirements engineering process mandates procedures and tools to support the phases of the requirements engineering process model and also takes into account other issues, e.g., social, political and cultural issues. There is a strong need for decision support throughout software development at the organizational, project and product levels. As new software developments approaches are emerging, such as agile methods, trends in business and technology force requirements engineering to expand its role in the software development life cycle.

1.7 Empirical Evidence

Empirical research aims to capture quantitative evidence and compares theory to reality, helping us to draw conclusions and to evaluate new methods and tools. Empirical research is important to the requirements engineering field because the results of such studies both help to characterize the potential problems (regarding requirements at the business, product and project levels) with which the field is concerned and evaluate new techniques in a relevant context. Empirical research provides valuable insight into aspects of requirements engineering. Furthermore, both academics and software practitioners need supporting evidence from case studies, field studies and experiments before adopting new technologies. Collecting empirical evidence from industry is often time consuming and can become very complicated. However, this is necessary to quantify and demonstrate their relative merits to the requirements engineering community.

Depending on the purpose of the evaluation, whether it is techniques, methods or tools, and depending on the conditions for the empirical investigation, the three most common types of quantitative investigations (strategies) are:

- Experiment [40]: Experiments are often highly controlled (and hence also occasionally referred to as controlled experiments) and often run in a laboratory setting. When experimenting, subjects are assigned to different treatments at random.
- Case study [41]: Case studies are normally conducted studying a real project and are used for monitoring projects, activities or assignments. Data is collected for a specific purpose throughout the study.
- Survey [3]: A survey is often an investigation performed in retrospect, when e.g. a tool or technique, has been in use for some time. The primary means of gathering qualitative or quantitative data are interviews or questionnaires.

1.8 Conclusion

This chapter has two key contributions: (a) from a theoretical point of view, it provides a brief introduction to the area of requirements engineering, and (b) from a practical point of view, it aims to provide the reader with guidelines to some important aspects of requirements engineering that are needed to obtain the full benefit of the other chapters of this book.

There are three parts in this book. Part 1 contains "state-of-the-art" chapters that address the key requirements engineering activities mentioned in Sect. 1.5, namely requirements elicitation, specification and modeling, prioritization, requirements dependencies, impact analysis, requirements negotiation and quality assurance issues. Part 2 is intended to address new trends in requirements engineering and pinpoints the advantages and pitfalls of these trends. Finally, Part 3 contains chapters focusing on empirical evidence from academic research as well industrial case studies.

References

1. Anthony RN (1965) Planning and control systems: a framework for analysis. Harvard University, Boston, USA

2. Aurum A, Wohlin C (2003) The fundamental nature of requirements engineering activities as decision making process. Journal on Information and Software Technology, 45(14): 945–954

3. Babbie E (1990) Survey research methods. Wadsworth, ISBN 0–524–12672–3

4. Berry DM, Lawrence B (1998) Requirements engineering. IEEE Software 25(2): 26–29

5. Boehm BW, (1988) A spiral model of software development and enhancement, Computer, May, 21(5): 61–72

6. Boehm BW, Papaccio, PN (1988) Understanding and controlling software costs. IEEE transactions on software engineering, 14 (10): 1462–1477

7. Boehm BW, Grünbacher P, Brigges RO (2001) Developing groupware for requirements negotiation: lessons learned. IEEE, Software, May/June, pp. 46–55

8. Boehm BW (2003) Value-based software engineering. ACM SIGSOFT, Software engineering notes, March, 28(2): 1–12

9. BSC'04 (2004) The challenges of complex IT projects. The report of a working group from the Royal academy of engineering and the British computer society. ISBN 1-903496-15-2. Access on 20th October 2004. http://www.bcs.org/BCS/News/ PositionsAndResponses/Positions/complexity.htm

10. Chaos'94 (1995) The Standish group. Access on 4th October 2004. http://standish group.com/sample_research/

11. Chaos'98 (1999) A recipe for success. The Standish group report. Access on 4th October 2004 http://www.standishgroup.com/sample_research

12. Chao'01 (2002) Extreme chaos. The Standish group report. Accessed on 4th October 2004 http://www.standishgroup.com/sample_research

13. Chatzoglou PD (1997) Factors affecting completion of the requirements capture stage of projects with different characteristics. Information and Software Technology, 39 (9): 627–640

14. Curtis B, Krasner H, Iscoe N (1988) A field study of the software design process for large systems. Communications of the ACM 31(11):1268–1287

15. Davis A (1990) System testing: Implications of requirements specifications. Information and Software Technology, 32 (6): 407–414

16. Edwards J, Coutts I, McLeod S (2000) Support for system evolution through separating business and technology issues in a banking system. In: Proceedings of international conference on software Maintenance, 11-14 October, pp. 271–276

17. El Emam K, Madhavji NH (1995) A field study of requirements engineering practices in information systems development. In: Proceedings of 2nd international symposium on requirements engineering, York, England, IEEE CS Press, pp.68–80

18. European Software Institute (1996) European user survey analysis. Report USV_EUR 2.1, ESPITI project, January

19. Faulk SR, Harmon RR, Raffo DM (2000) Value-base software engineering: A value-driven approach to product-line engineering. In: Proceedings of 1st international conference on software product-line engineering, Colorado, August 28, 2000

20. Hall T, Beecham S, Rainer A (2002) Requirements problems in twelve companies: an empirical analysis. IEE proceedings software, 149 (5): 153–160

21. Hofmann HF, Lehner F (2001) Requirements engineering as a success factor in software projects. IEEE Software, 18 (4): 58–66

22. Houdek F, Pohl K (2000): Analyzing requirements engineering processes: a case study. In: Proceedings of the 11th international workshop on database and expert systems applications, Greenwich, UK, 6-8 September, pp.983–987

23. Hunter A, Nuseibeh B (1997) Analyzing inconsistent specifications. In: Proceedings of 3rd international symposium on requirements engineering, RE'07, Annapolis, Md, pp.78–86

24. IEEE-STD 610.12-1990, Standard Glossary of Software Engineering Terminology, 1990, Institute of Electrical and Electronics Engineers

25. Kotonya G, Sommerville I (1998) Requirements engineering – processes and techniques, John Wiley & Sons UK

26. Lauesen, S (2002) Software requirements: styles and techniques, Addison-Wesley, London, UK

27. Loucopoulos P, Karakostas V (1995): System requirements engineering. McGraw-Hill Book company Europe

28. Lowe D, Eklund J (2001) Development issues in specification of web systems. In: Proceedings of 6th Australian workshop on requirements engineering, 22–23 November, University of New South Wales, Sydney, Australia, pp. 4–13

29. Lubars M, Potts C, Richter C (1993) A review of the state of the practice in requirements modelling. In: Proceedings of the IEEE international symposium on requirements engineering, IEEE Computer Society, San Diego, USA, pp. 2–14

30. Macaulay LA (1996) Requirements engineering. Springer-Verlag, New York, London

31. Madhavji NH, Holtje D, Hong W, Bruckhaus T (1994) Elicit: a method for eliciting process models. In: Proceedings of CAS conference, Toronto, Canada, 31 October–3 November, pp.11–122

32. Martin S, Aurum A, Jeffery R, Paech B (2002) Requirements engineering process models in practice. In: Proceedings of 7th Australian workshop on requirements engineering, AWRE'02, 2-3 December, Melbourne, pp. 41–47

33. Menzies T, Easterbrook S, Nuseibeh B, Waugh S (1999) An empirical investigation of multiple viewpoint reasoning in requirements engineering. In: Proceedings of IEEE international symposium on requirements engineering, 7-11 June, pp.100–109

34. Miller E (2002) For survival, start thinking lifecycle management. Computer-aided engineering, 21 (1): 15–18

35. Nguyen L, Swatman P (2003) Managing the requirements engineering process. Requirements engineering, 8 (1): 55–68

36. Pouloudi A, Whitley EA (1997) Stakeholder identification in inter-organizational systems: Gaining insights for drug use management systems. European journal of information systems, 6: 1–14

37. Sommerville I (2001) Software engineering. Pearson Education Ltd, UK

38. Tveito A, Hasvold P (2002) Requirements in the medical domain: Experiences and pre-scriptions. IEEE Software, Nov-Dec, pp.66–69

39. van Lamsweerde A (2000) Requirements engineering in the year 00: a research per-spective. In: Proceedings of 22nd International conference on software engineering, pp.5–19

40. Wohlin C, Runeson P, Höst M, Ohlsson MC, Regnell B, Wesslén A (2000) Experimen-tation in software engineering – An introduction. Kluwer Academic Publishers, Boston, MA, USA

41. Yin RK (1994) Case study research design and methods. Sage Publications, Beverly Hills, California, USA

Author Biography

Aybüke Aurum is a senior lecturer at the School of Information Systems, Tech-nology and Management, University of New South Wales. She received her BSc and MSc in geological engineering, and MEngSc and PhD in computer science. She is the founder and group leader of the requirements engineering Research Group (ReqEng) at the University of New South Wales. She also works as a visit-ing researcher in National ICT, Australia (NICTA). She is on the editorial board of *Journal of Requirements Engineering* published by Springer. She edited three books, including *"Managing Software Engineering Knowledge"* and *"Value-Based Software Engineering"*, and published over 70 articles. Her research interests in-clude management of software development process, software inspection, re-quirements engineering, decision making and knowledge management in software development. She is on the editorial boards of Requirements Engineering Journal and Asian Academy Journal of Management.

Claes Wohlin is a professor in software engineering at the School of Engineering at Blekinge Institute of Technology in Sweden. He is also pro vice chancellor of the institute. Prior to this, he has held professor chairs in software engineering at Lund University and Linköping University. He has a M.Sc. in Electrical Engineer-ing and a Ph.D. in Communication Systems both from Lund University, and he has five years of industrial experience. Dr. Wohlin is co-editor-in-chief of the journal of Information and Software Technology published by Elsevier. He is on the editorial boards of Empirical Software Engineering: An International Journal, and Software Quality Journal. Dr. Wohlin received the Telenor Nordic Research Prize in 2004 for his achievements in software engineering and improvement of software reliability in telecommunications.

Part 1
State-of-the-Art Surveys of Requirements Engineering Process Research

This part provides an introduction to some state-of-the-art in the requirements engineering process, as well as presenting literature surveys in the field. The objective is to give the reader an in-depth look at key areas of concern, otherwise covered only briefly in most textbooks to date on requirements engineering. This part contains seven chapters. The process of engineering and managing software requirements starts with the *elicitation* and *capturing* of the requirements (Chap. 2). Then the requirements must then be carefully *specified* (Chap. 3). When a sufficient understanding of the requirements has been obtained it is possible to *prioritize* them (Chap. 4). One important consideration when handling requirements is the *dependencies* between them, so that this can be taken into account when taking decisions in relation to the requirements (Chap. 5). When requirements are to be implemented, it is important that *impact analysis* is carried out, i.e. to predict the impact of the requirements on any existing software (Chap. 6). Different stakeholders most likely have different views of what the requirements are and hence it may be necessary to perform *negotiations* (Chap. 7). Once requirements have been implemented, it is crucial to be able to work with *quality assurance* (Chap. 8). On the above mentioned considerations regarding the engineering and managing of requirements are addressed in the chapters of Part 1. Thus, in summary this part contains an introduction to state-of-the-art practices in the following areas:

- Chapter 2: Elicitation and capturing of requirements
- Chapter 3: Modeling and specification of requirements
- Chapter 4: Prioritization of requirements
- Chapter 5: Dependencies between requirements
- Chapter 6: Impact analysis of requirements
- Chapter 7: Negotiation of requirements
- Chapter 8: Quality assurance of requirements

These seven chapters highlight some of the main issues related to engineering and managing software requirements. The chapters have been written by internationally recognized researchers from around the world who specialize in the above listed areas.

The seven chapters are by Didar Zowghi and Chad Coulin from University of Technology Sydney, Australia; Richardo J. Machado, Isabel Ramos and João M. Fernandes from University of Minho, Portugal; Patrik Berander from Blekinge Institute of Technology, Sweden and Anneliese Andrews from Washington State University, USA; Anne Persson and Åsa G. Dahlstedt from University of Skövde, Sweden; Per Jönsson from Blekinge Institute of Technology, Sweden, and Mikael Lindvall from Fraunhofer Centre for Experimental Software Engineering, Maryland, USA; Paul Grünbacher and Norbert Seyff from Johannes Kepler University Linz, Austria; Christian Denger and Thomas Olsson from Fraunhofer Institute for Experimental Software Engineering, Germany.

2 Requirements Elicitation: A Survey of Techniques, Approaches, and Tools

Didar Zowghi and Chad Coulin

Abstract: Requirements elicitation is the process of seeking, uncovering, acquiring, and elaborating requirements for computer based systems. It is generally understood that requirements are elicited rather than just captured or collected. This implies there are discovery, emergence, and development elements in the elicitation process. Requirements elicitation is a complex process involving many activities with a variety of available techniques, approaches, and tools for performing them. The relative strengths and weaknesses of these determine when each is appropriate depending on the context and situation. The objectives of this chapter are to present a comprehensive survey of important aspects of the techniques, approaches, and tools for requirements elicitation, and examine the current issues, trends, and challenges faced by researchers and practitioners in this field.

Keywords: Requirements, Elicitation, Techniques, Approaches, Tools, Issues, Challenges, Trends, Survey.

2.1 Introduction

The importance of requirements engineering (RE) within software systems development has long been established and recognized by researchers and practitioners (Chap. 1). The elicitation of requirements represents an early but continuous and critical stage in the development of software systems. The requirements for a software system may be spread across many sources. These include the problem owners, the stakeholders, documentation, and other existing systems. Because of the communication rich nature of requirements elicitation activities, many of the effective techniques do not originate from the traditional areas of software engineering or computer science research. Techniques for requirements elicitation are derived mostly from the social sciences, organizational theory, group dynamics, knowledge engineering, and very often from practical experience.

The process of requirements elicitation is generally accepted as one of the critical activities in the RE process. Getting the right requirements is considered a vital but difficult part of software development projects [36]. A recent field study of fifteen RE teams carried out by Hofmann and Lehner [31] identified key RE practices that should lead to project success. Effective elicitation of requirements was arguably among the most important of the resulting recommended good RE practices.

Requirements elicitation itself is a very complex process involving many activities, with multiple techniques available to perform these activities. The multidisciplinary nature of requirements elicitation only adds to this complexity. Elicitation is subject to a large degree of error, influenced by key factors ingrained in communication problems. Despite the importance of requirements elicitation within software development, insufficient attention has been paid to this area in industry and software engineering research to date.

In reality requirements elicitation is a multifaceted and iterative activity that relies heavily on the communication skills of requirements engineers and the commitment and cooperation of the system stakeholders. One of the main problems facing software development project teams is communication barriers and agreement about the requirements. The main point is that concepts that are clearly defined to one community of participants can be entirely opaque to members of another. The fact that this situation exists often goes unnoticed in the course of elicitation unless specific attention is paid to the problem. The type of the system and the purpose of the project significantly affect the way in which requirements elicitation is conducted. For example, it can be said that the method employed for a custom built embedded control system is likely to be substantially different to that of a commercially available inventory management system. The elicitation of requirements can be performed in a variety of settings including the development of web based information systems (Chap. 15) and market driven product lines (Chap. 13), the implementation of large enterprise systems, the selection of commercial off the shelf products (COTS), and the maintenance of existing and legacy systems. Furthermore, project teams may be spread across different geographical locations and from diverse cultural backgrounds. The specific elicitation techniques used for a particular situation often depend on a variety of additional factors including time and cost, the availability of resources, the safety criticality of the system, and any legal or regulatory constraints.

In this chapter we present the state of the art and practice in requirements elicitation through an extensive review and analysis of the relevant literature bearing in mind the interdisciplinary and practical nature of this important activity. The aim is to inform the reader of the strengths and weaknesses of some of the current techniques, approaches, and tools used in requirements elicitation today.

The chapter is structured as follows: Sect. 2.2 introduces the process of requirements elicitation, the activities associated with it, and the roles performed during elicitation by the analyst. Sect. 2.3 surveys a wide variety of techniques and approaches used for requirements elicitation, and includes a comparison of these with respect to each other and the activities they are used for. Sect. 2.4 provides some examples of methodology based requirements elicitation, and Sect. 2.5 presents the types of available tool support for this process. Sect. 2.6 describes some of the most common issues and pitfalls experienced during requirements elicitation, and Sect. 2.7 is dedicated to the current trends and challenges in this field. Sect. 2.8 offers some suggestions for future directions in requirements elicitation research, and finally Sect. 2.9 contains a brief summary of the chapter.

2.2 What is Requirements Elicitation?

Currently there is very little uniformity in RE research and practice concerning a standard definition for requirements elicitation. Requirements elicitation is concerned with learning and understanding the needs of users and project sponsors with the ultimate aim of communicating these needs to the system developers. A substantial part of elicitation is dedicated to uncovering, extracting, and surfacing the wants of the potential stakeholders. Robertson and Robertson [54] refer to this process as "trawling for requirements" to highlight the fact that through this process you are likely to get more requirements than expected. This implies that gathering a few extraneous requirements initially is always better than gathering less. This is one of the reasons why prioritization (Chap. 4) and negotiation (Chap. 7) are important parts of RE, especially within market driven RE (Chap. 13) where an overload from the constant influx of large amounts of requirements is a serious issue (Chap. 10). More recently the concepts of *inventing* and *creating* requirements have been used to highlight the role of creativity and to emphasize what really goes on during requirements elicitation [43].

2.2.1 The Process of Requirements Elicitation

The requirements elicitation process involves a set of activities that must allow for communication, prioritization, negotiation, and collaboration with all the relevant stakeholders. It must also provide strong foundations for the emergence, discovery, and invention of requirements as part of a highly interactive elicitation process. Requirements elicitation involves activities that are intensely communicative. These activities increase in significance when one considers the "culture gap" [62] or basic semantic differences dividing the problem owning and the problem solving communities when attempting to engage in meaningful dialogue [7]. Once again there is very little uniformity in the research literature and practice concerning the names given to the activities often performed during requirements elicitation. However what is generally accepted is that elicitation is the initial stage within the RE process albeit an iterative and integrated one. Typical activities of the requirements elicitation process can be divided into five fundamental types as described below:

- **Understanding the Application Domain** – It is important when beginning the process of requirements elicitation to investigate and examine in detail the situation or "real world" in which the system will ultimately reside (sometimes called the application domain) [34, 68]. The current environment needs to be thoroughly explored including the political, organizational, and social aspects related to the system, in addition to any constraints they may enforce upon the system and its development. Existing work processes and the related problems to be solved by the system need to be described with respect to the key business goals and issues.

- **Identifying the Sources of Requirements** – Requirements may be spread across many sources and exist in a variety of formats [41]. In all software development projects a number of possible sources for requirements may be identified. Stakeholders represent the most obvious source of requirements for the system. Users and subject matter experts are used to supply detailed information about the problems and user needs. Existing systems and processes represent another source for eliciting requirements, particularly when the project involves replacing a current or legacy system. Existing documentation about the current systems and business processes including manuals, forms, and reports can provide useful information about the organization and environment, as well as requirements for the new system and their supporting rationale and importance.

- **Analyzing the Stakeholders** – Stakeholders are people who have an interest in the system or are affected in some way by the development and implementation of the system and hence must be consulted during requirements elicitation. Typically stakeholders include groups and individuals internal and external to the organization. The customer, and more specifically the project sponsor, is usually the most apparent stakeholder of the system. In some cases however the actual users of the system may be the most important. Other parties whose sphere of interest may extend to some part of the system operations, such as those responsible for work process standards, customers, and partners, should also be regarded as stakeholders if affected. One of the first steps in requirements elicitation therefore is to analyze and involve all the relevant stakeholders. An extensive list of potential project stakeholders that should be consulted during this activity is available in the literature (e.g., [3, 54]). The process of analyzing the stakeholders also often includes the identification of key user representatives and product champions.

- **Selecting the Techniques, Approaches, and Tools to Use** – Although some may advocate that just one elicitation technique or a single methodology is sufficient and may be applied to all cases, it is generally accepted that an individual requirements elicitation technique or approach cannot possibly be suitable for all projects. The choice of techniques to be employed is dependent on the specific context of the project and is often a critical factor in the success of the elicitation process [48]. Hickey and Davis [27, 29] have investigated the elicitation technique selection and state that a particular elicitation technique may be selected for a variety of reasons. These include (a) the technique selected is the only one the analyst knows, (b) the technique selected is the analyst's favorite, (c) the selected technique is the one prescribed by a specific methodology that is being followed for the system development, and (d) the choice of technique is governed solely by the intuition of the analyst to be effective in the current context. Clearly requirements elicitation is best performed using a variety of techniques. In the majority of projects several methods are employed during and at different stages in the software development life cycle, often in cooperation where complementary.

- **Eliciting the Requirements from Stakeholders and Other Sources** – Once the sources of requirements and the specific stakeholders have been identified, the actual elicitation of the core requirements then begins using the selected elicitation techniques, approaches, and tools. During this activity it is important to establish the level of scope for the system and investigate in detail the needs and wants of the stakeholders, especially the users. It is also essential to determine the future processes the system will perform with respect to the business operations, and examine the ways in which the system may support them in order to satisfy the major objectives and address the key problems of the business.

It is important to remember that requirements elicitation does not occur in a vacuum. It is strongly related to the context in which it is conducted and specific characteristics of the project, organization, and environment [11]. In practice the budget and schedule of the project have a significant effect on the process and the way in which it is performed. The structure and maturity of the organization will determine how requirements are elicited, as will the way in which the system will interact with users and other systems. The level of volatility within a project must also be considered, as this will directly affect the quality of requirements and the elicitation process itself.

Typically the process begins with an informal and incomplete high-level mission statement for the project [69]. This may be represented by a set of fundamental goals, functions, and constraints for the target system, or as an explanation of the problems to be solved. In order to develop this description, stakeholders and other sources of requirements are identified and used for elicitation. These preliminary results form the basis of further investigation and refinement of requirements in a typically iterative and incremental manner.

Over the years a number of process models have been proposed for requirements elicitation [13, 39, 58]. For the most part these models provide only a generic roadmap of the process with sufficient flexibility to accommodate the basic contextual differences of individual projects. The inability of these models to provide definitive guidelines is a result of the wide range of task that may be performed during requirements elicitation, and the sequence of those activities being dependent on specific project circumstances. The variety of issues that may be faced and the number of techniques available to use only makes it more complex. In most cases the process of requirements elicitation is performed incrementally over multiple sessions, iteratively to increasing levels of detail, and at least partially in parallel with other system development activities. In reality its completion is often determined by time and cost constraints rather than achieving the required level of requirements quality and completeness. Typically the result of this process is a detailed set of requirements in natural language text and simple diagrammatic representations with additional information including descriptions of the sources, priorities, and rationales.

2.2.2 Roles of the Requirements Engineer During Elicitation

During requirements elicitation the requirements engineer (also sometimes referred to as the systems analyst or business analyst) may play a variety of roles and assume different responsibilities. These responsibilities and roles are dependent on the project, people, context and organization involved. A substantial part of elicitation involves *exploring* the problem domain and the requirements that are situated in that domain. Furthermore, the requirements engineers often need to perform some typical aspects of project management. Not only do they have to manage the process of elicitation, but they also have to communicate it effectively to the stakeholders. This involves among other things, decision-making (Chap. 12), prioritization (Chap. 4), and negotiation (Chap. 7).

Requirements engineers often play the important role of *facilitator*. When eliciting requirements by group work sessions, they are not only required to ask questions and record the answers, but must guide and assist the participants in addressing the relevant issues in order to obtain correct and complete requirements information. They are also responsible for ensuring that participants feel comfortable and confident with the process, and are given sufficient opportunity to contribute. This role represents a significant part of the skill and expertise required by the analyst in order to perform effective requirements elicitation. During elicitation conflicts between elicited requirements and stakeholders themselves are inevitable. In many cases the prioritization of requirements from different stakeholders groups is a source of much debate and dispute. When these situations occur the analyst is often playing the role of a *mediator* and is responsible for finding a suitable resolution through negotiation and compromise. It is important that the analyst is sensitive to all the political and organizational aspects of the project when mediating discussions related to the system.

Frequently requirements engineers are responsible for *documenting* the requirements elicited. This role is particularly important as it represents the production of results from the elicitation process, and forms the foundation for the subsequent project phases. Evaluation of the elicitation process and the work performed by the analyst is based on these resultant artifacts, which in some cases may form the basis of contractual agreements.

Analysts are often required to assume the various roles of the *developer* community during requirements elicitation. This includes system architects, designers, programmers, testers, quality assurance personnel, implementation consultants, and system maintenance administrators. This is often due to the fact that these stakeholders have not yet been assigned to the project at the requirements elicitation stage. Despite this the decisions made during this phase of the project will significantly affect these stakeholders and the subsequent phases of development.

All the requirements elicited must be *validated* against the other stakeholders, other systems, each other, and then compared with previously established goals for the system. By this it is meant that the requirements describe the desired features of the system appropriately, and that those requirements will provide the necessary functions in order to fulfill the specified objectives of the target system.

This process typically involves all the identified stakeholder groups, and results in further elicitation activities.

2.3 Techniques and Approaches for Requirements Elicitation

For over two decades now much of the research and practice within RE for software systems has been largely directed towards improving the complex process known as elicitation through the application and development of various techniques, approaches, and tools. Many of these methods have been borrowed and adapted from other disciplines such as the social sciences, and only a select few have been developed specifically for eliciting software requirements [14]. It is important to explain what we mean by the terms "technique" and "approach" as there exists a number of different uses for each of them in practice and multiple definitions in the literature. A "technique" is a way of doing something or a practical method applied to some particular task. An "approach", on the other hand is a systematic arrangement, usually in steps, of ideas or actions intended to deal with a problem or situation. In reality there are literally hundreds of different techniques and approaches from a variety of sources that can and have been employed for requirements elicitation. Below we present only some of those that are more widely used. Although not exhaustive, we believe this selection is representative of the range described in literature and practiced in industry today.

Interviews
Interviews [1, 32] are probably the most traditional and commonly used technique for requirements elicitation. Because interviews are essentially human based social activities, they are inherently informal and their effectiveness depends greatly on the quality of interaction between the participants. Interviews provide an efficient way to collect large amounts of data quickly. The results of interviews, such as the usefulness of the information gathered, can vary significantly depending on the skill of the interviewer [23]. There are fundamentally three types of interviews being unstructured, structured, and semi-structured, the latter generally representing a combination of the former two.

Unstructured interviews are conversational in nature where the interviewer enforces only limited control over the direction of discussions. Because they do not follow a predetermined agenda or list of questions, there is the risk that some topics may be completely neglected. It is also a common problem with unstructured interviews to focus in too much detail on some areas, and not enough in others [45]. This type of interview is best applied for exploration when there is a limited understanding of the domain, or as a precursor to more focused and detailed structured interviews. Structured interviews are conducted using a predetermined set of questions to gather specific information. The success of structured interviews depends on knowing what are the right questions to ask, when should they be asked, and who should answer them. Templates that provide guidance on structured interviews for requirements elicitation such as Volere [54] can be used to support this technique. Although structured interviews tend to limit the investigation of new ideas, they are generally considered to be rigorous and effective.

Questionnaires

Questionnaires [21] are mainly used during the early stages of requirements elicitation and may consist of open and/or closed questions. To be effective, the terms, concepts, and boundaries of the domain must be well established and understood by the participants and questionnaire designer. Questions must be focused to avoid gathering large amounts of redundant and irrelevant information. They provide an efficient way to collect information from multiple stakeholders quickly, but are limited in the depth of knowledge they are able to elicit. Questionnaires lack the opportunity to delve further on a topic, or expand on new ideas. In the same way they provide no mechanism for the participants to request clarification or correct misunderstandings. Generally questionnaires are considered more useful as informal checklists to ensure fundamental elements are addressed early on, and to establish the foundation for subsequent elicitation activities.

Task Analysis

Task analysis [9, 53] employs a top-down approach where high-level tasks are decomposed into subtasks and eventually detailed sequences until all actions and events are described. The primary objectives of this technique is to construct a hierarchy of the tasks performed by the users and the system, and determine the knowledge used or required to carry them out. Task analysis provides information on the interactions of both the user and the system with respect to the tasks as well as a contextual description of the activities that take place. In most cases considerable effort is required to perform thorough task analysis, and it is important to establish what level of detail is required and when components of the tasks need to be explorer further.

Domain Analysis

Examining the existing and related documentation and applications is a very useful way of gathering early requirements as well as understanding and capturing domain knowledge, and identification of reusable concepts and components. These types of investigations are particularly important when the project involves the replacement or enhancement of an existing legacy system. Types of documentation that may be useful for eliciting requirements include design documents and instruction manuals for existing systems, and hardcopy forms and files used in the current business processes. Application studies often also include looking at both upstream and downstream systems, as well as competitive or like solutions. In most cases these studies involve other elicitation techniques such as observing the exiting system in use and interviewing the current users. Domain knowledge in the form of detailed descriptions and examples plays an important part in the process of requirements elicitation. Approaches based on this type of information are often used in conjunction with, and as the input to other elicitation techniques. For example, analysts use previous experience in similar domains as a discussion template for facilitating group work and conducting interviews. Analogies and abstractions of existing problem domains can be used as baselines to acquire specific and detailed information, identify and describe possible solution systems, and assist in creating a common understanding between the analyst and stakeholders. These approaches also provide the opportunity to reuse specifications and validate new requirements against other domain instances [61]. Problem Frames [35] in particular provide a method for detailed problems examination in order to identify patterns that could provide links to potential solutions.

Introspection
The technique of introspection [23] requires the analyst to develop requirements based on what he or she believes the users and other stakeholders want and need from the system. Despite being employed to some extent by most analysts, this technique is mainly used only as a starting point for other requirements elicitation efforts. Introspection is only really effective when the analyst is not only very familiar with the domain and goals of the system, but also expert in the business processes performed by the users. In cases where the analyst is forced to use this technique more, for example when the users have little or no previous experience with software systems in their work environment, a type of facilitation introspection should take place via other elicitation techniques such as interviews and protocol analysis.

Repertory Grids
Repertory grids [38] involve asking stakeholders to develop attributes and assign values to a set of domain entities. As a result the system is modeled in the form of a matrix by categorizing the elements of the system, detailing the instances of those categories, and assigning variables with corresponding values to each one. The aim is to identify and represent the similarities and differences between the different domain entities. These represent a level of abstraction unfamiliar to most users. As a result, this technique is typically used when eliciting requirements from domain experts. Although more detailed than card sorting, and to a lesser degree laddering, repertory grids are somewhat limited in their ability to express specific characteristics of complex requirements.

Card Sorting
Card sorting requires the stakeholders to sort a series of cards containing the names of domain entities into groups according to their own understanding. Furthermore, the stakeholder is required to explain the rationale for the way in which the cards are sorted. It is important for effective card sorting that all entities are included in the process. This is possible only if the domain is sufficiently understood by both the analyst and the participants. If the domain is not well established then group work can be used to identify these entities. Class Responsibility Collaboration (CRC) cards [5] are a derivative of card sorting that is also used to determine program classes in software code. In this technique cards are used to assign responsibilities to users and components of the system. Because entities represent

such a high level of system abstraction, the information obtained from this technique is limited in its detail.

Laddering

When using laddering [30] stakeholders are asked a series of short prompting questions, known as probes, and required to arrange the resultant answers into an organized structure. A primary assumption when employing laddering is that the knowledge to be elicited can actually be arranged in a hierarchical fashion. For this technique to be effective, the stakeholders must be able to express their understanding of the domain and then arrange it in a logical way. This knowledge, which is often displayed using tree diagrams, is reviewed and modified dynamically as more is added. Like card sorting, laddering is mainly used as a way to clarify requirements and categorize domain entities.

Group Work

Group work such as collaborative meetings is a very common and often default technique for requirements elicitation. Groups are particularly effective because they involve and commit the stakeholders directly and promote cooperation. These types of sessions can be difficult to organize due to the number of different stakeholders that may be involved in the project. Managing these sessions effectively requires both expertise and experience to ensure that individual personalities do not dominate the discussions. Key factors in the success of group work are the makeup of participants and the cohesion within the group. Stakeholders must feel comfortable and confident in speaking openly and honestly, and therefore group work is less effective in highly political situations.

Brainstorming

Brainstorming [50] is a process where participants from different stakeholder groups engage in informal discussion to rapidly generate as many ideas as possible without focusing on any one in particular. It is important when conducting this type of group work to avoid exploring or critiquing ideas in great detail. It is not usually the intended purpose of brainstorming sessions to resolve major issues or make key decisions. This technique is often used to develop the preliminary mission statement for the project and target system. One of the advantages in using brainstorming is that it promotes freethinking and expression, and allows the discovery of new and innovative solutions to existing problems.

Joint Application Development (JAD)

Joint Application Development (JAD) [65] involves all the available stakeholders investigating through general discussion both the problems to be solved, and the available solutions to those problems. With all parties represented, decisions can be made rapidly and issues resolved quickly. A major difference between JAD and brainstorming is that typically the main goals of the system have already been established before the stakeholders participate. Also JAD sessions are typically well structured with defined steps, actions, and roles for participants (including a specialist facilitator). The focus of this type of meeting tends to often be on the needs and desires of the business and users rather than technical issues.

Requirements Workshops

Requirements workshop [25] is a generic term given to a number of different types of group meetings where the emphasis is on developing and discovering requirements for a software system. There are many different forms of requirements workshops, including cross functional which involves different types of stakeholders from various areas of the business, Co-operative Requirements Capture (CRC) [42] (where like JAD, there is a defined set of activities and the development community is especially involved), and Creativity [43] which encourages innovative thinking and expression. Another variation of requirements workshops often used in market analysis is the Focus Group [40].

Ethnography

Ethnography [4, 60], being the study of people in their natural setting, involves the analyst actively or passively participating in the normal activities of the users over an extended period of time whilst collecting information on the operations being performed. These techniques are especially useful when addressing contextual factors such as usability, and when investigating collaborative work settings where the understanding of interactions between different users with the system is paramount. In practice, ethnography is particularly effective when the need for a new system is a result of existing problems with processes and procedures, and in identifying social patterns and complex relationships between human stakeholders.

Observation

Observation is one of the more widely used ethnographic techniques. As the name suggests the analyst observes the actual execution of existing processes by the users without direct interference. This technique is often used in conjunction with others such as interviews and task analysis. As a general rule ethnographic techniques such as observation are very expensive to perform and require significant skill and effort on the part of the analyst to interpret and understand the actions being performed. The effectiveness of observation and other ethnographic techniques can vary as users have a tendency to adjust the way they perform tasks when knowingly being watched.

Protocol Analysis

Protocol analysis [23, 46] is where participants perform an activity or task whilst talking it through aloud, describing the actions being conducted and the thought process behind them. This technique can provide the analyst with specific information on and rationale for the processes the target system must support [45]. In most cases however talking through an operation is not the normal way of performing the task, and as a result may not necessarily represent the true process completely or correctly. Likewise minor steps performed frequently and repetitively are often taken for granted by the users, and may not be explained and subsequently recorded as part of the process.

Apprenticing

Apprenticing [54, 6] involves the analyst actually learning and performing the current tasks under the instruction and supervision of an experienced user. In this technique the analyst is taught the operations and business processes by observing, asking questions, and physically doing, rather than being informed of them, as is the case with protocol analysis. Similar to Role Playing but more involved, apprenticing is very useful where the analyst is inexperienced with the domain, and when the users have difficulty in explaining their actions. The technique of Emersion takes apprenticing one step further whereby the analyst becomes actively involved in the real life activities of the business.

Prototyping

Providing stakeholders with prototypes of the system to support the investigation of possible solutions is an effective way to gather detailed information and relevant feedback [60]. It is common that prototypes are used in conjunction with other elicitation techniques such as interviews and JAD. Prototypes are typically developed using preliminary requirements or existing examples of similar systems. This technique is particularly useful when developing human-computer interfaces, or where the stakeholders are unfamiliar with the available solutions. There are a number of different methods for prototyping systems such as storyboards, executable, throwaway and evolutionary, with varying levels of effort required. In many cases prototypes are expensive to produce in terms of time and cost. However, an advantage of using prototypes is that they encourage stakeholders, and more specifically the users, to play an active role in developing the requirements. One of the potential hazards when using prototypes for requirements elicitation is that users may become attached to them, and therefore become resistant to alternative solutions from then on. Despite this, the technique is extremely helpful when developing new systems for entirely new applications.

Goal Based Approaches

The fundamental premise of goal modeling (Chap. 9) and goal based approaches is that high-level goals that represent objectives for the system are decomposed (e.g. usually using AND and OR relationships) and elaborated (e.g. with "Why" and "How" questioning) into sub goals and then further refined in such a way that individual requirements are elicited. The result of this process is significantly more complicated and complete than the traditional methods of representing system goals using tree structure diagrams. These approaches are able to represent detailed relationships between domain entities, requirements, and the objectives of the system. In general one of the risks when using goal based approaches is that errors in the high-level goals of the system made early on can have a major and detrimental follow on effect, and that changing goals are difficult to manage. In recent times significant effort has been devoted to developing these types of approaches for requirements elicitation such as the F^3 project [8], the KAOS meta model [16] and the i* framework [67]. The use of goals in conjunction with scenarios to elicit requirements has also attracted considerable attention [55, 51, 26]. In practice these approaches have been particularly useful in situations where only the high-level needs for the system are well known, and there exists a general lack of understanding about the specific details of the problems to be solved and their possible solutions.

Scenarios
Scenarios are widely used in requirements elicitation and, as the name suggests, are narrative and specific descriptions of current and future processes including actions and interactions between the users and the system. Like use cases, scenarios do not typically consider the internal structure of the system, and require an incremental and interactive approach to their development. Naturally, it is important when using scenarios to collect all the potential exceptions for each step. A substantial amount of work from both the research and practice communities has been dedicated to developing structured and rigorous approaches to requirements elicitation using scenarios including CREWS [15], The Inquiry Cycle [15], SBRE [37], and Scenario Plus [56]. Scenarios are additionally very useful for understanding and validating requirements, as well as test case development.

Viewpoints
Viewpoint approaches aim to model the domain from different perspectives in order to develop a complete and consistent description of the target system. For example, a system can be described in terms of its operation, implementation and interfaces. In the same way systems can be modeled from the standpoints of different users or from the position of related systems. These types of approaches are particularly effective for projects where the system entities have detailed and complicated relationships with each other. Viewpoints are also useful as a way of supporting the organization and prioritization of requirements. One common criticism of viewpoint approaches is that they do not enable non-functional requirements to be represented easily, and are expensive to use in terms of the effort required. Some viewpoint approaches [59, 47] provide a flexible multi-perspective model for systems, using different viewpoints to elicit and arrange requirements from a number of sources. Using these approaches analysts and stakeholders are able to organize the process and derive detailed requirements for a complete system from multiple project specific viewpoints.

2.3.1 Comparison of Techniques and Approaches

Two important questions that need to be addressed during requirements elicitation are: (1) Which techniques and approaches should be used for a given requirements elicitation activity? and (2) Which of the these techniques and approaches are complementary or can be used as alternatives? Ultimately, each situation is unique and the answers to these questions are highly dependant on the context of the project and system. We acknowledge that because of this there is always the possible for exceptions to any rule made along these lines; however, the following two tables in this section are presented as a way of offering some high level support to this end. The intention is to provide an overview of how different techniques and approaches can be used for each of the requirements elicitation activities, and which of the commonly used techniques and approaches often employed for requirements elicitation can be used in cooperation with, or instead of each other. Rather than including all the techniques and approaches previously presented in Sect. 2.3 of this chapter, we have selected a core group of eight techniques and approaches which we believe provide suitable coverage across the spectrum of available techniques and approaches (for example ethnography includes observation, and JAD is an example of groupwork), and that are also appropriately representative of those that are currently both state of the art and state of practice. The information contained in these tables is based largely on our assessment of the literature as well as practical experience and observation in requirements elicitation research and practice.

Table 2.1 Techniques and approaches for elicitation activities.

	Interviews	Domain	Groupwork	Ethnography	Prototyping	Goals	Scenarios	Viewpoints
Understanding the domain	X	X	X	X		X	X	X
Identifying sources of requirements	X	X	X			X	X	X
Analyzing the Stakeholders	X	X	X	X	X	X	X	X
Selecting techniques and approaches	X	X	X					
Eliciting the Requirements	X	X	X	X	X	X	X	X

Techniques and Approaches for Elicitation Activities

We have seen that different techniques and approaches have different and relative strengths and weaknesses, and may be more or less suited to particular types of situations and environments. Likewise, some techniques and approaches are more appropriate for specific elicitation activities and the types of information that needs to be acquired during those activities. Table 2.1 below presents a selected core group of techniques and approaches best suited (marked with an "X") for the specific requirements elicitation activities described earlier on in Sect. 2.2 of the chapter.

We can see from Table 2.1 above that for each of the requirements elicitation activities there are a number of suitable techniques and approaches that can be used. Apart from interviews, domain analysis, and group work, which are generic and flexible enough to provide support for all the listed elicitation activities, goal, scenario, and viewpoint based approaches can also be used extensively throughout the process. Given that we have already classified them as requirements elicitation techniques and approaches, it is natural that all the core techniques and approaches presented in the table can be used for activity of actually eliciting the requirements.

Table 2.2 Complementary and alternative techniques and approaches

	Interviews	Domain	Group work	Ethnography	Prototyping	Goals	Scenarios	Viewpoints
Interviews		C	A	A	A	C	C	C
Domain	C		C	A	A	A	A	A
Group-work	A	C		A	C	C	C	C
Ethnography	A	A	A		C	C	A	A
Prototyping	A	A	C	C		C	C	C
Goals	C	A	C	C	C		C	C
Scenarios	C	A	C	A	C	C		A
Viewpoints	C	A	C	A	C	C	A	

Complementary and Alternative Techniques and Approaches
In most projects more than one requirements elicitation technique and approach will need to be used, therefore it is useful to select those techniques and approaches that are complementary to achieve the best possible results from the requirements elicitation process. In the same way alternative requirements elicitation techniques and approaches enables greater flexibility to the process, and more choice for the analysts and stakeholders. Table 2.2 below provides some guidance with respect to which of the selected core group of techniques and approaches can be used in cooperation (marked with a "C"), and which can be used as alternatives (marked with an "A").

We can see from Table 2.2 above that for each of the core requirements elicitation techniques and approaches there are both alternatives and those that are complementary. In some cases, such as when prototypes are operated by users under the observation of the analyst, the combination of these techniques has the potential to provide much richer and more detailed requirements information on both the business processes and the needs of the users. Alternative techniques and approaches are useful if for some reason a selected techniques or approach is not being as effective as expected, or when the analyst is unfamiliar, uncomfortable, or unable to use a particular technique or approach. For example, it may not be possible to observe users perform their normal business operations due to the physically hazardous environment in which they work. In this case the analyst may choose to use scenarios to elicit that type of information instead.

2.4 Methodology Based Requirements Elicitation

Methodology and model driven approaches (Chap. 3) provide ways of representing the existing or future processes and systems using analytical techniques with the intention of investigating their characteristics and limits. Goal, scenario, and agent based modeling techniques as detailed later in this chapter are also used for requirements elicitation in addition to the two approaches described below.

Structured Analysis and Design (SAD) [19, 66] has been around since the mid-1970s and has been widely written about, promoted, and used. The approach is largely function oriented. It comprises of a collection of techniques such as Data Flow Diagrams (DFD) which detail the functional decomposition with the emphasis on the data in and out of the system and related components, and Entity Relationship Diagrams (ERD) that facilitate the representation of system entities, their attributes, and their relationships to each other. Other SAD techniques used during requirements elicitation include Data Dictionaries and Event Lists.

Object Oriented (OO) approaches, and specifically the Unified Modeling Language (UML) contain several techniques often used for requirements elicitation with established yet flexible notations and formats such as Use Cases diagrams, Use Case descriptions, and Class Diagrams. Use Cases [12] are essentially abstractions of scenarios that describe the functional behavior of the system, and have become especially accepted in both research and practice despite their shortcomings such as impreciseness. The diagrammatic and tabular representations make them easy to understand and flexible enough to accommodate some context specific information. These techniques are especially effective in projects where there is a high level of uncertainty or when the analyst is not an expert in that particular domain.

Several attempts have been made to develop methodologies that combine a number of techniques with supporting roadmaps and guidelines as a way of addressing requirements elicitation. One such approach of combining techniques suggests that the process should begin with an ethnographic study to discover fundamental aspects of existing patterns and behavior, followed by structured interviews to gain deeper insight into the needs of the stakeholders and the priorities of requirements [23]. Furthermore, it is proposed that the more extensive requirements elicitation techniques are used to examine in greater detail those needs deemed important.

In other examples of methodology based approaches, requirements elicitation is a defined but closely integrated activity within other aspects of the software development process, such as is the case with Soft System Methodology (SSM) [10], which addresses organizational problems and change, and Quality Functional Deployment (QFD) [2], which focuses on achieving customer satisfaction through quality based development. Gause and Weinberg [22], on the other hand, have developed a methodology centered on requirements elicitation, and provide useful and practical techniques for the process including concepts such as Starting Points and Context-Free Questions.

Agile Methods (Chap. 14) for the most part enforce very little upfront requirements elicitation but instead advocate incremental and iterative discovery throughout and integrated with the software development lifecycle [44]. In addition to interview and prototypes, Agile Methods supports the use of Customer or User Stories. These provide basic descriptions of the business processes and what the system needs to do to support them. Typically, these are written on index cards by the customer and used as starting points for the development process. Additional requirements elicited as a result of the process from the ever-present customer are added to a Product Backlog, which represents a living requirements document consisting of prioritized system features and functions.

2.5 Tool Support for Requirements Elicitation

A wide variety of tools exist that have been developed and used to support requirements elicitation. These range from shallow to deep with respect to the level of detail and formality, and from generic to specific in purpose and operation. Tools can support a specific technique or process, and may have varying levels of task automation and assistance. Much like the techniques and approaches described above, some of the tools detailed below have been developed for purposes other than requirements elicitation but applied to it, whereas other have been designed specifically for it. By "tool" we refer to an implement, such as software or an artifact, used in practice to accomplish some act, in this case being requirements elicitation. For the most part the use of tools for requirements elicitation has been relatively limited and the more successful applications have tended to be domain or approach specific, with the exception of process guidelines and prototyping utilities. Templates such as IEEE Std 830 Software Requirements Specification [33] and Volere Requirements Specification Template [54] represent the most basic type of tool used by analysts to support the process of requirements elicitation. In a similar way requirements management tools like DOORS, CaliberRM and RequisitPro provide format based support for the elicitation of requirements. Many analysts also utilize specific modeling tools to assist the process of requirements elicitation. These typically have an easy to use graphical or tabular notation.

A number of tools have been developed to support specific requirements elicitation approaches, however, so far the mainstream software engineering community has largely not adopted these. Examples include Objectiver for goal based modeling and ART-SCENE for scenario elicitation. Several tools have been developed with cognitive support for the requirements elicitation analyst in mind such as The Requirements Apprentice [52], ACME/PRIME [20], and AbstFinder [24]. Enhanced multimedia support for this process and distributed stakeholders was also identified and addressed by several tools including AMORE [64].

Groupware represents a very wide range of tools that has been applied to requirements elicitation. This covers everything from basic support tools such as discussion boards and video conferencing to generic meeting tools like mind mapping and idea capture software, all the way through to virtual collaboration environments specifically designed groups sessions such as developed by TeamWave [27] and GroupSystems [63].

2.6 Issues and Pitfalls of Requirements Elicitation

There has been little doubt in the past about the complexity and difficulty of requirements elicitation in most situations, but the question is: why is this still the case today? Part of the reason is the number of problems that may need to be addressed and overcome during the process of requirements elicitation. In general terms there are a large number of contextual, human, economic, and educational factors which effect and may inhibit effective requirements elicitation. For the sake of explanation we have categorized some of the more commonly occurring issues and pitfalls in requirements elicitation faced by both practitioners and researchers according to the aspect of requirements elicitation that they most relate to. These have been collected from a variety of sources in the literature [11, 28, 49] as well as from practical experience and observation.

Process and Project
Each project is unique and no two requirements elicitation situations are ever exactly the same. The process can be performed as part of a custom software development project, COTS selection activity, product line definition, and existing system maintenance operation. Projects can range all the way from simple bespoke web-based applications to large and complex enterprise information system product lines. The environment in which the process takes place can also vary greatly including the geographic distribution of stakeholders and the familiarity of users with software systems. Furthermore, the process of requirements elicitation is inherently imprecise as a result of the multiple variable factors, vast array of options and decision, and its communication and socially rich nature. Arguably the most common project based requirements elicitation issue is that the initial scope of the project has not been sufficiently defined, and as such is open to interpretations and assumptions. Projects like all functions of a business are subject to change and in-

fluence from internal or external factors including economic, political, social, legal, financial, psychological, historical and geographical.

Communication and Understanding
It is common that stakeholders have difficulty articulating their requirements. In some cases this may be a result of the analyst and stakeholders not sharing a common understanding of concepts and terms, or the analyst is unfamiliar with the problem. Often stakeholders will have difficulty seeing new ways of doing things, or do not know the consequences of their requirements and as such may not know what is feasible or realistic. Stakeholders may understand the problem domain very well, but are unfamiliar with the available solutions and the way in which their needs could be met. Alternatively, stakeholders sometimes suggest solutions rather than requirements. Things that are trivial or constantly repeated by stakeholders are often assumed and overlooked although they may not be apparent to the analyst and other stakeholders.

Quality of Requirements
The requirements elicited may not be feasible, cost-effective, or easy to validate. In other cases they can be vague, lacking specifics, and not represented in such a way as can be measured or tested. Furthermore, requirements may be defined at different and insufficient levels of detail. Because the process of elicitation is informal by nature, a set of requirements may be incorrect, incomplete, inconsistent, and not clear to all stakeholders. The context in which requirements are elicited and the process itself is inherently volatile. As the project develops and stakeholders become more familiar with the problem and solution domains, the goals of the system and the wants of the users are susceptible to change. In this way the process of elicitation can actually cause requirements volatility and therefore affect the quality of the requirements as a whole.

Stakeholders
Conflicts between stakeholders and their requirements are common and almost inevitable. Furthermore, stakeholders may not want to compromise or prioritize their requirements when these conflicts occur. Sometimes stakeholders do not actually know what they want or what their real needs are, and are therefore limited in their ability to support the investigation of possible solutions. Likewise, stakeholder can be adverse to the change a new system may introduce and therefore have varying levels of commitment and cooperation towards the project. Often stakeholders do not understand or appreciate the needs of the other stakeholders and might only be concerned with those factors that affect them directly. Like all humans, stakeholders can change their minds independently, or as a result of the elicitation process itself.

Analyst

Analysts may not be equipped with sufficient implementation expertise and experience to prepare for and perform effective requirements elicitation including appropriate technique selection and the identification of all requirements sources. This may be as a result of lack of education in terms of theory behind techniques and approaches, or the practice of using soft skills such as listening, communicating, and questioning. Analyst from traditional software engineering backgrounds may sometimes focus on the solution not the problem, and reply on only those techniques they are familiar with for all situations. It is also the case that many analysts do not employ any structured or rigorous processes within software development projects to address requirements elicitation.

Research

It is arguable that many of the available techniques are not sufficiently useful or practical, and the transfer of knowledge required to introduce these methods and approaches to industry is too difficult. In fact, the quantity of detailed process guidelines with appropriate tool support is very limited, especially with respect to technique selection and addressing the contextual factors in different situations. This can largely be attributed to the absence of sufficient empirical research, case studies and experience reports on the specific topic of requirements elicitation in the literature. Furthermore, there are no agreed metrics by which to measure the performance of the requirements elicitation process within a software development project.

Practice

In general terms there is still a lack of sufficient awareness, understanding, and expertise in requirements elicitation practice. Large gaps exist between requirements elicitation theory and practice, as well as novice and expert analysts. The result of which is that many are still making the same mistakes time and time again with respect to requirements elicitation and do not acknowledge the real issues and their subsequent effects. It is unfortunate that in many cases organizations and particularly customers are resistant to investing the appropriate time and effort into the process despite an increased need for project success.

2.7 Trends and Challenges in Requirements Elicitation

Over the years a number of important trends and challenges have emerged within the field of requirements elicitation in research and practice although not necessarily the same for both. For that reason we have divided the following section into four areas, namely (1) trends in research, (2) trends in practice, (3) challenges in research, and (4) challenges in practice. These trends and challenges show how the field has progressed and changed, and what still needs to be done to further evolve this process in research and practice.

2.7.1 Trends in Requirements Elicitation Research

As the field of RE began to develop, researchers and practitioners identified that the elicitation of requirements for software-based systems had some unique and complicated characteristics, and therefore needed to be addressed as a new and separate topic from traditional knowledge acquisition [17, 23]. As a result, and for a time, attention was directed to the development of specific tools and techniques to support this process in the hope of reducing its complexity and resolving some of the key challenges in its execution [52, 20]. In the mid to late 1990s the focus of requirements elicitation research however was strongly on developing structured and rigorous manual approaches based on new and different paradigms as opposed to tools. These included those based on goals [16], scenarios [51], viewpoints [59], and domain knowledge [61], which continues to be used today.

Recently the development of much needed support for this process has once again been focused on creating tools, but this time for the implementation of those newly developed manual approaches, in addition to adapting generic applications to requirements elicitation such as template-driven documentation generation and assistive groupware applications. This has evolved as a result of the continuing need for improvement and the enduring complexity of the process. Furthermore, new approaches to requirements elicitation are being developed to support current and specific topics in software engineering such as agent and aspect oriented methodologies, web based systems, and product lines. Agile methods continue to gain interest and support, and subsequently work has been directed to investigating how the requirements elicitation process can be effectively implemented with these techniques whilst still maintaining the fundamental principles.

2.7.2 Trends in Requirements Elicitation Practice

Unfortunately, RE is not universally practiced as a distinct phase in software development; however its adoption has been on the steady increase particularly over the past decade or so. Many software organizations have discovered that it is in their best interests and the interests of their customers to invest the required time and effort into this phase by implementing a sufficient degree of structure and rigor to the process. However, for the most part this is only true for the larger and more technically mature organizations.

Overall the majority of analysts assigned the responsibility of eliciting requirements for software systems still use generic and traditional techniques such as interviews and group meetings, and only attempt to use others that they are familiar and comfortable with regardless of the circumstances. In recent times, however, approaches that have been developed specifically for requirements elicitation, such as JAD, Use Cases, Goal and Scenario based approaches, have grown in popularity and usage at least among experienced practitioners. The adoption of Agile Methods and modeling approaches such as UML continues to grow with widespread acceptance of use case diagrams and descriptions. The concept of just enough requirements engineering and subsequently elicitation as proposed by

Davis [18] has been readily accepted by industry and will hopefully lead to the adoption of robust requirements elicitation without unnecessarily committing to expensive and overly detailed processes.

2.7.3 Challenges in Requirements Elicitation Research

One of the key challenges for researchers remains the development of ways to reduce the infamous gap [57] between research and practice in terms of awareness, acceptance, and adoption. This can only be achieved by establishing the results in practice and making the approaches more attractive, thereby providing the proof and motivation for practitioners to use them. In order to make this happen, researchers need to reduce the complexity of approaches and the expertise required to integrate them into practice. Packaging them into manageable and flexible components with appropriate tool support can facilitate this process.

It is important to work towards reducing the gap between experts and novices through practical roadmaps, frameworks, and guidelines that can be easily taught to students and novices. Finding more efficient and effective ways to transfer expert knowledge is certainly part of this effort. Furthermore, educators need to adequately address the wide range of skills and expertise required to produce effective requirements engineers, and provide authentic learning environments for gaining realistic experiences. Overall research needs to continue to develop ways of improving the process and quality of requirements elicitation, and quantifying its success. Only through application to practice can the true value of new techniques, approaches, and tools be determined.

2.7.4 Challenges in Requirements Elicitation Practice

Industry, like academia, must also look for ways to reduce the gap between experts and novices by investing time and effort in education on what is currently available, and developing new procedures and process for the transfer of knowledge from senior analyst to juniors. Knowing when and which techniques, approaches and tools to use combined with the knowledge of how, will ultimately improve the chances of customer satisfaction and project success.

Practitioners need to be able to allocate sufficient time and resources to requirements elicitation. This can be partly achieved by educating customers of the value of being diligent in the process, and presenting the risks of not doing so. It is also important that stakeholders themselves understand the benefits and are committed to process. Organizations in practice need to be more open to accepting the research results, and prepared to join forces, pool resources, and share information to collaboratively produce improved methods of working, and better results for customers. Industry should be more prepared to address the social and organizational factors involved in requirements elicitation, and focus on building software systems that achieve both the business goals and satisfy the users' needs by using the appropriate techniques.

2.8 Future Directions in Requirements Elicitation Research

Despite the successes and progress to date, many important topics remain open for investigation with respect to providing appropriate techniques, approaches, and tools for requirements elicitation, including specific assistance for novice analysts, cognitive support through intelligent tools, and methods that involve direct interaction with stakeholders. Below we have listed some of the potential requirements elicitation research areas not completely resolved to date that we believe deserve appropriate attention in the coming years:

- Reducing the gap between the theory and practice, and experts and novices
- Increasing the awareness and education of analysts and stakeholders in industry
- Developing guidelines for technique selection and managing the impact of factors on the process
- Investigating ways of collecting and reusing knowledge about requirements elicitation
- Integration and use of new technologies including web and agent based architectures into the next generation of support tools
- Producing and publishing case studies and industrial experience reports on how requirements elicitation contributed to successes and failures of projects
- Exploring how requirements elicitation activities relates to new and developing fields of software engineering such as agent based systems, agile development methodologies, and web systems

More collaboration is still required between research and practice in order to fully evaluate the existing approaches, and develop new ones for emerging problems. Many of the best results in requirements elicitation research achieved so far have come from this type of joint work with industry. Awareness and education remain two of the biggest issues faced for those working in requirements elicitation. Students need to be given practical experience as well as a sound theoretical foundation. Practitioners need to be equipped with a variety of techniques, approaches, and tools to use where appropriate depending on what is best suited to the situation. Customers need to understand the importance of the process, believe in it, and support the efforts involved in doing it right.

2.9 Summary

The process of requirements elicitation, including the selection of which techniques, approach, or tool to use when eliciting requirements, is dependant on a large number of factors including the type of system being developed, the stage of the project, and the application domain to name only a few. Because of the relative strengths and weaknesses of the available methods and the type of information they provide, the reality is that in almost all projects a combination of several different techniques will be necessary to achieve a successful outcome. This is supported by the fact that many of the techniques are intended to be used in conjunction with each other, and have complementary attributes as discussed throughout the chapter. Most of the approaches require a significant level of skill and expertise from the analyst to use effectively. However, from the range of existing techniques, variations of interviews, group workshops, observation, goals, and scenarios are still the most widely used and successful in practice. Despite attempts to automate parts of the process and develop frameworks and guidelines, requirements elicitation still remains more of an art than a science.

References

1. Agarwal R, Tanniru, MR (1990) Knowledge acquisition using structured interviewing: An empirical investigation. Journal of Management Information Systems, 7(1): 123–140
2. Akao Y (1995) Quality function deployment: Integrating customer requirements into product design. Productivity press: Cambridge, MA
3. Alexander IF, Stevens R (2002) Writing better requirements. Addison Wesley, Great Britain
4. Ball LJ, Ormerod TC (2000) Putting ethnography to work: The case for a cognitive ethnography of design. International Journal of Human–Computer Studies, 53(1): 147–168
5. Beck K, Cunningham W (1989) A laboratory for teaching object-oriented thinking. In: Proceedings of the conference on object-oriented programming systems languages and applications, October 1-6, New Orleans, LA, pp. 1–6
6. Beyer HR, Holtzblatt K (1995) Apprenticing with the customer. Communications of the ACM, 38(5): 45–52
7. Bostrum RP (1989) Successful application of communication techniques to improve the systems development process. Information and Management, 16(5): 279–295
8. Bubenko JA, Jr., Wangler B (1993) Objectives driven capture of business rules and of information systems requirements. In: Proceedings of the international conference on systems, man and cybernetics, October 17-20, Le Touquet, France, pp. 670–677
9. Carlshamre P, Karlsson J (1996) A usability-oriented approach to requirements engineering. In: Proceedings of the 2nd International conference on Requirements Engineer-ing, April 15-18, Colorado Springs, CO, pp. 145–152
10. Checkland P, Scholes J (1990) Soft systems methodology in action. John Wiley & Sons: New York, NY
11. Christel MG, Kang KC (1992) Issues in requirements elicitation. Carnegie Mellon University Technical report, CMU/SEI-92-TR-012
12. Cockburn A (2001) Writing effective use cases. Addison Wesley: Reading, MA
13. Constantine L, Lockwood LAD (1999) Software for use: A practical guide to the models and methods of usage-centered design. Addison Wesley: Reading, MA
14. Coulin C, Zowghi D (2004) Requirements elicitation for complex systems: Theory and practice. In: Requirements Engineering for Socio-Technical Systems, Mate JL, Silva A (Eds.), Idea Group: USA
15. CREWS, http://sunsite.informatik.rwth-aachen.de/CREWS/, Accessed 15 November 2004

16. Dardenne A, van Lamsweerde A, Fickas S (1993) Goal-directed requirements acquisition. Science of Computer Programming, 20(1-2): 3–50
17. Davis AM (1994) Software requirements: Analysis and specification. Prentice Hall: New Jersey
18. Davis AM (2004) Just enough requirements management: Where marketing and development meet. Dorset House: New York
19. DeMarco T, Plauger PJ (1979) Structured analysis and system specification. Prentice Hall, New York, NY
20. Feblowitz M, Greenspan S, Reubenstein H, Walford R (1996) ACME/PRIME: Requirements acquisition for process-driven systems. In: Proceedings of the 8th International workshop on software specification and design, March 22–23, Paderborn, Germany, pp. 36–45
21. Foddy W (1994) Constructing questions for interviews and questionnaires. Cambridge University Press, Cambridge
22. Gause DC, Weinberg GM (1989) Exploring requirements: Quality before design. Dorset House, New York
23. Goguen JA, Linde C (1993) Techniques for requirements elicitation. In: Proceedings of the IEEE International symposium on Requirements Engineering, January 4-6, San Diego, CA, pp. 152–164
24. Goldin L, Berry DM (1994) AbstFinder: A prototype natural language text abstraction finder for use in requirements elicitation. Automated Software Engineering 4 (4): 375–412
25. Gottesdiener E (2002) Requirements by collaboration. Addison Wesley: Boston, MA
26. Haumer P, Pohl K, Weidenhaupt K (1998) Requirements elicitation and validation with real world scenes. IEEE transactions on Software Engineering, 24 (12): 1036–1054
27. Herela D, Greenberg S (1998) Using a groupware space for distributed requirements engineering. In: Proceedings of the 7th workshop on enabling technologies: Infrastructure for collaborative enterprises, June 17-19, Stanford, CA, pp. 57–62
28. Hickey AM, Davis AM (2002) The role of requirements elicitation techniques in achieving software quality. In: Proceedings of the 8th International workshop of requirements engineering: Foundation for software quality, September 9-10, Essen, Germany
29. Hickey AM, Davis AM (2003) Elicitation technique selection: How do experts do it? In: Proceedings of the 11th IEEE International requirements engineering conference, Sep-tember 8-12, Monterey Bay, CA, pp. 169–178
30. Hinkle D (1965) The change of personal constructs from the viewpoint of a theory of implications. Doctoral Dissertation, Ohio State University, USA
31. Hofmann HF, Lehner F, (2001) Requirements engineering as a success factor in software projects. IEEE Software, 18 (4): 58–66
32. Holtzblatt K, Beyer HR (1995) Requirements gathering: The human factor. Communications of ACM, 38 (5): 30–32
33. IEEE (1998) IEEE Std 830-1998 Software Requirements Specification, The Institute of Electrical and Electronics Engineers, Inc. 345 East 47th Street, New York, NY 10017–2394, USA
34. Jackson M (1995) The world and the machine. In: Proceedings of the 17th IEEE International conference on software engineering, April 24-28, Seattle, WA, pp. 283–292

35. Jackson M (2000) Problem frames: Analyzing and structuring software development problems. Addison Wesley: Boston, MA

36. Jones C (1996) Applied software measurement: Assuring productivity and quality. McGraw-Hill: New York

37. Kaufman LD, Thebaut S, Interrante MF (1989) System modeling for scenario-based requirements engineering. SERC Technical Report, SERC-TR-33-F

38. Kelly G (1955) The psychology of personal constructs, Norton, New York

39. Kotonya G, Sommerville I (1998) Requirements engineering: Processes and techniques, John Wiley & Sons, Great Britain

40. Krueger RA (1994) Focus groups: A practical guide for applied research, Sage, Thousand Oaks, CA

41. Loucopoulos P, Karakostas V (1995) Systems requirements engineering, McGraw-Hill: London

42. Macaulay LA (1993) Requirements as a cooperative activity. In: Proceedings of the IEEE Symposium on Requirements Engineering, January 4–6, San Diego, CA, pp. 174–181

43. Maiden N, Gizikis A, Robertson S, (2004) Provoking creativity: Imagine what your requirements could be like. IEEE Software, 21(5): 68–75

44. Martin RC (2003) Agile software development: Principles, patterns and practices, Prentice Hall: Upper Saddle River

45. McGraw KL, Harbison-Briggs K (1989) Knowledge acquisition: Principles and guidelines, Prentice Hall: New Jersey

46. Nielsen J, Clemmensen T, Yssing C (2002) Getting access to what goes on in people's heads: Reflections on the think-aloud technique. In: Proceedings of the 2nd Nordic Con-ference on Human-Computer Interaction, October 19–23, Aarhus, Denmark, pp. 101–110

47. Nuseibeh B, Finkelstein A, Kramer J (1996) Method engineering for multi-perspective software development. Information and Software Technology Journal, 38(4): 267–274

48. Nuseibeh B, Easterbrook S (2000) Requirements engineering: A roadmap. In: Proceedings of the conference on the future of software engineering, June 4-11, Limerick, Ireland, pp. 35–46

49. OPEN Process Framework, http://www.donald-firesmith.com/, Accessed 15 November 2004

50. Osborn AF (1979) Applied imagination. Charles Scribner's Sons: New York

51. Potts C, Takahashi K, Anton AI (1994) Inquiry-based requirements analysis. IEEE Software, 11 (2): 21–32

52. Reubenstein H, Waters R (1991) The requirements apprentice: Automated assistance for requirements acquisition. IEEE Transactions on Software Engineering, 17(3): 226–240

53. Richardson J, Ormerod TC, Shepherd A (1998) The role of task analysis in capturing requirements for interface design. Interacting with Computers, 9(4): 367–384

54. Robertson S, Robertson J (1999) Mastering the requirements process, Addison Wesley: Great Britain

55. Rolland C, Souveyet C, Ben Achour C (1998) Guiding goal modeling using scenarios. IEEE Transactions on Software Engineering, 24(12): 1055–1071

56. Scenario Plus, http://www.scenarioplus.org.uk/, Accessed 15 November 2004

57. Siddiqi J, Shekaran C (1996) Requirements engineering: The emerging wisdom. IEEE Software, 13(2): 15–19
58. Sommerville I, Sawyer P (1997) Requirements engineering: A good practice guide, John Wiley & Sons, Great Britain
59. Sommerville I, Sawyer P, Viller S (1998) Viewpoints for requirements elicitation: A practical approach. In: Proceedings of the IEEE International Conference on Requirements Engineering, April 6-10, Colorado Springs, CO, pp. 74–81
60. Sommerville I (2001) Software engineering. 6th edition, Addison Wesley, USA
61. Sutcliffe A, Maiden N (1998) The domain theory for requirements engineering. IEEE Transactions on Software Engineering, 24(3): 174–196
62. Taylor-Cummings A (1998) Bridging the user-IS gap: A study of major systems projects. Journal of Information Technology, 13(1): 29–54
63. Weatherall A (1998) Creative problem solving using Group Systems. In: Proceedings of the 31st Hawaii International Conference on System Sciences, January 6-9, Hawaii, 1, pp. 588–595
64. Wood D, Christel M, Stevens SM (1994) A multimedia approach to requirements capture and modeling. In: Proceedings of the 1st International Conference on Requirements Engineering, April 18-22, Colorado Springs, CO, pp. 53–56
65. Wood J, Silver D (1995) Joint application development. John Wiley & Sons, New York
66. Yourdon E (1989) Modern structured analysis. Prentice Hall, Englewood Cliffs, NJ
67. Yu ESK (1997) Towards modeling and reasoning support for early-phase requirements Engineering. In: Proceedings of the 3rd IEEE International Symposium on Requirements Engineering, January 5-8, Washington, D.C, pp. 226–235
68. Zave P, Jackson M (1997) Four dark corners of requirements engineering. ACM Transactions on Software Engineering and Methodology, 6(1): 1–30
69. Zowghi D (1999) A logic-based framework for the management of changing software requirements. Doctoral Dissertation, Macquarie University, Australia

Author Biography

Didar Zowghi is Associate Professor of Software Engineering and the Director of Requirements Engineering Research Laboratory in the Faculty of Information Technology at University of Technology, Sydney. She holds a Bachelor of Science (Hons) and a Masters of Science in Computer Science, and PhD in Software Engineering. She serves on the program committee of many national and international conferences, in particular the IEEE International Conferences on Requirements Engineering since 1998. She is the regional editor (and the editor of the Viewpoints column) of the International Requirements Engineering Journal and the associate editor of the Journal of Research and Practice in Information Technology (JRPIT). She has published extensively on many aspects of Requirements Engineering.

Chad Coulin is a PhD candidate and member of the Requirements Engineering research group in the Faculty of Information Technology at the University of Technology, Sydney. He holds a Bachelors of Engineering (Hons.) in Microelectronics, and is currently working on the development of new and innovative methods to support requirements elicitation for software-based systems. His other research interests include Computer Supported Cooperative Work (CSCW) and the development of interactive and intelligent Computer Assisted Software Engineering (CASE) tools. Previously he has worked as a project and product manager in the USA and Europe developing and implementing large-scale industrial software systems.

3 Specification of Requirements Models

Ricardo J. Machado, Isabel Ramos and João M. Fernandes

Abstract: The main aim of this chapter is to present and discuss a set of modeling and specification techniques, in what concerns their ontology and support in the requirements representation of computer-based systems. A systematic classification of meta-models, also called models of computation, is presented. This topic is highly relevant since it supports the definition of sound specification methodologies in relation to the semantic definition of the modeling views to adopt for a given system. The usage and applicability of Unified Modeling Language (UML) diagrams is also related to their corresponding meta-models. A set of desirable characteristics for the specification methodologies is presented and justified to allow system designers and requirements engineers to more consciously define or choose a particular specification methodology. A heuristic-based approach to support the transformation of user into system requirements is suggested, with some graphical examples in UML notation.

Keywords: Modeling, Specification, Meta-Models, Requirements, Model transformation.

3.1 Introduction

Computer-based systems integrate, as information processing sub-systems, one or more computing systems able to capture, store, process, transfer, present and manage information. Within the design of computer-based systems, this justifies the need for the incorporation of several technological entities: (1) software, firmware, and (analog and digital) hardware, to process and store information; (2) communication network services to transport information; (3) sensors and actuators to interact with the physical environment; and (4) human-machine interfaces to exchange information with human operators. Although computer-based systems can be strictly based on computer technologies, they normally include other entities such as human operators, organizational subsystems, documentation, and manuals.

Since computer-based systems are, by nature, heterogeneous, modeling and specifying their requirements demands a holistic approach.

A requirement can be defined as "something that a client needs." From the point of view of the system designer or the requirements engineer, a requirement could also be defined as "something that must be designed." The IEEE 610 standard [21] defines a requirement as: (1) a condition or capability needed by a user to solve a problem or achieve an objective; (2) a condition or capability that must be met or possessed by a system or system component to satisfy a contract, standard, specification or other formally imposed documents; (3) a documented representation of a condition or capability as in (1) or (2).

Clients and developers (system designers and requirements engineers) have, naturally, different points of view towards requirements, which imply that requirements can be divided into two different categories: user and system requirements.

User requirements result directly from the requirements elicitation task (see Chap. 2 for further details on requirements elicitation techniques), as an effort to understand the clients' needs. They are, typically, described in natural language and with informal diagrams, at a relatively low level of detail. User requirements are focused in the problem domain and are the main communication medium between the clients and the developers, at the analysis phase. System requirements result from the developers' efforts to organize the user requirements at the solution domain. They, typically, comprise abstract models of the system, at a relatively high level of detail, and constitute the first system representation to be used at the beginning of the design phase. The correct derivation of system requirements from user requirements is an important objective because it assures that the design phase is based on the effective clients' needs. This also guarantees that no misjudgment is arbitrarily introduced by the developers during the process of system requirements specification.

The aim of this chapter is to present and discuss a set of modeling and specification techniques, in what concerns their ontology and support in the requirements representation of computer-based systems. This chapter is not intended to be used as an exhaustive survey and summary of existing modeling approaches. It provides some guidelines to system designers and requirements engineers so that they select the modeling approach that best fits their problems. The intended audience of this chapter is system designers and requirements engineers who wish to expand their background knowledge on meta-modeling and improve their development strategy options.

Section 3.2 discusses the differences between the modeling and the specification activities. In this chapter, specification is only related to models, and not to other possible forms. Sect. 3.3 presents a systematic classification of meta-models as a key issue for the semantic definition of the modeling views to adopt for a given system. Some authors use the term "modeling techniques", instead of "meta-models". Sect. 3.4 describes a set of desirable characteristics for specification methodologies, so that system designers and requirements engineers can more consciously define or choose a particular specification methodology. Sect. 3.5 briefly describes a heuristic based approach to support the transformation of user into system requirements. This section shows that model continuity is a key issue and highlights the importance of having a well defined process to relate, map and transform requirements models.

3.2 Modeling vs. Specification

The first decision of developers, when they want to specify a system, is to select which part of the system they wish to take into account. The selection of that part defines the system view, i.e., the system perspective that needs to be represented

[5]. This view has a merely conceptual existence in the human mind, and, according to an unstructured and informal representation, at least at the conscious level of the developers.

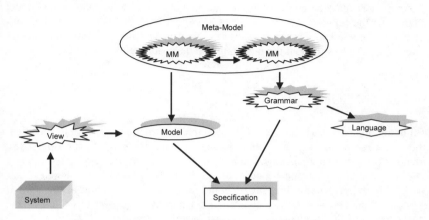

Fig. 3.1 Specification of systems

The formalization of the system view occurs when it originates a model. This model consists in a representation, still conceptual, of the view of the system, according to a particular meta-model. This meta-model corresponds to a set of (functional or structural) composition elements and of composition rules that permits to build a model representing the system view. This model serves the purpose of explaining and sharing the conceptual view held in the human mind. In this way, developers make their view available to the judgment of others and to further reformulation.

The accuracy of a particular modeling approach depends on its capability to select the meta-model that semantically supports the characteristics of the system to be modeled. The selected meta-model defines the semantic limits of the system representation at the model level. Meta-models characterization is of central importance due to its impact on the systems modeling accuracy.

Although the system model is already the result of a formalization effort of the system view, its existence is still at the conceptual level. To become "tangible" it must be transformed into a concrete representation called "specification", i.e., a real representation of the system model in a given language [41]. The conceptual model adopted in the definition of the language corresponds to the language meta-model, which allows the description of the system model by means of a graphical, textual or other kind of representation; see Fig. 3.1.

According to the terminology used here, the difference between modeling and specification, activities that are often misunderstood, is now clearer. Modeling corresponds to the activity of selecting a meta-model to formalize, at the conceptual level, a given system view, while specification is related to the adoption of a language to make a system model tangible. Obtaining a specification that adequately represents the system depends both on the characteristics of the selected meta-model for the modeling activity and on the meta-model of the chosen representation language. Thus, to avoid semantic mismatches, the two adopted meta-models must be compatible. Whenever possible, the language meta-model should be the same as the one used in the system modeling activity. In this context, it becomes clear that the characterization of meta-models is a fundamental issue for accomplishing both the modeling and the specification activities.

3.3 Meta-Models Categories

Although the two meta-models involved in the construction of a system specification may not be exactly the same, one can assume, for simplification purposes, that the representation language has been consciously selected taking into account the characteristics of its meta-model (which is not always true).

Ideally, representation languages should allow the specification of the desired system characteristics, in a non ambiguous way. This is possible, if the meta-model of the language is: (1) formal (accurate, rigorous), to avoid ambiguities in the interpretation of the system representation; (2) complete, to allow the construction of a representation that totally describes the system view. These are not absolute properties, since they depend on the particular system to be specified. In [17], Gajski *et al.* organize the most common meta-models into five distinct groups. A brief description of each meta-model category is presented next.

3.3.1 State Oriented Meta-Models

State oriented meta-models allow modeling a system as a set of states and a set of transitions. The transitions between states evolve according to some external stimulus. These meta-models are adequate to model systems in which temporal behavior is the most important aspect to be captured. Finite state machines (FSMs), finite state machines with data paths (FSMDs), StateCharts and Petri nets are examples of state oriented meta-models.

FSMs [32], also known as "finite state automata", correspond to the most used meta-model in the description of control systems, since the temporal behavior of these systems is naturally represented in the form of states and transitions between states. The two basic alternatives to construct state machines (Mealy or Moore) differ only in the output function. On Mealy machines the output function depends both on the state and the inputs, while on Moore machines the output function depends only on states. Graphical diagrams that represent state machines are usually called "state transition diagrams" (STDs).

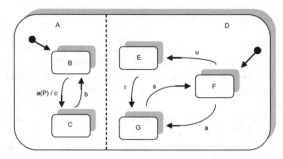

Fig. 3.2 Example of a StateChart

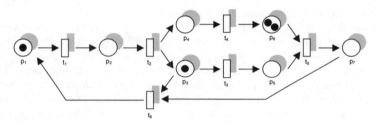

Fig. 3.3 Example of a Petri net

FSMDs [16] are an evolution of FSMs to solve, in a simple way, the problem of state explosion. FSMDs extend FSMs by using integer or floating variables to replace thousands of states in the corresponding FSM. While FSMs can only represent control systems, FSMDs are also able to represent computing systems. These meta-models are not able to capture complex behaviors, since they lack the ability to deal with concurrency and hierarchy.

HCFSMs are another FSM extension, since they support the representation of concurrency and allow the construction of hierarchical models. HCFSMs are relatively limited in dealing with complex data structures. The meta-model behind HCFSMs is the same as Harel's StateCharts graphical representation language [18]; see Fig. 3.2. UML's state diagrams have their origins in Harel's StateCharts.

Petri nets [34, 35] constitute another state oriented meta-model. Petri nets are appropriate to model concurrent actions, since they can deal with parallelism, synchronization, resource sharing and memorization; see Fig. 3.3. Petri nets enclose a solid mathematical base, enabling models to be formally analyzed. Additionally, Petri nets are one of the meta-models that offer more extensions, allowing an enormous variety of utilizations, from system specification and performance analysis to system synthesis and implementation. Several Petri net extensions include powerful semantic mechanisms, such as hierarchical approaches and object orientation, allowing to cope with complex system modeling [24, 31]. There are some languages that directly support some of the existing Petri net extensions [25, 28].

3.3.2 Activity Oriented Meta-Models

Activity oriented meta-models allow modeling a system as a set of activities related by data or by execution dependencies. These meta-models are well suited to model systems where data are affected by a sequence of transformations at a constant rate. Data flow diagrams (DFDs) and flowcharts are two examples of activity oriented meta-models.

A DFD [10], also known as a "data flow graph" (DFG), consists in a set of interconnected activities or processes with arcs representing the data flow among them. DFDs support hierarchy, since each activity can be further detailed by another DFD. DFDs can not express temporal behavior, or action control. UML does not have any kind of diagram based on this meta-model [12]. Neither UML's use case diagrams nor UML's activity diagrams are DFDs, although some developers argue that there are some graphical resemblances.

Flowcharts [9], also known as "control flow graphs" (CFGs), model control flow among activities. While in FSMs transitions are activated by external events, in flowcharts transitions are activated as soon as an activity is complete. This meta-model is suitable for modeling systems with well defined activities and that do not depend on external stimulus, allowing the representation of sequences of activities related by control flow. UML's activity diagrams are essentially based on this meta-model. However, fork and join primitives of activity diagrams are inspired by Petri net transitions.

3.3.3 Structure Oriented Meta-Models

Structure oriented meta-models allow the description of system physical modules and their interconnections. These meta-models are dedicated to the characterization of the physical composition of a system, instead of its functionality. Block diagrams, also called "component-connectivity diagrams" (CCDs), are the most frequently used structure oriented meta-model. UML's deployment and component diagrams are based on this meta-model.

3.3.4 Data Oriented Meta-Models

Data oriented meta-models allow modeling a system as a collection of data related by some kind of attribute. These meta-models dedicate more importance to the organization of data than to the system functionality. UML does not have any kind of diagram exclusively based on these meta-models, since it favors object oriented systems and does not promote the usage of diagrams mainly dedicated to data modeling. Nevertheless, it is possible to argue that UML's class diagrams are partially data oriented meta-models.

Data oriented meta-models are, typically, used within methodologies based on the traditional structure analysis and design techniques [46]. Entity relationship diagrams (ERDs) and Jackson's structured diagrams (JSDs) are two examples of data oriented meta-models. ERDs [6] describe a system as a collection of entities and the existing relationships among them. Each entity corresponds to a unique type of data with one or more specific attributes. This meta-model is useful when developers want to organize complex relationships between different data types. ERDs cannot model functional or temporal characteristics.

JSDs [42] model the structure of each data type, through subtype decomposition. Decomposition is performed in a tree structure in which the leaves correspond to the basic data types and the other nodes to the composite data, obtained through various operations such as composition (AND), selection (OR), and iteration (*). While ERDs are suitable to model different data entities with complex inter-relations, JSDs are adequate to model complex data structures. The limitations of JSDs are similar to the ones referred for ERDs.

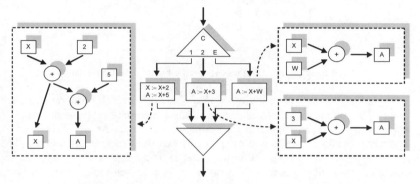

Fig. 3.4 Example of a control/data flow graph

3.3.5 Heterogeneous Meta-Models

Heterogeneous meta-models allow the usage, in the same system representation, of several characteristics from different meta-models, namely the four categories described before. These meta-models are a good solution when relatively complex systems must be modeled. Control/data flow graphs (CDFGs), object process diagrams (OPDs) and program state machines (PSMs) are examples of heterogeneous meta-models.

CDFGs [16] embody DFDs (to model data flow between system activities) and flowcharts (to impose the sequence of DFDs execution). CDFGs succeed in modeling, in a single representation, data dependencies and system control sequence, simultaneously benefiting from DFDs and flowcharts advantages; see Fig. 3.4.

Within the Object Process Methodology (OPM), the combined usage of objects and processes is recommended [11]. An OPD can include both processes and objects, which are viewed as complementary entities that together describe the structure and behavior of the system. Objects are persistent entities and processes transform the objects by generating, consuming or affecting them. In addition, states are also integrated in OPDs to describe the objects.

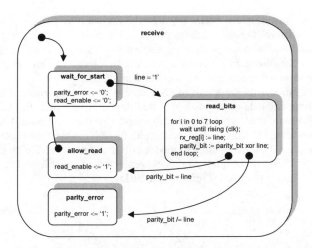

Fig. 3.5 Example of a PSM model specified in the SpecCharts language

PSMs [33] allow the integration of HCFSMs with a textual programming language. This meta-model basically consists in a hierarchy of program states, in which each state represents a distinct computation mode. At any instant, only a subset of the program states is simultaneously executing their computations. PSMs are more powerful than HCFSMs to model systems that possess complex data structures, since they are able to incorporate, in a unique model, data, activities and states. HCFSMs and programming languages delimit the two opposite extremes of using PSMs. A program may be considered a PSM with only one specified state, and a HCFSM may be viewed as a PSM in which none of their states possess descriptions in the programming language. SpecCharts is a representation language for the PSM meta-model; see Fig. 3.5.

If PSMs are considered a heterogeneous meta-model, it is also acceptable to consider programming languages as a meta-model themselves. There exits a considerable number of developers that make use of programming languages to specify systems, usually, their behavior and data structures. This approach to specification imposes a considerable amount of design and implementation decisions at the analysis phase, which can have an undesired effect on the specifications.

Programming languages allow the modeling of data structures, activities and control. The modeling "style" imposed by a particular programming language is called paradigm in computer science terminology. The meta-model behind a programming language is its paradigm and not the language itself. Programming languages should be considered representation languages at the implementation level.

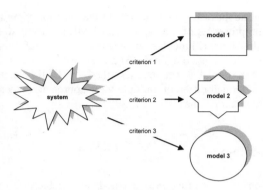

Fig. 3.6 The multiple view approach

Historically, there are two different meta-models (paradigms) for programming languages: imperative and declarative. The imperative paradigm (where C and Pascal are included) follows von Neumann's computational model, since it adopts the sequential execution of the computing primitives. The declarative paradigm (where Lisp and Prolog are included) does not define an explicit order of execution of the primitives, focusing in defining the target of computation, through functions and logic rules declaration. More recently, the object oriented paradigm has emerged, which is based on the heterogeneous object oriented meta-model. Object oriented meta-models evolved from data oriented meta-models, being characterized by its tendency in describing the system as a collection of cooperating objects. Each object consists in a data collection and in operations to transform its data. This meta-model supports data abstraction (information hiding), through encapsulation of data in each object, making data invisible to other objects. They can easily represent concurrency, since each object coexists with the others and can potentially execute its tasks in parallel with tasks in other objects.

3.3.6 Multiple-View Approach

With the increasing complexity of systems, the use of different meta-models to represent different kinds of system characteristics is becoming a common practice. A system is modeled by a set of different models, each one corresponding to a different view of the system, devoted to represent a well delimited set of the system characteristics, see Fig. 3.6, where the criteria shown are related to the characteristics each view is intended to capture. This multiple view approach does not correspond to the usage of a heterogeneous meta-model, since the information in different views may not be explicitly related through common information structures. On the contrary, in a heterogeneous meta-model the different views must hold common information structures within a unique integrated representation. UML notation permits the adoption of multiple view approaches.

Multiple view modeling can adopt orthogonal views: (1) the function view is responsible for representing the processes of the system and UML's activity diagrams can be used to support this view; (2) the data view defines system information, that can be supported by UML's class diagrams; (3) the control view characterizes the system dynamic behavior that can be described by UML's state diagrams. Several authors have defined different multiple view approaches where views are vehicles for separation of concerns [1, 14, 27, 29].

3.4 Specification Methodology

Formal description, comparison, and construction of methods and techniques for systems development are the main goals of the method engineering community [19]. Meta-models of the development process are also called "meta-process models" and meta-models of the development products, or deliverables, are called 'meta-data models' (in this chapter we call these just "meta-models"). Some well known approaches to the method engineering are: ISO/IEC 12207 [22], OPEN [15] and PIE [8].

The act of defining our own specification methodology is called "situational method engineering" [44] and it is in this context that it is important to take into consideration the following three key issues [39]: specification language, complexity control, and model continuity.

3.4.1 Specification Language

Specification languages must allow the representation of a particular system view, without ambiguities. This is the main purpose of specification languages, and their relation with the meta-models has already been discussed. Additionally, specification languages must offer support for analyzing and reasoning about the specification. The available analysis mechanisms depend on the specification language itself. However, there are essentially two different kinds of mechanisms: formal analysis and specification execution. Formal analysis is important to verify if a specification is incoherent, but its existence is only possible if the specification language owns a solid mathematical base. Executable specifications allow an early testing of system prototypes for requirements validation, rendering a more robust and understandable specification process.

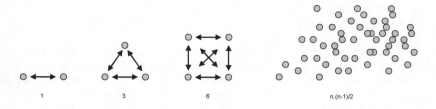

Fig. 3.7 Complexity

3.4.2 Complexity Control

The control of the complexity of the specification process can be carried out within two different dimensions: representational complexity and development complexity. The complexity of a system does not only depend on the cardinality of its parts, but mainly on the way its parts interact among them; see Fig. 3.7, where systems are represented by circles and interactions by arrows.

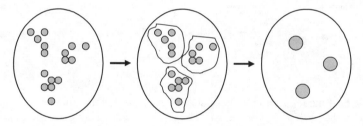

Fig. 3.8 Abstraction levels

The first dimension of complexity control refers to the representational complexity. It essentially depends on the specification language and, if correctly managed, permits concise and comprehensible specifications to be obtained. Complexity control at the representation level can be achieved by making use of three different techniques: hierarchy, orthogonality, and representation scheme. Developers must be able to decide the appropriate abstraction level to be used. Typically, the adoption of higher levels of abstraction improves the understanding of the system as a whole, while details are being hidden.Model hierarchization corresponds to grouping similar (structural or behavioral) system parts together into a new element that represents the group; see Fig. 3.8. Model orthogonalization consists in describing a set of system behaviors independently from each other (whenever possible). In what concerns the representation scheme, complexity control effort can decide either for textual representations or for graphical representations. Graphical representation schemes imply visual formalisms where both syntactic and semantic interpretations are assigned to graphical entities. Graphical approaches are usually easier to understand than textual ones and thus improve the readability and the understandability of system view. UML adopts a graphical approach.

The second dimension of complexity control (development complexity) refers to the control of the evolution of the system specification from initial conceptualization of requirements. This control can be accomplished by deferring certain details to the next phases of system development and by adopting different specification evolutions throughout the specification process (top-down, bottom-up or middle-out).

3.4.3 Model Continuity

Models obtained in the initial phases of the development must be persistent, avoiding their rewriting at each step. To support design and implementation methodologies, this model continuity concern must assure conformity in models evolution throughout the whole development process. This is possible by allowing models to be refined through the inclusion of new behavioral and structural attributes acquired along the design and implementation phases; see Fig. 3.9.

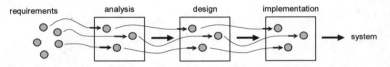

Fig. 3.9 Model continuity

The first model must be independent of implementation, allowing developers to focus in the system behavioral modeling. When constructing the first specification, design or implementation decisions and unnecessary restrictions should be avoid. Within a full model continuity approach, it is desirable that the automatic synthesis of the solution is completely based on the system specification. This synthesis technique, carried out at the system level, is not yet sufficiently efficient. It is usually based on the structural characteristics of the specifications and it has the disadvantage of limiting the design space exploration, generating non-optimal solutions for system implementation.

3.4.4 Non-Functional Requirements

Non-functional requirements limit the design space exploration, since they typically impose, at early stages of development, particular design and implementation solutions. This kind of requirements can be classified into three different groups: design objectives, design decisions, and design constraints.

Design objectives are related to general requirements of qualitative system performance. Typical design objectives appear in the form of "it must be as fast as possible," "it must be cheap" or "it must be easy to adapt." Although, these design objectives are not really requirements, they can be transformed into design constraints if some metrics can be devised. Otherwise, design objectives should only be used to select amongst functional equivalent alternatives, when there is no firmer criterion for the decision; see Chap. 12 for further details on decision support in requirements engineering.

Design decisions can be related, for example, to the inclusion of the system in a given family of commercial products or with the incorporation into a bigger product. These non-functional requirements can affect the technological decisions or interfere with the functionality of the system, so they should always be questioned and justified. UML's OCL (Object Constraint Language) can be used to describe architectural or functional design decisions. Design constraints include, for example, performance, reliability, cost and size. Timing requirements can be classified as reply time, repetition rate and correlation time. This kind of non-functional decisions is typically quantifiable and syntactically incorporated in the system models as tagged values or object stamps. UML's sequence diagrams can support the inscription of timing and performance requirements.

In [7, 36] non-functional requirements are thoroughly treated both on how to discover and on how to specify them.

3.5 Requirements Transformation

The problem of obtaining system requirements models from user requirements that can be directly used within the design phase is not simple and easy and faces several difficulties [26]. Generically, it involves several decisions that can not be made by a method or a tool, due to the natural discontinuity between functional and structural models. Holland and Lieberherr consider that the identification of objects and the description of the relationships between them are two of the three challenges of object oriented design in the construction of object oriented models [20].

There are many authors that propose solutions to tackle this problem, namely by guiding the transformation of use case models into object/class models [2, 3, 23, 37]. Some approaches [30, 38] propose a use case rationale based on goal identification and can be used to better support the transition for the architectural design issues. However, they lack an explicit scenario framework for capturing the semantic intentionality of each use case. This could be incorporated by adopting some scenario based requirements engineering techniques, such as those suggested in [43, 45]. See Chap. 5 for further details on requirements interdependencies.

In this section, we describe an approach for defining the system objects based on use cases and their respective textual descriptions. The strategy uses the object categories (interface, data and control) defined in [23] and incorporates some mechanisms that allow each object to be related to the use cases that gave origin to it. Due to the relatively weak support of UML 1.5 to component based design, UML object concept was chosen to represent system level entities or components.

UML 2.0 was not used here since its final approval as an ISO standard was not taken at the time of writing.

3.5.1 User Requirements Modeling

The identification of the system components requires the definition of a model to capture the system functionalities offered to its users. Use cases are one of the most suitable techniques for that purpose, since they are simple and easy to read. In fact, they only include three main concepts (use cases, actors and relations). This low number of concepts is a fundamental characteristic for involving non-technical stakeholders in the requirements capture process.

Although use cases are used in several object oriented projects, they do not hold any intrinsic characteristic that can be classified as "pure" object oriented. However, there is a large consensus on the recognition that use cases are a proper technique for object oriented projects [4], namely for discovering (and later specifying) the behavior of the system, during the analysis phase. This is also highlighted by the fact that use cases are part of UML. Thus, adopting use cases for user requirements is undoubtedly a valid technique, but poses the problem related to the transformation of use cases into objects or components.

The requirements for the case study used in this chapter were acquired using requirements engineering techniques, and the end-result was a collection of artifacts, including UML diagrams. Some of the artifacts are presented in Fig. 3.10-3.11. After identifying all the use cases of the system, the next step is to describe their behavior. There are some alternatives for describing use cases, namely informal text, numbered steps with pre- and post-conditions pseudo code and activity diagrams [40]. As an example, the description of the top level use case {U0a.1} with informal text is presented. Similar descriptions were created for the other top-level use cases.

{U0a.1} **send alert:** Send domain alert or disseminating domain information to the users informing of domain related events and situations or unexpected domain situations that are happening in the region. Only users that have previously subscribed this e-service will receive the alert messages (subscription made via {U0a.4} user profile subscription). This is an asynchronous e-service. If technically possible, the system acquires user context raw information (location, time, etc) from external context sources. Also, a contextualization process will assist the system in making the level of granularity of the information adequate to the geographic location of the user context (geographic location context, time context and activity context). Examples: an alert of a dangerous hole in a street should only be sent to the users geographically located in that street; an alert of a street obstructed should be sent to the users geographically located in that street or in any of the incident streets; an alert of weather storm should be sent to all the users in the region. The information associated to the alert should always be up-to-date and match the user-specific request, excluding any extra information or undesired advertisements. For those users that require personalized information, a subscription must be made via {U0a.4} user profile and e-service subscription.

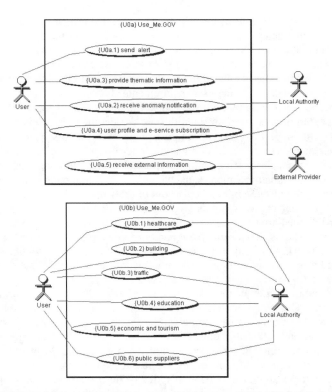

Fig. 3.10 UML top level use case diagram according to two orthogonal criteria; top: functionality criterion; bottom: domain criterion

3.5.2 4SRS Technique

Transforming use cases into architectural models representing system requirements is a difficult task. A technique called 4 step rule set (4SRS) was proposed to help with that task in [13]. The 4SRS technique is organized as four steps to transform use cases into objects: object creation (step 1), object elimination (step 2), object packaging and aggregation (step 3) and object association (step 4).

In step 1 (object creation), each use case must be transformed into three objects (one interface, one data, and one control). Each object receives the reference of its respective use case appended with the suffix (i, d, c) that indicates the object's category (in this approach, object references start with an "O"). This is a fully "automatic" step, since there is no need to any kind of particular decisions or rationale for the specific context of each use case. From this step on, there are only objects as design entities. Use cases are still used in the following steps to allow the introduction of requirements into the object model.

In step 2 (object elimination), it must be decided which of the three objects must be maintained to fully represent, in computational terms, the use case, taking into account the whole system and not each use case in isolation. These decisions must be based on the textual description for each use case. This step aims at deciding which of the objects created in step 1 must be kept in the object model. It also eliminates redundancy in the user requirements elicitation and detects missing requirements. Object elimination is the most important step of the 4SRS technique, since the definitive system level entities are decided here. To cope with the complexity of the step, it has been decomposed into seven micro-steps: use case identification (micro-step 2i), local elimination (micro-step 2ii), object naming (micro-step 2iii), object description (micro-step 2iv), object representation (micro-step 2v), global elimination (micro-step 2vi) and object renaming (micro-step 2vii). The description of these micro-steps is out of the scope of this chapter.

In step 3 (object packaging and aggregation), the remaining objects (those that were maintained after step 2) for which there is an advantage in being treated in a unified way should give origin to aggregations or packages of semantically consistent objects. This step supports the construction of a truly coherent object model, since it introduces an additional semantic layer at a higher abstraction level, that works as a "functional glue" for the objects.

Packaging is technique that can introduce a very light semantic cohesion among the objects. This cohesion can be easily reversed within the design phase whenever needed. This means packaging can be flexibly used to obtain more comprehensive and understandable object models. In the opposite way, aggregation imposes a strong semantic cohesion among the objects. The level of cohesion in aggregations is more difficult to reverse in subsequent stages, which suggests a more scrupulous approach in using this kind of functional glue. Thus, aggregation should only be used when it is explicitly assumed that the set of considered objects is affected by a conscious design decision. Typically, aggregation is used when there is a part of the system that constitutes a legacy subsystem, or when the design has a pre-defined reference architecture that constricts the object model.

Step 4 (object association) of the 4SRS technique supports the introduction of associations in the object model, completely based on the information from the use case model and generated in micro-step 2i. Regarding the information in the use case model, if the textual descriptions of use cases possess hints on the kind of sequences use cases are inserted in, this information must be used to include associations in the object model.

Alternatively, the use case model can include other kinds of information to support associations, when there are UML relations between use cases. As an example, use case {U0a.1.1} «uses» use case {U0a.1.2}, which justifies the association between objects {O0a.1.1.d} and {O0a.1.2.c}, and between objects {O0a.1.1.i} and {O0a.1.2.d}; see Fig. 3.12.

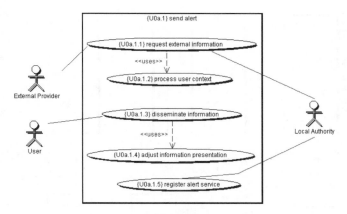

Fig. 3.11 Refinement of UML use case {U0a.1}

3.5.3 System Requirements Modeling

The system architectural model expresses the system requirements, but also an informal description of the objects. 4SRS helps to define a logical architecture for the system by capturing all its functional requirements and its non-functional intentions. The former gives origin to textual descriptions for each object in the model and the later has been classified as design decisions and design constraints. Design objectives are not allowed at system requirements models generated by the 4SRS technique.

The generated object model shows how significant properties of a system are distributed across its constituent parts. The 4SRS technique generates a raw object diagram that identifies the system level entities, their responsibilities and the relationships among them. Its purpose is to direct attention at an appropriate decomposition of the system without delving into details. Each one of the used packages defines one different decomposition region that contains several tightly semantically connected objects. Within the next design phases, these packages must be further specified concerning its architectural structure, by using design patterns.

The resulting raw object diagram can be used in the following development phases to support the definition of specific sub-projects, by using collapsing and filtering techniques. These techniques allow the redefinitions of the system boundary, giving origin, for instance, to the database project, services formalization, or platform pattern analysis. Fig. 3.12 shows the collapsed object diagram that was obtained from the raw object diagram by hiding packages details. Therefore, associations appear at a higher level of abstraction and the resulting object diagram is more readable.

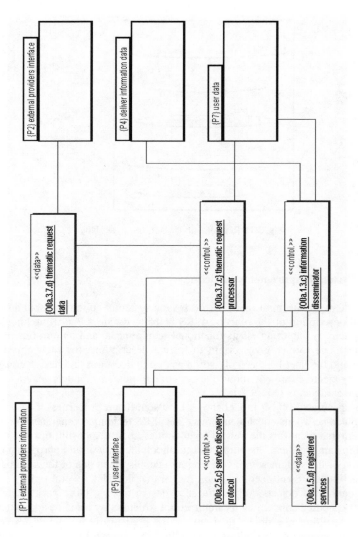

Fig. 3.12 Collapsed UML object diagram representing system requirements

3.6 Conclusion

The correct derivation of system requirements from user requirements is an important topic in requirements engineering research. This activity assures that the design phase is based on the effective clients' needs without any misjudgment arbitrarily introduced by the developers during the process of system requirements specification. One approach to support this derivation is by transforming user requirements models into system requirements models, by manipulating the corresponding specifications. User requirements are, typically, described in natural language and with informal diagrams, at a relatively low level of detail and are focused in the problem domain. System requirements comprise abstract models of the system, at a relatively high level of detail, and constitute the first system representation to be used at the beginning of the design phase.

This chapter deals with the characteristics of different modeling techniques for the specification of systems requirements. It presents various classes of modeling and specification techniques that can be used in different circumstances during development projects. Here, meta-models play an important role, since they define the semantic capability of the modeling views to adopt for a given system. The chapter ends with a brief description of a heuristic based approach to support the transformation of user into system requirements. This transformational approach shows that model continuity is a key issue and highlights the importance of having a well defined process to relate, map and transform requirements models.

The topics presented in this chapter emphasize the fact that system design is a highly abstract task that focuses on the functional and non-functional requirements of computer-based systems. Both system designers and requirements engineers benefit from a model based approach to requirements specification to allow the correct evolution of system representations during development projects.

References

1. Ainsworth M, Cruickshank AH, Groves LG, Wallis PJL (1994) Viewpoint specification and Z. Information Software Technology, , February 36: 43–51
2. Back RJ, Petre L, Porres I (1999) Analyzing UML use cases as contracts: Beyond the standard. In: Proceedings of 2nd International Conference on the Unified Modeling Language (UML'99), Fort Collins, CO, USA, pp.518–33
3. Becker LB, Pereira CE, Dias OP, Teixeira IM, Teixeira JP (2000) MOSYS: A methodology for automatic object identification from system specification. In: Proceedings of 3rd International Symposium on Object-Oriented Real-Time Distributed Computing (ISORC 2000), Newport Beach, CA, USA, pp.198–201
4. Booch G (1996) Best of booch: Designing strategies for object technology. SIGS, New York, NY, USA
5. Calvez JP (1996) A system specification model and method. In: High Level System Modeling: Specification and Design Methodologies. Waxman R, Bergé JM, Levia O, Rouillard J. (Eds.), Kluwer Academic, Dordrecht, The Netherlands
6. Chen PS (1977) The entity relationship approach to logical data base design. Q.E.D. Information Sciences, Wellesley, MA, USA
7. Chung L, Nixon B, Yu E, Mylopoulos J (2000) Non-functional requirements in software engineering. Kluwer Academic, Boston, MA, USA
8. Cunin PY, Greenwood R, Francou L, Robertson I, Warboys B (2001) The PIE methodology: Concept and application. In: Proceedings of 8th European Workshop on Software Process Technology, Witten, Germany, pp.3–26

9. Davis WS (1983) Tools and techniques for structured systems analysis and design. Addison-Wesley, Reading, MA, USA

10. De Marco T (1979) Structured analysis and system specification. Yourdon Press, New York, NY, USA

11. Dori D (2002) Object-process methodology: A holistic systems paradigm, Springer, Berlin, Germany

12. Fernandes JM, Lilius J (2004) Functional and object-oriented views in embedded software modeling. In: Proceedings of 11th International Conference on the Engineering of Computer Based Systems (ECBS 2004), Brno, Czech Rep., pp.378–87, IEEE CS Press, May

13. Fernandes JM, Machado RJ (2001) From use cases to objects: An industrial information systems case study analysis. In: Proceedings of 7th International Conference on Object-Oriented Information Systems (OOIS'01), Calgary, Canada, August pp.319–28

14. Finkelstein A, Kramer J, Nuseibeh B, Finkelstein L, Goedicke M (1992) Viewpoints: A framework for integrating multiple perspectives in system development. International Journal of Software Engineering and Knowledge Engineering, 2: 31–57

15. Firesmith D, Henderson-Sellers B (2002) The OPEN process framework: An introduction. Addison-Wesley, Harlow, UK

16. Gajski D, Dutt N, Wu A, Lin S (1992) High level synthesis: Introduction to chip and system design, Kluwer Academic, Boston, MA, USA

17. Gajski D, Vahid F, Narayan S, Gong J (1994) Specification and design of embedded systems. Prentice Hall, Englewood Cliffs, NJ, USA

18. Harel D (1988) On visual formalisms. Communications of the ACM, 31(5): 514–30

19. Henderson-Sellers B (2003) Method engineering for OO systems development. Communications of the ACM, 46(10): 73–8

20. Holland IM, Lieberherr KJ (1996) Object-oriented design. ACM Computing Surveys, 28(1): 273–5

21. IEEE (1990) IEEE Standard glossary of software engineering terminology, 610.12-1990

22. International Standards Organization (1995) Information technology: Software life-cycle processes (ISO/IEC12207). Geneva, Switzerland

23. Jacobson I, Christerson M, Jonsson P, Overgaard GÄ (1992) Object-oriented software engineering: A use case driven approach. Addison Wesley, Reading, MA, USA

24. Jensen K (1997) Colored Petri nets: Basic concepts, analysis methods and practical use. Vol.1, Basic concepts. Monographs in Theoretical Computer Science, Springer, New York, NY, USA

25. Jensen K, Christensen S, Huber P, Holla M (1992) Design/CPN: A reference manual. MetaSoftware Corporation

26. Kaindl H (1999) Difficulties in the transition from OO analysis to design. IEEE Software, 16(5): 94–102

27. Kotonya G, Sommerville I (1992) Viewpoints for requirements definition. Software Engineering Journal, 7(6): 375–87

28. Lakos C, Keen C (1994) LOOPN++: A new language for object oriented Petri Nets. In: Proceedings of European Simulation Multi-conference, Barcelona, Spain, pp.369 74, Society for Computer Simulation

29. Leite JCSP, Freeman PA (1991) Requirements validation through viewpoint resolution, IEEE Transactions on Software Engineering, 12(12): 1253–1269

30. Liang Y (2003) From use cases to classes: A way of building object model with UML. Information and Software Technology, 45: 83–93

31. Machado RJ, Fernandes JM (2001) A Petri Net meta-model to develop software components for Embedded Systems. In: Proceedings of 2nd IEEE International Conference on Application of Concurrency to System Design (ACSD'01), Newcastle, UK, pp.113–22, IEEE CS Press

32. Moore EF (1964) Sequential machines: Selected papers. Addison Wesley, Reading, MA, USA

33. Narayan S, Vahid F, Gajski D (1991) System specification and synthesis with the speccharts language. In: Proceedings of International Conference on Computer-Aided Design (ICCAD '91), Santa Clara, CA, USA, pp.266–9, IEEE CS Press

34. Peterson J (1981) Petri Net theory and the modeling of systems. Prentice Hall, Upper Saddle River, NJ, USA

35. Reisig W (1985) Petri Nets: An introduction, EATCS Monographs on Theoretical Computer Science, Vol.4, Springer, Berlin, Germany

36. Robertson S, Robertson J (1999) Mastering the requirements process, Addison Wesley, Reading, MA, USA

37. Rosenberg D, Scott K (1999) Use case driven object modeling with UML: A practical approach. Addison Wesley, Reading, MA, USA

38. Saeki M, Kaiya H (2003) Transformation based approach for weaving use case models in aspect-oriented requirements analysis. 4th Workshop on AOSD Modeling with UML, within the UML 2003 Conference, San Francisco, CA, USA, October

39. Sarkar A, Waxman R, Cohoon J (1995) Specification modeling methodologies for reactive systems design. In: High Level System Modeling: Specification Languages. Bergé JM, Levia O, Rouillard J. (Eds.), Kluwer Academic, Dordrecht, The Netherlands

40. Schneider G, Winters JP (1998) Applying use cases: A practical guide. Addison Wesley, Reading, MA, USA

41. Stevens R, Brook P, Jackson K, Arnold S (1998) Systems engineering: Coping with complexity. Prentice Hall Europe, Hertfordshire, UK

42. Sutcliffe A (1988) Jackson system development. Prentice Hall, Hertfordshire, UK

43. Sutcliffe A, Maiden M, Minocha S, Manuel D (1998) Supporting scenario-based requirements engineering. IEEE Transactions on Software Engineering, 24(12): 1072-88

44. ter Hofstede AHM, Verhoef TF (1997) On the feasibility of situational method engineering. Information Systems, 22(6/7): 401-22

45. van Lamsweerde A, Willemet L (1998) Inferring declarative requirements specifications from operational scenarios. IEEE Transactions on Software Engineering, 24(12): 1089–114

46. Yourdon E, Constantine L (1978) Structured design: Fundamentals of a discipline of computer program and systems design. Yourdon Press, New York, NY, USA

Author Biography

Ricardo J. Machado is an assistant professor of Software Engineering and coordinator of the Software Engineering and Management Research Group (SEMAG) at the Department of Information Systems, Universidade do Minho (Guimarães, Portugal). He holds a PhD and an MSc degrees in Informatics and Computer Engineering (both from U.Minho), and a DEng degree in Electronics and Computer Engineering (from FEUP). He is the president of the Portuguese technical committee responsible for analyzing the documents produced by JTC1/SC7 from ISO/IEC and by TC311 from CEN/CENELEC in the software and system engineering domain, and he is one of the founding members of IFIP WG10.3 SIG-ES special interest group. He is a regular scientific reviewer of IEEE Transactions on CAD and IEEE Transactions on Software Engineering. He acted as general chair of ACSD'03 conference, as co-organizer of MOMPES series workshops, and has been appointed as general chair of DIPES'06 conference. He has also served as a PC member of ETFA'03, ACSD'03/'04/'05, MOMPES'04, and INDIN'05. His current research interests include software engineering, embedded software, and pervasive information systems.

Isabel Ramos holds a doctorate degree in Information Technologies and Systems, specialization in Information Systems Engineering and Management, since 2001. She also holds a master degree in Informatics for management. Isabel Ramos is an assistant professor at the Department of Information Systems, Universidade do Minho (Guimarães, Portugal). She is a researcher in the Algoritmi Research Center and coordinates the interest group in Knowledge Management of the department. She is also responsible for the Requirements Engineering modules in the Master course on Information Systems. She integrates the steering committee of a Master on Business Information. Isabel is author of several scientific publications presented at international conferences and published in scientific and technical journals. Her main areas of interest are requirements engineering, knowledge management, organizational theory, sociology of knowledge, history of science, research methodology.

João M. Fernandes is an assistant professor at the Department of Informatics, Universidade do Minho (Braga, Portugal). He received a DEng degree in Informatics and Systems Engineering in 1991, MSc degree in Computer Science in 1994, and a PhD degree in Computer Engineering in 2000, all from U. Minho. From Sep/2002 until Feb/2003, he was a post-doctoral researcher at the TUCS Embedded Systems Laboratory (Turku, Finland). He is a (co-)author of several scientific publications with peer revision on international conferences, journals and chapters of books. He has already served as a scientific reviewer for an Addison-Wesley book, for several international conferences, and for IEEE, Elsevier, and Springer international journals. He has also served as a member of the Program and Organizing Committees of international workshops and conferences, namely DSOA 2004, CPN 2004, MOMPES 2004, ETFA 2003, and ACSD 2003. His research interests focus on embedded software, hardware/software co-design, methodologies for system development, software modeling, software process and management, and history of computing.

4 Requirements Prioritization

Patrik Berander and Anneliese Andrews

Abstract: This chapter provides an overview of techniques for prioritization of requirements for software products. Prioritization is a crucial step towards making good decisions regarding product planning for single and multiple releases. Various aspects of functionality are considered, such as importance, risk, cost, etc. Prioritization decisions are made by stakeholders, including users, managers, developers, or their representatives. Methods are for combining individual prioritizations based on overall objectives and constraints. A range of different techniques and aspects are applied to an example to illustrate their use. Finally, limitations and shortcomings of current methods are pointed out, and open research questions in the area of requirements prioritization are discussed.

Keywords: Requirements analysis, Software product planning, Requirements prioritization, Decision support, Trade offs.

4.1 Introduction

In everyday life, we make many decisions, e.g. when buying a DVD-player, food, a telephone, etc. Often, we are not even conscious of making one. Usually, we do not have more than a couple of choices to consider, such as which brand of mustard to buy, or whether to take this bus or the next one. Even with just a couple of choices, decisions can be difficult to make. When having tens, hundreds or even thousands of alternatives, decision-making becomes much more difficult.

One of the keys to making the right decision is to prioritize between different alternatives. It is often not obvious which choice is better, because several aspects must be taken into consideration. For example, when buying a new car, it is relatively easy to make a choice based on speed alone (one only needs to evaluate which car is the fastest). When considering multiple aspects, such as price, safety, comfort, or luggage load, the choice becomes much harder. When developing software systems, similar trade-offs must be made. The functionality that is most important for the customers might not be as important when other aspects (e.g. price) are factored in. We need to develop the functionality that is most desired by the customers, as well as least risky, least costly, and so forth.

Prioritization helps to cope with these complex decision problems. This chapter provides a description of available techniques and methods, and how to approach a prioritization situation. The chapter is structured as follows: First, an overview of the area of prioritization is given (Sect. 4.2). This is followed by a presentation and discussion of different aspects that could be used when prioritizing (Sect. 4.3). Next, some prioritization techniques and characteristics are discussed (Sect. 4.4), followed by a discussion of different stakeholders' situations that affect prioritization in Sect. 4.5. Section 4.6 discusses additional issues that arise when prioritizing software requirements and Section 4.7 provides an example of a prioritization. Section 4.8 discusses possible future research questions in the area. Finally, Sect. 4.9 summarizes the chapter.

4.2 What is Requirements Prioritization?

Complex decision-making situations are not unique to software engineering. Other disciplines, such as psychology, and organizational behavior have studied decision-making thoroughly [1]. Classical decision-making models have been mapped to various requirements engineering activities to show the similarities [1]. Chapter 12 in this book provides a comprehensive overview of decision-making and decision support in requirements engineering. Current chapter primarily focuses on requirements prioritization, an integral part of decision-making [49]. The intention is to describe the current body of knowledge in the requirements prioritization area.

The quality of a software product is often determined by the ability to satisfy the needs of the customers and users [7, 53]. Hence, eliciting (Chap. 2) and specifying (Chap. 3) the correct requirements and planning suitable releases with the right functionality is a major step towards the success of a project or product. If the wrong requirements are implemented and users resist using the product, it does not matter how solid the product is or how thoroughly it has been tested.

Most software projects have more candidate requirements than can be realized within the time and cost constraints. Prioritization helps to identify the most valuable requirements from this set by distinguishing the critical few from the trivial many. The process of prioritizing requirements provides support for the following activities [32, 55, 57, 58]:

- for stakeholders to decide on the core requirements for the system
- to plan and select an ordered, optimal set of software requirements for implementation in successive releases
- to trade off desired project scope against sometimes conflicting constraints such as schedule, budget, resources, time to market, and quality
- to balance the business benefit of each requirement against its cost
- to balance implications of requirements on the software architecture and future evolution of the product and its associated cost
- to select only a subset of the requirements and still produce a system that will satisfy the customer(s)
- to estimate expected customer satisfaction
- to get a technical advantage and optimize market opportunity
- to minimize rework and schedule slippage (plan stability)
- to handle contradictory requirements, focus the negotiation process, and resolve disagreements between stakeholders (more about this in Chap. 7)
- to establish relative importance of each requirement to provide the greatest value at the lowest cost

The list above clearly shows the importance of prioritizing and deciding what requirements to include in a product. This is a strategic process since these decisions drive the development expenses and product revenue as well as making the difference between market gain and market loss [1]. Further, the result of prioritization might form the basis of product and marketing plans, as well as being a driving force during project planning. Ruhe et al. summarize this as: "The challenge is to select the "right" requirements out of a given superset of candidate requirements so that all the different key interests, technical constraints and preferences of the critical stakeholders are fulfilled and the overall business value of the product is maximized" [48].

Of course, it is possible to rectify incorrect decisions later on via change management (more about change impact analysis in Chap. 6), but this can be very costly since it is significantly more expensive to correct problems later in the development process [5]. Frederick P. Brooks puts it in the following words: "The hardest single part of building a software system is deciding precisely what to build. [...] No other part of the work so cripples the resulting system if done wrong. No other part is more difficult to rectify later." [10]. Hence, the most cost effective way of developing software is to find the optimal set of requirements early, and then to develop the software according to this set. To accomplish this, it is crucial to prioritize the requirements to enable selection of the optimal set.

Besides the obvious benefits presented above, prioritizing requirements can have other benefits. For example, it is possible to find requirements defects (e.g misjudged, incorrect and ambiguous requirements) since requirements are analyzed from a perspective that is different from that taken during reviews of requirements [33].

Some authors consider requirements prioritization easy [55], some regard it of medium difficulty [57], and some regard prioritization as one of the most complex activities in the requirements process, claiming that few software companies have effective and systematic methods for prioritizing requirements [40]. However, all these sources consider requirements prioritization a fundamental activity for project success. At the same time, some text books about requirements engineering [9, 47] do not discuss requirements prioritization to any real extent.

There is no "right" requirements process and the way of handling requirements differs greatly between different domains and companies [1]. Further, requirements are typically vaguer early on and become more explicit as the understanding of the product grows [50]. These circumstances imply that there is no specific phase where prioritization is made, rather, it is performed throughout the development process (more about this in Sect. 4.6.2) [13, 38]. Hence, prioritization is an iterative process and might be performed at different abstraction levels and with different information in different phases during the software lifecycle.

Prioritization techniques can roughly be divided into two categories: methods and negotiation approaches. The methods are based on quantitatively assigning values to different aspects of requirements while negotiation approaches focus on giving priorities to requirements by reaching agreement between different stakeholders [39]. Further, negotiation approaches are based on subjective measures and are commonly used when analyses are contextual and when decision variables are strongly interrelated. Quantitative methods make it easier to aggregate different decision variables into an overall assessment and lead to faster decisions [15, 50]. In addition, one must be mindful of the social nature of prioritization. There is more to requirements prioritization than simply asking stakeholders about priorities. Stakeholders play roles and should act according to the goals of that role, but they are also individuals with personalities and personal agendas. Additionally, many organizational issues like power, etc. need to be taken into account. Ignoring such issues can raise the risk level for a project. Negotiation and goal modeling are described in detail in Chaps. 7 and 9, respectively, while this chapter focuses primarily on quantitative methods for prioritizing requirements.

4.3 Aspects of Prioritization

Requirements can be prioritized taking many different aspects into account. An aspect is a property or attribute of a project and its requirements that can be used to prioritize requirements. Common aspects are importance, penalty, cost, time, and risk. When prioritizing requirements based on a single aspect, it is easy to decide which one is most desirable (recall the example about the speed of a car). When involving other aspects, such as cost, customers can change their mind and high priority requirements may turn out to be less important if they are very expensive to satisfy [36]. Often, the aspects interact and changes in one aspect could result in an impact on another aspect [50]. Hence, it is essential to know what effects such conflicts may have, and it is vital to not only consider importance when prioritizing requirements but also other aspects affecting software development and satisfaction with the resulting product. Several aspects can be prioritized, and it may not be practical to consider them all. Which ones to consider depend on the specific situation, and a few examples of aspects suitable for software projects are described below. Aspects are usually evaluated by stakeholders in a project (managers, users, developers, etc.)

4.3.1 Importance

When prioritizing importance, the stakeholders should prioritize which requirements are most important for the system. However, importance could be an extremely multifaceted concept since it depends very much on which perspective the stakeholder has. Importance could, for example, be urgency of implementation, importance of a requirement for the product architecture, strategic importance for the company, etc. [38]. Consequently, it is essential to specify which kind of importance the stakeholders should prioritize in each case.

4.3.2 Penalty

It is possible to evaluate the penalty that is introduced if a requirement is not fulfilled [57]. Penalty is not just the opposite of importance. For example, failing to conform to a standard could incur a high penalty even if it is of low importance for the customer (i.e. the customer does not get excited if the requirement is fulfilled). The same goes for implicit requirements that users take for granted, and whose absence could make the product unsuitable for the market.

4.3.3 Cost

The implementation cost is usually estimated by the developing organization. Measures that influence cost include: complexity of the requirement, the ability to reuse existing code, the amount of testing and documentation needed, etc. [57]. Cost is often expressed in terms of staff hours (effort) since the main cost in software development is often primarily related to the number of hours spent. Cost (as well as time, cf. Sect. 4.3.4.) could be prioritized by using any of the techniques presented in Sect. 4.4, but also by simply estimating the actual cost on an absolute or normalized scale.

4.3.4 Time

As can be seen in the section above, cost in software development is often related to number of staff hours. However, time (i.e. lead time) is influenced by many other factors such as degree of parallelism in development, training needs, need to develop support infrastructure, complete industry standards, etc. [57].

4.3.5 Risk

Every project carries some amount of risk. In project management, risk management is used to cope with both internal (technical and market risks) and external risks (e.g. regulations, suppliers). Both likelihood and impact must be considered when determining the level of risk of an item or activity [44]. Risk management can also be used when planning requirements into products and releases by identifying risks that are likely to cause difficulties during development [41, 57]. Such risks could for example include performance risks, process risks, schedule risks etc. [55]. Based on the estimated risk likelihood and risk impact for each requirement [1], it is possible to calculate the risk level of a project.

4.3.6 Volatility

Volatility of requirements is considered a risk factor and is sometimes handled as part of the risk aspect [41]. Others think that volatility should be analyzed separately and that volatility of requirements should be taken into account separately in the prioritization process [36]. The reasons for requirements volatility vary, for example: the market changes, business requirements change, legislative changes occur, users change, or requirements become clearer during the software life cycle [18, 50]. Irrespective of the reason, volatile requirements affect the stability and planning of a project, and presumably increase the costs since changes during development increase the cost of a project (see more about this issue in Chap. 6). Further, the cost of a project might increase because developers have to select an architecture suited to change if volatility is known to be an issue [36].

4.3.7 Other Aspects

The above list of aspects has been considered important in the literature but it is by no means exhaustive. Examples of other aspects are: financial benefit, strategic benefit, competitors, competence/resources, release theme, ability to sell, etc. For a company, we suggest that stakeholders develop a list of important aspects to use in the decision-making. It is important that the stakeholders have the same interpretation of the aspects as well as of the requirements. Studies have shown that it is hard to interpret the results if no guidelines about the true meaning of an aspect are present [37, 38].

4.3.8 Combining Different Aspects

In practice, it is important to consider multiple aspects before deciding if a requirement should be implemented directly, later, or not at all. For example, in the Cost-Value approach, both value (importance) and cost are prioritized to implement those requirements that give most value for the money [30]. The Planning Game (PG) from eXtreme Programming (XP) uses a similar approach when importance, effort (cost), and risks are prioritized [2]. Further, importance and stability (volatility) are suggested as aspects that should be used when prioritizing while others suggest that dependencies also must be considered [12, 36] (more about dependencies in Chap. 5). In Wiegers' approach, the relative value (importance) is divided by the relative cost and the relative risk in order to determine the requirements that have the most favorable balance of value, cost, and risk [57]. This approach further allows different weights for different aspects in order to favor the most important aspect (in the specific situation).

There are many alternatives of combining different aspects. Which aspects to consider depends very much on the specific situation and it is important to know about possible aspects and how to combine them efficiently to suit the case at hand.

4.4 Prioritization Techniques

The purpose of any prioritization is to assign values to distinct prioritization objects that allow establishment of a relative order between the objects in the set. In our case, the objects are the requirements to prioritize. The prioritization can be done with various measurement scales and types. The least powerful prioritization scale is the ordinal scale, where the requirements are ordered so that it is possible to see which requirements are more important than others, but not how much more important. The ratio scale is more powerful since it is possible to quantify how much more important one requirement is than another (the scale often ranges from 0–100 percent). An even more powerful scale is the absolute scale, which can be used in situations where an absolute number can be assigned (e.g. number of hours). With higher levels of measurement, more sophisticated evaluations and calculations become possible [20].

Below, a number of different prioritization techniques are presented. Some techniques assume that each requirement is associated with a priority, and others group requirements by priority level. When examples are given, importance is used as the aspect to prioritize even though other aspects can be evaluated with each of the techniques. It should be noted that the presented techniques focus specifically on prioritization. Numerous *methods* exist that use these prioritization techniques within a larger trade-off and decision making framework e.g. EVOLVE [24], Cost-Value [30] and Quantitative Win-Win [48].

4.4.1 Analytical Hierarchy Process (AHP)

The Analytic Hierarchy Process (AHP) is a systematic decision-making method that has been adapted for prioritization of software requirements [45, 51]. It is conducted by comparing all possible pairs of hierarchically classified requirements, in order to determine which has higher priority, and to what extent (usually on a scale from one to nine where one represents equal importance and nine represents absolutely more important). The total number of comparisons to perform with AHP are $n \times (n-1)/2$ (where n is the number of requirements) at each hierarchy level, which results in a dramatic increase in the number of comparisons as the number of requirements increases. Studies have shown that AHP is not suitable for large numbers of requirements [39, 42]. Researchers have tried to find ways to decrease the number of comparisons (e.g. [26, 54]) and variants of the technique have been found to reduce the number of comparisons by as much as 75 percent [31].

In its original form, the redundancy of the pair-wise comparisons allows a consistency check where judgment errors can be identified and a consistency ratio can be calculated. When reducing the number of comparisons, the number of redundant comparisons are also reduced, and consequently the ability to identify inconsistent judgments [33]. When using other techniques (explained below) a consistency ratio is not necessary since all requirements are directly compared to each other and consistency is always ensured. Some studies indicate that persons who prioritize with AHP tend to mistrust the results since control is lost when only comparing the requirements pair-wise [34, 39]. The result from a prioritization with AHP is a weighted list on a ratio scale. More detailed information about AHP can be found in [30], [51] and [52].

4.4.2 Cumulative Voting, the 100-Dollar Test

The 100-dollar test is a very straightforward prioritization technique where the stakeholders are given 100 imaginary units (money, hours, etc.) to distribute between the requirements [37]. The result of the prioritization is presented on a ratio scale. A problem with this technique arises when there are too many requirements to prioritize. For example, if you have 25 requirements, there are on average four points to distribute for each requirement. Regnell et al. faced this problem when there were 17 groups of requirements to prioritize [45]. In the study, they used a fictitious amount of $100,000 to have more freedom in the prioritizations. The subjects in the study were positive about the technique, indicating the possibility to use amounts other than 100 units (e.g. 1,000, 10,000 or 1,000,000). Another possible problem with the 100-dollar test (especially when there are many requirements) is that the person performing the prioritization miscalculates and the points do not add up to 100 [3]. This can be prevented by using a tool that keeps count of how many points have been used.

One should only perform the prioritization once one the same set of requirements, since the stakeholders might bias their evaluation the second time around if they do not get one of their favorite requirements as a top priority. In such a situation, stakeholders could put all their money on one requirement, which might influence the result heavily. Similarly, some clever stakeholders might put all their money on a favorite requirement that others do not prioritize as highly (e.g. Mac compatibility) while not giving money to requirements that will get much money anyway (e.g. response time). The solution could be to limit the amount spent on individual requirements [37]. However, the risk with such an approach is that stakeholders may be forced to not prioritize according to their actual priorities.

4.4.3 Numerical Assignment (Grouping)

Numerical assignment is the most common prioritization technique and is suggested both in RFC 2119 [8] and IEEE Std. 830-1998 [29]. The approach is based on grouping requirements into different priority groups. The number of groups can vary, but in practice, three groups are very common [37, 55]. When using numerical assignment, it is important that each group represents something that the stakeholders can relate to (e.g. critical, standard, optional), for a reliable classification. Using relative terms such as high, medium, and low will confuse the stakeholders [57]. This seems to be especially important when there are stakeholders with different views of what high, medium and low means. A clear definition of what a group really means minimizes such problems.

A further potential problem is that stakeholders tend to think that everything is critical [36, 55]. If customers prioritize themselves, using three groups; *critical*, *standard*, and *optional*, they will most likely consider 85 percent of the requirements as critical, 10 percent as standard, and 5 percent as optional [4, 57]. One idea is to put restrictions on the allowed number of requirements in each group (e.g. not less than 25 percent of the requirements in each group) [34]. However, one problem with this approach is that the usefulness of the priorities diminishes because the stakeholders are forced to divide requirements into certain groups [32]. However, no empirical evidence of good or bad results with such restrictions exists. The result of numerical assignment is requirements prioritized on an ordinal scale. However, the requirements in each group have the same priority, which means that each requirement does not get a unique priority.

4.4.4 Ranking

As in numerical assignment, ranking is based on an ordinal scale but the requirements are ranked without ties in rank. This means that the most important requirement is ranked 1 and the least important is ranked n (for n requirements). Each requirement has a unique rank (in comparison to numerical assignment) but it is not possible to see the relative difference between the ranked items (as in AHP or the 100-dollar test). The list of ranked requirements could be obtained in a variety of ways, as for example by using the bubble sort or binary search tree algorithms [33]. Independently of sorting algorithm, ranking seems to be more suitable for a single stakeholder because it might be difficult to align several different stakeholders' views. Nevertheless, it is possible to combine the different views by taking the mean priority of each requirement but this might result in ties for requirements which this method wants to avoid.

4.4.5 Top-Ten Requirements

In the top-ten requirements approach, the stakeholders pick their top-ten requirements (from a larger set) without assigning an internal order between the requirements. This makes the approach especially suitable for multiple stakeholders of equal importance [36]. The reason to not prioritize further is that it might create unnecessary conflict when some stakeholders get support for their top priority and others only for their third priority. One could assume that conflicts might arise anyway if, for example, one customer gets three top-ten requirements into the product while another gets six top-ten requirements into the product. However, it is important to not just take an average across all stakeholders since it might lead to some stakeholders not getting any of their top requirements [36]. Instead, it is crucial that some essential requirements are satisfied for each stakeholder. This could obviously result in a situation that dissatisfies all customers instead of satisfying a few customers completely. The main challenge in this technique is to balance these issues.

4.4.6 Which Prioritization Technique to Choose

Table 4.1 summarizes the presented prioritization techniques, based on measurement scale, granularity of analysis, and level of sophistication of the technique.

Table 4.1 Summary of presented technique

Technique	Scale	Granularity	Sophistication
AHP	Ratio	Fine	Very Complex
Hundred-dollar test	Ratio	Fine	Complex
Ranking	Ordinal	Medium	Easy
Numerical Assignment	Ordinal	Coarse	Very Easy
Top-ten	-	Extremely Coarse	Extremely Easy

A general advice is to use the simplest appropriate prioritization technique and use more sophisticated ones when a more sensitive analysis is needed for resolving disagreements or to support the most critical decisions [42]. As more sophisticated techniques generally are more time consuming, the simplest possible technique ensures cost effective decisions. The trade-off is to decide exactly how "quick and dirty" the approach can be without letting the quality of the decisions suffer. It should also be noted that there exist several commercial tools that facilitate the use of more sophisticated techniques (e.g. AHP) and that it is possible to construct simple home-made tools (e.g. in spreadsheets) to facilitate the use of different prioritization techniques.

4.4.7 Combining Different Techniques

The techniques in Table 4.1 represent the most commonly referenced quantitative prioritization techniques. It is possible to combine some of them to make prioritization easier or more efficient. Some combinations of the above techniques exist and probably the best known example is Planning Game (PG) in eXtreme Programming (XP) [2] (more about agile methods in requirements engineering in Chap. 14). In PG, numerical assignment and ranking are combined by first dividing the different requirements into priority groups and then ranking requirements within each group [34]. Requirements triage is an approach where parallels are drawn to medical treatment at hospitals [17]. Medical personnel divide victims into three categories: those that will die whether treated or not, those who will resume normal lives whether treated or not, and those for whom medical treatment may make a significant difference. In requirements prioritization, there are requirements that must be in the product (e.g. platform requirements), requirements that the product clearly need not satisfy (e.g. very optional requirements), and requirements that need more attention. This means that the requirements are assigned to one of three groups (numerical assignment) and requirements that need more attention are prioritized by any of the other techniques (AHP, ranking, 100 points etc.). In this approach, not all requirements must be prioritized by a more sophisticated technique, which decreases the effort.

The two examples above show that it is possible to combine different techniques for higher efficiency or to make the process easier. Which method or combination of methods is suitable often depends on the individual project.

4.5 Involved Stakeholders in the Prioritization Process

In Chap. 13, market-driven software development is discussed and similarities and differences between market-driven and bespoke software development are presented. As can be seen in Chap. 13, similarities and differences also apply when prioritizing software requirements. In a bespoke project, only one or a few stakeholders must be taken into consideration while everyone in the whole world might serve as potential customers in market-driven development. Table 4.2 outlines some of the differences between market-driven and bespoke development that affects requirements prioritization.

Table 4.2 Differences between market-driven and bespoke development [11]

Facet	Bespoke Development	Market-driven Development
Main stakeholder	Customer organization	Developing organization
Users	Known or identifiable	Unknown, may not exist until product is on market
Distance to users	Usually small	Usually large
Requirements Conception	Elicited, analyzed, validated	Invented (by market pull or technology push)
Lifecycle	One release, then maintenance	Several releases as long as there is a market demand
Specific RE issues	Elicitation, modeling, validation, conflict resolution	Steady stream of requirements, prioritization, cost estimating, release planning
Primary goal	Compliance to specification	Time-to-market
Measure of success	Satisfaction, acceptance	Sales, market share

As can be seen in Table 4.2, there are large differences between these two extremes and different projects have to consider different ways to handle, and hence prioritize, requirements. Table 4.2 shows the two extremes in software development; a real case probably falls somewhere in between. For example, it is possible that a company delivers for a market, but the market is limited to a small number of customers (e.g. telecommunication systems are only bought by telephone operators). The discussion here focuses on three different "general" scenarios: one customer, a number of "known" customers, and a mass-market.

4.5.1 One Customer

In a one customer situation, there is only one customer's priorities that need to be considered (from the customer/user perspective). Many of the present software development processes are based on one customer and assume that this customer is available throughout the project [11]. For example, eXtreme Programming has an "on-site customer" as one of the core practices (the focus is on having one customer even though this customer could represent a market) [2]. One important issue to consider when having a one-customer situation is that the customer and the end-user(s) are not always the same. In this case, the person who prioritizes and the persons who will use the system may not have the same priorities [24]. Such situations are of course undesirable since it may result in reduced use of the product. In this case, it would be better to involve the end-users in prioritizing the requirements since they are the ones who know what they need. For example, if the customer is an employer, and the user is an employee of the company buying the product, this may result in conflicts. It is possible to imagine features that are desirable to an employer, but not an employee.

4.5.2 Several Known Customers

When having several customers, the issue of prioritization becomes more difficult since the customers may have conflicting viewpoints and preferences [1]. This introduces the challenge of drawing these different customer views together [38]. The ultimate goal in these situations is to create win-win conditions and make every stakeholder a "winner" [6]. If one perspective is neglected the system might be seen as a failure by one or several of the stakeholders [1]. Hence, it is of tremendous importance that all stakeholders are involved in this process since the success of the product ultimately is decided in this step. A discussion on how to make trade-offs between different stakeholders is provided in Sect. 4.5.5.

4.5.3 Mass-Market

When developing for a mass-market, it is not possible to get all customers to prioritize. When eliciting information for prioritization in a mass-market situation, different sources exist [35]: internal records (e.g. shipments, sales records), marketing intelligence (e.g. information from sales force, scientists), competitor intelligence (e.g. information about competitors' strategies, benchmarking competitors' products) and marketing research (e.g. surveys, focus groups). When conducting marketing research, the sample must be representative for the intended market segment (group of consumers with similar needs) [35]. For example, if developing products for large companies, it is meaningless to involve small companies in the focus groups or the surveys. Hence, it is very important to decide which market segments should be the focus of the product before performing the prioritization.

The result from a prioritization for a mass-market product could provide a good base for analyzing which requirements are high priorities for all different market segments. By using this information, it is possible to identify which parts of a system should be common for all market segments and which parts should be specifically developed for specific market segments. This way of dealing with requirements is valuable when developing software product lines [14].

One way of dealing with the problem that all possible users are not known or accessible is to use the concept of "personas" that originated in marketing and has been used in system design [25]. These personas are fictional persons, representing market segments. They have names, occupations, possessions, age, gender, socioeconomic status, etc. They are based on and inspired by real people that are supposed to use the developed product. This information is gathered from ethnographies, market research, usability studies, interviews, observations, and so forth. The intention is to help the developing organization focus the attention on personas that the system is and is not designed for, and to give an understanding of these target personas. Further, personas enhance engagement and reality by providing fictional users of the system. The developing organization can use the personas in decision-making (and prioritization) by asking questions like: Why are we building this feature (requirement)? Why are we building it like this? When having such explicit but fictitious users of the system, the organization can get an understanding of which choices the personas would make in different situations.

4.5.4 Stakeholders Represented in the Prioritization

Since requirements can be prioritized from several different aspects, different roles must also be involved in the prioritization process to get the correct views (e.g. product managers prioritize strategic importance and project managers prioritize risks). At least three perspectives should always be represented: customers, developers, and financial representatives [17]. Each of these stakeholders provides vital information that the other two may neglect or are unable to produce since customers care about the user/customer value, developers know about the technical difficulties, and financial representatives know and care for budgetary constraints and risks [17]. Nevertheless, it is of course suitable to involve all perspectives (beside these three) that have a stake in the project or product.

4.5.5 Trade-Off between Different Stakeholders

In both market-driven and bespoke projects, there can be several different stakeholders with different priorities and expectations of the system. How to make trade-offs between several stakeholders with different priorities is an issue that is commonly mentioned as a problem by product managers in software organizations. First, this could be a problem when having one or a few very strong stakeholders since their wishes are often hard to neglect (i.e. when the big customer says jump, the company jumps). Second, "squeaky wheel" customers often get what they want [38, 58].

In such situations, it is important to have a structured way of handling different stakeholders. Regnell et al. adjust the influence of each stakeholder by prioritize for different aspects [45]. This can be done by weighting market segments based on for example: revenue last year, profit last release, size of total market segment, number of potential customers, etc. The weighting aspect depend on the strategy most suitable in the current market phase ([43], cited in [45]). Priorities are then used to weigh each stakeholder in the prioritization process. This approach is also possible when dealing with specific stakeholders even though the aspects on which the priorities are based might be different. The weighting of the stakeholders could be performed in the same way as ordinary prioritization, and the techniques described in Sect. 4.4 could be used to provide the weights (preferably the techniques based on a ratio scale since these will provide distances of importance between the stakeholders).

4.6 Using Requirements Prioritization

Requirements prioritization needs to consider several different aspects, techniques, and stakeholder situations. This section presents additional issues to consider and ways of dealing with such issues.

4.6.1 Abstraction Level

Requirements are commonly represented at different levels of abstraction [23], which causes problems when prioritizing requirements. One reason is that requirements on higher abstraction levels tend to get higher priority in pair-wise comparisons [39]. For example, if prioritizing requirements in a car, a lamp in the dashboard cannot be compared with having a luggage boot. Most customers would probably prefer a luggage boot over a lamp in the dashboard but if one had to compare a lamp in the luggage boot and a lamp in the dashboard, the lamp in the dashboard might have higher priority. Hence, it is really important that the requirements are not mixed at different abstraction levels [57].

Deciding on the level of abstraction can be difficult and depend very much on the number of requirements and their complexity. With a small number of requirements, it might be possible to prioritize the requirements at a low level of abstraction while it might be a good idea to start with requirements at a high level and prioritize lower levels within the higher levels later when having many requirements to prioritize [57]. AHP supports this approach of decomposing requirements into different hierarchical levels in order to decrease the number of comparisons. In other cases, it might even be a good idea to just prioritize the high level requirements, and then letting the subordinate requirements inherit the priorities. If choosing this approach, it is important that all stakeholders are aware of this inheritance [57].

Regnell et al. discuss the problem of having a lot of requirements to prioritize [45]. They grouped the requirements to make the prioritization easier. The requirements were divided into a low level (original requirements) and a higher level (requirements were grouped based on relationships). This approach not only reduces the number of requirements to prioritize but also deals with dependencies of requirements [50]. Grouping requirements based on requirements dependencies (e.g. which requirements must be implemented together) would make further analysis of the requirements easier since requirements that are grouped together would not compete for priorities (issues related to dependencies are further discussed in Chap. 5). According to the result of the study, forming coherent groups was easy and the stakeholders successfully prioritized at both levels.

4.6.2 Reprioritization

When developing software products, it is likely that new requirements will arrive, requirements are deleted, priorities of existing requirements change, or that the requirements themselves change [24, 39]. Hence, it is of tremendous importance that the prioritization process is able to deal with changing requirements and priorities of already prioritized requirements. When prioritizations are on an ordinal (e.g. ranking and numerical assignment) or absolute scale (estimating cost) this does not introduce any major problems since the new or changed requirement just need to be assigned a value, or a correct priority. Such iterations of the numerical assignment technique have been used successfully [17].

When using prioritization on a ratio scale (such as AHP), the situation becomes more complex since all requirements should be compared to all others to establish the correct relative priorities. However, it is possible to tailor this process by comparing new or modified requirements with certain reference requirements and thereby estimating the relative value. For example, when using the 100-dollar test it is possible to identify the two requirements with higher and lower *ranking*, and then establish the relative value in comparison to these and normalize the weights (of the complete requirements set). However, this means that the original process is not followed and the result might differ from a complete reprioritization even though the cost versus benefit of such a solution might be good enough. Cost and benefit must be taken into consideration when choosing a prioritization technique.

Further, it is important to not forget that priorities of already implemented requirements can change; especially non-functional requirements. Techniques such as gap-analysis (see Sect. 4.6.5) could be successfully used to prioritize already implemented requirements in order to take these into account in a reprioritization.

4.6.3 Non-Functional Requirements

Previously in this chapter, no differences in analyzing functional and non-functional (quality attributes) requirements have been discussed. The previously presented methods can be used with both kinds of requirements and sometimes it is preferable to prioritize them together. Nevertheless, it is not *always* advisable to prioritize functional and non-functional requirements together, for the same reasons that requirements at different abstraction levels should not be prioritized together. Differences between functional and non-functional requirements include, but are not limited to [36, 47, 56]:

- Functional requirements usually relate to specific functions while non-functional requirements usually affect several functions (from a collection of functions to the whole system).
- Non-functional requirements are properties that the functions or system must have, implying that non-functional requirements are useless without functional requirements.
- When implemented, functional requirements either work or not while non-functional requirements often have a "sliding value scale" of good and bad.
- Non-functional requirements are often in conflict with each other, implying that trade-offs between these requirements must be made.

Thus, it is not always possible or advisable to prioritize both types of requirements together. For example, if there is one functional requirement about a specific function and one non-functional requirement regarding performance, it could be hard to prioritize between them. In such cases, it is possible to prioritize them separately with the same or even with different techniques. Some techniques are especially suitable for prioritizing non-functional requirements. One such approach (originating from marketing) is conjoint analysis where different product alternatives are prioritized based on the definition of different attribute levels [22]. It should be noted that there does not seem to be a need to include all levels of all attributes (e.g. faster response time is always preferable). Since trade-offs often are present with such attributes (e.g. maintainability vs. performance), one idea is to only include comparisons where trade-offs are taken into consideration.

4.6.4 Introducing Prioritization into an Organization

As with other technology transfer situations, it is recommended to start small with one or a few of the practices (e.g. using numerical assignment to prioritize importance and cost) and then add more sophistication (and thereby complexity) as need and knowledge increase. Since introducing and improving prioritization is a form of process improvement, rules and guidelines for software process improvement should be applied (e.g. changes should be done in small steps and should be tested and adjusted accordingly [28]). A good idea could be to monitor future extensions by measuring process adherence and satisfaction of the involved stakeholders (both internally and externally). This way, it is possible to continuously measure the process and thereby determine when the process gets too heavy by calculating the cost versus benefit of each extension.

4.6.5 Evaluating Prioritization

Both for the reasons of improving and adjusting the prioritization process, and for improving and adjusting a product, it is necessary to evaluate the result of prioritizations in retrospect. For both purposes, it is important that information about the priorities is kept since these provide the best information for analyzing both the product and the process [38]. This includes information about both selected and discarded requirements from a release [46]. When having access to this information, it is possible to do post mortem analysis to evaluate if the correct requirements were selected and if they fulfilled the stakeholders' expectations. If they did not, it is possible to change the process and the product for subsequent products/releases to get better prioritizations and more satisfied stakeholders. One way of evaluating if the correct priorities were assigned is through gap-analysis where the "gap" between perceived levels of fulfillment of a requirement and the importance of the requirement is calculated [27]. The result shows how well each requirement, or type of requirement, is fulfilled according to how important the stakeholders think the requirements are. In this case, the requirements with the largest gaps get the highest priorities for improvement (PFI) [27]. This makes it possible to improve parts of the product with a low level of fulfillment, but it could also be used to tune the process to avoid such situations again.

4.6.6 Using the Results of Requirements Prioritization

The results of a prioritization exercise must be used judiciously [39]. Dependencies between requirements should be taken into consideration when choosing which requirements to include. Dependencies could be related to cost, value, changes, people, competence, technical precedence, etc. [16, 49]. Such dependencies might force one requirement to be implemented before another, implying that it is not possible to just follow the prioritization list (dependencies are further discussed in Chap. 5). Another reason for not being able to solely base the selected requirements on the priority list is that when the priority list is presented to the stakeholders, their initial priority might have emerged incorrectly [39]. This means that when the stakeholders are confronted with the priority list, they want to change priorities. This is a larger problem in techniques where the result is not visible throughout the process (e.g. AHP).

The product may have some naturally built-in constraints. For example, projects have constraints when it comes to effort, quality, duration, etc. [50]. Such constraints makes the selection of which requirements to include in a product more complex than if the choice were solely based on the importance of each requirement. A common approach to make this selection is to propose a number of alternative solutions from which the stakeholders can choose the one that is most suitable based on all implicit context factors [24, 38, 48, 50, 57]. By computerizing the process of selecting nominated solutions, it is possible to focus the stakeholders' attention on a relatively small number of candidate solutions instead of wasting their time by discussing all possible alternatives [19]. In order to automate and to provide a small set of candidate solutions to choose from, it is necessary to put some constraints on the final product. For example, there could be constraints that the product is not allowed to cost more than a specific amount, the time for development is not allowed to exceed a limit, or the risk level is not allowed to be over a specific threshold.

4.7 An Example of a Requirements Prioritization

To illustrate the different aspects, prioritization techniques, trade-offs between stakeholders, and combinations of prioritization techniques and aspects, an example of a prioritization situation is given. The method used in this example is influenced by a model proposed by Wiegers but is tailored to fit this example [57]. The example analyses 15 requirements (R1-R15) in a situation with three known customers (see 4.5.2). The analysis is rather sophisticated to show different issues in prioritization but still simple with a small amount of requirements. While many more requirements are common in industry, it is easier to illustrate how the techniques work on a smaller example. Each of the 15 requirements is prioritized according to the different aspects presented in Sect. 4.3. Table 4.3 presents the aspects that are used in the example together with the method that is used to prioritize the aspect and from which perspective it is prioritized.

Table 4.3 Aspects to prioritize

Aspect	Prioritization Technique	Perspective
Strategic importance	AHP	Product Manager
Customer importance	100-dollar / Top-ten[1]	Customers
Penalty	AHP	Product Manager
Cost	100-dollar	Developers
Time	Numerical Assignment (7)	Project Manager
Risk	Numerical Assignment (3)	Requirements Specialist
Volatility	Ranking	Requirements Specialist

As can be seen in Table 4.3, all prioritization techniques presented in Sect. 4.4 are used. However, two clarifications are in order. First, numerical assignment for time (7) and risk (3) uses a different number of groups to show varying levels of granularity. The customer importance is prioritized both by the top-ten technique and the 100-dollar technique depending how much time and cost the different customers consider reasonable.

To make the prioritizations more effective, requirements are further refined. First, requirements R1 and R2 are requirements that are absolutely necessary to get the system to work at all. Hence, they are not prioritized by the customers but they are estimated when it comes to cost, risk, etc. since R1 and R2 influence these variables no matter what. This is a way of using the requirements triage approach presented in Sect. 4.4.7. Further, two groups of requirements have been identified as having high dependencies (must be implemented together) and

---

[1] The top-ten technique is modified to a top-four technique in this example due to the limited number of requirements.

should hence be prioritized together. Requirements R3, R4, and R5 are grouped together as R345, and requirements R6 and R7 are grouped into R67.

Table 4.4 Prioritization results of strategic and customer importance. Priority, $P(R_X) = RP_{C1} \times W_{C1} + RP_{C2} \times W_{C2} + RP_{C3} \times W_{C3} + RP_{PM} \times W_{PM}$, where RP is the requirement priority, and W is the weight of the stakeholder

Requirement	C1 (0.15)	C2 (0.30)	C3 (0.20)	PM (0.35)	Priority:
R8	0.25	0.24	0.16	0.15	0.19
R9		0.07	0.14	0.03	0.06
R10	0.25	0.05	0.13	0.29	0.18
R11		0.05	0.01	0.02	0.02
R12		0.16	0.04	0.01	0.06
R13		0.05	0.16	0.02	0.05
R14	0.25	0.02	0.10	0.10	0.10
R15		0.03	0.04	0.05	0.03
R345		0.04	0.18	0.17	0.11
R67	0.25	0.29	0.04	0.16	0.19
Total:	1	1	1	1	1

Table 4.5 Descending priority list based on importance and penalty (IP). $IP(R_X) = RP_I \times W_I + RP_P \times W_P$, where RP is the requirement priority, and W is the weight of Importance (I) and Penalty (P)

Requirement	Importance (0.7)	Penalty (0.3)	IP	Cost	Time	Risk	Volatility
R1	1	1	1	0.11	3	1	2
R2	1	1	1	0.13	4	2	1
R8	0.19	0.2	0.20	0.07	1	3	7
R67	0.19	0.09	0.16	0.10	6	3	5
R10	0.18	0.01	0.13	0.24	2	3	11
R14	0.10	0.16	0.12	0.01	1	3	10
R345	0.11	0.02	0.08	0.03	3	2	8
R9	0.06	0.12	0.08	0.09	3	2	9
R15	0.03	0.17	0.08	0.05	5	1	4
R12	0.06	0.06	0.06	0.11	4	2	6
R11	0.02	0.14	0.06	0.02	3	1	3
R13	0.05	0.03	0.05	0.04	7	1	12
Total / Median:	3	3	3	1	3	2	

The next step is to prioritize the importance of the requirements. In the case at hand, the three known customers and the product manager prioritize the requirements. Furthermore, these four stakeholders are assigned different weights depending on how important they are deemed by the company. This is done by using the 100-dollar test to get the relative weights between the stakeholders (see Sect. 4.5.5). Table 4.4 presents the result of the prioritization. In the table, the three customers are denoted C1–C3 and the product manager is denoted PM.

As can be seen in this table, the different stakeholders have different priorities, and it is possible to combine their different views to an overall priority. The weights (within parenthesis after each stakeholder) represent the importance of each customer and in this case, the product manager is assigned the highest weight (0.35). This is very project dependent. In this case, the mission of this product release is to invest in long-term requirements and attract new customers at the same time as keeping existing ones. As also can be seen, C1 used the top-ten technique and hence the priorities were evenly divided between the requirements that this customer regarded as most important. The list to the far right presents the final priority of the requirements with the different stakeholders and their weights taken into consideration. This calculation is possible since a ratio scale has been used instead of an ordinal scale.

The next step is to prioritize based on the other aspects. In this case, the Priority from Table 4.4 is used to express Importance in Table 4.5. It should also be noted that requirements R1 and R2 (absolutely necessary) have been added in Table 4.5.

Table 4.6 Selected requirements based on IP and cost

Requirement	IP	Cost	IP/Cost	Time	Risk	Volatility
R1	1	0.11	9.09	3	1	2
R2	1	0.13	7.69	4	2	1
R8	0.20	0.07	2.80	1	3	7
R67	0.16	0.1	1.59	6	3	5
R10	0.13	0.24	0.54	2	3	11
Total / Median:	2.48	0.65	21.71	3	3	

Table 4.5 shows a prioritized list of the requirements (based on IP). With this information there are two options: 1) pick prioritized items from the top of the list until the cost constraints are reached, 2) analyze further based on other prioritized aspects, if prioritizations of additional aspects are available. The example has two major constraints: 1) the project is not allowed to cost more than 65% of the total cost of the elicited requirements, and 2) the median risk level of the requirements included is not allowed to be higher than 2.5. Based on this, we first try to include the requirements with the highest IP. The result of this is presented in Table 4.6 where the list was cut when the sum of costs reached 65% of the total cost of elicited requirements.

Table 4.6 shows that we managed to fit within the cost constraints but could not satisfy the risk constraint. As a result, the project becomes too risky. Instead, another approach is taken to find a suitable collection of requirements. In this approach, we take the IP/Cost ratio into consideration. This shows which requirements provide most IP at the least cost. In this case, we try to set up a limit of only selecting requirements that have an IP/Cost-ratio higher than 1.0. The result is presented in Table 4.7. Table 4.7 shows the cost constraints are still met (even nine percent less cost) while also satisfying the risk constraint. Comparing tables 4.6 and 4.7 shows that the IP-value of the second candidate solution is higher which indicates that the customers are more satisfied with the product and the IP/Cost ratio is almost doubled. The second candidate solution satisfies 91 percent (2.73/3) of the IP aspect, compared to 83 percent in the first candidate solution. The fact that the second alternative costs less and is less risky also favors this choice. Nevertheless, the above example is not optimal since cost was constrained at 0.65 and other combinations of requirements may be more optimal for the selection.

Table 4.7 Selected requirements based on cost and IP/cost ratio.

Requirement	IP	Cost	IP/Cost	Time	Risk	Volatility
R1	1	0.11	9.09	3	1	2
R2	1	0.13	7.69	4	2	1
R8	0.20	0.07	2.80	1	3	7
R67	0.16	0.1	1.59	6	3	5
R14	0.12	0.01	11.70	1	3	10
R345	0.08	0.03	2.71	3	2	8
R15	0.08	0.05	1.50	5	1	4
R11	0.06	0.02	2.94	2	1	3
R13	0.05	0.04	1.17	7	1	12
Total / Median:	2.73	0.56	41.19	3	2	

This type of release planning is known in operational research as the binary knapsack problem [13]: maximize value when the selection is bounded by an upper limit. However, the difference between a classical knapsack problem and the problem faced above is that release planning is a "wicked problem" [13]. This means that an optimal solution may not exist, that every release planning is unique, and that no objective measure of success exists, etc. [13]. In addition, the values of the aspects in the above example are estimates and subjective measures in comparison to objective measures such a length, weight, and volume. Instead of finding the optimal set, different alternative solutions should be discovered and the alternative that seems most suitable should be chosen [13]. This implies that the purpose with prioritization is not to come up with a list of final requirements, but rather to provide support for good decisions. In comparison to the above example, real projects generally have more requirements, and more complex dependencies [13]. However, this example was meant to show how different aspects can be used to handle trade-offs between different (sometimes conflicting) aspects. It is also possible, as illustrated, to fine-tune an existing technique or method to suit a company specific situation.

4.8 Future Research in the Area of Requirements Prioritization

Requirements engineering is a field with much research activity. One journal, several workshops, and one large annual international conference are devoted to requirements engineering. Nevertheless, the existing work in the area of requirements prioritization is limited even though the need for prioritizing software requirements is acknowledged in the research literature [32]. Especially, few empirical validations of different prioritization techniques and methods exist. Instead, it is common that new techniques and methods are introduced and they seem to work well, but the scalability of the approach has not been tested [48]. However, there exist some studies that have evaluated different prioritization techniques [33,

34]. Unfortunately, such empirical evaluations most often focus on toy systems with a few requirements (seldom more than 20). This is not really providing any evidence of whether one technique is better than another even though some preliminary evidence could be found. One of the few industry studies, for example, found that AHP was not usable with more than 20 requirements since the number of comparisons became too many for the practitioners [39]. Hence, more studies are needed when prioritization methods are used in industry.

A further question that seldom is addressed in requirements prioritization research is the question of how much sophistication is actually needed. Many techniques and methods are developed and they become more and more complex with the goal to provide more help for practitioners but the results are seldom used in industry. Instead, professionals use simple methods such as numerical assignment. Practitioners live in a different environment than experimental subjects (often students) and are more limited by time and cost constraints [4]. Hence, an important question to answer is how much sophistication (and thereby complexity) is actually necessary and desirable by practitioners?

The above issues lead to another open question about when a technique or method is suitable. Existing empirical studies seldom discuss factors such as company size, time-to-market limitations, number of stakeholders, domain, etc. Instead, focus is on whether a technique or method is better than another one. A more sound approach would be to test different approaches in various environments to get some understanding when different prioritization techniques, aspects, etc. are suitable. In [21] a framework for evaluating pair programming is suggested and independent (e.g. technique), dependent (e.g. quality), and context variables (e.g. type of task) are proposed for evaluating programming techniques. A similar framework for requirements prioritization would be beneficial.

Another important question in the area of requirements prioritization concerns dependencies between requirements. Dependencies are not covered in this chapter since Chap. 5 discusses this in detail. Nevertheless, the impact of dependencies can be tremendous. For example, prioritization techniques (such as AHP) assume that requirements are independent even though we know that they seldom are [46]. We need to find better ways to handle dependencies in an efficient way.

As could be seen in Sect. 4.6.3, functional and non-functional requirements are very different even though they have a serious impact on each other. Prioritizing these two entirely together or separately might not be the best solution. Approaches where prioritizations of functional and non-functional could be combined in an efficient way are necessary. Different methods that seem suitable for prioritizing non-functional requirements are available (e.g. Conjoint Analysis [22], and Quality Grid [36]) and it would be interesting to evaluate these empirically in industrial settings. Further, finding ways to combine such approaches with approaches more directed to functional requirements would be a challenge.

4.9 Summary

This chapter has presented a number of techniques, aspects, and other issues that should be thought of when performing prioritizations. These different parts together form a basis for systematically prioritizing requirements during software development. The result of prioritizations suggests which requirements should be implemented, and in which release. Hence, the techniques could be a valuable help for companies to get an understanding of what is important and what is not for a project or a product. As with all evaluation methods, the results should be interpreted and possibly adjusted by knowledgeable decision-makers rather than simply accepted as a final decision.

References

1. Aurum A, Wohlin C (2003) The fundamental nature of requirements engineering activities as a decision-making process. Information and Software Technology 45(14): 945–954
2. Beck K (1999) Extreme programming explained. Addison-Wesley, Upper Saddle River
3. Berander P, Wohlin C (2004) Differences in views between development roles in software process improvement – A quantitative comparison. In: Proceedings of the 8th International Conference on Empirical Assessment in Software Engineering (EASE 2004). IEE, Stevenage, pp.57–66
4. Berander P (2004) Using students as subjects in requirements prioritization. In: Proceedings of the 2004 International Symposium on Empirical Software Engineering (ISESE'04). IEEE Computer Society, Los Alamitos, pp.167–176
5. Boehm BW (1981) Software engineering economics. Prentice Hall, Englewood Cliffs
6. Boehm BW, Ross R (1989) Theory-W software project management: Principles and examples. IEEE Transactions on Software Engineering 15(7):902–916
7. Bergman B, Klefsjö B (2003) Quality from customer needs to customer satisfaction. Published by Studentlitteratur AB, Lund, Sweden
8. Bradner S (1997) RFC 2119. http://www.ietf.org/rfc/rfc2119.txt (24 November 2004)
9. Bray IK (2002) An introduction to requirements engineering. Pearson Education, London
10. Brooks FP (1995) The mythical man-month: Essays on software engineering. Addison-Wesley Longman, Boston
11. Carlshamre P (2001) A usability perspective on requirements engineering – From methodology to product development. Ph.D. thesis, Linköping Institute of Technology, Sweden
12. Carlshamre P, Sandahl K, Lindvall M, Regnell B, Natt och Dag J (2001) An industrial survey of requirements interdependencies in software release planning. In: Proceedings of the 5th IEEE International Symposium on Requirements Engineering (RE'01). IEEE Computer Society, Los Alamitos, pp 84–91
13. Carlshamre P (2002) Release planning in market-driven software product development: provoking an understanding requirements engineering 7(3):139–151
14. Clements P, Northrop L (2002) Software product lines – Practices and patterns. Addison-Wesley, Upper Saddle River

15. Colombo E, Francalanci C (2004) Selecting CRM packages based on architectural, functional, and cost requirements: Empirical validation of a hierarchical ranking model. Requirements Engineering 9(3):186-203

16. Dahlstedt Å, Persson A (2003) Requirements interdependencies – Molding the state of research into a research agenda. In: Proceedings of the 9th International Workshop on Requirements Engineering: Foundation for Software Quality (REFSQ '03). Universität Duisburg-Essen, Essen, pp. 71–80

17. Davis AM (2003) The art of requirements triage. IEEE Computer 36(3):42–49

18. Ecklund EF, Delcambre LML, Freiling MJ (1996) Change cases: Use cases that identify future requirements. In: Proceedings of the 11th ACM SIGPLAN Conference on Object-Oriented Programming, Systems, Languages, and Applications (OOPSLA '96). ACM, USA, pp. 342–358

19. Feather MS, Menzies T (2002) Converging on the optimal attainment of requirements. In: Proceedings of the IEEE Joint International Conference on Requirements Engineering (RE'02). IEEE Computer Society, Los Alamitos, pp. 263–270

20. Fenton, NE, Pfleeger SL (1997) Software metrics – A rigorous and practical approach, 2nd Edition. PWS Publishing Company, Boston

21. Gallis H, Arisholm E, Dybå T (2003) An initial framework for research on pair programming. In: Proceedings of the 2003 International Symposium on Empirical Software Engineering (ISESE'03). IEEE Computer Society, Los Alamitos, pp.132–142

22. Giesen, J, Völker A (2002) Requirements interdependencies and stakeholders preferences. In: Proceedings of the IEEE Joint International Conference on Requirements Engineering (RE'02). IEEE Computer Society, Los Alamitos, pp.206–209

23. Gorschek T (2004) Software process assessment & improvement in industrial requirements engineering. Licentiate Thesis, Blekinge Institute of Technology

24. Greer D, Ruhe G (2004) Software release planning: An evolutionary and iterative approach. Information and Software Technology 46(4): 243–253

25. Grudin J, Pruitt J (2002) Personas, participatory design and product development: An infrastructure for engagement. Participation and Design Conference (PDC2002), Computer Professionals for Social Responsibility, Palo Alto, pp.144–161

26. Harker PT (1987) Incomplete pairwise comparisons in the analytic hierarchy process. Mathematical Modeling 9(11): 837–848

27. Hill N, Brierly J, MacDougall R (1999) How to measure customer satisfaction. Gower Publishing, Hampshire

28. Humphrey WS (1989) Managing the software process. Addison-Wesley, USA

29. IEEE Std 830-1998 (1998) IEEE recommended practice for software requirements specifications. IEEE Computer Society, Los Alamitos

30. Karlsson J, Ryan K (1997) A cost-value approach for prioritizing requirements. IEEE Software 14(5): 67–74

31. Karlsson J, Olsson S, Ryan K (1997) Improved practical support for large-scale requirements prioritizing. Requirements Engineering 2(1): 51–60

32. Karlsson J (1998) A systematic approach for prioritizing software requirements. Ph.D. Thesis, Linköping Institute of Technology

33. Karlsson J, Wohlin C, Regnell B (1998) An evaluation of methods for prioritizing software requirements. Information and Software Technology 39(14-15): 939–947

34. Karlsson L, Berander P, Regnell B, Wohlin C (2004) Requirements prioritisation: An experiment on exhaustive pair-wise comparisons versus planning game partitioning. In: Proceedings of the 8th International Conference on Empirical Assessment in Software Engineering (EASE 2004). IEE, Stevenage, pp.145–154

35. Kotler P, Armstron G, Saunders J, Wong V (2002) Principles of marketing, 3rd European Edition. Pearson Education, Essex

36. Lausen S (2002) Software requirements – styles and techniques. Pearson Education, Essex

37. Leffingwell D, Widrig D (2000) Managing software requirements – A unified approach. Addison-Wesley, Upper Saddle River

38. Lehtola L, Kauppinen M, Kujala S (2004) Requirements prioritization challenges in practice. In: Proceedings of 5th International Conference on Product Focused Software Process Improvement, Lecture Notes in Computer Science (vol. 3009), Springer-Verlag, Heidelberg, pp.497-508

39. Lehtola L, Kauppinen M (2004) Empirical evaluation of two requirements prioritization methods in product development projects. In: Proceedings of the European Software Process Improvement Conference (EuroSPI 2004), Springer-Verlag, Berlin Heidelberg, pp.161–170

40. Lubars M, Potts C, Richter C (1993) A review of the state of practice in requirements modeling. In: Proceedings of IEEE International Symposium on Requirements Engineering, IEEE Computer Society, Los Alamitos, pp.2-14

41. Maciaszek LA (2001) Requirements analysis and system design – Developing information systems with UML. Addison Wesley, London

42. Maiden NAM, Ncube C (1998) Acquiring COTS software selection requirements. IEEE Software 15(2):46–56

43. Moore G (1991) Crossing the chasm. HarperCollins, New York

44. Nicholas JM (2001) Project management for business and technology: Principles and Practice. Prentice Hall, Upper Saddle River

45. Regnell B, Höst M, Natt och Dag J, Beremark P, Hjelm T (2001) An industrial case study on distributed prioritization in market-driven requirements engineering for packaged software. Requirements Engineering 6(1):51-62

46. Regnell B, Paech B, Aurum A, Wohlin C, Dutoit A, Natt och Dag J (2001) Requirements mean decisions! – Research issues for understanding and supporting decision-making in requirements engineering. In: Proceedings of 1st Swedish Conference on Software Engineering Research and Practise (SERP'01). Blekinge Institute of Technology, Ronneby, pp. 49–52

47. Robertson S, Robertson J (1999) Mastering the requirements process. ACM Press, London

48. Ruhe G, Eberlein A, Pfahl D (2002) Quantitative WinWin – A new method for decision support in requirements negotiation. In: Proceedings of the 14th International Conference on Software Engineering and Knowledge Engineering (SEKE'02), ACM Press, New York, pp. 159–166

49. Ruhe G (2003) Software engineering decision support - A new paradigm for learning software organizations. Advances in learning software organization, Lecture Notes in Computer Science, Springer-Verlag, Vol. 2640, pp.104–115

50. Ruhe G, Eberlein A, Pfahl D (2003) Trade-off analysis for requirements selection. International journal of Software Engineering and Knowledge Engineering 13(4): 345–366

51. Saaty TL (1980) The analytic hierarchy process. McGraw-Hill, New York
52. Saaty TL, Vargas LG (2001) Models, methods, concepts & applications of the analytic hierarchy process. Kluwer Academic Publishers, Norwell
53. Schulmeyer GG, McManus JI (1999) Handbook of software quality assurance, 3rd Edition. Prentice Hall, Upper Saddle River
54. Shen Y, Hoerl AE, McConnell W (1992) An incomplete design in the analytical hierarchy process. Mathematical computer modeling 16(5):121–129
55. Sommerville I, Sawyer P (1997) Requirements engineering – A good practice guide. John Wiley and Sons, Chichester
56. Sommerville I (2001) Software engineering, 6th Edition. Pearson Education, London
57. Wiegers K (1999) Software requirements. Microsoft Press, Redmond
58. Yeh AC (1992) REQUirements engineering support technique (REQUEST) – A market driven requirements management process. In: Proceedings of 2nd Symposium of Quality Software Development Tools. IEEE Computer Society, Piscataway, pp.211–223

Author Biography

Patrik Berander is a Ph.D. student in Software Engineering at the School of Engineering at Blekinge Institute of Technology in Sweden. He received his degree of Master of Science with a major in Software Engineering – with a specialization in Management in 2002. His research interests are requirements engineering in general and decisions related to requirements and products in particular. Further research interests include software product management, software quality, economic issues in software development, and software process management.

Dr. Anneliese Amschler Andrews is the Huie Rogers Endowed Chair in Software Engineering at Washington State University. Dr. Andrews is the author of a textbook and over 130 articles in the area of Software Engineering, particularly software testing and maintenance. Dr. Andrews holds an MS and PhD from Duke University and a Dipl.-Inf. from the Technical University of Karlsruhe. She served as Editor in Chief of the IEEE Transactions on Software Engineering. She has also served on several other editorial boards including the IEEE Transactions on Reliability, the Empirical Software Engineering Journal, the Software Quality Journal, the Journal of Information and Software Technology, and the Journal of Software Maintenance. She was Director of the Colorado Advanced Software Institute from 1995 to 2002. CASI's mission was to support technology transfer research related to software through collaborations between industry and academia.

5 Requirements Interdependencies: State of the Art and Future Challenges

Åsa G. Dahlstedt and Anne Persson

Abstract: It is well acknowledged in practice as well as in research that requirements are related to each other and that these relationships affect software development work in various ways. This chapter addresses requirements interdependencies, starting from a traceability perspective. The focus of the chapter is on giving an overview of requirements interdependency research and on synthesizing this into a model of fundamental interdependency types and a research agenda for the area. Furthermore, a description of how knowledge about requirements interdependencies can facilitate various activities within software engineering is provided. The main challenges for the future are to understand the nature of requirements interdependencies and to develop approaches that enable to identify, describe and effectively deal with them in the software development process.

Keywords: Requirements traceability, Requirements interdependencies, Requirements dependencies, Requirement coupling.

5.1 Introduction

Most individual requirements, developed during the requirements engineering (RE) process, cannot be treated in isolation during software development. Instead they are related to and affect each other in complex manners [5, 33]. A recent study has shown that only approximately a fifth of the requirements in any set of requirements are truly singular, i.e., are not related to or influence any other requirements [5]. Examples of how requirements may affect each other are when one requirement:

- Constrains how other requirements can be designed or implemented
- Affects the cost of implementation of other requirements, or
- Increases or decreases the customer satisfaction of other requirements

Requirements interdependencies are not problematic per-se, but they influence a number of development activities and decisions made during the software engineering process, e.g. in release planning [5, 20], change management [22, 37], requirements design and implementation [35], testing [8], and requirements reuse [38]. These activities or decisions may be based on one or several requirements and may affect other requirements in ways not intended or not even anticipated. For example, a change made to one requirement may affect several other requirements making them to change as well [22, 26]. Neglecting these dependencies when assessing the impact of a change may result in neglecting some of the actual impact of a change. Consequently, the cost of implementing a requirement may become several times higher than expected, and in turn cause budget or schedule problems (see Chap. 6). A similar example is within release planning, where an optimal set of requirements is selected for implementation in the next release of a software system. It is not always possible to select the requirements with highest priority, due to requirements interdependencies. Implementing a high priority requirement may, e.g., require that a requirement with low priority and high cost must be implemented first [5, 20]. Understanding and knowing about these relationships is important in order to avoid selecting a set of requirements that must be changed later, which may potentially cause costly modifications of the software.

Knowing about the existence and consequences of requirements interdependencies is hence essential in order to avoid costly mistakes. The purpose of systematically dealing with requirements interdependencies is to improve decisions made during software development and also to support early detection of potential problems due to requirements interdependencies. Managing requirements interdependencies is about identifying, storing, and maintaining information about how requirements relate to and affect each other. This also involves deciding which interdependency information is needed in various situations in the software development process and how that information should be presented.

Despite the need for and potential benefits of systematically taking requirements interdependencies into account, there is little research invested in this topic and more is needed [4, 5, 20]. In addition, existing literature tends to address the topic based on a specific problem or development activity [5, 20, 35, 28]. As a consequence, current knowledge about requirements interdependencies is spread throughout the literature into different segments dealing with specific aspects and development activities. It is certainly important to address the area focusing on specific development activities, but the literature about the common characteristics of requirements interdependencies is scarce. The objective of this chapter is hence to synthesize existing knowledge regarding requirements interdependencies in order to give an overall view of the area through describing the state of the art and presenting a research agenda for future research in the area.

In the following we outline requirements traceability, in order to place requirements interdependencies into a context (Sect. 5.2). This is followed by an overview of fundamental types of interdependencies that can exist between requirements (Sect. 5.3). A discussion on how knowledge about requirements interdependencies can facilitate software engineering is given in Sect. 5.4. Section 5.5 outlines a research agenda for the area, and finally, a summary is given in Sect. 5.6.

5.2 Requirements Traceability: A Basis for Understanding Requirements Interdependencies

There are several different definitions of the term requirements traceability (see e.g. [16, 18, 26, 34]). In this chapter, we have chosen to define it as the "ability to describe and follow the life of a requirement, in both forward and backward direction, ideally through the whole system life cycle" ([17], p. 32, based on [13]). This definition is one of the most frequently used within the field. Requirements traceability is, generally speaking, achieved through associating related information objects such as:

- Requirements and related system components satisfying those requirements
- System objectives and requirements derived from those requirements
- Change proposals and requirements which they intend to change
- A decision and the rationales and assumptions on which they are based
- Test cases and the requirements which fulfillment they intend to ensure, and
- System components and the resources needed to implement those requirements

The topic of requirements interdependencies is viewed as a specific aspect of traceability, since it is about associating related information of a specific type – namely requirements (see the shaded area in Fig. 5.1). Therefore, in order to place requirements interdependencies into a context this section aims at providing an overview of the area of requirements traceability.

5.2.1 Why Requirements Traceability?

Requirements traceability is nowadays considered as important support for developing high quality software systems. In order to avoid costly mistakes, traceability information is needed as a basis for decisions and tasks in most phases of the software development process [12, 26]. One example is within change integration, where traceability information enables identification of the impact of a proposed change [22, 30, 37]. Identifying how requirements and other artifacts are affected by the change proposal facilitates more accurate cost and schedule analysis. Requirements traceability also supports the understanding of why a certain object has been created, modified and evolved [30]. This motivates and explains the decisions and trade-offs made during development work, and is also a valuable input for process improvement [26, 27]. Traceability also provides a possibility to ensure that all requirements are fulfilled by the system components and that no features have been added [29, 32] since all components or features within the system should be related to one or several requirements. Comprehensive traceability supports producing a better quality product, improving both the development and maintenance of software, and potentially lowering system life cycle costs [32]. It is emphasized in [11] that poor traceability practice, where traceability is neglected or where insufficient and unstructured traces are captured, leads to "a decrease in system quality, causes revisions, and thus, increases project cost and time. It results in loss of knowledge if individuals leave the project, leads to wrong decisions, misunderstanding, and miscommunications" (p. 54).

Capturing and maintaining traces is hence seen as an important activity during requirements engineering as well as other parts of software engineering. The topic is well-explored, judging by the large amount of literature describing both theoretical and empirical studies (see e.g. [11, 13, 14, 17, 19, 27, 30, 31, 32]).

5.2.2 Different Types of Requirements Traceability

Figure 5.1 presents an overview of requirements traceability and shows what is meant by forward and backward direction mentioned in the definition. However, it is a simplified view of what type of information that should be related in order to ensure requirements traceability, as is indicated by the examples above. As the figure shows, requirements traceability can be divided into two major types: pre-traceability and post-traceability [13].

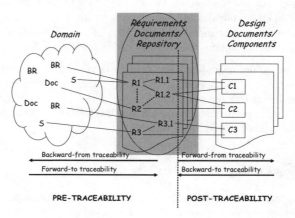

Fig. 5.1 Different types of traceability (based on [13] and [22])

Pre-traceability refers to those aspects of a requirement's life before it is included in the requirements specification [13] and is focused on enabling a better understanding of *requirements*. Pre-traceability includes tracing the elicitation and definition of the requirements, as well as their evolution [26]. The requirements should be related to their origin e.g. stakeholder (S), business rule (BR), or previous documentation (Doc), but also to other associated requirements e.g. through requirements decomposition. Requirements pre-traceability is the foundation for managing evolution of a system, because it enables elicitation of the parts of the specification that are affected by a particular raised change request, e.g. by organizational policies, business processes, or the usage of the system.

Post-traceability refers to those aspects of a requirement's life from the point in time when it has been included in the requirements specification and forward [13] and is focused on enabling a better understanding and acceptance of the current *system/software*. Post-traceability is concerned with ensuring that all requirements are fulfilled by the system, through the design and implementation of the system, by relating the requirements to the component (C), which helps satisfying that particular requirement. No requirements should be lost and none added [26]. It also involves relating requirements to test cases, which should be used to ensure that components fulfill those requirements. Requirements post-traceability is also important for change integration by enabling identification of the impact that changes have on design and implementation [22].

Requirements pre-traceability is hence concerned with *requirements production* and focuses on the domain with which we interact when requirements are developed and in which the systems is to be installed. Requirements post-traceability is concerned with *requirements deployment* and is focused on the software that is developed based on the requirements. A more refined categorization can be found in [10], together with four types of requirements traceability (see Fig. 5.1) related to the direction of the tracing. Traceability can also be divided into horizontal and vertical traceability [12, 29] which refers to whether the related information objects belong to the same type or not. *Horizontal* traceability deals with relating versions or variants of the same type of information, e.g. between requirements or between system components. *Vertical* traceability is concerned with tracing information between previous and subsequent phases in the development process i.e. between information objects of different types. One example is relating a requirement to the design made based on the requirement, and further to the system component that fulfils the requirement.

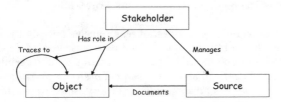

Fig. 5.2 Traceability meta-model [32]

5.2.3 A Meta-Model of Requirements Traceability

The meta-model presented in Fig. 5.2 shows the major perspectives of requirements traceability [32] and also indicates that there are several dimensions of the traceability information. The *source* is the physical artifact where the information is maintained, e.g. requirements specification document, design document, memorandum, and telephone call. This perspective emphasizes the document management part of traceability, which is important because trace objects available in persistent sources constitute long-term traceability. The *stakeholder* is the agent involved in the management of traceability, e.g. the customer, system analyst, and project manager. This perspective emphasizes the importance of different usage roles when designing and implementing a traceability system. It also provides the ability to define who is responsible for various products and decisions during the development process. *Object* refers to the type of information objects that should be related to each other, e.g. requirement, rationale, decision, and system component. Several reference models for traceability have been presented in [30]. They focus on the object aspect and describe the different types of objects that should be related to each other as well as the different types of traceability links offered to carry out this linking.

These three perspectives are related to each other in such a way that the sources are used to document objects. The stakeholders are involved in managing the different sources, i.e. they create, use and maintain them. They also have different roles in the establishment and use of various objects and traces between objects. This meta-model can be used to represent several dimensions of traceability, including (see [30]):

- What information is represented
- Where it is represented and how
- Who are the stakeholders and what are their roles in the creation and use of the information, and
- Why certain object is created or modified

5.2.4 Some Concluding Remarks on Requirements Traceability

In this chapter, we focus on the *object aspect* of requirements traceability and the dimension concerning what information that should be represented. More specifically, we focus on objects of one specific type –requirements –and traceability between requirements. This is defined above as mainly a *pre-traceability* issue (see Fig. 5.1) belonging to the *horizontal traceability* category, since we relate information objects of the same type.

The different types of traceability information discussed above support different phases and activities during the development and maintenance of a software system (see [22]). The information that needs to be captured varies between projects, organizations, and domains, and must be adjusted to the situation at hand [11]. Organizations hence need support for defining traceability strategies that are suitable for their project-specific needs. In addition, traceability information tends to take enormous proportions resulting in large additional costs for collecting, storing and maintaining it [13, 22, 23]. This further emphasizes the need to carefully consider what information that is needed based on the situation at hand.

5.3 An Overview of Interdependency Types

In Sect. 5.2 requirements interdependencies was described as a specific issue in requirements traceability. As for traceability in general, there are several ways in which requirements can relate to each other. This section provides an overview of currently known interdependency types, which can be used to describe relationships between requirements.

As stated in Sect. 5.1, current literature which explicitly addresses types of re-quirements interdependencies approaches the subject from different perspectives. This has resulted in several more or less different views on existing interdependency types. None of these include all dependency types presented in the litera-ture. In addition, many of the interdependency types found are overlapping or similar, and are hence difficult to distinguish from each other. This problem is also identified in a survey on requirements interdependencies, where practitioners were asked to find interdependencies between a given set of requirements and to iden-tify which type should be used to describe how they related to each other [5]. Fur-thermore, the meanings of certain terms used to denote the types clear and distinct among the different sources. Even when the interdependency types appear to be fairly different they can be difficult to separate in practice. One example is the re-lationship between two requirements in the sense that one requirement should be implemented before the other. This can be described as a temporal dependency, i.e. that one should be implemented before the other. On the other hand, it can also be viewed as the second requirement requiring the first one, i.e. that one cannot function without the other [5].

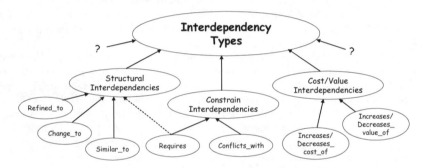

Fig. 5.3 A classification of fundamental interdependency types

We aim to provide an overall view of existing interdependency types presented in the literature, but due to the selection problem mentioned above we focus on identifying the fundamental interdependency types. We have therefore compiled overlapping or similar interdependency types into more generic types and hence kept the number of interdependency types as low as possible, without losing any of the core intentions behind the types presented in literature. The result is a model of fundamental interdependencies types (Fig. 5.3.). The types in this model can, of course, be further elaborated due to project-specific needs. Furthermore, the ques-tion marks in the model emphasize that the model needs further research, where more fundamental categories and interdependency types may be found. The model is based both on the literature and an interview study. For more detail concerning how the model has been developed, we refer to [7, 8]. The literature used is the following, all explicitly presents various interdependency types [4, 5, 20, 26, 30,

35, 37, 38]. An overview of all interdependency types presented in the literature can be found in [9].

5.3.1 Structural Interdependencies

Structural interdependencies are concerned with the fact that given a specific set of requirements, they can be organized in a structure where relationships are of a hierarchical as well as of a cross-structure nature. High-level business requirements are gradually decomposed into more detailed software requirements, forming a hierarchy. Also, there can be structural relationships between requirements within different parts of the overall hierarchy. We find that the following interdependency types fall into this category:

Refined_to. A higher-level requirement is refined by a number of more specific requirements. This dependency type is used to describe hierarchical structures, where more detailed requirements are related to their source requirements. In this sense, these requirements provide further explanation, detail or clarification about the source requirement. The source requirement can hence be seen as an abstraction of the detailed requirements. If a detailed requirement is derived from a higher-level requirement, but is not a prerequisite for this requirement, the relationship is of the dependency type refined_to.

In the literature there are many variants of this interdependency type. We have chosen to compile these into one group, due to the difficult task of clearly distinguishing them from one another (see discussion above). This dependency type hence covers situations where one requirement is elaborated by another, where a more detailed requirement is derived from a high level requirement, or where one or several requirements are based on a source requirement. It also includes dependencies were one requirement has been divided into several parts, i.e., several simpler requirements are considered as part of a complex source requirement. Other situations here are if one requirement formalizes another requirement or if one high-level requirement is a generalization of one or several more detailed requirements. All these types are used to describe some kind of hierarchical relationships, where high level requirements are refined into more detailed ones by several more detailed requirements. They are therefore compiled into one type, refined_to.

> EXAMPLE: A requirement stating that "The system should support a following up of the customer orders after their delivery," could be refined by requirements stating e.g. during a following up it should be possible to compare the cost of producing the products related to a given customer order with the manufacturing budgets for those products, and the system should facilitate changing the manufacturing budgets when following up the products within a customer order.

Changes_to. One requirement changes to another requirement if a new version of that requirement is developed which replaces the old one.

This dependency type is used to describe the history of a requirement, i.e., how it has evolved over time since it enables to relate the different versions of a single requirement. A new version of a requirement may be developed for several reasons. It may, for example, be the result of making the requirement more comprehensive, changing details within the requirement, or expressing it more formally.

> EXAMPLE: The requirements "It should take no longer than 10 seconds to perform a search for contact information" could be changed to a new version of that particular requirements stating that "It should take no longer than 15 seconds to perform a search for contact information."

Similar_to. One stated requirement is similar to or overlapping with one or more other requirements.

This interdependency type describes situations where one requirement is similar to or overlapping with another in terms of how it is expressed or in terms of a similar underlying idea of what the system should be able to perform. It can also be used to describe similar solutions, from which one has to be selected to be part of the system. It can hence be used to describe similarities both within the requirements and their potential solutions. This topic is further discussed in Chap. 10.

> EXAMPLE: The requirements "The system shall support the management of library items" and "The system shall provide means to handle books and journals within the library" are similar since both books and journals could be considered as library items.

5.3.2 Constraining Interdependencies

Some literature introduces fairly broad and general interdependency types such that there are some requirements that are dependent on or that constrain others [26, 38]. Our hypothesis is that more detailed interdependencies can be identified here in order to describe how requirements can constrain each other or be dependent on each other, especially if this classification is further elaborated with respect to different development activities or decisions. However, at this stage we choose to include this general interdependency category, being aware of the need for further research. We have, so far, identified two types within this category.

Requires. The fulfillment of one requirement depends on the fulfillment of another requirement. This type is used to describe that if one requirement is to be included into the system, it requires another requirement to be included as well. It can also be used to describe hierarchical relations between two requirements of a stronger nature than refined_to. Requires in this sense means that one or more detailed requirements are required, i.e. not optional, in order to fulfill a requirement on a higher level. Requires can hence be seen as partly belonging to the structural category as well.

This type is also fairly common in the literature, only the term used to describe it differs. It includes dependencies where one requirement must exist among the selected ones in order to implement another requirement and describes a situation where one requirement cannot work without another. This means that one requirement is a pre-requisite or pre-condition for another. Because of that, requires can also be used to describe a temporal interdependency, where one requirement needs to be implemented before another.

There are also interdependency types of a weaker nature than requires, where requirements which support or enhance each other's fulfillment are related. Requires can hence be used to describe relations where one requirement must be implemented in order for another to be implemented, but also where one requirement have a positive effect on the fulfillment of another.

> EXAMPLE: If the system should be able to include emailing and web-access, a network connection is required.

Conflicts_with. A requirement is in conflict with another requirement if they cannot exist at the same time or if increasing the satisfaction of one requirement decreases the satisfaction of another requirement.

This interdependency type both includes situations were it is impossible to implement both requirements, and situations where requirements have a negative influence on each other's achievement and a trade-off between the resolution of the requirements must be made. Conflict is also one of the most frequently mentioned interdependency types. [35] has a strong focus on conflict dependencies, and presents some relations, which can be interpreted as reasons for the conflict, e.g. in terms of needing the same resources, one requirement describing a task that is depending on another requirement, or in terms of one requirement describing a consequence of another. The concept of conflict between requirements is further discussed in Chap. 7.

> EXAMPLE: If one requirement states that "All personnel should be able to search for information about both products and customers" and another states that "Only personnel with security status A should be able to search for customers classified as military related," these two contradict each other, and cannot be simultaneously satisfied.

5.3.3 Cost/Value Interdependencies

Cost/value interdependencies are concerned with the costs involved in implementing a requirement in relation to the value that the fulfillment of that requirement will provide to the perceived customer/user. The following interdependency types fall into this category (both these are also mentioned in relation to negotiation in Chap. 4):

Increases/Decreases_cost_of. If one requirement is chosen for implementation, then the cost of implementing another requirement increases or decreases.

It is used to relate requirements that somewhat influence the implementation, cost of each other, e.g., by making it more expensive or cheaper to implement another requirement.

> EXAMPLE: If a requirement states that no response time should be longer than 5 seconds, it will most likely increase the cost of implementing many other requirements.

Increases/Decreases_value_of. If one requirement is chosen for implementation, then the value to the customer of another requirement increases or decreases.

This type focuses on the effect relations between requirements may have on the perceived customer value. Some requirements may have a positive influence on the customer value of each other, while others have a negative influence, e.g., by making functionality more complex.

> EXAMPLE: The customer satisfaction of including a planning calendar into a mobile phone will probably increase if it is possible to synchronize this with planning calendars used on PCs.

5.4 How can Knowledge about Requirements Interdependencies Facilitate Software Engineering?

We have argued that requirements are interdependent and that these dependencies influence different activities in the software engineering process. This section presents an overview of situations during software engineering where interdependencies may influence the tasks carried out. It aims at providing an insight into how requirements interdependencies influence activities within software engineering and how knowledge about dependencies can facilitate software development. For each activity described, the interdependency types relevant to the activity are discussed.

5.4.1 Requirements Management

Requirements Management (RM) is concerned with managing the large amount of requirements-related information elicited during the RE process [15]. RM includes, among other things, keeping track of and maintaining the decomposition of requirements, i.e. how high level requirements and objectives are decomposed into more refined requirements describing the software system in more detail. Knowledge about the decomposition is important in order to understand why these derived requirements exist and how they have been developed, especially since the decomposition is often based on assumptions made by developers and other stakeholders [30]. This knowledge also provides means to ensure that all low level requirements are related to higher level requirements or goals, i.e. that they exist for a good reason. Most often, there are tight budget and time schedule constraints to meet in a software project. This means that requirements that support the business strategies and objectives of the system should have high priority and be included in the requirements specification. Therefore, all requirements should come from an approved source and be based on customers' and users' real needs [21]. In addition, tracking the decomposition provides a historical view of the evolution of the requirements in the sense that they show how the high-level requirements have been decomposed into more detail. The RM issue here is to provide traceability between the source requirements, and the more detailed requirements explaining them. Finally, managing the decomposition is also a way of managing the fast increasing number of requirements, since the requirements are often grouped into hierarchies.

Managing requirements in the manner described above relies heavily on the ability to identify, document and maintain information about requirements interdependencies. The focus here is particularly on the structural interdependency types, namely *refines_to*, and *changed_to*, and also *requires*.

5.4.2 Change Management and Impact Analysis

One of the major challenges in software development is the constant evolution and change of requirements [30]. Change management and impact analysis are concerned with systematically managing changes, and assessing the effect of change requests. Research into impact analysis has traditionally been focused on program code [1] which may explain the limited amount of literature discussing the influence of requirements interdependencies in this context. However, requirements interdependencies are useful here since they show the evolution of requirements, i.e. how a certain requirement has changed over time. They also show the major assumptions behind a requirement, by relating it to the original requirement, which can indicate the importance of the requirement. Moreover, one of the more important benefits of requirements interdependencies is that they show if requirements influence each other. This facilitates the accuracy of impact analysis since other requirements that need to be changed due to a change request can be identified [22, 37]. More detail on impact analysis can be found in Chap. 6.

The interdependency types that are useful in this context consequently belong to constrain category as well as the *change_to* interdependency type. *Refined_to* together with *requires* are also relevant interdependency types because they enable showing the major assumptions behind a requirement.

5.4.3 Release Planning

In market-driven development, software suppliers usually release new versions of their software products on a more or less regular basis. Release planning is the activity concerned with selecting an optimal collection of requirements for implementation in the next version of a software system. More often than not, software suppliers have a large number of requirements to choose from during this task. The aim is to identify the set of requirements that maximizes the value added for customers, but also to select the requirements that can be developed within the constraints of the resources available and the fixed release date [5]. The selection is usually based on requirements priority (see Chap. 4) and the estimated cost of implementing the requirement. However, due to the fact that requirements are related to and affect each other, this cannot be the only basis for requirements selection [5, 20]. The selection of one requirement may imply that several other requirements have to be selected as well or at least considered for selection. For example, the selection of a highly prioritized requirement A may imply that the costly but not so highly prioritized requirement B has to be selected as well, since A cannot be implemented without having B in place. Requirements interdependencies hence increase the complexity of requirements selection for a certain release. Knowledge about how requirements relate to, affect and depend on each other is, therefore, an important basis for these decisions since these dependencies demonstrate the impact of including or excluding requirements [20]. For more information about release planning, we refer to Chap. 13.

The interdependency types that are useful to take into consideration during release planning are *requires*, *similar_to*, *conflicts_with*, and the whole *cost/value category*. The *requires* category is useful in order to show that if one requirement is selected, another must be included as well. If similar requirements are shown, situations can be avoided where two similar requirements are included in a release. Then resources are not calculated twice for the same functionality or property of the system. Such double-calculation could potentially have hindered the inclusion of other requirements due to resource limitations. Knowledge about conflicting requirements is useful during release planning since these conflicts can be either solved before inclusion or be avoided, e.g. by only including one of the conflicting requirements. The interdependency types in the *cost/value category* are useful here since this knowledge enables to maximize the requirements selected for implementation with respect to available recourses.

5.4.4 Reuse of Components

Traceability supports the process of reusing components on a requirements level [26]. If similarities between requirements are documented, this information can be used to identify reusable components by comparing the stated requirements with the requirements of the existing system. These can then be traced down to design and implementation, using traceability information, and identify the component used to implement the requirement. Moreover, the traceability information can also be used to recognize the adjustment needed to change the components to the new application.

The interdependency type useful in this situation is *similar_to*.

5.4.5 Reuse of Requirements

Knowledge about requirements interdependencies can also be useful not only when reusing components, but also when reusing requirements (see also Chap. 10 which discusses this topic). When variants of software products are developed, part of the requirements may be the same since products are often built on the same basic functionality. The requirements documents hence have many similarities. When requirements are recycled, e.g., when building a new variant of a product, this is usually carried out ad-hoc which is both time consuming and error prone [38]. One reason is the difficulty to identify the requirements that can potentially be reused and another is the difficulty to ensure that all requirements related to the once recycled ones are included. It is also a problem that too many requirements are included in the new requirements document. Knowledge about the relationships and dependencies between the requirements can clearly support the task of requirements recycling.

Not all related requirements can be included without analysis [38]. There are more complex recycling steps where adaptation is taken into consideration, i.e. changes to the recycled requirements may occur. In addition to this, the refinement of a high level requirement into more detailed requirements is a negotiation process (see Chap. 7), where the details concerning, e.g., the functionality are decided. Consequently, it is not self-evident that all these details should be part of the functionality of the new version of the system. For example, a search function can be further explained by a number of detailed requirements, which describes how this function should behave in detail. When this functionality is recycled, some advanced details regarding this search function may be excluded due to budget constraints, i.e. some of the requirements are excluded from the specification of the new version.

The interdependency types relevant to take into consideration in this context are both the *refined_to* and the *requires* interdependency types, and also the *constrain category* as a whole.

5.4.6 Design and Implementation

Software design is to a large extent concerned with decision-making. Many trade-offs are made e.g. to decide the scope and functionality of the system as well as between implementation cost and other resources [30]. A common trade-off is between conflicting or inconsistent requirements [6]. A challenging issue is hence to analyze to what extent multiple requirements can be satisfied simultaneously. This is beneficial in order to detect potential problems prior to system construction [35]. An area called requirements interaction management has been developed to answer this need. It is defined as "the set of activities directed toward the discovery, management, and disposition of critical relationships among sets of requirements." ([35], p. 132). The aim is to find dependencies between requirements and to show those that cannot be simultaneously satisfied. This knowledge is utterly important to take into consideration in order to identify and solve problems when the system is being designed. Chap. 7 presents several conflict resolutions strategies for resolving conflicts among stakeholders.

Requirements interdependencies can also be used to plan the implementation of requirements, e.g. in which order the requirements should be implemented due to testing constraints and efficiency, or allocation of requirements to developers.

Identifying and showing conflicts between requirements is hence important in this context, which makes *conflicts_with* a fundamental interdependency type here. Other relevant interdependency types are *requires* and *increase/decrease_cost_of*.

5.4.7 Testing

Testing is, among other things, about ensuring that all the requirements of the system have been met [36] and includes tasks such as test planning, selecting and designing test cases, executing test cases, and reporting on the result of the execution. For more information about testing and how it relates to requirements, see Chap. 8.

The order in which test cases are executed is essential, since some system functionality cannot be tested before other functionality is in place and verified. In addition, the order is essential for efficiency reasons. Functionality, on which much other functionality is based, should be tested first in order to avoid or reduce unnecessary re-execution of test cases if errors are discovered within that base functionality. The ideal situation is to be able to identify and test this base information first, and then after that test related functionality. These types of relationships can be discovered based on dependencies between requirements. This issue is also related to regression tests, where related test cases are selected for re-execution when errors are found and corrected. In that case, already tested functionality must be tested again in order to ensure that the system functions the way it should and did before the correction.

During testing, test cases are developed based on the requirements to ensure the fulfillment of the requirements. Since requirements are related, knowledge about requirements interdependencies certainly affects the ability to create purposeful and complete test cases. Test cases are related to one or several requirements, which means that requirements interdependencies are useful for deciding which requirements should be grouped into one test case.

The interdependency types relevant in this situation are mainly *requires* and the *constrain category*. However, it is also important to have a good structure and overview of the requirements set which makes the *structural category,* foremost the *refined_to* interdependency type important as well.

5.5 Research Issues

The topic of requirements interdependencies is fairly unexplored and diverse. There are some parts where more research has been carried out, e.g. within requirements interaction management and requirements conflict management, but on the whole a substantial amount of additional research is needed in order to provide a comprehensive view of the area as such. More research is also needed into interdependency-related problems and their solutions. This section introduces a research agenda consisting of four major areas.

5.5.1 What is the Nature of Requirements Interdependencies?

Due to the fact that requirements interdependencies are fairly unexplored, there is not much known about the phenomenon as such. There are many issues to consider here. How frequently are requirements interdependent? Why are requirements interdependent and how exactly do they affect each other? Which type of dependency is most common/frequent? Does our model of fundamental interdependency types cover the most common relationships between requirements? We believe that resolving these questions is essential for improving the understanding of the nature of requirements interdependencies and in particular for developing approaches to address the three issues identified below.

5.5.2 How can we Identify Requirements Interdependencies?

The problems within requirements interdependencies are not only concerned with how to record and maintain links between related requirements. These relationships must also be identified somehow. Some interdependencies may be easy to identify when analyzing the requirements set, but there are interdependencies that are more difficult to discover. In addition, it can also be difficult to identify how requirements affect each other, especially when it comes to non-functional requirements.

Another problem concerning identification is that interdependencies are not necessarily static with respect to the software development life cycle. For example, if a change is to be made to one requirement R1, this may not affect requirement R2, but in release planning, R1 may have an important impact on the customer value of R2. The dynamics of requirements interdependencies is hence an area for future research.

A potential risk with introducing the task of identifying requirements interdependencies is that it could be seen as yet another task that has to be done within a tight schedule within the software development process. A possible solution is to combine this analysis with other existing activities, such as prioritization or inspections, in order to achieve benefits from work already performed (as in [5]). We believe that this could be a sound starting point when an approach for identifying requirements interdependencies is developed.

Work on using language tools to analyze requirements sets is presented in [25], but only for identifying similarities between requirements (see also Chap. 10). [26] has proposed a method for automatically recording traceability links and [5] describes how to use pair-wise analysis of the requirements to discover interdependencies. The later also discusses several alternatives how to decrease the time required to carry out this analysis. These two approaches assume that the developers know how the requirements affect each other but none of them deals with dynamic dependencies. There is also a need for approaches focusing on how to explore the consequences of a particular interdependency type in a given situation, i.e. *how* the requirements affect each other and not only *that* they affect each other.

5.5.3 How can we Describe Requirements Interdependencies?

When the different relationships between requirements have been identified we must also provide support for storing and managing them. A common problem in current traceability tools is that they provide means to store a relationship between requirements but they provide very little guidance regarding the semantics and inherent meaning and consequences of a relationship.

In order to develop an effective as well as efficient approach to storing and managing requirements interdependencies, there are several issues that should be addressed. Firstly, large amounts of interdependencies are difficult and time-consuming to maintain. How can we develop an approach that scales up? Should we delimit the amount of interdependencies? If so, should we focus on the most critical ones, or the most critical requirements [30] or is better to bundle requirements and store relations between bundles? Also, how do we know which interdependencies are most critical in different development situations and what is meant by critical in various contexts? Secondly, there could be a need to store the strength of the dependency, since the impact may be small or large [5, 30]. Thirdly, we must consider dynamic interdependencies. How can we show under which conditions a dependency exists? Finally, the difficulties in choosing which dependency type to use should also be addressed, e.g. by prioritizing the interdependency types perhaps based on development situation.

This list of requirements for a tool supporting the management of interdependencies must, of course, be elaborated. In fact, we have just scratched the surface of the topic. A first step would be the evaluation of existing approaches which may be suitable for storing and managing interdependencies. We would like to really emphasize the need for improving way beyond the current trend towards using dependency matrixes to store and manage interdependencies. Current traceability matrix approaches lack support for specifying the nature of dependencies and provide poor visualization capabilities. Finally, it is not clear on which abstraction level interdependencies should be described. In some situations it is relevant to relate autonomous requirements, in other situations it is more appropriate to bundle requirements and to relate groups of requirements.

Requirements traceability research includes several alternative approaches for recording and managing traceability links. One important research issue is to investigate which of these are suitable for recording and managing requirements interdependencies. [5] presents one approach for describing requirements interdependencies. This approach is built on visualization, which is considered to be an important feature involved in this issue. It could also be relevant in this context to look at other areas for new ideas. Goal modeling could be a potential area to investigate here (see e.g. [2, 3, 39] as well as Chap. 9 which discusses how goal driven approach supports RE), since requirements could be considered to be low-level goals.

5.5.4 How Do we Address Requirements Interdependencies in the Software Development Process?

According to [30], literature and standards within requirements traceability provide few guidelines regarding what type of information must be captured and used in what context. An important research issue is, therefore, to investigate what it means in different contexts when stating that an inter-dependency exists. As indicated by the literature, different types of interdependencies are important in different development activities or as a basis for various decisions. Another important research issue is to explore which types of interdependencies are critical to consider in different situations. The first step towards this is to investigate which activities are affected by requirements interdependencies (see Sect. 5.3 for a starting point regarding this issue).

It has been suggested that management of interdependencies should be based on strength rather than type [5]. We believe that selecting which interdependencies to store and manage depends on several factors. The potential usage of the knowledge about interdependencies is one relevant factor, i.e. what we need to know when making various decisions and/or with respect to different development situations. Other factors are the strength of the dependencies, but also the criticality and significance of the requirements [27].

5.5.5 Relations Between the Research Issues

The issues discussed above are, of course, related. For example, being able to discover and identify interdependencies is a prerequisite for having something to store and manage. If we want to be able to effectively support the management of interdependencies we need to understand how this knowledge should be used in, development activities and decisions during software development. In order to make the identification more efficient and effective we need to know more about what we should identify, i.e. how interdependencies affect different development situations. Therefore, we believe that there is no obvious starting point for research among these three issues. There are, for example, ways to identify interdependencies, but they could most likely be improved. However, it could be beneficial to know more about what we should identify before we start this investigation. On the other hand, if we had better techniques for exploring potential relationships it would support the work of finding out more about what types of dependencies there are. Addressing all three issues is hence essential, and improving the understanding of the very nature of requirements interdependencies is clearly a necessity.

5.6 Summary

Most individual requirements, developed during the requirements engineering (RE) process, cannot be treated in isolation during software development. Instead they are related to and affect each other in complex manners. We call these relationships requirements interdependencies. The objective of this chapter is to provide an overview of this area, by synthesizing existing knowledge about the phenomenon.

In this chapter we have identified requirements interdependences as being part of a larger topic, namely requirements traceability. We have developed a model describing the fundamental types of interdependencies, which can be used to describe how requirements relate to and affect each other. Dependencies between requirements is not a problem per se, but interdependencies affect many decisions and activities in the software development process, e.g. requirements management, change management and impact analysis, release planning, reuse of components and requirements, design and implementation, and testing. Failure to address requirements interdependencies in these situations will most likely cause problems in terms of poor functionality as well as budget and schedule overruns.

The topic of requirements interdependencies is fairly unexplored and diverse. There are some parts where more research have been carried out, e.g. within requirements interaction management and requirements conflict management, but on the whole much more research is needed in order to provide a comprehensive view of the area as such. More research is also needed into interdependency-related problems and their solutions. More specifically, the main challenges for the future are to understand the nature of requirements interdependencies and to develop approaches that enable to identify, describe and effectively deal with them in the software development process.

References

1. Briand LC, Labiche Y, O'Sullivan L (2003) Impact analysis and change management of UML models. In: Proceedings of the International Conference on Software Maintenance, Amsterdam, The Netherlands, pp.256–265
2. Bubenko jr., JA (1993) Extending the scope of information modeling. In: Proceedins of 4th International Workshop on the Deductive Approach to Information Systems and Databases, Department de Llenguatges i Sistemes Informatics, Universitat Politecnica de Catalunya, Report de Recerca LSI/93–25, Barcelona
3. Bubenko jr JA, Persson A, Stirna J (2001) User guide of the knowledge management approach using enterprise knowledge patterns. Deliverable D3, IST Programme project HyperKnowledge - Hypermedia and Pattern Based Knowledge Management for Smart Organisations, Project no. IST-2000-28401, Dept. of Computer and Systems Sciences, Royal Institute of Technology, Stockholm, Sweden available on http://www.dsv.su.se/~js/ekd_user_guide.html

4. Carlshamre P, Regnell B (2000) Requirements lifecycle management and release planning in market-driven requirements engineering processes. In: Proceedings of 2nd International Workshop on the Requirements Engineering Process, Greenwich, London, pp.961-966

5. Carlshamre P, Sandahl K, Lindvall M, Regnell B, Natt och Dag J (2001) An industrial survey of requirements interdependencies in software product release planning. In: Proceedings of the 5th International Symposium on Requirements Engineering, 27-31 August, Toronto, Canada, pp. 84-91

6. Curtis B, Krasner H, Iscoe N (1988) A field study of the software design process for large systems. Communications of the ACM, 31(11): 1268-1286

7. Dahlstedt ÅG (2004) Requirements interdependencies – Towards an understanding of their nature and context of use. Licentiate thesis, Department of Computer and Systems Science, Stockholm University/Royal Institute of Technology, Sweden

8. Dahlstedt ÅG, Persson A (2003a) Requirements interdependencies - Molding the state of research into a research agenda. In: Proceedings of the 9th International Workshop on Requirements Engineering: Foundation for Software Quality, Klagenfurt/Velden, Austria, pp. 71-80

9. Dahlstedt ÅG, Persson A (2003b) An overview of requirements interdependency types. http://www.ida.his.se/ida/~asa/ReqInterdependencies.pdf.

10. Davis AM (1990) The analysis and specification of systems and software requirements. Systems and Software Requirements Engineering, IEEE Computer Society Press, pp.119-144

11. Dömges R, Pohl K (1998) Adapting traceability environment to project-specific needs. Communication of the ACM, 41(12): 54-62

12. Gotel O (1995) Contribution structures for requirements traceability. PhD Thesis, Department of Computing Imperial College of Science, Technology and Medicine, University of London

13. Gotel O, Finkelstein A (1994) An analysis of the requirements traceability problem. In: Proceedings of the 1st international Conference on Requirements Engineering, Colorado Springs, Colorado, USA, pp. 94-102

14. Gotel O, Finkelstein A (1997) Extended requirements traceability: Results of an industrial case study. In: Proceedings of the 3rd International Symposium on Requirements Engineering, Annapolis, MD, IEEE Computer Society Press, pp. 169-178

15. Grehag Å (2001) Requirements management in a life-cycle perspective - A position paper. In: Proceedings of the 7th International Workshop on Requirements Engineering: Foundation for Software Quality, Interlaken, Switzerland, pp.183-188

16. IEEE Standard 830 (1984): IEEE guide to software requirements specifications. Institute of Electrical and Electronics Engineers, New York, USA

17. Jarke M (1998) Requirements tracing. Communication of the ACM, 41(12): 32-36

18. Johnson WL, Feather MS, Harris DR (1991) Integrating domain knowledge, requirements and specifications. Journal of Systems Integration, 1: 283-320

19. Kaindl H (1993) The missing link in requirements engineering. ACM SIGSOFT Software Engineering Notes, 18(2): 30-39

20. Karlsson J, Olsson S, Ryan K (1997) Improved practical support for large-scale requirements prioritization. Requirements Engineering, 2(1): 51-60

21. Kirkman DP (1998) Requirements decomposition and traceability. Requirements Engineering, 3(2): 107-114

22. Kotonya G, Sommerville I (1998) Requirements engineering – Processes and techniques, John Wiley & Sons

23. Maciaszek LA (2001) Requirements analysis and system design – Developing information systems with UML, Addison Wesley

24. Moran TP, Carroll JM (1996) Design rationale concepts, techniques, and use. Lawrence Erlbaum Associates, Publisher, Mahwah, New Jersey

25. Natt och Dag J, Regnell B, Carlshamre P, Andersson M, Karlsson J (2002) A feasibility study of automated natural language requirements analysis in market-driven development, Requirements Engineering, 7(1): 20–33

26. Pohl K (1996) Process-centered requirements engineering, John Wiley & Sons Inc.

27. Ramesh B (1998) Factors influencing requirements traceability practice. Communications of the ACM, 41(12): 37–44

28. Ramesh B, Dhar V (1992) Supporting systems development by capturing deliberations during requirements engineering, IEEE Transactions on Software Engineering, 18(6): 498–510

29. Ramesh B, Edwards M (1993) Issues in the development of a requirements traceability model. In: Proceedings of the IEEE International Symposium on Requirements Engineering, San Diego, California, USA, pp. 256–259

30. Ramesh B, Jarke M (2001) Toward reference models for requirements traceability. IEEE Transactions on Software Engineering, 27(1): 58–93

31. Ramesh B, Powers T, Stubbs C, Edwards M (1995) Implementing requirements traceability: A case study. In: Proceedings of the 2nd International Symposium on Requirements Engineering, York, England, pp. 89–93

32. Ramesh B, Stubbs C, Powers T, Edwards M (1997) Requirements traceability: Theory and Practice. Annals of Software Engineering, 3: 397–415

33. Regnell B, Paech B, Aurum A, Wohlin C, Dutoit A, Natt och Dag J. (2001) Requirements mean decisions! – Research issues for understanding and supporting decision-making in requirements engineering. In: Proceedings of 1st Swedish Conference on Software Engineering Research and Practice (SERP'01), October 25–26, Ronneby, Sweden

34. Robertson S, Robertson J. (1999) Mastering the requirements process, Addison-Wesley

35. Robinson WN, Pawlowski SD, Volkov V (2003) Requirements interaction management. ACM Computing Surveys, 35(2): 132–190

36. Sommerville I (1996) Software engineering, Addison-Wesley, UK

37. von Knethen A, Grund M (2003) QuaTrace: A tool environment for (semi-) automatic impact analysis based on traces. In: Proceedings of the International Conference on Software Maintenance, Amsterdam, The Netherlands, pp. 246–255

38. von Knethen A, Peach B, Kiedaisch F, Houdek F (2002) Systematic requirements recycling through abstraction and traceability. In: Proceedings of IEEE Joint International Conference on Requirements Engineering, 9-13 September, Essen, Germany, pp.273–281

39. Yu E (1995) Modeling strategic relationships for process reengineering. Ph.D thesis, Department of Computer Science, University of Toronto, Canada

Author Biography

Åsa G. Dahlstedt is a Ph.D. Student at the University of Skövde. Her research interests are within the area of Requirements Engineering, with a focus on how requirements are related to and affect each other as well as how that influences the software development work e.g. regarding release planning and testing. She is currently working on her Ph.D. thesis related to this issue.

Anne Persson is a senior lecturer in Information Systems Engineering at the University of Skövde. She holds an MSc in computation from the University of Manchester Institute of Science and Technology (UMIST), UK, a licentiate and a PhD in computer and systems science from Stockholm University. Research areas include Enterprise Modeling, Requirements Engineering and methods for Information Systems Engineering.

6 Impact Analysis

Per Jönsson and Mikael Lindvall

Abstract: Software changes are necessary and inevitable in software development, but may lead to software deterioration if not properly controlled. Impact analysis is the activity of identifying what needs to be modified in order to make a change, or to determine the consequences on the system if the change is implemented. Most research on impact analysis is presented and discussed in literature related to software maintenance. In this chapter, we take a different approach and discuss impact analysis from a requirements engineering perspective. We relate software change to impact analysis, outline the history of impact analysis and present common strategies for performing impact analysis. We also mention the application of impact analysis to non-functional requirements and discuss tool support for impact analysis. Finally, we outline what we see as the future of this essential change management tool.

Keywords: Impact analysis, Software change, Traceability analysis, Propagation of change, Non-functional requirements, Metrics.

6.1 Introduction

It is widely recognized that change is an inescapable property of any software, for a number of reasons. However, software changes can, and will, if not properly controlled, lead to software deterioration. For example, when Mozilla's 2,000,000 Source Lines of Code (SLOC) were analyzed, there were strong indications that the software had deteriorated significantly due to uncontrolled change, making the software very hard to maintain [17].

Software deterioration occurs in many cases because changes to software seldom have the small impact they are believed to have [40]. In 1983, some of the world's most expensive programming errors each involved the change of a single digit in a previously correct program [38], indicating that a seemingly trivial change may have immense impact. A study in the late 90s showed that software practitioners conducting impact analysis and estimating change in an industrial project underestimated the amount of change by a factor of three [26]. In addition, as software systems grow increasingly complex, the problems associated with software change increase accordingly. For example, when the source code across several versions of a 100,000,000 SLOC, fifteen-year-old telecom software system was analyzed, it was noticed that the system had decayed due to frequent change. The programmers estimating the change effort drew the conclusion that the code was harder to change than it should be [13].

Impact analysis is a tool for controlling change, and thus for avoiding deterioration. Bohner and Arnold define impact analysis as "the activity of identifying the potential consequences, including side effects and ripple effects, of a change, or estimating what needs to be modified to accomplish a change before it has been made" [3]. Consequently, the output from impact analysis can be used as a basis for estimating the cost associated with a change. The cost of the change can be used to decide whether or not to implement it depending on its cost/benefit ratio.

Impact analysis is an important part of requirements engineering since changes to software often are initiated by changes to the requirements. In requirements engineering textbooks, impact analysis is recognized as an essential activity in change management, but details about how to perform it often left out, or limited to reasoning about the impact of the change on the requirements specification [20, 23, 27, 32, 35]. An exception is [40], where Wiegers provides checklists to be used by a knowledgeable developer to assess the impact of a change proposal.

Despite its natural place in requirements engineering, research about impact analysis is more commonly found in literature related to software maintenance. In this chapter, we present impact analysis from a requirements engineering perspective. In our experience, impact analysis is an integral part of every phase in software development. During requirements development, design and code do not yet exist, so new and changing requirements affect only the existing requirements. During design, code does not yet exist, so new and changing requirements affect only existing requirements and design. Finally, during implementation, new and changing requirements affect existing requirements as well as design and code. This is captured in Fig. 6.1. Note that in less idealistic development processes, the situation still holds; requirements changes affect all existing system representations.

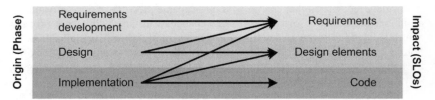

Fig. 6.1 Software life-cycle objects (SLOs) affected (right) due to requirements changes in different phases (left)

The chapter is organized as follows. In the remainder of this section, we define concepts, discuss software change and outline the history of impact analysis. In Sect. 6.2, we present common strategies for impact analysis. Sect. 6.3 discusses impact analysis in the context of non-functional requirements. We explore a number of metrics for impact analysis and give an example of an application of such metrics in Sect. 6.4. In Sect. 6.5, we look at tool support for impact analysis and discuss impact analysis in requirements management tools. Finally we outline the future of impact analysis in Sect. 6.6 and provide a summary of the chapter in Sect. 6.7.

6.1.1 Concepts and Terms

Throughout this chapter, we use several terms and concepts that are relevant in the field of impact analysis. In this section, we briefly visit these terms and concepts, and explain how each relates to impact analysis and to other terms and concepts.

Software life-cycle objects (SLOs –also called software products, or working products) are central to impact analysis. An SLO is an artifact produced during a project, such as a requirement, an architectural component, a class and so on. SLOs are connected to each other through a web of relationships. Relationships can be both between SLOs of the same type, and between SLOs of different types. For example, two requirements can be interconnected to signify that they are related to each other. A requirement can also be connected to an architectural component, for example, to signify that the component implements the requirement.

Impact analysis is often carried out by analyzing the relationships between various entities in the system. We distinguish between two types of analysis: dependency analysis and traceability analysis [3]. In dependency analysis, detailed relationships among program entities, for example variables or functions, are extracted from source code. Traceability analysis, on the other hand, is the analysis of relationships that have been identified during development among all types of SLOs. Traceability analysis is thus suitable for analyzing relationships among requirements, architectural components, documentation and so on. Requirements traceability is defined and discussed in Chap. 5. It is evident that traceability analysis has a broader application within requirements engineering than dependency analysis; it can be used in earlier development phases and can identify more diverse impact in terms of different SLO types.

It is common to deal with sets of impact in impact analysis. The following sets have been defined by Arnold and Bohner [3]:

- The System Set represents the set of all SLOs in the system – all the other sets are subsets of this set.
- The Starting Impact Set (SIS) represents the set of objects that are initially thought to be changed. The SIS typically serves as input to impact analysis approaches that are used for finding the Estimated Impact Set.
- The Estimated Impact Set (EIS) always includes the SIS and can therefore be seen as an expansion of the SIS. The expansion results from the application of change propagation rules to the internal object model repeatedly until all objects that may be affected are discovered. Ideally, the SIS and EIS should be the same, meaning that the impact is restricted to what was initially thought to be changed.
- The Actual Impact Set (AIS), finally, contains those SLOs that have been affected once the change has been implemented. In the best-case scenario, the AIS and EIS are the same, meaning that the impact estimation was perfect.

In addition to the impact sets, two forms of information are necessary in order to determine the impact of a change: information about the dependencies between objects, and knowledge about how changes propagate from object to object via dependencies and traceability links. Dependencies between objects are often captured in terms of references between them (see Chap. 5). Knowledge about how change propagates from one object to another is often expressed in terms of rules or algorithms.

It is common to distinguish between primary and secondary change. Primary change, also referred to as direct impact, corresponds to the SLOs that are identified by analyzing how the effects of a proposed change affect the system. This analysis is typically difficult to automate because it is mainly based on human expertise. Consequently, little can be found in the literature about how to identify primary changes. It is more common to find discussions on how primary changes cause secondary changes, also referred to as indirect impact.

The indirect impact can take two forms: Side effects are unintended behaviors resulting from the modifications needed to implement the change. Side effects affect both the stability and function of the system and must be avoided. Ripple effects, on the other hand, are effects on some parts of the system caused by making changes to other parts. Ripple effects cannot be avoided, since they are the consequence of the system's structure and implementation. They must, however, be identified and accounted for when the change is implemented.

We have previously mentioned architectural components as an example of SLOs. The software architecture of a system is its basic structure, consisting of interconnected components. There are many definitions of software architecture, but a recent one is "the structure or structures of the system, which comprise software elements, the externally visible properties of those elements, and the relationships among them" [2]. Several other definitions exist as well (see [34]), but most echo the one given here. Software architecture is typically designed early in the project, hiding low-level design and implementation details, and then iteratively refined as the knowledge about the system grows [10]. This makes architecture models interesting from a requirements engineering and impact analysis point-of-view, because they can be used for early, albeit initially coarse, impact analysis of changing requirements.

6.1.2 Software Change and Impact Analysis

Software change occurs for several reasons, for example, in order to fix faults, to add new features or to restructure the software to accommodate future changes [28]. Changing requirements is one of the most significant motivations for software change. Requirements change from the point in time when they are elicited until the system has been rendered obsolete. Changes to requirements reflect how the system must change in order to stay useful for its users and remain competitive on the market. At the same time, such changes pose a great risk as they may cause software deterioration. Thus, changes to requirements must be captured, managed and controlled carefully to ensure the survival of the system from a technical point of view. Factors that can inflict changes to requirements during both initial development as well as in software evolution are, according to Leffingwell and Widrig [23]:

- The problem that the system is supposed to solve changes, for example for eco-nomic, political or technological reasons.
- The users change their minds about what they want the system to do, as they understand their needs better. This can happen because the users initially were uncertain about what they wanted, or because new users enter the picture.
- The environment in which the system resides changes. For example, increases in speed and capacity of computers can affect the expectations of the system.
- The new system is developed and released leading users to discover new re-quirements.

The last factor is both real and common. When the new system is released, users realize that they want additional features, that they need data presented in other ways, that there are emerging needs to integrate the system with other systems, and so on. Thus, new requirements are generated by the use of the system itself. According to the "laws of software evolution" [24], a system must be continually adapted, or it will be progressively less satisfactory in its environment.

Problems arise if requirements and changes to requirements are not managed properly by the development organization [23]. For example, failure to ask the right questions to the right people at the right time during requirements develop-ment will most likely lead to a great number of requirements changes during sub-sequent phases. Furthermore, failure to create a practical change management process may mean that changes cannot be timely handled, or that changes are im-plemented without proper control.

Maciaszek points out: "Change is not a kick in the teeth, unmanaged change is" [27]. In other words, an organization that develops software requires a proper change management process in order to mitigate the risks of constantly changing requirements and their impact on the system. Leffingwell and Widrig discuss five necessary parts of a process for managing change [23]. These parts, depicted in Fig. 6.2, form a framework for a change management process allowing the project team to manage changes in a controlled way.

Fig. 6.2 Change management process framework [23]

Plan for change involves recognizing the fact that changes occur, and that they are a necessary part of the system's development. This preparation is essential for changes to be received and handled effectively.

Baseline requirements means to create a snapshot of the current set of require-ments. The point of this step is to allow subsequent changes in the requirements to be compared with a stable, known set of requirements.

A *single channel* is necessary to ensure that no change is implemented in the system before it has been scrutinized by a person, or several persons, who keep the system, the project and the budget in mind. In larger organizations, the single channel is often a change control board (CCB).

A *change control system* allows the CCB (or equivalent) to gather, track and assess the impact of changes. According to Leffingwell and Widrig, a change must be assessed in terms of impact on cost and functionality, impact on external stakeholders (for example, customers) and potential to destabilize the system. If the latter is overlooked, the system (as pointed out earlier) is likely to deteriorate.

To *manage hierarchically* defeats a perhaps too common line of action: a change is introduced in the code by an ambitious programmer, who forgets, or overlooks, the potential effect the change has on test cases, design, architecture, requirements and so on. Changes should be introduced top-down, starting with the requirements. If the requirements are decomposed and linked to other SLOs, it is possible to propagate the change in a controlled way.

This framework for the change process leaves open the determination of an actual change process. Requirements engineering textbooks propose change management processes with varying levels of detail and explicitness [27, 32, 35]. The process proposed by Kotonya and Sommerville is, however, detailed and consists of the following steps [20]:

1. Problem analysis and change specification
2. Change analysis and costing, which in turn consists of:
    1.   Check change request validity
    2.   Find directly affected requirements
    3.   Find dependent requirements
    4.   Propose requirements changes
    5.   Assess costs of change
    6.   Assess cost acceptability
3. Change implementation

Impact analysis is performed in steps 2b, 2c and 2e, by identifying requirements and system components affected by the proposed change. The analysis should be expressed in terms of required effort, time, money and available resources. Kotonya and Sommerville suggest the use of traceability tables to identify and manage dependencies among requirements, and between requirements and design elements. We discuss traceability as a strategy for performing impact analysis in Sect. 6.2.1.1.

6.1.3 History and Trends

In some sense, impact analysis has been performed for a very long time, albeit not necessarily using that term and not necessarily resolving the problem of accurately determining the effect of a proposed change. The need for software practitioners to determine what to change in order to implement requirement changes has always been present. Strategies for performing impact analysis were introduced and discussed early in the literature. For example, Haney's paper from 1972 on a technique for module connection analysis is often referred to as the first paper on impact analysis [18]. The technique builds on the idea that every module pair of a system has a probability that a change in one module in the pair necessitates a change in the other module. The technique can be used to model change propagation between any system components including requirements. Program slicing, which is a technique for focusing on a particular problem by retrieving executable slices containing only the code that a specific variable depends on, was introduced already in 1979 by Weiser [39]. Slicing, which is explained in Sect. 6.2.1.2, can be used to determine dependencies in code and can be used to minimize side effects. Slicing can also be used to determine dependencies between sections in documents, including requirements, which is described below. Requirements traceability was defined in ANSI/IEEE Standard 830-1984 in 1984 [1]. Traceability describes how SLOs are related to each other and can be used to determine how change in one type of artifact causes change in another type of artifact. The notion of ripple effect was introduced by Yau and Collofello in 1980 [41]. Their models can be used to determine how change in one area of the source code propagates and causes change in other areas.

Impact analysis relies on techniques and strategies that date back a long time. It is however possible to identify a trend in impact analysis research over the years. Early impact analysis work focused on source code analysis, including program slicing and ripple effects for code. The maturation of software engineering among software organizations has led to a need to understand how changes affect other SLOs than source code.

For example, Turver and Munro [37] point out that source code is not the only product that has to be changed in order to develop a new release of the software product. In a document-driven development approach, many documents are also affected by new and changed requirements. The user manual is an example of a document that has to be updated when new user functionalities have been provided. Turver and Munro focus on the problem of ripple effects in documentation using a thematic slicing technique. They note that this kind of analysis has not been widely discussed before. The same approach can be applied to the requirements document itself in order to determine how a new or changed requirement impacts the requirements specification.

In 1996, Arnold and Bohner published a collection of research articles called Software Change Impact Analysis [3]. The purpose of the collection was to present the current, somewhat scattered, material that was available on impact analysis at the time. Reading the collection today, nearly ten years later, it becomes apparent that it still is very relevant. Papers published after 1996 seem to work with the same ideas and techniques. We do not mean to depreciate the work that has been done, but it indicates that the field is not in a state of flux. Rather, the focus remains on adapting existing techniques and strategies to new concepts and in new contexts. Impact analysis on the architectural level is an example of this.

When the year 2000 approached, the Y2K problem made it obvious that extensive impact analysis efforts were needed in order to identify software and parts of software that had to be changed to survive the century shift. This served as a revelation for many organizations, in which the software process previously had not included explicit impact analysis [4].

Today, software systems are much more complex than they were 25 years ago, and it has become very difficult to grasp the combined implications of the requirements and their relationships to architecture, design, and source code. Thus, a need for impact analysis strategies that employ requirements and their relationships to other SLOs has developed. Still, dependency webs for large software systems can be so complex that it is necessary to visualize them in novel ways. Bohner and Gracanin present research that combines impact analysis and 3D visualization in order to display dependency information in a richer format than is possible with 2D visualization [5]. Bohner also stresses the need to extend impact analysis to middleware, COTS software and web applications. The use of these types of software is becoming more common, moving the complexity away from internal data and control dependencies to interoperability dependencies. Current impact analysis strategies are not very well suited for this type of dependencies [4].

6.2 Strategies for Impact Analysis

There are various strategies for performing impact analysis, some of which are more germane to the requirements engineering process than others. Common strategies are:

- Analyzing traceability or dependency information
- Utilizing slicing techniques
- Consulting design specifications and other documentation
- Interviewing knowledgeable developers

We divide these impact analysis strategies into two categories: *automatable* and *manual*. With automatable strategies, we mean those that are in some sense algorithmic in their nature. These have the ability to provide very fine-grained impact estimation in an automated fashion, but require on the other hand the presence of a detailed infrastructure and result at times in too many false positives [30]. With manual strategies, we mean those that are best performed by human beings (as opposed to tools). These require less infrastructure, but may be coarser in their impact estimation than the automatable ones. We recognize that the two categories are not entirely orthogonal, but they do make an important distinction; the manual strategies are potentially easier to adopt and work with because they require less structured input and no new forms of SLOs need to be developed.

A previous study indicated that developers' impact analyses often result in optimistic predictions [26], meaning that the predicted set of changes represents the least possible amount of work. Thus, the work cannot be easier, only more difficult. The study also identified the need for conservative predictions and establishing a "worst level" prediction. The real amount of work will lie between the optimistic and the conservative level. An improvement goal would be to decrease variation as the impact analysis process stabilizes and becomes more mature.

The cost associated with producing a conservative prediction depends on its expected accuracy. Since conservative predictions identify such a large part of the system, developers often cannot believe they are realistic. The benefit of having a conservative prediction is the ability to determine a most probable prediction somewhere between the optimistic and the conservative prediction. An ideal impact analysis approach would always provide an optimistic and a conservative estimate. By collecting and analyzing empirical data from the predictions as well as the actual changes, it can be established where in that span the correct answer lies.

6.2.1 Automatable Strategies

Automatable impact analysis strategies often employ algorithmic methods in order to identify change propagation and indirect impact. For example, relationship graphs for requirements and other SLOs can be used with graph algorithms to identify the impact a proposed change would have on the system. The prerequisite for automatable strategies is a structured specification of the system. By structured, we mean that the specification is consistent and complete, and includes some semantic information (for example, type of relationship). Once in place, such a specification can be used by tools in order to perform automatic impact analysis. Requirements dependency webs and object models are examples of structured specifications.

The strategies presented here, traceability and dependency analysis and slicing, are typically used to assess the Estimated Impact Set by identifying secondary changes made necessary because of primary changes to the system. They are not well suited for identifying direct impact.

6.2.1.1 Traceability/Dependency Analysis
Traceability analysis and dependency analysis both involve examining relationships among entities in the software. They differ in scope and detail level; traceability analysis is the analysis of relationships among all types of SLOs, while dependency analysis is the analysis of low-level dependencies extracted from source code [3]. Requirements traceability is discussed further in Chap. 5.

By extracting dependencies from source code, it is possible to obtain call graphs, control structures, data graphs and so on. Since source code is the most exact representation of the system, any analysis based on it can very precisely predict the impact of a change. Dependency analysis is also the most mature strategy for impact analysis available [3]. The drawback of using source code is that it is not available until late in the project, which makes dependency analysis narrow in its field of application. When requirements traceability exists down to the source, it can, however, be very efficient to use source code dependencies in order to determine the impact of requirements changes. A drawback is that very large systems have massive amounts of source code dependencies, which make the dependency web difficult to both use and to get an overview of [5].

Traceability analysis also requires the presence of relationship links between the SLOs that are analyzed. Typically, these relationships are captured and specified progressively during development (known as pre-recorded traceability). The success of traceability analysis depends heavily on the completeness and consistency of the identified relationships. However, if traceability information is properly recorded from the beginning of development, the analysis can be very powerful.

A common approach for recording traceability links is to use a *traceability matrix* (see, for example, [20], [23] and [40]). A traceability matrix is a matrix where each row, and each column, corresponds to one particular SLO, for example a requirement. The relationship between two SLOs is expressed by putting a mark where the row of the first SLO and the column of the second SLO intersect. It is also possible to add semantic information to the relationship between SLOs. For example, the relationship between a requirement and an architectural component can be expanded to include information about whether the component implements the requirement entirely, or only partially.

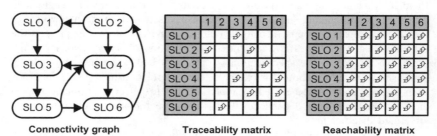

| Connectivity graph | Traceability matrix | Reachability matrix |

Fig. 6.3 Three views of the relationships among SLOs

Ramesh and Jarke report that current requirement practices do not fully embrace the use of semantic information to increase the usefulness of relationships between SLOs [31]. A relationship stating that two SLOs affect each other but not how, will be open to interpretation by all stakeholders. According to Ramesh and Jarke, different stakeholders interpret relationships without semantic information in different ways. For example, a user may read a relationship as "implemented-by," while a developer may read the same relationship as "puts-constraints-on."

To further illustrate the need for semantics in traceability links, we have created an example with six interconnected SLOs. Figure 6.3 shows the SLOs in a connectivity graph (left), where an arrow means that the source SLO affects the destination SLO. For example, SLO 2 affects, or has an impact on, SLO 1 and SLO 4.

The connectivity graph corresponds exactly to a traceability matrix, shown next in the figure. An arrow in the traceability matrix indicates that the row SLO affects the column SLO. Both the connectivity graph and the traceability matrix show direct impact, or primary change needed, whereas indirect impact, or secondary change needed, can only be deduced by traversing the traceability links. For systems with many SLOs, the amount of indirect impact quickly becomes immense and hard to deduce from a connectivity graph or a traceability matrix. In order to better visualize indirect impact, the traceability matrix can be converted into a reachability matrix, using a transitive closure algorithm[1]. The reachability matrix for our example is also in Fig. 6.3, showing that all SLOs eventually have impact on every other SLO. Consequently, the reachability matrix for this example is of limited use for assessing indirect impact. Bohner points out that this problem is common in software contexts, unless some action is taken to limit the range of indirect impact [4].

One way of limiting the range of indirect impact is to add distances to the reachability matrix. By doing so, it becomes possible to disregard indirect impacts with distances above a predefined threshold. This is a simple addition to the normal creation of reachability matrices, but it fails to address the fact that different types of traceability relationships may affect the range of indirect impact differently. Another solution is to equip the traceability matrix with traceability semantics and adjust the transitive closure algorithm to take such information into account. The algorithm should consider two SLOs reachable from each other only if the traceability relationships that form the path between them are of such types that are expected to propagate change.

Traceability analysis is useful in requirements engineering, which we view as an activity performed throughout the entire software lifecycle. Initially, traceability links can only be formed between requirements, but as design and implementation grow, links can be created from requirements to other SLOs as well.

6.2.1.2 Slicing Techniques

Slicing attempts to understand dependencies using independent slices of the program [16]. The program is sliced into a *decomposition slice*, which contains the place of the change, and the rest of the program, a *complement slice*. Slicing is based on data and control dependencies in the program. Changes made to the decomposition slice around the variable that the slice is based on are guaranteed not to affect the complement slice. Slicing limits the scope for propagation of change and makes that scope explicit. The technique is, for example, used by Turver and Munro [37] for slicing of documents in order to account for ripple effects as a part of impact analysis. Shahmehri *et al.* [33] apply the technique to debugging and testing. Pointer-based languages like C++ are supported through the work of Tip et al. and their slicing techniques for C++ [36]. Slicing tools are often based on character-based presentation techniques, which can make it more difficult to analyze dependencies, but visual presentation of slices can be applied to impact analysis as shown by Gallagher [15].

Architectural slicing was introduced by Zhao [42], and is similar to program slicing in that it identifies one slice of the architecture that is subject to the proposed change, and one that is not. As opposed to conventional program slicing, architectural slicing operates on the software architecture of a system. As such, it can be employed in early development, before the code has been written. The technique uses a graph of information flows in order to trace those components that may be affected by the component being changed. In addition, those compo-

---

[1] The **transitive closure** of a graph is a graph where an edge is added between nodes A and B if it is possible to reach B from A in the original graph.

nents that may affect the component being changed are also identified. This means that there must be a specification of the architecture that exposes all the information flows that it contains.

Slicing techniques can be useful in requirements engineering to isolate the impact of a requirements change to a specific part of the system. In order to provide a starting point for the slicing technique, the direct impact of the change must first be assessed.

6.2.2 Manual Strategies

Manual impact analysis strategies do not depend as heavily on structured specifications as their automatable counterparts do. Consequently, there is a risk that they are less precise in their predictions of impact. On the other hand, they may be easier to introduce in a change management process and are, in our experience, commonly employed in industry without regard to their precision.

The strategies presented here, using design documentation and interviewing, are primarily used for assessing the Starting Impact Set by identifying direct impact. The identification of secondary impact is possible, but is better handled by automatable strategies. Note that manual strategies, like the ones described here, can be used to capture traceability links between SLOs to be used in traceability analysis.

6.2.2.1 Design Documentation

Design documentation comes in many different forms, for example as architecture sketches, view-based architecture models, object-oriented UML diagrams, textual descriptions of software components and so on. The quality of design documentation depends on the purpose for which it was written, the frequency with which it is updated, and the information it contains. It is far too common in industry that design documentation is written early in a project only to become shelfware, or that the documentation is written after the project, just for the sake of writing it. To perform impact analysis and determine how a new or changed requirement affect the system based on design documentation requires the documentation to be up-to-date and consistent with any implementation made so far. In addition, a prerequisite for using design documentation to assess direct impact is the possibility of relating requirements to design SLOs found in the documentation. The success and precision of this activity depends on a number of factors:

- *The knowledge and skills of the persons performing the analysis.* Persons with little insight into the system will most likely have problems pinpointing the impact of changed requirements in the system.
- *The availability of the documentation.* Documentation that is "hidden" in personal computers or stored in anonymous binders may be overlooked in the analysis.
- *The amount of information conveyed in the documentation.* Simple design sketches are common, but fail to express the semantics in connections between

classes or architectural components. Ill-chosen naming schemes or inconsistent notation makes the analysis task arduous.

- *Clear and consistent documentation.* Ambiguous documentation is open for interpretation, meaning, for example, that the impact of a proposed change is coupled with great uncertainty, simply because another interpretation would have yielded different impact.

If the factors above have been taken into account, impact analysis of a requirements change can be performed by identifying the design SLOs that implement or in any other way depend on the requirements affected by the change. Additional measures that can be taken in order to alleviate the impact analysis effort are:

- *Keep a design rationale.* A design rationale is documentation describing why decisions are made the way they are. Bratthall et al. performed an experiment on the effect of a design rationale when performing impact analysis [7]. The results from the experiment suggest that a design rationale in some cases can shorten the time required for impact analysis, and increase the quality of the analysis.
- *Estimate impact of requirements as soon as the requirements are developed.* The estimated impact is necessarily coarse to begin with, but can be improved incrementally as knowledge about the system increases.

Of course, structured design documentation can also be used with traceability analysis (see Sect. 6.2.1.1) to identify indirect impact. For example, Briand et al. propose a method for performing impact analysis in UML models, where they use a transitive closure algorithm to find indirect impacts in the models [8]. They do point out, however, the essential criterion that the UML models are updated as the system undergoes changes.

6.2.2.2 Interviews

Interviewing knowledgeable developers is probably the most common way to acquire information about likely effects of new or changed requirements according to a study on impact analysis [25]. The study found that developers perceive it as highly cost-effective to ask a knowledgeable person instead of searching in documents or other forms of information sources. Extensive communication between developers was also mentioned by developers as a success factor for software development projects. Analysis of source code was the second most common way of acquiring information about the likely impact of new or changed requirements. While all developers said they interviewed other developers and consulted source code, about half of the developers answered that they also consulted information, such as use-case models and object models, stored in the CASE tool in use. When asked why information in object models was not used more extensively, the developers answered that the information in object models was not detailed enough for impact analysis. In addition, they did not believe that the information in the models was up-to-date. "Source code, on the other hand, is always up-to-date." Among some developers, especially newcomers, the attitude towards using object models as the basis for determining change as an effect of new or changed requirements was less than positive. Object models (and the particular CASE tool that was used) were, however, mentioned as a good tool for documenting impact analysis and for answering questions about the relation between requirements and design objects using the support for traceability links.

6.3 Non-Functional Requirements

Requirements are often divided into *functional* and *non-functional requirements*. Non-functional requirements, or quality requirements, are those requirements "which are not specifically concerned with the functionality of the system" [20]. Non-functional requirements are often harder to deal with than functional ones, because their impact is generally not localized to one part of the system, but cuts across the whole system.

A non-functional requirement that, for example, relates to and calls for high security, often requires fundamental support in the software architecture, as it may constrain data access, file management, database views, available functionality and so on. Changes to functional requirements may also affect non-functional requirements. For example, if a change involves replacing a data transfer protocol to one that is more data intensive, overall system performance may be degraded. One approach for dealing with non-functional requirements is to convert them into one or more functional requirements [6]. For example, a requirement stating that "no unauthorized person should be allowed access to the data" may be broken down into the more tangible requirements "a user must log into the system using a password" and "the user's identity must be verified against the login subsystem upon data access." Not all non-functional requirements can be converted in this way, however, which means that changes to them still have system-wide impact. Unfortunately, most impact analysis techniques deal exclusively with changes that can be initially pinpointed to a specific component, class or the like.

Lam and Shankararaman stress the distinction between functional impact analysis and quality impact analysis, i.e. impact analysis for functional and quality requirements, respectively [21]. They suggest the use of Quality Function Deployment (QFD) for dealing with changes to both functional and non-functional requirements. In QFD, a matrix connecting customer requirements with design features is constructed. A change to a requirement can be mapped to design features through the QFD matrix.

Cleland-Huang et al. accomplish performance-related impact analysis through event-based traceability [9]. In their approach, requirements are interconnected as event publishers to subscribing performance models. Whenever a change to a requirement is proposed, the relevant performance models are re-calculated. The resulting impact analysis is subsequently compared to constraints in the requirements specification. If several requirements are linked to the same performance model, they will all be verified against the impact analysis.

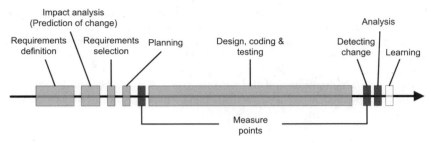

Fig. 6.4 Measuring impact using metrics

The impact of non-functional requirements is commonly dealt with in software architecture evaluation. Bosch has created a software architecture design method with a strong focus on non-functional requirements [6]. In the method, an initially functional architecture is progressively transformed until it is capable of meeting all non-functional requirements posed on the system. Parts of the method lend themselves well to impact analysis, since they deal with the challenge of assessing the often system-wide impact that non-functional requirements have. For most operational non-functional attributes (for example performance and reliability), a profile consisting of usage scenarios, describing typical uses of the system-to-be is created. The scenarios within the profile are assigned relative weights, in accordance with their frequency or probable occurrence. In scenario-based assessment, an impact analysis is performed by assessing the architectural impact of each scenario in the profile. For performance, the impact may be expressed as execution time, for example. Based on the impact and the relative weights of the scenarios, it is possible to calculate overall values (for example, throughput and execution time) for the quality attribute being evaluated. These values can be compared to the non-functional requirements corresponding to the quality attribute, in order to see whether they are met or not. Furthermore, they serve as constraints on the extent to which non-functional requirements can change before an architectural reorganization is necessary. Also, should a functional requirement change, it is possible to incorporate the change in a speculative architecture, re-calculate the impact of the scenarios in the scenario profile, and see whether the non-functional requirements are still met or not.

6.4 Impact Analysis Metrics

Metrics are useful in impact analysis for various reasons. They can, for example, be used to measure and quantify change caused by a new or changed requirement at the point of the impact analysis activity. Metrics can also be used to evaluate the impact analysis process itself once the changes have been implemented. This is illustrated in Fig. 6.4, in which two measure points are depicted; one after the requirements phase has ended and design is about to start, and one when testing has been completed. Using these measure points, one can capture the predicted impact (the first point) and compare it to the actual impact (the second point). This kind of measurement is crucial for being able to do an analysis and learn from experiences in order to continuously improve the impact analysis capability. The figure is simplified and illustrates a learning cycle based on a waterfall-like model. As discussed earlier, impact analysis can be used throughout the life cycle in order to analyze new requirements and the measure points can be applied accordingly: whenever a prediction has been conducted and whenever an implementation has been completed.

6.4.1 Metrics for Quantifying Change Impact

Metrics for quantifying change impact are based on the SLOs that are predicted to be changed as an effect of new or changed requirements. In addition, indicators of how severe the change is can be used. Such measures of the predicted impact can be used to estimate the cost of a proposed change or a new requirement. The more requirements and other SLOs that are affected, the more widespread they are and the more complex the proposed change is, the more expensive the new or changed requirement will be. Requirements that are costly in this sense but provide little value can, for example, be filtered out for the benefit of requirements that provide more value but to a smaller cost.

Change impact can be measured based on the set of requirements that is affected by the change. For example, the number of requirements affected by a change can be counted based on this set. The affected requirements' complexity often determines how severe the change is and can be measured in various ways. Examples are the size of each requirement in terms of function points and the dependencies of each requirement on other requirements. For other SLOs, the metrics are similar. For architecture and design, measures of impact include the number of affected components, the number of affected classes or modules, and number of affected methods or functions. For source code, low-level items such as affected lines of code can be measured and the level of complexity for components, classes, and methods can be measured using standard metrics such as cyclomatic complexity and regular object-oriented metrics.

In determining how severe or costly a change is, it is useful to define the *impact factor*. Lindvall defined the impact factors in Table 6.1 to measure the impact of a suggested change [25]. The impact factor is based on empirical findings in which it was determined that changes to different types of SLOs can be used as an indicator of the extent of the change. The higher the impact factor, the more severe the change. For example, changes that do not affect any other type of SLO but the design object model are relatively limited in scope. Changes that affect the use-case model are instead likely to require changes that are related to the fundamentals of the system and are therefore larger in scope. In addition, changes to the use-case model most likely also involve changes of all other SLOs making this kind of changes even more severe.

Table 6.1 Impact factors

Impact Factor	Impact	Description
M1	Change of the design object model.	These changes regard the real or physical description of the system and may generate change in the software architecture about the size of the change in the model.
M2	Change of the analysis object model.	These changes regard the ideal or logical description of the system. A small change here may generate change in the software architecture larger than the change in this model.
M3	Change the domain object model.	These changes regard the vocabulary needed in the system. A small change here may generate large change in the software architecture.
M4	Change the use-case model.	These changes require additions and deletions to the use-case model. Small changes here may require large change in the software architecture

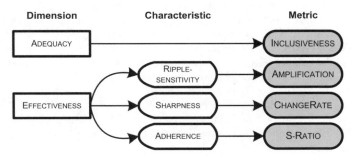

Fig. 6.5 Tree of impact analysis metrics

6.4.2 Metrics for Evaluation of Impact Analysis

Bohner and Arnold proposed a number of metrics with their introduction of impact sets [3]. These metrics are relations between the cardinalities of the impact sets, and can be seen as indicators of the effectiveness of the impact analysis approach employed (# denotes the cardinality of the set):

1. #SIS / #EIS, i.e. the number of SLOs initially thought to be affected over the number of SLOs estimated to be affected (primary change and secondary change). A ratio close to 1 is desired, as it indicates that the impact is restricted to the SLOs in SIS. A ratio much less than 1 indicates that many SLOs are targeted for indirect impact, which means that it will be time-consuming to check them.
2. #EIS / #System, i.e. the number of SLOs estimated to be affected over the number of SLOs in the system. The desired ratio is much less than 1, as it indi-

cates that the changes are restricted to a small part of the system. A ratio close to 1 would indicate either a faulty impact analysis approach or a system with extreme ripple effects.

3. #EIS / #AIS, i.e. the number of SLOs estimated to be affected over the number of SLOs actually affected. The desired ratio is 1, as it indicates that the impact was perfectly estimated. In reality, it is likely that the ratio is smaller than 1, indicating that the approach failed to estimate all impacts. Two special cases are if AIS and EIS only partly overlap or do not overlap at all, which also would indicate a failure of the impact analysis approach.

Fasolino and Visaggio also define metrics based on the cardinalities of the impact sets [14]. They tie the metrics to properties and characteristics of the impact analysis approach, as per the tree in Fig. 6.5.

Adequacy is the ability of the impact analysis approach to estimate the impact set. It is measured by means of the binary metric *Inclusiveness*, which is strictly defined to 1 if all SLOs in AIS also are in EIS and 0 otherwise. *Effectiveness* is the ability of the approach to provide beneficial results. It is refined into *Ripple-sensitivity* (the ability to identify ripple effects), *Sharpness* (the ability not to overestimate the impact) and *Adherence* (the ability to estimate the correct impact).

Ripple-sensitivity is measured by *Amplification*, which is defined as (#EIS - #SIS) / #SIS, i.e. the ratio between the number of indirectly impacted SLOs and the number of directly impacted SLOs. This ratio should preferably not be much larger than 1, which would indicate much more indirect impact than direct impact. Sharpness is measured by *ChangeRate*, which is defined as #EIS / #System. This is the same metric as the second of Arnold and Bohner's metrics presented previously. Adherence is measured by *S-Ratio*, which is defined as #AIS / #EIS. S-Ratio is the converse of the third of Arnold and Bohner's metrics presented previously.

Lam and Shankararaman propose metrics that are not related to the impact sets. These metrics are more loosely defined and lack consequently recommended values [21]:

- *Quality deviation*, i.e. the difference in some quality attribute (for example, performance) before and after the changes have been implemented, or between actual and simulated values. A larger than expected difference could indicate that the impact analysis approach failed to identify all impact.
- *Defect count*, i.e. the number of defects that arise after the changes have been implemented. A large number of defects could indicate that some impact was overlooked by the impact analysis approach.
- *Dependency count*, i.e. the number of requirements that depend on a particular requirement. Requirements with high dependency count should be carefully examined when being subjected to change.

Lindvall [25] defined and used metrics in a study at the Swedish telecom company Ericsson AB in order to answer a number of questions related to the result (prediction) of impact analysis as conducted in a commercial software project and performed by the project developers as part of the regular project work. The study was based on impact analysis conducted in the requirements phase, as Fig. 6.4 indicates, and the term *requirements-driven impact analysis* was coined to capture this fact. The results from the impact analysis was used by the Ericsson project to estimate implementation cost and to select requirements for implementation based on the estimated cost versus perceived benefit. The study first looked at the collected set of requirements' predicted and actual impact by answering the following questions: "How good was the prediction of the change caused by new and changed requirements in terms of predicting the *number* of C++ classes to be changed?" and "How good was this prediction in terms of predicting *which* classes to be changed?" The last question was broken down into the two sub questions: "Were changed classes predicted?" and "Were the predicted classes changed?"

There were a total of 136 C++ classes in the software system. 30 of these were predicted to be changed. The analysis of the source code edits showed that 94 classes were actually changed. Thus, only 31.0% (30 / 94) of the number of changed classes were predicted to be changed.

In order to analyze the data further, the classes were divided into the two groups *Predictive group* and *Actual group*. In addition, each group was divided into two subgroups: *Unchanged* and *Changed*. The 136 classes were distributed among these four groups as shown in Table 6.2.

Table 6.2 Predicted vs. actual changes

		Predictive Group		
		Unchanged	Changed	
Actual Group	**Unchanged**	A: 42 (30.9%)	B:0 (0.0%	A+B: 42 (30.9%)
	Changed	C; 64 (47.1%)	D: 30 (22.1%)	C+D: 94 (69.1%)
		A+C: 106 (77.9%)	B+D: 30 (22.1%)	N: 136 (100.0%)

Cell A represents the 42 classes that were not predicted to change and that also remained unchanged. The prediction was correct as these classes were predicted to remain unchanged, which also turned out to be true. The prediction was implicit as these classes were indirectly identified –they resulted as a side effect as complement of predicting changed classes.

Cell B represents the zero classes that were predicted to change, but actually remained unchanged. A large number here would indicate a large deviation from the prediction.

Cell C represents the 64 classes that were not predicted to change, but turned out to be changed after all. As with cell B, a large number in this cell indicates a large deviation from the prediction.

Cell D, finally, represents the 30 classes that were predicted to be changed and were, in fact, changed. This is a correct prediction. A large number in this cell indicates a good prediction.

There are several ways to analyze the goodness of the prediction. One way is to calculate the percentage of correct predictions, which was $(42 + 30) / 136 =$

52.9%. Thus, the prediction was correct in about half of the cases. Another way is to use Cohen's Kappa value, which measures the agreement between two groups ranging from -1.0 to 1.0. The -1.0 figure means total discompliance between the two groups, 1.0 means total compliance and 0.0 means that the result is no better than pure chance [11]. The kappa value in this case is 0.22, which indicates a fair prediction. We refer to [26] for full details on the Kappa calculations for the example. A third way to evaluate the prediction is to compare the number of classes predicted to be changed with the number of classes actually changed. The number of classes predicted to be changed in this case turned out to be largely underpredicted by a factor of 3. Thus, only about one third of the set of changed classes was identified. It is, however, worth noticing that all of the classes that were predicted to be changed were in fact changed.

The study then analyzed the predicted and actual impact of each requirement by answering similar questions for each requirement. The requirements and the classes that were affected by these requirements were organized in the following manner: For each requirement, the set of classes predicted to be changed, the set of changed classes and the intersection of the two sets, i.e. classes that were both predicted and changed. In addition, the sets of classes that were predicted but not changed and the set of classes that were changed but not predicted were identified.

The analysis showed that in almost all cases, there was an underprediction in terms of number of classes. In summary, the analysis showed that the number of changed classes divided by the number of predicted classes ranged from 1.0 to 7.0. Thus, up to 7 times more classes than predicted were actually changed.

Estimating cost in requirements selection is often based on the prediction like it was in the Ericsson case, which means that requirements predicted to cause change in only a few entities are regarded as less expensive, while requirements predicted to cause change in many entities are regarded as more expensive. This makes the rank-order of requirements selection equal to a requirements list sorted by the number of items predicted. By comparing the relative order based on the number of predicted classes with the relative order based on the number of actually changed classes, it was possible to judge the goodness of the prediction from yet another point of view. In summary, the analysis on the requirements level showed that a majority of the requirements were underpredicted. It was also clear that it is relatively common that some classes predicted for one requirement are not changed because of this particular requirement, but because of some other requirement. This is probably because the developers were not required to implement the changed requirements exactly as was specified in the implementation proposal resulting from the impact analysis. The analysis of the order of requirements based on number of predicted classes showed that the order was not kept entirely intact; some requirements that were predicted to be small proved to have a large change impact, and vice versa.

In order to try to understand the requirements-driven impact analysis process and how to improve it, an analysis of the various characteristics of changed and unchanged classes was undertaken. One such characteristic was size, and the questions were: "Were large classes changed?", "Were large classes predicted?" and "Were large classes predicted compared to changed classes?"

The analysis indicated that large classes were changed, while small classes remained unchanged. The analysis also indicated that large classes were predicted to change, which leads to the conclusion that class size may be one of the ingredients used by developers, maybe unconsciously, when searching for candidates for a new or changed requirement.

6.5 Tool Support

The complexity of the change management process makes it necessary to use some sort of tool support [27, 35]. A change management tool can be used to manage requirements and other SLOs, manage change requests, link change requests to requirements and other SLOs, and monitor the impact analysis progress. A simple database or spreadsheet tool may be used as basic change management support, but still requires a considerable amount of manual work, which eventually may lead to inconsistencies in the change management data. If the tool support is not an integral part of the change management process, there is always a risk that it will not be used properly. A change management system that is not used to its full extent cannot provide proper support to the process.

A problem with many change management tools is that they are restricted to working with change and impact analysis on the requirements level. Ideally, a change management tool would support impact analysis on requirements, design, source code, test cases and so on. However, that would require the integration of requirement management tools, design tools and development environments into one tool or tool set. In a requirements catalog for requirements management tools, Hoffmann *et al.* list both *traceability* and *tool integration* as high-priority requirements, and *analysis functions* as a mid-priority requirement, confirming the importance of these features [19].

In a survey of the features of 29 requirements management tools supporting traceability, we could only find nine tools for which it was explicitly stated on their web sites that they supported traceability between requirements and other SLOs, such as design elements, test cases and code. Depending on the verbosity and quality of the available information, this may not be an exact figure. However, it indicates that in many cases it is necessary to use several different tools to manage traceability and perform impact analysis, which can be problematic depending on the degree of integration between the tools.

There are tools that extract dependency information from existing system representations, for example source code and object models, but the task of such tools is nonetheless difficult and often requires manual work [12]. Higher-level representations may be too coarse, and source code may have hidden dependencies, for instance due to late binding. Egyed, for example, proposes an approach for extracting dependencies primarily for source code [12]. Input to the approach is a set of test scenarios and some hypothesized traces that link SLOs to scenarios. The approach then calculates the footprints of the scenarios, i.e. the source code lines they cover, and based on footprints and hypothesized traces generates the remaining traces. The approach can also be used when no source code exists, for example by simulating the system or hypothesizing around the footprints of the scenarios.

Tools that deal with source code are mostly used in software maintenance contexts, and are obviously of limited use within the development project. Natt och Dag et al. have studied automatic similarity analysis as a means to find duplicate requirements in market-driven development [29]. In addition to the original field of application, they suggest that their technique can be used to identify dependency relationships between requirements, for example that two requirements have an "or" relation, or that several requirements deal with similar functionality. How to deal with natural language requirements is further explored in Chap. 10. Tools that aid in performing impact analysis can be synonymous with the underlying methods. Methods that rely on traceability analysis are well suited for inclusion in tools that try to predict indirect impact. For example, Fasolino and Visaggio present ANALYST, a tool that assesses impact in dependency-based models [14]. Lee *et al.* present another tool, ChAT, which calculates ripple effects caused by a change to the system [22]. Many such tools are commonly proof-of-concept tools, constructed to show or support a particular algorithm or methodology. What is lacking is the integration into mainstream change management tools.

6.6 Future of Impact Analysis

Most strategies for impact analysis work under the assumption that changes only affect functionality. It is thus more difficult to assess the impact of changes to non-functional requirements, or changes where non-functional requirements are indirectly affected. Some work on this topic exists (see [9] and [21]), but a stronger focus on impact analysis for non-functional requirements is needed.

As we have pointed out, impact analysis is mostly referred to in software maintenance contexts. We have argued that impact analysis is an essential activity also in requirements engineering contexts, and that standard impact analysis strategies apply in most cases (for example, traceability approaches are commonly exercised for requirements). There is still, however, a need for more research focusing on the requirements engineering aspects of impact analysis, for example, how to relate requirements to other SLOs and how to perform change propagation in this context. Most automatable strategies for impact analysis assume complete models and full traceability information. Since it is common in industry to encounter models that are not updated and traceability information that is only partial, there is a need for more robust impact analysis strategies that can work with partial information. Egyed has proposed one such approach [12]. Existing tools for impact analysis are often proof-of-concept tools, or work only with limited impact analysis problems, such as the extraction of dependencies from system representations. Some mainstream requirements management tools incorporate impact analysis of not only requirements, but also design, code and test, but far from all these things. Full-scale impact analysis must be an integral part of requirement management tools in order for change to be dealt with properly. Impact analysis needs to be adapted to the types of systems that become increasingly common today, such as web applications and COTS software. Web applications, for example, often consist of standalone components that connect to a central repository, such as a database. Thus, there are few control dependencies between components, and instead rich webs of data dependencies towards and within the central repository. The fact that such repositories can be shared among several distinct systems introduces interoperability dependencies that impact analysis strategies especially tailored for these technologies must address in order to be effective.

6.7 Summary

Impact analysis is an important part of requirements engineering since changes to software often are initiated by changes to the requirements. As the development process becomes less and less waterfall-like and more of new and changed requirements can be expected throughout the development process, impact analysis becomes an integral part of every phase in software development. In some sense, impact analysis has been performed for a very long time, albeit not necessarily using that term and not necessarily fully resolving the problem of accurately determining the effect of a proposed change. The need for software practitioners to determine what to change in order to implement requirement changes has always been present. Classical methods and strategies to conduct impact analysis are dependency analysis, traceability analysis and slicing. Early impact analysis work focused on applying such methods and strategies onto source code in order to conduct program slicing and determine ripple effects for code changes. The maturation of software engineering among software organizations has, however, led to a need to understand how change requests affect other SLOs than source code, including requirements, and the same methods and strategies have been applied. Typical methods and strategies of today are based on analyzing traceability or dependency information, utilizing slicing techniques, consulting design specifications and other documentation, and interviewing knowledgeable developers. Interviewing knowledgeable developers is probably the most common way to acquire information about likely effects of new or changed requirements. Metrics are useful and important in impact analysis for various reasons. Metrics can, for example, be used to measure and quantify change caused by a new or changed requirement at the point of the impact analysis activity. Metrics can also be used to evaluate the impact analysis process itself once the changes have been implemented. In determining how severe or costly a change is, it is useful to determine the impact factor as it indicates the likely extent of a change to a certain type of SLO. To summarize: Impact analysis is a crucial activity supporting requirements engineering. The results from impact analysis feed into many activities including estimation of requirements' cost and prioritizing of requirements. These activities feed directly into project planning, making impact analysis a central activity in a successful project.

Acknowledgements

We would like to thank Jen Dix for proof reading, and the anonymous reviewers for helping to improve the chapter.

References

1. ANSI/IEEE Std 830-1984 (1984) IEEE guide to software requirements specifications, Institute of the Electrical and Electronics Engineers
2. Bass L, Clements P, Kazman R (2003) Software architecture in practice, Addison Wesley
3. Bohner SA, Arnold RS (1996) Software change impact analysis, IEEE Computer Society Press
4. Bohner SA (2002) Extending software change impact analysis into COTS components. In: Proceedings of the 27th Annual NASA Goddard Software Engineering Workshop, December 4-6, Greenbelt, USA, pp.175-182
5. Bohner SA, Gracanin D (2003) Software impact analysis in a virtual environment. In: Proceedings of the 28th Annual NASA Goddard Software Engineering Workshop, December 2-4, Greenbelt, USA, pp.143-151
6. Bosch J (2000) Design & use of software architectures - Adopting and evolving a product-line approach. Pearson Education, UK
7. Bratthall L, Johansson E, Regnell B (2000) Is a design rationale vital when predicting change impact? - A controlled experiment on software architecture evolution. In: Proceedings of the 2nd International Conference on Product Focused Software Process Improvement, June 20-22, Oulo, Finland, pp.126-139
8. Briand LC, Labiche Y, O'Sullivan L (2003) Impact analysis and change management of UML models. In: Proceedings of the International Conference on Software Maintenance, September 22-26, Amsterdam, Netherlands, pp 256-265
9. Cleland-Huang J, Chang CK, Wise JC (2003) Automating performance-related impact analysis through event based traceability. Requirements Engineering 8(3):171-182
10. Clements P, Bachmann F, Bass L, Garlan D, Ivers J, Little R, Nord R, Stafford J (2003) Documenting software architectures: Views and beyond. Addison Wesley, UK
11. Cohen J (1960) A coefficient of agreement for nominal scales, educational and psychological measurement 20(1):37-46
12. Egyed A (2003) A scenario-driven approach to trace dependency analysis. IEEE Transactions on Software Engineering 29(2):116-132
13. Eick SG, Graves L, Karr AF, Marron JS (2001) Does code decay? Assessing the evidence from change management data. IEEE Transactions on Software Engineering 27(1):1-12
14. Fasolino AR, Visaggio G (1999) Improving software comprehension through an automated dependency tracer. In: Proceedings of the 7th International Workshop on Program Comprehension, May 5-7, Pittsburgh, USA, pp 58-65
15. Gallagher KB (1996) Visual impact analysis. In: Proceedings of the International Conference on Software Maintenance, November 4-8, Monterey, USA, pp 52-58
16. Gallagher KB, Lyle JR (1991) Using program slicing in software maintenance. IEEE Transactions on Software Engineering 17(8):751-761

17. Godfrey LW, Lee EHS (2000) Secrets from the monster - Extracting Mozilla's software architecture. In: Proceedings of the 2nd International Symposium on Constructing Software Engineering Tools, Limerick, Ireland, pp 15–23

18. Haney FM (1972) Module connection analysis - A tool for scheduling software debugging activities. In Proceedings of AFIPS Joint Computer Conference, pp 173–179

19. Hoffmann M, Kühn N, Bittner M (2004) Requirements for requirements management tools. In: Proceedings of the 12th IEEE International Requirements Engineering Conference, September 6–10, Kyoto, Japan, pp 301–308

20. Kotonya G, Sommerville I (1998) Requirements engineering - Processes and techniques. Wiley and Sons, UK

21. Lam W, Shankararaman V (1999) Requirements change: A dissection of management issues. In: Proceedings of the 25th EuroMicro Conference, September 8–10, Milan, Italy, Vol. 2, pp.244–251

22. Lee M, Offutt JA, Alexander RT (2000) Algorithmic analysis of the impacts of changes to object-oriented software. In: Proceedings of the 34th International Conference on Technology of Object-Oriented Languages and Systems, July 30–Aug 4, Santa Barbara, USA, pp 61–70

23. Leffingwell D, Widrig D (1999) Managing software requirements - A unified approach. Addison Wesley

24. Lehman MM, Ramil JF, Wernick PD, Perry DE, Turski WM (1997) Metrics and laws of software evolution - The nineties view. In: Proceedings of the 4th International Software Metrics Symposium, November 5-7, Albuquerque, USA, pp 20–32

25. Lindvall M (1997) An empirical study of requirements-driven impact analysis in object-oriented systems evolution. Ph.D. thesis no. 480, Linköping Studies in Science and Technology, Sweden

26. Lindvall M, Sandahl K (1998) How well do experienced software developers predict software change?, Journal of Systems and Software 43(1):19–27

27. Maciaszek L (2001) Requirements analysis and system design - Developing information systems with UML, Addison Wesley

28. Mockus A, Votta LG (2000) Identifying reasons for software changes using historic databases. In: Proceedings of the International Conference on Software Maintenance, October 11-14, San Jose, USA, pp 120–130

29. Natt och Dag J, Regnell B, Carlshamre P, Andersson M, Karlsson J (2002) A feasibility study of automated support for similarity analysis of natural language requirements in market-driven development. Requirements Engineering 7:20–33

30. O'Neal JS, Carver DL (2001) Analyzing the impact of changing requirements. In: Proceedings of the International Conference on Software Maintenance, November 6-10, Florence, Italy, pp.190–195

31. Ramesh B, Jarke M (2001) Towards reference models for requirements traceability. IEEE Transactions on Software Engineering 27(1): 58–93

32. Robertson S, Robertson J (1999) Mastering the requirements process. Addison Wesley, UK

33. Shahmehri N, Kamkar M, Fritzson P (1990) Semi-automatic bug localization in software maintenance. In: Proceedings of the Conference on Software Maintenance, November 26-29, San Diego, USA, pp 30–36

34. Software Engineering Institute (2004): How do you define software architecture?, http://www.sei.cmu.edu/architecture/definitions.html, Accessed November 19, 2004.

35. Sommerville I, Sawyer P (1997) Requirements engineering - A good practice guide. John Wiley and Sons, London

36. Tip F, Jong DC, Field J, Ramlingam G (1996) Slicing class hierarchies in C++. In: Proceedings of Object-Oriented Programming, Systems, Languages & Applications Conference, October 6-10, San Jose, USA, pp 179–197

37. Turver RJ, Munro M (1994) An early impact analysis technique for software maintenance. Journal of Software Maintenance Research and Practice 6(1):35–52

38. Weinberg GM (1983) Kill that code. Infosystems 30: 48–49

39. Weiser M (1979) Program slices: formal, psychological, and practical investigations of an automatic program abstraction method. Ph.D. thesis, University of Michigan, Michigan, USA

40. Wiegers KE (2003): Software requirements. Microsoft Press

41. Yau SS, Collofello JS (1980) Some stability measures for software maintenance. IEEE Transactions on Software Engineering 6(6): 545–552

42. Zhao J (1998) Applying slicing technique to software architectures. In: Proceedings of the 4th IEEE International Conference on Engineering of Complex Computer Systems, August 10-14, Monterey, USA, pp.87–98

Author Biography

Per Jönsson is a Ph.D. student in Software Engineering at the School of Engineering at Blekinge Institute of Technology in Sweden, where he also received his Degree of Master of Science in Software Engineering in 2002. His main research interest is impact analysis on a software architecture level. This touches the boundary between requirements engineering and software architecture, and includes questions about how requirements affect the architecture, but also how architectures are created, changed, maintained and merged.

Dr. Mikael Lindvall is a scientist at Fraunhofer Center Maryland. He manages the center's participation in NASA's High Dependability Computing Project. He heads test bed development for experimenting with and determining technologies' impact on software dependability and studies how best practices, lessons learned and other experience and knowledge management strategies are best applied in software engineering. He studies software architecture evaluation and evolution to efficiently understand software architectures and to identify architectural violations. Lindvall received a Ph.D. from Linköping University, Sweden 1997, on impact analysis and evolution of object-oriented systems at Ericsson Radio in Sweden.

7 Requirements Negotiation

Paul Grünbacher and Norbert Seyff

Abstract: Negotiation is regarded as crucial in many disciplines, and negotiation methods and tools are increasingly studied by requirements engineering researchers and practitioners. The objectives of this chapter are to motivate the need for negotiation in requirements engineering, to introduce fundamental concepts and terminology, and to provide an overview about negotiation research. We structure the existing research (a) by presenting a general negotiation process highlighting typical negotiation stages; (b) by introducing a framework covering important dimensions of requirements negotiation comprising the conflict resolution strategy, the collaboration situation of the stakeholders, and the degree of negotiation tool support; and (c) by discussing and classifying existing negotiation tools using the general process and framework.

Keywords: Negotiation, Negotiation process, Conflict resolution, Collaboration, Negotiation tools, Stakeholder win-win.

7.1 Introduction

Conflicts play an important role in software engineering although they are often neglected or badly handled by existing development methods. Conflicts arise almost inevitably as project stakeholders such as future system users, acquirers, developers, or maintainers frequently pursue mismatching goals [10]. For example, future system users are typically interested in many features, high level of service, or early availability. Acquirers focus on cost effectiveness, compliance with standards, or budget/schedule constraints. Developers typically want flexible contracts and stable requirements. Although studies show that conflict is extensive in software engineering [15], many existing methods neglect or do not explicitly address conflict handling and resolution. Nevertheless, negotiation techniques and tools have gained increased attention in software engineering research. As a result, methods and tools have been developed supporting the requirements negotiation process, some of them are also available commercially.

Software engineering is a highly collaborative process and identifying shared or opposed interests is a necessity for project success [41, 60]. The objectives of customers, users, or developers have to be understood and reconciled to develop mutually acceptable agreements [5]. This obviously does not mean that stakeholders will always agree. The result of negotiation is also to understand why stakeholders disagree. Identified disagreements represent major risks and need to be addressed by project management.

Requirements negotiation is not a one time episode in a project, but should be used early on and repeated in later stages [9]. In each cycle new stakeholders and new objectives have to be considered often leading to negotiations. In iterative software life cycles such as the spiral model [3] the achieved agreements are evolved into more detailed requirements, development plans, architectures, etc. The primary purpose of requirements negotiation is to identify and resolve conflicts among stakeholders. It contributes to the goal of defining feasible and mutually satisfactory requirements that accommodate all stakeholder goals and expectations [6, 41, 60]. Beyond this primary purpose, research and evidence from practitioners show further benefits:

Understanding project constraints. It has been shown in many studies that software projects often fail to meet critical project constraints such as budget and schedule [58]. Negotiation makes stakeholders aware of these constraints and supports finding solutions for meeting them.

Adapting to changes. Because of rapid chances of market competition, technology, personnel, etc. requirements (and sometimes even constraints) are highly volatile. As a result stakeholders are forced to frequently adapt to new situations. Negotiation helps to deal with such changes more easily as stakeholders are aware of existing issues and alternatives. Should agreements become obsolete they can be re-negotiated and revised to accommodate the evolving requirements and constraints.

Fostering team learning. Different stakeholders come to a project with their experiences, backgrounds, and expectations and bring their goals to the table. Developing requirements is a cognitive process, in which stakeholders collaboratively find out what has to be done [60] by understanding problems and domains, learning from other stakeholders, and by negotiating and discussing different viewpoints. Stakeholders share information and search for mutually beneficial solutions. Developers, for example, learn more about the customer's and user's world, while customers and users learn more about what is technically and economically feasible.

Surfacing tacit knowledge. People know more than they can ever tell. Tacit stakeholder goals, hidden assumptions and expectations often lead to problems in software projects. Negotiation supports people bringing hidden issues and assumptions to the table [27].

Managing complexity. Establishing software requirements is fraught with complexity. In a typical non-trivial project with 10+ stakeholders one has to deal with hundreds of individual goals, and dozens of issues and alternatives that need to be understood. Complex interdependencies among requirements and between requirements and related development artifacts are another source of complexity as described in Chap. 5. Further things complicating negotiations are cognitive overflows, conflicting strategies of negotiators, or unforeseen interventions by third parties [57]. Handling that complexity is supported by negotiation techniques [14].

Dealing with uncertainty. Specifying software requirements without negotiation is difficult, because users do not know exactly what they need and what is technologically feasible [4, 60]. Negotiation helps to reduce uncertainty by highlighting things needing attention and fosters a shared vision among stakeholders.

Finding better solutions. Without negotiation techniques stakeholders often try to persuade others to accept a suggested solution instead of jointly seeking for new solutions that are beneficial to all parties [52]. For example, the main disadvantage of sequential negotiation of issues is that trade-offs between issues cannot be considered adequately. Negotiation techniques help to see the full picture instead of dealing with issues sequentially, which can help to avoid suboptimal solutions.

The benefits of negotiation are obvious, and many researchers have pointed out its usefulness for requirements engineering [42, 46]. However, establishing a requirements negotiation process is not trivial and important issues have to be addressed: How can conflicts be identified? How can the identified conflicts be resolved? How can stakeholders find feasible alternatives? Who is in charge of the negotiation, the stakeholders themselves or a facilitator? How can the negotiation be supported with tools or other means? Requirements negotiation can make use of negotiation methods and tools from a wide range of disciplines and domains. Negotiation is a phase in the decision making process and there is a strong body of knowledge on decision making. Consequently, negotiation in group decisions have been investigated from multiple perspectives, such as decision theory [36], management theory and social sciences [19, 50, 59], organizational psychology [61], and game theory [49]. Giving an overview about the start-of-the-art in requirements negotiation is challenging, as a thorough discussion of all these aspect is certainly beyond the scope of this chapter. We therefore discuss the existing research from the perspective of software requirements negotiation instead of negotiation in general.

The chapter is structured as follows: In Sect. 7.2 we review several definitions for requirements negotiation, define basic terminology, and present a general negotiation process highlighting typical negotiation stages. Section 7.3 introduces our framework covering important dimensions of requirements negotiation such as conflict resolution strategy, the collaboration situation of the stakeholders, and the level of negotiation tool support. The purpose of the framework is to help understand and classify existing and future research approaches and to increase awareness of the issues involved in defining and implementing requirements negotiation processes in practice. In Sect. 7.4, we use the framework to present examples of existing requirements negotiation approaches. Conclusions round out the chapter in Sect. 7.5.

7.2 The Negotiation Process

Negotiation is widely adopted and has been investigated by multiple disciplines. Consequently, there are different perspectives on negotiation and different aspects are emphasized [14, 16, 31, 47]. Negotiation is traditionally viewed as "the actual interactions among participants that lead to mutual commitment" starting "when participants begin communicating their goals, and ending (successfully) when all agree to a specified contract." [52]

Other definitions have a slightly different flavor. Easterbrook [20] defines negotiation as "a collaborative approach to resolving conflict by exploration of the range of possibilities. It is characterized by the participants attempting to find a settlement which satisfies all parties as much as possible." The author emphasizes conflict as the fundamental reason for negotiation and points out that negotiation often involves some sort of compromise when saying that parties should be satisfied "as much as possible."

In another definition Curtis et al. [15] take a requirements engineering perspective when stating that "in general terms, requirements negotiation can be seen as an iterative process through which stakeholders make tradeoffs between requested system functions, the capabilities of existing or envisioned technology, the delivery schedule and the cost." Robinson and Volkov [52] argue that beyond the actual negotiation one should also consider pre- and post-negotiation phases as part of the negotiation process covering activities such as initial problem recognition, participant solicitation and communication, or solution maintenance. This broader view is also confirmed by different negotiation approaches. The negotiation support system Inspire [40], for example, uses the phases pre-negotiation, negotiation, post-settlement. The EasyWinWin negotiation approach is embedded in processes of preparing the actual negotiation and post-negotiation analyses and quality assurance [28]. The identification of stakeholders in EasyWinWin is covered by the win-win spiral model. Our discussion of the negotiation process follows these approaches and therefore discusses the general stages of pre-negotiation, negotiation, and post-negotiation.

7.2.1 Pre-Negotiation

Important activities of this phase are the definition of the negotiation problem, the identification and solicitation of stakeholders, the elicitation of goals from stakeholders, and the analysis of goals to find conflicts. The results of this phase are the issues and conflicts involved. According to [40] an issue is "a topic of discussion that is of particular interest in a negotiation. Each issue has a range of alternatives or options, one of which must ultimately be agreed upon by the negotiators in order to achieve a compromise."

Problem Definition. Before the actual negotiation can start it is important to identify the problem by analyzing the situation and defining the purpose of the negotiation. For example, in a software project the problem depends on both the overall objectives of the project and the current stage of the project. Early stage requirements negotiations involve high-level issues while later negotiation might focus on specific aspects or subprojects. Requirements gathered in early stages of a project express a wider range of possibilities in general terms and become more precise later on [22]. Defining the negotiation problem is essential for stakeholder identification and for adjusting the negotiation method and techniques.

Stakeholder Identification. The success-critical stakeholders have to be identified. Finding the people (or appropriate representatives) whose interests must be accommodated is often a challenging task itself [32, 56] but essential for the success of the requirements negotiation. The success-critical stakeholders are the people that can make agreements about requirements and can make those agreements stick. Identifying the right people can accelerate the negotiation process.

Goal Elicitation. Before conflicts can be identified stakeholders have to bring their individual goal to the table. A goal is an objective the system under consideration should achieve [43]. All success-critical stakeholders need to express their individual goals or the goals of people they represent. Depending on the identified problem and stakeholder characteristics such as role, domain knowledge, experience, etc. goals are formulated at different levels of granularity, ranging from high-level aspects such as general system capabilities, budgets, or schedules to lower level technical concerns such as development environments or target platforms. Many of the elicitation and prioritization techniques presented in Chaps. 2 and 4 support this activity.

Goal analysis. The elicited goals are examined to identify conflicts, i.e., by analyzing stakeholder goals and preferences. For example, there might be a conflict between the level of service required by users and budget constraints imposed by acquirers. Identifying conflicts is typically a manual process and relies on the knowledge and expertise of the involved stakeholders and the capabilities of the facilitator. Goal analysis does not only reveal conflicts among stakeholder goals but typically also reveals inconsistencies, risks, uncertainties, and hidden assumptions [27]. Prioritization techniques presented in Chap. 4 support this task.

Different authors have tried to automate or partially automate the task of understanding requirements conflicts. For example, Egyed and Grünbacher [21] recently presented an approach for identifying conflicts and cooperation among requirements based on software attributes and automated traceability. Another example of this kind of support are sophisticated visualization techniques to identify conflicting goals and requirements [33].

7.2.2 Negotiation

This phase involves the actual conduct of the negotiation and the definition of agreements. Based on the elicited goals and the identified conflicts stakeholders seek mutually beneficial solutions that are acceptable to all parties. This activity is about structuring issues and developing alternatives to solve problems, for example by exchanging offers and counteroffers, or proposing alternatives for mutual gain. After developing possible solutions stakeholders eventually agree on the "best" one. The explanation of possible solutions is a prerequisite before stakeholders can agree on a decision and requires the establishment of judgment criteria, a common set of rules agreed by all stakeholders [60]. If these rules are missing, the merits of different options will be inconsistent. It might therefore be necessary to carry out a preparatory negotiation session in order to agree on these judgment criteria.

Depending on the type of conflict and problem at hand different strategies can be adopted [48] for dealing with the conflicts (see also Sect. 7.3). This involves trade-offs in which stakeholders give up partly on some issues so as to gain on other issues, for example, by making concessions to ease gaining an agreement; problem-solving by identifying and adopting solutions that satisfy the goals of the parties; or persuading other negotiators to concede. Apparently, negotiators might also decide to drop out of a negotiation. Some authors have developed automated approaches for resolving conflicts. An example is the Oz system developed by Robinson and Fickas [51].

7.2.3 Post-Negotiation

In this phase stakeholders (or automated tools) analyze and evaluate the negotiation outcomes and suggest re-negotiation if necessary. For example, it can be determined if the current agreement satisfies the preferences of the counterparts and if a better solution would be possible for one negotiation party, without causing loss to the other side [37]. It can also involve quality assurance reviews of the negotiation results [28]. The importance of early quality assurance in RE is also emphasized in Chap. 8. Another important aspect of post-negotiation is to secure commitment of stakeholders over time. For example, by monitoring existing agreements and initiating re-negotiation in case agreements become obsolete due to new developments. Especially in iterative life cycle models [2, 3, 7] negotiation results need to be constantly evolved as new goals can always arise and potentially cause new conflicts [8]. Understanding the impacts of changing goals is typically non-trivial as also discussed in Chap. 6.

7.3 Dimensions of Requirements Negotiation

The negotiation process presented in the previous section defines the scope and purpose of activities relevant in requirements negotiation. It does, however, not address more specific aspects of negotiations. We therefore present a simple framework which describes important dimensions of requirements negotiation in more detail. By explaining the dimensions of the framework we give a survey of relevant research. The purpose of the framework is twofold: (a) It can be used for classifying and understanding existing negotiation approaches and tools by using well-defined and relevant dimensions; (b) it addresses issues important for organizations wishing to design and implement effective negotiation processes.

The dimensions of the framework address (1) the conflict resolution strategy, (2) the collaboration situation of stakeholders, and (3) the degree of negotiation tool support. The dimensions are derived by analyzing literature and negotiation tools from different fields. Although the chosen dimensions are important we do not claim that the framework is complete and covers all aspects relevant in requirements negotiations. Also, dependencies between the dimensions are not explicitly addressed. For example, a certain collaboration situation may imply certain conflict resolution strategies and specific kinds of negotiation support. The dimensions cover key questions in requirements negotiation: How are conflicts resolved? How do stakeholders collaborate? Which tools are used to support the process?

Conflict resolution strategy. Conflict is an inevitable part of system design and the reason for negotiation. The first dimension thus addresses the different conflict resolution strategies based on the conflict handling modes developed by Thomas [61] in the field of organizational psychology.

Collaboration situation. The second dimension addresses the collaboration setting defined by the location of stakeholders and the time of negotiation. Synchronous/co-located negotiations, where people work together face to face, are fundamentally different from asynchronous/dislocated forms of negotiations that make interaction more difficult. This dimension is informed by research done in CSCW (Computer Supported Cooperative Work) [35].

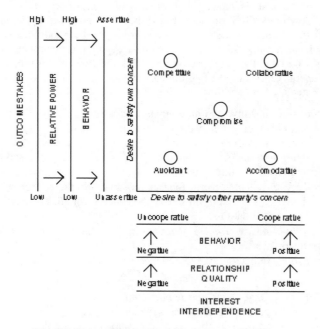

Fig. 7.1 Determinants of conflict behavior [1, 61]

Negotiation support tools. Negotiations can be supported with different kinds of tools ranging from manual guidelines to sophisticated tools and environments. Understanding these types and levels of automation is important to choose the appropriate level of support for a given situation. Authors in the field of negotiation support systems (NSS) have done research to classify the different options for tool support [34, 37, 44].

7.3.1 Conflict Resolution Strategy

Software engineering projects face conflicts of interests and needs in important decisions. Theoretically, such situations can be framed as mixed-motive, where parties experience partly common ground (joint goals and objectives of the project) but also face considerable differences in preferences for specific issues. It has been shown that conflict is not the exception but very common in group interactions. A study by Curtis et al. [15] reveals three major sources of conflict in software engineering: the thin spread of application domain knowledge; fluctuating and conflicting requirements; and breakdowns in communication and coordination. Conflicting requirements have many causes, including changes in the organizational setting and business environment. Also, software will be used by different people with different goals and needs. Further sources of conflicts listed by Easterbrook [20] include conflicts between suggested solution components; conflicts between stated constraints; conflicts between perceived needs; conflicts in resource usage; and discrepancies between evaluations of priority.

A well-known model of conflict behavior has been proposed by Thomas in the field of organizational psychology [61]. According to this model a stakeholders' orientation has two dimensions: the focus on satisfying their own concerns (unassertive, assertive) and the emphasis on satisfying the concerns of others (uncooperative, cooperative). Using the two dimensions one can define five dominant orientations of dealing with conflicts (see Fig. 7.1):

- *Competing (forcing)* involves an emphasis on winning one's own concerns at the expense of another, often leading to "win-lose" situations.
- *Accommodating (smoothing)* involves trying to satisfy the other's concerns without attention to one's own concerns. This can mean that one stakeholder is self-sacrificing and yielding to the other.
- *Collaborating (problem-solving)* focuses on satisfying the concerns of all parties to find alternatives that try to satisfy the concerns of all. The emphasis is on finding "win-win" situations.
- *Avoiding (withdrawing from)* a negotiation could be a result of indifference, denial, or apathy.
- *Compromising (sharing)* involves concessions to find a satisfactory middle ground.

Figure 7.1 shows that choosing the best conflict handling strategy depends on factors such as the outcome stakes, the interdependence of interests, the relative power of parties, and their quality of relationship. For example, if the outcome stakes for a stakeholder is high (which is the case in many software projects) and people want to maintain a good quality of relationship, a collaborative conflict handling mode is preferred over accommodative behavior. Another model for comparing different negotiation styles has been proposed by Fisher and Ury [23]. The authors distinguish between soft, hard, and principled negotiation strategies. In the *soft strategy* the underlying assumption is that parties are willing to collaborate to seek mutually satisfactory agreements. Stakeholders cooperate in a consensus-oriented, problem-solving team process. In the *hard strategy* parties are seen as competitors that not necessarily want to arrive at a win-win situation. It can also be seen as an interaction of competing stakeholders, where conflicts are will occur inevitably. Instead of focusing on these two extremes Fisher and Ury propose a combined approach called *principled strategy* [23].

Table 7.1 Characteristics of soft, hard and principled strategies [23]

Soft	Hard	Principled
Participants are friends.	Participants are adversaries.	Participants are problem-solvers.
The goal is agreement.	The goal is victory.	The goal is a wise outcome reached efficiently and amicably.
Make concessions to cultivate the relationship.	Demand concessions as a condition of the relationship.	Separate the people from the problem.
Be soft on the people and the problem.	Be hard on the problem and the people.	Be soft on the people, hard on the problem.
Trust others.	Distrust others.	Proceed independent of trust.
Change your position easily.	Dig into your position.	Focus on interests, not positions.
Make offers.	Make threats.	Explore interests.
Disclose your bottom line.	Mislead as to your bottom line.	Avoid having a bottom line.
Accept one-sided losses to reach agreement.	Demand one-sided gains as the price of agreement.	Invent options for mutual gain.
Search for the single answer: the one they will accept.	Search for the single answer: the one you will accept.	Develop multiple options to choose from; decide later.
Insist on agreement.	Insist on your position.	Insist on using objective criteria.
Try to avoid a contest of will.	Try to win a contest of will.	Try to reach a result based on standards independent of will.
Yield to pressure.	Apply pressure.	Reason and be open to reason; yield to principle, no to pressure.

Table 7.1 compares the three strategies using a set of negotiation characteristics. The combined strategy focuses on four principles printed in bold in Table 7.1. These are separating the people from the problem; focusing on interests, not positions; generating a variety of possibilities before deciding what to do; and insisting that the result is based on some objective standard.

7.3.2 Collaboration Situation

The negotiation process discussed in Sect. 7.2 has to consider different collaboration situations depending on the time and place of interaction. For example, a team might decide to organize a face to face meeting for the definition of agreements, while the elicitation of preferences is carried out in a dislocated manner. The time of the negotiation and location of stakeholders have a strong impact on the actual interactions during a negotiation and pose additional challenges. The field of Computer-Supported Cooperative Work has developed the CSCW matrix, a simple classification scheme that distinguishes four different scenarios (see Table 7.2):

Table 7.2 Collaboration situations of negotiating stakeholders [35]

	Co-located	Dislocated
Synchronous communication	**Same time/Same place**	**Same time/Different place**
Asynchronous communication	**Different time/Same place**	**Different time/Different place**

Same time/Same place. Face to face meetings are still a common way to elicit and negotiate requirements. In requirements engineering, many approaches still work best or even necessitate continuous, synchronous team work [32]. Newer approaches such as agile methods strongly advocate face to face meetings. A popular example is the "on-site customer", a practice in eXtreme Programming [2]. Especially when trying to resolve conflicts the richness of face to face interactions makes it easier to build trust and jointly seek for solutions. The facilitator guidelines of the EasyWinWin approach, for example, suggest to organize the "negotiation of agreements" activity as a face to face meeting to benefit from the richness of non-verbal cues, which make it easier to understand people and therefore to reduce negotiation time.

Different time/Same place. Organizing an entire negotiation with face to face meetings is typically not possible even if stakeholders are co-located at the same site. The duration of negotiations often exceeds the time of typical workshops and meetings are generally difficult to arrange due to time constraints. Also, information needed to take a final decision is often not available during a meeting. It is then necessary to carry out certain steps in an asynchronous manner, supported by shared workspaces allowing all stakeholders to contribute to ongoing negotiations and to keep track of the progress [26].

Same time/Different place. Even if it is impossible to bring together stakeholders in a face to face meeting, it is frequently possible to gather them at the same time, with some of them participating remotely. The use of audio and video conferencing provides a reasonable interaction bandwidth and the team benefits from same-time interaction. For example, group decision support systems have been successfully used to support synchronous/dislocated brainstorming or voting sessions [45].

Different time/Different place. Requirements engineering is increasingly carried out in an asynchronous and dislocated setting as more and more projects span globally or affect multiple organizations [12]. In such a situation advanced technology for collaboration is a necessity to allow stakeholders to contribute from different parts of the world. However, little research exists to investigate the impact of different time/different place interactions on the success of requirements negotiation. Damian et al. [18] have explored the role of facilitation in such a situation.

The four collaboration situations described by the CSCW matrix do, however, not address all important issues that impact requirements negotiations such as the number of stakeholders involved, the difference between multiple individual sites verses multiple group sites, as well as cultural differences among negotiating parties.

7.3.3 Negotiation Tool Support

The third dimension of our framework deals with the type and degree of tool support. Negotiations are often supported by traditional means such as guidelines and handbooks for facilitation as well as general meeting tools for all stakeholders such as whiteboards, flipcharts etc. [25]. The scale and complexity of real-world projects however suggest the use of more sophisticated forms of negotiation support ranging from software tools for communication to intelligent software agents. In a recent paper Kersten [37] provides an insightful classification for negotiation support tools:

Passive Support. Such tools provide an infrastructure for negotiation and support all different collaboration situations discussed above. They allow all parties involved to express their preferences, to communicate about ideas, offers and arguments, and to share intermediate and final results. Examples are email, chat, or multimedia rooms [17]. Passive systems do not support the production of content with hints and guidance.

Active facilitative support. Tools of this kind are capable of guiding the stakeholders towards an agreement, for example, by identifying situations for mutual gain. Such systems can aid the users in the formulation, evaluation, and solution of difficult problems. They also support concession-making and construction of offers, as well as the assessment of the process. Active negotiation support systems typically follow a negotiation process. Group decision support systems [45] fall in this category especially if the collaborative tools are integrated with facilitation guidelines [13].

Pro-active interventive support. These systems are additionally capable of coordinating the activities of stakeholders. For example, they critique their actions or suggest what agreement to accept. To provide such capabilities the systems access and use knowledge-bases and employ intelligent software agents that monitor the negotiation process and the negotiators' individual activities. An example is the Atin intelligent software agent augmenting the Inspire system (see Sect. 7.4.1) [39].

7.4 Examples of Negotiation Systems

Researchers and practitioners have been developing different types of negotiation systems supporting stakeholders in conducting a negotiation. However, some of them are particularly targeted at software requirements negotiation while most tools provide more general negotiation support. Examples of negotiation tools include DealMaker, Inspire, MeetingOne, Negoisst, SimpleNS, SmartSettle, and WebNS. In this section we use the negotiation process and framework to characterize existing negotiation support systems. We have selected four examples: Aspire is a pro-active negotiation support system supporting bilateral negotiations which is based on Inspire; EasyWinWin, a system targeted at software requirements negotiation; Negoisst, an electronic business-to-business negotiation system; and SmartSettle, a commercially available negotiation support system for complex negotiations.

7.4.1 Aspire

Aspire is a recent extension to the Inspire system and provides pro-active level support with the Atin software agent [39]. The agent advices the negotiators by analyzing an ongoing negotiation using rules derived from literature. This could, for example, involve warning the user about implications of actions he intends to undertake. The tool [37, 38] is a web-based negotiation support system supporting asynchronous, dislocated negotiations and is targeted at bilateral negotiations.

Aspire implements a three phase negotiation model comprising pre-negotiation, conduct of negotiation, and post-settlement. The key activities during the *pre-negotiation phase* are the analysis of the current situation regarding issues and options, and the identification of key stakeholders. In the pre-negotiation phase Aspire assists stakeholders in understanding the negotiation case by providing a detailed description of the initial situation. Stakeholders are invited to express their preferences regarding the issues and alternatives. During the *negotiation phase* the opponents exchange messages and offers to present their viewpoints. The negotiation ends when an agreement is achieved or one of the opponents stops the negotiation. Aspire supports the opponents by providing capabilities for sending messages and offers. Also, for analyzing the ongoing negotiation the two opponents can view a history of the negotiation processes, which is tracked by the tool. The *post-settlement phase* is used to analyze and evaluate the negotiation outcomes and if necessary to re-negotiate an already existing agreement. Based on the preference information entered in the pre-negotiation phase, Aspire determines if the current agreement satisfies the preferences of the counterparts. It checks if there is a better solution possible for one negotiation party, without loss to the other side. Aspire has a strong support for the solution generation stage by analyzing the negotiation and giving active hints.

7.4.2 Negoisst

The Negoisst system for negotiation has its focus on supporting business-to-business electronic commerce. Based on theories of communication and information systems it combines communication and document management [54]. Teams can use natural language to exchange semi-structured messages and jointly compose the terms of a complex contract. Negotiation systems for e-commerce transactions typically support general phases of business-to-business e-commerce: finding potential partners; negotiating and finding agreements; and fulfilling the contractual obligations [53]. In this context, the aim of the Negoisst system is to support the negotiation phase by providing intuitive, unambiguous, efficient, and process-oriented negotiation support between human negotiators. Using semi-structured message exchange the negotiators can choose from various message types to make intentions explicit. The Negoisst system provides the following types of messages, which also outline the negotiation process: request, offer, counter-offer, accept, reject, question, and clarification.

7.4.3 EasyWinWin

EasyWinWin is a requirements negotiation approach that combines the win-win spiral model of software engineering [9] with collaborative knowledge techniques and automation of a Group Support System. It is based on Boehm's negotiation model [11]. The individual objectives of stakeholders are captured as *win conditions*. Conflicts among win conditions, risks, and uncertainties are recorded as *issues*. *Options* are proposed to reconcile issues. *Agreements* are developed out of win conditions and out of options by taking into account the preceding decision process and rationale. EasyWinWin helps a team of stakeholders to gain a better and more thorough understanding of the problem and supports co-operative learning about others' viewpoints. It is an example of an active negotiation support system. The EasyWinWin requirements negotiation approach also includes steps for elicitation and analysis. For example, in a brainstorming step all stakeholders are invited to post their ideas. A facilitator analyzes the ideas and forms win conditions jointly with the team of stakeholders. EasyWinWin is based on a Group Support System (GSS). Within the vast number of groupware technologies Group Support Systems (GSS) focus on supporting group decision-making. A GSS is not just a single piece of software, but a collection of computer-based collaborative tools that a team may use to focus and structure their mental effort as they work together toward a goal. Extensive research in the lab and in the field reveals that, under certain circumstances, teams can use GSS to become substantially more productive than would otherwise be possible. Fjermestad et al. [24] provide an exhaustive compendium of GSS field research.

Typical examples of such tools are Electronic Brainstorming tools for support idea generation, group outlining tools for idea organization, or voting tools for idea evaluation. In EasyWinWin participants use a multi-criteria polling tool to prioritize win conditions regarding business importance and ease of implementation. The brainstorming capability is used to gather stakeholder interests. There is an electronic page for each stakeholder. Whenever a stakeholder contributes a comment to a page the system takes that page away and randomly replaces it with a different page containing comments from other stakeholders. As the activity progresses, the pages swap among the participants, picking up a new comment at each stop. This process tends to broaden the scope of the discussion, resulting in breadth, rather than depth. It is a useful way to identify many concepts in a short amount of time. The major area of application of EasyWinWin is software requirements negotiation. Teams use EasyWinWin throughout the development cycle to develop a shared project vision, high-level requirements definitions, detailed requirements for features, functions, and properties, requirements for transitioning the system to the customer and user. The goal elicitation aspect is strongly supported; the solution generation support is weaker and relies on the help of a facilitator. EasyWinWin follows mainly a collaboration-oriented conflict resolution strategy. There are no limitations with respect to the number of stakeholders and collaboration situations, although most groups have used EasyWinWin in same time (synchronous or asynchronous) settings. The level of tool support is active, the collaborative tools provide an infrastructure for negotiation and the negotiation model and the explicit process guide stakeholders.

7.4.4 SmartSettle

SmartSettle is a negotiation support system that uses the Internet to enable the interaction among project stakeholders with conflicting objectives that wish to reach an agreement. A facilitator is required to model the problem and to represent preferences in way that can be used by the adopted optimization algorithms. SmartSettle uses a joint session area to compose a Framework for Agreement with natural language messages. Preferences can be represented using satisfaction graphs. The SmartSettle negotiation process further uses optimization algorithms to transform conflicting objectives into fair and efficient solutions and to generate suggestions before an agreement is reached. After a tentative agreement is reached, SmartSettle looks to improve the situation by fairly distributing gains to both parties. The use of these built-in optimization algorithms leads to solutions maximizing the mutual satisfaction for all stakeholders.

A facilitator guides stakeholders through the stages of the SmartSettle process, including the following stages: Prepare for negotiation, qualify interests (the elicitation of stakeholder objectives and draft of framework for agreement), qualify satisfaction (preference elicitation), establish equity (suggestion of solutions and acceptance of tentative agreement), maximize benefits (refinement of preferences including optimization), and secure commitment.

In Sect. 7.2 we discussed a general negotiation processes and explained important activities done during pre-negotiation, the actual conduct of the negotiation, and during post-negotiation. Table 7.3 shows that specific implementations of this general process emphasize different stages. For example, Negoisst provides a strong message model supporting the actual negotiation. EasyWinWin supports both pre-negotiation and negotiation activities but its negotiation model is less rigorously enforced.

Table 7.3 Comparison of negotiation tools

Dimen-sion/Tool	Aspire	Negoisst	EasyWinWin	SmartSettle
Specific implementa-tions of ne-gotiation process	**Pre-Negotiation** * Negotiation preparation	**Pre-Negotiation** * Define catego-ries for negotia-tion	**Pre-Negotiation** * Define nego-tiation purpose, negotiation top-ics, and glossary of terms * Identify suc-cess-critical stakeholders * Elicit win conditions * Prioritize win conditions * Reveal issues & constraints	**Pre-Negotiation** * Negotia-tion prepara-tion * Qualify in-terests * Qualify satisfaction
	Negotiation * Conduct of negotiation (of-fers and counter-offers)	**Negotiation** * Conduct of negotiation (re-quest, offer, counter-offer, accept, reject, question, clari-fication)	**Negotiation** * Identify issues and options * Negotiate agreements	**Negotiation** * Establish equity * Maximize benefits
	Post-Negotiation *Post-settlement	**Post-Negotiation** * Definition of contract	**Post-Negotiation** * QA reviews * Win-win spi-ral model itera-tions	**Post-Negotiation** * Secure commit-ments
Conflict resolution strategy	Competing	Competing	Collaborative compromising	Competing compromis-ing
Collabora-tion situation	* Different time – different place	* Different time – different place	* Same time – same place * Same time – different place	* Different time – dif-ferent place
Negotiation support	Pro-active interventive	Active facilitative	Active facilitative	Active facilitative

Similarly, differences can be seen in the conflict handling dimension: Aspire supports a conflict-oriented approach where two stakeholders can exchange offers and counters, whereas EasyWinWin emphasizes a collaborative conflict resolution based on problem-solving by a team. The chosen negotiation tools support different time/different place interaction with the exception of EasyWinWin, which is weaker in this respect and assumes synchronous interaction in most of its negotiation steps. With respect to the degree of negotiation tool support, Aspire is the only tool that can be classified as pro-active interventive as its Atin agent continuously monitoring negotiations and giving guidance to stakeholders.

7.5 Conclusions

In this chapter our aim was to give an overview of the state-of-the art by explaining important negotiation steps; introducing a three-dimensional framework that covers the conflict resolution strategy, the collaboration situation of stakeholders involved, and the degree of negotiation support; and by discussing existing negotiation approaches in the context of this framework. Beyond its value for classifying existing and future research the purpose of the framework is to assist practitioners to understand important issues when implementation negotiation processes. Although some progress has been made in the area of requirements negotiation by researchers and practitioners, there are still many open issues requiring further research. The discussion of the requirements negotiation dimensions already defined some candidate areas. In particular, investigating the complex interdependencies between the dimensions leads to some interesting questions. For example, finding the most effective negotiation processes for a given negotiation problem, expected conflict behavior, collaboration situation, and adopted tools. For the future, we expect several developments for requirements negotiation which pose some interesting research challenges:

Scalability. Researchers have been developing numerous methods and tools supporting negotiations. Often, these systems are applicable to small problems only and do not scale up to real-world situations which are characterized by many stakeholders and many issues (which is the case in most real-world software projects).

Integration of fields. Software engineering researchers have been developing approaches, often not aware of research going on in the NSS community. While pragmatic approaches such as EasyWinWin work quite well in real-world settings, complementing it with techniques and tools from the NSS community would be beneficial. We hope to see the better integration approaches from different fields.

Novel tools. New technological developments will result in more sophisticated negotiation support. For example, mobile computing enables stakeholders to participate in negotiations in new collaboration situations more easily. First prototypes of such tools have already been developed [55].

Multi-stakeholder distributed systems. A further challenge comes from the fact that more and more applications, especially those that are developed and deployed over the web, represent so-called multi-stakeholder distributed systems, "... in which subsets of the nodes are designed, owned, or operated by distinct stakeholders." [30] These nodes are often designed or operated in ignorance of one another or with different, possibly conflicting goals. Negotiation approaches will become even more important in such a context as the requirements placed by diverse stakeholders are often ephemeral and conflicting. Furthermore, details about the elements of such a dynamic system are largely unknown to single stakeholders and outside their sphere of control [29].

Handling cultural differences. Negotiation is a complex decision process which is influenced by political, psychological, sociological and organizational aspects and cannot be formally represented. For example, there is currently only limited understanding of the impact of corporate and national culture on requirements negotiation. Some approaches exist [40], but we have mostly only tacit expertise and anecdotal evidence. A research challenge is to develop negotiation processes, techniques, and tools that better understand and handle the impact of corporate and national culture.

References

1. (2002) Workbook on international negotiation. Netherlands institute of international relations Clingendael, 69p.
2. Beck K (1999) Extreme programming explained: Embrace change. Addison-Wesley
3. Boehm BW (1988) A spiral model of software development and enhancement. IEEE Computer. 21(5): 61–72
4. Boehm BW (2000) Requirements that handle IKIWISI, COTS, and rapid change. IEEE Computer. 33(7): 99–102
5. Boehm BW (2000) Spiral development: Experience, principles and refinements. Han-sen WJ, Editor, CMU/SEI-00-SR-08
6. Boehm BW, Abi-Antoun M, Port D, Kwan J, Lynch A (1999) Requirements engineering, expectations management, and the two cultures. In: Proceedings of IEEE International Symposium on Requirements Engineering, pp.14–22
7. Boehm BW, Bose P (1994) A collaborative spiral software process model based on Theory W. In: Proceedings of Conference on the Software Process, pp.59–68
8. Boehm BW, Bose P, Horowitz E, Lee MJ (1994) Software requirements as negotiated Win conditions. In: Proceedings of IEEE CS 1st International Conference on Requirements Engineering. Colorado Springs, Colorado, USA
9. Boehm BW, Egyed AF, Kwan J, Port D, Shah A, Madachy R (1998) Using the Win-Win spiral model: A case study. IEEE Computer. 31(7): 33–44
10. Boehm BW, Port D, Al-Said M (2000) Avoiding the software model-clash spiderweb. IEEE Computer, pp.120-123
11. Boehm BW, Ross R (1989) Theory-W software project management: Principles and examples. IEEE Transactions on Software Engineering, 15(7): 902–-916
12. Bose P, Zhou X (1999) WWAC: WinWin abstraction based decision coordination. In: Proceedings of International Conference on Work activities Coordination and Collaboration. San Francisco, California, United States: ACM Press, pp.127–136
13. Briggs RO, de Vreede GJ, Nunamaker JF (2003) Collaboration Engineering with ThinkLets to pursue sustained success with group support systems. Journal of Man-agement Information Systems, 19(4): 31–63

14. Briggs RO, Grünbacher P (2002) EasyWinWin: Managing complexity in requirements negotiation with GSS. In: Proceedings of the 35th Annual Hawaii International Conference on System Sciences (HICSS-35.02). Big Island, Hawaii

15. Curtis B, Krasner H, Iscoe N (1988) A field study of the software design process for large systems. Communications of the ACM, 31: 1268–1287

16. Damian D (2001) Negotiation behavior and group interaction in face-to-face and distributed requirements negotiations: four case studies. In: Proceedings of the 6th Australian Workshop on Requirements Engineering. Sydney, Australia, pp.22–31

17. Damian D, Eberlein A, Shaw M, Gaines BR (2000) Using different communication media in requirements negotiation. IEEE Software. 17(3): 28–36

18. Damian DE, Eberlein A, Shaw MLG, Gaines BR (2003) An exploratory study of facilitation in distributed requirements engineering. Requirements Engineering Journal 8(1): 23–41

19. Deutsch M (1973) The resolution of conflict. Yale University Press, New Haven

20. Easterbrook S (1991) Handling conflict between domain descriptions with computer-supported negotiation. Knowledge Acquisition: An International Journal, 3: 255–289

21. Egyed A, Grünbacher P (2004) Identifying requirements conflicts and cooperation: How quality attributes and automated traceability can help. IEEE Software, November/December, pp.50–54

22. Fickas S, Feather M (1995) Requirements monitoring in dynamic environments. In: Proceedings of 2nd IEEE International Symposium on Requirements Engineering, pp.140–147

23. Fisher R, Ury W (1983) Getting to yes: Negotiation agreement without giving in. New York. Penguin Books

24. Fjermestad J, Hiltz R (2000) Case and field studies of group support systems: An empirical assessment. In: Proceedings of 33rd International Hawaii Conference on System Science, January, Mauii, Hawaii, 1: 4–7

25. Galin A, Gross M, Gosalker G (1993) E-negotiation versus face-to-face negotiation. What has changed - If anything? , Tel Aviv University: Tel Aviv, Accessed on 3rd December 2004, http://www.recanati.tau.ac.il/research/IIBR/obhr/amira_miron.doc

26. Grünbacher P, Braunsberger P (2003) Tool support for distributed requirements negotiation. In: Cooperative methods and tools for distributed software processes. De Lucia A, Gall H (Eds.) FrancoAngeli: Milano, Italy, pp.56–66.

27. Grünbacher P, Briggs RO (2001) Surfacing tacit knowledge in requirements negotiation: Experiences using easy WinWin. In: Proceedings of 34th Hawaii International Conference on System Sciences, 3-6 January, Maui, Hawaii, Vol.1, pp.1024

28. Grünbacher P, Halling M, Biffl S, Kitapci H, Boehm BW (2004) Integrating collaborative processes and quality assurance techniques: Experiences from requirements negotiation. Journal of Management Information Systems, 20(4): 9–29

29. Grünbacher P, Stallinger F, Maiden NAM, Franch X (2003) A negotiation-based framework for requirements engineering in multi-stakeholder distributed systems. Requirements Engineering and Open Systems (REOS). Monterey, CA, Accessed on 3rd December 2004, http://www.cs.uoregon.edu/~fickas/REOS/

30. Hall RJ (2002) Open modeling in multi-stakeholder distributed systems: requirements engineering for the 21st Century. In: Proceedings of 1st Workshop on the State of the Art in Automated Software Engineering. U.C. Irvine, Institute for Software Research

31. Herlea DE (1998) Computer supported collaborative requirements negotiation. In: Proceedings of KAW'98. Banff, Alberta, Canada, Accessed on 3rd December, 2004, http://ksi.cpsc.ucalgary.ca/KAW/KAW98/herlea/

32. Herlea DE (1999) User participation in requirements negotiation. ACM SIGGROUP Bulletin. 20(1): 30−35

33. In H, Roy S (2001) Visualization issues for software requirements negotiation. In: Proceedings of Computer Software and Applications Conference, pp. 10−15

34. Jelassi MT, Foroughi A (1989) Negotiation support systems: An overview of design issues and existing software. Decision Support Systems, 5: 167−181

35. Johansen R (1988) Groupware: Computer support for business teams, New York. The Free Press

36. Keeney RL, Raiffa H (1976) Decisions with multiple objectives: Preferences and value tradeoffs. J. Wiley & Sons, NY

37. Kersten G (2004) E-negotiation systems: Interaction of people and technologies to resolve Conflicts. In: Proceedings of 3rd Annual Form on Online Dispute Resolution 5-6 July, Melbourne Australia

38. Kersten G, Noronha SJ (1997) Negotiation via the World Wide Web: A cross-cultural study of decision making. An Interim Report, Access on 3rd December 2004, http://www.iiasa.ac.at/Publications/Documents/IR-97-052.pdf

39. Kersten GE, Lo G (2003) Aspire: Integration of Negotiation Support System and Software Agents for E-Business Negotiation. International Journal of Internet and Enterprise Management, 1(3): 293−315

40. Kersten GE, Noronha SJ (1999) Negotiations via the World Wide Web: A cross-cultural study of decision making. Group Decision and Negotiations, 8(3): 251−279

41. Kotonya G, Sommerville I (1996) Requirements engineering with viewpoints. Software Engineering Journal, 11: 5−18

42. Lamsweerde Av (2000) Requirements engineering in the year 00: A research perspective. In: Proceedings of the 22nd International Conference on Software Engineering. Limerick, Ireland, pp.5−19

43. Lamsweerde Av (2001) Goal-oriented requirements engineering: A guided tour. In: Proceedings of International Conference on Requirements Engineering'01 Tutorial Notes

44. Lim LH, Benbasat I (1992-93) A Theoretical Perspective of Negotiation Support Systems. Journal of Management Information Systems, 9(3): 27−44

45. Nunamaker JF, Briggs RO, Mittleman DD, Vogel DR, Balthazard PA (1997) Lessons from a dozen years of group support systems research: A discussion of lab and field findings. Journal of Management Information Systems, 13(3): 163−207

46. Nuseibeh B, Easterbrook S (2000) RE: A Roadmap. In: Proceedings of 22nd International Conference on Software Engineering, Special Issue: ACM-IEEE, pp.37−46

47. Park J, Port D, Boehm BW (1999) Supporting distributed collaborative prioritization. in Software Engineering Conference, pp. 560−563

48. Pruitt DG, Carnevale PJ (1993) Negotiation in social conflict. Buckingham. Open University Press

49. Rapoport A (1974) Game theory as a theory of conflict resolution. D. Reidel Publ. Co., Dordrecht, Holland

50. Robbins S (1989) Organizational behavior: Concepts, controversies and applications. 4th edition, Prentice Hall, NJ

51. Robinson WN, Fickas S (1994) Supporting multi-perspective requirements engineering. In Proceedings of IEEE Conference on Requirements Engineering, pp.206–215

52. Robinson WN, Volkov V (1998) Supporting the negotiation life cycle. Communications of ACM, 41(5): 95–102

53. Schmid B, Lindemann M (1993) Elements of a reference model for electronic markets. In: Proceedings of the 31st Hawaii International Conference on System Sciences, IEEE Computer Society Press, pp.193–200

54. Schoop M, Jertila A, List T (2003) Negoist: a negotiation support system for electronic business-to-business negotiations in e-commerce. Data & Knowledge Engineering, 47(3): 371–401

55. Seyff N, Grünbacher P, Maiden NAM, Tosar A (2004) RE Tools Go Mobile. In: Proceedings of the 26th IEEE International Conference on Software Engineering (Research Demo), IEEE Computer Society Press.

56. Sharp H, Finkelstein A, Galal G (1998) Stakeholder identification in the requirements engineering process. In: Proceedings of 10th International Workshop on Database & Expert Systems Applications. Florence, Italy, pp.387–391

57. Souren P (2001) Collective memory support in negotiation: A theoretical framework. In: Proceedings of the 34th Hawaii International Conference on System Sciences, pp.1–8

58. Standish Group (2001) Extreme CHAOS report. The Standish Group, 196 Old Townhouse Road, West Yarmouth, MA 02673 -- http://www.standishgroup.com

59. Strauss A (1978) Negotiations: Varieties, contexts, processes and social order. Jossey-Bass Publishers, San Francisco, CA

60. Sutcliffe AG (2002) User-Centred Requirements Engineering. Springer, London

61. Thomas K (1976) Conflict and conflict management. In: Handbook of industrial and organizational psychology. Dunnette MD (Ed.) Rand McNally College Publishing Company, Chicago, pp.889–935

Author Biography

Paul Grünbacher is an Associate Professor at Johannes Kepler University Linz, Austria and a research associate at the Center for Software Engineering (University of Southern California, Los Angeles). He studied Business Informatics and holds a Ph.D. from the University of Linz. Paul's research focuses on applying collaborative methods and tools to support and automate complex software and system engineering activities such as requirements acquisition and software inspections. He is a member of ACM, ACM SIGSOFT, and IEEE.

Norbert Seyff is a Research Assistant at the Johannes Kepler University Linz, Austria where he received his Master's degree (Dipl.-Ing.) in Computer Science. Within the scope of his ongoing Ph.D. research Norbert is developing and evaluating innovative methods and tools supporting mobile stakeholders and analysts in acquiring and negotiating requirements.

8 Quality Assurance in Requirements Engineering

Christian Denger and Thomas Olsson

Abstract: This chapter presents a survey of the state of the art for quality assurance for requirements. The meaning of quality in the requirements context is discussed, as is the influence of the quality assurance during requirements on other parts of the development. Different quality assurance approaches are categorized as either constructive (e.g., standards, guidelines, elicitation techniques) or analytical (e.g., inspections) and discussed with respect to their impact on the requirements quality. Based on the approaches, future challenges are discussed. The main future challenges lie in investigating the return on investment of quality assurance in the requirements context and to provide more empirical results which approach that effectively prevent or detect which problems.

Keywords: Quality assurance, Requirements, Quality characteristics, Inspections, Analytical approaches, Constructive approaches.

8.1 The Importance of Early Quality Assurance

Continuously increasing complexity, ever-increasing market pressure, and customers' demands for higher quality require a combination of carefully selected validation and verification techniques to deliver a software product on time, within budget and with the desired quality. Requirements engineering is the initial part of a software development process, and all later steps of the development are influenced by the requirements, making the quality of the requirements an important factor for the overall quality of the developed system.

Independent of the domain, quality assurance (QA) is an important but elusive part of software development. Traditionally, QA techniques have mainly focused on the later development phases such as the implementation phase and the related testing activities. However, QA can and should start earlier. This chapter addresses exactly this aspect by discussing QA activities that can be applied in the requirements engineering phase.

Why it is important to detect defects as early as possible? An issue that originates in the requirements runs the risk of affecting not only other requirements but also later phases and can cause follow-up defects in architecture, design, coding and testing, see Fig. 8.1.

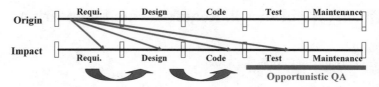

Fig. 8.1 Impact of requirements issues

If the quality assurance is only performed in the test and maintenance phase, one is dependent on the ability of the requirements engineers, designers and programmers to produce good working products, suitable for the rest of the development. That is, you rely on their ability not to make any crucial mistakes. However, this would reflect an ideal case that in almost all cases cannot be achieved (it is natural that humans make errors). Having no intermediate QA, i.e. a quality gate for the intermediate work products, it is most likely that the design and implementation are based on the wrong requirements. This, in consequence, leads to high rework effort as not only the code but most often the overall system architecture and design have to be revised due to requirements defects. Nevertheless, it seems to be quite common to do QA only by means of testing (and maintenance approaches), which, therefore, is an opportunistic approach.

Many studies show that late, opportunistic QA leads to a stressful and costly test and maintenance phases. Issues should be resolved in the phase of their origin to avoid costly testing and rework. Testing and rework can account for up to 40–50 % of the development effort [10]. In addition, removing defects early in the development process is more cost effective than addressing the defects during testing or maintenance [7]. Correcting a defect late in the process gets more expensive as development effort has already been spent and more artifacts are affected. A requirements issue can become up to 100 times more expensive if it is detected in operation, compared to detecting it in the requirements phase [10].

Based on these data, the knowledge that requirements deficiencies are the prime source of project failures [21], and that over 40% of problems in the software development cycle result from low quality requirements [47], QA techniques for requirements are one of the most promising and cost effective techniques to ensure successful development and to prevent avoidable rework in later phases. Independently of whether high quality is required or not, QA in the requirements phase pays of. But it does, of course, become even more important if high quality is a key success factor.

The remainder of the chapter discusses quality of and quality assurance for requirements. Techniques to assure the specified quality aspects are discussed and a framework on how to integrate the different QA techniques is presented (Sect. 8.2). The subsequent sections deal with concrete QA approaches. A general introduction to constructive apaches is described in Sect. 8.3, together with examples of constructive approaches. The analytical approaches, such as inspections and early test case creation, are presented in Sect. 8.4. In Sect. 8.3 and Sect. 8.4 the issue of traceability and how it can be used to facilitate QA is elaborated. The final sections, Sect. 8.7 and Sect. 8.8, summarize the important future work and conclude the chapter, respectively.

8.2 Requirements and Quality Assurance

Quality is hard to define as it is a complex concept, dependent on organizational viewpoints and context characteristics [32]. For example, do fewer defects per lines of code equal high quality? What if one of these defects causes the loss of life? Quality has a very different meaning in different situations. In a word processor, different quality criteria are important than in an electronic control unit of a car or an airplane.

With requirements, this becomes even more difficult, as the notion of quality often depends on the opinions of various stakeholders. For example, if you have not understood the stakeholders' needs correctly, you are bound to end up with a system that is not considered to be of good quality as it might not support the user in fulfilling certain tasks. This section introduces how quality and quality assurance can be defined for requirements and presents aspects of defining a quality strategy for early QA.

First of all, it is important to define what is meant by a defect in the requirements phase. In this chapter, the term *issue* is used as an umbrella term for all matters that should be resolved in the requirements context. The terms defects, errors, faults or problems are other words used with a similar meaning. However, in the case of requirements, it is sometimes unclear whether an issue really is a defect. For example, if two stakeholders disagree on one aspect of a requirement, this is an issue that should be resolved, but would usually not be referred to as a defect in the traditional sense. If it is not resolved, at least one stakeholder will reject the system in acceptance test. However, contradicting requirements are closer to the conventional interpretation of a defect. Therefore, the matters mentioned in the examples are summarized as requirements issues that need to be resolved through the QA activities on the requirements.

8.2.1 Quality of Requirements

The quality of requirements is dependent on various stakeholders and their perspective. Several different views need to be considered in order to define what quality means in a certain context [32]. The first view on quality is the transcendental view. Therein, quality is considered as something that we always strive for as an ideal but we will never be able to implement this ideal. The goal of this viewpoint is to express the complexity of the concept quality in general. Second, the user view evaluates the quality of a software product with respect to its fitness of purpose to fulfill certain user tasks. The third view, the manufacturing view, focuses on the product view during production and after delivery. It is focused on the adherence of standards and evaluates whether the product was build right the first time. The fourth view is the product view. The focus for this view is on internal quality aspects of the product that can be measured. It is assumed that ensuring certain internal quality aspects has an impact on the external quality and the quality in use of the product. Finally, the value-based view relates quality to cost. It considers quality as something the customer is willing to pay for [32].

Mapping these views on the quality of requirements reveals relevant stakeholders and needed QA for the requirements. The requirements should, for example, describe what the user requires of the final system (user-view). Furthermore, they should be described in a way that allows the developers to produce the software effectively and efficiently (product-view). The requirements engineers have to follow certain standards when specifying the requirements to ensure the quality of the requirements right from the start (manufacturing view). Finally, the customers have to decide on the value of each requirement and whether the implementation cost is motivated (value-based view).

All these aspect have to be considered when discussing the quality of requirements. The inherently human based nature of requirements engineering and the necessity to consider not only technical but also social aspects when eliciting, negotiating and specifying requirements makes the definition of quality characteristics for requirements even harder. Standards are a starting point for defining the quality of requirements and requirements specifications [24, 25]. Further, there exist a number of processes, guidelines, and best practices on how to perform good requirements engineering [8, 11, 14, 41, 46, 50]. The advocates of these approaches argue that, for example, adhering to the process facilitates requirement engineering and minimizes later quality problems. In order to specify an initial set of quality criteria, the IEEE standard for requirements specification [24] is used as a starting point (see Table 8.1). The standard is extended to provide a more complete picture of relevant quality aspects of requirements (e.g. [16]), especially to address customer and user needs (value-based and user view on requirements quality). Moreover, we extended the definition of the quality attributes beyond the quality of a requirements specification. In accordance to the different views on quality in general, the definitions of the quality attributes were adapted (see also [13]). In consequence, the quality aspects consider technical and human related aspects, which both are relevant for the overall quality of the requirements.

The information in brackets behind the attribute name specifies whether the attribute is originally defined in the IEEE standard or whether the attribute is part of the extension (IEEE/new). The second information specifies which view on the requirements' quality is addressed with the attribute.

Table 8.1 Quality attributes for requirements (1 of 2)

Quality Attribute	Definition
Correctness (IEEE, user-view)	The requirements that are implemented have to reflect the expected (intended) behavior of the users and customers. That is, everything stated as a requirement is something that shall be met by the final system to fulfill a certain purpose (suitability).

Table 8.1 *(cont.)* Quality attributes for requirements (2 of 2)

Quality Attribute	Definition
Unambiguity (IEEE, product-view)	The requirements should only have one possible interpretation. Note that one requirement might be unambiguous to a certain group of stakeholder but has a different meaning in another. It is important to involve all stakeholders in the requirements engineering process to gain a common understanding (see Chaps. 2 and 3)
Completeness (IEEE, product-view)	All important elements that are relevant to fulfill the different user's tasks should be considered. This includes relevant functional and non-functional requirements and interfaces to other systems, the definition of responses to all potential inputs to the system, all references to figures and tables in the specification, and a definition of all relevant terms and measures.
Consistency (IEEE, product, manufacturing view)	The stated requirements should be consistent with all other requirements, and other important constraints such as hardware restrictions, budget restrictions, etc.
Ranked for Importance / Stability (IEEE, product, value-based, user view)	Each requirement specifies its importance and/or its stability. Stability expresses the likelihood that the requirement changes, while importance specifies how essential the requirement is for the success of the project (from a value-based and a user point of view). See also Chap. 5
Verifiability (IEEE, product view)	All requirements should be verifiable. That is, there exists a process for a machine or a human to check (in a cost effective way) whether the requirement is fulfilled or not.
Modifiable (IEEE, product view)	All requirements should be modifiable, that is the structure of the requirements and the requirements specification allow the integration of changes in an easy, consistent and complete way.
Traceable (IEEE, manufacturing view)	All requirements should be traceable, that is, it should be possible to reference the requirement in an easy way. Moreover, it is possible to identify the origin of a requirement (see also Chap. 4)
Comprehensibility (New, manufacturing, user, value-based view)	The requirements are specified and phrased in a way that is understood by all involved stakeholders.
Feasibility (New, value-based, product view)	All requirements can be implemented with the available technology, human resources and budget. Moreover, all requirements contribute to the monetary success of the system, that is, they are worth to include in the system.
Right Level of Detail (New, user, manufacturing, value-based view)	The information given in the requirements is suitable to gain the right understanding of the system and to start implementation. There are no unnecessary implementation or design details specified in the requirements.

The IEEE Standard was extended to give a more complete way of describing the quality of requirements:

- *Comprehensibility* is essential, as there are many different stakeholders involved in the requirements engineering process. It is important that the requirements can be easily understood by all of these stakeholders and that they all have a common understanding of the requirements.
- *Feasibility* is especially important to consider as a requirement and is only of value if it can be transformed into a design and an implementations with reasonable effort and cost.
- Finally, the requirements should be specified on an *adequate level of detail,* that is, concrete enough to allow that design and implementation can be started ,but that is on the other hand abstract enough to allow discussion between all involved stakeholders (which have in many cases technical and non-technical backgrounds).

Note that there are relationships among the attributes. For example, ambiguous requirements are also difficult to understand. Further, if the requirements are not traceable, the verifiability, modifiability and the comprehensibility can be affected. Even though the classification is not orthogonal, each attribute refers to a special aspect of requirements' quality that should be considered. A more detailed analysis is needed regarding how the different quality attributes impact each other and how this information can be used to balance QA activities on the requirements (see Sect. 8.5).

8.2.2 Requirements Quality Strategy

Developing software without any defects is impossible (see, for example [32], specifically the transcendental view of quality). It is, however, possible to achieve an optimal compromise between the desired quality and available resources, considering the specific context factors and quality need of a company or a project. Many factors influence the importance of different quality attributes in a specific context. For example, in certain domains, it is more important to be the first on the market than to have high quality products in the sense of few defects. There is a lot of software being tremendously successful, from a commercial point of view, which is anything but of high quality. On the other hand, the cost of a single defect can be fatal and incredibly expensive, for example the Ariane 5 disaster [33]. Thoroughness and budget for quality assurance need to be related to the cost of erroneous implementation, leading to financial or human costs.

During the requirements engineering phase, it is important to define a quality strategy that addresses those quality issues that can easily be verified and validated in the requirements phase. Other quality aspects that cannot be efficiently addressed during the requirements phase should be left for later phases.

A *quality strategy* defines how, when and where different QA approaches, in combination with other approaches in the software development process, are used to assure high quality. This includes the planning of resources (which approach is applied when and how much effort should be spent) and the definition of an optimized combination of the different QA approaches with the aim of achieving the desired quality at the desired cost. The definition of such a strategy is not a trivial task. It requires detailed knowledge about the context of the company and the project, the required level of assurance of the different quality attributes (i.e. to which degree we can be sure the requirement are fulfilled) and which QA approaches are applicable. Figure 8.2 summarizes the elements impacting a quality strategy. At the top of the picture are context related elements, at the bottom technically oriented elements. There are five context elements relevant for QA strategies:

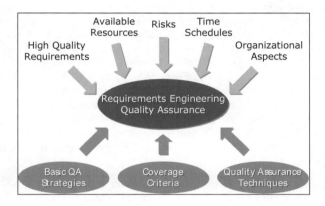

Fig. 8.2 Elements important to define a quality assurance strategy for requirements

1. *The quality of requirements* specifies the quality criteria for good requirements, as described in the previous section. These criteria can vary from company to company and from project to project. They impact the strategy in that they specify what should be achieved with the quality strategy. It is important to define optimal and minimal sets of quality characteristics of requirements [32].
2. The *available resources* describe the available effort, budget, hardware, and personnel to perform QA during the requirements activities. In addition, the availability of additional experts has to be considered, as for certain quality assurance approaches, certain stakeholders beyond the requirements engineering processes might be essential (e.g. lead architect during requirements reviews). The available resources have also a direct impact on the applicable QA approaches. For example, if only a small effort is available to perform requirements reviews it is not possible to fulfill a full Fagan inspection with many participants but only a peer review or desk-checking approach [49].
3. *Risks* related to certain requirements, especially risks of not realizing a requirement or implementing a requirement in the wrong way, are an additional factor influencing the quality strategy. Risk is defined as not being able to live up to the quality goals and is an important factor for deciding on which part of the requirements which QA approach should focus. For example, not meeting a requirement important to protect human lives bears a high risk and should therefore be checked extra carefully. Moreover, risks can be used to plan the

limited quality assurance resources. For example, with the help of risk analysis, it is possible to identify the most critical requirements in the sense of loss of lives or loss of money. The QA approaches should then be focused exactly on these aspects (see also Chap. 5 for related approaches).

4. The overall *time schedule* is related to the available resources and defines the time available for QA in general and within the requirements phase in particular. Time resources are especially important as they relate the requirements QA activities with other development activities.

5. Finally, the *organizational aspects*, such as development process, e.g., plan-driven or agile development, or product domain, (e.g., desktop software or airplane control system) influence the decision on which QA approaches to use. Moreover, it is important to take the various stakeholders into account. Dependent on the domain, different sets of stakeholders are varying importance (see also Chaps. 2 and 3). These aspects impact the quality strategy in that certain QA approaches might not be applicable due to the organizational constraints. For example, in an agile process, requirements reviews are almost impossible to perform as in the most agile processes requirements are not documented in a way that would allow an inspection (e.g. user stories in extreme-programming often are not longer than one sentence that specifies a general feature [5]).

The context elements are important to consider as they define in which way the QA approaches can be applied and which restrictions and constraints must be adhered to. Beside the context in which the quality strategy is embedded, it is also important to consider technical aspects of quality assurance:

1. *The basic strategies* represent those strategies in place in a company or a project that define how to perform QA in the requirements phase. In that sense they represent the current state of the practice in a certain context. Due to the lack of sophisticated quality strategies, ad-hoc approaches are most frequently applied. For example, the simplest but also the least systematic strategy is to state that everything in the requirements specification should be verified or that all quality issues should be tackled in later development phases. Experience based strategies give hints on what to address in the requirements based on the experience of earlier projects. Such basic strategies should be considered when creating a more sophisticated quality strategy. They provide valuable input on where to start from and what has paid of in the past.

2. The *coverage criteria* define which aspects of the requirements should be covered by the QA approach. One example of a coverage criterion is that all requirements are covered by at least one test case. An aspect related to coverage that should be considered is the depth of the QA approach [35]. Depth defines the level of detail to which the requirements are verified or validated or, in other words, the quality level to be achieved. The greater the depth, the more resources are required for QA and the more sophisticated QA approaches are required.

3. The most important element of a requirements quality strategy is the potential *quality assurance approaches* and methods that can be used to ensure the dif-

ferent quality characteristics of the requirements. As discussed, the context elements and the technical elements impact the applicability of QA approaches. The QA approaches are the technical core element of the quality strategy as they represent the means of achieving good requirements quality.

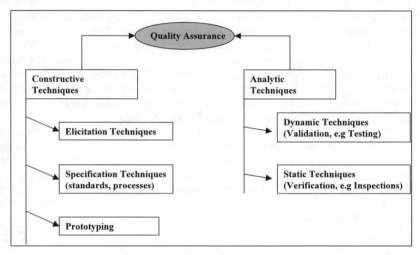

Fig. 8.3 Excerpt of quality assurance approaches

The framework presented in this section supports the definition of a good quality assurance strategy. It specifies which elements are important to consider when talking about quality assurance in the requirements engineering phase. It is important that all these elements are considered in the specific context of a specific company and have to be instantiated accordingly. To instantiate the framework into a concrete quality assurance strategy, it is essential to stress the continuous collection of data. Such a measurement approach should address the question which requirements issues are the most expensive ones and which quality assurance techniques work best in the specific context. The most essential element in the framework is the QA techniques (QA approaches) that can be applied. This is the element that should be considered first, i.e. before defining a detailed QA strategy, it is important to investigate potential approaches to verify the quality attributes of the requirements.

8.2.3 Quality Assurance Approaches for Requirements

In this report the quality assurance approaches are divided into one of two classes: constructive and analytical approaches. Figure 8.3 provides some examples of QA approaches of the different classes.

Constructive approaches ensure that mistakes are minimized during the creation of a work product (e.g. the requirements specification). That is, they prevent issues from being introduced. Examples of constructive approaches in the requirements phase are style guidelines on how to specify requirements, templates for the requirements specification, elicitation approaches and prototyping.

Analytical approaches are performed on the completed artifact or a self contained part of it with the aim to detect issues. Analytical quality assurance approaches can be further divided into *static quality assurance approaches, dynamic quality assurance approaches* (including formal methods) [36]. The difference between the two classes is that dynamic approaches require an executable version of the system. Testing approaches are examples of dynamic quality assurance. Static quality assurance approaches can be performed without executing code. Inspections and formal verifications are an examples of static approaches. There is in most cases no executable code available during the requirements engineering phase. Hence, usually only static approaches are applicable.

It is important to distinguish between QA in the requirements analysis phase and in the requirements validation phase [46]. QA in the analysis phase means that requirements issues are prevented from being introduced (i.e. during elicitation) with the help of constructive approaches omissions and ambiguous requirements are addressed. The validation process of requirements is based on a requirements document and tries to resolve issues within this document. Here, the analytical approaches are applied.

8.3 Constructive Approaches

Constructive approaches ensure quality during the creation of the requirements. In that sense, constructive approaches are preventive, as they aim to minimize mistakes from being made. These approaches are called constructive as they are applied while developing the requirements. Different ways constructing requirements and eliciting them from the various stakeholders are discussed in Chap. 2 and Chap. 3 of the book. How these approaches contribute to higher quality of the requirements in this section.

Requirements engineering is largely a human-based activity. Even if formal methods are used, at some point you will be interacting with customers and other stakeholders. As we humans are fallible, we are bound to make mistakes. Therefore, even if constructive methods are applied according to all the rules, there will still be a need to check the results, that is, apply analytical approaches. In this section, the impact of constructive approaches is presented. In Sect. 8.4, the analytical approaches are presented.

8.3.1 Elicitation Techniques

The elicitation step is important to the overall quality of the requirements and the acceptance of the final system [35, 46]. During the elicitation step, requirements are captured from various sources, such as the customer, the users, earlier projects, market studies etc. In this process, various stakeholders such as the customers, the technical staff (developers), and end users work together to derive an appropriate set of requirements. Requirements engineers can apply different techniques to support the various stakeholders in discovering the requirements, e.g. interviews, questionnaires, workshops and focus groups (see Chap. 2 for more details).

By means of elicitation techniques, the following quality attributes can be ensured:

- Comprehensibility: by developing a common terminology and ensuring that the different stakeholders speak the same language, comprehensibility is improved.
- Completeness: if the elicitation is performed correctly, all the (relevant) stakeholders, and their individual stakes, should be identified. Here, elicitation activities contribute to higher quality in that they support the requirements engineers in the identification processes.
- Verifiability and feasibility: again, by involving the relevant stakeholders, quality can be assured. By involving the testers the attribute verifiability is improved, and by involving the developers feasibility is improved.
- Correctness: the elicitation process should be driven by the business concerns [46]. Suitability, as part of correctness, is supported by this, as it is then more likely that the developed software will bring a real financial benefit in the context of use.

8.3.2 Specification Techniques

The main objective of the specification step is to document the requirement in such a way that they can be used as a basis for development (see Chap. 3). Usually, the output of the specification activity is a requirements document that captures the relevant aspect of the system to be built (i.e. functional, non-functional aspects, restrictions, etc.). In the section it is outlined how certain specification techniques, best practices and standards can help to ensure the quality of the requirements.

Standards, such as IEEE 830-1998 and IEEE 1233-1998 [24, 25], describe which elements a "good" requirements specification should have and which quality attributes the requirements should fulfill. Templates also provide elements that should be specified when documenting the requirements. Examples include templates on how to specify use cases or how to structure the requirements document.

With respect to the quality characteristics defined in Sect. 8.2.1, standards and templates contribute to better requirements in the following way:

- Completeness: in the case that the requirement engineers adhere to the recommendations in the standards and apply the pre-defined templates it can be ensured that all relevant aspects of a requirements document are considered, i.e. completeness of the document.
- Understandability and modifiability: the structure provided by templates and standards ensures that requirements document look similar over different projects in a company. Standardization of requirements documents prevents ambi-

guities within the documents and improves the understandability as well as the modifiability, as elements that need to be changed can be found more easily.

In addition to standards and templates, there is a huge collection of best practices showing how different steps in the requirements engineering process should be performed in order to gain high quality output of each of these steps only to mention some of them: [8, 11, 14, 17, 25, 35, 41, 46, 50].

Specifying functional requirements using, for example, use cases and related scenarios ensures also the comprehensibility of the requirements right from the start, as use cases and scenarios are easy to understand for technical and non-technical stakeholders. This also supports the attribute right level of detail. In addition, use cases seem to be valuable source for the definition of acceptance and system test cases (see Sect. 8.4.2). Therefore, specifying the requirements in a structured, scenario-oriented way improves their verifiability.

Basically, it would be possible to address almost all of the quality attributes in a constructive way if certain processes and standards are rigorously followed and applied. However, practice shows, that such rigorous approaches are not always reasonable or feasible (e.g. due to time restrictions, budget restrictions, regulations, etc.).

8.3.3 Prototyping

Another constructive approach that can be used to support elicitation is prototyping. A prototype is an executable version of the system under development, though restricted in one way or another. For example, a user interface prototype implements parts of the user interface, the structure and navigation, but will not have all the functionality, while a performance prototype focuses on memory and CPU load and might have no user interface at all.

The goal of a prototype is for the stakeholders to be able to try the system and make improvement suggestions [46]. By doing this, they get a better feeling of whether the system represents what they required, and thus it helps to identify missing requirements and detect misconceptions. The most important value of a prototype is that it crosses the gap between the description and implementation [17]. Further, a quite common issue with the requirements is that the customer does often not exactly know what they want.

In general, developing a prototype requires a careful study of the requirements [46]. A prototype typically target the following quality attributes:

- Inconsistencies and incompleteness: the process of developing a prototype will, in it self, reveals inconsistencies and incompleteness of the requirements and thus improves their quality.
- Correctness: correctness is improved by letting the different stakeholders work with and evaluate a concrete object rather than the abstract requirements.
- Feasibility: by trying out different solutions, already in the requirements phase, feasibility is improved. A lot of time and money can be saved if dead-ends are detected at an early stage.

To underline the benefits of prototyping in the context of QA, an experiment showed that prototyping can significantly reduce requirements and design errors, especially for the user interfaces [9].

8.4 Analytical Approaches

The analytical quality assurance approaches assess the requirements specification to check whether the requirements specified in there fulfill the quality criteria specified. The main challenge of the analytical approaches is that there are no reference documents against which the requirements can be checked, i.e. there is no documented source of truth against to compare. This emphasizes that QA of requirements has to involve all relevant stakeholders of the requirements. In the following, two analytical approaches requirements inspections and test case creation (as a part of acceptance testing) are presented in more detail.

8.4.1 Requirements Inspections

Inspections are a valuable means to ensure the quality of a software product right after its creation. There are many experimental and industrial results that show the value of inspection in general and requirements inspection in particular [2, 3, 4, 9, 17, 19, 20, 34, 37, 40, 43, 44, 48, 49]. Inspections in general aim at minimizing the issues of a certain product being propagated to later phases, as the issues are addressed in the same phase in which they are introduced. Considering the costs of an requirement issue (see Sect. 8.1), requirements inspections are one of the most cost effective QA approaches, as they prevent issues from being propagated from the requirements to other artifacts and cause follow-up defects and avoidable rework [7, 17, 37, 44, 49].

A second important benefit of early QA is that many organizations report an improved knowledge transfer achieved when performing early QA activities such as inspections and test case creation. For example, with the help of the reading scenarios and the checklist questions it is possible to transfer knowledge about defect patterns, best practices and known pitfalls from experts to less experienced people.

An inspection is characterized by a process, the roles involved in the process, reading techniques used, and the information on how the results of the inspection are documented. These elements can be seen as the four dimensions of an inspection [34].

The Inspection Process
A basic inspection process contains four main steps: planning (managing the organizational issues of an inspection), detection (inspectors search for issues in the document under inspection), collection or meeting step (moderated meeting merging the results of the inspectors into approved defect list) and correction (where the author has to resolve all the identified issues). These steps are common for al-

most all instantiations of the inspection process. However, several inspection processes mention additional steps such as the overview meeting or the follow-up meeting [18, 49]

Each phase of the process can be implemented in different ways depending on the level of detail with which the requirements should be inspected. For example, in the case that the requirements should be checked only from an abstract viewpoint, the individual preparation phase of the process could be skipped and the requirements would be discussed during a meeting with certain experts. According to the IEEE Standard 1028-1997 [26], such a process would be similar to a walkthrough of the requirements document. The company applying the inspection approach has to decide to which level of detail the requirements should be inspected [49]. This mainly depends on the requirements quality strategy as discussed in Sect. 8.2.2 (see discussion on how different elements of the framework impact the QA approaches). The above-mentioned process steps are the four most essential steps that should be performed in case the requirements are to be inspected in a more detailed way.

Reading Techniques
The most important, but also the most difficult step, in a requirements inspection is the detection step. In this step, the inspectors identify requirements issues. A reading technique supports the inspectors in performing this step. A reading technique represents a series of steps or procedures that guide an inspector in acquiring a deeper understanding of the requirements under inspection and detecting issues in them [34].

There are different kinds of reading techniques that can be used during a requirements inspection: ad-hoc reading (reading without further guidance based on ones experience), checklist-based reading (using a list of questions to point to potential issues in the requirements) and scenario-based reading (using a step-wise description to guide the inspector during the defect detection step). Again, depending on the desired level of depth and coverage, one of these techniques might be more suitable for verifying the requirements than another. A more detailed summary of different reading techniques can be found in [34].

Checklist based reading (CBR), as the name indicates, is based on checklists containing questions that should be answered during the defect detection. These questions focus on certain quality aspects that are relevant for the requirements under inspection. The checklist approach tells an inspector what to check. However, an often cited weakness of CBR is that it provides little support for how to perform the analysis [34, 48]. The reviewers get no guidance or hints on how to answer the questions in the checklist.

A checklist for use cases, for example, is presented in [2]. Many other checklists for requirements can be found on the Internet. However, it is important to note that there exist no standard checklist that can be applied in all contexts. A checklist has to be company- and sometimes even project-specific. Thus, the checklist has to be tailored to the context and characteristics of the company and the project. It is important to consider the elements of the requirements quality framework as it provides input for defining valuable checklist questions (e.g. input on quality goals, existing checklists (basic techniques), quality characteristics of importance, organizational restrictions, etc.). In addition, one should consider known defects or problems and, of course, expert knowledge, as further sources for checklists questions.

Checklists have three basic weaknesses [34]. First, the checklist questions are often extremely general. That is, concrete guidance on how to use the checklist is missing. Further, the checklist questions are often not up to date. To overcome these drawbacks, alternative approaches were developed. One class of alternative approaches is called scenario-based approaches. For requirements, the following scenario-based approaches are applicable: Perspective-based reading (PBR) [4, 34, 43, 45], traceability-based reading [45], defect-based reading [40] and usage-based reading [48].

The basic idea of the scenario-based reading techniques is that inspectors are guided by a scenario that tells them what to look for during the inspection and how to perform the inspection. Furthermore, the scenario guides the inspector to actively work with the requirements, resulting in a deeper understanding of the requirements and their interrelationships [34, 43]. Having such a deep understanding of the requirements is a prerequisite for finding more subtle and logical defects, which are often critical to the final system. Finally, the scenarios focus the attention of the inspectors on the essential quality aspects and on the essential parts of the requirements under inspection that need the most thorough investigation [34]. This input should be taken for example from prioritization techniques (see Chap. 5).

The special aspect of PBR is that the requirements are inspected from the viewpoint of different stakeholders, see Fig. 8.4. Different stakeholders have different interests in the requirements. The assumption behind PBR is that the requirements are of good quality if all stakeholders who use the requirements for their specific tasks, agree on the requirements quality (find no serious issues in them).

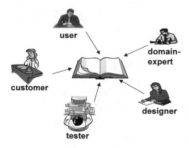

Fig. 8.4 Some perspectives to inspect the requirements

In each company context, the involved perspectives are different. Therefore, the first essential step when applying the PBR approach is identification of the potential perspectives and the quality concerns these perspectives are interested in.

During an inspection traceability links (see Chap. 5) can help to guide the inspectors through the requirements. For example, the quality attribute of consistency (see Sect. 8.2.1) is directly related to the ability to trace one requirement to another. The problems with inconsistency are well documented and are often one reason for quality problems and project delays [35]. With well defined links between the requirements it is possible for the inspector to follow these links and check that the requirements work together in a consistent and correct way. In that sense, the defect detection step gets more efficient as the inspectors do not have to think of potential relationships between requirements but can follow the links between them. Beside the consistency issue, it is also possible for the inspector to judge whether certain functions are completely realized with the different requirements described in the specification by following the traceability links and judging whether the sum of the requirements results in the desired support for the user. Finally, the traceability links indicate requirements that are highly related to each other and therefore help the inspectors to judge the maintainability and understandability of the requirements.

But also without the support of traceability, inspections can address many of the quality attributes specified in Sect. 8.2.1 (assuming that the inspection is performed thoroughly): correctness, completeness, unambiguity, comprehensibility, feasibility, modifiability, verifiability. This can be achieved with the right set of questions in the reading scenarios and checklists.

8.4.2 Requirements-Based Testing

Testing is usually performed at the end of the development process when executable system parts are available. Test cases are usually defined and run on the system to validate whether the system fulfills its specification. For example, the test cases derived from the requirements are used during the acceptance and system test phase. Testing is often perceived as the pure execution of the test cases at the end of the development cycle. This perception has led to the myth that testing can start only at the end of the software development process [22]. However, testing is more than running the test cases and looking for failures in the final software. At least the two steps test planning and test case creation can and should be integrated in the development process much earlier than they are usually integrated.

It is recommended that test planning and test case creation should be performed as soon as the requirements, or a self-contained sub-set, are defined [22, 51]. The idea of early test case creation is similar to the idea of perspective-based inspections. Through the early construction of the test cases, the test engineers gain a better understanding of the requirements and are able to identify weaknesses and potential issues within the requirements. Moreover, test engineers bring in a completely new perspective on the requirements which also contributes to identify requirements issues during the early test case creation. For example, if the test engineers have difficulties in deriving the acceptance test case from requirements it might be necessary to refine the requirements, to add missing information or to remove/restate the requirement as it is not possible to test them.

The principle of early test case creation helps to improve the quality of the requirements by identifying correctness, completeness, ambiguity, consistency and verifiability issues during the specification of the test cases. If this is done at the very end of the project, these issues are propagated from the requirements to all later phases and the test engineers might base their test cases on the wrong requirements, as the requirements are taken for granted (a fixed source of truth which is different at the beginning of the process).

An overview on requirements based testing approaches can be found in [15]. Special approaches that work on use cases are described in [6, 12, 30, 42]. General approaches that can be applied on the requirements specification to define detailed test cases are, for example, defined in [31, 39].

Again, it is possible to use traceability links to facilitate this activity (see Chap. 5). They provide a better understanding of which aspects in the requirements have to be tested together (e.g. in a test scenario) and which requirements are already covered by the defined test cases. Depending on the granularity of the traceability links, it is then possible to judge which requirements as a whole are covered by one ore more test cases, which test cases test more than one requirement, or whether there are test cases that cover only a single requirements. This information helps to identify points that need further consideration and special attention. Furthermore, traceability can help to select those parts that need regression testing by identifying which requirements are affected by a certain change [1, 33].

8.4.3 Automated Approaches and Formal Methods

Due to the abstract and informal nature of most requirements documents it is difficult to apply any automated tools to ensure their quality. For simple issues, such as grammar or spelling defects, there are tools available. Removing such issues from the requirements typically improve their comprehensibility.

For one quality attribute, unambiguity, more tool support is available. The idea of tools that address ambiguity flaws is the identification of certain patterns and keywords in the requirements that point to potential risk areas (i.e. areas where more than one interpretation of the requirements is possible). These tools identify, based on a glossary, phrases that are marked as weak or subjective, for example, "if possible", "may", "could", "optionally", etc. The tools parse the requirements document based on the pre-defined glossary and provide a list of all occurrences of the weak-phrases in the document [19, 52]. Even though the tools automatically detect certain quality issues in the requirements, the applicability of these tools in industrial practice has to be further investigated.

Further automation is possible when the requirements are defined in a formal way. The use of formal languages copes with requirements issues by avoiding the imprecise nature of natural language. Requirements are specified in a semantically well-defined way, typically mathematically based. Several benefits can be gained by using formal methods. The communication between the stakeholders is more precise, and thus, misunderstandings and ambiguities can be reduced. It is possible to check the completeness and the consistency of the requirements document, and automated proof of safety properties is possible. Finally, the requirements engineer can perform simulations of the future system, when the language is supported by a tool. Examples for such languages are SCR [23], SDL [27], and VDM [29].

However, formal methods also have drawbacks. They are difficult to learn and difficult to understand for a person without the necessary background. Specifically, the customer is often not interested in learning the formal language, and a compromise needs to be found. The first version of the requirements might be formulated in natural language, in the language of the customer. The requirements must then be translated into the formal version.

8.5 Open Research Questions

Based on the current state of the practice, some open questions with respect to quality assurance in the requirements engineering phase are identified. First, some open issues with respect to testing are discussed and afterwards, inspections are further elaborated on.

The survey on existing approaches for early test case creation and the involvement of testing during requirements engineering reveals that there are many promising approaches and that the need of early tester involvement is clearly recognized. However, the survey also shows that there is a lack of empirical evidence that the proposed approaches do, in fact, save money, improve the quality of the requirements, and to improve the overall system quality by means of better acceptance and system test cases that are more related to the requirements. Future research should focus on gathering this data as these results are important to transfer the approaches into industry (convince practitioners of the benefits).

Related to this aspect is the fact that test case creation for system and acceptance testing is performed without the involvement of the final system user. Almost all of the research papers explicitly mention that the user should be involved during test case creation but do not state how this should be done. Here, research is necessary to define ways to involve the system end users in this process in a most efficient and beneficial way.

Many test case creation approaches provide only little guidance on how to derive the test cases from the requirements or intermediate models of the requirements (e.g. sequence or state charts that represent the requirements). Often, there are only high level descriptions on how to come up with good test cases. Therefore, more research activities should focus on the relationships between requirements and other artifacts such as certain types of models and, of course, test cases. Guidelines that provide a stepwise approach on how to derive intermediate models should be defined to further facilitate the test case creation activity and, of course, any further development steps (e.g., analysis and high level design would also benefit from such guidelines).

Finally, it is a common fact that within requirements specifications, more and more various notations are used (e.g., pure text, tables, use case diagrams, sequence diagrams, etc.). How to deal with this variety of notations during test case creation is an unresolved question. Each notation provides relevant input and has to be considered during test case creation.

Concerning requirements inspections, most of the above-mentioned open issues with respect to requirements based testing also apply to inspections. Approaches for inspecting heterogeneous requirements documents need to be developed, and a process needs to be defined on how to most efficiently integrate the various stakeholders of the requirements in the inspection process. Here, it is especially important to define decision support for inspections that gives guidance on when to include which stakeholders (e.g., when to include which perspectives) and when it is necessary to perform which process steps. More research is therefore needed that investigates the factors influencing a good inspection process and to develop guidelines to customize the inspections in an optimal way to the quality needs that should be addressed during requirements engineering.

One part of this decision support should be a guideline on which inspection technique (checklist, scenario-based reading, including usage based reading, perspective-based reading, defect-based reading, etc.) should be used to verify the requirements. Past research focused only on the question of which of the techniques outperforms the other technique with respect to efficiency and effectiveness of the inspection process. The more relevant question seems to be how the different reading techniques should be combined to gain a more efficient inspection of the requirements. Thus, one should address the question of which of the reading techniques is more suited in detecting certain types of requirements issues. A second part of such a customization approach should be a guideline that provides hints on which questions or reading scenarios should be used during the inspection in order to address certain quality issues in a most efficient way. Therefore, it is up to future research to investigate what kind of inspection questions (for requirements) have an impact on which qualities the customer is interested in.

Finally, the question of tool support for inspections should be further addressed. With respect to requirements inspections, it should be investigated which quality issues could be automatically checked by a tool (e.g., application to certain structural restrictions) and how the inspection of other quality aspects could be facilitated, e.g. by providing support in checking certain checklist questions.

The most important open question that should be addressed in future research activities is how the different quality assurance approaches (constructive and analytic ones) of the requirements engineering phase can be combined into a comprehensive quality assurance strategy. There are some initial results that address this question [13], but these results need to be further investigated. In [9], it is stated that different quality assurance approaches help to address different quality issues. Unfortunately, neither the state of art nor the state of the practice can explicitly state which approaches are most efficient to address which quality issues, i.e. it is important to evaluate which of the approaches is more effective and consumes less effort in addressing certain requirements quality issues. In other words, future research has to investigate which qualities of the final system and the requirements are most efficiently assured by means of which approach (constructive, testing, inspections). Here, especially, more research is needed on the impact of applying constructive approaches such as certain elicitation techniques or specification techniques on the quality of the requirements. A second important step is the definition of external or system quality characteristics that should be addressed (e.g. safety, security, reusability, maintainability, etc.) and how these qualities manifest in the requirements. If this connection can be drawn, it is possible to customize the different QA approaches in that way that they focus on those system qualities that are most relevant for the customer.

These are all cornerstones that need to be investigated for the definition of a requirements quality strategy. And we should force our efforts as a well-defined requirements quality strategy would help to minimize the costs for quality assurance and, in parallel, increase the effectiveness and efficiency of the different approaches.

8.6 Conclusion

Quality is an elusive but important subject for requirements, especially since the quality of the requirements will more or less affect all other artifacts in the development. This chapter presents ideas on a framework for quality assurance (QA) in the requirements phase. The framework describes a set of attributes that are used to define quality. In addition, the framework describes what has to be considered when defining a QA strategy, to achieve the defined quality characteristics of requirements and requirements documents.

Further, an overview of state of art constructive and analytical QA approaches is presented. The theoretical contribution consists of an overview of state of the art QA approaches for requirements, as well as a more detailed description of a selected set. The QA approaches addressed are inspections, test case creation, and the impact of elicitation specification, and prototyping on quality. Moreover, some initial ideas are sketched on when to apply a specific type of QA approach by means of a mapping the QA approach to requirements quality characteristics.

Looking at the state of the art, it is clear that there are certain gaps in our understanding of how high quality requirements can be achieved and how the costs of the QA activities on the requirements affect the cost of the rest of the development. It is, however, a fair amount of research performed on individual QA approaches, but the combination and wider effects need more investigation.

Acknowledgements

This work has been partly supported by the ForPICS project, funded by the Provincia Autonoma di Trento, Italy. The authors also would like to thank the anonymous reviewers, as well as colleagues, specifically Sonnhild Namingha, for helpful comments on draft version of this chapter.

References

1. Ahlowalia N (2002) Testing from use cases using path analysis technique. In: Proceedings of the International Conference on Software Testing, Analysis & Review, Anaheim, CA, USA

2. Anda B, Sjøberg D I K (2002) Towards an inspection technique for UC models. In: Proceedings of the 14th International Conference on Software Engineering and Knowledge Engineering (SEKE), Italy, pp 127–134

3. Aurum A, Petersson H, Wohlin C (2002) State-of-the-Art: Software Inspections Turning 25 Years. Journal on Software Testing, Verification and Reliability 12(3): 133–154

4. Basili V R, Green S, Laitenberger O, Lanubile F, Shull F, Sorumgard S, Zelkowitz M (1996) The empirical investigation of perspective-based reading. Empirical Software Engineering 1(2): 133–164

5. Beck K (1999) Extreme programming explained. Boston: Addison-Wesley

6. Binder RV (1999) Testing object-oriented systems: Patterns, models and tools. Boston: Addison-Wesley Object Technologies Series

7. Briand L, Freimut B, Vollei F, (2000) Assessing the cost-effectiveness of inspections by combining project data and expert opinion. In: Proceedings of the 11th International Symposium on Software Reliability Engineering, pp.124–135

8. Bittner K, Spence I (2003) Use case modeling. Boston: Addison-Wesley

9. Boehm BW, Gray TE (1984) Prototyping versus specifying: A multi-project experiment. IEEE Transaction on Software Engineering 10(3):290–302

10. Boehm BW, Basili VR (2001) Software defect reduction top 10 list. IEEE Computer 34(1):135–137

11. Cockburn, A (2001) Writing effective use cases. Boston: Addison-Wesley

12. Collard R (1999) Test design: Developing test cases from use cases. Software Testing and Quality Engineering July/August 1(4): 31–36

13. Denger C, Paech B (2004) An integrated quality assurance approach for use case based requirements. In: Proceedings of the German conference of Modellierung, pp.59–74

14. Denger C, Paech B, Benz S (2003) Guidelines -- Creating use cases for embedded systems. IESE-Report, 078.03/E, Kaiserslautern, Germany

15. Denger C, Medina M (2003) Test cases derived from user requirements specifications: Literature survey. IESE Report No. 033.03/E, Kaiserslautern, Germany

16. Denger C, Kerkow D, Knethen Av, Paech B (2003) A comprehensive approach for creating high-quality requirements and specifications in automotive projects. In: Proceedings of the International Conference Software and Systems Engineering and their Applications, 2-6 December, Paris, France

17. Endres A, Rombach H D (2003) A handbook of software and systems engineering. Empirical Observations, Laws and Theories. New York: Addison-Wesley

18. Fagan ME, (1976) Design and code inspections to reduce errors in program development. IBM Systems Journal 15(3):182–211

19. Fantechi A, Gnesi S, Lami G, Maccari A (2002) Application of linguistic techniques for use case analysis. In: Proceedings of the International Conference on Requirements Engineering, pp 157-164, Essen, Germany

20. Gilb T, Graham D (1993) Software inspection. Boston, Addison-Wesley

21. Glass RL (1998) Software runaways. Lessons learned from massive software project failures. Upper Saddle River, NJ: Prentice Hall

22. Graham D (2002) Requirements and testing: Seven missing-link myths. IEEE Software 19(9):15-17

23. Heitmeyer CL, Jeffords RD, Labaw BG, (1996) Automated consistency checking of requirements specifications. ACM Transactions on Software Engineering and Methodology 5(3): 231–261

24. IEEE Recommended practice for software requirements specification. IEEE Standard 830-1998, 1998

25. IEEE guide for developing system requirements specification. IEEE Standard 1233-1998, 1998

26. IEEE standard for software reviews. IEEE Standard 1028-1997, 1997

27. ITU-T (1993) Recommendation Z.100. Specification and description language (SDL) ITU-International Communication Unit, Geneva

28. Jalote P (1989) Testing of completeness of specifications. IEEE Transactions on Software Engineering 15(5): 526–531

29. Jones CB, (1990) Systematic software development using VDM. Upper Saddle River, NJ, Prentice Hall

30. Kamsties E, Pohl K, Reis S, Reuys A (2004) Szenario-basiertes systemtesten von software-produktfamilien mit ScenTED. In: Proceedings of Modellierung, Marburg, Germany, pp.169–186

31. Keese P, Meyerhoff D (2003) Tutorial on requirements-based testing (SQS). Held in conjunction of the International Conference on Software Testing, Cologne, Germany

32. Kitchenham B, Pfleeger S (1996) Software quality: the elusive target. IEEE Software, 13(1): 12–21

33. Le Lann G (1996) The Ariane 5 Flight 501 Failure - A case study in system engineering for computing systems. Research report RR-3079, INRIA

34. Laitenberger O (2000) Cost-effective detection of software defects through perspective-based inspections. PhD Thesis in Experimental Software Engineering; Fraunhofer IRB Verlag

35. Leffingwell D, Widrig D (2000) Managing software requirements – A unified approach. Boston: Addison-Wesley

36. Liggesmeyer P (1990), Modultest und modulverifikation – State of the art. Mannheim, Wien Zürich, BI-Wissesverlag

37. Briand LC, Freimut B, Vollei F (2000) Assessing the cost-effectiveness of inspections by combining project data and expert opinion. In: Proceedings of the 11th International Symposium on Software Reliability Engineering, pp 124–135

38. Musa J (1993) Operational profiles in software-reliability engineering. IEEE Software 10:(2): 14–32

39. Ostraned T J, Balcer M J (1988) The category-partition method for specifying and generating functional tests. Communications of the ACM 31(6):676–686

40. Porter A, Votta LG (1998) Comparing detection methods for software requirements specification: A replication using professional subjects. Empirical Software Engineering 3(4): 355–379

41. Robertson S, Robertson JH (1999) Mastering the requirements process. Boston: Addison-Wesley

42. Rupp C, Queins S (2003) Vom use-case zum Test-Case. OBJEKTspektrum, Vol.4

43. Shull F, Rus I, Basili V (2000) How perspective-based reading can improve requirements inspections. IEEE Computer 33(7):73–79

44. Shull F, Basili V, Boehm B, Brown AW, Costa P, Lindvall M, Port D, Rus I, Tesoriero R, Zelkowitz M (2002) What we have learned about fighting defects. In: Proceedings of 8th International Metrics Software Metrics Symposium: p 249ff., Ottawa, Canada

45. Shull F, Travassos G H, Carver J (1999) Evolving a set of techniques for OO inspections. Technical Report CS-TR-4070, UMIACS-TR-99-63; University of Maryland

46. Sommerville I, Sawyer P (1997) Requirements engineering. A good practice guide. Chichester: John Wiley & Sons

47. http://www.standishgroup.com/chaos_chronicles/index.php Accessed on 3rd December 2004

48. Thelin T, Runeson P, Wohlin C (2003) An experimental comparison of usage-based reading and checklist-based reading. IEEE Transactions on Software Engineering, 29(8): 687–704

49. Wiegers K E (2002) Peer reviews in software. A practical guide. Boston: Addison-Wesley

50. Wiegers K E (1999) Writing quality requirements. Software Development Magazine, 7(5): 44–48

51. Wiegers K E (2000) Karl Wiegers describes 10 requirements traps to avoid. Software Testing & Quality Engineering Journal, January/February, 2(1)

52. Wilson WM, Rosenberg LH, Hyatt LE (1996) Automated quality analysis of natural language requirements specifications. NASA Software Assurance Technology Center, USA

Author Biography

Christian Denger studied computer science at the University of Kaiserslautern, Germany, with a minor in economics. He received his master in computer science in 2002. Since then, he has been working as a scientist at the Fraunhofer Institute for Experimental Software Engineering in Kaiserslautern, Germany. His research interests are software inspections in the context of defect cost reduction approaches in early development phases and the combination of quality assurance techniques in the context of embedded systems. Currently, he is involved in several German and international projects as a team member and project leader and is pursuing a PhD degree at the University of Kaiserslautern.

Thomas Olsson works as a scientist at the Fraunhofer Institute for Experimental Software Engineering in Kaiserslautern, Germany. He received a Licentiate of Engineering in Software Engineering in 2002 and a Master of Science in Computer Science and Engineering in 1999, both from Lund University, Sweden. His research interests lie in heterogeneous information and documentation models, especially in the context of requirements. Currently, he is leading one European and one German project, and is at the same time pursuing a PhD degree at Lund University.

Part 2
The Next Practice in Requirements Engineering

This part provides descriptions of some specific ways of addressing the challenges in requirements engineering as well as presenting various areas where requirements engineering plays a key role in the success of a software project. There are seven chapters in this Part. Chapter 9 addresses the possibility of using goal modeling in requirements engineering and, in particular, how to reason with goals. Chapter 10 recognizes that software requirements are often represented in natural language, which results in some challenges when it comes to the management of large repositories of requirements. Natural language also raises the challenge of overcoming ambiguity in the wording of requirements. Chap. 11 presents an introduction and some empirical results in relation to ambiguity. Part I has established that decision-making is an important aspect of engineering and managing requirements. Thus Chap. 12 is devoted to decision-support. Requirements engineering is all too often focused on bespoke software development. In many cases, software is developed for markets. A market-driven approach to requirements engineering is presented in Chap. 13. Software development methods evolve over-time. One such family of methods is agile methods. The handling of requirements within agile development is presented in Chap. 14. Finally, requirements engineering in a web-based context is presented in Chap. 15.

Thus, in summary, this part contains chapters on the following topics:

- Chapter 9: Goal modeling
- Chapter 10: Use of natural language
- Chapter 11: Ambiguity in requirements
- Chapter 12: Decision support
- Chapter 13: Market-orientation
- Chapter 14: Agile methods
- Chapter 15: Web-based development

These seven chapters highlight some of the main issues related to engineering and managing software requirements. The chapters are written by researchers from around the world that have conducted extensive and reputable research in the above areas.

The seven chapters are by Collette Rolland and Camille Salinesi from University of Paris, France; Johan Natt och Dag from Lund University, Sweden and Vincenzo Gervasi from University of Pisa, Italy; Erik Kamsties from University of Essen, Germany; An Ngo-The and Günther Ruhe from University of Calgary, Canada; Björn Regnell from Lund University, Sweden and Sjaak Brinkkemper from Utrecht University, The Netherlands; Alberto Sillitti and Giancarlo Succi from the Free University of Bozen, Italy; Jacob L. Cybulski from Deakin University, Australia and Pradip K. Sarkar from Central Queensland University, Australia.

9 Modeling Goals and Reasoning with Them

Colette Rolland and Camille Salinesi

Abstract. The concept of goal has been used in many domains such as management sciences and strategic planning, artificial intelligence and human computer interaction. Recently, goal-driven approaches have been developed and tried out to support requirements engineering activities such as requirements elicitation, specification, validation, modification, structuring and negotiation. This chapter first review various research efforts undertaken in this line of research and presents the state-of-the-art in using goals to engineer requirements. It then presents a particular goal model, the goal/strategy map, and shows that maps can help with facing the challenge of new emerging multi-purposes systems, i.e. systems imposing variability in requirements elaboration and customization in the requirements engineering process.

Keywords: Goal, Goal modeling, Goal specification, Reasoning with goals, Elicitation, Variability, User, Scenario.

9.1 Introduction

Goals have long been recognized to be an essential component involved in the Requirements Engineering (RE) process. In their seminal paper, Ross and Schoman stated "requirements definition must say why a system is needed, based on current and foreseen conditions, which may be internal operations or external market. It must say what a system features will serve and satisfy this context. And it must say how the system is to be constructed" [77]. Typically, the current system is analyzed; problems are pointed out and opportunities are identified; high level strategic goals are elicited and refined to address such problems and meet such opportunities; requirements are then elaborated to meet these goals. Goals are thus the driving force of the requirements engineering process.

Goal-driven approaches have proved to be an effective way to elicit requirements [64, 76] and also to support a systematic exploration of design choices [41, 74, 90] to check requirements completeness [91], to ensure requirements pre-traceability [26, 66] and to help in the detection of threats [31] such as conflicts [68] and obstacles [41, 64] and their resolution. The leading role played by goals in the RE process led to a whole stream of research on goal modeling, goal specification/formulation and goal-based reasoning for the multiple aforementioned purposes.

This chapter aims first to provide a state-of-the-art review in the three key topics of goal modeling, goal specification and reasoning with goals. Thereafter, we will discuss a particular goal model, the *goal/strategy map* [73] and show how comprehensive guidelines, drawn from our research and our practical experience, help to model and specify maps and to reason with them. A special emphasis will be put to demonstrate how goal/strategy maps are well suited to deal with new challenges raised by the emerging conditions of systems development leading to variability in requirements capture and customization in the requirements process. Variability is imposed by the *multi-purpose* nature of software systems of today. These systems must meet the purpose of several organizations and must be adaptable to different usage situations sets of customers. In contrast, earlier software systems were concerned with the purpose of a single organization and of a single set of customers. Variability is defined in software development as the ability of a software system to be changed, customized or configured to a specific context [87]. Therefore, it can be seen that variability affects both goal models, which must make variability explicit, and the process of goal-based reasoning that must help selecting the right variant for the project at hand.

The rest of this chapter is organized in two main sections. Section 2 is an overview of the state-of-the-art in using goals to engineer requirements. Section 3 presents the goal/strategy map model and its contribution to deal with variability requirements.

9.2 State-of-the-Art Review

According to Axel van Lamsweerde [40], RE is "concerned with the identification of goals to be achieved by the envisioned system, the operationalization of such goals into services and constraints, and the assignment of responsibilities of resulting requirements to agents as humans, devices, and software". In this view which is largely shared by the RE community, goals drive the RE process which focuses on goal centric activities such as goal elicitation, goal modeling, goal operationalization and mapping goals onto software objects, events and operations. This section provides an overview of research efforts undertaken in this line. It is organized in three parts. The first one provides the "big picture", the second overviews contributions of goal modeling approaches and the third one discusses their weaknesses.

9.2.1 The Big Picture

This section presents a motivation for goal-driven RE, briefly defines what a goal is and introduces the roles of goals in the RE process and the difficulties encountered in their use.

9.2.2 Motivation for Goal-Based RE Approaches

Goal-driven RE approaches have emerged as a means to overcome the major drawback of traditional approaches, that is, to lead to systems technically good but unable to respond to the needs of users in an appropriate manner. Indeed, several field studies show that a requirement misunderstanding is a major cause of system failure. For example, a survey of 800 projects undertaken by 350 US companies revealed that one third of the projects were never completed and one half succeeded only partially; poor requirements were identified as the main source of problems [81]. Similarly, a survey over 3800 organizations in 17 European countries shows that most of the perceived problems are related to requirements specification (>50%), and requirements management (50%) [23]. More recently, a 2003 survey of the Meta Group [54] shows even more pessimistic figures attributing 60 to 70% of system failures to poor requirements capture, validation and management. If we want better quality systems to be produced, i.e. systems that meet the requirements of their users, RE needs to explore the objectives of different stakeholders and the activities carried out by them to meet these objectives in order to derive purposeful system requirements. Goal-driven approaches aim at meeting this objective.

The framework of Fig. 9.1 shows that goal-based RE approaches are motivated by establishing an *intentional relationship* between the usage world and the system world [34]. The *usage world* describes the tasks, procedures, interactions etc. performed by agents and how systems are used to do work. It can be looked upon as containing the objectives that are to be met in the organization and achieved by the activities carried out by agents. The *subject world* contains knowledge of the real world domain about which the proposed system has to provide information. Requirements arise from both of these worlds. However, the subject world imposes domain-requirements, which are facts of nature and reflect domain laws, whereas the usage world generates user-defined requirements, which arise from people in the organization and reflect their goals, intentions and wishes.

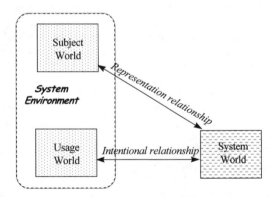

Fig. 9.1 Relationships between the worlds of usage, subject and system

The *system world* is the world of system specifications in which the requirements arising from the other two worlds must be addressed. These three worlds are interrelated as shown in Fig. 9.1. User-defined requirements are captured by the intentional relationship. Domain-imposed requirements are captured by the representation relationship. Understanding the *intentional relationship* is essential to comprehend the reason why a system should be constructed. The usage world provides the rationale for building a system. The purpose of developing a system is to be found outside the system itself, in the enterprise, or in other words, in the context in which the system will function. The relationship between the usage world and the system world addresses the issue of the system purpose and relates the system to the goals and objectives of the organization. This relationship explains why the system is developed. Modeling this establishes the conceptual link between the envisaged system and its changing environment.

Goal-driven approaches have been developed to address the semiotic, social link between the usage and the system world with the hope to construct systems that meet the needs of the organization and fulfill their purpose.

9.2.2.1 What Are Goals?

According to Axel van Lamsweerde [43] "a goal corresponds to an objective the system should achieve through the cooperation of agents in the software to be and in the environment". Goals refer to intended or *optative* [32] properties of envisioned system or of its environment. They are expressions of intent and thus declarative with a *prescriptive* nature, by opposition to descriptive statements [32] which describe real facts. For instance, *Transport passengers fast* is a goal whereas *If doors are closed, they are not open* is a descriptive statement. Goals can be formulated at different levels of abstraction ranging from high-level, e.g. strategic results that an enterprise wants to achieve, down to low-level, e.g. technical concerns on precise situations that a system component should help to reach. *Transport passengers safely* is an example of a high level goal whereas *Keep doors closed when moving* is a goal of a lower level of abstraction.

Goals cover different types of concerns, functional and quality (also called non functional). *Functional goals* refer to services that will be provided by the system or its environment whereas *quality goals* refer to qualities of the system behavior in its environment. *Provide cash* is a functional goal whereas *Serve customer quickly* is a quality goal.

Unlike requirements, goals are usually achieved by the cooperation of multiple agents. The goal *Transport passengers safely* requires, for example, the cooperation of multiple agents such as the train transportation system, the software system, the tracking system and the passengers. A goal under the responsibility of a single agent in the software becomes a requirement. One important decision in the RE process is therefore to decide which goals will be automated and which ones will not. Whereas the actual situations met in the system environment (e.g. physical laws, regulations, norms and behaviors, etc) are usually not controlled by the system, it is possible to control the satisfaction of requirements by implementing them into the system. *Maintain doors closed while moving* is a goal leading to a requirement for the system that will ensure its satisfaction whereas *Get in when doors open* is an assumption [15] about agents out of the system control. Such a statement cannot be used as a requirement.

9.2.2.2 Roles of Goals

As a driving force of the requirements engineering process, goals play a number of roles which are introduced in the following.

- *Requirements elicitation*: goal modeling proved to be an effective way to elicit requirements [4, 15, 20, 35, 43, 64, 76]. The pros of goal-based requirements elicitation being that the rationale for developing a system must be found outside the system itself, in the enterprise [49] in which the system shall function.

- *Exploration of design choices*: RE assumes that the envisioned system might function and interact with its environment in many alternative ways. Alternative goal refinement proved helpful in the systematic exploration of system choices [30, 43, 64, 74].

- *Requirements completeness* is a major RE issue. Yue [91] was probably the first to argue that goals provide a criterion for requirements completeness: the requirements specification is complete if the requirements are sufficient to achieve the goal they refine.

- *Requirements traceability*: goals provide a means to ensure requirements pre-traceability [26, 60, 66]. They establish a conceptual link between the system and its environment, thus facilitating the propagation of organizational changes into the system functionality. This link provides the rationale for requirements [11, 56, 64, 77, 80] and facilitates the explanation and justification of requirements to the stakeholders.

- *Requirements negotiation*: Stakeholders provide useful and realistic viewpoints about the system to be. Negotiation techniques have been developed to help choosing the prevalent one [9, 29]. Prioritization techniques aim at providing means to compare the different viewpoints on the basis of costs and value [36, 55]. Chapters 7 and 4 respectively provide a more detailed survey of requirements negotiation and prioritization methods.

Conflicts detection and resolution: Multiple viewpoints are inherently associated to conflicts [59] and goals have been recognized to help in the detection of conflicts and their resolution [41, 68, 70, 78].

9.2.3 Contributions of Goal Modeling Approaches

For goals to play the aforementioned roles, a whole stream of research led to contributions on goal modeling, goal formulation and goal-based reasoning that we review in turn.

9.2.3.1 Modeling Goals

Goal modeling is central to RE Goal-driven approaches; its benefit are to support heuristic, qualitative or formal reasoning schemes during the RE process. Goals are modeled by intrinsic features such as types and by links with other goals or other elements in the requirements model. We consider them in turn.

Goal Taxonomies: Goals can be of different types. Several classification schemes have been proposed in the literature. Functional versus non-functional is the first one. Functional goals underlie services that the system is expected to deliver whereas non-functional goals refer to expected system qualities such as security, safety, performance, usability, flexibility, customizability, interoperability, and so forth. A rich taxonomy for non-functional goals can be found in [12]. Another distinction often made in the literature is between *soft goals*, whose satisfaction cannot be established in a clear-cut sense [57], and *hard goals* whose satisfaction can be established through verification techniques [7, 11, 16]. Soft goals are especially useful for comparing alternative goal refinements and choosing one that contributes the "best" to them.

Another classification axis is based on types of temporal behavior prescribed by the goal. In [15], achieving (respectively cease) goals generates system behaviors; maintaining (respectively avoid) goals restricts behaviors; optimizing goals compares behaviors to favor those, which better ensure some soft target property. In a similar way, [82] proposes a classification according to desired system states (e.g., positive, negative, alternative, feedback, or exception-repair) and to goal level (e.g., policy level, functional level, domain level). In [6] Antòn makes a distinction between objective goals that refer to objects in the system, and adverbial goals, that refer to ways of achieving objective goals. Goal types and taxonomies are used to formulate a goal [2, 22, 57, 76] and to define heuristics for goal acquisition, goal refinement, requirements derivation, and semi-formal consistency/completeness checking [2, 5, 12, 15, 82].

Goal Links: Many different types of relationships among goals have been introduced in the literature. They can be classified in two categories to relate goals: (1) to each other and (2) with other elements of requirements models. We consider them in turn in the next sub-sections. Chapter 5 of this book deals with similar expressions.

a) Goal Links Among Goals: The most common form of a goal model is an AND/OR graph. AND/OR relationships [11, 15, 50, 58, 76] inspired from AND/OR graphs in Artificial Intelligence are used to capture goal decomposition into more operational goals and alternative goals, respectively. In the former, all the sub-goals must be satisfied for the parent goal to be achieved, whereas in the latter if one of the alternative goals is achieved, then the parent goal is satisfied. For example, in a book lending system, the goal *Satisfy borrower request* is *ANDed* (has an AND relationship) with *Satisfy Bibliography request, Satisfy book request* and *Provide long borrowing period*. These three goals are sub-goals of the former that will be satisfied if its sub-goals are themselves satisfied. *Maintain as many copies as needed* and *Maintain regular availability* are alternatives to satisfy the goal *Satisfy customer request*. The former is *ORed* (has an OR relationship) with the latter and will be satisfied if one of the two alternative goals is satisfied.

In [12, 57, 58], the inter-goal relationship is extended to support the capture of negative/positive influence between goals. A sub-goal is said to contribute partially to its parent goal. This leads to the notion of goal *satisfycing* instead of goal *satisfaction.* For example, *Ensure confidentiality of accounts* and *Ensure security of accounts* are ANDed to *Secure accounts.* Both contribute positively to satisfycing the parent goal *Secure accounts.* By opposition to goal satisfaction, which can be verified quantitatively, using some criterion [69], goal satisfycing cannot be established in a clear-cut sense. Goal satisfaction expressed in AND/OR graphs of hard goals is referred to as the *quantitative framework* whereas goal satisfycing expressed with soft goals is part of the so-called *qualitative framework.* The "motivates" and "hinders" relationships among goals in [11] are similar in the sense that they capture positive/negative influences among goals.

In [76], goal-scenario pairs (called requirement chunks, RC) can be assembled together through *composition, alternative and refinement* relationships. The first two lead to AND and OR structures of RCs whereas the last leads to the organization of the collection of RCs as a hierarchy of chunks of different granularity. *AND relationships* among RCs link complementary chunks in the sense that every one requires the others to define a completely functioning system. RCs linked through *OR relationships* represent alternative ways of fulfilling the same goal. RCs linked through a *refinement relationship* are at different levels of abstraction. The goal *Fill the ATM with cash* is an example of ANDed goal to *Withdraw cash from the ATM* whereas *Withdraw cash from the ATM with two invalid code capture* is ORed to it. Finally *Check the card validity* is linked to the goal *Withdraw cash from the ATM* by a refinement relationship.

Conflict relationships are another kind of relationship among goals. These relationships have been introduced [11][15][59][21] to capture the fact that one goal might prevent the other from being satisfied. For example, in the book lending system considered above, *Provide long borrowing period* which is a sub-goal of *Satisfy borrower request* in the AND/OR graph has a conflict relationship with the alternative goal *Maintain regular availability* of the parent goal *Satisfy customer request* in the same goal graph.

b) Goal Links with Other Elements of Requirements Models: In addition to inter-goal relationships, goals are also related to other elements of requirements models. In his keynote talk [37], Lamsweerde introduced the magic RE triangle as composed of goal, scenario and agent. Obviously goals have privileged relationships with the two other concepts of scenario and agent. Many authors suggest combining goals and *scenarios* [2, 13, 28, 35, 38, 46, 62, 85]. This is understandable because scenarios and goals complement each other. Goals are declarative whereas scenarios are procedural. Intentions are made explicit by goals whereas they are implicit in scenarios. Goals are abstract whereas scenarios are concrete. Combining goals and scenarios can be therefore, seen as a way to mitigate limitations that each concept has when used in isolation. Potts [62] for example, says that it is "unwise to apply goal based requirements methods in isolation" and suggests complementing them with scenarios. This combination has been used mainly, to make goals concrete: scenarios can be interpreted as containing information on how goals can be achieved. In [14, 33, 46, 61], a goal is considered as a contextual property of a use case [33] i.e. a property that relates the scenario to its organizational context. Therefore, goals play a documenting role only. [13] goes beyond this view and suggests to use goals to structure use cases by connecting every action in a scenario to a goal assigned to an actor. In this sense a scenario is discovered each time a goal is. Clearly, all these views suggest a unidirectional relationship between goals and scenarios. [76] further extends this view by suggesting a "bi-directional relationship between goals and scenarios". In the forward direction from goal to scenario, the scenario represents a possible behavior of the system to achieve the goal, and therefore, scenarios help make the goal concrete and detect unrealistic goals. In the backward direction, from scenario to goal, the relationship is used to discover new goals using mining techniques. As the scenario represents a concrete, realistic behavior of the system to be, the goals inferred from it should themselves be realistic ones.

As mentioned before, goal satisfaction requires cooperation among agents. Relationships with *agents* have been emphasized in [89, 90] where a goal is the object of the dependency between two agents. Such type of link is introduced in other models as well [15, 42, 47] to capture who is responsible of a goal. Aside from the golden relationships with scenarios and agents, goals might have links with other concepts of requirements models. For example, as a logical termination of the AND/OR decomposition, goals link to *operations* which operationalize them [2, 15, 35, 38]. Relationships between goals and system *objects* have been studied in [45] and are for instance, inherently part of the KAOS model [15, 42]. In [11] goals are related to a number of concepts such as *problem, opportunity* and *threat* with the aim to better understand the context of a goal. Finally the interesting idea of *obstacle* introduced by [62] leads to obstructions and resolution relationships among goals and obstacles [41, 85].

9.2.3.2 Formulating Goals: Goal formulation is necessary to document the goal model and to support some form of reasoning. Goal formulation can be informal, semi-formal or formal. Goal statements are often texts in natural language [7, 13] and may be supplemented as suggested by [92] with an informal specification to make precise what the goal name designates.

The motivation for semi-formal or formal goal expressions is to support some form of automatic analysis. Typical *semi-formal formulations* use some goal taxonomy and associate the goal name to a predefined type [2, 15]. This helps clarifying the meaning of the goal. For instance, in [57] a non-functional goal can be specified. *Accuracy[account.balance]* is an example of such a goal formulation. Similarly, in Elektra [22], goals for change are pre-fixed by one of the seven types of change: *Maintain, Cease, Improve, Add, Introduce, Extend, Adopt* and *Replace*. Graphical notations [12][57][43] can be used in addition to a textual formulation. L'Ecritoire [76] proposes to formulate each goal as a clause with a main verb and several parameters, where each parameter plays a different role with respect to the verb. For example in the goal statement *Withdraw $_{verb}$ (cash)$_{target}$ (from ATM)$_{means}$, Withdraw* is the main verb, *cash* is the parameter target of the goal, and *from ATM* is a parameter describing the means by which the goal is achieved. The linguistic approach of Fillmore's Case grammar [24], and its extension [19] was used to define goal parameters [65]. Each type of parameter corresponds to a case and plays a different role with respect to the verb, e.g. target entities affected by the goal, means and manner to achieve the goal, beneficiary agent of the goal achievement, destination of a communication goal, source entities needed for goal achievement etc.

Formal specifications of goals like in Kaos [15][43] require a higher effort but yield more powerful reasoning. Achieve [BookRequestSatisfied]: ($\forall$bor: Borrower, b: Book, lib: Library) Requesting (bor, b) $\land$ b.subject $\in$ lib.coverageArea $\Rightarrow \Diamond$ ($\exists$ bc:BookCopy) (Copy(bc, b) $\land$Borrowing(bor, bc)) is an example of such formal specification.

9.2.3.3 Reasoning with Goals: The ultimate purpose of goal modeling is to support some form of goal reasoning for RE sub-processes such as requirements elicitation, consistency and completeness checking, obstacle discovery, conflict resolution and so forth. We consider some of these in the following.

a) Eliciting Goals by Reuse: Although goals can sometimes be spontaneously expressed by stakeholders and therefore available to requirements engineers at early phases of the requirements process, most goals are implicit. Therefore, eliciting goals is not always an easy task, and reasoning techniques can be usefully employed for better performance. *Reuse techniques* are some of these. Chap. 2 is devoted to elicitation problems. For example, Massonet [53] proposes to retrieve goals that have semantically and structurally similar specifications in a repository of reusable specification components, and then transpose the specifications found according to the matching that emerged from the retrieval process. An attempt to retrieve cases from a repository of process cases was developed in [44]. The software tool captures traces of RE processes using the NATURE contextual model [44] and develops a case-based technique to retrieve process cases similar to the situation at hand.

b) Eliciting Goals from Scenarios: A goal inductive elicitation technique based on the analysis of conceptualized scenarios is proposed in [76]. Scenarios can be conceptualized owing to powerful analysis and transformation linguistic techniques based on a Case Grammar inspired by Fillmore's Case Grammar [19, 24]. The pay-off of the scenario conceptualization process is the ability to perform powerful induction on conceptualized scenarios. In [38], a similar approach is developed that takes scenarios as examples and counter examples of the intended system behavior and generates goals that cover positive scenarios and exclude the negative ones. [5] takes similar position to derive goals from use-case specifications.

c) Eliciting Goals by Refinement: Many approaches suggest formulating goals at different levels of abstraction. By essence, goal centric approaches aim to help in the move from strategic concerns and high level goals to technical concerns and low abstraction level goals. Therefore, it is natural for approaches to identify different levels of goal abstraction where high level goals represent business objectives and are refined in system goals [2, 3] or system constraints [41]. Inspired by cognitive engineering, some Goal-driven RE approaches deal with means-end hierarchy abstractions, where each hierarchical level represents a different model of the same system. The information at any level acts as a goal (the end) with respect to the model at the next lower level (the means) [48, 67, 88]. In [76] the refinement strategy helps discovering goals at a lower level of abstraction. This is a way to support goal decomposition. Another obvious technique to perform refinement is to decompose it by asking the HOW question [39]. Other decomposition based goal elicitation heuristics have been developed in [50] and [47].

d) Obstacle Driven Elaboration: Goal models seem to be powerful instruments to perform hazard reasoning. Several RE approaches have already been developed to deal with obstacles and conflicts [4, 31, 41]. Both concepts relate to the goals that users have in mind when they use the facilities offered by software systems. An obstacle is defined as a phenomenon that occurs in the system and/or its environment and obstructs the achievement of the goal [4, 41]. A conflict is when the achievement of two different goals obstructs each other [21, 68]. A similar principle is used to build misuse case descriptions. A *misuse case* is as a use case described from the point of view of a hostile actor. The goal of this actor is to use the system functions for a different purpose than the one initially intended [1, 79].

e) Conflict Resolution: Reasoning with goals can also help to resolve conflicts among stakeholders. A conflict is when the achievement of two different goals obstructs each other. [59, 68, 78] explain how conflicts arise from multiple viewpoints and concerns. Various forms of conflict have also been studied in [17]. Ivankina [31], and Sutcliffe [83, 84], generalize the notions of obstacle, conflict and other system menace into the notion of threat because they all correspond to the partial or total hindering of one or several system goals.

9.2.4 Weaknesses of Goal-Driven Approaches

Despite their contributions to the performance of a number of RE activities, several authors [39][2][28] also acknowledge the fact that dealing with goals is not an easy task. This sub-section discusses weaknesses of goal driven approaches.

- *Mitigating goal abstractness*: Our own experience in several domains such as air traffic control, electricity supply, human resource management, tool set development is that it is difficult for domain experts to deal with the abstract concept of a goal [75]. Scenario authoring is one of the rare ways used in goal driven approaches to make a goal more concrete. More mechanisms are needed to mitigate the abstract nature of a goal.
- *Finding the right goal*: It is often assumed that systems are constructed with some goals in mind [18]. However, practical experiences show that goals are not given and therefore, the question of where they originate from [2] acquires importance. In addition, enterprise goals, which initiate the goal discovery process, do not reflect the actual situation, but an idealized one. Therefore, pro-

ceeding from spurious goals may lead to ineffective requirements [63]. Thus, finding the right goal is rarely an easy task and more support is needed.

- *Removing goal fuzziness*: The initial goal statement is usually rather imprecise and sketchy and can be interpreted in many ways. The exact meaning of the goal gets clearer and clearer as the elicitation process proceeds. However, experience shows [72] that it is best to make a precise, formal statement of the goal as early as possible in the RE process and that the informal goal statement must be brought into a form that is conducive to performing goal analysis. Goal driven approaches must better support goal formulation avoiding nevertheless the burden of formal languages.
- *Supporting goal operationalization*: Additionally, it has been shown that the application of goal reduction methods to discover the components goals of a goal, is not as straight-forward as literature suggests [15][7]. Our own experience in the F3 [11] and ELEKTRA [75] projects confirms this. It is thus evident that help is needed to achieve meaningful goal modeling.
- *Guiding alternative goals discovery*: Finding alternative goals to a parent goal is crucial for the envisionment of the future system and therefore, crucial to RE. However, experience shows that the process is manual, adhoc and unsatisfactory. This is similar to observations made in the discovery of use case variants [13]. Providing automated support is needed to facilitate the discovery of a large number of alternative designs as an exhaustive generation of alternatives is very difficult to practice manually.

9.3 Goal/Strategy Maps

In this section, we discuss the case of particular type of goal model, the goal/strategy map. We first justify the move from traditional AND/OR goal models to goal/strategy maps as a response to the challenge posed by new multi-purpose emerging systems and by the need to swerve from goal modeling to model goal achievement through strategies to fulfill goals. We introduce the concept of map, illustrate it with an ERP system example and discuss how the model meets the aforementioned challenge. Thereby we consider the customization process implied by multi-purpose systems and discuss the way it can be handled with maps.

9.3.1 Facing the Multi-Purpose System Challenge with Maps

9.3.1.1 Motivations for Maps

Goal modeling approaches have been conceived with the traditional software system life cycle in mind: high strategic goals are captured to elicit software requirements and build the software functionality that fulfils these requirements. However, in recent years, development "from scratch" became the exception and a new context in which software systems are developed has emerged. Whereas earlier, a system met the purpose of a single organization and of a single set of customers, a system of today must be conceived in a larger perspective, to meet the purpose of several organizations and to be adaptable to different usage situations/customer sets. The former is typical of an ERP-like development situation whereas the latter is the concern of product-line development [86], [10] and adaptable software [30]. In the software community, this leads to the notion of software variability, which is defined as the ability of a software system to be changed, customized or configured to a specific context [87]. Whereas the software community studies variability as a design problem and concentrates on implementation issues [8], [10], [86], we believe like Halmans [27] that capturing variability at the goal level is essential to meet the multi-purpose nature of new software systems.

Our position is that variability implies a move from systems with a *mono-facetted purpose* to those with a *multi-facetted purpose*. Whereas the former concentrates on goal discovery, the multi-facetted nature of a purpose extends it to consider the many different ways of goal achievement. For example, for the goal Purchase Material, earlier it would be enough to know that an organization achieves this goal by forecasting material need. Thus, Purchase material was mono-facetted: it had exactly one strategy for its achievement. However, in the new context, it is necessary to introduce other strategies as well, say the Reorder Point strategy for purchasing material. Purchase Material now is multi-facetted, it has many strategies for goal achievement. These two strategies, among others, are made available, for example, in the SAP Materials Management module[72].

The foregoing points to the need to balance goal-orientation with the introduction of strategies for goal achievement. This is the essence of goal/strategy maps.

A *goal/strategy map*, or *map* for short, is a graph, with intentions as nodes and strategies as edges. An edge entering a node identifies a strategy that can be used for achieving the intention of the node. The map therefore, shows which intentions can be achieved by which strategies once a preceding intention has been achieved. Evidently, the map is capable of expressing goals and their achievements in a declarative manner.

9.3.1.2 The Map Representation Formalism

In this section we introduce the key concepts of a map and their relationships and bring out their relevance to model multi-facetted purposes. A map provides a representation of a multi-facetted purpose based on a non-deterministic ordering of intentions and strategies. The key concepts of the map and their inter-relationships are shown in the map meta-model of Fig. 9.2, which is drawn using UML notations.

- As shown in Fig. 9.2, a map is composed of several sections. A *section* is an aggregation of two kinds of intentions, *source* and *target*, linked together by a strategy.
- An *intention* is a goal, 'an optative' statement [32] that expresses what is wanted i.e. a state that is expected to be reached or maintained. *Make Room Booking* is an intention to make a reservation for rooms in a hotel. The

achievement of this intention leaves the system in the state, *Booking made.* Each map has two special intentions, *Start* and *Stop*, associated with the initial and final states respectively.

- A *strategy* is an approach, a manner, a means to achieve an intention. Let us assume that bookings can be made *on the Internet.* This is a means of achieving the *Make Room Booking* intention, and is a strategy. *by visiting a travel agency* is another strategy to achieve the same intention.
- A *section* is an aggregation of the source intention, the target intention, and a strategy. As shown in Fig. 9.2 it is a triplet $<I_{source}, I_{target}, S_{source\text{-}target}>$. A section expresses the strategy $S_{source\text{-}target}$ using which, starting from I_{source}, I_{target} can be achieved. The triplet *<Start, Make Room Booking, on the Internet>* is a section; similarly *<Start, Make Room Booking, by visiting a travel agency>* constitutes another section.

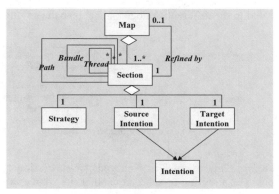

Fig. 9.2 The map meta-model

A section is the basic construct of a map which itself can be seen as an assembly of sections. When a map is used to model a multi-facetted purpose, each of its sections represents a facet. The set of sections models the purpose in its totality and we will see below that the relationships between sections and between a section and a map lead to the representation of the multi-facetted perspective. A facet highlights a consistent and cohesive characteristic of the system that stakeholders want to be implemented in the software system through some functionality. A facet in our terms is close to the notion of feature, which can be defined as a "prominent or distinctive user-visible aspect, quality or characteristic of a software system or systems". We believe that a facet is a useful abstraction to express variability in intentional terms. A map is drawn as a directed graph from *Start* to *Stop*. Intentions are represented as nodes of the graph and strategies as edges between these. The graph is directed because the strategy shows the flow from the source to the target intention (see Fig. 9.5).

- Three kinds of relationships can be defined between sections, namely the thread, path and bundle. These relationships generate multi-thread and multi-path topologies in a map.
- *Thread relationship*: It is possible for a target intention to be achieved from a source intention in many different ways. Each of these ways is expressed as a section in the map. Such a map topology is called a *multi-thread* and the sections participating in the multi-thread are said to be in a thread relationship with one another. Assume that *Accept Payment* is another intention in our example and that it can be achieved in two different ways, *By electronic transfer* or *By credit card*. This leads to a thread relationship between the two sections shown in Fig. 9.3.

It is clear that a thread relationship between two sections regarded as facets represents directly the variability associated to a multi-facetted purpose. Multi-faceting is captured in the different strategies to achieve the common target intention.

Fig. 9.3 An example of thread relationship

- *Path relationship*: This establishes a precedence/succession relationship between sections. For a section to succeed another, its source intention must be the target intention of the preceding one. For example the two sections *<Start, Make Room Booking, By the Internet Strategy>*, *<Make Room Booking, Accept Payment, By credit card>* form a path.

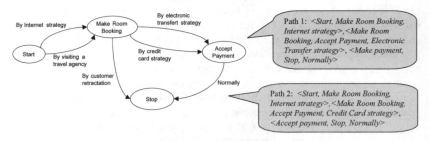

Fig. 9.4 The multi-path of the map *Make Confirmed Booking*

From the point of view of modeling facets, the path introduces a composite facet whereas the section based facet is atomic. Given the thread and the path relationships, an intention can be achieved by several combinations of sections. Such a topology is called a *multi-path*. In general, a map from its *Start* to its *Stop* intentions is a multi-path and may contain multi-threads. Let us assume in our example that it is possible to *Stop* either because a customer retracts from making the booking (*By customer retraction*) or after payment (*Normally*). Fig. 9.4 shows the entire map with the purpose to *Make Confirmed Booking*. This map contains 6 paths from Start to Stop out of which two are highlighted in the Figure.

Clearly, the multi-path topology is yet another way of representing the multi-facetted perspective. Multi-faceting in this case is obtained by combining various sections together to achieve a given intention of the map. Consider for instance the intention Accept payment in Fig. 9.4; there are four paths from Start to achieve it; each of them is a different way to get the intention achieved and in this sense, participates to the multi-faceting. Each path is a composite facet composed of two atomic facets. This can be extended to the full map which can be seen as composed of a number of paths from Start to Stop. This time these paths introduce multi-faceting but to achieve the intention of the map which in our example, is Make Confirmed Booking.

- *Bundle relationship*: Several sections having the same pair $<I_{source}, I_{target}>$ which are mutually exclusive are in a *bundle relationship*. The group of these sections constitutes a *bundle*. Notice that the difference between a thread and bundle relationship is the exclusive OR of sections in the latter versus an OR in the former.
- *Refinement relationship*: The map meta model also shows that a section of a map can be refined as another map through the refinement relationship. The entire refined map then represents the section. Refinement is an abstraction mechanism by which a complex assembly of sections at level i+1 is viewed as a unique section at level i. As a result of refinement, a section at level i is represented by multiple paths & multiple threads at level i+1.

From the point of view of multi-faceting, refinement allows to look to the multi-facetted nature of a facet. It introduces levels in the representation of the multi-facetted purpose which is thus completely modeled through a hierarchy of maps. To sum up:

- The purpose of the system is captured in a *hierarchy of maps*. The intention associated to the root map is the highest level statement about the purpose. Using the refinement mechanism, each section of the root map can be refined as a map and the recursive application of this mechanism results in a map hierarchy. At successive levels of the hierarchy the purpose stated initially as the intention of the root map is further refined.
- At any given level of the hierarchy, the multi-facetted dimension is based on multi-thread and multi-path topologies. Multi-thread introduces local faceting in the sense that it allows to represent the different ways for achieving an intention directly. Multi-path introduces global faceting by representing different combinations of intentions and strategies to achieve a given map intention. Any path from Start to Stop represents one way of achieving the map intention, therefore the purpose represented in this map.

9.3.1.3 Illustrating Map with the SAP R3 Material Management Map

In this section we show the use of the Map to capture the multi-facetted purpose of a system and take the SAP R/3 Materials Management (MM) module to illustrate this. This module provides automated support for the day-to-day operations of any type of business that entails the consumption of materials. It consists of five key components starting from materials planning (MM-MRP Materials Requirements Planning), through purchasing (MM-PUR Purchasing), managing inventory (MM-IM Inventory Management), managing warehousing (MM-WM Warehouse Management), to invoice verification (MM-IV Invoice Verification). It also includes two support components, MM-IS Information System and MM-EDI Electronic Data Interchange.

In its totality, the MM module can be seen to meet the purpose, *Satisfy Material Need Efficiently*. This is the intention of the root map shown in Fig. 9.5. The map shows that to meet this purpose two intentions have to be achieved, namely *Purchase Material* and *Monitor Stock*. These reflect the conventional view of materials management as "procuring raw material and ensuring effectiveness of the logistics pipeline through which materials flow" [72]. Evidently, there is an ordering between these two intentions: stock cannot be monitored unless it has been procured. This is shown in the Figure by the section *<Purchase Material, Monitor Stock, Out-In strategy >*.

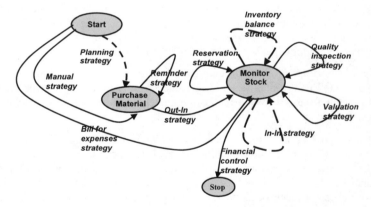

Fig. 9.5 The material management map. Intermittent lines represent bundles.

The map of Fig. 9.5 has 25 paths from *Start* to *Stop*, 5 following the *Bill for expenses strategy*, 10 following the *Planning Strategy*, and 10 following the *Manual strategy*. Thus, the map is able to present a global perspective of the diverse ways of achievement of the main purpose. When a more detailed view is needed, then it becomes necessary to focus more specifically on the multi-facetted nature of each intention found in the "global" map. The detailed view of the intentions contained in Fig. 9.5 is brought out in turn below.

The Multiple Facets of Purchase Material: The multi-facetted nature of *Purchase Material* is shown in Fig. 9.5 by including three strategies for its achievement (a) *Planning strategy*, (b) *Manual strategy* and (c) *Reminder strategy*. The three facets are *<Start, Purchase Material, Planning strategy>*, *<Start, Purchase Material, Manual strategy>* and *<Purchase Material, Purchase Material, Reminder strategy>*. Subsumed in the first facet are two mutually exclusive facets, one that allows purchase to be made when stock falls to the reorder point and the other for purchasing as per the planned material need. These two are captured in a bundle consisting of two strategies not shown in the figure, namely the *Reorder point strategy* and *Forecast based strategy*. The second facet, *<Start, Purchase Material, Manual strategy>*, allows the buyer to manually enter a purchase requisition leading to the generation of the purchase order. The third facet is used to remind the vendor to deliver material when the delivery is not made in due time. The bundled strategies correspond to the SAP functions of MM-MRP Forecast Based Planning and Reorder Point Planning respectively whereas the manual strategy is part of the MM-PUR component. It can be seen that the component structure of SAP does not directly reflect the alternative functionality of achieving the same goal.

The Multiple Facets of Monitor Stock: *Monitor Stock* is the second key intention of the material management map. The intention represents the management goal of ensuring proper posting of procured material and effectiveness of material logistics while maintaining financial propriety. This suggests that Monitor Stock has three classes of facets (a) the procurement/posting class, (b) the logistics class, and (c) the financial class. The facets in each class are as follows:

a) Procurement/Posting Facets
Procurement of material can be done either against a purchase order or without a formal purchase order, directly from the market. In the latter case, material is immediately ready for posting, whereas in the former case, posting is done after delivery is made against the purchase order. Thus, we have two facets of this class:

- Posting of material delivery against a purchase order
- Posting of material procured through direct purchase

These correspond in the map of Fig. 9.5 to the *Out-in strategy* and *Bill for expenses strategy*, respectively. In SAP, the facet represented by the section *<Purchase Material, Monitor Stock, Out-In strategy>* is covered by functions of the MM-IM and MM-WM components whereas *<Start, Monitor Stock, Bill for expenses strategy>* is a function of MM-IV, the Invoice Verification component.

The facet *<Purchase Material, Monitor Stock, Out-In strategy>* is, in fact, a compound one. It represents the variety of ways in which compliance of delivered material with the purchase order can be ensured and material posting made. Therefore, its refinement reveals a complex assembly of facets that can be represented through a map at a lower level. This refinement is shown in Fig. 9.6. Since *<Purchase Material, Monitor Stock, Out-In strategy>* does not permit stock posting unless material delivery complies with the purchase order, its refinement contains an ordering of the two intentions, *Accept Delivery* and *Enter Goods in Stock*. The former has four facets, one for the case where delivery is strictly according to the purchase order and three facets that allow delivery to be accepted within specified tolerances from that in the purchase order. The four facets are as follows:

- The delivery complies with the purchase order
- Reconciliation against the purchase order has to be done
- Reconciliation between the different units used by the supplier and the receiver has to be done
- Reconciliation of under/over delivery has to be done

These correspond in Fig. 9.6 to the four multi-threads identified by the strategies Okay strategy, Reconciliation by PO recovery, Reconciliation of unit difference, and Reconciliation of under/over delivery. The nature of the three Reconciliation facets is such that one or more can be simultaneously used. Therefore, these strategies do not form a bundle but are each represented as a thread.

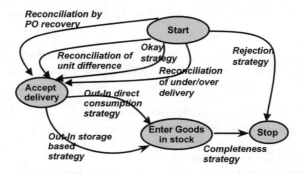

Fig. 9.6 Refinement of *<Purchase Material, Monitor Stock, Out-In strategy>*

Now consider the intention *Enter Goods in Stock*. This displays two facets for entering goods in stock (a) when delivery is made directly to the consumption location and (b) when delivered goods are stored in a warehouse. As shown in Fig. 9.6, these two ways of achieving *Enter Goods in Stock* correspond to the two strategies, *Out-In direct consumption* and *Out-In storage based strategy*. The target intention, *Monitor Stock*, of the facet under refinement is achieved in the map when the intention *Stop* is achieved. Evidently, this happens when either the material delivered is rejected and no stock entry is made or when, after entering the accepted delivery in stock, all subsequent housekeeping is done to take into account the consequences of entering goods in stock. These two facets of *Stop* are represented in Fig. 9.6 by *Rejection strategy* and *Completeness strategy* respectively.

b) Material Logistics Facets

Facets in this class enter the picture only after initial posting of stock has been made by the class of procurement/posting facets of *Monitor Stock*. The interesting question now is about the movement of stock and how this movement is kept track of. That is, *Monitor Stock* has to be repeatedly achieved after each movement to/from warehouses, to consumption points or for quality inspection. This gives us the three facets:

- Control of material movement to/from warehouses
- On-time transfer of material to consumption points
- Quality control of the material transferred

These correspond in the map of Fig. 9.5 to the *In-In, Reservation,* and *Quality inspection strategies.* These strategies have *Monitor Stock* as both their initial as well as their target intentions. This represents the repeated achievement of *Monitor Stock.* Of the three foregoing facets, the first, represented by the section *<Monitor Stock, Monitor Stock, In-In strategy>* needs further explanation. In fact, subsumed in this facet are two mutually exclusive facets of *Monitor Stock.* These correspond to the cases when the stock to be moved spends a long time in transit or when immediate transfer is possible. As before, the section *<Monitor Stock, Monitor Stock, In-In strategy>* is represented as a bundle of two sections having strategies *One-step transfer* and *Two-step transfer.* The former corresponds to immediate transfer and the latter to delayed transfer. In SAP, this bundled section is covered partly by MM-IM and MM-WM and has a relationship with Financial Accounting, Assets Management, and Controlling.

c) Financial Propriety Facets

The third class of facets of *Monitor Stock* deals with financial propriety. Not only must it be ensured that stock on hand is physically verified but also it should be financially valued. Thus, we have two facets in this class

- Physical stock taking of the material
- Valuing the stock for balance sheets

These are represented in the map of Fig. 9.5 by the *Inventory balance* and *Valuation* strategies respectively. As for the material logistics class of facets, these are also concerned with the repeated achievement of *Monitor Stock.* Therefore, both the source and target intentions of these strategies is *Monitor Stock.* The facet corresponding to the *<Monitor Stock, Monitor Stock, Inventory balance strategy>* section subsumes three different ways of physical stock taking: by periodic inventory verification, by continuous verification and by verifying a sample of the total inventory. Any of these three can be mutually exclusively deployed. Therefore, we represent it as a bundle of the three strategies, *periodic, continuous* and *sampling* strategies. This bundle is handled by the MM-IM component in SAP.

The facet represented in Fig. 9.5 by the section *<Monitor Stock, Monitor Stock, Valuation strategy>* can itself be treated as a bundle of mutually exclusive facets represented by strategies such as LIFO and FIFO. In SAP, only LIFO valuation is available as a function in MM-IM.

Completing Satisfy Material Need Effectively: The complete fulfillment of *Satisfy Material Need Effectively* requires that the financial aspects of material procurement are properly handled. Thus completion, corresponding to the achievement of *Stop* of Fig. 9.5 is done by the *Financial control strategy* allowing the flow from *Monitor Stock* to *Stop*. In SAP, this takes the form of the Invoice Verification component, MM-IV. When a multi-facetted product like the SAP MM is to be adopted, then the task of the adoption process is to select the facets of the MM map that are of relevance. This leads us to the issue of the process dimension which we consider in the next section.

9.3.2 Matching Maps to Support Multi-Purpose System Customization

The multi-purpose view of emerging systems that leads to the representation of variability in *product models* has a counterpart on the *process dimension* which implies a change of the traditional RE process. Whereas the latter corresponds merely to a move from an *As-Is* to a *To-Be* model (Fig. 9.7a), the former leads to producing the *To-Be* model by a model-match centered process. As shown in Fig. 9.7b the organizational goals are expressed in the *As-Wished* model. The *Might-Be* model reflects the functional capability of the multi-purpose system (e.g. an ERP) and the *To-Be* model needs to be defined as the best match between the *As-Wished* and the *Might-Be*. This process leads to customizing the *Might-Be* model to tailor it to the organizational requirements expressed in the *As-Wished* model.

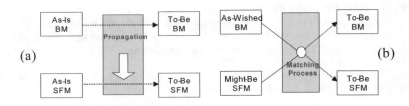

Fig. 9.7 Multi-purpose system customization process (BM stands for Business Models, SFM stands for System Functionality Models)

We believe that maps can help in facing the challenge raised by the customizing activity required in the RE process of multi-purpose systems in two ways: (a) by offering a uniform representation of the involved models, namely the *As-Is*, *As-Wished*, *Might-Be* and *To-Be* and (b) by providing a formalism to model the matching process in a multi-purpose dimension. Our position is that the multi-facetted perspective on product modeling has implications on process modeling as well. First, there cannot be a mismatch between the process modeling paradigm and the product modeling paradigm. Instead, the former must be aligned to the latter. Thus, the process modeling paradigm should be Goal-driven. Secondly, it is unlikely that product variability can be discovered with a monolithic way of working. This implies that the process model should provide many different strategies to achieve the same process goal. The foregoing points to the desirability of the process to be looked upon as a multi-facetted purpose process. This multi-facet aspect implies a process model that has the capability to integrate in it the many strategies found in different methodologies for achieving the same process goal.

For example, to *Elicit a Goal*, different methodologies follow different strategies, top-down, bottom-up, what-if, participative etc. These get integrated in one multi-facetted purpose process model.

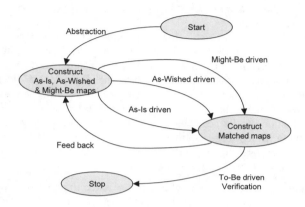

Fig. 9.8 Process model for ERP customization.

This position was confirmed by our experience in different projects where we observed that people have specific expectations and requirements about these process models. First, they are facing an issue and have a goal in mind and would like process models to let them easily situate both and to suggest different alternative paths to achieve the goal and solve the issue. Second, they want freedom and flexibility in their ways of working; one single imposed way-of-working is not acceptable. They expect to learn about the different ways by which each of their goals can be achieved and each issue can be solved. Third, they want advice on how to choose between the different alternative solutions that shall be proposed to solve a given issue. The first two points lead to a multi-purpose driven process model and the third point raises the requirement of a model able to offer guidance in process enactment. Maps can be used to model a methodological process and to capture *process goals* as map nodes and *strategies* to achieve those as edges. For maps to provide guidance we introduced guidelines that can be associated to sections in a process map to guide the selection of process goals as well as to guide strategy selection, situation identification and section achievement.

Fig. 9.8 shows a process model that was developed for an ERP customization project. As the figure shows the process model is represented as a map. The root purpose of this map is *Elicit ERP Installation Requirements*. Achieving the purpose leads to the *Matched-map* which expresses the requirements that the ERP installation shall be met. Many of the intentions/strategies of the *Matched Map* are obtained from the *Might-Be map* (the ERP map) and match the *As-Wished* organizational requirements. Others may not be available in the *ERP map* and will require in-house development. In such a case, the *Matched Map* makes them explicit. Again, all the intentions and strategies of the *ERP map* may not be included in the *Matched Map*. This corresponds to the ERP functionality that is not matching the requirements in the *As-Wished map*. Thus, the *Matched Map* is the input to the installation process. The multi-facetted nature of the process is shown by the sub-purposes embedded in the map, namely the two main intentions *Construct As-Is, As-Wished, Might-Be maps* and *Construct Matched Map* and the various strategies to achieve them.

There are three ways of achieving it by three different strategic drives, *As-Wished*, *Might-Be* and *As-Is* drives. Each drive considers the intentions and strategies of its corresponding map from *Start* to *Stop* in order to decide if these (a) match the requirements exactly and so must be included in the *Matched map,* (b) need adaptation before their inclusion in the *Matched map*, or (c) are irrelevant.

These three strategies have the same initial and target intentions showing that the target intention can be achieved in a non-deterministic way. This reflects the possibility that different organizations may interleave these strategies in different combinations thereby following different processes to *Construct Matched Map*. Findings from our experience are summed up as follows:

1. If the context is that of a well-defined business requirements to which the system should fit, and in-house development is not a problem, then the As-Wished driven matching strategy can be used.
2. If on the contrary, the system is less likely to change than the business (e.g. because customizing the system has become too expensive [72], or if the system customization is an opportunity to change the business (e.g. because it allows to generalize its associated best practice in the business) then the matching process should be driven by the system. This is what the Might-Be driven strategy proposes.
3. If it is particularly important to preserve the functionality provided by the existing system in the To-Be system functionality model, then an As-Is driven matching is required. We encountered such functional non regression requirements when we studied the introduction of software components for selling electricity in the PPC company at the occasion of European electricity market deregulation [71].

Construct As-Is, Might-Be, As-Wished maps is also multi-facetted. It can be achieved in two ways, by the *Abstraction strategy* or the *Feedback strategy*. The latter has *Construct Matched Map* as its source intention and allows an incremental achievement of *Construct As-Is, Might-Be, As-Wished maps*. This extends to *As-Is* and *ERP maps* the view of Anthony Finkelstein and colleagues [25] that starting with complete requirements specification is not always needed in software package requirements engineering. Finally, the *Stop* intention achieves completion of *Elicit ERP Installation Requirements* through the *To-Be driven verification strategy* that verifies the accuracy of the *Matched Map*.

9.4 Conclusion

Goal-driven requirements engineering are intended to provide the rationale of the system to be. Beyond this objective, we have seen that there are some other advantages:

- Goals bridge the gap between organizational strategies and system requirements thus providing a conceptual link between the system and its organizational context
- Goal decomposition graphs provide the pre-traceability between high level strategic concerns and low level technical constraints; therefore facilitating the propagation of business changes onto system features
- ORed goals introduce explicitly design choices that can be discussed, negotiated and decided upon
- AND links among goals support the refinement of high level goals onto lower level goals till operationalizable goals are found and associated to system requirements
- Powerful goal elicitation techniques facilitate the discovery of goal and requirements;
- Relationships between goals and concepts such as objects, events, operations etc. traditionally used in conceptual design facilitates the mapping of goal graphs onto design specification

We have also discussed the fact that goal driven RE approaches suffer from a number of weaknesses partly due to the nature of the concept of a goal and partly to the lack of modeling and support of the goal driven RE process. The belief of the authors is that goal-driven approaches are now facing the challenge of forthcoming multi-purpose systems, i.e. systems that incorporate variability in the functionality they provide and will be able to self adapt to the situation at hand. The goal/strategy maps have been introduced and discussed as an example of goal model that has been conceived to meet the aforementioned challenge.

References

1. Alexander I (2002) Initial industrial experience of misuse cases in trade-off analysis. In: Proceedings of IEEE Joint International Requirements Engineering Conference, 9-13 September, Essen, pp.61–68
2. Antòn AI, Potts C (1998) The use of goals to surface requirements for evolving systems. In: Proceedings of International Conference on Software Engineering (ICSE'98), Kyoto, Japan, pp.157–166
3. Antòn AI, Earp JB, Potts C, Alspaugh TA (2001) The role of policy and stakeholder privacy values in requirements engineering. In: Proceedings of IEEE 5th International Symposium on Requirements Engineering (RE'01), Toronto, Canada, pp.138–145
4. Antòn AI, Potts C, Takahanshi K (1994) Inquiry based requirements analysis. IEEE Software 11(2): 21–32

5. Antòn AI, Carter R, Dagnino A, Dempster J, Siege DF (2001) Deriving goals from a use-case based requirements specification. Requirements Engineering Journal, 6: 63–73

6. Antòn AI, McCracken WM, Potts C (1994) Goal decomposition and scenario analysis in business process reengineering. CAISE'94, LNCS 811, Springer-Verlag, pp.94–104

7. Antòn AI (1996) Goal based requirements analysis. In: Proceedings of 2nd International Conference on Requirements Engineering ICRE'96, pp.136–144

8. Bachmann F, Bass L (2001) Managing variability in software architecture. ACM SIGSOFT Symposium on Software Reusability (SSR'01), pp.126–132

9. Boehm B, Bose P, Horowitz E, Ming-June L (1994) Software requirements as negotiated win conditions. In: Proceedings of 1st International Conference on Requirements Engineering, USA, pp.74–83

10. Bosch J, Florijn G, Greefhorst D, Kuusela J, Obbink JH, Pohl K (2001) Variability issues in software product lines. In: Proceedings of 4th International Workshop on Product Family Engineering (PEE-4), Bilbao, Spain, pp.22–37

11. Bubenko J, Rolland C, Loucopoulos P, de Antònellis V (1994) Facilitating 'fuzzy to formal' requirements modelling. In: Proceedings of IEEE 1st Conference on Requirements Engineering, ICRE'94 pp.154–158

12. Chung KL, Nixon BA, Yu E, Mylopoulos J (1999) Non- functional requirements in software engineering. The Kluwer international series in software engineering. 1st edition, Kluwer Academic Publishers

13. Cockburn A (1995) Structuring use cases with goals. Technical report. Human and Technology, HaT.Technical Report.1995.01, Accessed on 3rd December 2004. http://alistair.cockburn.us/crystal/articles/sucwg/structuringucswithgoals.htm.

14. Dano B, Briand H, Barbier F (1997) A use case driven requirements engineering process. Journal of Requirements Engineering, Springer-Verlag, 2(2): 79–91

15. Dardenne A, Lamsweerde A, Fickas S (1993) Goal-directed requirements acquisition. Science of Computer Programming, Elsevier.20: 3–50

16. Darimont R, Lamsweerde A. (1996) Formal refinement patterns for goal-driven requirements elaboration. In: Proceedings of 4th ACM SIGSOFT Symposium on the Foundations of Software Engineering, San Francisco, pp.179–190

17. Darimont R, Lamsweerde A, Letier E (1998) Managing conflicts in goal-driven requirements engineering. IEEE Transactions on Software Engineering, 24(11): 908–926

18. Davis AM (1993) Software requirements objects, functions and states. Prentice Hall, UK

19. Dik SC (1989) The theory of functional grammar. Part 1: The structure of the clause. Functional Grammar Series, Fories Publications Dordrecht, Holland

20. Dubois E, Yu E, Pettot M (1998) From early to late formal requirements: a process-control case study. In: Proceedings of 9th International Workshop on software Specification and design. IEEE CS Press, pp. 34–42

21. Easterbrook SM, Finkelstein ACW, Kramer J, Nuseibeh BA (1994) Coordinating conflicting view points by managing inconsistency. Workshop on Conflict Management in Design, International Conference on Artificial Intelligence in Design, Lausanne, Switzerland, pp. 15–18

22. ELEKTRA consortium (1997) Electrical enterprise knowledge for transforming applications. ELEKTRA Project Reports No 22927

23. European Software Institute (1996) European user survey analysis. Report USV_EUR 2.1, ESPITI Project

24. Fillmore C (1968) The case for case. In: Universals in linguistic theory, Bach E, Harms RT (Eds.), Holt, Rinehart & Winston New York, pp.1–90

25. Finkelstein A, Spanoudakis G, Ryan M (1996) Software package requirements and procurement. In: Proceedings of 8th International workshop on Software Specification and Design, IEEE Computer Society Press, Washington, DC, pp.141–145

26. Gotel OCZ, Finkelstein ACW (1994) Modelling the contribution structure underlying requirements. In: Proceedings of 1st International Workshop on Requirements Engineering: Foundations of Software Quality, Utrecht, The Netherlands, pp. 71–81

27. Halmans J, Pohl K, (2003) Communicating the variability of a software product family to customers. Journal of Software and System Modeling, 2(1): 15–36

28. Haumer P, Pohl K, Weidenhaupt K (1998) Requirements elicitation and validation with real world scenes. IEEE Transactions on Software Engineering, Special Issue on Scenario Management, Jarke M, Kurki-Suonio R (Eds.), 24(12): 11036–1054

29. Hoh P (2002) Multi-criteria preference analysis for systematic requirements negotiation. In: Proceedings of 26th Annual International Computer Software and Applications Conference, Oxford, England pp.887

30. Hui B, Liaskos S, Mylopoulos J (2003) Requirements analysis for customizable software: A goals-skills-preferences framework. In: Proceedings of IEEE Conference on Requirements Engineering, Monterey Bay, USA, pp.117–126

31. Ivankina E, Salinesi C (2004) An approach to guide requirement elicitation by analyzing the causes and consequences of Threats. In: Proceedings of14th European - Japanese Conference on Information Modelling and Knowledge Bases, Skövde, Sweden

32. Jackson M (1995) Software requirements & specifications – a lexicon of practice. Principles and Prejudices, ACM Press, Addison-Wesley

33. Jacobson I (1995) The use case construct in object-oriented software engineering. In Scenario-Based_Design: Envisioning Work and Technology in System Development, J.M. Carroll (Ed.), pp.309–336.

34. Jarke M, Pohl K (1993) Establishing visions in context: Towards a model of requirements processes. In: Proceedings of 12th International Conference on Information Systems, Orlando (ICIS), Orlando, pp.23–34

35. Kaindl H (2000) A design process based on a model combining scenarios with goals and functions. IEEE Transactions on Systems, Man and Cybernetic, 30(5): 537–551

36. Karlsson J, Olsson S, Ryan K (1997) Improved practical support for large-scale requirements prioritizing. Journal of Requirements Engineering, 2(1): 51–60

37. Lamsweerde A. (2004) Goal-oriented requirements engineering: A roundtrip from research to practice. In: Proceedings of 12th IEEE International Symposium on Requirements Engineering, Kyoto, Japan

38. Lamsweerde A, Willemet L (1998) Inferring declarative requirements specifications from operational scenarios. IEEE Transactions on Software Engineering, Special Issue on Scenario Management 24(12): 1089–1114

39. Lamsweerde A, Darimont R, Massonet P (1995) Goal-directed elaboration of requirements for meeting schedulers: Problems and lessons learnt. In: Proceedings of the 2nd IEEE International Symposium on Requirements Engineering (RE'95), pp.194–203

40. Lamsweerde A (2000) Requirements engineering in the year 2000: A research perspective. In: Proceedings of 22nd International Conference on Software Engineering, (ICSE'2000): Limerick, Ireland, Invited Paper, ACM Press, pp. 5–19

41. Lamsweerde A, Letier E (2000) Handling obstacles in goal-oriented requirements engineering. IEEE Transactions on Software Engineering, Special Issue on Exception Handling, 26(10): 978–1005

42. Lamsweerde A, Dardenne B, Delcourt F (1991) The KAOS project: Knowledge acquisition in automated specification of software. In: Proceedings of AAAI Spring Symposium Series, Stanford University, pp.59–62

43. Lamsweerde A (2001) Goal-oriented requirements engineering: A guided tour. In Proceedings of International Joint Conference on Requirements Engineering, Toronto, IEEE, pp.249–263

44. Le TL (1999) Guidage des processus d'ingénierie des besoins par un approche de réutilisation de cas, Master Thesis, CRI, Université Paris-1, Panthéon Sorbonne

45. Lee SP (1997) Issues in requirements engineering of object-oriented information system: A review. Malaysian Journal of computer Science, 10(2)

46. Leite JCS, Rossi G, Balaguer F, Maiorana A, Kaplan G, Hadad G, Oliveros A (1997) Enhancing a requirements baseline with scenarios. In: Proceedings of 3rd IEEE International Symposium on Requirements Engineering, Antapolis, Maryland, pp.44–53.

47. Letier E (2001) Reasoning about agents in goal-oriented requirements engineering. Ph. D. Thesis, University of Louvain

48. Leveson NG (2000) Intent specifications: an approach to building human-centred specifications. IEEE Transactions on Software Engineering 26: 15–35

49. Loucopoulos P (1994) The f³ (from fuzzy to formal) view on requirements engineering. Ingénierie des systèmes d'information, 2(6): 639–655

50. Loucopoulos P, Kavakli V, Prekas N (1997) Using the EKD approach, the modelling component. ELEKTRA project internal report, UMIST, Manchester, UK

51. Maiden N, Ncube C (1998) Acquiring COTS software selection requirements. IEEE Software, 15(2): 46–56

52. Maiden N, Kuim H, Ncube C (2002) Rethinking process guidance for software component selection. In: Proceedings of 1st Int. Conf. of Component Based Eng, pp.151–164

53. Massonet P, Lamsweerde A, (1997) Analogical reuse of requirements frameworks. In: Proceedings of 3rd International Symposium on Requirements Engineering, Annapolis, pp.26–37.

54. META Group (2003) Research on requirements realization and relevance, Meta Group report

55. Moisiadis F (2002) The fundamentals of prioritising requirements systems engineering. Systems Engineering, Test & Evaluation Conference, Sydney, Australia, October

56. Mostow J (1985) Towards better models of the design process. AI Magazine, 6: 44–57

57. Mylopoulos J, Chung KL, Nixon BA (1992) Representing and using non- functional requirements: a process-oriented approach. IEEE Transactions on Software Engineering, Special Issue on Knowledge Representation and Reasoning in Software Development, 18(6): 483–497

58. Mylopoulos J, Chung KL, Yu E (1999) From object-oriented to goal-oriented requirements analysis. Communications of the ACM, 42(1): 31–37

59. Nuseibeh B, Kramer J, Finkelstein A (1994) A framework for expressing the relationships between multiple views in requirements specification. IEEE Transactions on Software Engineering, 20: 760–773

60. Pohl K (1996) Process centred requirements engineering, J. Wiley and Sons.

61. Pohl K, Haumer P (1997) Modelling contextual information about scenarios. In: Proceedings of the 3rd International Workshop on Requirements Engineering: Foundations of Software Quality REFSQ'97, Barcelona, Spain, pp.187–204

62. Potts C (1995) Using schematic scenarios to understand user needs. In: Proceedings of ACM Symposium on Designing interactive Systems: Processes, Practices and Techniques, University of Michigan, USA, pp.247–256

63. Potts C (1997) Fitness for use: The system quality that matters most. In: Proceedings of International Workshop on Requirements Engineering: Foundations of Software Quality REFSQ'97, Barcelona, pp.15–28

64. Potts C, Takahashi K, Antòn AI (1994) Inquiry-based requirements analysis. IEEE Software 11(2): 21–32

65. Prat N (1997) Goal formalisation and classification for requirements engineering. In: Proceedings of 3rd International Workshop on Requirements Engineering: Foundations of Software Quality REFSQ'97, Barcelona, Spain, pp.145–156

66. Ramesh B, Powers T, Stubbs C, Edwards M (1995) Implementing requirements traceability: a case study. In: Proceedings of the 2nd Symposium on Requirements Engineering (RE'95), UK, pp.89–95

67. Rasmussen J (1990) Mental models and the control of action in complex environments. In: Mental Models and Human--Computer Interaction, Ackermann D, Tauber MJ (Eds.) North-Holland: Elsevier, pp.41–69

68. Robinson WN, Volcov S (1996) Conflict oriented requirements restructuring, Georgia State University, Atlanta, GA, Technical Paper CIS-96-15, October 8,

69. Robinson WN, (1989) Integrating multiple specifications using domain goals. In: Proceedings of 5th International Workshop on Software Specification and Design, IEEE, pp.219–225

70. Robinson WN, Volkov S (1998) Supporting the negotiation life-cycle. Communications of the ACM, 41(5): 95–102

71. Rolland C (2000) Intention driven component reuse. In: Information Systems Engineering, Brinkkemper S, Lindencrona, E, Solvberg A (Eds.) Springer, pp.197–208

72. Rolland C, Prakash N (2000) Bridging the gap between organizational needs and ERP functionality. Requirements Engineering Journal, 4(1): 180–193

73. Rolland C, Salinesi C, Etien A (2004): Eliciting gaps in requirements change. Requirements Engineering Journal, 9(1): 1–15

74. Rolland C, Grosz G, Kla R (1999) Experience with goal-scenario coupling. In Proceedings of 4th IEEE International Symposium on Requirements Engineering, Limerik, Ireland, pp.74–81

75. Rolland C, Nurcan S, Grosz G (1997) Guiding the participative design process. In Proceedings of Association for Information Systems Americas Conference, Indianapolis, Indiana, pp.922–924

76. Rolland C, Souveyet C, Salinesi C (1998) Guiding goal modelling using scenarios. IEEE Transactions on Software Engineering, Special Issue on Scenario Management, 24(12): 98–27

77. Ross DT, Schoman KE (1977) Structured analysis for requirements definition. IEEE Transactions on Software Engineering, 3(1): 6–15

78. Easterbrook SM (1994) Resolving requirements conflicts with computer-supported negotiation. In Requirements Engineering: Social and Technical Issues, Jirotka M, Goguen J (Eds.) London: Academic Press, pp.41–65

79. Sindre G, Opdahl L (2001) Templates for misuse case description. In Proceedings of 7th International Workshop on Requirements Engineering, Foundation for Software Quality (REFSQ'2001): Interlaken, Switzerland

80. Sommerville I, Sawyer P (1997) Requirements engineering. Worldwide Series in Computer Science, Wiley

81. Standish Group (1995) Chaos, Standish Group Internal Report, www.standishgroup.com/chaos.html

82. Sutcliffe A, Maiden N (1993) Bridging the requirements gap: Policies, goals and domains. In: Proceedings of 7th International Workshop on Software Specification and Design, IEEE Computer Society Press, pp.52–55

83. Sutcliffe A, Minocha S (1999) Analyzing socio-technical system requirements. CREWS project Report 98-37, Accessed on 5th December 2004, http://sunsite.informatik.rwth-aachen.de/CREWS/reports.htm

84. Sutcliffe AG, Galliers J, Minocha S (1999) Human errors and system requirements. In: Proceedings of 4th IEEE International Symposium on Requirements Engineering, Limerick, Ireland, pp.23-30

85. Sutcliffe AG, Maiden N, Minocha S, Darrel M (1998) Supporting scenario-based requirements engineering. IEEE Transactions Software Engineering, 24(12): 1072–1088

86. Svahnberg M, Gurp J, Bosch J (2001) On the notion of variability in software product lines. In: Proceedings of the Working IEEE/IFIP Conference on Software Architecture (WICSA 2001) pp.45–55

87. Van Gurp J (2000) Variability in software systems: The key to software reuse. Licentiate Thesis, University of Groningen, Sweden

88. Vicente KJ, Rasmussen J (1992) Ecological interface design: Theoretical foundations. IEEE Transactions on Systems, Man and Cybernetics, 22(4): 589–606

89. Yu E (1997) Towards modeling and reasoning support for early-phase requirements engineering. In: Proceedings of 3rd IEEE International Symposium on Requirements Engineering -RE97, pp.226–235

90. Yu E (1994) Modeling strategic relationships for process reengineering. Ph.D. Thesis, Department Computer Science, University of Toronto, Canada

91. Yue K (1987) What does it mean to say that a specification is complete? In: Proceedings of 4th International Workshop on Software Specification and Design, Monterey, CA, USA, pp.34–41

92. Zave P, Jackson M (1997) Four dark corners of requirements engineering. ACM Transactions on Software Engineering and Methodology, 6(1): 1–30

Author Biography

Colette Rolland is Professor of Computer Science and head of CRI at University of Paris 1 - Panthéon Sorbonne. Her research interests lie in the areas of information modeling, object-oriented analysis and design, requirements engineering, CASE and CAME tools, change management and enterprise knowledge development. She has supervised 62 PhD theses and was author/co-author of 5 textbooks and of over 170 invited and refereed papers. She also has extensive experience in leading research projects funded by French institutions (CNRS, INRIA, Ministry of Research and Technology) as well as by ESPRIT programs, including

NATURE (N° 6353) - *ESPRIT 3*, ELEKTRA (N° 22927), and CREWS (N° 21903) - *FRAMEWORK 4*.

Dr. Camille Salinesi is a senior lecturer of Computer Science at the University of Paris 1 Panthéon - Sorbonne. His research works deal with Requirements Engineering, Systems Engineering, and Process Engineering. He has published more than 40 refereed papers and organized several conferences (OOIS'98, REP'99, REFSQ'01'02'03, RE'05) in these domains. His recent works showed significant results on the topics of the use of Use Cases, Goals, and Scenarios in Requirements Engineering and about Information System evolution and ERP implementation. Dr Salinesi was involved in several fundamental research projects such as ESPRIT NATURE and CREWS, and was consultant for several national and international companies. Camille Salinesi is a member of the INCOSE and belongs to the RE group of the French association of Systems Engineering.

10 Managing Large Repositories of Natural Language Requirements

Johan Natt och Dag and Vincenzo Gervasi

Abstract: An increasing number of market and technology driven software development companies face the challenge of managing an enormous amount of requirements written in natural language. As requirements arrive at high pace, the requirements repository easily deteriorates, impeding customer feedback and well-founded decisions for future product releases. In this chapter we introduce a linguistic engineering approach in support of large-scale requirements management. We present three case studies, encompassing different requirements management processes, where our approach has been evaluated. We also discuss the role of natural language requirements and present a survey of research aimed at giving support in the engineering and management of natural language requirements.

Keywords: Large-scale requirements management, Linguistic engineering, Natural language processing, Relationships, Redundancy, Duplicates.

10.1 Introduction

Market and technology driven companies developing increasingly complex software products eventually face the challenge of dealing with huge information flows that may overwhelm their management and analysis capabilities. Requirements are particularly difficult to manage effectively due to their unstructured nature. The requirements also have a potential to grow to such volumes and arrive at such rates that specific information and knowledge management challenges emerge: deterioration of the requirements repository and an increasing difficulty to identify and maintain requirements inter-relationships.

A major reason for these problems is that requirements are communicated in natural language, which induces several problems like imprecision, ambiguity, incompleteness, conflict, and inconsistency, which take time to resolve (see Chap. 11 for a separate discussion on ambiguity). Requirements management processes may be very different in design. Nevertheless, companies that acknowledge both customer involvement and their own innovative potential as rewarding means for discovering successful product services and functionality are faced with a common challenge: analyzing and evaluating every incoming requirement, customer wish and technical suggestion as soon and as thoroughly as possible.

In traditional requirements management [49] there is an implicit focus on isolated monolithic requirements specifications. The new challenge of managing enormous amounts of requirements that continuously must be analyzed, re-analyzed and consolidated is generally left untouched. This is also reflected by current requirements management tools, which do provide the functionality to assign links between requirements, but give no assistance in the actual matching of thousands of incoming requirements with those already analyzed. Requirements management tools could do better than providing simple keyword search facilities to alleviate the manual burden of consolidating large amounts of requirements.

Companies facing these challenges may arrive at a cross-road where the choice is to reduce the flow of incoming requirements or to assign more resources to handle them [24]. However, seen from a business perspective, neither of these approaches is particularly rewarding (and in many situations impossible). Choking the elicitation and invention of new requirements will increase the risk of missing potential business opportunities [28], and adding more people to do the job has been shown to be too costly and at times counter-productive [3, 24].

In this chapter we present a linguistic engineering approach that may give considerable support in the continuous management of large amounts of textual requirements. The approach is based on techniques from information retrieval where similarities between requirements are calculated to indicate the semantic overlap. This gives a possibility for product managers to more quickly find relationships between requirements based on their textual content.

In Sect. 2 we will first discuss the general role that natural language requirements play in large-scale software development. Section 3 provides an in-depth survey of the current research in linguistic engineering applied to requirements engineering and management. Section 4 introduces the idea of calculating similarity between requirements as a means for identifying semantically related requirements. In Sects. 5 through 7 we present three case studies conducted at three software developing companies, while Sect. 8 concludes the chapter.

10.2 The Role of Natural Language Requirements

A recent survey supports our own research experience that requirements to a very large extent are written and communicated in natural language (NL) [34]. Still, after years of rewarding research that has helped us understand and improve the way requirements may be specified and formulated [Chaps 3 & 11], the state of the practice is generally that requirements quality guidelines are rarely applied. There is a large gap between the formal models advocated by many researchers and the informality that dominates in industry. Several reasons can be identified to why requirements are initially specified in natural language and in many cases kept in that form throughout the development process:

- NL is the primary communication language, which is shared by all stakeholders and participants in the development process. Formal languages require specific training, which is unrealistic to expect from every stakeholder and in particular from customers or end-users.
- Requirements engineering (RE) is a social and evolutionary process where requirements are elicited and specified at different levels of abstraction at different points in the development process. NL is universal, meaning that it can be

used to talk about arbitrary domains and at arbitrary levels of abstraction. Many formal languages do not have this strength.

- In large-scale development there are comparatively few of the proposed requirements that are actually selected for implementation (see for example Chap. 4 on prioritization and Chap. 13 on market-driven RE). Since not all requirements are expected to be implemented, there is little motivation for spending time formalizing them. In particular, our experience tells us that companies which value close interaction with their customers and rapid reaction to changing market conditions do not find it cost-beneficial to translate all requirements into formal specifications.

- Many formal methods do not offer any support for the management and analysis of erroneous, incomplete, or partially-specified requirements. In contrast, NL techniques adapt naturally to such situations, which in practice make up a large part of a requirement life cycle.

- While formal languages can improve our ability to check internal consistency and completeness of requirements (a process often referred to as *verification*), they cannot capture external properties of the requirements, e.g. correspondence between the requirements and the actual user intentions. It requires good communication and interaction with the stakeholders to verify such properties (*validation*) – and to this end, NL is a more suited language.

Thus, despite its recognized and infamous deficiencies, there are few incentives to avoid natural language. We should therefore expect that its use cannot be escaped. This is also elucidated by M. Jackson stating that RE is where the informal meets the formal [25]. The gap between the users' needs and a new release of the software system must therefore be bridged using methods and techniques that acknowledge, in some form, communication in natural language.

An increasing number of software development companies move away from isolated contract development projects (also called bespoke software development) towards development for a broader market. This is, for example, also indicated by the growing interest in commercial off the shelf (COTS) development in the RE research community [52]. Companies developing for a broader market face distinct challenges, of which one crucial is to stay ahead of competitors and reduce time-to-market [Chap. 13]. After an initial version of a product has been released, there is a need for a dynamic process of elicitation and prioritization. In this dynamic environment where requirements arrive from many different sources and stakeholders (customers, sales representatives, developers, support personnel), the decision of which requirements are to be included in the next release of the product must in most cases be made based on the NL requirements available in the repository, in addition to the experience and skill of the product manager and certain nonnegotiable requests by key customers.

In essence, these companies face an information overload problem. But, as we already pointed out in the introduction, the most apparent solutions (reducing the inflow of requirements or adding personnel) are not satisfying. Another approach has therefore been examined, which aims at supporting requirements analysis activities through automation. The proposed solution is to use the techniques from *natural language processing* (NLP) [26].

10.3 State of the Research Addressing NL Requirements

As pointed out in the well-referenced paper by Ryan [46], there have been many unrealistic expectations on NLP techniques given the desire for a system that could support the currently expensive activities within RE. These expectations are typically based on misconceptions about what the communication problem in industrial RE really is and to what extent the requirements on a system are available in textual form (e.g. see [51] on linguistic problems with requirements elicitation). Ryan concludes that RE is a social process and that linguistic techniques can succeed only in a supporting role to this process –not by trying to replace it.

A pragmatic approach is suggested by Garigliano, who points out a range of criteria for applied systems dealing with natural language [18]. The criteria elucidate the possible variation points for the usefulness of an NLP-based system. In essence, it is a matter of systematic cost-benefit analysis.

To relate our work to the current body of knowledge, we present here a survey of research aimed at supporting RE activities using linguistic engineering techniques, grouped by three major RE process activities addressed:

- *Domain and requirements understanding*, which is a fundamental success factor in all systems and software development.
- *Requirements verification and validation*, which are carried out to ensure that a specification is internally consistent and to certify that the requirements are a correct representation of the users' intentions [2, Chap. 8].
- *Requirements management,* dealing with storage, change management and traceability issues. This is within the scope of this paper.

We encourage the interested reader to look into the work of each author. In many cases the industrial applicability and scalability is yet to be determined through larger case studies with real data. Also, although most approaches acknowledge ambiguity and inconsistencies, seldom is it reported how any other pollution in the data is treated (e.g. misspellings and non-information carrying characters). A combination of different techniques would likely be the most rewarding and the research surveyed provides an excellent basis for this acquisition.

10.3.1 Domain and Requirements Understanding

A central task in domain and requirements understanding is to identify and understand *domain concepts*, also called *domain abstractions*. Domain abstractions are general concepts that are formed to represent common features of specific instances in the domain. Domain abstractions make communication more efficient within the domain, but developers must nevertheless take into account not only the general concept, but also the specific instances, in order to fully understand the abstractions. Domain abstractions are typically represented in NL through sets of terms (often nouns and noun phrases). Researchers have therefore investigated linguistic engineering techniques to extract these terms, representing the abstractions, from the discourse generated from interview transcripts and customer wishes expressed in natural language. Following is a survey of the major research efforts addressing abstractions.

Goldin and Berry [21] presents an original approach and a prototype tool for suggesting requirement abstractions to the human elicitor. Their method compares sentences using a sliding window approach on a character-by-character basis and extracts matching fragments that are above a certain threshold in length. The approach can properly handle arbitrary lengths, gaps and permutations and avoids some specific weaknesses in confidence and precision when using only parsers or counting isolated words.

Rayson et al. [44] present two experiments in probabilistic NLP using tools they have developed (part-of-speech and semantic taggers integrated into an end-user tool). The results suggest that the tools are effective in helping to identify and analyze domain abstractions. This is further supported by a later study by Sawyer and Cosh [47] where ontology charts of key entities are produced using collocation analysis.

10.3.2 Requirements Verification and Validation

It is generally acknowledged that spending more time in the verification and validation stages and finding errors early is more rewarding than proceeding too soon to coding [1, 9, 10]. Therefore, considerable research effort has been put applying natural language processing to support requirements verification and validation. The two activities are not carried out separately. Checking a set of requirements may reveal internal inconsistencies that may as well be external, which must be resolved with a stakeholder. Therefore, requirements verification and validation are here addressed together.

Gervasi and Nuseibeh [19] treat validation as a decision problem on whether a given software model, generated by parsing the requirements text, satisfies certain properties. Their experiment with the use of lightweight formal methods shows that even subtle errors, not discovered by human inspection, may be identified.

An approach to improve the quality of written requirements is proposed by The Goddard Space Flight Center's Software Assurance Technology Center (SATC) [53]. They have derived seven quality indicators used for measuring the quality of requirements specifications. These have been used to develop a tool which is used by NASA to improve their requirements specifications. Fabbrini et al. [11, 12] also propose a quality model and have implemented a tool to show the quality model's industrial applicability. Fantechi et al. [13] have applied both the tool by Fabbrini et al. and SATC to evaluate the quality of 100 use cases. They conclude that although the techniques may support quality evaluation, they are not sufficient to completely address correctness and consistency. Cybulski and Reed [6, 7] describe an elicitation method and a supporting management tool that help in analyzing and refining requirements A set of NLP components are used to force the requirements engineer to rephrase requirements in order to unify the terminology.

Burg and van de Riet [4] have developed an approach and a supporting environment for specification, verification, and validation of functional requirements. Verification is supported graphically, lexically, and logically, while validation is supported through paraphrasing (transforming models into language readable by the user or customer) and simulation of the dynamic behavior. In several different ways they show how the approach enhances the quality of the specification. Park et al. [42] present an implementation of a requirements analysis supporting system, which may help to identify conflicts, inconsistencies, and ambiguities in requirement. Their approach to combine syntactic parsing with a sliding window method gives more accurate similarity measures than using them separately.

To further adapt the language to formal validation, several researchers have proposed to explicitly restrict the language used in requirements. The suggested advantage is that it may be used by domain specialists that want the benefits from formal languages but who lack the required training. Fuchs and Schwertzel [16] and Macias and Pulman [31, 32] use a subset of English to forbid the expression of ambiguous sentences. Cyre and Takar [8] define a syntax and grammar of restricted English. Somé et al. [50] go one step further and restrict the language and semantics to a scenario style, albeit more understandable by the user than formal specification. Osborne and MacNish [41] suggest using extensions to a parser with a wide-coverage grammar in order to identify and present syntactic and semantic ambiguities to the requirements analyst.

Towards formalization, Fliedl et al. [14] suggest the use of a conceptual pre-design model to bridge the gap between the NL representations and enable formal validation. The pre-design model is not as technical as common conceptual modeling languages, while still supporting the general principles behind several different conceptual models (e.g. use cases, state charts, etc.) and the mapping to more formal model.

Nanduri and Rugaber [38] use object modeling technique guidelines and a link grammar parser for transforming high level specifications into object charts. Although their tool produces object diagrams that may help identify omissions, the approach suffers from several common problems when trying to transform natural language requirements into object models: parser limitations, ambiguity, incompleteness and insufficient domain knowledge and transformation rules. A similar approach is taken by Mich and Garigliano [35]. Rolland and Proix [45] describe a prototype that aims at providing support to problem-statement acquisition, elicitation, modeling and validation. It has not been validated but likely also suffers from the common problems listed above. In a recent paper García Flores [17] proposes to use NLP techniques to extract relevant sentences from and identify inconsistencies within large requirements corpora. The approach uses shallow parsing and contextual exploration networks, based on the presence of certain textual markers in the text. It has not yet been evaluated.

10.3.3 Requirements Management

As previously noted, large-scale software systems development involves a considerable flow of requirements. Requirements are elicited and arrive from many different sources and constantly change [49]. When numerous requirements arrive each month, either in bursts of thousands or continuously 3-5 requirements each day, the importance of proper requirements management activities becomes very apparent. Although requirements management is intertwined with the traditional software development process (i.e., where requirements are further analyzed and successively formalized into specifications, ending in executable and tested code), there are requirement management activities that take place before actual development starts [Chap. 13]. But, although it may be clear what must be done, the requirements management process easily becomes overloaded due to the sheer number of requirements. Thus, there is a strong need for more supportive tools.

Current requirements management tools provide facilities for storing and recalling requirements, annotating them with metadata (usually consisting in arbitrary attribute/value pairs, where standard sets of attributes are offered as libraries), and for managing relationships between requirements. Indexing, keyword-based search, and search on metadata are normally provided. Unfortunately, the management of relationships is most often limited to manually establishing links (typically used for traceability) between pairs of requirements. Some link types can be declared as fragile, in that any change in one of the linked requirements marks the link as broken until manually verified and re-established by the user.

Surprisingly, there are, beside the cases presented later on in this chapter, no specific attempts that directly try to tackle the management challenges by using natural language requirements processing. In particular, the following specific hands-on requirements management activities are open for scrutinized research:

- Matching incoming (potentially new) requirements to previously elicited, planned, and already implemented requirements
- Maintaining a separation and finding relationships between customer requests and requirements invented within the organization
- Identifying dependencies and other interrelationships between requirements [5]
- Supporting the extraction of requirements from the repository that fit strategic areas (e.g. invoicing capabilities, decision-making features)

Difficulties in performing these activities are a major obstruction in the efficient management of elicited, invented and implemented requirements. Any technique that may support requirements maintenance and management activities, even if partially, can be expected to be warmly accepted in industry.

10.4 Requirements Similarity

In this section we introduce a fundamental concept in our discussion, that of *requirements similarity*. As we will see in the following, a number of problems in the management of large volumes of requirements can be solved or at least alleviated by using a measure of how similar two requirements are. Naturally, many different notions of similarity can be used. In most problems, what is needed is a notion of *semantic similarity*: a measure of whether two requirements convey the same meaning, and to what extent. However, other notions of similarity can also be used. A few of these are listed in Table 10.1; more measures can easily be obtained by considering other metadata about the requirements (e.g., priority assigned, system version targeted, approval responsibility, implemented status, etc.).

Table 10.1 A listing of some similarity measures

Similarity measures	Description
Semantic	Similarity in meaning
Syntactic	Similarity in grammatical structure
Lexical	Similarity in words used
Structural	Similarity in sectional structure
Extensional	Similarity in size
Argumentative	Similarity in rationale
Goal	Similarity in objective
Source	Similarity in the proponent
Function	Similarity in function addressed
Object	Similarity in system parts affected
Temporal	Similarity in time of origin

Whatever measure is chosen, in order to be applicable to the management of large repository it must possess a fundamental property: it has to be computable in a relatively inexpensive way. Any measure requiring significant human intervention will be too costly to be used on large requirement repositories; we are thus forced to focus on similarity measures that can be computed in a totally automatic way. Unfortunately, given the current state of the art in natural language processing and in knowledge representation, it is not feasible to extract meaning in a reliable way from totally unrestricted natural language text as that found in most requirements. We therefore focus on *lexical similarity* as a way of approximating semantic similarity.

On a lexical level, we consider a requirement as a sequence of *words*. The exact definition of what a word is varies with the language and the application. More refined approaches distinguish the various lexical (and at times, morphological) constituents of requirements with more precision, e.g., punctuation (as in ","), contraction markers (as the apostrophe in "can't"), parenthetical structures (as "(") etc. can be considered as words on their own. We refer to the process of separating the lexical constituents of a requirement as *tokenization*, and each word (in this extensive definition) is called a *token*. In the upcoming case studies, a token is regarded as sequence of letters and/or digits. Any other characters are regarded as delimiters and thus discarded.

$$sim(p,r) = \frac{\sum_i w_p(v_i) \cdot w_r(v_i)}{\sqrt{\sum_i w_p(v_i)^2 \cdot \sum_i w_r(v_i)^2}}$$

Fig. 10.1 The Cosine measure

Tokens can be further processed in various ways. Most typically, tokens are reduced to their base form, removing morphological inflections (e.g., reducing plural nouns to their singular form, or removing person, mood or aspect information from verbs). This process is called *stemming* and is usually performed with the help of general morphological rules, and a dictionary listing exceptions to those rules. In Case 1 we have used the well-known Porter stemmer [43], but in Cases 2 and 3 we have switched to a newer one, reported to perform better [37].

Another common operation is *stop word removal*. It consists in dropping from the sequence of tokens all those words that have a purely grammatical role. The grammatical information they convey may be stored in some other form (e.g., in parsing trees) before removing the stop words, if so desired. Again, the details of the process depend on the language at hand, and on the kind of analysis that is to be performed on the requirements. In most cases, stop words coincide with so-called *closed class words*, e.g. articles and prepositions. Also in this case, a special-purpose dictionary can list exceptions. In the presented cases we have used a stop word list comprising 425 words derived from the Brown corpus [15].

Further various processing steps are possible, but for the sake of brevity we return now to the problem of measuring requirements similarity. We can formally consider a requirement r taken from a requirement set $\square$ as a finite sequence $r = \langle v_{i_1}, v_{i_2}, ..., v_{i_m} \rangle$ of tokens drawn from a given alphabet $V = \{v_1, v_2, ... v_n\}$, which includes all the tokens that appear in our requirements database. Using the preprocessing steps described above, V would consequently contain stemmed tokens that do not appear in the stop word list. If order is not considered important, an alternative representation is possible: a requirement r can be considered as a vector $a_r = [w_r(v_1), w_r(v_2), ... w_r(v_n)]$, where $w_r(v_i)$ denotes the weight, or relative importance, of the token v_i in requirement r. Different weighting schemes are possible. As requirements expressed in feature style are more focused than literary text, we assume that the tokens remaining after the preprocessing step are all equally valuable. In Case 1, we apply the simplest weighting scheme, assuming that weight coincides with frequency. However, as it is considered that the importance of a token is not linearly proportional to the number of times it occurs, in Cases 2 and 3 we also use the well-known weighting formula *1+log₂(term frequency)* [33]. Case 2 explicitly compares the results obtained by using the two schemes.

Once requirements have been encoded as vectors, it becomes possible to apply standard similarity measures. In Case 1 we chose to compare the performance of the Dice, Jaccard, and Cosine measures [33]. Their most significant difference is how they treat different lengths of the compared requirements. In Case 2 and 3, the Cosine measure was selected as it was considered to generally perform better than the other two. This measure got its name from calculating the cosine of the angle between the vectors that represent the requirements in a vector-space model.

Formally, given two requirements, p and r, we have that the similarity between p and r is given by the formula in Fig. 10.1 (An example of applying the measure can be found in [39]). The definition assumes that the vector space employed has a Euclidean distance, uniform across all dimensions. This is of course a gross over-simplification: in practice, the presence or absence of certain terms may be much more important and revealing of true semantic similarity than that of other terms. However, since we are mainly interested in techniques that work irrespective of the exact domain and language used, and for the sake of generality, we will accept this simplification, keeping in mind that more refined techniques can be employed in specific domains.

In the following sections we present three case studies in which the technique of calculating similarity between requirements has been evaluated. For the evaluation we utilize the widely adopted measures of recall, precision, and accuracy. Since their usage and interpretation is dependent on the application we leave the definitions and explanations of the measures to each individual case.

10.5 Case 1: Keeping the Repository in Shape

Telelogic AB develops a software development environment for real-time systems called Telelogic Tau, which supports standardized graphical languages and code generation. Telelogic Tau is marketed globally and requirements are collected continuously from several different sources (e.g. marketing, support, development, testing, usability evaluations, and technology forecasting). The requirements are collected into a repository and assigned the status of "New". Each requirement then undergoes a series of evaluations and refinements, such as checking for appropriate detail level, and assignment of cost, impact, and priority. Each requirement has a lifecycle progressing through specific states in the development process. So, for example, when a requirement has been implemented and verified, it is assigned the status "Applied". Thus, all requirements are kept in the repository, which continuously grows.

In its initial state a requirement is checked for three related properties: (1) whether or not the requirement is regarded as a duplicate of another requirement already in the repository, (2) if it is possible to merge the requirement with another requirement, or (3) if the requirement should be split into two or more requirements before further analysis. If a requirement has one of these properties, it is assigned the "Duplicate" status and an appropriate action is taken. When a requirement is merged, all the information is added to the requirement it is merged with. When a requirement is split, the information is distributed over two or more new requirements. When a requirement is a pure duplicate, no further action is taken.

As requirements arrive at an average rate of three per day, and as the requirements repository unendingly increases in size, these activities are causing congestion in the requirements process [24]. Automated support in this situation, using similarity measures to identify duplicates, is suggested to help avoiding deterioration of the repository and enable a quicker way of checking arriving requirements against the ones stored in the repository.

10.5.1 Case Study Requirements Data

A snapshot of the state of the requirements and the repository by the year 2000 is shown in Table 10.2. Of the 1,920 requirements in the repository, 130 had been identified by the analysts as being duplicates, merges, or split sources (i.e. assigned the status 'duplicate'). Example requirements may be found in [40].

Table 10.2 Number of requirements in the database.

New	Assigned	Classified	Implemented	Rejected	Duplicates	**Total**
406	428	601	252	103	130	**1,920**

10.5.2 Evaluation

Of the 130 requirements marked as duplicates, we only consider the 101 that were real duplicates for evaluation purposes, as merges and split sources would match partially and thus bias the results. Moreover, we use the standard measures of *recall, precision* and *accuracy*. Let $sim(r_i, r_j)$ be a function that takes a pair of requirements and gives a similarity measure between 0 and 1, and t be a threshold value, which acts as a selection criteria. If $sim(r_i, r_j) \geq t$ then (r_i, r_j) are considered to be a suspected duplicate pair. Recall is calculated as the percentage of the actual duplicate pairs that fall above the similarity threshold. Precision is calculated as the percentage of actual duplicates above the similarity threshold in relation to all pairs above the similarity threshold. Finally, accuracy is the percentage of all duplicate pairs that fall on the correct side of the threshold (i.e. correctly suggested duplicate pairs and non-duplicate pairs respectively).

The textual information used to represent each requirement was collected from the "Summary" field, which corresponds to a short requirement title, and the "Description" field, which corresponds to a further explanation (see the examples in Table 10.6 and Table 10.7 in the appendix). These fields were then pre-processed according to the steps described in Sect. 10.4. To investigate the impact of different similarity measures we calculated recall, precision, and accuracy curves for the three different measures in Sect. 10.4. The results are presented in Fig. 10.2, which shows that recall decreases from around 80% at threshold level 0+ to just below 20% at threshold level 1. At threshold levels 0+ and 1 the similarity measures perform exactly the same (as expected considering the formula) but between these two extremes the curves differ. The Dice measure gives slightly worse recall compared to the Cosine measure and may thus be discarded. The best choice between the Jaccard and the Cosine measure is not obvious. The Cosine gives higher recall but lower precision than Jaccard. The choice would thus depend on the application.

The low precision at threshold level 0+ may at first seem very discouraging. However to properly evaluate the feasibility of the approach in an industrial setting, a deeper investigation of the requirement pairs is needed. Taking any two suggested pairs, they may or may not involve the same particular requirements. For example, the requirement pairs (A, F) and (C, F) share the requirement F. If the analyzer assigns similarity values above zero to each of these pairs and a similarity value equal to zero to the pair (A, C) it would nevertheless be interesting to look at the three involved requirements together. We denote these preferred groupings of requirements as *n-clusters*, where n is the number of requirements in the cluster. The two single pairs in the previous example will thus form a 3-cluster. The cluster distribution can be derived by calculating the transitive closure of a graph in which the nodes correspond to requirements and edges correspond to pairs of requirements (r_i, r_j) with $sim(r_i, r_j) \geq t$.

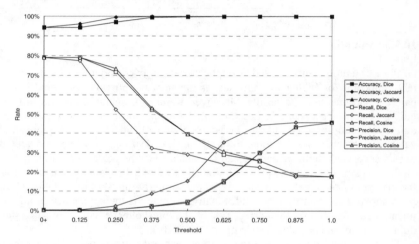

Fig. 10.2 Performance of the similarity measures

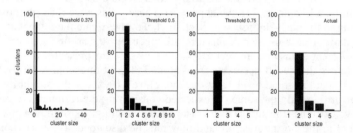

Fig. 10.3 Requirements cluster distribution using the cosine measure on the *Summary* and the *Description* fields. The three leftmost graphs show the number of clusters of different sizes for various thresholds compared to the actual cluster distribution on the right

The cluster distributions at three different threshold levels are shown in Fig. 10.3. The last graph shows the cluster distribution for the actual duplicates found by the experts. The graphs show that with increasing threshold the number of clusters of larger size decreases. For example, at threshold level 0.375 there is one very large cluster involving 42 different requirements.

Noteworthy is that the presented evaluation is made on a snapshot of a reasonably large set of requirements. However, at Telelogic, the requirements arrive continuously, a few at a time. The similarity analysis can thus be made incrementally on a smaller set of requirements, avoiding the need for interpreting the results of similarity analysis of the entire set of requirements at one time. The cluster distribution shows that if we analyze one randomly selected requirements from the database (which may represent a newly submitted requirement), the worst case would be that the analyzer suggests a cluster of 42 requirements to be identical. This is thus the maximum number of requirements the requirement analyst must handle simultaneously. As the number may seem too high for the lower thresholds, it is reasonable to suggest that such large clusters may be ignored as they are probably irrelevant.

Table 10.3 Expert reanalysis of requirements presumed to be incorrectly classified

Relationship	Count
Duplicates	28
Similar	13
Related	8
Part of	5
Not related	21

Another interesting issue is whether the automated analyzer reveals duplicate pairs that the experts missed. To explore this we let an expert analyze 75 requirements that were suggested as duplicates using the Cosine measure at threshold level 0.75, but had not been assigned as duplicates by the experts. Table 10.3 shows the surprising result from the analysis. It turned out that 37% of the suggested duplicate pairs had been actually missed by the experts! For that threshold level, recall would increase from 25% to 40%, precision from 30% to 56% and the already high accuracy would become even higher. The analyst did not regard two requirements in a pair as duplicate or similar if they were to be implemented in different parts of the software. The table also shows the additional relationships identified, which thus imply that only 21 of the 75 pairs identified would be completely wrong. These 21 erroneously identified pairs should be put in relation to the several thousand potential suggestions. In an industrial setting it is better to have a few extra suggestions that may be discarded rather than missing any actual duplicates. Stated differently, it is (to a certain extent) of greater interest to increase recall at the expense of precision.

10.6 Case 2: Linking Customer Wishes to Product Requirements

Baan, now part of SSA Global, develops large complex applications aimed for enterprise resource planning, customer relationship management, supply chain management, product lifecycle management, and business intelligence. Continuously, new customer wishes, called *Market Requirements* (MR), and product requirements, called *Business Requirements* (BR), are inserted into the *Baan Requirements Database* (BRD) upon their receipt or creation, respectively. Periodically, the company management decides to start a new release project, and a number of BRs are selected for implementation –preferably, in such a way as to maximize the number of MRs that are satisfied in the new release, compatibly with time and budget constraints. Customers receive informative messages when a MR is accepted in the BRD and when it is satisfied in an upcoming release. Thus, establishing complete and correct MRs-BRs links is paramount to maintaining good relationships with the customers.

MRs and BRs that cover the same underlying functional requirement are linked to each other in a many-to-many relationship; a single MR can span several BRs (e.g., to split a huge work package into manageable pieces), and a BR can satisfy several MRs (e.g., when several customers are requesting the same functionality). MRs are copied into the BRD as-is, i.e. without altering the original text as specified by the customer. Linking MRs to BRs and the other way round is a daily routine for product managers. Each time a new MR is inserted into the BRD, it is first checked by searching whether there are one or more BRs that already include the specified functionality. This process is very time consuming, as the current tool only allows text search in the requirement description. Similarly, when a new BR is created, the corresponding MRs need to be found in the BRD, since the objective is to satisfy as many customers as possible. Finding all MRs that are covered by the BR at hand is virtually impossible, because of the large number of MRs and due to the time-consuming understanding of MR content. Advanced automated assistance to the MRs-BRs linking can improve the quality of the requirements management process and save costly man-hours of the product managers.

Given the favorable lexical features of the requirements, that use mostly terms from a restricted domain, we propose a tool-supported linking process that integrates well with the existing practices and technologies, while at the same time reducing the cost and improving on the effectiveness of manual linking. Based on the similarity calculations, a tool can suggest which requirements already in the BRD could be linked to an incoming MR or BR. The human expert can then decide whether to accept these suggestions or not, or can decide to resort to keywords-based search (as in the original process) for further options. Our expectation is that relevant suggestions will be provided faster this way than if a human would have to select several different search terms and, for each of these, search through the database.

10.6.1 Case Study Requirements Data

The total number of business and market requirements elicited at Baan between 1996 and 2002 and manually linked to each other is found in Table 10.4. Overall, the analyzed corpus contained almost one million words, with MRs contributing approximately two thirds of the total, and BRs constituting the remaining third. Representative examples of each of the two kinds of requirements may be found in [39].

Table 10.4 Requirements elicited and linked at Baan, 1996

Year	Business Requirements		Market Requirements	
	Elicited	Linked	Elicited	Linked
1996	0	0	183	113
1997	5	4	683	262
1998	275	169	1,579	388
1999	709	261	2,028	502
2000	669	167	1,270	397
2001	1,000	153	864	224
2002	1,121	340	1,695	514
Total	**3,779**	**1,094**	**8,302**	**2,400**

In current practice, the association between the two presented requirements would be found by emanating from the submitted BR in Table 10.9, searching for the term *container* among the MRs. Such a search returns 37 hits if searching only in the label field and 318 hits if searching the description field. Experts would then have to browse through all the MRs returned by the search. However, historical data shows that only five MRs were actually linked by the experts (all five were submitted earlier than the BR).

Of these, four could be found by searching for *container*, but the last relevant MR was not returned by the search, and required a new search (for example, on *statistics*, which however adds another 40 hits on the label field and 99 hits on the description field to the already daunting set of candidates to examine). Based on this and similar cases, we estimate that significant time can be saved by replacing the search procedure based on designated keywords with a more sophisticated one based on lexical similarity of the requirements.

A potential hurdle to be overcome is the varying linguistic quality of the text of the requirements. As in Case 1, requirements are often typed in haste, and may contain acronyms, spelling errors, code snippets, colloquial language, etc. We investigated these occurrences for a subset of all terms (those starting with "a"), finding that non-word entities represent around 2–3% of the whole corpus, with spelling errors (the only real threat to lexical matching) only accounting for 0.3%-0.4%. We can therefore assume that the calculation of lexical similarity will not be significantly affected by occasional typing errors in the requirements. The investigation also showed that the two sets of requirements (MRs and BRs) have very similar composition in terms of statistical features. A more detailed comparison can be obtained by considering the two lists of distinct term occurrences, ranked by frequency. The two lists have a 4,660 terms intersection (most of them in the topmost ranking positions); 1,899 terms only occur in BRs, with 8,234 terms only occurring in MRs. Overall, the Spearman rank order correlation coefficient for the two lists is $r_s \cong 0{,}78$, significant at the $p < 0.00003$ level (see [48] and [27] for a discussion on statistics for corpora comparison). The correlation coefficient gives a good indication that a shared lexicon is being used in the two kinds of requirements. This is not surprising, as both MRs and BRs are discussing issues in a restricted domain. In turn, this gives support to our assumption that in this context lexical similarity can be a good approximation for semantic similarity.

10.6.2 Evaluation

In order to evaluate how well the approach presented above performs for identifying correct links, we use the links established manually by the various product managers as the "presumably correct" answer. Our goal is to find out how many of these links the automatic approach can retrieve.

In our industrial setting, we can expect user interaction to consist in the following steps:

1. A new requirement (MR or BR) is submitted to the BRD.
2. A tool computes the similarity score between the new requirement and the pre-existing ones of the opposite type (i.e., BRs or MRs, respectively), and ranks all the requirements according to the similarity score.
3. The top-ranking n requirements are presented to the user for manual verification and, optionally, for establishing links in the BRD.
4. Optionally, the user can "scroll down" the list, and check the next page of results.

The size of the top list n will thereby represent our similarity threshold. A top list size of 7 ± 2 could be a good compromise [36], as such a size would enable the user to quickly spot one or more correctly related requirements, while taking into account that we are not able to reach 100% recall or precision anyway. In this situation it is not critical that a correct suggestion is presented at position 1 but, of course, the higher the position the better. We could then use the ranked recall measure [26], but as we would like to relate the recall to a threshold (i.e. the top list size) we choose to compute recall for different top list sizes. Recall is in this case the proportion of the target items that a system gets right (i.e., true positives divided by the total number of answers returned) and we use the following adapted procedure to compute it:

1. Compute the complete similarity matrix
2. For each requirement of one type, sort the requirements of the other type by similarity
3. Calculate the overall recall for a top list of size n as the ratio between the number of correct links identified among the top n ones and the total number of correct links

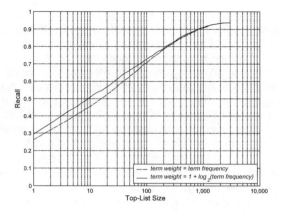

Fig. 10.4 Recall for linking a MR to BRs

The recall curve as a function of the top list size is shown in Fig. 10.4. The figure shows the recall curve for the top lists of suggested BRs for each MR. The dashed line represents the recall curve for calculating the similarity using just the *term frequency* as weight; the solid line represents the recall curve using $1+\log_2(\textit{term frequency})$, which provides slightly better recall.

The figure reveals that we only reach a maximum recall of approximately 94% (though with an unreasonable top list of 3,000 requirements). This is due to 204 requirements that have been linked manually but have no terms in common at all. The 204 links are particularly interesting to look at, as they represent cases where our assumption about the validity of lexical similarity as an approximation of semantic similarity does not hold. In particular, we found that:

- The links comprised 101 BRs and 158 MRs.
- The majority of the requirements were sparingly described, consisting of just a single line of text. In some cases there was no description at all. This is not necessarily wrong in the Baan RM process perspective (an empty BR is allowed to be created and directly linked to an MR). These special cases do, however, affect the results negatively.
- Some requirements were completely written in languages other than English, while the requirements they were linked to were written in English. This should not be allowed without an additional English description, and of course makes automatic matching practically infeasible.
- Some of the linked BRs and MRs seemed to us to describe completely different things. They could have been erroneously linked, or perhaps be related in a way that escaped our understanding. For a more thorough analysis of these cases further work would be required, which is beyond the scope of this analysis.

On the positive side, Fig. 10.4 shows that, for a very reasonable top list size of 10, we reach a recall of 51%, which is good considering the pragmatic approach taken and the impact on the saving of time that could be made in industry.

To get an impression of the time that could be saved, we can make a rough estimate based on the statistics presented and on another measure reflecting how many requirements could be completely linked just by browsing a top-10 list. We found that for 690 of the BRs, the recall rate would be 100% using a top list size of 10, i.e. every related MR for each of the BRs would be found within a top-10 list. These 690 BRs are linked to 1,279 MRs, giving an average of 1.85 MRs per BR, but in order not to exaggerate the gain we assume that, in the manual case, one search term would be enough to find all the links for one requirement. Supported by the search hit example in [Sect. 10.6.1], we further assume that a search would return approximately 30 hits. Thus, in the manual setting the average case scenario would be to browse 30 requirements. With a top list size of 10, the worst case scenario with automated support would be to browse 10 requirements. Up to 66% effort could consequently be saved. If we assume that it takes about 15 seconds to read a requirement and either accept or reject it as a link, we find that the overall gain is 57.5 hours.

The critical reader might observe that in a real setting it is not possible to know when to stop perusing the list, as more relevant links could be found by further browsing. The same applies to the manual case: searching for more keywords could yield more links. Nevertheless, the data from our case study show that a similar level of coverage can be reached more efficiently (i.e., with less effort) by applying lexical similarity when compared to keywords search. If so desired, the time saved can be spent in increasing the level of coverage, by examining more candidates, or devoted to other RE activities if the coverage attained is deemed acceptable.

10.7 Case 3: Managing Redundant Customer Requests

Sony Ericsson Mobile Communications AB (SEMC) develops mobile phones for a global market. As such, they must handle requirements from many different sources in the RE process. SEMC's primary customers are the mobile phone operators, who sell the phones to the end user, either directly or through a third party. In order for the operators to acquire knowledge in the technical capabilities of SEMC's phones, so called Requests for Information (RFI) are submitted to SEMC by the operators. Two kinds of RFI's can be identified: *general requests for information* and requests for *statement of compliance* (SoC). SoCs, which are the most common ones, comprise specific requirements and are replied upon using simple standardized statements on whether or not a certain product complies, i.e. whether or not a stated requirement is fulfilled by the product.

The RFI process is depicted in Fig. 10.5. Each year each operator submits a couple of RFIs. The RFIs arrive to the Key Account Managers (KAM), one for each major operator, in different document formats (PDF, Excel, MSWord, etc) and at different times. The main specification technique for the RFI requirements is feature style, i.e. function specification in natural language [30]. The KAM passes the RFI on to a Bid Support Specialist (BSS), who reviews the RFI from a

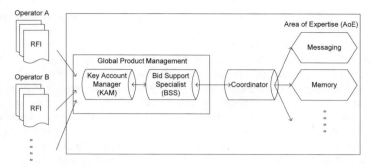

Fig. 10.5 The request for information process at Sony Ericsson

market point of view and decides which products shall be considered when dealing with the RFI. The BSS then passes the documents on to the coordinator, who analyzes the RFI and accompanying instruction and then distributes relevant parts of the RFI to Areas of Expertise (AoE). An AoE consists of a Function Group (FG) and a Technical Work Group (TWG). The TWG works with roadmaps (i.e. future functions) and the FG works with implementation and testing. When the AoEs have stated the compliance to each requirement, they send the RFI reply back to the coordinator. He reviews the answers and sends the replies on to the Bid Support Specialist, who also checks the answers. If the RFI originates from a major operator, a meeting is held with Global Product Management, the coordinator, and experts from the AoE in order to discuss the answers which are to be submitted back to the operator. The RFI reply is then sent back to the operator by the KAM.

The RFIs play a important role in the operator's strategic planning. The RFIs also provide SEMC with vital business intelligence information as the features prioritized by the operators may be used as a guideline when developing future phones. The operators thus have a great deal of influence on the final requirements for a product and a good relationship with the operators, based on timely and correct replies to the RFI's, is therefore of utmost concern.

The efficiency of the RFI process, in which requirement are analyzed and checked against product features, is however severely impeded. The AoE are concerned with their primary assignment in development and testing and have trouble finding the time required to analyze the RFIs. Furthermore, they get particularly frustrated as they have to state the compliance to the same or very similar requirements over and over again. Large parts of new versions of RFIs arriving from the same operator are typically the same as previous versions. Unfortunately, the revision history of the operators requirements cannot be trusted as there have been cases where requirement IDs have been reused and where requirements have been changed without indication. Current requirements management tools give no automated assistance in merging thousands of requirements. Furthermore, it is often the case that the same and very similar requirements occur in the RFIs from different operators. Consequently, there is much unnecessary redundant work required by the AoE.

As the RFIs are written in natural language, we have investigated the possibility of providing automated support to the RFI process using linguistic engineering techniques in order to find similar and related requirements. When RFIs arrive they are converted into a standardized format, where atomic requirements may be identified using unique identifiers. Of course, there is a desire to get the operators to use a standardized format when submitting their RFIs. The manual conversion step could then be removed and more time could be saved –which is of mutual interest for the operators. The standardized RFI is matched against a database of previous RFIs, which have been analyzed for compliance. For each requirement in the RFI, matches are provided based on a similarity measure. The KAM or the Bid Support Specialist may then mark the new RFI requirements as duplicate or similar, or not at all. The RFIs may then be passed on to the AoEs as before, but this time the AoEs only have to check those that are marked as similar or not marked at all. The hypothesis is that it is quicker to judge how similar two requirements are, than to reanalyze each for compliance. Additional benefits are automatically provided through this process:

- All business intelligence is gathered in one place.
- Similarities between different operator requirements may be identified and maintained.
- Contradictions between different operators requirements may be identified more easily.

At the time of writing, a central repository has been put in place comprising approximately 11,000 previously collected requirements. The goal is now to give support in the RFI process as explained above. Furthermore, it has been suggested that the similarity measuring techniques are used to clean the repository by identifying duplicates as described in Case 1.

10.7.1 Evaluation

The technique of using lexical similarity for matching incoming requirements to those already in the repository is currently undergoing further investigations. A support tool, based on our prototype presented in [39] is being developed. The decision to go further was based on an initial pre-study, which is presented here.

At the time of this evaluation, the envisioned repository was unfortunately not yet in place. This put constraints on the number of requirements that could be used in the evaluations. Furthermore, due to the resource constraints at SEMC, there was no possibility to do a full experimentation with experts. SEMC could not allow the AoE to perform the same compliance check twice on the same set of requirements. Instead, indication on potential time to be saved using the proposed approach was made by comparing the work and performance of experts and non-experts and let the expert's judgment decide if the approach is worthwhile. For the case where requirement only were checked for similarity, an expert performed the

Table 10.5 Evaluation results from Sony Ericsson

Run	RFI	# reqs.	Manual (h)	# identical requirements	Semi-automatic (h)
1	A rev. 2	434	AoE: 20	175 (40%)	Non-expert: 8
	A rev. 1	242			
2	B rev. 2	63	Expert: 3		Expert: 2
	A rev. 2	434			

compliance check both manually and with automated supported, below referred to as the *semi-automatic approach,* in which a simple software script was used to calculate similarity between requirements sets and suggest, for each requirement in one set, the five most similar in the other set. The evaluation results are shown in Table 10.5 and discussed in the following.

Run 1. Two revisions of requirements from Operator A were selected to see to what extent the approach could save time by supporting an early process of sifting out similar requirements in order to reduce the redundant work currently required by the AoE. Revision 1 comprised 242 requirements that previously had been checked for compliance. Revision 2 comprised 434 requirements and was sent to an AoE for compliance check by experts. They were thus checking compliance on all requirements in Revision 2 (the revision history from the operator could not be relied upon). The non-expert used the semi-automatic approach and was within 8 hours able to identify that, compared to revision 1, 209 requirements were new, 50 were changed, and 175 were identical. Only 259 requirements would thus have required attention by the AoE. However, the AoE estimated that 65% of the requirements were identical or very similar to revision 1, implying that the KAM and BSS would likely only send 152 requirements to the AoE for compliance check. Assuming that experts within 8 hours (but likely quicker) would find 282 requirements to be already checked according to revision 1 and thus forward the remaining 152 requirements for compliance check, 5 hours could be saved (i.e. $20-(8+(152*20/434))$ h).

Run 2. Two revisions from two different operators were selected to see how the approach may support the experts to sift out requirements that had already been checked for compliance. Furthermore, the requirements were chosen to see how the approach performs on requirements originating from different sources and which are thus expected to be stated differently. In this case, an expert made both a fully manual comparison between the two requirements sets and a comparison supported by the semi-automatic approach. The evaluation suggests a 33% increase in performance, but as a learning effect is expected the exact figure should not be taken too seriously. However, a discussion with the expert revealed that the semi-automatic approach did give relevant support to be valuable in the process.

Given the full picture from the evaluation, knowledge in the requirements, and an understanding of the non-expert's lacking domain knowledge, it was concluded that it was worthwhile to proceed with further studies, which are now in progress. The lack of a streamlined, user-friendly support tool was identified as a performance killer when using the semi-automatic approach. The next logical step is thus the development of a tool that interactively supports the initial check for similar requirements. It has been estimated that 20% of the time spent on checking the products' compliance to the RFIs may be saved. Even a lower expectation motivates further investigations and improvements.

10.8 Conclusions

An increasing number of market- and technology-driven companies realize that requirements are better managed continuously, and therefore best stored, in larger repositories. Unfortunately, as indicated by the same companies' struggle with their requirements repositories, it seems that pure information management challenges are becoming increasingly apparent in large-scale requirements management. This may be an indication that currently available requirements management tools do not meet the demands. The presented approach of calculating similarity between requirements on a lexical level gives reasonably high accuracy, considering its simplicity. Most importantly, it provides added support to the management of large repositories of natural language requirements. The support is not aimed at replacing the current way of working, but to complement it in order to save time. The simplicity of the technique is a deliberate choice. As such, it is robust and requires no or little maintenance or attention, which is important for acceptance in industry. Minor adaptations may be required to align the techniques with the current tools used and with the requirements process. Still, our experience from the three case studies is that the major obstacle is on the implementation level as there are no ready solutions. Until commercial solutions are available, the cost of adopting the technique would correspond to a general in-house development project.

For research purposes, the presented evaluations acts as a baseline to which further research may be compared. Based on the three case studies we suggest an incremental improvement approach. Additional research must be made at a linguistic level, e.g. understanding how requirements are written and communicated, in order to fully understand the limitations and potential of linguistic engineering support. The current state is that twenty-five years of research in corpus linguistics has just recently and very briefly touched the new corpus of software requirements. The technique, as suggested by the three case studies, is relatively easy to implement and could be incorporated by most tool vendors. One vendor, Focal Points AB, already provide a "Find Similar"-functionality based on our earliest results, and our own recent prototype tool, ReqSimile, is freely available and may be adapted to fit the needs (http://reqsimile.sourceforge.net). In addition to the activities presented in the cases, the following other information intensive activities could be supported by the approach:

- Requirements tracing. For several purposes, a requirements traceability matrix should be maintained. A study by Hayes et al. suggests using similarity measuring techniques for easy "after-the-fact" requirements tracing [22].

- Defect tracking. As new defects are reported, a similarity check can help testers to identify if similar defects have been reported earlier, and avoid spending time on duplicate "bug reports".
- Support issues. Call center personnel browse support issues on a daily basis and could be supported by similarity measuring techniques.

Linguistic engineering techniques are widely used in information intensive support systems; for some reason most CASE tools excluded. The techniques are available and may be successfully adapted and further exploited. With the increase in the amount of information written in natural language that large software development companies need to manage, taking advantage of these techniques is definitely worthwhile.

References

1. Boehm BW (1976) Software engineering. IEEE Transactions on Computers 25:1226–1241
2. Boehm BW (1984) Verifying and validating software requirements and design specifications. IEEE Software 1(1): 75–88
3. Brooks FP, Jr. (1995) The mythical man-month: essays on software engineering, Addison-Wesley, Boston
4. Burg JFM (1997) Linguistic instruments in requirements engineering. Ph.D. thesis, Vrije Universiteit, Amsterdam, the Netherlands
5. Carlshamre P, Sandahl K, Lindvall M, Regnell B, Natt och Dag J (2001) An industrial survey of requirements interdependencies in software product release planning. In: Proceedings of the 5th IEEE International Symposium on Requirements Engineering, Los Alamitos pp.84–91
6. Cybulski JL, Reed K (1998) Computer assisted analysis and refinement of informal software requirements documents. In: Proceedings of 1998 Asia-Pacific Software Engineering Conference, Los Alamitos, pp.128–135
7. Cybulski JL, Reed K (1999) Automating requirements refinement with cross-domain requirements classification. In: Proceedings of the 4th Australian Conf on Requirements Engineering. Macquarie University, Sydney, pp 131–145
8. Cyre WR, Thakar A (1997) Generating validation feedback for automatic interpretation of informal requirements. Formal Methods in System Design 10: 73–92
9. Daly EB (1977) Management of software development. IEEE Transactions on Software Engineering 3:229–242
10. Davis AM, Jordan K, Nakajima T (1997) Elements underlying the specification of requirements. Annals of Software Engineering 3: 63–100
11. Fabbrini F, Fusani M, Gervasi V, Gnesi S, Ruggieri S (1998) On linguistic quality of natural language requirements. In: Proceedings of the 4th Workshop on Requirements Engineering: Foundations for Software Quality, Les Presses Universitaires de Namur, Namur, pp 57–62
12. Fabbrini F, Fusani M, Gnesi S, Lami G (2001) The linguistic approach to the natural language requirements quality: benefits of the use of an automatic tool. In: Proceedings of the NASA Goddard Space Flight Center Software Engineering Workshop, Los Alamitos, pp.97–105

13. Fantechi A, Gnesi S, Lami G, Maccari A (2003) Application of linguistic techniques for use case analysis. Requirements Engineering 8: 161–170

14. Fliedl G, Kop C, Mayr HC (2003) From scenarios to KCPM dynamic schemas: aspects of automatic mapping. In: Proceedings of the 8th International Conference on Applications of Natural Language to Information Systems. Bonn, Germany, pp.91–105

15. Francis WN, Kucera H (1982) Frequency analysis of English usage: lexicon and grammar. Houghton Mifflin, Boston

16. Fuchs NE, Schwertel U (2003) Reasoning in Attempto Controlled English. In: Proceedings of the International Workshop on Principles and Practice of Semantic Web Reasoning, Lecture Notes in Computer Science 2901, pp.174–188

17. Garcia Flores JJ (2004) Linguistic processing of natural language requirements: The contextual exploration approach. In: Proceedings of the 10th Anniversary International Workshop on Requirements Engineering: Foundation for Software Quality, Riga, Latvia, Essener Informatik Beiträge, 7-8 June

18. Garigliano R (1995) JNLE editorial. Natural Language Engineering, 1:1–7

19. Gervasi V, Nuseibeh B (2002) Lightweight validation of natural language requirements. Software: Practice & Experience 32: 113–133

20. Gervasi V, Zowghi D (2005) Reasoning about inconsistencies in natural language requirements. ACM Transactions on Software Engineering and Methodology (to appear)

21. Goldin L, Berry DM (1997) AbstFinder, a prototype natural language text abstraction finder for use in requirements elicitation. Automated Software Engineering 4: 375–412

22. Hayes, JF, Dekhtyar A, Sundaram SK, Howard S (2004) Helping analysts trace requirements: an objective look. In: Proceedings of the 12th IEEE International Requirements Engineering Conference, Los Alamitos, pp.249–259

23. Hearst M (1995) TileBars: visualization of term distribution information in full text information access. In: Proceedings of the ACM SIGCHI Conf on Human Factors in Computing Systems, ACM Press, New York, pp.59–66

24. Höst M, Regnell B, Natt och Dag J, Nedstam J, Nyberg C (2001) Exploring bottlenecks in market-driven requirements management processes with discrete event simulation. Systems and Software 59: 323–332

25. Jackson M (1995) Requirements and specifications: a lexicon of software practice, principles and prejudices. Addison-Wesley, New York

26. Jackson P, Moulinier I (2002) Natural language processing for online applications: text retrieval, extraction and categorization. John Benjamins, Amsterdam

27. Kilgariff A (2001) Comparing corpora. Int J Corpus Linguistics 6: 97–133

28. Kristensson P, Magnusson P, Matthing J (2002) Users as a hidden resource for creativity, findings from an experimental study on user involvement. Creativity and Innovation Management 11: 55–61

29. Landauer TK, Foltz PW, Laham D (1998) An introduction to latent semantic analysis. Discourse Processes 25: 259–284

30. Lauesen S (2002) Software requirements: Styles and techniques. Addison-Wesley, UK

31. Macias B, Pulman SG (1993) Natural language processing for requirement specifications. In: Safety Critical Systems, Redmill F, Anderson T (Eds). Chapman and Hall, London, pp.57–89

32. Macias B, Pulman SG (1995) A method for controlling the production of specifications in natural language. The Computer Journal 38: 310–318

33. Manning CD, Schütze H (2001) Foundations of statistical natural language processing. MIT Press, Cambridge

34. Mich L, Franch M, Novi Inverardi P (2004) Market research for requirements analysis using linguistic tools. Requirements Engineering, 9: 40–56

35. Mich L, Garigliano R (2002) NL-OOPS: A requirements analysis tool based on natural language processing. In: Proceedings of the 3rd International Conference on Data Mining. WIT Press, Wessex, pp 321–330

36. Miller GA (1956) The magical number seven, plus or minus two: some limits on our capacity for processing information. The Psychological Review 63: 81–97

37. Minnen G, Carroll J, Pearce D (2001) Applied morphological processing of English. Natural Language Engineering, 7: 207–223

38. Nanduri S, Rugaber S (1996) Requirements validation via automated natural language parsing. Management Information Systems, 12: 9–19

39. Natt och Dag J, Gervasi V, Brinkkemper S, Regnell B (2005) A linguistic engineering approach to large-scale requirements management. IEEE Software 22(1):(to appear)

40. Natt och Dag J, Regnell B, Carlshamre P, Andersson M, Karlsson J (2002) A feasibility study of automated natural language requirements analysis in market-driven development. Requirements Engineering, 7(1): 20-35

41. Osborne MC, MacNish K (1996) Processing natural language software requirements specifications. In: Proceedings of the 2nd International Conference on Requirements Engineering, IEEE CS Press, Los Alamitos, pp.229–236

42. Park S, Kim H, Ko Y, Seo J (2000) Implementation of an efficient requirements-analysis supporting system using similarity measure techniques. Information and Software Technology 42: 429–438

43. Porter MF (1980) An algorithm for suffix stripping. Program, 14: 130–137.

44. Rayson P, Emmet L, Garside R, Sawyer P (2000) The REVERE project: experiments with the application of probabilistic NLP to systems engineering. In: Proceedings of 5th International Conference on Applications of Natural Language to Information Systems, Lecture Notes in Computer Science 1959. Springer-Verlag, Heidelberg, pp.288–300

45. Rolland C, Proix C (1992) A natural language approach for requirements engineering. In: Proceedings of the 4th International Conference on Advanced Information Systems Engineering. Lecture Notes in Computer Science 593, pp.257–277

46. Ryan K (1993) The role of natural language in requirements engineering. In: Proceedings of the IEEE International Symposium on Requirements Engineering. Los Alamitos, pp.240–242

47. Sawyer P, Cosh K (2004) Supporting MEASUR-driven analysis using NLP tools. In: Proceedings of the 10th Anniversary International Workshop on Requirements Engineering: Foundation for Software Quality Riga, Latvia, Essener Informatik Beiträge, 7-8 June

48. Siegel S, Castellan NJ, Jr. (1988) Nonparametric statistics for the behavioral sciences, 2nd edition. McGraw-Hill, Singapore.

49. Sommerville I (2001) Software Engineering, 6th edition, Pearson Education, Harlow

50. Somé S, Dssouli R, Vaucher J (1996) Toward an automation of requirements engineering using scenarios. J Computing and Information, 2: 1110–1132

51. Sutton DC (2000) Linguistic problems with requirements and knowledge elicitation. Requirements Engineering 5: 114–124

52. Wieringa R, Ebert C (2004) RE'03: Practical requirements engineering solutions. IEEE Software 21(2): 16–18

53. Wilson WM, Rosenberg LH, Hyatt LE (1996) Automated quality analysis of natural language requirement specifications. In: Proceedings of the 14th Annual Pacific Northwest Software Quality Conference, Portland, pp.140–151

Author Biography

Johan Natt och Dag is a Licentiate Engineer in Software Engineering at the Department of Communication Systems of Lund University, Sweden. His main interests are in requirements engineering, software product management, software quality, and usability engineering. He received an MSc in Computer Science and Technology from Lund Institute of Technology. He is a member of the ACM and of the Swedish Requirements Engineering Research Network.

Vincenzo Gervasi is a Research Associate at the Dipartimento di Informatica of the University of Pisa, Italy, where he is a member of the Software Engineering group, and Honorary Associate at the Faculty of Information Technology of the University of Technology, Sydney. His main interests are in requirements engineering, natural language processing, specification techniques, and design and evaluation of distributed algorithms. He received his MSc and PhD in Computer Science from the University of Pisa.

11 Understanding Ambiguity in Requirements Engineering

Erik Kamsties

Abstract: This chapter illustrates that ambiguity is a serious problem of natural language requirements documents, which is not limited to simple language problems such as multiple referents of an "it". The results of two empirical studies are presented, which indicate that on one hand ambiguity problems are not solved by formalization during further software development activities, and, on the other hand, it is difficult to detect all ambiguities, even if the reader is aware of all the facets of ambiguity. A combination of the results of both studies indicated that most ambiguities that slip through formalization can be detected by a previous inspection using a tailored reading technique. Based on these results, recommendations are made on how to live with the inevitable ambiguity in the RE process.

Keywords: Natural language requirements, Ambiguity, Disambiguation, Inspection, Formalization, Empirical study.

11.1 Introduction

In industrial requirements engineering (RE), natural language is the most frequently used representation in which to state requirements that are to be met by information technology products or services. Diagrams and other semi-formal representations are often used to supplement informal requirements specifications. Fully formalized requirements specifications are rare. A recent on-line survey indicates that 79% of the requirements documents are written in common natural language, 16% are written in structured natural language, and only 5% are written in a formalized language [20].

The use of natural language to specify requirements has many benefits, although it bears also some problems, as Chap. 10 has argued. A major, well-recognized problem is the inherent ambiguity of natural language. Stakeholders are often not even aware that there is an ambiguity in a requirement, i.e., the ambiguity is unintentional. Each stakeholder gets from reading the requirements an understanding that differs from that of others, without recognizing this difference. Consequently, the software developers design and implement a system that does not behave as intended by the users, but the developers honestly believe they have followed the requirements. Also, components fail to interact properly, because the same requirement was allocated to different components, and the different developers of the components have interpreted the requirement differently.

Ambiguity is also a feature of natural language. It can be intentionally used, e.g., to postpone decisions, because they are considered design decisions. This chapter focuses on unintentional ambiguity.

We distinguish between *linguistic ambiguity* and *software engineering ambiguity*. The former is context independent and can be observed by any reader who has a tone for language. An example, taken from [25], is:

(1) The product shall show the weather for the next 24 hours.

The phrase *for the next twenty-four hours* can be attached to the verb *show* or to the noun *weather*. Thus, the requirement can be interpreted as the product shall show the current weather and continue to do so for the next 24 hours or the product shall show the projected weather for the forthcoming 24 hours.

A software engineering (SE) ambiguity is context dependent and can be observed only by a reader who has knowledge of the particular project's domain. Parnas, Asmis, and Madey give an example of such an ambiguity in a requirement that happens to be about a continually varying water level in a tank [22]:

(2) Shut off the pumps if the water level remains above 100 meters for more than 4 seconds.

The authors claim that this type of ambiguity is very common in informal requirements documents. One can find four interpretations: Shut off the pumps if the *mean/median/root mean square/minimum* water level over the past 4 seconds was above 100 meters. However, the software engineers did not notice this ambiguity and quietly assumed the fourth interpretation. Unfortunately, under this interpretation, with sizable rapid waves in the tank, the water level can be dangerously high without triggering the shut off. In general, the interpretation of the ambiguity is very much a function of the reader's background. For example, in many other engineering areas, the standard interpretation would be the third.

SE ambiguities are more important than linguistic ones. Although a requirements sentence may be ambiguous because of multiple word senses, syntactic sentence readings, or referenced items, psycho-linguistic experiments show that there is often one preferred sentence reading after semantics and the context are considered [23]. In the requirements documents that we have investigated, SE ambiguities account for the majority of ambiguities, while purely linguistic ambiguities played a less significant role. The requirements document used throughout the studies described in this chapter contains 4 linguistic but 34 SE ambiguities.

This chapter provides a comprehensive analysis of ambiguity in requirements engineering. First, the related work on how to deal with ambiguity in RE is discussed. Then, a definition of linguistic and SE ambiguity is provided to increase awareness for the multi-facetted issues of ambiguity. Next, the results of an empirical study on the effect of unintended ambiguity on further formalization during the RE process are reported. An ambiguity also conveys the intended meaning, i.e., it is only a *potential* defect and the question is: which types of ambiguity really cause problems? Afterwards, a reading technique tailored to ambiguity and empirical results of its application are presented. Finally, we show that formalization accompanied with inspection in the RE process can lead to the conscious resolution of most of the unintended ambiguities. This chapter concludes with recommendations how to deal with ambiguity in the RE process.

11.2 Related Work

The most recommended solution to the ambiguity problem is the use of a formal requirements specification language, such as SCR [11], or a semi-formal requirements specification language, such as UML, rather than natural language. Such a language has a more-or-less well-defined semantics. Thus, the degree of ambiguity in requirements is at least significantly diminished if not eliminated. However, even when such a language is used, there is no escape from natural language as the initial requirements are written in natural language. Even if one directly moves to a formal language, ambiguity may strike when the transition is made. An ambiguous informal requirement ends up becoming an unambiguously right or wrong formal or semi-formal requirement. A misinterpretation can slip through undetected, because the client's domain experts are often not able to read the formal or semi-formal language well enough to detect a meaning different from their experiences or intentions. Finally, it is usually not cost efficient to formalize an entire specification.

An ambiguous requirement is often defined in the RE literature as a requirement that has more than one interpretation. Terms, pronoun references, and certain sentence structures are shown to be sources of ambiguity [25]. Occasionally, the broader RE context behind the written requirements has been recognized as a source of ambiguity [27]. Also, it has been recognized that the RE context can help to disambiguate a requirement and that a certain amount of contextual knowledge is required from the reader; otherwise every requirement appears ambiguous [25, 4].

Several inspection techniques have been proposed for spotting ambiguities. See, for example, references [8, 7, 26]. The most effective approach is to hand requirements to several different stakeholders, to ask each for an interpretation, and to compare these interpretations afterwards. If the interpretations differ, the requirements are ambiguous [8]. This approach is economically feasible only for small sets of requirements. Second, specific checklists have been proposed. A detailed checklist of ambiguous words often used in requirements is provided in reference [7], and a checklist derived from Neuro-Linguistic Programming is provided in reference [26]. These checklists help to find many linguistic ambiguities, but they do not address SE ambiguities. Some other inspection techniques assume that inspectors are able to detect ambiguities just by reading; no guidance is provided on how to find an ambiguity. There is usually one checklist item asking, "is the requirement ambiguous?" The major problem of ambiguity is not being aware of it. Thus, simply asking whether there is an ambiguity is not much help. Ambiguities can be detected also by a Natural Language Processing (NLP) tool, but their use is not without difficulties. First, they sometimes require restricting the syntax of natural language requirements. Second, they sometimes require expert programming to be made able to parse arbitrary text [9]. Third, they tend to raise many more ambiguities than are really perceived by a human.

11.3 A New Definition of Requirements Ambiguity

We define a requirement as *ambiguous if it has multiple interpretations despite the reader's knowledge of the context* [14]. It does not matter whether the author unintentionally introduced the ambiguity, but knows what was meant, or he/she intentionally introduced the ambiguity to include all possible interpretations. The context is important to be taken into account, because a requirements document cannot be expected to be self-contained in a way that an arbitrary naïve reader could understand it.

Based on this definition, we proposed taxonomy of types of ambiguities that appear in requirements [14, 3]. In this section we present the linguistic effects that can make a requirements statement ambiguous, and we classify the SE ambiguities.

11.3.1 Linguistic Ambiguity

Most linguistic ambiguities do not cause trouble, because they can be easily resolved by the surrounding requirements, as it is likely the case in Example (1). Thus, we restrict ourselves to those types of linguistic ambiguity that were not discussed deeply enough in the RE literature.

Polysemy occurs when a word has several related meanings, e.g., *green* (the color green, pleasantly alluring, youthful, vigorous, not ripened, or not matured). In contrast, a word is homonymous when it has unrelated meanings, e.g., *bank* (an establishment for custody, loan, exchange, or issue of money or a rising ground bordering a lake, river, or sea). In the context of the example,

(3) When the user inserts the paper strip, the Tamagotchi is set to its defaults,

the word *Tamagotchi* is used both as the name of a toy, i.e., an electro-mechanical device, as well as a creature simulated by this toy. Thus, Example 3 can mean that the whole toy or just the creature can be set to its defaults. Polysemies are a much larger problem in requirements documents than are homonyms. The meanings of a polysemy are related, i.e., more detailed contextual information is necessary to disambiguate it than, e.g., in the case of *bank*.

Systematic polysemy applies to a class of words. The *volatile–persistent ambiguity*, for instance, arises when a word of a requirement refers to either a volatile or a persistent property of an object. In the requirement,

(4) When the user presses the L- and R-button simultaneously, the alarm is turned off,

the phrase *turned off* can refer to an alarm that is currently sounded by the system or to the general ability of the system to raise alarms.

11.3.2 Software Engineering Ambiguity

SE ambiguities arise from the context that must be considered when considering requirements statement. This context can be subdivided into several domains:

- The *requirements document* of which the considered requirement is part
- The *application domain*, e.g., the organizational environment and the behaviors of external agents
- The *system domain*, e.g., conceptual models of the software systems and their behaviors
- The *development domain*, e.g., conceptual models of the development products and processes

This understanding of context is inspired by the WRSPM (World, Requirements, Specifications, Program, and Machine) model [10] and by the Four-World model [13].

A *requirements document ambiguity* occurs if a requirement allows several interpretations with respect to what is known about other requirements in the requirements document. A single requirement is rarely self-contained. Usually, it has implicit or explicit references to other requirements. That is, the reader must know the related requirements in order to understand a requirement correctly. Requirements document ambiguity can arise from pronoun references, e.g., *it*, and definite noun phrases like the one below. The requirement

(5) The product shall show all roads predicted to freeze.

suffers from requirements-document ambiguity. The definite noun phrase *roads* can refer to more than one set of roads that are specified earlier in the requirements document.

An *application domain ambiguity* occurs if a requirement allows several interpretations with respect to what is known about the application domain. The requirement of Example (2) is an example of such an ambiguity. As discussed above, it is observable only to a person who has application domain knowledge.

A *system domain ambiguity* occurs if a requirement allows several interpretations with respect to what is known about the system domain. The requirement

(6) If the timer expires before receipt of a disconnect indication, the SPM requests transport disconnection with a disconnect request. The timer is cancelled on receipt of a disconnect indication.

is ambiguous. The ambiguity arises from the system domain. It is ambiguous whether or not the second sentence is part of the if-statement in the first sentence. This particular requirement could be disambiguated by the application of common sense; the cancellation of an expired timer probably makes little sense, but the sentence illustrates the issue nicely.

A *development domain ambiguity* occurs if a requirement allows several interpretations with respect to what is known about the development domain.

(7) The doors of the lift never open at a floor unless the lift is stationary at that floor.

It remains open as to whether the statement is a requirement to be implemented in the software or the statement can be assumed as already provided by the hardware. That is, the statement can be interpreted as either indicative or optative [12]. In U.S. requirements documents, the word *shall* is often used to identify requirements, in the optative mood, reserving the word *will* for statements, in the indicative mood, that will be true about the environment in the future. SE ambiguities are context-specific. Requirements for an information system suffer from SE ambiguities different from those of requirements for an embedded system. We developed an approach for systematically identifying the SE ambiguities that are specific to a particular context, which is described in [14, 3, 5]. This approach leads to a context-specific refinement of the above-mentioned ambiguity types.

11.4 Ambiguity in RE Processes

This section discusses the *sources* of ambiguity and the *impact* of ambiguity on the progress of the RE process.

11.4.1 Sources of Ambiguity

Requirements engineering can be understood as a process along three dimensions, specification, agreement, and representation [24]. Initially, requirements are informal, incomplete, and represent personal views. A final requirements specification is formal, complete, and represents a common view. We use this model to discuss sources and impacts of ambiguity.

Ambiguity is a cross-cutting phenomenon, which straddles all three dimensions, specification, agreement, and representation. Ambiguity is typical for the initial phases of the RE process.

The first source of ambiguity is lack of completeness in specification. Incomplete requirements can lead to ambiguity about what is meant [8]. The more complete requirements are the less ambiguous they are. The second source of ambiguity is lack of agreement. Conflicting individual views can result in ambiguity, i.e., the diverging expectations and goals of individuals lead to different interpretations. The third source is representation [8]. Informal requirements are inevitable ambiguous, while formal requirements are significantly less ambiguous, but still leave some room for ambiguity. This kind of ambiguity is caused by weaknesses of the natural language, in particular, in its power to express technical concepts and the lack of proper usage of the language. The focus of this chapter is on ambiguity due to weaknesses in the representation of requirements.

11.4.2 Impacts of Ambiguity

The level of ambiguity decreases when the RE process is making progress. Requirements become more complete, more agreed, and more formal. Thus, the deliberate ambiguities are decreasing, but what is about the unconscious ambiguities? We separate several effects of ambiguities and other defects in the initial requirements on the RE process and the final, formal requirements model:

- *Identified and removed*. The defect was recognized by a specifier and was reported to the customer while *reading* an informal requirement or while *formalizing* an informal requirement. Based on the customer's response, the defect is removed.
- *Self-resolved*. The defect has been removed, but it has not been discussed with the customer, it has been removed by the specifier, e.g., using his or her background knowledge.
- *Forwarded*. The same defect of the informal requirements is included in the requirements model. For instance, an incomplete informal requirement has not been recognized and has become an incomplete statement in the requirements model.
- *Transformed*. A defect in the informal requirements has been *transformed* into another type of defect in the requirements model. For instance, an ambiguous requirement has been misinterpreted and has become an incorrect statement in the requirements model.

We present in the remainder of this section an empirical study about the impact of the unconscious ambiguities on the RE process based on the above classification. This empirical study aimed at answering two research questions about the ambiguities compared to other defects. We restrict ourselves to the representation dimension of the RE process and analyze the effects on the formalization of informal requirements using some kind of semi-formal requirements specification language (RSL):

Are there differences in the numbers of conflicts, incompleteness, and ambiguities:

- That are found during creation of a requirements model?
- That are not found and, thus, are contained in the final requirements model?

In the following we describe the design of the study and the main results.

11.4.3 Design of Formalization Study

We present in this subsection an informal summary of an empirical study, the detailed description of formal hypotheses, experimental design, statistical analysis, and discussion of threats to validity can be found in [17].

The study as described here was part of a larger effort to compare different RSLs [16]. Thus, we used several RSLs, namely Focus, SCR, SDL, OCTOPUS, ROOM, Statemate, and UML. The selection of these languages was driven by the availability of CASE tools, availability of experts for supervising the subjects, and practical relevance of languages. Furthermore, the languages should represent a good balance between emerging object-oriented RSLs, and traditional structural RSLs. All employed CASE tools offer simulation of requirements models or full code generation.

The task was to develop a requirements model for a given set of informal requirements of a consumer electronics product, namely the Tamagotchi toy [1]. We limited the types of defects considered in the study to defects that can be identified without knowledge of the application domain, because we did not expect the subjects to have deep knowledge about the application domain. In particular, we were interested in incompleteness (only those detectable without domain knowledge), conflicts, and ambiguities. For the same reason, we did not consider incorrect, unrealistic, or extraneous requirements.

A requirements document is *incomplete* if information is missing such as a function or a definition of a response to particular input data. A requirement is *ambiguous* if it has several interpretations as discussed before. An ambiguous requirement can be considered as *potentially* deficient, because it conveys also the right meaning. Incompleteness defects and ambiguities can be clearly distinguished by the type of required correction activity. The former require adding information, while the latter just require rephrasing the present information so that a requirement unambiguously conveys its meaning. Two requirements are *inconsistent* if they state facts that cannot both be true, or if they express actions that cannot be carried out at the same time. This type of defect is also called *conflict*.

The empirical study was performed at the University of Kaiserslautern (UKL) and the TU München (TUM).

Hypotheses. We assume that there are no significant differences between the investigated RSLs in spotting defects, because they all address behavioral requirements and provide some state-machine-based language to describe them. Rather, we expect differences between the defect *types*, because a RSL forces the requirements engineer to be precise, i.e., to resolve ambiguities before creating a requirements model. Thus, ambiguities might be spotted during formalization, but nevertheless become unambiguously right or wrong statements in a requirements model. On the other hand, the structure imposed by the RSL on the requirements helps detecting inconsistencies and incompleteness (recall that we limited the considered kinds of incompleteness to those that are detectable without domain knowledge. A requirements model can be inconsistent and incomplete to some degree, even if it is checked by a CASE tool.

There was a difference in the *customer participation* between the sites UKL and TUM. At UKL, the customer was involved from the beginning of the formalization process. At TUM, the customer was involved only at the end of the formalization process, when the final requirements model was evaluated by an interview with the team. This allows us to investigate another hypothesis regarding ambiguities. We expect a significant difference between UKL and TUM in the numbers of removed and transformed ambiguities. Humans are naturally skilled in resolving ambiguity. Thus, the ambiguities that were reported at UKL are those that need clarification. If there is no customer participation, as in the case of TUM, the likeliness of misinterpretations raises. The general fact that customer and user participation can influence the RE process and the quality of its outcome was shown by El Emam et al. in an empirical study [6].

Subjects. Ten computer science students from UKL and nine from TUM participated in the empirical study. All students were enrolled in a joint seminar. The students were from the third year and above and had knowledge of the principles underlying the RSLs such as finite state machines and object-orientation, but no experience with the particular languages or CASE tools.

Design. The students worked together in teams of two or three students. This means that each team performed the same task, the development of a requirements model based on a set of informal requirements, but using a different RSL. Six teams were formed such that there is a one-to-one relation between team and RSL.

Instrumentation. The teams received an informal requirements document of about nine pages. This document described a consumer electronics product, the Tamagotchi toy, which is an event-driven system (note that all selected RSLs are well-suited for specifying event-driven systems). The requirements document had two parts, a problem description of four pages that defines the background of a fictional software development project, and the customer requirements of five pages that describe the desired behavior of the Tamagotchi toy. The customer requirements consist of 42 textual requirements; each requirement has on average two or three sentences. Some requirements were derived from a book describing the Tamagotchi [1], others were reverse engineered from the original toy, and some were invented.

The requirements document contained 57 known defects of which 38 were ambiguities, 13 incompleteness defects, and 6 conflicts. These defects were not seeded after the document was written; instead they were a result of writing. Thereby, we relied on the observation that the first versions of a requirements document contain lots of defects even if they are written carefully [27]. We have identified the defects through an intensive review by several experts. The document may contain more defects. However, the experimenters agreed upon these 57 defects. Only these defects were considered in the data collection.

Data Collection. Data collection was performed in several steps. The teams were required to write a brief report about each issue they encountered in the informal requirements and received a solution. This solution was *not sent* to the other teams. At the end of the seminar, we interviewed each team about its requirements model using the list of 57 known defects in the informal requirements. For each defect, it was checked whether the defect has been removed, forwarded, or transformed.

Preparation. During the preparation phase, the students read material about their RSL and produced a tiny requirements model for a simple event-driven system. Then, each team wrote a one-to-two-page essay about the RSL. At the end of this phase, the students had an opportunity to discuss all the problems they encountered with the RSL or CASE tool with their supervisor. The outcome of this phase was the requirements model and the essay. Based on these two deliverables, the supervisor got an impression of the students' current understanding of the treatment. In case a team's understanding was poor, the team could have discussed the problems with the supervisor. However, this case actually did not occur.

Execution. In the execution phase, the participants developed a requirements model of the Tamagotchi toy. All issues and defects that were detected during the formalization of informal requirements were reported and then answered in such a way that if two teams encountered the same issue or defect, they received the same answer.

11.4.4 Results of Formalization Study

The quantitative results are shown in Table 11.1. The before-mentioned difference in customer participation makes it necessary that we block the analysis of this study with respect to the site (UKL, TUM). To test our hypotheses, we tested whether the reported numbers of ambiguities, incompleteness, and conflicts depart significantly from the expected numbers of those defects (Chi-Square test, $\alpha=0.05$). Based on the numbers of known defects in the requirements document (38 ambiguities, 13 incompleteness defects, and 6 conflicts), the theoretical probabilities of detecting an ambiguity, incompleteness, and conflict were 0.67 (38 ambiguities divided by 57 defects in total), 0.23, and 0.1, respectively. The underlying assumption is that the difficulty of detecting a defect is homogenous for each defect type. We were able to show this assumption [14, pp. 47-48] for the given requirements document. The expected number of defects of a particular type $f_{e(j)}$ is defined as $f_{e(j)} = n \times p_j$, where n is the total number of reported defects and p_j, is the probability of detecting a defect of type j.

Table 11.1 summarizes the observed ("O") and the expected ("E") numbers of identified and removed, self-resolved, forwarded, and transformed defects for each site. Note that the data presented in the table is the average team score, statistical tests were performed on individual team data.

Identified and Removed Defects. The observed numbers of reported incompleteness defects, ambiguities, and conflicts differ significantly from the expected ones. The application of a RSL leads to *higher numbers* of detected incompleteness defects and conflicts and *lower numbers* of detected ambiguities, as one would expect based on the defect numbers in the document. A UKL team reported on average 14% of the known ambiguities, but 39% of the known incompleteness defects. This result is noticeable. It shows that ambiguities are not detected just because the informal requirements are formalized. If the requirements engineer is not aware of an ambiguity while developing a requirements model, then a RSL does not help to detect the ambiguity. On the other hand, a RSL seems to help detect incompleteness defects and conflicts, because they were reported more frequently than expected.

Self-Resolved Defects. We found a significant difference between the numbers of defects that are self-resolved and their expected numbers. On average, a UKL team resolved 57% of the known ambiguities, but it resolved only 16% of the known incompleteness defects without asking the customer. During the final interviews, it became apparent that the teams often did not recognize ambiguities as such. Therefore, we conclude that ambiguities are more often *unconsciously* removed than are other types of defects. Unconscious disambiguation is a serious problem, because implicit assumptions are more likely than in our study to be wrong when the system is more complex.

Table 11.1 Aggregated data and results of chi-square tests

Defect Class	Site	Obs. Exp.	Incompl.	Confl.	Ambig.	Chi-square Test
Identified and Removed Defects	UKL	O	5.0	1.7	5.3	**significant**
		E	2.8	1.2	8.0	
Self-resolved Defects	UKL	O	3.6	1.6	22.0	**significant**
		E	6.3	2.7	18.2	
Removed Defects	TUM	O	7.3	2.3	21.0	Non
		E	7.0	3.1	20.5	significant
Forwarded Defects	UKL	O	2.6	2.3	3.3	**significant**
		E	1.9	0.8	5.5	
	TUM	O	4.0	3.3	3.0	**significant**
		E	2.4	1.0	6.9	
Transformed Defects	UKL	O	1.0	0.3	7.3	**significant**
		E	2.0	0.8	5.8	
	TUM	O	1.6	0.3	14.0	**significant**
		E	3.7	1.6	10.6	

Removed Defects. When a RSL is applied, there is no difference between the numbers of removed incompleteness defects, conflicts, and ambiguities and what one would expect based on the defect numbers in the document. 56% ambiguities and incompleteness defects were removed on average by a TUM team. 72% ambiguities and incompleteness defects were removed on average by a UKL team if identified and self-removed defects are counted together.

Forwarded Defects. The observed numbers of forwarded incompleteness defects, ambiguities, and conflicts both at UKL and at TUM differ significantly from the expected ones. In accordance to our expectation, the application of an RSL leads to *higher numbers* of forwarded incompleteness defects and conflicts and to a *lower number* of forwarded ambiguities, as one would expect based on the defect numbers in the document. On average, a UKL team forwarded only 9% of the known ambiguities, but it forwarded 21% of the known incompleteness defects. In the case of the TUM teams, this difference is even bigger. On average, a TUM team forwarded only 8% of the known ambiguities, but it forwarded 31% of the known incompleteness defects. This result confirms that the applied RSLs significantly reduce the level of ambiguity; however, they do not eliminate ambiguity.

Transformed Defects. The observed numbers of transformed incompleteness defects, ambiguities, and conflicts at UKL and at TUM differ significantly from the expected ones. The application of a RSL leads to more transformed ambiguities and fewer transformed incompleteness defects than one would expect based on the defect numbers in the document. On average, a UKL team (except for the UML team) transformed 20% of the known ambiguities, but it transformed only 4% of the known incompleteness defects. Again, the difference is bigger for the TUM teams. On average, a TUM team transformed 37% of the known ambiguities, but it transformed only 13% of the known incompleteness defects.

Customer Participation. There is a significant difference between the numbers of removed ambiguities at UKL and TUM. The UKL teams removed 72% of the known ambiguities, while the TUM teams removed only 55% as shown in Table 11.2. Consequently, there is also a significant difference between the number of transformed ambiguities at UKL and TUM. The TUM teams resolved twice as many ambiguities, 37%, the wrong way as did the UKL teams. The fact that there are no significant differences between UKL and TUM in the numbers of forwarded ambiguities shows the homogeneity of the two groups. Recall that a forwarded defect is a defect that was not observed. Therefore, the customer participation should not have an effect on the numbers of forwarded ambiguities.

We analyzed the single ambiguities that were removed by the two groups. Each ambiguity that was reported and removed by an UKL team was also recognized and removed by a TUM team. The difference lies in the frequency; more UKL teams were able to remove an ambiguity, because they had access to the customer, than did the TUM teams. Any ambiguity that is removed by one team without a report, can be misinterpreted unconsciously by another team, and can raise a question for a third team. If this question is not answered, the number of transformed ambiguities grows.

Table 11.2 Effect of customer participation

	Removed Ambiguities	Forwarded Ambiguities	Transformed Ambiguities
UKL	27.3 (72%)	3.3	7.2 (20%)
TUM	21.0 (55%)	3.0	14.0 (37%)
Chi-square Test	significant	non-significant	significant

Threats to Validity. The investigated requirements document might not be representative in terms of size, complexity, and numbers of defects. The Tamagotchi system already exists, i.e., the requirements were well understood and the document might expose a different defect profile compared to one describing a completely new system. However, we strongly believe that our results can be generalized to other requirements documents describing well understood systems, as far as ambiguities and incompleteness defects are concerned. The number of conflicts in the Tamagotchi requirements document is too low to draw significant conclusions on them.

Summary of Study. Ambiguities are not detected just because informal requirements are formalized. If not identified, incompleteness defects and conflicts tend to become forwarded, while ambiguities tend to become transformed (i.e., misinterpreted). This behavior of ambiguities is a serious problem, since such a misinterpretation can slip through undetected, because of the customers' reluctance to read requirements written in artificial language. Ambiguities, if noticed, need immediate clarification. Otherwise, the number of misinterpretation rises.

11.5 Detection of Ambiguity in Requirements Inspection

The previous section has illustrated that ambiguity is inevitable and we cannot rely on formalization to surface all ambiguities. Therefore, we need a technique for spotting ambiguities before the formal requirements are developed.

Ambiguities depend on the context, i.e., an effective technique must be tailored towards a particular application domain. We present in this section a reading technique for event-driven systems.

11.5.1 A Scenario-Based Reading Technique for Ambiguity

Reading techniques help an inspector to detect defects in a software artifact, e.g., in a requirements document. Reading is a fundamental technique for achieving quality software [2]. Usually, ad-hoc, checklist-based, and scenario-based reading are distinguished. Ad-hoc reading is not really a technique as it does not provide any instructions for the inspector on how to proceed during defect detection activity. Thus, it is not well-suited for ambiguities, as the reader is often unaware of them and needs some kind of support. Checklist-based reading is effective and frequently used for requirements documents [28].

The previously identified ambiguity types can be mapped easily into a checklist. We recommend creating a separate checklist for ambiguity and putting important types of SE ambiguity into the list. As mentioned before, linguistic ambiguities, except for lexical and referential ambiguity, can usually be resolved by the reader. Table 11.3 shows an ambiguity checklist.

Checklists provide support for spotting ambiguities, but there are a number of different and subtle kinds of ambiguity, not all of which fit on an effective checklist. Therefore, we use scenario-based reading in addition to checklist-based reading. The overall idea of *scenario-based reading* is to provide an inspector with an operational scenario, which requires him or her to first create an abstraction of the product, i.e., the requirements document in our case, and then answer questions based on analyzing the abstraction with a particular emphasis or role that the inspector assumes. For example, the operational scenario requires the inspector to create test cases as an abstraction of the requirements document and a question could be "Do you have all information necessary to develop a test case?" If there is information missing, then the inspector may have detected a defect in the requirements document.

Table 11.3 Checklist for Ambiguity

Checklist Item	Description
Lexical Ambiguity	Does a word in a requirement have several meanings? Check for homonymy and polysemy (a word with similar meanings). Be aware that lexical ambiguity arises in particular from the actual usage of a word in an RE context (i.e., in the requirements document, application domain, or system domain).
Systematic Polysemy	A systematic polysemy applies to a class of words: (1) The object-class ambiguity arises when a word in a requirement can refer either to a class of objects or to just a particular object of the same class. (2) The process-product ambiguity arises when a word can refer either to a process or to a product of the process. (3) The volatile-persistent ambiguity arises when a word refers to either a volatile or a persistent property of an object.
Referential Ambiguity	Can an anaphor in a requirement refer to more than one element introduced earlier in the sentence or in a sentence before? Anaphora are pronouns (e.g., it), definite noun phrases (e.g., the roads), and some forms of ellipses (e.g., *If A... If B ... If not ...*).
Domain Ambiguity	Is the requirement ambiguous with respect to what is known about the application or development domain?

We use in our reading technique the black-box specification from the Box Structure Method by Harlan Mills [21] as abstraction. We have selected this formalism, because of its conceptual simplicity and its lack of states. Most other formalisms for describing event-driven systems have a more complex notation or rely on state machines. However, the identification of useful states is a non-trivial task that takes time; black-box specifications allow postponing the identification of states.

A black-box specification is a completely external view of a system; the behavior of the system is described by assigning a response to every possible stimulus history. Informally, one can think of a black box as a mechanism which accepts a sequence of stimuli and, for each stimulus accepted, issues a response [21]. For any history of stimuli, the next response, that is, the response to the most recent stimulus, is the value of the black-box function. The function represented using a table; the skeleton of this table is shown in Table 11.4.

Table 11.4 Black-box table

Tag	Stimulus	Response	Condition	Trace
	s_n	r	$f(s_1, s_2, ...,s_{n-1})$	
T7	L-Button and R-Button pressed	/BuzzerEnabled = no	menu=deselected, BuzzerEnabled = yes	R2,R3

Table 11.5 Scenario for spotting ambiguities

Black-Box Table Scenario
Create a black-box table for the requirements document by using the provided form. The goal is to detect ambiguities in the requirements. Follow the procedure below to create the black-box table and answer the provided questions to detect ambiguities.
Step 1: Create Black-Box Table   For each requirement, create one or more transitions. Introduce variables to capture state data when necessary. For each transition, record the stimulus, response, and condition in the form. Use previously identified stimuli and responses as much as possible.   **Questions:**   *Stimulus*: Can a phrase in a requirement be interpreted as a stimulus in several ways? This can happen when: − The phrase describes a period of time, not an instant.   − The quantifiers, negations, or logical connectives (i.e., *and, or*) are used to describe a complex logical condition within a stimulus.   − The stimulus is described relative to another stimulus, by using words such as *after* and *before*, and more than one stimulus is referenced.   − The name of a stimulus is lexically ambiguous and denotes more than one previously introduced stimulus.   *Response*: Can a phrase in a requirement be interpreted as a response in several ways? This can happen when: − A verb phrase describes a response that can be interpreted as an response that is executed (1) once, i.e., it is an action or (2) until the next response, i.e., it is a do-activity.   − The name of a response is lexically ambiguous and denotes more than one previously introduced response.   *Condition*: Can a phrase in a requirement be interpreted as a historical condition in several ways? This can happen when: − Various historical conditions can be derived due to generality or vagueness.   − The quantifiers, negations, or logical connectives are used to describe a complex historical condition.   − The historical condition ambiguously refers to conditions described in other requirements.
Step 2: Check Black-Box Table   Compare the requirements document with your black-box table. Make sure that you have mapped all requirements to transitions of the black-box table.   **Questions:**   − Are there requirements that you interpret now differently after you have created the black-box table?   − Are there two transitions that are not disjoint? If so, check whether the respective requirements can be interpreted in several ways: (1) Particular properties of the application domain prevent both conditions from becoming true at the same time. (2) The requirements describe non-deterministic behavior, that is, both transitions can occur. (3) In the case that both conditions are true, both responses are desired.

Each row of a black-box table is called a *transition*. The *tag* is a unique ID of a transition to enable forward traceability. The *stimulus* is a particular input to the system. The *response* is the output of the system when this stimulus occurs and the *condition* is true. The condition describes the historical conditions under which the response is generated, i.e., a particular stimulus history. The description of the condition can be simplified to a great extent by referring to other responses [21]. The *trace* is used for backwards traceability; it is the ID of the related informal requirement, from which the transition was derived. Thus for the history of stimuli $s_1, s_2,...,s_n$ giving response r, the row of the table would be as shown in the skeleton; f is some function on the history evaluating to a Boolean value.

To make black-box specification more convenient, we assume that each response concerns a particular object, e.g., an actuator or a variable. A variable can be introduced to capture essential state data, e.g., "BuzzerEnabled" captures whether some buzzer is enabled or disabled. With regard to a response we separate an *action* from a *do-activity*. An action is instantaneous, and a do-activity starts when the stimulus occurs and stops either by itself or when the next response regarding that particular object occurs, whichever comes first. An action is denoted by "/*action name*" and a do-activity by "do/*activity name*".

The scenario for creating a black-box table and the questions to uncover ambiguities are depicted in Table 11.5. The questions were derived from ambiguity that appears in event-driven systems. How to systematically derive these ambiguity types is shown in [14, 15]. We call the combination of scenario- and checklist-based reading *extended scenario-based reading* (ESBR). The effectiveness of ESBR is discussed in the following section.

11.5.2 Design and Results of Inspection Study

In this section, we provide descriptive statistics for ESBR introduced in the previous section. We evaluated several alternative reading techniques for spotting ambiguities in a series of controlled experiments; ESBR proved most efficient [14].

The data comes from an experiment that was part of the course "Software Engineering I" taught by Prof. Julio Leite in English at the University of Kaiserslautern (UKL) in the winter term 1999/2000. From the students enrolled in this course, 18 applied the ESBR technique. The participants were randomly assigned to 6 teams. Each team consisted of three subjects. Each subject inspected the whole requirements document. The experiment required two lectures of 90 minutes each during the hosting course. The preparation was done in the first lecture. The preparation consisted of a motivational lecture explaining why reviewers should care about ambiguity, an introduction to and a practice run with the ESBR technique. For the practice run, the subjects received all experimental materials which were used later in the experiment, except the requirements document. For training purposes, a small scale requirements document was used. These requirements were inspected by the subjects using ESBR. Problems with ESBR and the ambiguities in the requirements were discussed at the end of the first lecture.

The Tamagotchi requirements document was used also in the inspection experiment, i.e., we are able to compare results between the two studies. The inspection took 90 minutes. The document was new to all subjects. The subjects received a printout of the requirements document, the materials for their reading technique, and a debriefing questionnaire. The participants were told not to report apparent ambiguities. The reviewers were told that they should spend only 45 minutes on the checklist. This was necessary in order to ensure that there was enough time for applying the scenario. These times were communicated to the subjects as a recommendation. We could not force them to stop with the checklist and to start with the scenario when these times expired.

Table 11.6 shows the average numbers of defects of different kinds that were spotted by an individual/team/all reviewers using ESBR. The first interesting experience was that the inspectors spotted defects that were not observed in the previous study. The series of experiments with the reading techniques led to the detection of 27 additional defects; most of them were ambiguities. We were compelled to accept all claims of ambiguity that are not spurious, if there was admittedly more than one interpretation to each of the concerned requirements, although we, the authors, knew the right interpretation. Actually, a team reported on average 14.6 ambiguities. However, in order to keep consistency with the first study we ignore these additional defects in this analysis.

Table 11.6 Results of inspection study

Mean values	False positives	Defects	Ambiguities	Incompleteness	Conflicts
Individual	7.8	7.6	5.1	2.4	0.1
Team (3 participants)	17.2	17.9	12.2	5.5	0.2
18 subjects (# defects)	-	40 (57)	27 (38)	12 (13)	1 (6)

The number of ambiguities reported by a team (12.2 ambiguities) is significantly higher than those spotted while formalizing requirements (5.0) [14]. A team of three reviewers was able to spot 12.2 ambiguities, while a single reviewer detected only 5.1 ambiguities. That is, teams seem to be useful when searching for ambiguities. However, even 18 reviewers were not able to find all 38 ambiguities, but only 27. As opposed to the first study, the reviewers reported false positives although they were told not to do so.

The ESBR technique seems to be useful to identify incompleteness as well, but ineffective to spot conflicts. The reason could be the black-box table used in ESBR, which makes it easy to spot certain types of incompleteness.

11.5.3 Combination of Specification and Inspection Results

The results of the inspection study indicate that we cannot expect to spot all ambiguities in a requirements document with realistic resources. The inspected requirements document contained 38 ambiguities. Given a team of three reviewers that spends a total of 4.5 hours, we can expect 12.2 of these ambiguities to be detected if ESBR is applied. However, there is no need to detect all ambiguities; the formalization study has shown that 72% of the ambiguities were interpreted correctly in the requirements model. Most of the remaining 28% of the ambiguities were misinterpreted.

The question which arises is: can inspection add to the formalization of requirements? That is, are inspection techniques capable of spotting defects that tend to become misinterpreted in requirements models? We cross-compared the data of our two studies to analyze if the inspectors spotted those ambiguities that were actually misinterpreted by the specifiers. For this purpose, we divided the 38 ambiguities contained in the requirements document into two groups. The first group of ambiguities, termed "never misinterpreted", contains those ambiguities that were interpreted correctly by each team of specifiers in the first study. The second group of ambiguities, termed "misinterpretable", contains those ambiguities that were misinterpreted by at least one team of specifiers. For each of the two groups, we determined how many ambiguities were detected on average by an inspection team and how many slipped through. Table 11.7 provides a comparison of results.

Table 11.7 Comparison of formalization and inspection results

Average number of ambiguities	detected by inspection team	not detected by inspection team	Total
correctly interpreted by specifiers ("never misinterpreted" and "misinterpretable"	2.5	24.8	27.3
actually misinterpreted by specifiers ("misinterpretable")	9.7	1.0	10.7
Total	12.2	25.8	38

To answer the above question, those ambiguities are of interest that were misinterpreted by the specifiers, but were detected by the inspectors. On average 28%, i.e., 10.7 ambiguities were not interpreted correctly by at least one team of specifiers. In total, 29 out of the 38 ambiguities in the requirements document were classified "misinterpretable". That is, not all of the misinterpretable ambiguities were really misinterpreted. An inspection team is able to find on average 9.7 ambiguities that are misinterpretable. However, by matter of fact, one cannot say whether these ambiguities detected by ESBR are a true subset of those 10.7 ambiguities that would be misinterpreted otherwise or if some portion belongs to those ambiguities that still would be correctly interpreted. In the table above, we assumed the optimistic case that all of those 9.7 misinterpretable ambiguities would be actually misinterpreted otherwise. Performing an inspection of the requirements document using ESBR before the document is used for developing requirements models, 33% (9.7 out of 29) of the misinterpretable ambiguities could have been detected.

In conclusion, the performance of ESBR when applied by a team of 3 reviewers seems to be sufficient to reach the percentage of ambiguities that are actually misinterpreted. In other words, up to 91% (9.7 out of 10.7) of the ambiguities actually misinterpreted by the specifiers could have been detected by the inspectors.

11.6 How to Live with Ambiguity

The first step to improve an RE process is to avoid unconscious ambiguity by different means.

Increasing the Precision of Natural Language. Glossaries, style guides, sentence patterns, and controlled languages increase the precision and decrease the ambiguity of natural language. A *glossary* or dictionary defines important terms and phrases used in a requirements document. Thus, it helps to avoid lexical ambiguity. It requires considerable effort to create and validate a glossary, but the effort pays off since it can be reused for future projects within the same application domain. A style guide helps an author to avoid ambiguities [7]. *Sentence patterns* have been proposed to give the requirements author support in articulating requirements, e.g., by Rupp and Goetz [26]. We developed patterns for event-driven systems [5]. Another approach to increase the precision of natural language is to use a *controlled language*, which is a precisely defined subset of natural language for use in specific environments. The inherent ambiguity of natural language is reduced through a restricted grammar and a fixed vocabulary.

Providing More Context Information. "Context gives meaning to descriptions by anchoring them in reality" [18]. Examples, comments, rationales, fit criteria, test cases, inverse requirements, and traceability information support the strategy of providing more context information. A *comment* can be used to explain the background of a requirement. A *rationale* describes why a requirement is needed. A *fit criterion* describes a condition that a software product must fulfill in order to satisfy a requirement. Each fit criterion thus provides contextual information and leaves less room for interpretation. A *test case*, a more elaborated form of a fit criterion, describes a possible input and its expected output explicitly. An *inverse requirement* describes functionality that the software product does not perform. Inverse requirements are often misused to express non-functional requirements, e.g., "*the system must not lose user data*", which is actually a reliability requirement. However, in its essence, an inverse requirement rules out possible interpretations of one or more functional requirements. *Traceability information* on the dependencies between requirements, i.e., requirements–requirements traceability, also helps to disambiguate a requirement, if the links help identify closely related requirements that provide enough contextual information.

Setting Up Conventions for Interpretation An example could be *The rules of Boolean logic apply to logical statements in requirements*. The conventions must be clear to both the writer and the reader. Otherwise, misinterpretations may occur.

Tool support is available to spot particular types of ambiguities. A parser-based tool such as CIRCE [9] attempts to parse the subject sentences to identify the component parts. Certainly the existence of more than one parse is a signal of an ambiguity. A pattern-matching tool searches for instances of a given set of particular words, phrases, and even lexical affinities considered ambiguous. For example, NASA has developed a pattern matching tool for checking requirements documents [29]. The LOLITA tool [19] identifies lexical ambiguity (concerning the meanings of a word or phrase) and syntactic ambiguity (concerning grammatical structures of sentences). All tools are able to find linguistic ambiguity, but they are unable to find most SE ambiguities. That is, tools may be used in a first pass, but inspections are inevitable to spot SE ambiguities. Based on the results of the inspection study, we make two recommendations.

Inspection of Informal Requirements Before their Formalization. Since RSLs enforce precision, an ambiguity can become an unambiguously wrong formal requirement, which can slip through undetected, because of the customers' reluctance to read requirements written in artificial language. We recommend the inspection of informal requirements with an emphasis on ambiguities to avoid these problems. Inspections should target on SE ambiguities. The size of the inspection team should be at least two to allow the inspectors to exchange their interpretations.

Participation of Customers and Users during Formalization. The development of requirements models from informal requirements is a task of requirements engineers, not customers or users. Nevertheless, we recommend participation of customers and users *during* the development of these models, not afterwards, in order clarify observed ambiguities as soon as possible.

11.7 Summary and Conclusion

Requirements ambiguity is not limited to simple linguistic ambiguities such as different readings of a sentence due to prepositional phrase ("She hit the man with the suitcase"). This chapter emphasized the role of the *context* in making requirements ambiguous and identified the major domains of the RE context, the requirements document, the application domain, the system domain, and the development domain. The results of an empirical study were presented on the effects of ambiguity on the RE process. Ambiguities are reported less often, but are resolved *unconsciously* more often than other types of defects. This is a serious problem, because the contextual knowledge of customers and software developers usually differ. Thus, implicit assumptions are likely to be wrong when a system is more complex than in our study. Moreover, ambiguities that were not recognized were misinterpreted more often than other types of defects. We conclude that a requirements engineer should not rely on the formalization of informal requirements to assist with spotting ambiguities. Ambiguities cannot be considered potential defects, because they also convey the right meaning, but they are *real defects*. As our study shows, a considerable number of ambiguities tend to become misinterpreted (20% to 37% depending on customer participation). This number is likely to rise if the domain is more complicated than a simple consumer electronics product the Tamagotchi toy. The results motivated us to develop a reading technique for requirements inspections targeting at ambiguity. This technique uses a combination of checklist and scenario-based reading. We presented empirical data indicating that on one hand one cannot expect that all ambiguities are detected with reasonable resources. On the other hand, most ambiguities are interpreted the right way as our first study has shown, i.e., there is no need to find all ambiguities. Our reading technique is capable of finding most of those ambiguities that could be misinterpreted otherwise. Finally, we discussed further techniques to reduce ambiguity and to improve the likeliness of detecting ambiguities.

References

1. Bandai (1997) Das Original Tamagotchi Buch. Tamagotchi & Bandai
2. Basili VR (1997) Evolving and packaging reading technologies. Journal of Systems and Software, 38: 3–12
3. Berry DM, Kamsties E (2003) Ambiguity in requirements specification. In: Perspectives on Software Requirements, Leite J, Doorn J (Eds.) Kluwer Academic Pub., pp.7–44
4. Davis A, Overmyer S, Jordan K, et al. (1993) Identifying and measuring quality in a software requirements specification. In: Proceedings of METRICS'93, Baltimore, USA, pp.141–152
5. Denger C, Berry DM, Kamsties E (2003) Higher quality requirements specifications through natural languages patterns. In: Proceedings of the IEEE International Conference on Software: Science, Technology & Engineering, Herzelia, Israel, pp.80–89
6. El Elmam K, Quintin S, Madhavji NH (1996) User participation in the requirements engineering process: An empirical study, Requirements Engineering Journal, 1(1):4–26
7. Freedman DP, Weinberg GM (1990) Handbook of walkthroughs inspections and technical reviews, Dorset House, New York, NY
8. Gause DC, Weinberg GM (1989) Exploring requirements: Quality before design. Dorset House, New York, NY
9. Gervasi V, Nuseibeh B (2000) Lightweight validation of natural language requirements, In: Proceedings of 4th IEEE International Conference on Requirements Engineering, June 19-23, Schaumburg, USA, pp. 140–148
10. Gunter CA, Gunter EL, Jackson M, Zave P (2000) A reference model for requirements and specifications. IEEE Software; 17(3): 37–43
11. Heitmeyer CL, Jeffords RD, Labaw BG (1996) Automated consistency checking of requirements specifications, ACM Transactions on Software Engineering and Methodology 5(3): 231–261
12. Jackson M, Zave P (1993) Domain descriptions. In: Proceedings of the 1st International Symposium on Requirements Engineering, January 4-6, San Diego, pp. 89–98
13. Jarke M, Rolland C, Sutcliffe A, Dömges R (1999) The NATURE of requirements engineering. Aachen, Germany: Shaker Verlag.
14. Kamsties E (2001): Surfacing ambiguity in natural language requirements, Ph.D. Dissertation, Fachbereich Informatik, Universität Kaiserslautern, Germany
15. Kamsties E, Berry DM, Paech B (2001): Detecting ambiguities in requirements documents using inspections. In: Proceedings of the 1st Workshop on Inspection in Software Engineering (WISE'01), July 23, Paris, France, pp. 68–80
16. Kamsties E, von Knethen A, Philipps J, Schätz B (1999) Eine vergleichende Fallstudie mit CASE-Werkzeugen für formale und semi-formale Beschreibungstechniken, Tagungsband des 9. GI/ITG-Fachgesprächs "Formale Beschreibungstechniken für verteilte Systeme", pp.103–112.

17. Kamsties E, von Knethen A, Philipps J, Schätz B (2004) An empirical investigation of requirements specification languages: Detecting defects while formalizing requirements. In Modelling Methods and Methodologies, Krogstie J, Siau K, Halpin T(Eds.), IDEA Book Group pp.125–147

18. Kovitz B (2002) Ambiguity and what to do about it. In: Proceedings of the 10th International Requirements Engineering Conference (RE'02), Essen, Germany, pp.213

19. Mich L (2001) On the use of ambiguity measures in requirements analysis. In: Proceedings of NLDB'01, June 28-29, Madrid, Spain, pp. 143–152

20. Mich L, Franch M, Novi Inverardi P (2002) Market research for requirements analysis using linguistic tools. Technical Report 66, University of Trento, http://eprints.biblio.unitn.it/view/department/informaticas.html.

21. Mills HD (1988) Stepwise refinement and verification in box-structured systems, IEEE Computer, 21(6): 22–36

22. Parnas DL, Asmis GJK, Madey J (1991) Assessment of safety-critical software in nuclear power plants. Nuclear Safety 32(2): 189–198

23. Poesio AM (1996) Semantic ambiguity and perceived ambiguity. Semantic Ambiguity and Under specification, Cambridge Univ. Press, No 55 in CSLI LN, Cambridge, UK.

24. Pohl K (1993) The three dimensions of requirements engineering. Technical report NATURE - 92-11, Informatik V, RWTH-Aachen, Germany

25. Robertson S, Robertson J (1999) Mastering the requirements process. Addison-Wesley

26. Rupp C, Goetz R (2000) Linguistic methods of requirements engineering (NLP), In: Proceedings of the European Software Process Improvement Conference (EuroSPI), 7-11 November, Copenhagen, Denmark

27. Schneider GM, Martin J Tsai WT (1992) An experimental study of fault detection in user requirements documents. ACM Transactions on Software Engineering and Methodology 1(2): 188–204.

28. Sommerville I, Sawyer P (1997) Requirements engineering – A good practice guide, John Wiley & Sons, UK

29. Wilson WM, Rosenberg LH, Hyatt LE (1997) Automated analysis of requirements specifications. In: Proceedings of International Conference on Software Engineering (IASTED), May 17-23, Boston, USA

Author Biography

Dr. Erik Kamsties is senior research assistant in the Institute for Computer Science and Business Information Systems (ICB) at the University of Duisburg-Essen since 2002. As group leader for software product lines, he is working in research and technology transfer. Prior to that he was leader of the RE competence team at the Fraunhofer Institute for Experimental Software Engineering in Kaiserslautern. He received a Ph.D in computer science from the University of Kaiserslautern and a MS degree (Diploma) in computer science from the Technical University of Berlin, Germany. His research interests include requirements engineering, in particular natural language requirements, object-oriented analysis, software product family engineering, requirements-based testing, and empirical software engineering. Dr. Kamsties is program co-chair of the Requirements Engineering: Foundation of Software Quality workshop series.

12 Decision Support in Requirements Engineering

An Ngo-The and Günther Ruhe

Abstract: Decisions are increasingly understood as the crystallization points of the software development process. Despite the abundance of the requirements engineering (RE) processes, little attention has been given to providing appropriate support for making RE decisions. In this chapter we analyze current research related to RE decision making. We study how and when decisions are made in RE and the underlying methodology. Our focus is not to provide solution approaches for particular decision problems in RE, but to discuss strategies for improving research and practice in the RE decision making process. We have performed an extensive analysis of related research. Our findings show the difficulties in RE decision making and the deficits of current research. We position decision support at the appropriate approach to handle incompleteness and uncertainty of information as is mostly the case in RE. Based on this, we propose an agenda for future research.

Keywords: Requirements engineering process, Requirements engineering decision, Decision making, Decision support, Research analysis, Classification scheme.

12.1 Introduction

As in any management activity, decision making plays a vital role in the value-generation process, being a kind of driving engine within the whole development process. DeGregorio [19], in a recent research at the Software & System Engineering Laboratory of Motorola Labs, has recognized the need to have an integrated approach for strategic decision making, requirement management, and road-mapping processes. According to this analysis [19], the most successful companies in the future will be the ones which leverage their intellectual capital generated by the decision making process and would link this process to the essential supporting information. Their premise would be "Requirements management is not possible without decision management".

In this chapter, we study how and when decisions are made in RE and the underlying methodology. There is a broad range of individual decision problems. However, the focus of this chapter is not to provide solution approaches for particular decision problems in RE but to discuss strategies for improving research and practice in the decision making process. Some of the most important RE decision problems have been addressed in different chapters of this book: requirements elicitation (Chap. 2), requirements prioritization (Chap. 4), requirements negotiation (Chap. 7), and release planning for market driven software products (Chap. 13).

As extensive research is undertaken to improve the RE process, the awareness of the role of decision support in the RE process has emerged. We will argue later in this chapter that requirements decisions are hard because of the uncertainty and incompleteness of the information available. We will provide arguments that any notion of strict optimality is not appropriate in this context. Instead, the whole philosophy of providing substantial support to the decision maker is developed as an approach to qualify the actual (human) decision making.

The importance of decisions in RE is discussed by Evans et al. [21]. The authors emphasize that it is important to recognize requirements as design decisions in order to achieve a fully integrated software system. Regnell et al. [44] further develop this idea with the claim "Requirements mean decisions!" and investigate issues and challenges for both descriptive and prescriptive research. Aurum and Martin [7, 8] point out the similarity between activities involved in organizational decision making and those in the RE process. Aurum and Wohlin [9] describe the fundamental nature of RE activities as a decision making process. They observe that the RE process is rich in complex decision problems ranging from the organization level to the project level. They also examine the integration of classical decision making models (Anthony's organization-oriented model [6], Mintzberg's process-oriented model [38]) into Macaulay's RE process [36]. Ruhe [52] describes the software planning, development and evolution process as a continuous problem-solving and decision making activity.

Despite the increasing awareness, decision support in RE is still in its infancy. More theoretical and empirical research is needed to improve the practice of RE. In this chapter, we address this issue through an analysis of research related to RE decisions. The contribution of this chapter is threefold:

- Understanding and classification of the current research around decisions to be made as part of RE
- Analysis of the deficits and difficulties in this research
- Proposal of an agenda for future research in this field

The chapter is organized as follows. In Sect. 12.2 we present basic concepts of decision problems in RE. In Sect. 12.3 we discuss the relationship between decision making and decision support and its implications for making decisions in RE. In Sect. 12.4, we analyze the literature related to RE decision support. Section 12.5 summarizes and concludes the chapter.

12.2 Basic Concepts

12.2.1 Formulation of Decision Problems

Decision science is a well-established discipline with strong links and interactions to many other disciplines such as economics, operations research, logic, organization theory, psychology and sociology. In this section, we present fundamental concepts and terminology of decision science to the extent necessary for the understanding of the rest of the chapter. There are numerous textbooks devoted to decision science, e.g., Simon [58]. For a deeper discussion of decision making models and their integration into RE process models, we refer to [9].

We start with a simple example of decision problem in RE. For that we assume that after the requirements elicitation phase, the project manager has a list of some hundred requirements. A rough estimation shows that the available resources are not sufficient to implement all of them. The project manager (PM) must take an action (i.e., make a decision) to keep the project on the right track. There are at least four different alternative actions possible: (a) renegotiate the requirements, (b) increase available resources, (c) ignore the fact and (d) abandon the project. The project manager has to evaluate the consequences of each action from different perspectives. Finally, he selects one action based on the consideration of all consequences. Two essential factors in this simple example are: There is a set of alternatives (if only one action is possible, there is nothing to decide) and a set of criteria to evaluate the consequences of each action (otherwise, it is just a random choice, not a decision). In its simplest form, a decision problem can be described by:

- Set $A=\{a_1, a_2, ...\}$ of alternatives (these alternatives are not necessarily described explicitly)
- Set $G = \{g_1, g_2, ...,g_n\}$ of criteria to evaluate each alternative $a \in A$ from different perspectives

Roy and Bouyssou [50] distinguish three main categories of decision problems:

- Selection (P_α): Select one alternative $a* \in A$ or a subset $A* \subset A$
- Triage (P_β): Assign each alternative $a \in A$
  to one of the classes $C_1, C_2, ..., C_k$
- Ranking ($P\gamma$): Arrange all alternatives in A according to an order
  $a_1 \geq a_2 \geq ...$ ($a \geq b$ means "alternative a is at least as good as b")

In the above example, the set of alternatives is $A = \{(a), (b), (c), (d)\}$, the type of the problem is P_α (selection) and the set of criteria can be $G = \{$time-to-market, cost, schedule, risk$\}$. During the decision process, set A can evolve. The PM might choose an action that is not initially listed such as "renegotiate first, then increase resources, only when everything fails, consider between ignore the fact or abandon the project". We can also observe that the description of a decision problem is never complete without its context as this factor strongly affects all the activities of the decision process.

12.2.2 Structured versus Unstructured Decision Problems

Simon [58] defines two categories of decisions: structured and unstructured. The former category refers to decisions that are repetitive with a clearly identified process for reaching a (good) decision. The latter refers to decisions that are novel and the associated process is still ambiguous. A typical example of structured decision problem in the area of finance is to approve or reject a mortgage loan request. A bank receives millions of such requests a year and has a well-established process to handle them. The decision is based on precise information.

A typical example of an unstructured decision is the decision of a software company to continue with the current software development process or adapt a new one. Many companies do not exist long enough to face such a decision. Only few companies face this decision more than once in its lifetime, and finally, no one has a clear idea of how to handle the problem.

Between these two extremes, there are many decision problems having different degrees of structure. In general, this degree depends essentially on our knowledge about the process to handle the problem. In the introductive example, another possible alternative is to select a subset of the requirements that can be implemented within the available resources (requirements selection problem). Since there is no established process that is widely accepted to solve the problem, we consider this as a semi-structured problem. The situation is typical in RE, where most of the important decision problems are not novel, but the associated processes are usually ambiguous due to our limited understanding. For many decisions certain criteria can be identified, but their evaluation and their aggregation are not straightforward. Therefore, in general, researchers agree that the RE process is a semi-structured or unstructured complex decision making process [7].

12.2.3 Strategic, Tactical and Operational Decisions

Anthony [6] identifies three levels of decisions: strategic, tactical and operational. Strategic decisions concern the objectives, the goals of an organization or a product. They have a large scope of impact (all the activities in an organization or a project) and a long-term time horizon (life-cycle of a product, duration of a project). A typical example is defining the product strategy (road-mapping) of a company for the next five years.

Tactical decisions address the planning (resources, time, tasks…) to achieve the goals (decided at the strategic level). They are usually made at the middle level of management with a smaller scope of impact and shorter time horizon. A typical example is "Project planning" and related decisions such as "How much effort should be allocated to each task?" or "How to schedule the tasks?"

Operational decisions are made at the operative level by requirement engineers, developers or testers while performing specific tasks to realize the project according to the plan. Decisions such as "When to stop testing", "How to design modules" or "Which architecture is most appropriate to achieve a target quality" belong to this category.

12.2.4 Requirement-Centric versus Activity-Centric Decision Problems

As an RE process consists of artifacts (requirements) and activities (elicitation, analysis), decision problems in RE can also be seen from two perspectives: requirement-centric and activity-centric. The requirement-centric perspective might be the position taken by a researcher in software engineering looking at the decision theory paradigm. The activity-centric perspective might be the position of a researcher in decision theory looking at the software engineering paradigm. It is of no surprise that the former is dominant in the software engineering community (Evan et al. [21], Regnell et al. [44], Aurum and Wohlin [9]). In this chapter, we choose the activity-centric perspective, believing that it will shed light on different aspects of RE decisions, and enrich and reinforce our understanding. The two perspectives are not conflicting but complementary. Together, they form a comprehensive framework for understanding the problems, contexts and research issues of RE decisions, as will be discussed in the rest of the section.

12.2.5 The Impact of the Context

The requirement-centric perspective identifies the contexts that are directly related to requirements. Regnell et al. [44] identify five possible contexts: (a) customer specific systems, (b) off-the-shelf systems, (c) embedded systems, (d) safety critical systems and (e) data-base centric systems. In customer specific systems, the client is an actual person (or group of people). On the other hand, in off-the-shelf systems, the client is just an abstract entity. This factor strongly affects the way we can support decision making for certain RE problems such as requirements negotiation. While EasyWinWin [12] can be used to help the negotiation with the client in a customer specific system, a more complicated approach must be used to consider the client in an off-the-shelf system.

The activity-centric perspective reveals different contexts that are more specific to the decision process: (f) maturity of the organization, (g) experience of the project manager, (h) availability of information, and (i) geographical distribution of stakeholders. These contexts affect the methodology of the support given to decision making. For a highly mature organization, it is very likely that requirements selection problem is considered more structured (than in other organizations) with a clear guiding procedure to solve it.

12.2.6 A Collection of Requirements Engineering Decision Problems

From the requirement-centric perspective, the identification of decision problems starts with the requirements. Some examples of the most important decisions are (Regnell et al. [44]): scope decisions (which requirement is consistent with the product strategy) and resource decisions (allocation of resources to RE). From the activity-centric perspective, the identification starts with the activities of the software development process and the RE process. Following these activities, as described by Kotonya and Sommerville in [35], we can identify decisions such as selection of RE process and requirements prioritization. Decision problems identified in one perspective are not excluded in the other, but they appear in a different order of importance. In the following, we will mention some typical decision problems in RE at each level.

Strategic decisions are not frequently encountered and are usually unstructured.

- *Identification of business goals*: This decision defines the scope of a product or an organization (client of the product). It is among the most important decisions in RE. Goal-driven RE (Chap. 9) provides a systematic approach in RE based on goals, showing that goals are the foundation of almost all other activities in RE. The results, business goals, are used to guide the elicitation process and to determine if a requirement is relevant. They can also serve as criteria in other problems such as: requirements prioritization, selection, project and release planning.
- *Selection of RE process*: This is another important decision to make at the organization level; still some organizations choose not to face it. This decision is guided by the business goals of the organization (that produces software products). This decision can have many sub-decisions: "Should the organization have an established RE process?", "Should it use an existing process or create its own process?", "Which process (among the existing ones) should it use?", "How should the selected process be adapted to the organization?", "Should the organization change the current process (to face new challenges)?"

Tactical decisions are mainly about planning and usually are semi-structured. Any project manager is likely to face tactical decisions in every project. This means that we have certain knowledge about these problems, but not enough to consider them as structured. For many of these problems, it is not very difficult to identify the set of alternatives. There is a general agreement about the set of criteria. However, there is no widely accepted procedure to evaluate each alternative against each criterion and to aggregate them to reach the final decision.

- *Identification of stakeholders*: The participation of stakeholders might be a key factor for the success of a project. The problem can be formulated as involving one or some of the following decisions: "Should this person be invited as a stakeholder?" (Each candidate is considered separately), "Who are stakeholders?" (All candidates are considered), "What level of participation should we expect from the stakeholders?", "Should we prioritize the stakeholders?".
- *Requirements selection*: The decision here is "Which requirements should be implemented?" This problem can be formulated as a "requirements prioritization problem" (so that the most wanted requirements can be selected), "requirements negotiation problem" (reaching a consensus among stakeholders about which requirements to implement), or simply "requirements selection" (picking out a subset of requirements to be implemented using a special procedure or an optimization procedure).
- *Release Planning*: The release planning problem is a generalization of the selection problem with an extended time horizon (two or more releases). The planning is of high importance, since it materializes long-term vision of the organization. The complexity of the problem is very high.

Operational decisions are frequently encountered and concern specific tasks in the RE process. We expect that they are more structured, less important than decisions at higher levels, therefore easier to handle. However, it is not always the case. Acceptance testing is an operational decision that is both difficult and important. For acceptance testing it is rarely the case that a product is perfect. We have to accept the product with a certain tolerance. We consider the problem to be semi-structured.

12.3 Decision Support versus Decision Making

12.3.1 The Two Schools of Thinking

As pointed out by Glass et al. [25], research in software engineering in general needs more references to other paradigms. While more and more research efforts in software engineering refer to decision theory, most of them concentrate on the application of specific methods to RE decision problems. The Analytical Hierarchy Process AHP [56] is the most widely referred to technique in RE decision making. We argue that given the challenge of RE decision making, the methods and algorithms alone are not enough. We believe that the clear distinction between decision support and decision making is a fundamental point we can learn from decision theory. This section gives only a brief description of the issue in the context of RE.

The main obstacle in decision-driven RE research resides in the desire to solve any problem formally and rigorously. This presumes that each problem can be properly described by a formal model and is "solved" just using this model. It equates decision making with finding the optimal solution. According to Roy [51] and Schärlig [57], such thinking was also once dominant in management science and operations research. The reality was that despite enormous progress in optimization and operational research, many questions in the real world could not be answered in a satisfactory way. In many real situations, insisting on establishing the ideal model and searching for the numerically optimal solution eventually ends in a deadlock. Such problems have been characterized as "wicked problems" by Rittel and Webber [47].

The above arguments are the starting point of the multi-criteria decision aiding (MCDA) school of thinking in decision theory. This school emphasizes studying decision support (or aid) rather than decision making. The following points summarize the main differences between the two schools of thought:

- *Finding "The" optimal decision versus constructing "A" satisfactory decision*: Decision making believes in the existence and relevance of an optimal solution. The mission of decision making is to find it or to help the decision maker to find it. Decision support realizes that such an optimal solution does not exist in many situations. The mission of decision support is to help the decision maker find a satisfactory decision for the actual problem.

- *Descriptive versus explorative model*: Decision making relies on models to describe a reality. The models should only be accepted when they are "good enough" to solve the problem. Decision support accepts that when no amount of effort can produce a realistic and "good enough" model, then models should be used as a means to explore the reality. In decision making we must understand the reality to in order to create the model, while in decision support we use models to understand the reality.
- *Process*: In decision making, once we have a model, we use it to solve the problem and obtain the optimal solution. In decision support, the understanding process continues with the evolution of models until a satisfactory solution is reached. This means that different models can be used iteratively during the decision process.
- *Comparing alternatives*: In decision making, the belief in the existence of the optimal solution means that there must exist a way to compare all alternatives through an evaluation. In decision support, when it is too difficult to compare two alternatives, it is accepted that they cannot be compared.
- *Types of decision problems*: As discussed in the previous point, decision making holds that there must be a way to rank all alternatives in a decision problem. Therefore, there is no need to distinguish three types of decisions (selection, triage and ranking) as mentioned at the beginning of this chapter. This distinction makes sense only for the decision support school of thinking.
- *Structured versus Unstructured*: If a model is proposed to solve a problem, it is assumed that the problem is already structured. If we have enough understanding, then the problem is structured and we can solve it using the decision making approach. When the problem is unstructured, we can still go forward by adopting the decision support approach and expect to find a satisfactory solution instead of the optimal solution.

12.3.2 Decision Making versus Decision Support for Software Release Planning

Coming back to RE decision problems, we see that our situation is not much different from that experienced by management research. This is no surprise since software engineering, particularly RE, has a strong component of management in it. To make this discussion more concrete, let's consider software release planning. A software release is a collection of new and/or changed features that form a new product. Release planning for incremental software development assigns features to releases such that most important technical, resource, risk and budget constraints are met.

In [15], Carlshamre provides an understanding of the release planning problem in which many points confirm the need to adopt the decision support point of view. Besides the analysis of the difficulty of describing the best solution (i.e. the value of a release). In [55] it is argued that neither the subtlety of human judgment nor the rigid strength of computational model alone is able to provide appropriate decision support for the wicked problem of software release planning. The advantage of the human judgment is the ability to handle soft and implicit objectives and constraints. The advantage of a computational model is exactly where human judgment fails: to cover a large portion of the solutions space. The computational complexity of the problem makes it impossible for the decision maker to have a reasonable perception of the set of possible solutions and to evaluate and prioritize different solution alternatives.

The approach of [55] provides a decision support where the advantages of both sides are integrated. This integration of human judgment and a computational model can be understood in two aspects. First, with the strength of a computational model, we can expect solutions of formally defined problems of large size and complexity. Second, decision support needs the inclusion of human judgment to include tacit and subjective components into the process of selecting the most promising solutions. Typically, from this involvement, new questions are raised leading to a better understanding of the project manager about different aspects of the problem.

12.4 Analysis of Research

12.4.1 Classification Scheme

To understand the current situation and the tendencies of research concerning RE decision problems, we have conducted a comprehensive but preliminary analysis of existing research results. For that, we were looking for an appropriate classification scheme. We followed the classification scheme proposed by Zave in [63] proposed for all research in RE. This choice seems reasonable to us since RE decision support is part of RE. The first two dimensions (problem, solution), suggested by [63], give us an overview of the research in RE decision problems: which problems are of concern, and which solutions are proposed. We use an additional dimension to characterize the current tendency in research. By analyzing the literature using this framework and the overview in the previous section, we will try to clarify the following points:

- Decision problems in literature. Which problems receive more attention and which ones are neglected?
- What are the proposed solutions? Which techniques are used?
- How much effort is devoted to descriptive research? The question is important since RE decision making is at its infancy and it is very important to get substantial knowledge (from descriptive research).

At this level we provide a simple scheme. More details will be provided in the analysis. The first dimension of our classification scheme involves describing the problem to be addressed.

- (1A) RE decision in general: We put into this category any paper discussing different aspects of RE decision making, but not any particular decision problem.
- (1B) Specific decision problems: This category includes papers discussing specific decision problems such as identification of stakeholders or requirements negotiation.

The second dimension describes the contribution of papers to the solution of the problem in consideration.

- (2A) Proposed process-oriented solution: Papers in this category propose a method in terms of a process or a guideline to deal with a particular problem. They do not present formal representation, modeling, or algorithmic manipulation.
- (2B) Proposed product-oriented solution: For papers in this category, the particular problem is formulated using a formal model and solved using some algorithm. A process can still be an essential part of the proposed solution, but a formal model or a software tool is the core contribution.
- (2C) Understanding of RE decision: Papers in this category report on the state of practice, research or discussion of a topic related to RE decision.

The third dimension describes the characteristic of research from the perspective of decision theory:

- (3A) Descriptive research: Papers in this category describe how RE decisions are actually made in reality.
- (3B) Prescriptive research: Papers in this category describe how RE decisions should be made.
- (3C) Other research: Papers in this category are neither descriptive nor prescriptive.

12.4.2 Scope

The analysis covers publications from the last five years (from 2000) in the following journals: Requirements Engineering, ACM Transactions on Software Engineering and Methodology, Annals of Software Engineering, Information and Software Technology, International journal of Software Engineering and Knowledge Engineering, IEEE Software, and Empirical Software Engineering; and the following conferences: Software Engineering and Knowledge Engineering (SEKE), Product Focused Software Process Improvement (PROFES), IEEE Requirements Engineering (ICRE). Since RE decision making is not yet an established research topic, we cannot determine the papers using keywords. A paper is selected if it satisfies at least one of the following three criteria:

- Discussing about decision in RE (e.g. decision process in RE).
- A decision question can be identified as the main topic (e.g. how to select requirements to implement).
- An issue that is directly involved in making decisions.

From the reading of the selected papers, we identified other papers discussing decision problems. We go through these new papers using the same criteria to extend the list of papers in consideration.

12.4.3 Classification

We have identified 44 papers and have classified them according to the three dimensions introduced above. The overall distribution of the papers is shown in Table 12.1. The list of papers is presented in Table 12.2.

Table 12.1 Distribution of papers along the three dimensions

	2A Process-oriented			2B Product-oriented			2C General understanding			Total			
	3A	3B	3C	3A	3B	3C	3A	3B	3C	3A	3B	3C	
1A	1	0	0	0	0	0	2	2	4	3	2	4	9
1B	0	10	0	0	16	0	4	3	2	4	29	2	35
Total	1	10	0	0	16	0	6	5	6	7	31	6	44

Table 12.2 List of Papers (1 of 2)

Paper	Contribution	Classification							
		1		2			3		
		A	B	A	B	C	A	B	C
[19]	Enterprise-wide Requirements, Decision Management	X		X			X		
[5]	Politics in RE	X				X	X		
[44]	Decisions in RE	X		X					X
[9]	Decisions in RE	X		X					X
[11]	Political ecology in RE	X		X					X
[24]	Socially mediated process in RE	X		X					X
[43]	Decision making under uncertainty to RE	X		X			X		
[52]	Decision Support in SE	X		X			X		
[61]	Subjectivity in RE decision making	X				X	X		
[59]	Identification of stakeholders		X	X				X	
[2]	Requirements negotiation using set diagrams		X	X				X	
[4]	Requirements elicitation using ethnography analysis		X	X				X	
[7]	Requirements elicitation with Solo Brainstorming		X	X				X	
[8]	Stakeholders participation in requirements elicitation		X	X				X	

Table 12.2 *(cont.)* List of Papers (2 of 2)

Paper	Contribution	Classification					
[40]	Prioritizing features for Agile	X	X			X	
[3]	COTS selection with goal-oriented approach	X	X			X	
[16]	Project planning	X	X			X	
[17]	Comparison of requirements elicitation methods	X	X			X	
[28]	New approach to acceptance test	X	X			X	
[12]	EasyWinWin supporting negotiation	X		X		X	
[13]	EasyWinWin supporting negotiation	X		X		X	
[23]	Quantitative risk support decision making in RE	X		X		X	
[31]	Cost-value trade off in requirements prioritization	X		X		X	
[32]	Cost value trade off in requirements prioritization	X		X		X	
[30]	Requirements negotiation – optimizing cost-value	X		X		X	
[41]	Requirements negotiation – soft approach	X		X		X	
[53]	Requirements negotiation – quantitative WinWin	X		X		X	
[10]	Algorithm of release planning	X			X		X
[14]	Influence diagrams in requirements selection	X		X		X	
[15]	Release planning – Understanding	X			X		X
[20]	Financial approach for release planning	X		X		X	
[1]	Release planning – case study	X		X		X	
[26]	Release planning – EVOLVE method	X		X		X	
[55]	Release planning – EVOLVE* method	X		X		X	
[42]	Release planning support based on effort estimation	X		X		X	
[37]	COTS selection - PORE method	X		X		X	
[54]	COTS selection – COTSIM method – simulation	X		X		X	
[18]	Requirements triage – Case studies – recommendations	X			X	X	
[29]	Requirements negotiation – Visualization issues	X			X		X
[22]	Stakeholders' involvement in RE	X			X	X	
[27]	Selection of requirements elicitation methods	X			X	X	
[33]	Comparison of requirements prioritization methods	X			X		X
[34]	AHP vs Planning Game for requirements prioritization	X			X		X
[45]	Case study – prioritization in market-driven RE	X			X	X	

12.4.4 Main Observations

We went through the selected papers to get an insight of research concerning decision problems in RE and present our observations. Our first four observations concern the first dimension (problem) that is resumed in Table 12.3.

Table 12.3 Decision problems in consideration

Problem	Papers	Total
1A General		
Non technical issues in RE	[5], [11], [24], [61]	4
Decision making in RE	[44], [9], [52	3
Others	[19], [43]	2
1B Specific		
Stakeholder identification	[59], [22], [8]	3
Requirements negotiation	[2], [12], [13], [30], [41], [53], [29]	7
Requirements elicitation	[4], [7]	2
Requirements prioritization	[40], [31], [32], [18], [45]	5
COTS selection	[3], [37], [54]	3
Planning	[16], [23], [14], [15], [20], [1], [26], [53], [42]	9
Comparison of methods	[17], [27], [33], [34]	4
Others	[10], [28]	2

1. The importance and challenge of RE decision making have not yet been widely considered in the RE research community. In all of these journals and conference publications, searches using the two keywords decision and requirements engineering gave very few results. These two keywords do not even appear in many selected papers. Furthermore, despite a large scope review, only 44 papers have been identified as having a significant relationship with decision problems.

2. There is a discrepancy between our claim that RE process is full of decisions (that are supposed to be difficult) and the fact that just a few decision problems are explicitly formulated in the literature. Perhaps because the perception of requirements as decisions is just recent and many decisions are not yet identified as important enough to be addressed as an explicit problem.

3. While papers addressing problems such as: project planning (including release planning), requirements prioritization and requirements negotiation are dominant (21 out of 35 papers addressing specific problems), there is just a modest number of papers related to requirements elicitation [4, 7], and to strategic decisions [17, 27, 33, 34]. The rarity of papers discussing requirements elicitation can be explained by that most of the papers addressing the problem discuss only the process and do not relate to decision making. Even in the two papers selected the role of decision making in RE is recognized but no specific formulation of a decision problem is mentioned. As an example, Andreou [4] promotes an elicitation process that emphasizes the role of non-technical factors such as human, social and organization (HSO). With regard to strategic decisions, the four related papers [17, 27, 33, 34] do not directly address any deci-

sion problems, but only contribute some necessary information. There can be many ways to explain this situation. However, without further research, we cannot give a reliable explanation. It might be because the awareness of decision making in RE is recent; or certain decisions are too easy (the guidance in the process is enough), and others are too difficult (even to formulate).

4. The awareness of the difficulties in RE decision making caused by non-technical issues [5, 11, 24, 61] has emerged with the awareness of the role of decision making in RE. Andriole [5] states that requirements management is indeed a political process. Strigini [61] emphasizes that in many cases, important decisions made in the software industry are subjective. Bergman et al. [11] point out that large-scale system requirements are constructed through a complex decision process in which political ambiguity (non-technical issues) can play a role that is as significant as that of domain complexity (technical issues). Galliers and Swan [24] state that RE should be addressed by an approach that goes beyond technical concerns, a "Socially Mediated Process".

5. This observation is related to the second dimension (proposed solution) which is resumed in Table 4. This table concerns only solutions having model/tool support to solve a decision problem that is explicitly identified, not just a process. From the table, the most popular approach is still optimization (maximizing profit, value, etc.). The application of new techniques such as simulation, artificial intelligence, and decision support systems is still limited.

Table 12.4 Techniques used in decision problems

Paper	Problem	Technique
[2]	Requirements negotiation	Set theory
[12,13]	Requirements negotiation	Group decision making
[30]	Requirements negotiation	Optimization
[41]	Requirements negotiation	Optimization
[53]	Requirements negotiation	Optimization
[14]	Requirements negotiation	Influence Diagram
[40]	Requirements prioritization	Finance
[31,32]	Requirements prioritization	Cost-value trade off
[16]	Planning	Artificial intelligence – Experience Base
[23]	Planning	Risk management
[42]	Planning	Effort based planning
[15]	Planning	Optimization
[20]	Planning	Finance – optimization
[1,26,55]	Planning	Optimization
[54]	COTS selection	Simulation

6. Our sixth observation concerns the third dimension (descriptive/prescriptive). The situation is particularly unbalanced with only seven descriptive papers [5, 18, 19, 22, 27, 45, 61]. DeGregorio [19] describes an enterprise-wide approach to requirements and decision management in industry. Davis [18], Hickey and Davis [27] give practical advice about requirements negotiation and elicitation based on their experience in industry. Andriole [5], Strigini [61] discuss some difficulties concerning socio-political issues in decisions in RE. Fakun and

Greenough [22] describe two industrial experiments to measure the influence of participants in the development of industrial hypermedia applications. Regnell et al. [45] describe an industrial case study on distributed prioritization. However, to some extent, some of these papers [19, 22, 45] are not completely "descriptive" since they are designed to validate a process, a method proposed by the authors. Therefore, they are somewhere between the description of the real world and the prescription of the model/process in consideration. The four other papers are not related to a particular experiment in industry. This analysis shows that the presence of descriptive research in RE decision making is very modest. Given the fact that research in RE decisions is still in its infancy, descriptive research is particularly important. Without a deep understanding of how the practitioners currently handle the problems and why they do what they do (descriptive research), we do not have a solid background to prescribe suitable solutions (prescriptive research) that can be accepted by practitioners. This might be one of the factors widening the gap between researchers and practitioners.

7. The last observation concerns the level of support provided to decision making in RE. We have seen that only a few problems are explicitly formulated as decision problems, of which release planning is perhaps the most important. There are many approaches addressing this problem, each of which represents an understanding from a different angle:

- Carlshamre [15] conducts a very comprehensive study to understand the problem and come to the conclusion that the problem is "wicked". From our point of view, this means unstructured.
- On the other extreme, Denne and Cleland-Huang [20] propose a model using financial data (cost and net present value) to solve the release planning problem by optimizing the return on investment. All we need to do is collect the data, apply the model and get the optimal solution. The fact that a formal model is proposed means that the problem is perceived as structured. At least, it can be true in the context where the method is used (the organization has high maturity and has enough data and knowledge to estimate the cost of development, as well as the cash flow of each marketable feature).
- In between, Conradi et al. [16] and Ruhe and Ngo-The [55] treat the problem as semi-structured. In [16], the proposed approach combining different techniques in artificial intelligence, experience bases, and evolution patterns to support the planning process.

12.5 Conclusion and Future Research

Decisions on software technologies, processes, resources and tools are the crystallization points to achieve quality of software-dependent products and services [19]. The impact of better decisions becomes stronger the earlier in the software life-cycle the decision has to be made. Decisions in software engineering should be based on both explicitly formulated and implicitly known objectives and constraints. The goal of decision support is not to replace human judgment and expertise, but to assist humans in making better decisions.

RE is a decision-driven process impacted by a high degree of uncertainty. Uncertainty can arise from organizations, people, technologies, functionality, time, budget, and resources. Under these circumstances, it does not make sense to look for optimal solutions, but rather to determine reasonable solution alternatives. Any formalized technique in isolation is unlikely to determine meaningful results because only a subset of the reality can be taken into account. Human intelligence provided by domain and/or solution experts is more likely to address hidden factors that are part of human decision making. This is why we have strongly argued in this chapter to follow the software engineering decision support paradigm and to apply it comprehensively in RE.

Based on the comprehensive analysis of research conducted in this chapter, an agenda for future research is proposed:

- Identification and study of further decision problems in the RE process. Researchers and practitioners should work together to identify important decision problems in the RE process.
- Advancing software engineering decision support methodology with emphasis on decisions under uncertainty. There is an existing portfolio of techniques for how to approach uncertainty known from other disciplines such as probability theory, statistics, Bayesian estimation, fuzzy sets and fuzzy logic and rough set theory.
- Development of innovative solution approaches exploiting the specific structure of requirements decision problems. Especially, there is a substantial lack in addressing strategic decision problem properly.
- Validate the impact of better decisions on software processes and products. More and qualified research is needed to determine the added value of following a more systematic way of making decisions.
- Further investigation of the influence of non-technical issues in RE decision making (political, social, technical, organizational and cultural). More research in this direction would be helpful for practitioners to deal with non-technical issues.
- Empirical studies have to be performed more comprehensively and more focused. They are excellent means to provide substantial input for decision support. The decision-prone character of software development and evolution is an excellent orientation for the selection of the most essential topics and questions addressed by empirical investigations.

Acknowledgements

The authors would like to thank the Alberta Informatics Circle of Research Excellence (iCORE) for its financial support of this research. Thanks also to all the reviewers for their valuable comments.

References

1. Amandeep A, Ruhe G, Stanford M (2004) Intelligent support for software release planning. In: Proceedings of PROFES'04, LN on Computer Science, Vol. 3009, 248–262

2. Al-Karaghouli W, Al-Shawi S, Fitzgerald G (2000). Negotiating and understanding information systems requirements: The use of set diagrams. Requirements Engineering 5(2): 93–102

3. Alves C, Finkelstein A (2002). Challenges in COTS decision making: A goal-driven requirements engineering perspective. In: Proceedings of 14th International Conference on Software Engineering and Knowledge Engineering, Ischia, pp.789–794

4. Andreou AS (2003) Promoting software quality through a human, social and organizational requirements elicitation process. Requirements Engineering 8(2): 85–101

5. Andriole S (1998) The politics of requirements management. IEEE Software, Nov-Dec: pp.82–84

6. Anthony RN (1965) Planning and control systems: A framework for analysis. Harvard University, Boston, USA

7. Aurum A, Martin E (1998) Requirements elicitation using solo brainstorming. In: Proceedings of 3rd Australian Conference on Requirements Engineering (ACRE'98), Melbourne, Australia, pp.29–37

8. Aurum A, Martin E (1999) Managing both individual and collective participation in software requirements elicitation process. In: Proceedings of 14th International Symposium on Computer and Information Sciences (ISCIS'99), Kusadasi, Turkey, pp.124–131

9. Aurum A, Wohlin C (2003) The fundamental nature of requirement engineering activities as a decision making process. Information and Software Technology 45(14): 945–954

10. Bagnall AJ, Rayward-Smith VJ, Whittley IM (2001) The next release problem. Information and Software Technology 43(14): 883–890

11. Bergman M, King JL, Lyytinen K (2002) Large-scale requirements analysis revisited: The need for understanding the political ecology of requirements engineering. Requirements Engineering 7(3): 152–171

12. Boehm B, Egyed A, Port D, Shah A, Kwan J, Madachy R (1998) A stakeholder Win-Win approach to software engineering education. Annals of Software Engineering 6: 295–321

13. Boehm B, Grunbacher P, Briggs RD (2001) Developing groupware for requirements negotiation: Lessons learned. IEEE Software, May-Jun pp.46–55

14. Burgess CJ, Dattani I, Hughes G, May JHR, Rees K (2001) Using influence diagrams to aid the management of software change. Requirements Engineering 6(3): 173–182

15. Carlshamre, P (2002) Release planning in market-driven software product development: Provoking an understanding. Requirements Engineering 7(3): 139–15

16. Conradi R, Nguyen MN, Wang AI, Liu C (2000) Planning support to software process evolution. International Journal of Software Engineering and Knowledge Engineering 10: 31–47

17. Coughlan J, Macredie RD (2002) Effective communication in requirements elicitation: A comparison of methodologies. Requirements Engineering 7(2): 47–60

18. Davis AM (2003) The art of requirements triage. IEEE Computer 36(3): 42–49

19. DeGregorio G (1999) Enterprise-wide requirements and decision management. In: Proceedings of 9th International Symposium of the International Council on System Engineering, Brighton

20. Denne M, Cleland-Huang J (2004) The incremental funding method: Data-driven software development. IEEE Software, May-Jun, pp.39–47

21. Evans R, Park S, Alberts H (1997) Decisions not requirements: Decision-centered engineering of computer-based Systems. In: Proceedings of International Conference on Engineering and Computer-Based Systems, pp.435–442

22. Fakun D, Greenough RM (2004) An exploratory study into whether to or not to include users in the development of industrial hypermedia applications. Requirements Engineering 9(1): 57–66

23. Feather MS, Cornford SL (2003) Quantitative risk-based requirements reasoning. Requirements Engineering 8(4): 248–265

24. Galliers RD, Swan JA (2000) There's more to information systems development than structured approaches: Information requirements analysis as a socially mediated process. Requirements Engineering 5(2): 74–82

25. Glass R, Vessay I, Ramesh V (2002) Research in software engineering: An analysis of the literature. Information and Software Technology 44(8): 491–506

26. Greer D, Ruhe G (2003) Software releasing planning: An evolutionary and iterative approach. Information and Software Technology 46(4): 243–253

27. Hickey AM, Davis AM (2003) Elicitation technique selection: How do experts do it? In: Proceedings of 11th IEEE International Conference Requirements Engineering (ICRE'03), pp.169–178

28. Hsia P, Kung D (1997) Software requirements and acceptance testing. Annals of Software Engineering 3: 291–317

29. In H, Roy S (2001) Visualization issues for software requirements negotiation. In: Proceedings of 25th International conference Computer Software and Applications Conference (COMPSAC), pp.10–15

30. Jung HW (1998) Optimizing value and cost in requirements analysis. IEEE Software, Jul-Aug, pp.74–78

31. Karlsson J (1996) Software requirements prioritizing. In: Proceedings 2nd IEEE International Conference Requirements Engineering (ICRE'96), pp.110–116

32. Karlsson J, Ryan K (1997) A cost-value approach for prioritizing requirements. IEEE Software, Sept-Oct, pp.67–74

33. Karlsson J, Wohlin C, Regnell B (1998) An evaluation of methods for prioritizing software requirements. Information and Software Technology 39: 939–947

34. Karlsson L, Berander P, Regnell B, Wohlin C (2004) Requirements prioritization: An experiment on exhaustive pair-wise comparisons versus planning game partitioning. In: Proceedings of EASE 2004, pp.145–154

35. Kotonya G, Sommerville I (1998) Requirements engineering processes and techniques. Wiley, Chichester, UK

36. Macaulay LA (1996) Requirements engineering, Springer Series on Applied Computing, Springer, London, UK

37. Maiden NA, Ncube C (1998) Acquiring COTS software selection requirements. IEEE Software, Mar-Apr, pp.46–56

38. Mintzberg H, Raisinghani D, Theoret A (1976) The structure of unstructured decision process. Administrative Science Quarterly, June, pp.246–275

39. Mumford E (2000) A socio-technical approach to systems design. Requirements Engineering 5 (2): 125–133

40. Nejmeh BA, Thomas I (2002) Business-driven product planning using feature vectors and increments. IEEE Software, Nov-Dec, pp.34–42

41. Ngo-The A, Ruhe G (2003) Requirements negotiation under incompleteness and uncertainty. In: Proceedings of 15th, International Conference on Software Engineering and Knowledge Engineering (SEKE'03), pp.586–593

42. Penny D (2002) An estimation-based management framework for enhancive maintenance in commercial software products. In: Proceedings of International Conference on Software Maintenance, pp.122–130

43. Pomerol JC (1998) Scenario development and practical decision making under uncertainty: Application to requirements engineering. Requirements Engineering 3(3-4): 174–181

44. Regnell B, Paech B, Aurum A, Wohlin C, Dutoit A, Natt och Dag J (2001) Requirements mean decisions! – Research issues for understanding and supporting decision making in requirements engineering. In: Proceedings of First Swedish Conference on Software Engineering Research and Practice (SERP'01), Ronneby, Sweden, pp.49–52

45. Regnell B, Höst M, Natt och Dag J, Beremark P, Hjelm T (2001) An industrial case study on distributed prioritization in market-driven requirements engineering for packaged software. Requirements Engineering 6(1): 51–62

46. Regnell B, Karlsson L, Höst M (2003) An analytical model for requirements selection quality evaluation in product software development. In: Proceedings of 11th IEEE International Conference Requirements Engineering, pp.254–263

47. Rittel H, Webber M (1984) Planning problems are wicked problems. In: Developments in Design Methodology, Cross N (Ed.), Wiley, Chichester, UK, pp.135–144

48. Rolland C, Souveyet C, Moreno M (1995) An approach for defining ways-of-working. Information Systems 20(4): 337–359

49. Rosca D, Greenspan S, Feblowitz M, Wild C (1997) A decision making methodology in support of the business rules lifecycle. In: Proceedings of 3rd IEEE International Symposium on Requirements Engineering, pp.236–246

50. Roy B, Bouyssou D (1993) Aide multicritère à la décision: méthodes et Cas. Economica, Paris, France

51. Roy B (1993) Decision science or decision aid science. European Journal of Operation Research 66(2): 184–203

52. Ruhe G (2003) Software engineering decision support – Methodology and applications. In: Innovations in Decision Support Systems. Advanced Knowledge International, Tonfoni G, Jain L (Eds.) Adelaide, Australia, pp.144–171

53. Ruhe G, Eberlein A, Pfahl D (2002) Quantitative WinWin - A quantitative method for decision support in requirements negotiation. In: Proceedings of 14th International Conference on Software Engineering and Knowledge Engineering, Ischia, Italy, pp.159–166

54. Ruhe G (2003) Intelligent support for selection of COTS products. In: Web, Web-Services, and Database Systems,. Chaudhri A, Jeckle M, Rahm E, Unland R (Eds.). Lecture Notes in Computer Science, Springer, Heidelberg, Germany, 2593: 34–45

55. Ruhe G, Ngo-The A (2004) Hybrid intelligence in software release planning. International Journal of Hybrid Intelligent System, 1: 99–110

56. Saaty T (1980) The analytic hierarchy process: Planning, priority setting, resource Allocation. McGraw-Hill, NY, USA

57. Schärlig A (1996) The case of the vanishing optimum. Journal of Multi-criteria Decision Analysis 5: 160–164

58. Simon HA (1960) The new science of management decisions. Prentice Hall, NJ, USA

59. Sharp H, Finkelstein A, Galal G (1999) Stakeholder identification in the requirements engineering process. In: Proceedings of 10th International Workshop on Database and Expert Systems Application, IEEE Computer Society, pp.387–391

60. Sommerville I, Sawyer P (1997) Requirements engineering: A good practice guide. Wiley, New York, USA

61. Strigini L (1996) Limiting the dangers of intuitive decision making. IEEE Software, Jan, pp.101–103

62. Wild C, Maly K, Zhang C, Roberts C, Rosca D, Taylor T (1994) Software engineering life cycle support – Decision based systems development. In: Proceedings of IEEE Region 10's 9th International Conference on Computer Technology, pp.781–784

63. Zave P (1997) Classification of research efforts in requirements engineering. ACM Computing Surveys 29(4): 315–321

Author Biography

Dr. An Ngo-The got his BSc in Mathematics and Computer Science at the University of Ho-Chi-Minh City, Vietnam in 1985 and his MBA at the French-Vietnamese Center for Management Education (Vietnam) in 1997. He received his DEA (equivalent to MSc) in Decision Support at the laboratory LAMSADE, University Paris Dauphine, France in 1998. He got his PhD in Computer Science (Decision Support in Operational Research) at the laboratory LAMSADE, France thanks to the scholarship of the ESSEC Doctoral Program. Since October, 2002, he is a post-doctorate fellow at the laboratory of Software Engineering Decision Support, University of Calgary, Canada.

Dr. Ruhe is an iCORE Professor holds an Industrial Research Chair in Software Engineering at University of Calgary. He is following an interdisciplinary research approach with main results and publications in the areas of software engineering decision support, software release planning, requirements engineering, COTS selection and project management. He received a doctoral degree in Mathematics with emphasis on Operations Research from Freiberg University, Germany and a doctorate habil.nat. degree from both the Technical University of Leipzig and University of Kaiserslautern, Germany. He got an Alexander von Humboldt research fellowship and was visiting scientist at the IBM Research Center in Heidelberg. From 1996 until 2001 he was deputy director of the Fraunhofer Institute for Experimental Software Engineering. Dr. Ruhe is the author of two books, several book chapters and more than 120 publications. He is a member of the ACM, the IEEE Computer Society and the German Computer Society GI.

13 Market-Driven Requirements Engineering for Software Products

Björn Regnell and Sjaak Brinkkemper

Abstract: An increasing part of software development is devoted to products that are offered to an open market with many customers. Market-driven development imposes special challenges for the requirements engineering process. This chapter provides an overview of the special characteristics of market-driven requirements engineering and describes the most important challenges of the area. Key elements of market-driven requirements engineering processes are presented together with a definition of process quality. Requirements state models and requirements repositories are also described and examples of typical solutions to progress tracking and data management are provided. The difficult problem of release planning is also discussed and an industrial example of a release planning process is given.

Keywords: Market-driven requirements engineering, Product software, Release planning, Requirements selection, Process quality, Process improvement.

13.1 Introduction

An increasing part of the software produced is aimed at being offered to an open marketplace rather than to one specific customer. This type of software development is often called market-driven and refers to the situation where the development costs of a generic product are divided among many buyers on an open market and where the potential profit is rewarded to the producer. Market-driven development is different from customer-specific development (also called bespoke development), where one single customer pays all development costs and the resulting product is specific to the needs and wishes of that one customer. This chapter explains the specific challenges of requirements engineering in a market-driven software development context, with focus on process issues and management concerns. It also describes some of the solutions provided by recent research in the area of Market-Driven Requirements Engineering (MDRE).

This chapter in particular, and MDRE in general, mainly takes the viewpoint of the developing organization and focuses on the producer's requirements engineering process, which is aimed at aligning the product content with the needs of the targeted market segments in order to create a profitable software product. There are a number of basic questions that need to be answered by an organization that is developing software products for an open market:

- *How to design and manage a MDRE process*? In order to maximize profit it is vital to outperform the competing software producers at requirements engineering. The developing organization needs to establish an efficient MDRE process that defines how to work with the classical RE activities, such as elicitation, specification and validation, but in a market driven context.

- *How to design and manage a MDRE repository?* The requirements produced during classical RE are often stored in a document denoted "the specification". In MDRE, it is often more useful to store information in a repository that is dynamically evolving with past and recent data of varying type and level of abstraction, such as: potential and current customer profiles, current and previous release contents, up-to-date status of both candidate requirements and requirements under development.
- *How to make profitable release planning?* A key result of the MDRE process is the strategic decision of what to deliver when. This decision takes into account the strategic assets of the developing organization such as the competence of its engineers, its software architecture investments to date, its current customer base, and combines this with the overall business strategy of the company in order to form a list of adequately detailed requirements that are to be released to the market at a carefully selected point in time.

This chapter has many relations to other chapters of this book. Elicitation (Chap. 2) is a very important part of MDRE but its focus is shifted from acquisition of one particular customer's wishes to a combination of market analysis and generation of new ideas based on opportunities provided by new technology. Specification techniques from Chap. 3 can be utilized, but it is important to realize that in the MDRE situation the set of requirements rapidly may get very large and not all requirements can be specified in detail. Often natural language is the main way of describing the major part of the requirements, and how to deal with large repositories of textual requirements is further discussed in Chapter 10.

Prioritization (Chap. 4) is a key element of decision-making in MDRE, and decision support (Chap. 12) can help in making better re-lease plans. Although each requirement is treated as a separate element of the MDRE process, intricate dependencies among requirements (Chap. 5) make release planning (Sect. 13.5) and impact analysis (Chap. 6) increasingly complex. Requirements-based estimations in general become more uncertain as the overwhelming number or potential dependencies must be excluded from in-depth analysis for practical reasons.

It is recommended that the reader first get a basic knowledge of the state-of-the-art part of the book (in particular Chaps. 2, 4, 5 and 6) before reading this chapter. It is also recommended that Chap. 13 is studied in conjunction with Chaps. 10 and 12, to get a broad view of the challenges and tools within the MDRE area.

The chapter is organized as follows. Sect. 13.2 is devoted to an in-depth description of the context and concepts of MDRE and describes what is particular to the market-driven situation compared to the customer-specific situation. Sect. 13.3 describes the main elements of the MDRE process and discusses various issues in relation to that process, such as process quality and process capacity, and Sect. 13.4 describes MDRE data management and the relation between requirements refinement states and the use of a requirements repository. Section 13.5 provides details of the special nature of elicitation in the MDRE context. Section 13.6 describes road mapping and release planning as a vehicle for profitable products. Finally, Sect. 13.7 concludes the chapter.

13.2 Concepts and Context

This section introduces the MDRE context in more detail. Firstly, a number of concepts are defined in order to establish a basic terminology for different types of variants of MDRE. Secondly, a characterisation of the differences between customer-specific RE and MDRE is given. Finally, a number of important challenges in MDRE are discussed.

13.2.1 Basic Concepts

Market-Driven Requirements Engineering (MDRE) covers the classical RE activities, such as elicitation, specification, and validation, adapted to the market-driven situation, where a software producer develops a product that is offered to an open market with many customers. MDRE also covers the specific activities needed in a market-driven context, such as release management and market analysis. MDRE is often conducted under the pressure of competition from other producers, and as the market and product evolve, the MDRE process enacted by a specific software developing organization also needs to be evolved in order to stay ahead of competition.

Of course, the buyer of a software product also has to do some careful requirements engineering in order to select the right product that matches the specific needs of that buyer. This selection process is out of direct control of the producer and a research area of its own (often called COTS selection, see e.g. [24, 18]) and is out of scope of this chapter. However, it is important for the producer to understand how potential buyers may think in their selection process. This type of information regarding customer priorities is subject to market analysis, as described in Sect. 13.4.

There are a number of variants of software products. Table 13.1 provides a classification and some examples of software products based on two dimensions: (1) the degree of customization and (2) the hardware/software content. The degree of customization is divided into three levels. A product is said to be *generic* if it is intended to be used as-is, out-of-the-box, perhaps with minor configurations that are possible to be done by the end-user. A product is said to be *customized* if the product is intended to be useful after it has been tailored to one specific customer's needs, e.g. through adding modules via an open application interface. A product is said to be *customer specific* if the entire product is developed with one particular customer's wishes in mind.

The hardware/software content is divided into three classes: *pure hardware* denotes products that are fixed through its hardware architecture and contains no software that can make the features of the product flexible; *embedded systems* imply products consisting of both a hardware platform and accompanying embedded software; *pure software* denote a product that is completely comprised of software and sold independently of its hardware platform(s).

In Table 13.1, the types of software products that are market-driven include generic/customized and embedded systems/pure software and have shaded cells. The cells with thick frame are *product software* (pure generic/customized software).

The acronym COTS (Commercial Off-The-Shelf) is sometimes used to denote software product, but we have deliberately not used this term subsequently, as it is overloaded with many meanings, see e.g., [20].

Table 13.1 Examples of variants of hardware and software products

	Pure Hardware	*Embedded Systems (HW+SW)*	*Pure Software*
Generic	Note sticks	Mobile phone	Firewall
Customized	Office furniture	Customized car	Enterprise resource planning systems
Customer-Specific	Portrait painting	Military vehicle	Web Site

The distinction between market-driven and customer-specific development is not strict. For example, it is not uncommon that the developing organisation both sells a generic product to an open market and at the same time sells consultancy hours for customizing the product. Some new and costly parts in product evolution are often developed as a customer-specific feature that is paid by a specific client and later generalized and included in the generic product to get more revenue from the investment. In these cases, the software producer has to deal with both MDRE and bespoke RE, as well as generalisation of custom parts.

There are, of course, other aspects that affect the nature of the MDRE context, not represented in Table 13.1. One additional aspect is the *type of buyer*, which can be divided into enterprise versus consumer. Some products are sold to only one of these segments, whereas some products are sold to both types. MDRE for enterprise products may differ in many respects compared to MDRE for consumer products, e.g. with respect to usability issues, product image, type of marketing channels and number of customer relations that need to be maintained.

The level of *complexity of the user interface* is also a factor that affects the MDRE process. Some products are almost invisible, e.g. an embedded Automatic Braking System in a car that has a simple user interface including a pedal and a lamp, but the software itself is very complex. End-users of systems with complex user interfaces of, for example, desktop applications are probably more likely to give extensive feedback on user interface issues, whereas transparent embedded systems perhaps only render attention by end-users when they do not work as intended. This in-turn may have strong implications on the elicitation process and how to treat software usability in MDRE. (A case study in usability engineering in a market-driven context is presented in [23].)

13.2.2 Characteristics of MDRE

Empirical evidence from a number of case studies and surveys show that MDRE is different from the RE that is conducted in customer-specific projects in many ways [5, 6, 19, 26, 15, 25, 12]. The primary objective of market-driven development is to deliver the right product at the right time, while the bespoke situation often is focused on fulfillment of a contract and compliance to a requirements specification. In the MDRE case, success is determined by sales, market share, product reviews etc., while in the bespoke case, customer satisfaction and user acceptance is directly determining whether the project is a failure or not. The life cycle of a bespoke system is often viewed as divided into development first and then maintenance. There is often one major release, whereas market-driven development often is a long series of releases, and the product is undergoing continuous evolution rather than maintenance.

In MDRE requirements elicitation is often devoted to innovation of new requirements combined with market analysis, whereas customer-specific elicitation is focusing on collecting information regarding one organizations wishes through, e.g., interviews with the known users. In MDRE, some of the features to be released may be confidential and the eventual users unknown, so elicitation cannot always rely on interviews with customers and end-users as the main source of information. Requirements specifications in the MDRE case are often less formal compared to the bespoke case, and natural language text is the dominating way of documenting the results of MDRE. (See also Chap. 15 on elicitation issues in web-based information systems.)

While much effort in bespoke RE is devoted to negotiation and conflict resolution (see Chap. 7), the MDRE case is more focused on prioritization, cost-estimation and release planning, and these activities are all conducted by the developing organization [5]. An example of a case study in market-driven prioritization is available in [28] and Chapter 4 includes an in-depth account of prioritization techniques.

In the bespoke case, validation can be made continuously through the contacts between the customer and the developers, but in the market-driven case validation is often delayed until a late stage in the development, e.g. at expositions during fairs or during beta tests with selected key customers.

Some of the most important characteristics of a typical MDRE context are summarized subsequently.

- The developing organization makes all decisions but also takes all risks.
- There is a continuous flow of requirements throughout the product lifetime.
- The requirements volume is potentially very large and continuously growing.
- A majority of the requirements are informally described.
- The product is evolving continuously and delivered in multiple releases.
- Release planning focuses on time-to-market and return-on-investment.

13.2.3 Challenges in MDRE

In a survey on market-driven requirements engineering [15], a number of challenges were identified. The study results are based on interviews with employees at five different companies of varying size and maturity. The purpose of the study is to provide insights into the special RE challenges in market-driven software development. Subsequently follows a short explanation of the most salient challenges found. For more details see [15].

- *Balancing market pull and technology push.* It is necessary to find a good trade-off between requirements corresponding to perceived user needs and new, inventive ones that may provide a competitive advantage through groundbreaking technology. Finding a good balance between technology-driven and needs-driven requirements may be a delicate challenge.
- *Chasm between marketing and development.* In some companies it can be observed that there is a gap between marketing and developers concerning the views on requirements engineering. Better communication and collaboration between these groups are needed, in order to increase the requirements quality and thereby the quality of the final product.
- *Organizational instability and market turbulence.* Companies without a defined process take a significant risk if key persons leave the organization, since they lack the necessary documentation and structure. In times of downsizing or rapid expansion it is very difficult to install a repeatable process.
- *Simple tools for basic needs.* Some companies requested simple and easy-to-use techniques for basic activities. For these companies it was a challenge to find solutions that are not too complex.
- *Requirements dependencies.* Dependencies among requirements make release planning difficult. Some companies treat dependencies in a basic way by bundling related requirements, but efficient ways of managing at least the most important dependencies are needed. (See further Chap. 5.) Different types of dependencies are reported in the case study by Carlshamre et al. [7].
- *Cost-value-estimation and release planning.* Release planning relies on accurate estimates; underestimation of cost may result in an exceeded deadline while over-estimation of cost may exclude valuable requirements; over- or underestimation of value may result in a product that is badly aligned with actual market needs and thus make the development investment a losing business.
- *Overloaded Requirements Management.* Requirements suggestions from developers and customers are essential. It is a challenge to prevent the requirements repository from being flooded with requirements and how to maintain throughput at times when the number of arriving requirements peak.

The challenges stated above reveal intrinsically difficult problems and it is unlikely that the challenges can be met by a single, simple solution. The key issue for a market-driven company is to continuously improve in managing these challenges in such a way that it stays ahead of competitors.

13.3 The MDRE Process

This section provides a definition of MDRE process quality in terms of decision outcomes in requirements selection. Process capacity and the importance of having a screening function is also discussed.

As described in Sect. 13.1, requirements are continuously generated during the entire lifetime of the product. The software is released in a series of releases as a result of product evolution, where new features are added and existing features are improved according to the advancement of the targeted market. In general, the MDRE process can be seen as a way of synchronizing the work with the continuous flow of candidate requirements and the work with the discrete release events. This synchronisation should enable all parts of development from RE to V&V to work in concert towards the same goals. The main vehicles for communicating these goals are the strategic roadmap together with the release plan of the product.

When designing an MDRE process for a specific company, it is important to realize that there are many situational factors that determine what the best concrete process implementation is. Such factors include: type of development process, type of distribution channels, price and licensing policy, type of market, what is the distinguishing customer value, product complexity, nature of competition, customer behaviour, requirements on product flexibility and adaptability, user interface complexity, predictions on sales, sales channels, etc. It is obvious that the maturity of the developing organization's development process with the competence of the developers, as well as the maturity of the market with customers' knowledge of how to apply technology for their own benefit, are major determining factors of what is most important to get right in the MDRE process. A further discussion on maturity issues in MDRE is provided in [16].

13.3.1 Process Quality

When designing a MDRE process that is adapted to a specific organisation's needs, it may be valuable to define criteria for process success and thus to have a concrete notion of process quality. Of course, the process quality is intimately related to the quality of the artefacts that are produced during the process, and MDRE processes typically generate requirements descriptions in various forms. However, a major process quality issue in MDRE is the quality of decisions that are made about produced artefacts. One way of capturing decision quality is by referring to the ratio of correct requirement selection decisions that are made during the recurring release planning activity, as in the *alfa/beta model* of MDRE selection quality [29], where the decision outcomes are divided into four cases, as described in Table 13.2.

An *alfa requirement* is a requirement that has such a high inherent quality that it ideally should be *selected*. The alfa requirements are thus the "golden grains" among all candidates that the MDRE process should bring forward. "High quality" can, for example, be interpreted as the actual added profit that the requirement is contributing with if included in the product. Correspondingly, *beta requirements* are those that ideally should be *rejected*, as they are of inherently low quality.

Table 13.2 Decision outcomes in requirements selection

		Decision	
		Selected	Rejected
Requirements Quality	alfa	A Correct selection ratio	B Incorrect selection ratio
	beta	C Incorrect selection ratio	D Correct selection ratio

In Table 13.2, the ratios of the different decision outcomes can be used to define metrics that can characterize the product and decision quality [29]. The *product quality* Q_p can be defined as $Q_p=A/(A+C)$, meaning the share of selected (and thus implemented) alfa requirements of the total selected requirements. The *decision quality* Q_d can be defined as $Q_d=(A+D)/(A+B+C+D)$, representing the share of correct decision in relation to the total number of decisions.

The main challenge of the MDRE process is to find and select alfa requirements, while rejecting beta requirements, and thus maximizing A and D while minimizing B and C. However, the problem is that it is not easy to know if a requirement is actually an alfa or a beta requirement, as the cost-benefit trade-off is very difficult. Estimations of both cost and value are inherently error prone and dependent on difficult forecasting of market and technology advancements as well as guesses about actions of competitors. Only post factum, when a product has been out on the market for a longer period, it is possible to say with some degree of certainty if it was a correct decision or not to select or reject a specific requirement [17]. Nevertheless, it is the quality of this uncertain decision-making that determines winners and losers on a software product marketplace.

The elicitation sub process of MDRE (see further Sect. 13.4) has a major impact on the process quality as it influences the fraction of incoming alfa requirements. The better the elicitation process is, the higher the share of alfa requirements, and thus representing an effective elicitation process that make the golden grains come forward. The *golden grain ratio*, defined as the number of issued alfa requirements divided by the total number of issued requirements, can thus be used for characterizing the outcome of the elicitation process.

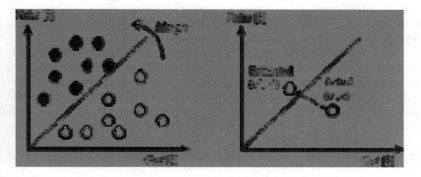

Fig. 13.1(a) Cost-value diagram with alfa-requirements (filled) and beta-requirements (empty)

Fig. 13.1(b) Estimated values are differing from actual values causing wrong selection decision

Figure 13.1 illustrates alfa and beta requirements using a cost-value diagram [13]. In Fig. 13.1 (a) the alfa requirements can be seen as those requirements that have values that are larger than their costs (filled circles in the figure). This means that they are above the *margin* line. If a higher margin of say 20% is requested, then the slope of the margin line is increased to the proportional factor of 1.2, which in turn increases the demand for a requirement to be of alfa type. It should be noted though, that the actual cost and value of a requirement is generally unknown. Furthermore, he decision-making is only based on uncertain estimates, resulting in the fact that beta requirements may end up above the margin line, as illustrated in Fig. 13.1 (b). Here the value is overestimated and the cost is underestimated so that a beta requirement is incorrectly judged to be an alfa requirement.

It should be noted that the value and cost of a requirement is not only depending on the requirement itself, but also on its relation to other requirements. As described in Chap. 5, requirements can have many different types of dependencies between pairs, or more generally among *n*-tuples of requirements, and the value and cost of one requirement may change depending on if other requirements are selected or not [7]. In addition, the value and cost of a requirement may also change over time, so that, e.g., an unanticipated delay in the implementation of a requirement may render another cost-value ratio than was expected at the point in time when the selection decision first was made.

In addition, the concept of "value" can be a complex combination of many different types of contributing values, e.g. value for a certain market segment, value for the internal architecture to enable future feature development, value for strengthening company image, value for entering new markets, etc. An example of how to visualize and balance several value estimates in a distributed marketing organisation is given in [28]. Examples of optimisation and trade-off analysis for release planning can be found in [9] and [31]. The alfa/beta model has been used as a basis for a survey among product managers [29], where it was found that a majority of the respondents that were able to consistently estimate process model parameters revealed that most of their implemented product requirements were incorrectly selected. This result indicates that the potential of process improvement in MDRE within the surveyed companies is great.

In a case study in MDRE process improvement using a method called PARSEQ (Post-release Analysis of Requirements SElection Quality) [17], it was shown that retrospective investigation of selection quality, including a root case analysis of decisions that were suspected to be wrong based on a re-estimation of cost and value, revealed many interesting process improvement proposals.

13.3.2 Process Capacity

In empirical studies of the MDRE process it has been found that there is a risk that the process gets in a state of congestion [27, 15], as a consequence of allowing more requirements to enter the MDRE process than can be handled with the available resources. This, in turn, results in throughput problems and eventually a negative impact on both time-to-market and product quality. The MDRE process capacity and the risk of overloading have been further studied using both analytical modelling with queuing theory [29] and discrete event process simulation [10, 1, 30]. These studies show that if the process gets overloaded, the throughput is severely hampered and the mean-time-to-market increases rapidly.

In [30] the alfa/beta quality model was used as a basis for measurement in process simulation experiments, and the results showed that an important means of reducing the risk of overloading is the introduction of a screening activity. During screening a quick assessment of each requirements value and cost is made before further effort is spent on analysing that requirement. This results in a rough judgement whether the requirement should be rejected upfront or if it should be allowed to enter subsequent stages of refinement. (See further the requirements state model in Sect. 13.4). Of course, there is a higher risk of making a wrong rejection decision based on a quick and rough analysis, but the benefit of not pushing too many requirements into the further stages of the process and thus avoiding overloading may be greater than the loss of a few golden grains, as taking on more work than the available process capacity allows for may damage the whole development and result in an unreasonably long mean-time-to-market [30].

Another means of speeding up MDRE is to support the manual and labour intensive analysis of natural language requirements descriptions by means of linguistic techniques [22, 21], which is further described in Chap. 10.

13.4 MDRE Data Management

This section provides a general description of two typical ingredients in MDRE data management, the requirements state model used for progress tracking of requirements refinement and the requirements repository where relevant attributes of candidate requirements are stored. The description here is based on previous studies of state models and repositories [6, 27] and our observation of industrial practice, but generalized and simplified in order to provide a broad and not too specific view of MDRE data management. One should therefore keep in mind that this perspective is quite different from tailor-made software, where the wishes and satisfaction of the customer are leading the requirements elicitation and capturing process. This implies that key principles are not the same in the processes and data management of MRDE.

13.4.1 Requirements State Model

At the conception of a requirement it is very uncertain whether it will finally get realized into a product release. Available resources and lead time until the planned date of the product release into the market limit the realization of any wish into the software product. Market-driven software implies that the vision and scope of the product are well established, thereby setting means to discern whether a requirement fits the standard or is to be rejected as it is too customer specific.

In keeping stock of the large volumes of requirements through the stages of the development a requirements state model is indispensable (see Fig. 13.2). We call this state model the requirements salmon ladder referring to the uncertainty of a salmon to get back upstream to the breeding currents.

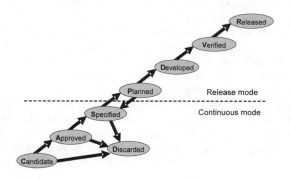

Fig. 13.2 Requirements state model, or requirements salmon ladder

Requirements are received at any time, but the development of a product is made in releases that are produced at discrete points in time. We therefore distinguish two modes: *continuous mode* and *release mode*. In the continuous mode, requirements are received and registered by the product manager from all kinds of submitters internal or external to the company, such as customers, sales representatives, or development teams.

The development of product releases is initiated at designated times according to the roadmap planning (see Sect. 13.6), and the requirements management activities are in release mode. During release development the product manager is in touch with other roles in the development team: project manager, software engineers, testers, technical authors, translators, etc. In release mode the content of the next release, also called the release scope, is then frozen in order to manage the release development project properly. Changes to the scope are then decided through a scope change procedure.

In order to monitor the progress of the work on the requirements the following statuses of the requirements salmon ladder are usually distinguished.

Candidate: Each requirement received gets the status of "Candidate". It is preferred that the description of the requirement follow the wording of the submitter as precisely as possible in order to keep commitment from the submitting party to the requirement. (For an overview of the requirements sources and elicitation, see Sect. 13.5.)

Approved: At regular time intervals the requirements with status Candidate are being reviewed for a possible inclusion into the future product releases. Accepted requirements get the status "Approved". This judgement process is a very difficult and responsible task. First, a long term vision of the product is required, which is usually expressed in product roadmap documents (see Sect. 13.6). Then a thorough functional and technical understanding of the product is required to determine the meaning and consequences of the often very detailed requirements of the existing customer base. Finally, the product managers should be able to cope with the political and strategic issues brought in by possible new contracts, important customers, and insisting sales people.

Specified: As the original description of the requirements is likely not very suitable for planning and development purposes, normally a more elaborate specification is created and linked to this requirement. The documentation type of the specifications may vary. In some organisations a text explaining the requirement in more depth is created, whereas in others a complete design document with Use Cases and Class diagrams is made. When the specification document is available the requirement gets the status "Specified".

Discarded: Rejected requirements get the status Discarded. A notification with the motivation of the rejection is send to the submitter. Discarded requirements are not deleted from the requirements database to enable future inquiries and analyses.

Planned: The planned release date and the available personnel resources determine the number of person days available for development, testing, and product completion. The product release planning can accommodate a maximum number of requirements based on the effort estimates and a prioritization. All requirements selected get the status "Planned", and are input for the design and coding processes. As the estimates are usually too optimistic, some of the planned requirements have an indication of lower priority and may be candidate to be taken out of the release plan in case of shortage of time to complete the release.

Developed: Development entails technical design, coding, unit tests, and production of collateral materials, such as brochures, marketing campaign, and training material. When all these activities have been successfully completed, the requirement gets the status "Developed". Note, that de-scoping, i.e. taking a requirement out of the release plan, can happen anytime, even when development is substantially under way. In this case the code has to be brought back to a state where the requirement was included. De-scoping usually happens if time runs out, or due to changing priorities.

Verified: Several tests are likely to be necessary in order to ensure an adequate level of quality before a developed requirement is released. Typical types of test are: functional unit tests for the small units performed by a tester not part of the development team; integration test focusing on dependencies between modules; system test for the complete software system; acceptance test for the complete product (software and collateral); and a final test of the installation files.

Released: When all activities for the product release have been completed the requirement finally gets the status of "Released", and the submitter is given a notification. Also released requirements are kept in the requirements repository for further analysis.

Most commercial requirement management tools allow the addition and definition of own statuses. The correspondence of status transfers with activities in the development, such as linkage to design and test documentation, can usually not be enforced by the tools, but require manual operation.

Table 13.3 Outline of a typical MDRE repository

Attribute	Value	Assigned in State
State	C / A / S / Di / P / De / V / R	-
ID	Unique identity	Candidate
Submitter	Who issued it?	Candidate
Company	Submitter's company	Candidate
Domain	Functional domain	Candidate
Label	Good descriptive name	Candidate
Description	Short textual description	Candidate
Contract	Link to sales contract enforcing requirement	Candidate
Priority	Importance category (1,2,3)	Approved
Motivation	Rationale: Why is it important?	Approved
Line of Business	Market segment for which requirement is important	Approved
Specification	Links to Use Case, Textual Specification	Specified
Decomposition	Parent-of / Child-of – links to other req's	Specified
Estimation	Effort estimation in hours	Specified
Schedule	Release for which it is planned for	Planned
Design	Links to design documents	Developed
Test	Links to test documents	Verified
Release version	Official release name	Released

13.4.2 Requirements Repository

In order to register the requirements properly many development teams use some kind of requirements repository. For smaller development efforts a simple spreadsheet may be sufficient. Larger-scale development is unlikely to be successfully executed without a requirements management tool due to the volume of requirements. Monolithic requirements specification documents are also considered problematic, as the document structure hinders the concurrent elaboration of different requirements by distinct teams. Individual registration of the requirements in an MDRE repository is indispensable. We present in Table 13.3 an outline of a typical MDRE repository in relation to the salmon ladder.

Aside from these generic attributes there are more attribute categories that are needed for specific markets. Country data is required for products that are sold internationally. Various countries have legal or financial rules that are required by law. Products sold on different technical platforms, such as operating systems, databases or multi-modal user interfaces, usually require specific requirements to cater with the particularities of these platforms. Some platforms may provide facilities that can be incorporated, whereas for other platforms these have to be completely developed.

Products with different product lines or being sold to different markets (line of business) require specific attributes related to the addressed functional domains. This is the case for products being sold in markets where safety is an important issue, such as the health care industry and in the avionics industry.

Tracing and tracking of requirements into the designs, code, and test reports is mainly an administrative task requiring proper support tools. As long as the tools employed in the requirements management and development lack proper means for interoperation, the tracing and tracking is condemned to be a labor-intensive error-prone manual task. Given the fact that developers often work at one requirement at a time, the tracing of changes made in the various work products would automatically provide insight into the requirements tracing process.

13.5 Market Analysis and Requirements Elicitation

Sources for requirements are numerous. When a new product is started, existing literature on the subject matter may provide insight in the domain. An efficient way to collect requirements in a structured manner is through the collaboration with key customers. In return for early knowledge transfer the key customer assist in requirements specification and in on-site testing. Care has to be taken that the focus of the product remains the full width of the market, and not deteriorate into a narrowing view of those key customer.

For larger enterprise applications markets, such as Enterprise Resource Planning (ERP) or Customer Relationship Management (CRM), analyst companies (e.g. Gartner, Forrester) provide functional and technical overviews of the underlying domains. A side effect of the analyst reports is the unification of the terminology in a domain. The positioning of the current product release on the complete domain overview is a good source for additional requirements.

Recently, facilitated workshops were proposed as a means for effective and efficient elicitation of requirements. In this setting a group of domain experts is brought together in an intensive work setting to specify the requirements managed by a facilitator. Schalken et al. [32] reported an investigation into the advantages of facilitated workshops compared to traditional one-on-one interviews. The comparison was in terms of required effort, in terms of calendar time required, and in terms of the quality of the requirements. About 50 projects in both categories in a large financial company in the Netherlands were analyzed. It turned out that requirements' gathering with facilitated workshops is less effective for small projects, but for large projects it is more effective. Surprisingly, the customers were less satisfied with the quality of the resulting requirements. Time and group pressure of the facilitated workshop might be reasons for this.

Customer involvement in requirements specification is to be performed in a careful manner. Expectations have to be managed as the development of the requirements may be spread over various releases and years. Some companies have organized *Customer Working Groups (CWG)*. A CWG is a team of customer representatives together with product managers, which develops a specification document for a whole new functional area. The customer representatives are experts in the domain, who can also judge the priorities of the must-have and the nice-to-have requirements very well. Establishing a CWG in an area also sets expectations regarding the future availability in releases. Strategic roadmap changes that exclude the CWG theme from the roadmap may set pressure on the vendor-customer relationship.

13.6 Roadmapping and Release Planning

A roadmap is a document that provides a layout of the product releases to come over a time frame of three to five years. Customers want to be sure that the future of the software product on which they depend is in line with their future plans. Especially in markets where the costs and consequences of a vendor change are large, the customer wants to have a stake in the roadmap decision-making.

Roadmaps are available in several segments of society to support decision makers in the route to innovation [3]. Based on a variety of roadmaps reported in the literature, Schaller [32] has established a taxonomy that classifies roadmaps according to their location in an applications-objectives space. This taxonomy scheme classifies the roadmaps broadly into the following four categories:

- Science and Technology Roadmaps
- Industry Technology Roadmaps
- Corporate or Product-Technology Roadmaps
- Product or Portfolio Management Roadmaps

The Product-Technology Roadmaps is the type of roadmap of the software industry according to the taxonomy. Software development is a technology development and a roadmap is made for each of the products. A technology roadmap is the document that is generated by the roadmapping process. It identifies the critical system requirement themes, the product and process performance targets and the technology alternatives and milestones for meeting these targets [8]. The roadmap helps identify precise objectives and helps focus the required resources on meeting those objectives. Roadmapping has several potential uses and resulting benefits at both the individual corporate and industry levels. According to Garcia [8] the three major uses of roadmapping are:

- Development of a consensus about a set of needs and the technologies required to satisfy those needs
- Provision of a mechanism to help experts forecast technology developments in target areas
- A framework to plan and coordinate developments either within an organization or in an entire industry

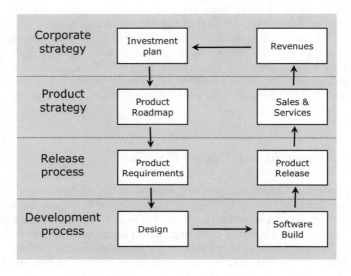

Fig. 13.3 Product roadmap in the investment cycle

The determination of the product roadmap in a MDRE context cannot be seen independent from the overall strategy of the company. As shown in Fig. 13.3 it serves best to distinguish a cyclic, four layer structure to stratify from strategy making to the development of the software product. First, on an annual basis the investment plan is devised based on revenues and forecast plans of the current product lines: an extension of the product line with a next release, a start of a new product line, and the termination of a product line. These plans also include the investment levels in terms of money or headcount, and some strategic issues regarding the content of the products.

The investment plan is then input for the management of the product development unit to create or update the current product roadmaps. In several product companies the main manager responsible for the product roadmap is called Chief Technology Officer. The roadmaps are created taking the views of the units for sales and consulting services into account, as these units know best what the strengths and weaknesses of the current products are, and what kind of market trends and functionality is appreciated by current and prospective customers.

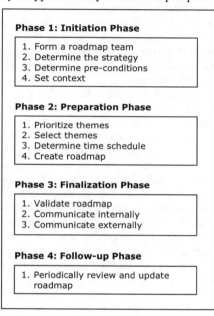

Phase 1: Initiation Phase

1. Form a roadmap team
2. Determine the strategy
3. Determine pre-conditions
4. Set context

Phase 2: Preparation Phase

1. Prioritize themes
2. Select themes
3. Determine time schedule
4. Create roadmap

Phase 3: Finalization Phase

1. Validate roadmap
2. Communicate internally
3. Communicate externally

Phase 4: Follow-up Phase

1. Periodically review and update roadmap

Fig. 13.4 Roadmap processes

Product managers are responsible for the release process at the next layer of operation. They elaborate the product roadmap into a set of product requirements for the various releases. Either they select the suitable requirements from the available candidate requirements in the requirements database (see Fig. 13.3), or they look for additional requirements (see Fig. 13.4) from various sources in the product domain. This step is especially needed when new product lines are initiated or when an existing product line is expanded with a new functional area. The set of product requirements is then input for the development process, which results into the kernel of the software product, the software build. The software build together with the auxiliary materials, such as user manuals, training material, marketing collateral, is then packaged as a new product release.

Example: Roadmapping at Baan

Recently, the roadmapping processes of Baan (now SSA Global) were evaluated and redesigned [3]. The process flow of the roadmap process, which resulted from this effort, is shown in Fig. 13.4 and explained subsequently.

The roadmapping effort starts in Phase 1 with the formation of the roadmap team. Obviously, some senior employees with in-depth product knowledge and access to the key people are candidates for this role. The strategy and preconditions are usually laid out by corporate management, e.g. time line (three or five years), products in scope, range of investment, and release frequency. The team then formulates its own plan and context. In the next phase the themes for functional and technical extension to the products are identified and prioritized. Themes can be seen as high-level requirements, usually well known generic issues in the product domain. The themes are elaborate in a set of coherent requirements to be planned in one or subsequent releases. Typical themes are "Enabling for Workflow", "Porting to Linux platform", and "Extensions for a new market". Themes should be so well defined and attractive, that they are candidates for the functional extensions to be listed on the brochures that cover the release products

Schedules of roadmaps are often expressed in quarters of a year. A timeline shows the various product lines with the releases plotted. The release frequency is dependent on the size of the product. For Baan ERP the frequency was about 1.5 year as the market is not receptive for too many disruptive system upgrades. Bookkeeping software is usually upgraded once a year. Changed legislation requires that the financial processes are brought up-to-date. When the roadmap has been drafted, it requires to be validated by the various stakeholders groups: general management, large customers, sales and consultancy teams, and development teams. Comments and feedback is integrated, and the roadmap is handed over to the general management, who is the owner and communicator of the roadmap. The formal communication of the roadmap is often launched at some large event where many customers meet.

Finally, in the Follow-up phase the roadmap team is thanked for its efforts and dissolved. Some product managers remain responsible for the maintenance of the product roadmap documentation and the updating with new themes. After about three years a new roadmap team is formed and the cycle of phases is repeated.

13.7 Conclusion

When the requirements engineering process is enacted in a market-driven context the developing organization faces special challenges. Continuously arriving requirement candidates provide input to the decision-making that should result in a strategic roadmap and a prioritized release plan. A major challenge is to cope with the potentially enormous amount of information and to represent and organize it in an efficient way so that it can provide a good basis for efficient and effective decision-making, which in-turn provides the basis for a profitable software business.

This chapter offers input to the design of a competitive MDRE process through the following elements as explained previously:

- A process quality model for assessing the goodness of requirements selection
- A typical requirements state model to be used in progress tracking
- A typical requirements repository to be used in data management
- An example of an industrial release management process

The MDRE has to be adapted to its specific context. The maturity of the organization and its products, as well as the market and its customers, are critical parameters that have to be considered when formulating and establishing a well-balanced process. It is also important that there is a built in mechanism for learning and improving in order to stay ahead even as the competition gets smarter. In [2], the following four research topics were identified based on a systematic assessment of research contributions in relation to the Capability Maturity Model Integration [4]:

- Release planning: means to select requirements for the next release based on priority, development effort estimates, and expected revenues
- Experience evaluations of industrial requirements management processes: a study in MDRE efforts in a variety of companies
- Tracking and tracing: tools to track and trace the requirements over the various work products of the development process, such as designs, code, tests, and manuals;
- Measuring requirements management efficiency and effectiveness: development of measurements to provide means to assess the efficiency and effectiveness of the requirements processes

Other important areas providing challenges to RE researcher in the market-driven context are: accurate prioritization, efficient management of dependencies, and tool support for handling very large requirement repositories, as well as the general area of RE decision support (see further Chaps. 4, 5, 10 and 12 respectively). Both descriptive and prescriptive research is needed to provide both a deeper understanding of the nature of MDRE as well as to offer solutions to industrial problems in combination with scientific evidence on how to best apply them.

Acknowledgements

We would like to thank all researchers that have been involved in the many projects that have formed the basis for this chapter. Special thanks to Johan Natt och Dag and Lena Karlsson, both at Lund University, who have during their PhD studies actively participated in the advancement of the research frontier within market-driven requirements engineering. We would also like to thank Dr. Joachim Karlsson and Per Beremark for providing rewarding opportunities of industrial collaboration. Thanks also to the product managers of Baan (now SSA Global) who participated in the company-wide requirements management processes. Especially thanks to Pierre Breuls, Mike Chouinard, Wim van Rijswijk and Shirley Bodegraven for their time and involvement.

References

1. Booth R, Regnell B, Aurum A, Jeffery R, Natt och Dag J (2001) Market-driven requirements engineering challenges: An industrial case study of a process performance declination. In: Proceedings of 6th Australian Workshop on Requirements Engineering (AWRE'01), Sydney, Australia, pp.41−47

2. Brinkkemper S (2004) Requirements engineering research the industry is (and is Not) waiting for. In: Proceedings of the 10th Anniversary International Workshop on Requirements Engineering: Foundation of Software Quality, Regnell B, Kamsties E, Gervasi V (Eds.), Essener Informatik Berichte, 9:251-264, ISBN 3-922602-91-6

3. Bodegraven S, Brinkkemper S (2004) Product software roadmap determination process: Where marketing and technology come together. Technical report, ICS, Utrecht University

4. Chrissis MB, Konrad M, Shrum S (2003) CMMI: Guidelines for process integration and product improvement. Addison-Wessley, ISBN: 0-321-15496-7

5. Carlshamre P (2002) A usability perspective on requirements engineering − From methodology to product development. Dissertation No. 726, Linköping University, Sweden

6. Carlshamre P, Regnell B (2000) Requirements lifecycle management and release planning in market-driven requirements engineering processes. International Workshop on the Requirements Engineering Process: Innovative Techniques, Models, and Tools to support the RE Process (REP'00), September 6-8, Greenwich UK, pp.961−965

7. Carlshamre P, Sandahl K, Lindvall M, Regnell B. Natt och Dag J (2001) An industrial survey of requirements interdependencies in software product release planning. In: Proceedings of 5th IEEE International Symposium on Requirements Engineering (RE'01), August 27-31, Toronto, Canada, pp.84-92

8. Garcia M, Bray O (1998) Fundamentals of technology roadmapping. Sandia National Laboratories, Technical Report, http://www.sandia.gov/Roadmap/home.htm

9. Greer D, Ruhe G (2004) Software release planning: an evolutionary and iterative approach. Information & Software Technology 46(4): 243−253

10. Höst M, Regnell B, Natt och Dag J, Nedstam J, Nyberg C (2001) Exploring bottlenecks in market-driven requirements management processes with discrete event simulation. Journal of Systems and Software, 59(3): 323−332

11. Hermann K, Brinkkemper S, Bubenko JA Jr, Farbey B, Greenspan SJ, Heitmeyer CL, Leite JCS, Mead NR, Mylopoulos J, Siddiqi J (2002) Requirements engineering and technology transfer: Obstacles and incentives. Requirements Engineering, 7(3):113−123

12. Kamsties E, Hörmann K, Schlich M (1998) Requirements engineering in small and medium enterprises. Requirements Engineering, 3, pp.84–90

13. Karlsson J, Ryan K (1997) A cost-value approach for prioritizing requirements. IEEE Software, Sept/Oct pp.67−74

14. Karlsson J, Wohlin C, Regnell B (1998) An evaluation of methods for prioritizing software requirements. Information and Software Technology, 39(14-15): 939−947

15. Karlsson L, Dahlstedt ÅG, Natt och Dag J, Regnell B, Persson A (2002) Challenges in market-driven requirements engineering - An industrial interview study. In: Proceedings of 8th International Workshop on Requirements Engineering: Foundation for Software Quality (REFSQ'02), September 09-10th, Essen, Germany, pp.37–49

16. Karlsson L, Regnell B (2004) Aligning the requirements engineering process with the maturity of markets and products. In: Proceedings of 10th International Workshop on Requirements Engineering: Foundation for Software Quality (REFSQ'04), June 7-8, Riga, Latvia, pp.69–74

17. Karlsson L, Regnell B, Karlsson J, Olsson S (2003) Post-release analysis of requirements selection quality - An industrial case study. In: Proceedings of 9th International Workshop on Requirements Engineering: Foundation for Software Quality (REFSQ'03), June 16 -17, Klagenfurt/Velden, Austria, pp.47–56

18. Lauesen S, Vium JP (2004) Experiences from a tender process - The customer's dreams and the supplier's frustrations. In: Proceedings of 10th International Workshop on Requirements Engineering: Foundation for Software Quality (REFSQ'04), June 7-8, Riga, Latvia, pp.29–46

19. Lubars M, Potts C, Richter C (1993) A review of the state of the practice in requirements modeling. In: Proceedings of IEEE International Symposium on Requirements Engineering (RE93), Los Alamitos, USA. IEEE Computer Society Press, pp.2–14

20. Morisio M, Torchiano M (2002) Definition and classification of COTS: A proposal. In: Proceedings of 1st International Conference on COTS Based Software Systems (ICCBBS), Orlando, February 4-6, pp.165–175

21. Natt och Dag J, Gervasi V, Brinkkemper S, Regnell B (2004) Speeding up requirements management in a product software company: Linking customer wishes to product requirements through linguistic engineering. In: Proceedings of 12th IEEE International Conference on Requirements Engineering (RE'04), Kyoto, Japan, pp.283–295

22. Natt och Dag J, Regnell B, Carlshamre P, Andersson M, Karlsson J (2002) A feasibility study of automated natural language requirements analysis in market-driven development. Requirements Engineering, 7(1): 20–33

23. Natt och Dag J, Regnell B, Madsen OS, Aurum A (2001) An industrial case study of us-ability evaluation in market-driven packaged software development. In: Proceedings of 9th International Conference on Human-Computer Interaction (HCII'2001), August 5-10, New Orleans, USA, pp.425–429

24. Maiden NA, Ncube C (1998) Acquiring COTS software selection requirements. IEEE Software, March/April, pp.46–56

25. Novorita RJ, Grube G (1996) Benefits of structured requirements methods for market-based enterprises. In: Proceedings of 6th Annual International INCOSE Symposium. Seattle, USA, INCOSE

26. Potts C (1995) Invented requirements and imagined customers: Requirements engineering for off-the-shelf software. In: Proceedings of Second IEEE International Symposium on Requirements Engineering (RE'95), pp.128–130 Los Alamitos, USA

27. Regnell B, Beremark P, Eklundh O (1998) A market-driven requirements engineering process: Results from an industrial process improvement programme. Requirements Engineering, 3(2):121–129

28. Regnell B, Höst M, Natt och Dag J, Beremark P, Hjelm T (2001) An industrial case study on distributed prioritization in market-driven requirements engineering for packaged software. Requirements Engineering, 6(1):51–62

29. Regnell B, Karlsson L, Höst M (2003) An analytical model for requirements selection quality evaluation in product software development. In: Proceedings of 11th IEEE International Conference on Requirements Engineering, (RE'03), September 8-12, Monterey Bay, California USA, pp.254–263

30. Regnell B, Ljungquist B, Thelin T, Karlsson L (2004) Investigation of requirements selection quality in market-driven software process using an open source discrete event simulation framework. In: Proceedings of 5th International Workshop on Software Process Simulation and Modeling (ProSim 2004), May 24-25, Edinburgh, UK

31. Ruhe G, Eberlein A, Pfahl D, (2003) Trade-off analysis for requirements selection. Software Engineering and Knowledge Engineering, 13(4): 345–366

32. Schalken J, Brinkkemper S, van Vliet H (2004) Assessing the effects of facilitated workshops in requirements engineering. In: Proceedings of 8th IEEE International Conference on Empirical Assessment in Software Engineering (EASE2004), pp.135–144

33. Kostoff RN, Schaller RR, (2001) Science and technology roadmaps. IEEE Transactions on Engineering Management, 48(2): 132–143

Author Biography

Dr. Björn Regnell is associate professor in Software Engineering at the Department of Communication Systems, Lund University, Sweden, and senior member of the Software Engineering Research Group (SERG). Dr. Regnell is the project leader of the requirements engineering research at SERG. His research interests include empirical software engineering, requirements engineering, and market-driven software development. He has published one book and more than 40 refereed papers in these areas. He was program co-chair of the International Workshop on Requirements Engineering – Foundation for Software Quality (REFSQ) in 2002–2004, and he is a member of the program committee of the International Conference on Requirements Engineering (RE) since 2002.

Dr. Sjaak Brinkkemper is professor in Organization and Information at the Institute of Information and Computing Sciences of the Utrecht University, the Netherlands. Previously he was a consultant at the Vanenburg Group and a Chief Architect at Baan Research and Development, where he was responsible for overall software process improvement initiatives in Requirements Management, Architecture and Design. He has published five books and more than 90 papers on software product development and information systems methodology. He is a member of the Editorial Board of the Requirements Engineering Journal, Journal of Database Management, and Journal on Information Systems and e-Business Management.

14 Requirements Engineering for Agile Methods

Alberto Sillitti and Giancarlo Succi

Abstract: Collecting, understanding, and managing requirements is a critical aspect in all development methods. This is true for Agile Methods as well. In particular, several agile practices deal with requirements in order to implement them correctly and satisfy the needs of the customer. These practices focus on a continuous interaction with the customer to address the requirements evolution over time, prioritize them, and deliver the most valuable functionalities first. This chapter introduces Agile Methods as the implementation of the principles of the lean production in software development. Therefore, Agile Methods focus on continuous process improvement through the identification and the removal of waste, whatever does not add value for the customer.

Keywords: Agile methods, Lean management, Process management, Requirements management, Variability management.

14.1 Introduction

Agile Methods (AMs) are a family of software development processes that have become popular during the last few years [1, 7, 14]. Their aim is to deliver products faster, with high quality, and satisfy customer needs through the application of the principles of the lean production to software development [25].

Lean production [36] has been conceived during the '50s at Toyota [23]. It involves several practices that are now part of most manufacturing processes, such as just-in-time development, total quality management, and continuous process improvement. The principle of lean production is the constant identification and removal of waste (*muda* in Japanese), that is, anything that does not add value for the customer to the final product. Being rooted on lean production, AMs focus on:

1. Delivering value for the customer
2. Ensuring that the customer understand such value and be satisfied by the project

Delivering value to the customer implies that the development team has to produce only what provides value and remove (or at least reduce to the minimum) everything else. AMs pose a lot of emphasis in producing and delivering to the customer only those features that are useful. Producing anything that is not required is considered a mistake. Adding a feature that is not needed not only consumes effort without adding customer value but also creates extra code, which may contain errors and make the code longer and more complex to maintain, to correct and to improve. This waste includes general architectures that are used only partially or reusable components with functionalities that are likely to be never used [25].

To achieve such elimination of waste, AMs claim to be [7] (a) adaptive rather than predictive, and (b) people-oriented rather than process-oriented. To ensure customer satisfaction, a close collaboration between the development team and the customer is sought, so that:

- Requirements are fully identified and correctly understood
- Final products reflects what the customer needs, no more and no less

Overall, requirement engineering is of paramount importance for AMs. This chapter introduces AMs and describes their approach to requirements engineering. It is mainly related to:

- Chapter 2: most of the techniques for requirements elicitation do not change much in an agile environment.
- Chapter 4: the prioritization of requirements is of paramount importance, since AMs focus on the implementation of the most valuable features for the customer.
- Chapter 5: in order to implement only high priority features, the identification of the interaction among features and their decoupling is extremely important.
- Chapter 7: the identification of the requirements to include in a single iteration is based on the negotiation between the customer and the development team.

The chapter is organized as follows: Section 14.2 briefly introduces Agile Methods. Section 14.3 identifies common problems in requirements engineering. Section 14.4 describes the agile approach to requirements engineering. Section 14.5 deals with the role and responsibility of customers, managers, and developers in an Agile environment. Section 14.6 briefly introduces tools for requirements management in Agile Methods. Section 14.7 draws the conclusions.

14.2 Agile Methods

AMs are a family of development techniques designed to deliver products on time, on budget, and with high quality and customer satisfaction. This family includes several and very different methods. The most popular include:

- eXtreme Programming (XP) [6]
- Scrum [28]
- Dynamic Systems Development Method (DSDM) [32]
- Adaptive Software Development (ASD) [17]
- The Crystal family [12]

14.2.1 The Agile Manifesto

The promoters of AMs have realized that the wide variety of such methods may refrain potential adopters, as they could not determine what to apply in their own operations [9, 15].

As a results, such promoters have analyzed the root of lean management and have defined a document containing a set of basic values common across all AMs. Such document is called "Agile Manifesto" [7]. Being rooted in lean management, such values focus on human resources and process management:

1. **Individuals and Interactions over Process and Tools:** The Agile approach emphasizes the importance of people and their interactions rather than focusing on structured processes and tools.
2. **Customer Collaboration over Contracts:** The relationship between the development team and the customer is regulated through the involvement of the customer in the development process rather than through detailed and fixed contracts (usually, contracts in agile projects are variable price-variable scope and not fixed price-fixed scope).
3. **Working Software over Documentation:** The goal of the development team is delivering working code, which is the artifact that provides value to the customer. Well-written code is self-documented and formal documentation is reduced to the minimum.
4. **Responding to Change over Planning:** The development team has to react quickly to requirements variability. Binding decisions affecting this ability are delayed as long as possible and the time spent in the planning activity is limited to what the customer needs. Any attempts to forecast future needs are forbidden.

From such values, a set of common practices and behaviors are identifies. The underlying claim is that they are not inventions of the Agile Community, but that they are the results of rationalizing the experience of successes and failures in software development. Some of these practices and behaviors are listed here below:

- **Adaptability:** Practices have to be adapted to the specific needs of both the development team and the customer. There is no *one size fits all* solution.
- **Incremental Development:** The different phases of software development (analysis, design, code, and testing) are compressed in very short iterations (from 2 weeks to 2 months) in order to focus on a few, well-defined problems that provide real value to the customer (Fig.14.1).
- **Frequent Releases:** At the end of every iteration, the application is released to the customer that tests it and provides feedback. This approach produces several benefits such as: (1) the customer can use the application very early, allowing the identification of potential problems in time for improving the product limiting the effect on the schedule; (2) the customer feels in control of the development process, since progresses are always visible; (3) the trust between

the customer and the development team increases, since the team is considered reliable because it able to deliver working versions of the application early.

- **Requirements Prioritization Before Every Iteration:** Before every iteration, the customer and the development team identify new requirements and reassign priorities to the old ones on the base of the customer actual needs.
- **High Customer Involvement**: The customer is involved in the development process through a continuous request of feedback in order to identify potential problems early in the development. In some cases, the customer is even a member of the development team (customer on site practice) and is always available to interact with the team and clarify requirements-related issues.

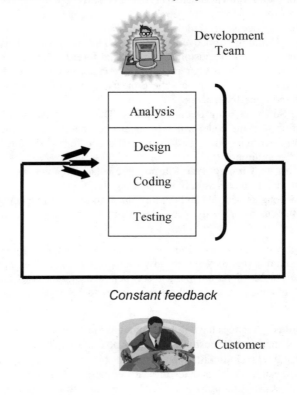

Fig. 14.1 Agile development cycle

As mentioned, the basic values and practices of all the AMs are very similar. Still, by "Agile Methods" we identify a diverse family of development methodologies with different focuses and related strengths and weaknesses. There are different levels of "agility" in AMs. A development methodology is more "agile" than another one if it requires less overhead, which is whatever does not produce value for the customer [12].

In each methodology, the development team has different priorities, processes, levels of overhead for the interaction of the team members, etc. Therefore, there is no single solution for all the contexts. AMs provide only guidelines and a basic background of practices and behaviors that have to be adapted to the specific problem [6, 9]. The applicability of the AMs is still a matter of research [4, 34]. Issues currently being discussed include:

1. The size of the problem that can be addressed
2. How people are managed in AMs
3. The application domains in which AMs are profitable.

14.2.2 Team Size in Agile Methods

Most AMs are specifically targeted to small teams, with up to 16 developers (e.g., eXtreme Programming). However, there are AMs supporting a wider range of team size (e.g. the Crystal family), but there are many problems under investigation, including the use of such methods and practices in a distributed environment [14].

The level of agility is often related to the size of the development team. Direct communication and limited documentation is possible only in small teams. On the contrary, when the team grows, the level of overhead grows as well. This overhead includes: (1) documentation and (2) mediated communication. More documentation is required to share knowledge and trace the status of the project because direct, many-to-many interaction is not possible anymore [12]. Therefore, the importance of the documentation increases and it becomes a way to improve knowledge sharing. In this case, the code itself is not enough and the direct communication between the development team and the customer is not possible with a large team.

Table 14.1 The Crystal family

Methodology	Team (Number of people)
Crystal Clear	2-6
Crystal Yellow	6-20
Crystal Orange	20-40
Crystal Red	40-80

For these reasons, small teams are more agile than large teams. However, the basic principles of the lean management are still valid and most of them can scale. One of these is the continuous process improvement through the reduction of waste. This principle is useful regardless the size of the development team. The Crystal family of AMs points out this concept [12]. Crystal includes different AMs fitting the needs of teams with different sizes (Table 14.1). The different levels of the Crystal family focus on different practices in order to manage the scalability. A limited scalability is achieved reducing the level of agility.

Developing large systems using AMs is difficult or even impossible. At present, the research effort in AMs focuses on small and medium size projects, since even in this area their effectiveness is sill under investigation. Many agile practices simply do not scale, others can. AMs are adaptive [7], therefore project managers have to identify the practices to use according to the specific environment. This decision is highly affected by the size and the domain of the problem.

14.2.3 Managing People in Agile Methods

AMs focus on the value of people to solve problems and share information [11], not on the process and a massive amount of documentation [2]. However, the people-orientation can represent a main weakness for AMs since skills required to build good agile teams are not common [11].

Team members have to be excellent developers, able to work in teams, communicate and interact with colleagues and customers, etc. All these skills are required, since the team is self-organizing and cannot refer to a predefined and detailed process to solve problems and share knowledge [10].

14.2.4 Applicability of Agile Methods across Application Domains

A key question is whether AMs can be applied in all application domains. This problem is still under investigation [4, 9, 34]. In particular, how and when using specific practices results in benefits [2, 8, 27]. In general, it seems that AMs are valuable for building applications that are not mission-critical and with a limited size. Researchers are studying other areas such as the embedded systems (e.g., mobile phones and PDAs) where performances, real-time behavior, and memory constraints are common problems.

AMs focus on producing only what provides value to the customer, which does not mean that building reusable artifact such as components. If the goal of the project is to develop a reusable artifact, the development team focuses on this problem and use AMs to address it. Reusable artifacts are not developed in projects with a different aim because developers have to include features that are not useful for the ongoing project. This approach is compliant to the principles of the AMs [7]. AMs are not the solution for developing every product. Their application is extremely hard or even impossible in many areas, such as safety-critical or very large and complex applications.

Several areas that have been analyzed in deep in traditional environments are not well understood in AMs. Often, there is a lack of research effort, especially in the area of requirements engineering [24, 34].

14.3 Traditional and Agile Requirement Engineering

Requirements are the base of all software products and their elicitation, management, and understanding are very common problems for all development methodologies. In particular, the requirements variability is a major challenge for all commercial software projects [29]. According to a study of the Standish Group [31], five of the eight main factors for project failure deal with requirements (Table 14.2) which are incomplete requirements, low customer involvement, unrealistic expectations, changes in the requirements and useless requirements.

Table 14.1 Main causes of project failure

Problem	%
Incomplete requirements	13.1
Low customer involvement	12.4
Lack of resources	10.6
Unrealistic expectations	9.9
Lack of management support	9.3
Changes in the requirements	8.7
Lack of planning	8.1
Useless requirements	7.5

Engineering requirements for software systems has been perceived as one of the key steps in a successful software development endeavor, since the early days of software engineering. As a result, traditional development processes have elaborated several standards, including:

- IEEE Standard 830: Recommended Practice for Software Requirements Specifications [18]
- IEEE Standard 1233: Guide for Developing System Requirements Specifications [19]
- IEEE Standard 1362: Guide for Information Technology – System Definition – Concept of Operations Document [20]

A detailed discussion of this topic is in Chap. 8. AMs do not rely on these standards for requirements elicitation and management but they have adapted many of the basic ideas to the new environment [3, 13, 16, 21, 24, 30, 37]. For instance, in AMs the whole development team is involved in requirements elicitation and management, while in traditional approaches often only a subset of the development team is involved.

This approach is feasible only if the size of the problem is limited. Only a small development team can interact directly with the customer. If the problem is bigger, the team can use other techniques for eliciting and managing requirements, as described in Chaps. 2 and 8. This is a strong limitation of AMs.

AMs are aware that requirements variability is a constant problem in nearly all software projects; therefore, the support to such changes is included in the process as a key strength [33]. Moreover, AMs do not try to forecast changes or future needs, they focus only on the features for which the customer is paying. This approach avoids the development of a too general architecture that requires additional effort [6]. The understanding of requirements variability has a strong impact on the ability of AMs to be "lean". Often, a larger and more comprehensive architecture is expected to handle better the variability of requirements that can be forecasted in advance. However, a more complex architecture costs more not only for the development but also for the maintenance and bug fixing. Therefore, such larger architecture may end up being an inhibitor of handling the variability in requirements that cannot be forecasted in advance. Not to mention that it is usually difficult to make correct predictions, therefore many features included in the early stages of the project are not used in the final product and new ones, not identified at the beginning, are required. This approach is likely to generate useless features that are waste and generate additional waste due to the increased complexity of the code and the additional effort required to the maintenance [6, 17]. AMs focus on the development of the minimal application able to satisfy all the needs of a specific customer. Developing reusable components or framework including functionalities that are not used in the current project is considered a mistake [6].

14.4 Agile Approaches to Requirements Engineering

AMs include practices focused on the key factors listed in Table 14.2 to reduce the risk of failure. In particular, the aim of incremental development, frequent releases, requirements prioritization before every iteration, and customer involvement is to address the main risk factors.

14.4.1 The Customer

In AMs, the customer assumes a paramount role. Usually, the term "customer" identifies a set of stakeholders that belongs to the organization that is paying for the development of a software product. In this case, the interaction between the development team and the stakeholders is complex due to the different perceptions of the problem that the stakeholders have [5].

In AMs, the problem of multiple stakeholders is solved reducing their number to one, a single person that represents all the stakeholders involved in the project. This customer should be a domain expert and able to make important decisions such as accepting the product, prioritize requirements, etc. In the case of mass-products for which there are no organizations paying directly for the product, the development team has to identify an expert in the area (e.g., a marketing expert) that is able to act as the customer and participate in the development of the product. This approach is feasible only if the size of the problem is limited and a single person can act as *customer*, representing all the stakeholders. If the size of the problem does not allow this approach, the team has to use other techniques to elicit and manage requirements, as described in Chaps. 2 and 8. In some AMs, the customer on site practice is common. This means that the customer is a member of the development team, is co-located with the team, and is always available to discuss issues related to the project with any team member [6]. The customer-on-site practice defines some specific requirements for the customer:

1. **Availability:** The customer has to be always available to answer questions coming from the development team. Any delay in the answer delays the development of the product.
2. **Complete Knowledge:** The customer is the representative for all the stakeholders. Therefore, he is able to answer all questions, since he is the domain expert and knows how the application should work and the input/output data required. Again, this is possible if the size of the project is limited.
3. **Decision Power:** The customer is able to make final decisions and commitments. Changes in requirements, acceptance of the features implemented, etc. can be decided directly by the customer, allowing a fast decision making process.

Having access to a customer able to satisfy all these requirements is not easy [26], since he has to be a very valuable member of staff. The availability of this kind of customer is of paramount importance in AMs, since most of their benefits (e.g., reduction of documentation, incremental delivery, etc.) are tightly coupled with the customer involvement [35]. However, there are attempts to extend requirements collection to involve more customers [22].

14.4.2 Waste in Requirements

AMs focus on the identification and reduction of waste in the development process [25]. In particular, identifying and reducing the waste from requirements assume a paramount role to avoid the creation of waste later in the process. In lean practices, the reduction of waste is extremely important because waste always generates further waste [23, 36]. For instance, if a factory produces more goods than required by the customers (first piece of waste) the system produces the following further waste:

- A warehouse
- People and processes to manage the warehouse
- People and processes to manage the interaction between the factory and the warehouse, etc

The introduction of waste in the early phases of the process causes the creation of further waste later on, the increment of the complexity, and the drain of resources available for the core business of the company. For this reasons, the optimization of a single activity produces more savings than the direct saving from the activity itself and contributes to the optimization of the whole process. Requirements engineering in AMs focuses on [7]:

1. Reduction of waste from requirements
2. Managing the requirements evolution

Waste in requirements deeply affects the development process and the ability to deliver a product able to satisfy the real needs of the customer. The main effects of waste in this area include:

- More source code to write and higher cost
- Increased complexity of the source code
- Delayed delivery of the final version of the application with all functionalities
- More complex and costly maintenance
- More resources required by the application, including: memory usage, processing power, network usage, etc
- Increased complexity of the application from the point of view of the customer (e.g., more complex user interface, more effort to learn how to use the application, etc.)
- Savings produced by the application in the production process of the customer are delayed

At the end, all the waste generated is a cost for the customer both directly and indirectly. Such costs are likely to generate further waste inside the customer organization due to the reduced amount of money available to its core business and the reduced revenues. Waste in requirements includes both wrong and useless requirements. A misunderstanding between the customer and the development team causes wrong requirements. In order to reduce the probability of such misunderstanding, AMs adopt several techniques focused on the interaction between the customer and the development team:

- **The whole Development Team Collects Requirements from the Customer:** Requirements elicitation (Chap. 2) is an activity in which the whole team is involved. In this way, the usage of documents to share the knowledge is reduced to a minimum and the probability of misunderstandings decreases.
- **Requirements are Collected using a Common Language:** Requirements are collected using the language of the customer, not a formal language for requirements specification. This means that developers have to be introduced to the domain of the customer in order to understand him/her.
- **Direct Interaction Between the Development Team and the Customer:** There are no intermediaries between the development team and the customer. This approach reduces both the number of documents required and the probability of misunderstanding due to unnecessary communication layers.
- **Requirements Splitting:** If the development team considers a requirement too complex, this technique helps the customer to split it in simpler ones. This splitting helps developers to understand better the functionalities requested by the customer (Chap. 5).

This approach does not scale, it is feasible only if the size of the development team is limited. Otherwise, the introduction of a representative and additional documentation is required. This means that if the team size grows, some agile practices cannot be used anymore while others are still useful. In case of large projects, AMs do not provide any specific solution. Even if the customer is an expert in its own domain, identifying the features that he really needs is not easy. Often, customers over specify the application, including a wide range of features that are not providing a real benefit for their business. Such requirements are useless, therefore, they are a source of waste. In order to reduce this kind of waste, AMs use the following techniques:

- **Requirements Prioritization:** The customer and the development team assign priorities to each requirement in order to identify more important features that have to be implemented first (Chaps. 4 and 7).
- **Incremental Releases:** Functionalities are released in small but frequent bunches (from 2 weeks to 2 months), in order to collect feedback from the customer.

After the identification of the functionalities to include into the system, the customer and the development team assign priorities to them. The prioritization activity is performed in four steps:

1. The development team estimates the time required to implement each functionality. If the effort required is too high, the requirement is split into simpler ones that can be implemented with less effort.
2. The customer specifies business priorities for each functionality.
3. According to the business priorities, the development team assign a risk factor to the functionalities.
4. The customer and the development team identify the functionalities to implement in the iteration.

The development team and the customer repeat requirements elicitation and these four steps at the beginning of every iteration. In this way, it is possible to identify requirements that do not provide enough value to the customer in order to discard them and focus on the most important ones.

14.4.3 Requirements Evolution

AMs assume that it is very hard to elicit all the requirements from the user upfront, at the beginning of a development project. They also assume that such requirements evolve in time as the customer may change its mind or the overall technical and socio-economical environment may evolve. Therefore, Agile companies are aware that changes are inevitable and they include the management of variability into the development process. AMs base the requirements collection and management on three main hypotheses [6]:

- Requirements are not well known at the beginning of the project
- Requirements change
- Making changes is not expensive

In particular, AMs assume that the cost of introducing changes in a product is nearly constant over the time (Fig. 14.2), but this hypothesis is not true in every context. Usually, the cost of implementing changes grows exponentially over the time. On the other hand, if development phases are grouped together in very short iterations (Fig. 14.1) and binding decisions are taken as late as possible, the growing of the costs is limited [6].

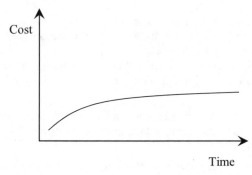

Fig. 14.2 Cost of changes

In order to manage requirements evolution, AMs use variable scope-variable price contracts [25]. This means that the features really implemented into the system and its cost evolve as well. Therefore, requirements are not specified in details at contract level but defined step by step during the project through a negotiation process between the customer and the development team. Managing variability is a challenge that AMs approach in two ways:

1. **Decoupling Requirements:** Requirements have to be as independent as possible in order to clearly identify what to implement and make the order of their implementation irrelevant.
2. **Requirement Elicitation and Prioritization:** At the beginning of every iteration, there is a requirements collection and prioritization activity. During that, new requirements are identified and prioritized. This approach helps to identify the most important features inside the ongoing project. Typically, if a requirement is very important is scheduled for the implementation in the upcoming iteration, otherwise it is kept on hold. At the following iteration, the requirements on hold are evaluated and, if they are still valid, they are included in the list of the candidate requirements together with the new ones. Then, the new list is prioritized to identify the features that will be implemented. If a requirement is not important enough, it is kept on hold indefinitely.

This approach is able to identify the most important requirements during the whole project, not just at the beginning. Requirements that are not considered very important at the beginning may become relevant at some stage of the project. Moreover, the decoupling of the requirements allows the implementation of the features in nearly any order; therefore, features are implemented mainly according to their prioritization, not to their functional dependences.

14.4.4 Non-Functional Requirements

AMs do not provide any widely accepted technique for eliciting and managing non-functional requirements [24]. Such requirements are collected implicitly during the requirements collection activity. The need of specifying non-functional requirements is less important than in other context due to the continuous interaction with the customer. After every iteration, the product is released and the customer is able to test the product. If he identifies problems related to non-functional qualities, the team can adapt the system to meet such requirements in the subsequent iteration without affecting the schedule too much.

Often, the customer does not perceive as high impact many non-functional requirements (e.g., scalability, security, etc.). This may affect deeply the release of the final version of the application, therefore the development team has to guide the customer in order to identify such hidden needs. This approach to non-functional requirements may represent a major risk for AMs, since they lack specific techniques for their management.

14.5 Role and Responsibility of Customers, Developers, and Managers

AMs require a high level of interaction among customers, managers, and developers. Usually, such interaction is unmediated and all the stakeholders meet frequently in working sessions to improve the mutual understanding, the quality of the final product, and keep the project under control (on time and on budget).

Roles and responsibilities of customers, managers, and developers assume a paramount importance and have a broad impact on the evolution of a software project.

14.5.1 The Customer

The customer is highly involved in the development process and often a member of the development team. The customer's presence is extremely important in AMs, since the amount of documentation is reduced to the minimum and the development team often asks for clarification regarding requirements. The constant presence of the customer replaces most of the documentation required to describe requirements in details and his/her contribution is a key factor for the success of the project. The customer provides feedback to the development team in order to identify potential problems early in the development and avoid a major impact on the project schedule.

As stated in Sect. 14.4.1, the customer-on-site practice has several benefits, but it is very difficult to implement. A poor implementation of this practice may reduce the effectiveness of several AMs, since many of them are tightly coupled with the involvement of the customer.

14.5.2 Developers

The whole development team is highly involved in the customer management collecting and negotiating requirements. Developers have to interact closely with the customer providing working software and collecting valuable feedback. For these reasons, the skills required by developers in agile teams are not common. They have to be very good developers, be able to work in teams, and interact with the customer using his/her own language [11]. Since AMs focus on this interaction, the development team has the responsibility to educate the customer. AMs require a high commitment of the customer in the project due to the frequent feedback required.

The trust between the development team and the customer assumes a paramount role. The team has to provide working and high quality software to the customer at every iteration in order to collect valuable feedback. This approach is valuable for both developers and customers. Developers can collect useful information to avoid the implementation of useless features that increase the level of waste; customers can use (or at least test) the product a few weeks after the project start.

14.5.3 Managers

In AMs, managers have to create and sustain a framework for the establishment of a productive interaction between the development team and the customer. They can achieve this goal identifying the best people to be included in an agile team, promoting collaboration, and negotiating contracts with the customer.

Usually, agile teams work with variable scope-variable price contracts rather than fixed price-fixed scope ones. This approach relies on the ability of the manager in the contracts definition in order to satisfy the customer and allow the maximum flexibility in the development process, as required by AMs.

14.6 Tools for Requirements Management in AMs

The most popular tools for requirements engineering in several AMs are paper, pencil, and a pin board. For instance, in Extreme Programming (XP) requirements are collected through user stories. User stories are extremely short descriptions of a single functionality that the development team has to implement. They are written on small pieces of paper with the size of a postcard and hang on a pin board.

The pin board is divided in three sections: user stories to be implemented, user stories under implementation, and user stories completed. This layout provides a visual representation of the project status. Even if many Agile teams do not use computer-based tools, some of them are useful. Among these, there are standard applications not focused on AMs and ad-hoc applications developed specifically to support some agile practices. Among the general purpose tools there are:

- **UML Modeling Tools:** Such tools are used in two ways: (1) to write a high level description of the application; (2) to reverse engineer the code to create documentation.
- **Requirements Negotiation Tools:** This kind of tools helps developers and customer to identify, prioritize, and manage requirements in different environments, including the Agile one (Chap. 7).
- **Instant Messaging Tools:** These tools are useful to keep in touch with the customer in order to discuss requirements when he is not on-site.

Among ad-hoc applications there are:

- **Project Management Tools:** Such tools focus on specific practices used in AMs and helps to store and retrieve requirements documents (e.g., user stories) in an electronic format.

14.7 Conclusions

This chapter has presented an introduction to the AMs and to their approaches to requirements elicitation and management. Since these methods are new, the subject is still evolving and many techniques are under investigation. AMs seem to be a valuable approach to software development for a relevant subset of projects, but their limits are not well defined yet.

The main difference between agile and traditional methods is the involvement of the customer in the development process. Both approaches present benefits and drawbacks. In particular, AMs seem to manage effectively requirements in small projects but not in large ones. AMs focus on the production of value for the customer reducing whatever does not add value from his point of view. Therefore, the involvement of the customer is of paramount importance to achieve this goal. On the contrary, traditional methods are able to manage effectively large project but their overhead is not suitable for smaller ones. At present, the research in this area is very active with several papers discussed in major software engineering conferences and two specific conferences: XP200x and Agile Universe.

Acknowledgements

This study has been partially funded by the Italian Ministry of Education, University, and Research under the Program FIRB, Project MAPS.

References

1. Abrahamsson P, Salo O, Ronkainen J, Warsta J (2002) Agile software development methods: Review and analysis. EPSOO 2002, VTT Publications 478

2. Ambler S (2001) Agile documentation. Accessed on 5th December 2004. http://www.agilemodeling.com /essays/agileDocumentation.htm

3. Ambler S (2002) Lessons in agility from Internet-based development. IEEE Software, 19(2): 66–73

4. Ambler S (2002) When does(n't) Agile modeling make sense? Accessed on December 5, 2004, http://www.agilemodeling.com/essays/whenDoesAMWork.htm

5. Bailey P, Ashworth N, Wallace N (2002) Challenges for stakeholders in adopting XP. In: Proceedings of 3rd International Conference on eXtreme Programming and Agile Processes in Software Engineering (XP2002), Alghero, Italy, 26-29 May

6. Beck K (1999) Extreme programming explained: Embrace change. Addison-Wesley, UK

7. Beck K, Beedle M, Bennekum A, Cockburn A, Cunningham W, Fowler M, Grenning J, Highsmith J, Hunt A, Jeffries R, Kern J, Marick B, Martin RC, Mellor S, Schwaber K, Sutherland J, Thomas D (2001) Manifesto for Agile software Development. Accessed on 5th December 2004, online at: http://www.agilemanifesto.org/

8. Cockburn A, Williams L (2000) The costs and benefits of pair programming. In: Proceedings of 1st International Conference on eXtreme Programming and Agile Processes in Software Engineering (XP2000), Cagliari, Italy, 21-23 June

9. Cockburn A (2000) Selecting a project's methodology. IEEE Software, 17(4): 64–71

10. Cockburn A, Highsmith J (2001) Agile software development: The business of innovation. IEEE Computer, September, pp.120–122

11. Cockburn A, Highsmith J (2001) Agile software development: The people factor. IEEE Computer, November, pp.131–133

12. Cockburn A (2002) Agile software development. Addison-Wesley, London, UK

13. Duncan R (2001) The quality of requirements in extreme programming. The Journal of Defence Software Engineering, June 2001 issue

14. Cohen D, Lindvall M, Costa P (2003) Agile software development. DACS State-of-the-Art Report. Accessed 5th December 2004, http://www.dacs.dtic.mil/techs/agile /agile.pdf

15. Cohn M, Ford D (2002) Introducing an Agile process to an organization. Access on 5th December 2004 http://www.mountaingoatsoftware.com/articles/IntroducingAnAgileProcess.pdf

16. Glass R (2001) Agile versus traditional: Make love, not war. Cutter IT Journal, December, 6(1): 12–18

17. Highsmith JA (1996) Adaptive software development. Dorset House Publishing, UK

18. IEEE Standard 830 (1998) IEEE recommended practice for software requirements

19. IEEE Standard 1233 (1998) IEEE guide for developing system requirements specifications

20. IEEE Standard 1362 (1998) IEEE guide for information technology: System definition, concept of operations document

21. Lee C, Guadagno L, Jia X (2003) An Agile approach to capturing requirements and traceability. In: Proceedings of 2nd International Workshop on Traceability in Emerging Forms of Software Engineering, Montreal, Canada, 7 October

22. Nawrocki J, Jasinski M, Walter B, Wojciechowski A (2002) Extreme programming modified: Embrace requirements engineering practices. In: Proceedings of International Conference on Requirements Engineering, 9-13 September, Essen, Germany

23. Ohno T (1988) Toyota production system: Beyond large-scale production. Productivity Press Cambridge, Mass

24. Paetsch F, Eberlein A, Maurer F (2003) Requirements engineering and Agile software development. In Proceedings of 8th International Workshop on Enterprise Security, Linz, Austria, 9-11 June

25. Poppendieck T, Poppendieck M (2003) Lean software development: An agile toolkit for software development managers. Addison-Wesley, London UK

26. Rasmusson J (2003) Introducing XP into Greenfield projects: Lessons learned. IEEE Software, May/June, 20(3): 21–28

27. Ronkainen J, Abrahamsson P (2003) Software development under stringent hardware constraints: Do Agile methods have a chance. In: Proceedings of 4th International Conference on eXtreme Programming and Agile Processes in Software Engineering (XP2003), Genoa, Italy, May 2003, pp.25–29

28. Schwaber K, Beedle M (2001) Agile software development with scrum. Prentice Hall PTR, Australia

29. Sommerville I, Sawyer P, (2000) Requirements engineering: A good practice guide. John Wiley & Sons, UK

30. Smith J. (2001) A comparison of RUP and XP. Rational software white paper. Accessed 5th December 2005 http://www.isk.kth.se/proj/2003/6b3403/sa3/www/RationalUnifiedProcess/papers/rupxp.htm

31. Standish Group, CHAOS Report 1994. Accessed 5th December 2004. http://www.standishgroup.com/sample_research/chaos_1994_1.php

32. Stapleton J (1995) DSDM –Dynamic system development method. Addison-Wesley, UK

33. Tomayko JE (2002) Engineering of unstable requirements using Agile methods. In: Proceedings of International Conference on Time-Constrained Requirements Engineering, Essen, Germany, 9-13 September

34. Turk D, France R, Rumpe B (2002) Limitations of Agile software processes. In: Proceedings of 3rd International Conference on eXtreme Programming and Agile Processes in Software Engineering (XP2002), Alghero, Italy, 26 - 29 May

35. Wells D (2003) Don't solve a problem before you get to it. IEEE Software, May/June, 20(3): 44–47

36. Womack JP, Jones DT (1998) Lean thinking: Banish waste and create wealth in your corporation, Simon & Schuster.

37. Young R (2002) Recommended requirements gathering practices, Accessed 5th December 2004, http://www.stsc.hill.af.mil/crosstalk/2002/04/young

Author Biography

Alberto Sillitti is Assistant Professor at the Free University of Bozen, Italy. His research areas include empirical software engineering, component-based software engineering, integration and measures of web services, and agile methods.

Giancarlo Succi, Ph.D., PEng is Professor of Software Engineering and Director of the Center for Applied Software Engineering at the Free University of Bozen. His research areas include agile methods, open source development, empirical software engineering, software product lines, software reuse, and software engineering over the Internet. He is author of more than 100 papers published in international conferences and journals, and of one book.

15 Requirements Engineering for Web-Based Information Systems

Jacob L. Cybulski and Pradip K. Sarkar'

Abstract: This chapter overviews the existing methods of requirements analysis as prescribed by some of the best-known web-development methods. It also discusses the pre-eminent importance of stakeholder analysis, identification of stakeholder views and concerns, and the processes governing elicitation of web systems requirements. The chapter finally derives a model of concern-driven requirements evolution from several case studies undertaken in the area of web-enabled employee service systems.

Keywords: Requirements engineering, Requirements evolution, Web-based information systems, Stakeholder analysis.

15.1 Introduction

Web-based information systems (WBIS) are often claimed to have a development process quite different to that of traditional software systems [10, 25, 65, 78, 79]. Requirements identification is one of the developmental stages where this difference is especially pronounced [54].

What makes web systems so different from the traditional software systems that their planning and construction requires a unique development process? The answers to this question are many, perhaps as many as the number of distinct types of WBISs themselves. Lawrence, Miletsky and their colleagues identify four major types of WBIS models, i.e. to deliver advertising and promotion, to assist business workflows, to facilitate inter-organizational interaction, and to support multi-participant trading (see Chap. 2 in [35] and Chap. 2 in [46]). Each kind of WBIS model emphasizes distinct aspects of site design depending on its purpose [16]. Some focus on supporting business to business transactions, the construction of online metaphors for business activity, and providing customer assistance, others look at promoting organizational brand, building market trust and credibility, yet some simply accentuate web contents, layout, navigation and search for organizational information. In the richness of web design issues, many directly concern WBIS customers and thus necessarily absorb requirements engineers. The customer preferences and wants, going well beyond the system function and performance, touch upon business organization and alliances, inter-organizational interactions, flow of supplies and products, business presence and access to customers (see Chaps. 4, 8-12 in [46]). In all of this business/system quagmire, marketing issues become dominant factors impacting web site's design –frequently ahead of its function –which includes web pages' style and color scheme, typography, graphic impression and multimedia, accessibility, internationalization and personalization, to name just a few (see Chaps. 9-14 in [43]). The WBIS development team often reflects the many issues that need to be taken into consideration during the system planning (see Chap. 5 in [46]). Apart from the obvious project stake-holders, such as sponsors, customers and users (see Chap. 2), the parties involved also include contents developers and copyright consultants, marketing and public relation specialists, media planner and strategies, creative and art directors, graphic designers, multimedia and interaction developers, and great many others, who are not often considered by requirements engineers as having input into the specification of a traditional software system. The fact that project stakeholders commonly hold conflicting opinions is well-known to the requirements engineer-ing community (see Chaps. 4 and 7). In WBIS systems, however, these conflicts are firmly embedded not only in the needs of the software systems to be developed but rather in the business processes and objectives of online buyers and sellers, and in the constraints imposed on the system by agencies regulating the financial transactions or determining compliance with the laws of the land and international treaties (see Chap. 5 in [80]).

While the scope of concerns to be considered in the earliest stages of web site construction can be significantly enlarged, due to the marketing-driven develop-ment process (also see Chap. 13), the delivery cycle for web-enabled applications is commonly very short, i.e. less than 3 month [17], which leaves very little time for any formal requirements gathering and their consolidation. The adequate de-velopment time-frame, so lacking in WBIS, is nevertheless critical for coping with the sheer diversity of web system users, in terms of their geographical locations, cultural and linguistic background, computer proficiency, and varying knowledge of business rules [10, 52, 78, 79]. Gordijn and associates [25] therefore criticize the currently practiced process of requirements gathering as largely inadequate for web development, failing requirements analysts in identification and characteriza-tion of the potential system users, their needs and preferences, and the features re-quired of the web systems under development [65]. All of these present major im-plications for the analysis of web systems requirements. Development of web-based information, thus, commonly relies on a step-wise prototyping approach [24, 74, 77] (see Chaps. 2 and 14). The iterative process of design, prototyping and evaluation is usually observed, and it commonly involves activities ranging from exploration, refinement, production, implementation, launch, maintenance and discovery (see Chaps. 3-5 in [16]). While prototype-based development re-sults in a shorter time to the market, due to the use of ad-hoc and unstructured de-velopment methods, it also leads to poor quality of web systems and services, and ultimately results in a great number of unsatisfied users [9, 17, 27, 79].

While acknowledging the necessity for requirements identification in the face of the continuing change of the web products [84], few of the established meth-odological approaches to WBIS development sheds much light on how require-ments for the web system could be fine-tuned and evolved along the various stages of system prototyping to improve the WBIS quality. To this end, Sarkar and Cybulski [68], as will be further elaborated in this chapter, emphasize the impact of stakeholder views and opinions on requirements evolution in web development. A stakeholder in this context is considered to be any individual, group, or organization whose actions can influence or be influenced by the development and use of the system whether directly or indirectly [55]. In case of information systems development process, the direct stakeholders are of special importance [73], and so Sarkar and Cybulski [69] place a particular attention to the concerns of users, developers, decision-makers and project initiators as the main drivers of the requirements establishment process. The remainder of the chapter is organized as follows. Section 15.2 outlines different approaches to requirements engineering to web development, with a special emphasis on the stakeholder issues. The following Sect. 15.3 discusses the significance of dealing with stakeholder concerns in the earliest stages of web development and the impact of these concerns on requirements engineering process. Special attention is placed on technical, organizational and inter-organizational impacts of stakeholder concerns. A model of concern-driven requirements evolution is subsequently developed in Sect. 15.4 based on the empirical study of several WBIS projects in the domain of employee service systems (ESS). Section 15.5 summarizes and concludes the chapter.

15.2 Approaches to RE for Development of WBIS

Review of WBIS literature reveals that the most commonly adopted development approach is incremental prototyping [28], which is often supplemented with a pilot development, in order to gather user feedback before the major development effort commences [22]. Subsequently, the web system prototype typically undergoes continuous evolution until it eventually becomes a fully-fledged web system [24, 74, 77]. The relative newness of WBIS, the incremental nature of the development approach, the rapid evolution of the underlying technology and the competitive pressure from other business units all seem to create a situation in which the requirements are in an almost constant flux [17] (also see Chap. 6).

Although there is no shortage of suggestions for the adoption of good WBIS design practices [see Chap. 4 in [35]], the fact that they are heavily interweaved with business strategy and marketing planning (see Appendix B in [46]), makes the disparate methods confusing in their vexed space of organizational, technical and social concerns. In recent times, however, the more systematic WBIS-specific methodologies have been slowly emerging. For example, Web Engineering [24], Relationship Management Methodology (RMM) [31], Howcroft's methodology [28], Internet Commerce Development Methodology (ICDM) [76] and Web IS Development Methodology (WISDM) [84] have all been proposed to deal with problems of web and e-commerce development.

15.2.1 Web Engineering

Ginige [24] argues that web development should be recognized as a process with all its structure and complexity, and not just as an atomic event considered by many web practitioners. In fact, the founders of the *web-engineering* concept [24,

51] go further to stress the importance of following a process where new functionality and information resources are iteratively added to the system over time. Furthermore, they assert that most of the current difficulties, with respect to the development of large web sites, can be attributed to a lack of suitable process models for the project teams to follow, suitable architecture, or a product model for the development of web-enabled applications. Another key aspect is that users could also be treated an integral part of a WBIS. Thus, when developing such systems, it is essential to have appropriate measures built into the development process that allow developers to cater for user related issues. One of the most significant points, at least from the point of view of this work, presented by Ginige [24] as a new and emerging trend associated with the development and evolution of web-enabled services, is the acknowledgement of the importance for project teams to improve by *learning through experience*.

15.2.2 Relationship Management Methodology (RMM)

RMM was introduced by Isakowitz [31] as a methodology for the development of hypermedia systems. RMM involves seven steps, of which the first three focus on design issues using entity-relationship diagrams. While acknowledging the importance of requirements analysis, RMM sheds little light on its mechanisms. Moreover, the steps prescribed by the methodology require a high level of specialized technical skills, which may not be a motivating factor for its adoption by web developers [65]. Another approach, proposed by Balasubramanian [4], an extension of RMM, is also a seven-stage iterative methodology. Though the methodology recognizes the complexity of stakeholder issues and consequent requirements setting, again as in RMM, it hardly sheds any light on the establishment of requirements, and focuses on document management over the web instead.

15.2.3 Howcroft's Methodology

In Howcroft's methodology [28], the first phase begins with a thorough analysis of the organizational web and competitive strategy. The project members need to be deeply involved with the formulation of the organization's strategies regarding the use of the web infrastructure. In the subsequent step the objectives or the business needs that are to be met through the adoption of the web infrastructure are defined. In the third step of the analysis phase, stakeholder analysis is conducted. Through *Information Analysis*, static and dynamic information required by the target users are identified. This is followed by an analysis of the skills of the project members, which are commonly multidisciplinary. The most critical process element, however, is the *User Analysis*, which for the most part is a complex process itself, as the intended users of the system have to be identified and analyses of their needs and characteristics carried out in advance. This step also includes an analysis of project risks.

Despite its thorough coverage of organizational objectives, business needs and user needs, the methodology does not propose any concrete means of how web developers could incorporate stakeholder issues into their work. Furthermore, there exists a dearth of empirical evidence about the experience of web developers with regards to their consideration of stakeholder issues.

15.2.4 Internet Commerce Development Methodology (ICDM)

Internet Commerce Development Methodology (ICDM) was proposed by Standing [76, 77]. ICDM combines the elements of business analysis as well as system development. Standing [77] contends that traditional information systems methodologies cover only the more technical aspects of information system development and do not look into the business aspects. Internet commerce is one of those fields, that necessitate intense business activity as part of their systems development, and thus it requires a thorough analysis of its place in the overall business strategy. Customers and suppliers (users of the systems) are encouraged to be involved at various stages of the e-Business operations, and participate in periodic reviews. Customer input is essential at the strategy development and business analysis stages and may involve the use of market research teams to obtain information on what customers require and on the potential barriers to using the web. More detailed requirements can be obtained in Group Requirements Sessions (GRS), telephone interviews or questionnaires. Customers can be involved in evaluating design issues through the use of prototype web systems and they should be included in testing and evaluation of the web site. Feedback is obtained from users once the web site is "live". The two requirements gathering techniques commonly used in ICDM are brainstorming and the Group Requirements Sessions (GRS). Standing [78] claims that brainstorming techniques are used to define alternative ways of undertaking Internet commerce, while GRS comprises of obtaining the detailed requirements within a relatively fast time frame with the involvement of customers, suppliers and internal staff [76-78].

Standing [76] also suggests that organizations implementing e-Business ventures should foster learning environments that enable the project executives to "learn" from the successes and failures of other organizations that have already adopted such ventures. This necessitates organizations investing in training programs for their staff. In fact, a web venture will not succeed if the users are not provided training in the usage of the system. Although clearly acknowledging the importance of stakeholder issues and "learning from experience" in requirements establishment for WBIS, ICDM is not prescriptive as to the use of any specific model or a process where these issues could be addressed.

15.2.5 Web Information Systems Development Methodology (WISDM)

The methodology, proposed by Vidgen [83], is an application of MultiView [3] to the development of web applications. WISDM was employed with the aim of evaluating the effectiveness of a pre-web methodology, such as MultiView, to a web-based application. The WISDM/MultiView approach begins with a thorough analysis of the system-hosting (owning or initiating) organizations to understand and articulate the strategic programs of the initiator. In the words of the author, "the overall aim of organizational analysis is the consideration of how value will be created." In the *Information Analysis* stage, the capture of system requirements is meant to take place; however, the recommended approach describes this development stage from a perspective of technical rationality.

The empirical testing of the WISDM methodology, actually on an electronic commerce project, indicates RAD (rapid application development) and prototyping as an effective approach to the WISDM project development. With this in mind, WISDM-developed websites are updated in an incremental manner to enhance them with new features. Disappointingly, WISDM, in its current form of definition, does not lay any explicit recommendations on the identification and analysis of stakeholders and their viewpoints and the project team's experience in dealing with user issues, though there is a clear indication of the future employment of an instrument (WebQual) to assess user satisfaction [82].

It is worth noting that other approaches to web design have also gained prominence in recent years, e.g., the *object-oriented hypermedia development methodology* (OOHDM) by Rossi [63]. Such methodologies are beyond the scope of this study as their primary focus is on the technical aspects of web systems rather than on stakeholder issues. Since we are dealing with the issue of stakeholder needs, examination of literature on stakeholder analysis in the disciplines of management, IS, and Requirements Engineering (RE) was warranted.

15.2.6 Comparison of Approaches

All the methodologies, with the exception of RMM, consider the organizational context to be a prime aspect associated with the adoption and implementation of WBIS. Furthermore, it can also be easily noted that by large the development of WBIS is iterative and incremental in nature. RMM is once again an approach that is structurally inclined. The importance of stakeholder issues is acknowledged in most of the discussed methodologies. However, none of the approaches explicitly incorporates stakeholder issues in the WBIS implementation process. Some of these proposed approaches have been offered in the form of mere suggestions [4, 24, 31], others have been evaluated by experts [28] or by focus groups [77]. WISDM has been empirically tested through an action research study [82], however, in the currently reported form of WISDM, the consideration of stakeholder issues has not been fully dealt with.

With regards to the existence of a mechanism for learning from experience, Ginige [24] (web engineering) and Standing [76] (ICDM) have mentioned that owing to the newness of web services dissemination within enterprises, project teams can *reuse* relevant aspects of their past experience or consult the experiences of their counterparts involved with similar projects in other institutions.

It should also be noted that the approaches discussed above, being methodologies, are naturally prescriptive, even to the extent that they could erect obstacles for project teams working in highly stressful and complex conditions [86]. Avoidance of such obstacles could possibly be the reason for the reviewed methodologies not to deal with the issue of stakeholders in a very structured, and thus restrictive manner. Web development methodologies, nevertheless, do act as frameworks guiding the construction of WBIS and are commonly found to be useful especially in organizations undertaking web projects across different organizational contexts, and which have different goals and thus distinct problems [28]. This trend is also reflected in a number of field studies where methodologies were adapted in order to cater to a particular organizational context [21, 66]. This is where the practical importance of project teams' consideration of the WBIS stakeholder needs is especially highlighted, though not adequately discussed in the existing methodologies. This very situation thereby triggered the motivation for this study to undertake further empirical investigation of real-life web projects.

Review of research into the development of web-enabled applications, and the implementation of web services, have uncovered a number of relevant facts and inadequacies, which are given in the following list.

Key Points:

- WBIS are acquired by organizations, from vendors, in order to web-enable (both intra-and inter-organizational) workflows.
- WBIS are developed or configured in an incremental manner using the evolutionary prototyping approach.
- New features are added to the WBIS with each development cycle iteration.
- The time frame for the development of WBIS is very short, i.e. about 3 months.
- A diverse and broad base of stakeholders are the potential users of web services, but it is not always possible to anticipate the constituent groups.
- The stakeholders are external to and thus beyond control of the project initiator.
- Due to this unanticipated large and relatively heterogeneous groups of stakeholders, system requirements for web applications are often "created from scratch", rather than elicited.
- The existence of a mechanism that enables web teams to learn from past experience, can aid the establishment of system requirements.

Issues inadequately covered by the current approaches

- Identification and description of stakeholders and their needs in the process of development and implementation of WBIS.
- Dealing with the needs and concerns expressed by a diverse and relatively large WBIS stakeholder base.
- Impact of the stakeholder needs and concerns on the requirement-driven features associated with the WBIS.
- Explanation of how the needs of the various potential users are inculcated in the further evolution and roll-over of web services.

The four issues pointing at the methodological inadequacies, as stated above, are associated with the existing research in the field of web-enabled workflow applications. Such issues fuel the need to probe further into the phenomenon of interest, as clearly outlined in the research objectives of this research. Thus, owing to the prominence of stakeholder issues in WBIS requirements engineering, aspects of stakeholder analysis, and the analysis of their viewpoints and concerns needs further elaboration.

15.3 Significance of Concerns in Requirements Engineering

The impetus for our research at this juncture came from the field of *stakeholder and viewpoint analysis*. In view of the impact of stakeholders concerns on the evolution of web systems, the review of relevant works of research was driven by the analysis of stakeholders and their needs and wants with regard to their future involvement with the system. The examination of stakeholder requirements and concerns led to the study of *viewpoints* or *multiple perspectives* in Requirements Engineering. The investigation of the concepts associated with the development and maintenance of multiple perspectives in the various disciplines, most notably in organization behavior and management, information systems, and requirements engineering, led to the revelation of an underlying body of knowledge about stakeholder resistance and conflict. The literature review moves to a discussion of conflict and stakeholder resistance in the context of information system development (ISD) and implementation.

15.3.1 Stakeholder Analysis

A review of literature in *information systems development* (ISD) and project management reveals that one of the major causes of project failures can be attributed to the dissatisfaction of stakeholders with either the way the project is undertaken or the final product of the project [6, 61, 62]. Indeed, stakeholder resistance to new technology adoption and their concerns over their association with it, and the prevailing power structures have a great impact on actual implementation of technological artifacts within the organization [40]. This fact has also been echoed by practitioners [41], who further assert that system development projects often fail because developers do not know who the "real" stakeholders are. The elevation of stakeholder analysis in system development projects, thus, seems imperative.

Stakeholder analysis originates from strategic management. Perhaps one of the most prominent works in the area is by Freeman [23], who argues that a prerequisite to effective strategic planning is the identification and analysis of those parties who can affect the implementation of the organization's strategic programs or be affected by them. This claim is strongly supported by Richardson [59], who affirms that stakeholder analysis should be carried out in business planning. Business *stakeholders*, or organizational members participating in common business processes, hold different perspectives on matters such as the setting of a group, organizational goals and values, allocation of resources, distribution of rewards, policies, procedures, and task assignments [23, 58, 72]. This reveals the idea of *multiple perspectives* held by the different stakeholders involved in organizational ventures. Freeman's [23] use of the concept enables an investigator to examine the external environment of an enterprise and to study how the enterprise manages multiple stakeholder relationships. In this way, a more comprehensive view is gained of the complexity of the business problems. Carroll and Nasi [8], on the other hand, stress the importance of considering multiple perspectives of stakeholders on moral grounds. In other words, the stakeholder analysis should be done not only to ensure the organization's survival and its profitability, but also because it is ethical to look into the viewpoints of the stakeholders who are affected or will be affected by the strategic decisions of the organization [14].

Over the years, information system researchers have discovered that the success of system development projects depends largely on the participation of all system stakeholders [40]. Ruohonen [64] argues that owing to the specialization in an enterprise, the existence of multiple perspectives with regard to system development and implementation projects is apparent. Therefore, as different stakeholders have different expectations with regards to an information system, the success or failure of the development project depends on how effectively managers address these expectations [6, 33]. Perhaps, the greatest proponents of the active involvement of end users in the development of information systems are Mumford and Weir [49]. In their approach to socio-technical system design, entitled the ETHICS (Effective Technical and Human Implementation of Computer-based Systems) approach, the authors contend that the effectiveness of system development projects can be brought about by the participation of stakeholders. A strong argument is put forward in favor of stakeholder participation in system development projects by warning that "systems designed without the active involvement of users may initially appear to be cost-effective on technical criteria, but in fact often incur high social costs, such as resistance to change, poor equipment utilization, high turnover, and absenteeism." Hence, the underlying premise behind ETHICS is the fact that for a system development project to be successful, there should be a close fit of the technology with social and organizational factors. Hwang and Thorn [29] speak in a similar strain with their assertion that stakeholder participation in the development of information systems can lead to higher levels of user satisfaction, system quality, and system usage. In a similar way, the socio-technical issues are prevalent in the analysis of *human activity* systems, as proposed by Checkland and Scholes [12] in their prominent work, *Soft Systems Methodology in Action*, in which identification of stakeholders and consideration of multiple perspectives is one of the most important aspects.

The concept of stakeholders with multiple perspectives is also relevant in the literature on inter-organizational systems (IOS). According to Cavaye [11], there are two key stakeholder perspectives in an IOS, namely those of the *sponsor* and of the *adopter*. Sponsors are firms leading the development and implementation of the IOS, while adopters are the intended users of IOS. Sponsors and adopters are referred to as *hubs* and *spokes*, respectively, by Murchland [50], and as *initiators* and *followers*, respectively, by Riggins and Mukhopadhay [60]. Even though a detailed look into IOS literature is beyond the scope of the study, we have adopted the term "initiator" to denote organizational units spearheading the implementation of WBIS.

One of the most significant contributions to the application of stakeholder theory in information system is by Pouloudi [55], who reiterates that the consideration of multiple stakeholder *viewpoints* will expose conflicting perspectives, and thus generate a greater understanding of stakeholder issues. This, in turn, will pave the way for the effective development and implementation of information systems. Pouloudi [57] proposes, within a specific organizational or inter-organizational context, a process of stakeholder identification and analysis that is iterative and evolutionary, thereby enabling a longitudinal and continuing approach of examining stakeholders and their viewpoints.

While placing considerable emphasis on the identification and analysis of stakeholders in information system development, how the multiple perspectives of stakeholders are examined in the process of building applications for organizational (or inter-organizational) workflows, and their reflection in the various software artifacts generated in the project is insufficiently explained. This indicates the value of a further investigation into the application of stakeholder theory and the resultant "multiple perspectives" to the requirements elicitation.

15.3.2 Viewpoint Analysis

Requirements engineers adopted the concept of stakeholder analysis for the purpose of identifying information sources and their characteristics, and the subsequent elicitation of requirements. This paved the way for the emergence of the concept of stakeholder *viewpoints* in RE. The concept of viewpoints was first introduced by Mullery [48] in his Controlled Requirement Specification (CORE) method. CORE recognizes the need for taking into account multiple perspectives of a system in the expression of requirements. The viewpoint approaches recognize that the development of a system involves the participation (in the form of expressing requirements) of multiple stakeholders with different perspectives, and conflict may erupt between these different perspectives

Finkelstein [20] and Nuseibeh [53] support the concept of multiple stakeholder perspectives with the statement that any requirements engineering activity in a project is likely to involve a "multiple development participants" with "multiple perspectives" on the system. They build on the concept of viewpoints as "a framework to structure, organize, and manage these perspectives" [20]. In their work, viewpoints are concerned with the role and responsibility of a particular participant or stakeholder in a software development process [19].

According to Leite [36] a viewpoint is a standing or mental position adopted by an observer of a phenomenon, with respect to his or her role in the observed situation. The viewpoints approach that is relevant to our research, in view of its disposition towards the organizational and human aspects of information systems development, is the *PREview (Process and Requirements Engineering Viewpoints)*

[75]. PREview provides an iterative process, based on the spiral model by Boehm [7], of identifying essential viewpoints, emergence of new requirements, and fine-tuning of existing ones with each cycle of the process. PREview places a significant emphasis on taking the strategic goals of an organization into account at the outset of the development process. These strategic issues affect every aspect of the system to be developed and are referred to as *concerns*, defined as a non-negotiable requirement, the compliance with which is critical to the success of the development process. Concerns reflect the goals of the organization, business objectives, beliefs, and policies, and can be represented with natural language statements. Thus, concerns need to be considered while designing a system. Concerns may impose constraints on requirements or translate into obligatory requirements.

Another prominent approach, which deals with multi-perspectives of stakeholders in Information Systems Development (ISD), is MultiView [2]. It comprises of a hybrid process involving both IT experts and users, thereby looking at both the technical and human aspects of ISD. The authors reiterate that the ISD should be considered as a social process, and be examined from a number of different perspectives, namely technical (system analysts), organizational (societal), and personal (individual) [Also see 37]. Organizational and personal perspectives reflect the human and social factors inherent in complex situations surrounding ISD projects [88]. Hence, an organization in which the IS project is being undertaken, can also hold a perspective, which essentially reflects its strategic goals and objectives. In this regard, it can be induced that the organizational viewpoint is similar to the notion of the concern offered by Sommerville [75].

At this juncture, it is appropriate to reflect on the fact that over time, while distinct stakeholders develop multiple viewpoints, the resulting divergence of views and objectives creates the potential for conflict [18, 53] (also see Chap. 7). In IS development, conflict is essentially a consequence of the scant attention paid by IS project managers to the resistance expressed by stakeholders [39] and when the needs and expectations of stakeholders are not being addressed [56], both of which are common in the realm of WBIS implementation [67].

15.3.3 Concern Analysis

It can be seen from the discussion so far that WBIS project could only be successful in terms of stakeholder satisfaction when the needs and expectations of the distinct (and non-homogenous) stakeholder groups could be complied with. Should the compliance not be achieved, the stakeholders will claim this situation as of great concern to them and perceive it as a serious problem. A clear distinction between the terms "concerns" and "problems" needs to be clearly articulated. Metcalfe [44] signals a warning against the use of the word "problem" to objectify facts. The objectification of facts to state problems implies an independence from human problem-owners, thereby legitimizing the universality of the issues, and thus preventing the subsequent claim by *elite* figures to be the sole producers of viable problem solutions, an argument strongly presented by Saul [71]. In reality, a problem does not exist independently of the problem-owner. According to

Landry [34], problems are perceptions in the minds of humans. Thus, it is more appropriate to refer to such issues as "concerns" rather than problems, as the former closely associates the issues with an owner. Furthermore, referring to issues as concerns also aligns the notion with the multiple perspectives or viewpoints approaches [88].

From this it can be induced that all stakeholders have concerns, which are expressed through their respective viewpoints. Similarly, the project team also has its own concerns, which are basically aligned with the related strategic concerns of the organization [15, 30, 32]. At this stage, one may wonder – if concerns are expressed through the different viewpoints of multiple stakeholders, how do we know that they are focused on the same issue? Churchman [13] enlightens us in this regard by advocating the splitting of the problem issue from the person who perceived it as such (i.e. separating the concern from the person who expressed it), and then asking other people to express their concerns over the problem issue. A stakeholder may express a range of concerns pertaining to a particular problem issue. Ultimately, the concerns can be analyzed and reconciled with the aim of generating a collective viewpoint on the problem, a perquisite to producing a collective solution [44]. Such an undertaking is in line with the Theory of Communicative Action by Habermas [26], who reiterated that members of society will jointly pursue actions to reach a rational consensus and mutual understanding, thereby bringing about the evolution of society. It should also be noted that if this consensus and mutual understanding cannot be reached, the concerns can potentially intensify [87], and result in full-blown conflict. Therefore, in concerns can be detected the seeds or antecedents of conflict [67].

Landry [34] and Metcalfe [44] supports the importance of stakeholder concerns in IS projects by maintaining that the perceptions of stakeholders with regards to the proposed information system are formed on the basis of their concerns. Therefore, project managers' understandings of the concerns of stakeholders are central to the "good design" of information system [45]. Metcalfe and Powell [45] further add that concerns provide the primary "lens" by which people process multitudes of information. In other words, they assign priorities to the messages on the basis of their concerns. Baskerville and Wood-Harper [5] employ the term "areas of concern", which warrants attention at the outset of an IS development process.

Our definition of a stakeholder concern is an amalgamation and an expansion of the previously discussed concepts, accordingly:

> A concern is an issue voiced by a particular stakeholder with regards to some aspect of the proposed information system, which impacts the stakeholder's involvement in this system and which when addressed will determine the need for further evolution of the system.

In a sense, concerns are related, albeit not directly, to the expectations and goals of stakeholders [38] (see also Chap. 9), i.e. both concerns and expectations are undoubtedly linked to their beliefs regarding what aspects of the proposed information systems will (or will not) motivate their involvement. Mazur [42] advises project managers to prompt customers and users to convey their main concerns regarding issues that prevent them from achieving their work-related and personal goals. They are also asked to state opportunities they are currently unable to avail, or reveal issues that consolidate their social position in the organization.

Key Points:

- Referring to issues of contention as "problems" objectify these issues, thereby ignoring the perspectives of people who expressed them and subsequently, restricting resolution in the hands of the elite.
- These issues are considered problems because people perceive them as such.
- Thus, the term "concern" is more appropriate as it relates the issue to the original perspective/viewpoint of the person.
- Concerns are expressed through the perspectives/viewpoints of stakeholders.
- Splitting the actual issue of concern from the perspective/viewpoint can enable other stakeholders to voice their concerns over the issue.
- Ultimately, concerns need to be analyzed and reconciled with the aim of generating a collective viewpoint on the problem and its solution.
- If the consensus and mutual agreement is not reached, the collective solution becomes impossible, thereby intensifying the concerns, and leading to conflict.
- Highly intense concerns signal the antecedents of conflict.
- Project managers' understandings of the concerns of stakeholders are central to the "good design" of information system.
- A concern is an issue voiced by a particular stakeholder with regards to some aspect of the proposed information system, which impacts the stakeholder's involvement in this system and which when addressed will determine the need for further evolution of the system.
- In line with the progression of a project, stakeholder concerns move from one stage to the other.

15.4 A Model of Concern-Driven Requirements Evolution

The impact of stakeholder concerns on the process of requirements elicitation in the development of WBIS has been studied by conducting a domain-wide study of six Melbourne-based organizations engaged in implementing web-based Employee Service Systems (ESS) [70]. Four of these organizations were universities and the other were the only two outsourced payroll companies in Melbourne adopting web technology to provide payroll services to their clients. In typical ESS projects, the stakeholders include project initiators, namely the HR divisions of the universities and the outsourced payroll providers, IT personnel (if separate from HR), clients of outsourced payroll companies, employees, and supervisors. Our interests were on project managers' experiences in dealing with concerns of the prime web-system stakeholders in the Human Resources (HR) environment and the impact of these concerns on the system requirements.

A set of semi-structured interviews were conducted with the participants who headed web projects. The interview protocol used for the interviews consisted of questions that were targeting elicitation of project managers experiences with the implementation and continual evolution of ESS, due to strategic initiatives of the organization and its business needs for a WBIS, characteristics of the baseline stakeholders, and the roll-over of the web-based solution. The questions were also directed at obtaining information about the project manager's experience with the concerns of stakeholders, their viewpoints regarding the issues of dissonance voiced by the users and the various players in the organization's power structures, as well as the perceived consequences of measures taken by the project team to alleviate discord or lessen user resistance toward the usage of web-enabled HR services. In companies that provided outsourced payroll services, the protocol also focused on the experience of project managers with the impact of promotional campaigns and incentives offered to clients in order to motivate their signing up for web services. In some cases, follow-up interviews were conducted either in person or by email communication to seek clarifications on narratives or to urge additional information.

As the primary focus of this study was views and opinions of individual project managers, the process of data collection and analysis followed phenomenological tradition [47, 81]. The phenomenological analysis has been employed in the study in order to fathom out the whole, and the relationship between stakeholders (project teams and the user-stakeholders), the organizations, and the web-enabled services. Through iterative reading and analysis of the transcribed interviews, a number of statements covering all explanations of the phenomena of interest were generated. When the iterative (hermeneutic) process was deemed to be complete, the statements were subjected to *phenomenological reduction* and *elimination* in order to identify their invariants. Statements that were irrelevant to the experience of the phenomena, overlapping, repetitive, or vague were removed, and the rest presented themselves as the textural meanings and invariant constituents. Through clustering and thematizing the invariants, forming the core themes of the experience, were generated. These included project manager's experience with stakeholder concerns in requirements establishment and system evolution, especially when dealing with WBIS data entry, workflow and other critical system functionality. The multidimensional account of project managers' experiences with the implementation of ESS revealed the social obstacles and fragility of intra-organizational relationships that demanded a cautious and tactful approach from project management.

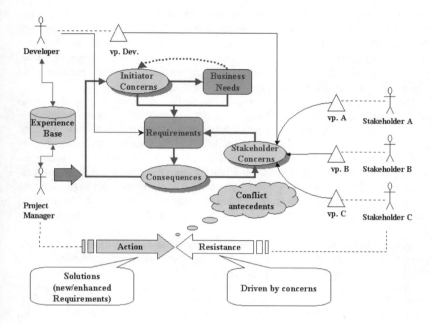

Fig. 15.1 The enhanced conceptual framework

The phenomenological method applied to this study led to the induction of factors that provide insights into the realm of ESS projects, and WBIS projects in general, especially with regards to the interactions between project managers and the other stakeholders as well as to the nature of the stakeholder concerns. Such insights indeed lead to the expansion and enhancement of the conceptual frameworks previously presented as part of stakeholder, viewpoint and concern analysis, as presented in Fig. 15.1.

Interestingly, the notion of concern-driven requirements evolution fits the conceptualization of the Concerns Based Adoption Model (CBAM), which originated from educational research in the 1970's and 1980's [1]. The CBAM model was aimed at conducting an in-depth study into the process of change as experienced by school teachers involved in the implementation of new curriculum and modes of teaching. One of the prime components of the model is the concept of the Stages of Concern (SoC), which provides a framework for elaborating the "feelings and motivations" of teachers with regards to the change in curriculum and instructional practices at different junctures in the implementation of new educational programs. The parallels between WBIS system requirements and educational curriculum are indeed striking. And so, the curriculum can be thought of as a specification of teaching practice, teachers as stakeholders, educational management as project managers, curriculum adoption as requirements refinement, etc. While the two models are not identical, the similarities provide opportunities to focus and guide the emerging model characteristics, and so we analyzed the WBIS requirements evolution process in terms of SoC stages of dealing with concerns, which include raising stakeholders' *awareness* of change, stakeholders' *informational* pursuits, *personal* and *management* engagement in the implementation, dealing with the *consequences* of change, *collaborative* improvement over change, and its possible *refocusing*.

In Fig. 15.1, the concept of stakeholders extends over the notions of an "organizational stakeholder" and "developer". The developer could either be the in-house IT division or the vendor from which the WBIS has been purchased. IT divisions have been also found to be the holders of WBIS project viewpoints, referred to in the figure as "vp. Dev", which are involved in the establishment of system requirements. However, it has not been affirmed from the phenomenological investigations in ESS that vendors make known their viewpoints with regards to the projects of their clients. However, vendors do play a role in the establishment of initial requirements as indicated by the arrow from the Developer to the Requirements.

Project managers, as revealed by the phenomenological inquiry of their experiences with ESS, are responsible for the entire process of implementation, and specify an initial set of system requirements for the WBIS, driven by their *personal* and *management* concerns [1]. These initial requirements are validated by the stakeholders through the feedback mechanism. Thus, the viewpoints "vp. A", "vp. B" and "vp. C" are expressed with regards to the requirements. However, the findings of the study uncovered the fact that the underlying concerns behind the viewpoints were linked to the actual or projected *consequences* of the requirements rather than the requirements themselves [1].

This is evident in Fig. 15.1 where the entire process of user validation is related to the consequences of the initiator requirements. In other words, stakeholders were primarily concerned with the situations resulting from the effects of the initiator requirements. Thus, they resist the initiator requirements in anticipation of such situations. To minimize the resistance, project managers interact and negotiate with the stakeholders, which is shown by the Action meeting the Resistance arrow in the figure (also see Chap. 7). This can give rise to *collaboration* concerns on the part of the project managers [1]. It is during these interactions that project managers should be able to detect the existence of conflict antecedents. As illustrated in the figure, the resistance is driven by the concerns of the stakeholders. Whenever project managers do not adequately address the concerns, the resistance may intensify, thereby increasing the likelihood of the antecedents manifesting into a full-blown conflict. On the other hand, project managers can alleviate the concerns and reduce resistance by introducing new requirements or enhancing or modifying the existing requirements, hence engaging in project and requirements *refocusing* [1]. This is indicated by the arrow leading back to the Requirements from the Stakeholder Concerns in Fig. 15.1. Evidently, the consequences of some of the new and enhanced/modified requirements are perceived negatively by the project managers, and give rise to their own concerns (arrow from Consequences back to Initiator concerns). Thus, the iterative nature of WBIS projects is demonstrated. It should be noted that the first two stages of concerns in the CBAM approach, namely *awareness*, and *informational*, could not be ascertained from the ESS managers' own experiences, though they implied that such concerns were voiced by some of the user groups.

The Experience Base, however implicit or semi-institutional, provides assistance to the IT developers and project managers alike. The arrow is double-headed to suggest the dual flow of information between the experience base, and the project managers and the developers, i.e. they also feed and augment the experience base with what they learnt from the current project, while availing the assistance provided by the knowledge infrastructure.

It is clear from the empirical data that stakeholder concerns, in this enhanced model of WBIS requirements evolution, are clearly the elemental precursors of system requirements.

It is therefore inconceivable that in the development of WBIS, and other similar software systems, stakeholder concerns should be left uncollected, unprocessed and unwanted. Requirements engineering methods must therefore be significantly enhanced and analysts retrained to place a special focus to their work with system requirements and stakeholder concerns.

15.5 Summary and Conclusion

Over an IS project duration, while distinct interdependent stakeholders develop multiple viewpoints, the resulting divergence of views and objectives creates the potential for conflict. The empirical evidence, as documented in the employee service system (ESS) projects described in this chapter, confirms that participation of stakeholders with multiple viewpoints can indeed lead to conflicts in requirements engineering for web-based information systems (WBIS).

The ESS case studies contribute to the formulation of a process governing the WBIS requirements evolution in response to stakeholder concerns, thereby creating the opportunity for the creation of a comprehensive, end-to-end, web development methodology. The studies also identify an explicit link between the stakeholder concerns, stakeholder resistance to change and the potential of conflict developing between concerned stakeholders and unresponsive project initiators. Web-based information systems are inherently complex, involving technological, enterprise and social concerns, and thus, a suitable iterative requirements engineering process model could enable WBIS project organization into more manageable, yet coherent, phases. The model of concern-driven web requirements evolution can be used as a solid basis for such a process model. Web engineering encompasses a number of activities from system conception and development to implementation, performance evaluation, and continual refinement. The enhanced conceptual framework of WBIS projects, covering prominent stages from strategic concerns to the formulation of business needs, and subsequent translation into system requirements and stakeholder validation of requirements, can indeed contribute in-depth substance to the web development methodology.

The advent of web-based information systems, quite unique in their features and development requirements, is only indicative of the new generation of software systems, as represented by enterprise-wide systems, commercial off-the-shelf systems, and reuse/component-based systems (also see Chap. 20). Such new types of software systems commonly involve the sophisticated enabling infrastructure, high business impact, short time to market and high level of stakeholder concerns. The new generation of software systems redefine the role of a requirements engineer and shift his or her attention from requirements management to stakeholder and concern management. By paraphrasing Wallnau's statement about component-based system paradigm [85, p 47], we observe that:

We cannot easily separate the real requirements from other desirable characteristic of the system. In fact, having collected the system requirements, the requirements engineer of the new generation systems, such as WBIS, still has a considerable task to accomplish. While the remainder of stakeholder needs may be no more than expression of preference, they still represent a large part, perhaps the majority, of the stakeholders' wants. These preferences will have conflicts, these preferences will have different communities that desire them, and most important, these preferences will be met in varying degrees by the delivered system.

This leads to an interesting requirements engineering paradox, again paraphrasing and refocusing Wallnau's original statement on the issues of concerns [85]:

The new requirements engineer now must spend a considerable amount of effort in dealing with nonrequirements. His traditional province –stakeholders' expression of what they wanted, what they needed, what would make their work improve - deals with those same needs, yet most of these things are now concerns.

And so ENTER the new generation of requirements engineers!

References

1. Anderson SE (1997) Understanding teacher change: Revisiting the concerns based adoption model. Curriculum Inquiry. 27(3): 331–367
2. Avison DE, Wood-Harper AT (1990) Multiview: An exploration in information systems development. Oxford, Blackwell Scientific Publications
3. Avison DE, Wood-Harper AT, Vidgen R, Wood JRG (1998) A further exploration into information systems development: The evolution of multiview 2. Information Technology & People. 11(2): 124–139
4. Balasubramanian V, Bashian A (1998) Document management and web technologies: Alice marries the mad hatter. Communications of the ACM, 41(7): 107–115
5. Baskerville R, Wood-Harper AT (1998) Diversity in information systems action research methods. European Journal of Information Systems, 7: 90–107
6. Bennet S, McRobb S, Farmer R (1999) Problems in information system development. Object-Oriented Analysis and Design using UML. McGraw-Hill Publishing Company

7. Boehm B (1986) A spiral model of software development and enhancement. Software Engineering Notes, 11(4): 22–32
8. Carroll AB, Nasi J (1997) Understanding stakeholder thinking: Themes from a Finish Conference. Business Ethics, A European Review, 6(1): 46–51
9. Carstensen PH, Vogelsang L (2001) Design of Web-based information systems: New challenges for systems development. In: European Conference on Information Systems, Bled, Slovenia, pp.536–547
10. Carter J (2002) Developing E-commerce systems. Prentice-Hall, Sydney Australia
11. Cavaye ALM (1995) The sponsor-adopter gap - Differences between promoters and potential users of Information Systems that link organizations. International Journal of Information Management, 15(2): 85–96
12. Checkland P, Scholes J (1990): Soft Systems Methodology in Action. Chichester: John Wiley & Son, Australia
13. Churchman CW (1971) The design of inquiring systems. New York, Wiley
14. Clarkson MBE (1995) A stakeholder framework for analyzing and evaluating corporate social performance. Academy of Management Review, 20(1): 92–117
15. Davenport TH (1993) Process innovation: Reengineering work through information technology. Boston, Harvard Business School Press
16. Duyne DK, Landay JA, Hong JI (2003) The design of sites: Patterns, principles and processes for crafting a customer-centered web experience. Boston, Addison-Wesley
17. Earl M, Khan B (2001) E-commerce is changing the face of IT. MIT Sloan Management Review. 43(1): 64–72
18. Easterbrook S (1991) Handling conflict between domain descriptions with computer supported negotiation. Knowledge Acquisition: An International Journal, 3(4): 255–289
19. Finkelstein A, Kramer J, Goedicke M (1990) ViewPoint oriented software development. In: Proceedings 3rd International Workshop on Software Engineering and its Applications. Toulouse, France
20. Finkelstein A, Kramer J, Nuseibeh B, Finkelstein L, Goedicke M (1992) Viewpoints: A framework for integrating multiple perspectives in system development. International Journal of Software Engineering and Knowledge Engineering, 2(1): 31–58
21. Fitzgerald B (1997) The use of system development methodologies in practice: A field Study. Information Systems Journal, 7(3):201–212
22. Fraternali P (1999) Tools and approaches for developing data-intensive web applications: A survey. ACM Computing Surveys, 31(3): 227–263
23. Freeman RE (1984) Strategic management: A stakeholder approach. Boston, Pitman
24. Ginige A (1998) Web engineering: Methodologies for developing large and maintainable web-based information systems. In: Proceedings of IEEE International Conference on Networking India and the World Ahmedabad, India
25. Gordijn J, Akkermans H, van Vliet H (2000) Value based requirements creation for electronic commerce applications. In: Proceedings of the 33rd Hawaii International Conference on Systems Sciences. Hawaii, pp.1915–1924
26. Habermas J (1984): The theory of communicative action. Cambridge, Polity Press
27. Hammar-Cloyd MH (2001) Designing user-centered web application in web time. IEEE Software. 18(1): 62–69
28. Howcroft D, Carroll J (2000) A proposed methodology for web development. In: Proceedings of 8th European Conference in Information Systems (ECIS), Vienna, Austria

29. Hwang MI, Thorn RG (1999) The effect of user engagement on system success: A meta-analytical integration of research findings. Information and Management. 35(4): 229–236

30. Irani Z (2002) Information systems evaluation: Navigating through the problem domain. Information and Management. 40(1): 11–24

31. Isakowitz T, Stohr EA, Balasubramanian V (1985) RMM: A methodology for structured hypermedia design. Communications of the ACM 38(8): 34–44

32. Jacobson I, Christerson M, Jonsson P, Overgaard G (1992) Object-oriented software engineering: A use case driven approach. Addison-Wesley, UK

33. Lacity MC, Hirschheim R (1995) Benchmarking as a strategy for managing conflicting stakeholder perceptions of information systems. Journal of Strategic Information Systems, 4(2): 165–185

34. Landry M (1995) A note on the concept of problem. Organizational Studies, 16(2): 315–327

35. Lawrence E, Newton S, Corbitt B, Braithwaite R, Parker C (2002) Technology of internet business. MIlton, Qld, Wiley & Sons, Australia

36. Leite JCSP, Freeman PA (1991) Requirements validation through viewpoint resolution. IEEE Transactions Software Engineering, 17(12): 1253–1269

37. Linstone HA (1989) Multiple perspectives: Concept, applications and user guidelines. Systems Practice. 2(3): 307–331

38. Lyytinen K, Hirschheim R (1987) Information system failures - A survey and classification of the empirical literature. Oxford Surveys in Information Technology, 4: 257–309

39. Marchewka JT (2003): Information technology project management: Providing measurable organizational value. John Wiley & Sons, UK

40. Markus ML (1983) Power, politics and MIS implementation. Communications of the ACM, 26(6): 430–444

41. May LJ (1998) Major causes of software project failures. Crosstalk, July

42. Mazur G (2003) Voice of the customer (define): QFD to define value. In: Proceedings of the 57th American Quality Congress. Kansas City, USA

43. McCracken DD, Wolfe RJ (2004) User-centered website development: A human-computer interaction approach. Upper Saddle River, NJ: Pearson-Prentice Hall

44. Metcalfe M (2000) Concern solving: Emancipating problem solving. Working Paper, University of South Australia, School of Accounting and Information Systems, Adelaide, Access 5th December 2004 http://business.unisa.edu.au/cobra /documents/concerns_IT&P.pdf

45. Metcalfe M, Powell P (1995) Perceiver's concerns: On the nature of information. European Journal of Information Systems, 4: 121–129

46. Miletsky J (2002) Planning, developing and marketing successful web sites. Australia: Thomson

47. Moustakas C (1994) Epoche, phenomenological reduction, imaginative variation, and synthesis. In: Phenomenological Research Methods. SAGE Publications, UK

48. Mullery GP (1979) CORE - A method for controlled requirements expression. In: Proceedings of 4th International Conference on Software Engineering. Munich, Germany, pp.126–135

49. Mumford E, Weir M (1979) Computer systems in work design, the ETHICS method: Effective technical and human implementation computer systems: A work design exercise book for individuals and groups. London: Associated Business Press.

50. Murchland P (1995) Inhibitors to adoption of electronic commerce. Electronic Markets(16-17): 11–12

51. Murugesan S, Deshpande Y, Hansen S, Ginige A (1999) Web engineering: A new discipline for development of web-based Systems. In: Proceedings of 1st ICSE Workshop on Web Engineering. Los Angeles, pp.1–9

52. Nazareth DL (1998) Designing effective websites: Lending structure to a chaotic process. In: Proceedings of 4th Americas Conference on Information Systems. Baltimore, Maryland, pp.1011–1013

53. Nuseibeh B, Finkelstein A, Kramer J (1994) A framework for expressing the relationships between multiple views in requirements specification. IEEE Transactions on Software Engineering, 20(10): 760–773

54. Overmeyer SP (2000) What's different about requirements engineering for web sites? Requirements Engineering Journal, 5(1): 62–65

55. Pouloudi A (1999) Aspects of the stakeholder concept and their implications for information systems development. In: Proceedings of 32nd Hawaii Conference on System Sciences. Hawaii

56. Pouloudi A, Whitley EA (1996) Discussing the role of information systems in the manifestation of organizational and inter-organizational conflict. The Systemist, 18: p. 217–238

57. Pouloudi A, Whitley EA (1997) Stakeholder identification in inter-organizational systems: Gaining insights for drug use management systems. European Journal of Information Systems, 15(2): 85–96

58. Putnam L, Poole M (1987) Conflict and negotiation. Handbook of Organizational Communication: An Interdisciplinary Perspective, Porter L (Ed.), pp.549–599

59. Richardson B, Richardson R (1992) Business planning: An approach to strategic management. Pitman, USA

60. Riggins FJ, Mukhopadhyay T (1999) Overcoming adoption and implementation risks of EDI. International Journal of Electronic Commerce 3(4): 103–115

61. Robey D, Farrow DL (1982) User involvement in information system development: A conflict model and empirical test. Management Science, 28(1): 73–87

62. Robey D, Farrow DL, Franz CR (1989) Group process and conflict in system development. Management Science, 35(10): 1172–1191

63. Rossi G, Schwabe D, Garrido A (1997) Design reuse in hypermedia application development. In: Proceedings of 8th ACM Conference on Hypertext Technology (HyperText'97). Southampton, Inglaterra, ACM Press

64. Ruohonen M (1991) Stakeholders of strategic information systems planning: Theoretical concepts and empirical examples. Journal of Strategic Information Systems. 1(1): 15–28

65. Russo NL (2000) Developing applications for the web: Exploring differences between traditional and world wide web application development. In: Managing Web-Enabled technologies in Organizations: A Global Perspective, Khosrowpour M (Ed.). Idea Group Publishing, pp.23–35

66. Russo NL, Wynekoop J, Walz D (1995) The use and adaptation of system development Methodologies. In: Proceedings of the Information Resources Management Association International Conference, Khosrowpour M (Ed.). Idea Group Publishing: Hershey, PA, USA

67. Sarkar PK, Cybulski JL (2002a) Analysis of stakeholder concerns with a view to avoid organizational conflict in B2B Systems. In: Proceedings of the 15th International Conference in Electronic Commerce. Bled, Slovenia

68. Sarkar PK, Cybulski JL (2002c) Consideration of stakeholder concerns in the development of web-enabled systems. In: Proceedings of the IADIS International Conference WWW/Internet. Lisbon, Portugal, pp.774–779

69. Sarkar PK, Cybulski JL (2003a) Process of requirements evolution in web-enabled employee service systems. In: Proceedings of 12th International Conference in Information System Development (ISD). Melbourne, Australia

70. Sarkar PK, Cybulski JL (2003b) Applying domain analysis to the investigation of web-enabled human resource Projects. In: Proceedings of 14th Australasian Conference in Information Systems (ACIS). Perth, Australia, paper No: 270

71. Saul JR (1997) The unconscious civilization, Penguin, UK

72. Schermerhorn Jr. JR, Hunt JG, Osborn RN (1997) Conflict and negotiation. In: Proceedings of Organization Behavior. John Wiley & Sons, Inc. pp. 377–398

73. Sharp H, Finkelstein A, Galal G (1999) Stakeholder identification in the requirements engineering Process. In Proceedings of Database and Expert Systems Applications (DEXA 99). Florence, Italy, IEEE Computer Society Press, pp.387–391

74. Siau K (1998) Method engineering for web information systems development: Challenges and issues. In: Proceedings of Fourth Americas Conference on Information Systems. Baltimore, Maryland, pp.1017–1019

75. Sommerville I, Sawyer P, Viller S (1997) Viewpoints for requirements elicitation: A practical approach. In: Proceedings of 3rd IEEE International Conference on Requirements Engineering. CO, USA, pp.74–81

76. Standing C (2000) Internet commerce development: Artech House Inc., USA

77. Standing C (2001) The requirements of methodologies for developing web applications. IN: Proceedings of European Conference on Information Systems, Bled, Slovenia, pp.548–556.

78. Standing C (2002) Methodologies for developing web applications. Information and Software Technology, 44(3): 151–159

79. Stevens KJ, Timbrell GT (2002) The implications of E-commerce for software project risk: A preliminary investigation. In: Proceedings of IFIP, Copenhagen, Denmark

80. Treese GW, Stewart LC (2003) Designing systems for Internet commerce. Addison-Wesley, Australia

81. van Manen M (1990) Researching lived experience. New York, USA University of New York Press

82. Vidgen R (2002) Constructing a web information system development methodology. Information Systems Journal, 12: 247–261

83. Vidgen R (2002) What's so different about developing web-based information systems? In: Proceedings of European Conference in Information Systems. Gdansk, Poland, pp.262-271

84. Vidgen R, Avison D, Wood B, Wood-Harper T (2002) Developing web information Systems. Elsevier, Amsterdam

85. Wallnau KC, Hissam SA, Seacord RC (2002) Building systems from commercial components. Addison-Wesley, Boston

86. Wastell DG, Newman M (1993) The behavioural dynamics of information systems development: A stress perspective. Accounting, Management and Information Technology, 3: 121–148
87. Wilson P (1983) Second hand knowledge. Greenwood Press, Westport, Connecticut, USA
88. Wood-Harper AT, Corder S, Wood J, Watson H (1996) How we profess: The ethical system analyst. Communications of the ACM, 39(3): 69–77

Author Biography

Associate Professor Jacob L. Cybulski is an Associate Head of School (Research) in Information Systems at Deakin University. His professional interests include requirements engineering, knowledge management and domain analysis. Jacob works as a consultant with organizations willing to introduce novel approaches to their development methods, e.g. domain analysis, design patterns and life-cycle support tools. Jacob's past projects range from mechanical engineering and telecommunications applications to developing software productivity environments and toolkits. Jacob also acted as an expert witness in the area of software development methodologies and process quality. His current work focuses on information systems alignment, e-commerce and web development.

Dr Pradip K. Sarkar is a Research Assistant in the School of Business Systems at Monash University. His research is aimed at improving current methods of requirements engineering for web-based application development to better service the diverse needs of a global user. In the past, Pradip has also worked in India, Thailand and Australia in the software industry and academia, which has given him the unique opportunity to gain first-hand experience with software development practices across national, language and cultural boundaries.

Part 3
Studies and Industrial Experience

Part 3 concludes the book with chapters on specific practical/industrial examples, empirical studies and an examination of trends in requirements engineering. Chapter 16 presents practical experiences from requirements engineering in the public sector. Chapter 17 discusses the experiences of a company using a tailored variant of the Rational Unified Process and, in particular, their experiences with requirements engineering. Chapter 18 present a study on requirements engineering across six different companies. A lot can be learned by trying to combine results obtained in different studies. One such attempt is presented in Chap. 19, where an analysis of surveys in requirements engineering is provided. Finally, this part is concluded with a chapter discussing possible solutions and trends in requirements engineering (Chap. 20).

Thus, in summary this part contains chapters on the following topics:

- Chapter 16: Requirements engineering in the public sector
- Chapter 17: Experiences from one company
- Chapter 18: A study of requirements engineering at six companies
- Chapter 19: A analysis of published surveys in requirements engineering
- Chapter 20: Solutions and trends

This part concludes with an outlook into the future trends in requirements engineering.

The five chapters are by Nigel Martin from Department of Defense, Australia and Shirley Gregor from Australian National University, Australia; Nur Yilmaztürk from ABB Corporate Research, Sweden; Tony Gorsheck and Mikael Svahnberg from Blekinge Institute of Technology, Sweden; Barbara Paech and Lars Borner from University of Heidelberg, Germany, Tom Konig from Fraunhofer Institute for Experimental Software Engineering, Germany, and Aybüke Aurum from University of New South Wales, Australia; Christof Ebert from Alcatel, France and Roel Wieringa from University of Twente, The Netherlands.

16 Requirements Engineering: A Case of Developing and Managing Quality Software Systems in the Public Sector

Nigel Martin and Shirley Gregor

Abstract: This chapter describes the managerial processes and governance frameworks that are used to develop software applications and software-intensive systems at the Australian Bureau of Statistics (ABS). The chapter focuses on the software requirements development activities against the backdrop of a dynamic operating environment and technically challenging Information and Communication Technology (ICT) infrastructure. Recognition of the importance of software requirements engineering at a strategic level is evident, supported by senior management and with ongoing user involvement and consultation An enterprise architecture provides a framework for the integration of requirements engineering with business drivers and subsequent development practices. The software and ICT outcomes are benchmarked at or near best practice and are accompanied by above average ABS corporate performance. The ABS practices show congruence with theoretical frameworks and international standards.

Keywords: Software development process, Enterprise architecture, Management involvement, Phases, Activities, Tasks, Prioritization.

16.1 Introduction

The Australian Bureau of Statistics (ABS) is Australia's official statistical organization, with a corporate charter to assist and encourage informed decision-making, research and discussion with governments and the community. It aims to provide high quality and objective statistics products and a responsive statistics service. The ABS organization is focused on understanding and attending to their clients' business requirements, providing a clear explanation of what clients must provide in order for the ABS to meet their information needs, and assisting the clients to understand ABS statistics. In a broader sense, the ABS is involved in delivering client services in the areas of current and historical statistics research; survey, sample, and questionnaire design; statistical training; and survey evaluation and methodology reviews.

The aim of this chapter is to examine and analyze the software requirements engineering practices within a public sector organization. The ABS was selected for its exemplary performance as a business agency of the Australian government, and its continuing outstanding record of achievement in the development and management of high quality ICT systems, particularly software required for delivering statistics products. The ABS is a unique government organization that internally generates sixty percent of its business software. The software generation effort includes the development of new software systems (where required), and the adaptation and integration of commercial and specialist statistics processing software packages into the existing ABS ICT infrastructure. The other elements of the ABS suite of software are commercially available ready-use products, such as operating systems and desktop productivity applications (e.g. word processors, spreadsheets, and electronic presentations).

The ABS data and information presented in this case study was gathered as part of a larger doctoral study in information systems, specifically the use of Enterprise Architectures in government agencies. The study used a qualitative research method, which included several data collection techniques, with the ABS organization as one case study. The opportunity was taken to speak directly with senior management and executives in semi-structured and unstructured interviews, collect and analyze archival documents and parliamentary reports, study public announcements and executive presentations, and participate in system demonstrations. The data collected include interviews with the ABS Director responsible for the Software Development Process (SDP) (including the Requirements Engineering phase) and a 'hands-on' test run of the Input Data Warehouse software application.

While this first section has provided a brief introduction, the balance of the chapter is organized as follows. In Sect. 16.2 the case background that describes the ABS organization and what it does, the ABS ICT systems, and how the ABS case has been evaluated from the specific quality and organizational perspectives is presented. In Sect. 16.3 the practical workings of the governance frameworks from the requirements engineering perspective, a discussion of the social mechanisms used to engineer requirements, and a view on how architecture can be used in drawing together and managing software requirements is presented. In Sect. 16.4 the ABS software development process, including a description of the five core development phases, is detailed. In Sect. 16.5 the requirements phase of the software development process, including contrasts with theory and internationally recognized standards, is discussed. In Sect. 16.6 three examples of ABS software requirements elicitation are presented. In Sect. 16.7 the chapter concludes with a summary of what has been observed about the requirements phase in the ABS case, including the connections with strategic and resource planning, the requirements engineering method and relationship with quality assurance, and how social mechanisms form an important part of the requirements phase.

16.2 The ABS Case Study Setting

The ABS is a unique agency of the Commonwealth government of Australia in that it is a public provider of statistical products, goods and services to the local and international community. The ABS mission, shows a concentration on the important service provider aspects of the agency [5], and is stated as follows: "Assisting and encouraging informed decision-making, research and discussion within governments and the community, by providing a high quality, objective and responsive national statistical service".

The ABS is an organization of 3,002 personnel covering the employment disciplines of mathematics, economics, statistics, information technology, finance and general business administration. In 2002-2003, the ABS expended over $272 million in primarily employee, and goods and service supplier costs. As a proportion, approximately 17 per cent of staff are engaged as ICT professionals, while around 20 per cent of the annual expenses are attributable to ICT activities and initiatives [11, 12]. The ABS offers statistical publications in the two major areas of economic (e.g., trade, business, national accounts, manufacturing, agriculture) and population (e.g., census, demography, labor, social conditions, crime) statistics, information consultancy services, statistical consultancy services, user funded surveys, and other products and services to local and international customers. The ABS delivered over 170 economic-statistic and over 160 population-statistic publication titles, covering over 690 separate publication releases, in the 2002-2003 period [10]. The statistics business has proven to be lucrative for the ABS with over AUD$26.1 million raised from statistics based operations in 2002-2003 [9].

In supporting these expansive business operations, the ABS is a diverse user of ICT with a complex array of software and hardware infrastructure that is primarily directed at meeting business needs and solving business-related problems. The ABS ICT environment is characterized by a desktop environment that includes a Windows XP operating system, Lotus Notes, Lotus SmartSuite, and 500 commercial software products, with a network of over 3,400 personal computers and over 1,100 laptop computers. The ABS network is built on a distributed client-server computing arrangement [13, 21].

ABS Hewlett Packard ProLiant servers provide the file, print, directory and naming services, with Transmission Control Protocol-Internet Protocol (TCP/IP) deployed over 100 Mbps switched Ethernet Local Area Networks (LANs) and Wide Area Network (WAN) IP. The ABS will operate a solely mid-range environment by 2006. The mid-range environment is based on Sun Microsystems servers and the Solaris operating systems. The majority of systems are deployed as Oracle database servers using SQL.NET over TCP/IP, including 20 Oracle databases that support over 150 software applications. The information storage solution is based on an IBM FastT900, 3584 Tape library and Tivoli Storage Manager Software [13, 21]. Some specific examples of agency software include security and encryption services software for external network devices, messaging software for conducting virtual meetings across the WAN, time series and tabulated data analysis software applications, and survey interview assistance software. Some further discussions on the requirements for time series analysis, survey interview assistance, and data warehousing software will follow later in the chapter.

The ABS aims to ensure that no matter how diverse its software needs, the requirements engineering and management phase, including all associated activities and component tasks, remain constant across ABS ICT activities. The ultimate goal of the ABS is to create software that enables business processes and the conduct of its three-year rolling-work programs. This approach to developing software, which is driven primarily by agency business requirements, is typified in the

ABS business practices and processes [14]. One of the core ABS beliefs provides a pointer as to how software requirements should be developed: Never lose the business focus. All information technology should a have a direct or indirect business value [31]. This is potentially a good axiom for all organizations whether they are in the private or public sector of business.

The ABS works with the community, the private sector and other government agencies in the three jurisdictions to develop and deliver information products and services. As examples, the ABS works with representatives from the community and health sector to develop statistical products, surveys and reports on Australia's national health industry sector, while also working with the Australian Taxation Office and Department of Family and Community Services to exchange collected government information and develop products related to business and social conditions statistics. The structured management of software requirements, and the associated delivery of business systems and outcomes, has seen the ABS attain a level of ICT systems performance that is comparable to many private and public sector organizations. Since mid 1994, the ABS Technology Services Division (TSD) has contracted the Gartner Group to benchmark a large range of functional areas within TSD, as part of a quality improvement program, and to test the efficiency of TSD against peer groups of selected similar organisations.

The ABS advised the Australian Parliament that by the end of 1999–2000, over 80 per cent of TSD activities have been covered by the benchmarking work, including applications and ICT infrastructure development work. The Gartner studies compare ABS TSD functions with a large number of other government and non-government organisations internationally, showing that the ABS information technology operations rate well above average in most areas, and above average in all areas [2]. This was followed up in 2000-2001 with a further report to the parliament that ongoing benchmarking studies with Gartner show that the ABS is "very efficient in its management and use of technology" [4]. The ABS case will be evaluated from two perspectives. First, we look at requirements engineering from the corporate management viewpoint, and examine how software requirements engineering assists the ABS in meeting its overall business objectives. Second, we look at the requirements engineering phase in more detail, and determine what this phase delivers to successful ABS software projects. The ABS was selected as an exemplary public organization that develops its software taking a strategic view, rather than developing stove-piped software solutions on a project-by-project basis.

16.3 Governance of ABS Software Development

In order to understand the more tactical requirements phase of software development, we consider that it is important to recognize that strategic management issues drive the business. The creation of software requirements does not simply start when an organization decides to buy a new desktop tool or operating system. The seeds of new software systems are sown very early in the higher levels of management. The non-executive Australian Statistics Advisory Councilors and senior ABS executive group members play a pivotal role in the early definition of core business needs and drivers.

The two most senior management groups in the ABS set the corporate directions that shape the business processes and the scope of the ICT systems, including software, that are to be developed during the rolling three-year forward-work Program. This means that the software requirements have their genesis and support in the executive ranks of the ABS. The management groups have directed that substantial user group consultations occur to ensure that business requirements are elicited, identified, and prioritized for action and development. These consultation processes are aimed at assisting the compilation of requirements that are consistent, feasible and testable [2]. ABS practices in the area of user consultation and advisory show that over 57 external advisory working groups and consultative committees are activated each year to test business directions, processes and practices. Corporate user groups are represented on project management boards, architecture panels (i.e., business managers and ICT architects), and the critical business unit customer groups [13, 15, 20]. User groups have an additional role later in the software development process test phase when the ABS conducts user testing. The ABS uses Hiser group documentation and user test protocols to conduct user testing and review of prototype and production systems, including software functionality. The Hiser Group is an ICT consultancy firm based in Melbourne, Australia that specializes in assisting organizations with the development and testing of user-centered information systems, particularly web-based applications, user interfaces and systems [18].

Importantly, the definition and development of requirements at the strategic and tactical levels of the ABS organization is evident. This approach suggests that non-executive boards and/or councils, government executives and operational managers should assume joint responsibilities for the development of ICT systems for the business. The vertical flow down of requirements from top level "business" to lower level "software" also provides the ABS with a traceability pathway that is defined in the relevant software standards and specifications. Software requirements must be traceable to the business needs, systems requirements and the system design objects [28].

The ABS Enterprise Architecture realizes the ABS vision for ICT, providing an integrative framework for business goals and the accompanying software and infrastructure related activities. The Enterprise Architecture is a description of all the elements of the ABS organization including the connective relationships between the various elements. These elements include the business process taxonomies, technologies and toolsets, software application architecture, data management architecture, and information technology infrastructure [13]. The Enterprise Architecture is driven by the business goals, strategies and corporate financing, and includes the taxonomy of human resources and systems that enable the conduct of agency work outputs. The architectural method shows a vision for the creation of an organization that has management decisions, business drivers and needs, and required ABS products (goods and services) as critical inputs and considerations [17] (see Fig. 16.1).

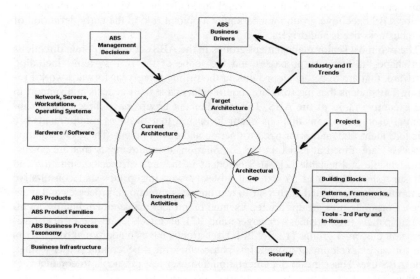

Fig. 16.1 ABS enterprise architecture method [17]

The Enterprise Architecture imposes strict strategic and tactical rules on the development of software systems. The architecture mandates that the agency "should assemble, before it buys, before it builds" new software systems. Project software programmers are encouraged to snap lock pre-developed or commercial software components together using service interfaces, rather than creating new software systems. Also, project managers are instructed to look at currently deployed software technologies in order to maintain technology control and discipline [13].

The architecture method enables the proliferation and evolution of an Enterprise Architecture (i.e., current to target architecture) where the ABS invests in hardware, software and infrastructure systems to serve the agency and its business needs. ABS software assets are intrinsic to the agency and its architecture and, at the strategic level, provide a source of competitive advantage in delivering goods and services to the community. Importantly, as we see in this case, software requirements have a strategic dimension that is often forgotten when placed in the frame of an individual ICT project.

16.4 The ABS Software Development Process

The effective engineering and dynamic management of software requirements is of critical importance in any organization that depends heavily on software systems for its business. In the past twenty years, the Australian Bureau of Statistics (ABS) has generated internally over sixty percent of its business software [9]. In order to bring a greater level of consistency, uniformity and overall quality to the development of software at the ABS, a business quality project was initiated and placed under the leadership of a senior ICT Director in mid 2001. The ABS SDP was officially launched and adopted in September 2002, effectively formalizing twenty years of software development practice at the ABS [8, 31] (Fig. 16.2).

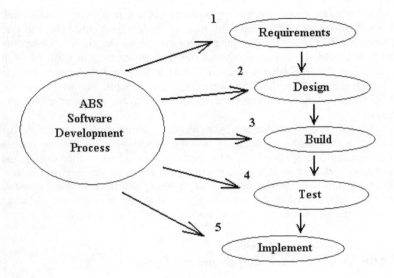

Fig. 16.2 ABS software development process [8, 31]

Some important terminology is briefly explained as follows. The ABS has purposefully adopted a specific hierarchy of phases, activities and tasks for the SDP. The software development process consists ideally of the five core phases with each phase broken into a series of integrated activities. The activities are then further sub-divided into a set of inter-related tasks [8]. The SDP consists of five major phases. First, the client requirements are identified, recorded, reviewed and prioritized. Second, an architecture panel consisting of business and technical representatives is initiated, the software analysis and design is conducted, and a specification of the system implementation is prepared. Third, all software units or components are selected or created (if necessary), and documentation is prepared, including the test plans. All unit software modules and procedures are individually tested. Fourth, the software systems and procedures are placed in a partitioned test and development environment for integration, prototype building, and system testing. User acceptance testing and client feedback on the prototype systems is also initiated. Systems changes are progressed in accordance with client feedback. Fifth, the software is released into the production environment. Users are trained and a post-implementation review conducted [8]. While this chapter deals specifically with the initial software requirements phase of the process, earlier in the book we saw that software requirements quality assurance can deliver significant business and ICT development benefits, such as an optimized system maintenance phase and the creation of good business conditions (see Chap. 8). Operating as a national statistics organization is a specialized business requiring specific skills, people and systems. Accordingly, the ABS has not been able to simply purchase and install commercial software to meet its role as a national statistics provider. The ABS has developed a process for software development, in particular engineering and managing requirements, in order to implement a consistent and uniform approach to software development projects across the ABS organization. However, of potentially greater significance is the improvement of software quality processes at the ABS corporate level. The ABS software development process enables coherent and integrated development processes while providing opportunities for collaborative and communicative software project work across the ABS enterprise.

The ABS ICT vision is enhanced by a complete and integrative Enterprise Architecture that combines a taxonomy of business processes and resources, various sub-architectures (eg, applications, data management, security, components and technologies), and a sound ICT infrastructure [13]. Software development is integral to this vision with the requirements engineering and management processes forming the primary means for addressing the systems requirements including business, technical, user, design, operations and maintenance aspects.

16.5 The ABS Software Requirements Phase

The software requirements phase is composed of the core identification, recording, reviewing and prioritization activities. The subordinate tasks can include identifying important inputs, outputs and functions, defining maintenance needs, recording dates, times, scopes or providers, checking consistency, and grouping or categorizing of requirements [8]. The core requirements activities are defined as follows:

- Identification of the software requirements (in accordance with the defined system requirements)
- Recording the software requirements
- Reviewing the software requirements with stakeholders
- Prioritization of the software requirements for development action

These activities not only form part of the software development process but also the larger ABS Enterprise Architecture. The context diagram is depicted in Fig. 16.3. The software development process phases play a vital part in building the ABS portfolio of systems and enabling the realization of the core business processes in statistics collection, processing, management, storage, production and service delivery. In employing best practice, the ABS uses a structured process of requirements engineering and management activities and tasks, for creating and managing its software requirements, which are discussed in the following sections.

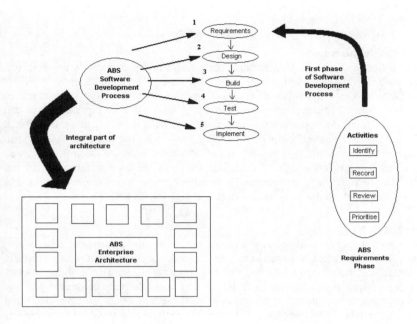

Fig. 16.3 ABS software development context [8, 13]

Identify Requirements

In developing software, the users or business unit customers are integrated into focus groups and user group workshops that are aimed at identifying the user specifications (e.g., inputs, outputs, functions). Use case models and analysis, undertaken with Unified Modeling Language (UML) tools such as Simply Objects, are also used in the requirements elicitation and communication process. The ABS sees the agency business units and client managers as paying customers who must identify and define "what they want the software system to do". There is an explicit consideration that the software products must represent "value for money" to the customer [8, 13].

Record Requirements

In ABS software projects, the project manager is responsible for recording the software system requirements on a Lotus Notes database application. The requirements database provides an up to date listing of the project requirements, including additional information such as the requirement identification number, proposing client, requirement priority, and cross reference to the software system specification. The project requirements database is the master record for all software system requirements [8].

Review Requirements

The follow-on software requirements review allows the customer's requirements to be objectively examined and amended, if required. The review activity typically includes business and financial trade-off analyses by stakeholder representatives on the project board and architecture panel. Users and their representatives can also be offered the opportunity to review the software requirements in the critical design phase; however, business customers tend to be more actively engaged in the requirements validation activity as part of the test phase of the software development. It is emphasized that the ABS deploys user-centered design practices and facilities (e.g., Hiser group techniques) for client feedback and review, particularly in the areas of web applications, services and user interfaces [18].

Prioritize Requirements

The final workflow activity is the prioritization of software requirements where the business critical requirements take precedence over what are commonly termed "the nice to haves" or optional requirements. Users give a higher priority to those requirements that are critical to the business delivery compared with the less important or optional functions. Typically, requirements are prioritized into critical, standard and optional categories. The critical and standard requirements are progressed into the design phase, while the optional requirements are held over for further client review and/or future software releases [8].

While the ABS software requirements phase appears to be built on sound practices and processes, it would be valuable to contrast their approach with peer inputs from practitioners, academics, and standards organizations. In particular, we consider there to be some value in contrasting ABS practice with a well-established requirements engineering process model [29], the views of academics who specialize in system requirements engineering [23, 41], and the content of recognized international software related standards [26, 27]. Requirements engineering has evolved as a distinct and important discipline, not just in the area of software, but in all forms of ICT systems. The "requirements" discipline has grown substantially in recent years, forming a body of knowledge that attracts regular and consistent inputs from academics and practitioners. Although dating back to the mid-1990s, the requirements engineering model developed by Loucopoulos and Karakostas (1995) is well established in requirements literature and uses an interactive process of elicitation, written specification, and a review or validation of the requirements products (see Fig. 16.4). The framework emphasizes the continuous interactions and inputs from system users and the importance of understanding the use case models that flow from the complete process. The ABS requirements phase encapsulates all of this theoretical framework's activities and tasks, including the discrete ABS requirements prioritization activity (as part of the specification activity). Importantly, the theoretical requirements framework and the ABS requirements phase show a high regard for proactive and continuous user involvement, and are wholly consistent with the user requirements elicitation processes outlined earlier in the book (see Chap. 2).

While some have considered customer-focused requirements a state of nirvana [36], other academic researchers have long championed the input from users and customers [27, 30, 33, 41]. Zowghi and Offen (1996) typified this view noting that "when aspects of the applications domain are being explored, the social order has to be biased towards the users beliefs since their understanding of the business domain is more valid that that of the requirements engineers". Earlier in the book, we noted the importance of this stakeholder communication, negotiation and collaboration from the business and technical perspectives (see Chap. 2). The ABS customer involvement activities, such as use case analysis and group work, clearly follows best practice in this aspect of requirements development.

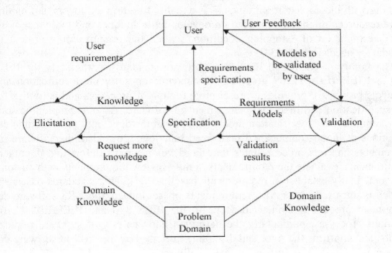

Fig. 16.4 Requirements engineering process model [31]

A more emergent element of the Requirements Engineering process is the prioritization of requirements in order that they meet the most important customer needs [25, 34]. This aspect was stressed by Siddiqi and Chandra Shekaran [34] who noted "competitive forces have reduced time to market, causing development organizations to speed development by deliberately limiting the scope of each (software) release. This forces developers to distinguish between desirable and necessary (and indeed, between levels of needed) features of an envisioned system. Further, modifying certain non-critical requirements may enable an envisioned system to be realized using one or more off-the-shelf components". Hofmann and Lehner [25] held a similar view on the value of software requirements prioritization noting that "requirements prioritized by stakeholders drive successful Requirements Engineering teams. This allows the Requirements Engineering team to decide which requirements to investigate when and to what degree of detail. To specify prioritized requirements, the Requirements Engineering team develops various models together with prototypes".

Earlier in the book the importance of prioritizing the requirements in order to make the right decisions and gain maximum value in the complex problem space was noted (see Chap. 4). In keeping with this theme, the ABS takes a strong position on the prioritization of requirements, using numerical assignment classifications and outputs from trade off analyses, albeit driven to some extent by ICT finance restrictions and human resource efficiencies. Prototype systems reflect the critical and standard priority requirements, while optional software requirements are identified for further client reviews, future software releases, and forward agency work programming. Interestingly, the evolving focus on requirements prioritization suggests that in some respects the software requirements specification will remain in a state of incompleteness. Some conventional thinking directs that "coping with incomplete requirements" is a reality for all practitioners, noting that more resources might be expended on developing techniques and tools that assist the determination of "stopping conditions" when the organization's critical or mandatory needs are met [34].

The family of IEEE and IEEE/EIA software standards, particularly the IEEE 830 and IEEE/EIA 12207 grouping of standards on software specification and lifecycle processes, provides a prescriptive regime of processes and activities for the specification and lifecycle management of software. As an example, the software requirements specification process states that the developer must include descriptions of inputs, outputs and performed functions [26]. Also, the software requirements analysis process states that the developer must define and document requirements, evaluate the requirements, jointly review requirements with customers, and finally establish a requirements baseline [27]. This standards-based approach is mirrored in the ABS requirements phase. Indeed, the ABS software development process is similar in scope to the IEEE 830 and IEEE/EIA 12207 standard processes, particularly the definition and analysis of software requirements, and confirms the rigor and discipline exercised by the ABS in software development activities. A further internationally recognized standard is the software Capability Maturity Model (CMM) developed by the Software Engineering Institute of Carnegie Mellon University [33, 35]. Specific to requirements management, level two on the maturity scale requires organizations to establish and maintain an agreement with the customer on the requirements for the software project. The business and technical requirements of the software project must be addressed, documented, controlled and managed [33]. In accordance with the CMM principles, the ABS ensures that the project requirements are reviewed with the clients through project board and architecture panel processes, while any changes to requirements are reflected in software plans, work activities and tasks [8].

What the comparative analysis shows is that the ABS requirements phase not only conforms to current academic and practitioner viewpoints, but also possesses the rigorous processes of well-established theoretical frameworks and international standards. The ABS has a practical approach to requirements engineering and management with high quality business processes that are grounded in well-established theory and widely adopted standards. The study suggests supports the view that this type of software requirements approach is valid for any organization whether they operate in the private or public sector.

16.6 Some Examples of ABS Software

While we have reviewed the software requirements process, and provided a contrast with theory and practice, we also consider it important to examine practical examples of business requirements and more specific lower level software requirements that have been developed by the ABS. The examples we have chosen are software used for computer assisted survey interviews, seasonal adjustment of statistics, and a data warehouse facility. The following sections provide some typical examples of business and technical requirements that have been developed for ABS software applications.

Computer Assisted Interviewing (CAI) Software
Our first example is the ABS adoption in 1994 of Computer Assisted Interviewing (CAI) software for conducting field survey work. In the software selection process, ABS field staff participated in focus groups that identified what the required CAI software should do and what benefits it should deliver.

During the elicitation process, ABS staff stated that CAI software should improve data quality and timeliness. Staff considered that the software should contribute to improved data quality through fewer transcription errors (greater than 20% reduction) and the single (one-off) entry of data into the computerized databases. ABS staff also stated that CAI software should lead to survey resource savings. Staff considered that the software should enable data collection and processing efficiencies. ABS staff stated that CAI software must be able to be introduced to an interviewer workforce with little computing experience. Most field staff were used to the manual collection of statistics data, and were unfamiliar with laptop computer data collection processes. From the operational perspective, ABS staff stated that CAI software must not cause concern to those being interviewed. Field staff were concerned that the use of laptop computers might frighten or intimidate some data providers. These requirements illustrate some of the typical needs of the user community. While the field user group identified the business requirements for CAI, the software also needed to meet some specific technical and functional requirements. For example, for ease of operations, maintenance and upgrade, ICT managers stated that the CAI software had to be written in a simple syntax and block structure language. Further, the CAI software data structures had to allow the data to be processed, transferred and shared among all ABS software tools. In order to support the previous data-sharing requirement, ICT management specified that the CAI software had to also possess data and metadata conversion interfaces as standard features.

Following a period of review and a design-based evaluation of the Blaise III software, the ABS took the decision to adopt Blaise as the data collection tool for CAI. Blaise was trialed by a field user group in July 1994 using a Household Expenditure Survey with 800 questions, 12,000 software code lines of Blaise, and platformed on a 486 processor laptop computer. The trial was conducted across 450 households using 10 field interviewers and included electronic mail data transmissions. Since this successful trial, Blaise III has been adopted for other survey work including population and employment related work programs, and has been successfully integrated into the use of telephone survey work [39].

Seasonal Adjustment Software

In 1983, the ABS adopted the X-11 Arima software package (the Statistics Canada variant), a knowledge-based seasonal analysis and adjustment tool, for adjusting estimated seasonal and calendar influences on an original statistical time series. The software was renamed "Seasonal Analysis to ABS Standards" or simply SEASABS, and includes a core X-11 processing system. SEASABS is one part of the ABS seasonal adjustment system that includes the ABSDB (ABS information warehouse) and FAME (Forecasting, Analysis and Modeling Environment) that is used to store and manipulate time series data. Before selecting the X-11 Arima software package, the business users were canvassed during workshops and were requested to define some of their more important requirements. For instance, the primary requirement for SEASABS was that it must be capable of adjusting any designated ABS time series for seasonal and other calendar-related influences. Business users also stated that ABS staff must be able to operate SEASABS with little, or no, detailed knowledge of the X-11 software package. This operator requirement was coupled to technical features where it was specified that the SEASABS software must possess an intelligent user interface (eg, specific input relationships, and screen, data and command formats) that guides users through the seasonal analysis process. Users also mandated that SEASABS must possess a function to store and perform diagnostics on previously collected and processed time series analyses. The SEASABS software had to meet some stringent business and technical requirements before deployment in the ABS environment [3, 19, 40]. Since its adoption, SEASABS has undergone evolutionary upgrades to improve the adjustment process and user functionality, including filter enhancements and graphical user interface developments (i.e., windows screen formats). After more than twenty years operation in a production environment, SEASABS is still successfully meeting users' needs, and forms the analytical backbone of the ABS statistical time series adjustment process [1, 3, 6, 19, 40].

Input Data Warehouse Software

In 2001, the ABS commenced the development of an Input Data Warehouse (IDW) facility to complement the ABS information environment, including the ABS Information Warehouse that is used for the production of ABS goods and services. The IDW was developed using a three phase process that included the construction of a "production pilot" warehouse, a "pilot" warehouse, and a "full production" warehouse that was completed in June 2004. The creation of an IDW was primarily aimed at capturing and aggregating statistical inputs for movement to the managed output/dissemination store (ABS Information Warehouse).

While it was expected that a high quality database management system would be an important component of the IDW, the ABS project team and business user groups were canvassed in focus groups and project workshops to elicit their key requirements. The new IDW was to enable reduced statistics provider workloads. Providers must have a single (one) database structure for data collection, hence reducing the multiple database workloads of the past. Also, the IDW was to integrate the previously separate data stores, enabling data integration beyond the single statistical unit integration to the three (3) sub-units of data definitions, concepts and items at the unit record level. The business users also specified that the new IDW should improve the capacity to support future analytical outputs and products. Ideally, the IDW was to support the delivery of current and future ABS products and publications. From the technical perspective, ICT management specified that the IDW software must be capable of accessing (linking) metadata from the Corporate Metadata Repository (CMR), and must include the three (3) mandatory update, query and data matching functions.

In meeting the various business and technical requirements for the IDW software, the ABS selected an SAS database product. The successful warehouse development holds over 400 million records and was put into full production in mid-2004. SAS is one of the key ICT suppliers to the ABS and provides products for the integrated portfolio of corporate databases and applications under the agency's Enterprise Architecture [13, 16, 18].

Summary
The three examples of ABS software shows that it is possible to combine high level business and more specific software requirements into an integrated set of requirements that enable software developments to be directed at the solving of important business problems. This approach to software is deliberate and lasting (over twenty years of quality practices), while being clearly underpinned by executive mandates and quality decisions. It was also observed that the ABS culture of teamwork and sharing views and experiences in the workplace plays an important role in governing the creation of business-oriented software systems [15].

16.7 What can We Learn From the ABS?

Having seen how the ABS works to develop its software requirements, there are a number of important observations that can be highlighted from this case study. A strengthening of the software development process capability is an important driver of the agency strategy and architecture. The ABS firmly believes that it cannot build future generations of ICT systems without fully understanding its current and future business requirements. ABS executives and management recognize that in order for the software applications to enable the business processes and outputs, the business and technical requirements must be clearly understood. Over the period 1999–2001, the ABS launched its Enterprise Architecture program to baseline its current business and system states and look to shaping its future through sound strategic planning, enlightened resource management, and disciplined corporate governance. Quality software development forms part of this larger program [7].

The ABS views software development as a key activity in the technical domain and has invested substantial human and financial resources in developing and implementing a well defined and end-to-end software development process. Software requirements development and on-going management is seen as a critical first step in the software journey, specifically the identification, recording, reviewing and prioritization of all user requirements. In the context of the broader organization, we have seen that the ABS software development process forms part of the fabric of an Enterprise Architecture, which assists with the shaping of the future state of ABS business and software systems.

The development of a rigorous software development process is also aimed at dealing with organizational dynamism and technical complexity. As we have seen, the ABS is a dynamic organization operating in a challenging technical environment, with a large base of demanding and varied business customers. The ABS deploys a large and complex ICT environment based on a client-server network coupled to a vast array of database storage devices and facilities. The annual publication rate of over 700 products, and the requirement to service customers across physical and electronic channels, has meant that the ABS has concentrated its efforts on carefully developing software and other technical systems that are integrated and aligned with the business requirements and delivery functions. Ultimately, the ABS has learned that its software intensive systems are a critical enabler of business value. While there has been a clear emphasis on establishing development processes that match the organization, the building of software requirements at the ABS is reflective of the organization's quality and the best practices across the public and private sector. When we compare ABS software requirements development and management practices with well established software process models (e.g., Loucopoulos and Karakostas [16]), academic literature (e.g., Siddiqi and Shekaran [34]), and the IEEE and IEEE/EIA families of software related standards, a consistent quality and standards-based approach emerges. One of the key lessons learned in studying ABS software practices is that the "prioritization of requirements' is very much about "the trade off of business and technical needs", "a focus on resource efficiency" and "the acceptance that a software specification may never be complete in all respects". The approach to software requirements development observed at the ABS serves as a practical example to other public and private sector organizations.

In some instances, organizations fail to recognize that building ICT systems, particularly those involving software, starts long before any programmers are hired or code is cut. The ABS displays a bi-directional governance process that draws together the high level business directions and executive decisions, with the more socially based working level processes and practices that form the cornerstone of software requirements documentation and user agreement. As we read earlier, the overall vision for ICT at the ABS is ultimately shaped by its Enterprise Architecture that integrates and aligns the business and technology domains of the agency. Other Australian government agencies, like the Centerlink social services agency and Department of Defense, have attempted to emulate the ABS with various levels of success [24, 38]. The examples of software application development show that the ABS has mastered the ability to combine business and technology requirements in order to meet internal and external customer demands. Much like the ABS, private companies and organizations of today will need to understand the intricacies of developing software using top-down and bottom-up perspectives and processes (see examples in Chap. 18).

In concluding this chapter, the software development practices and processes at the ABS meet world class performance benchmarks according to successive Gartner Group comparative surveys, confirming that organizational ICT systems, especially the software, meets "best practice" guidelines. In a very clear vote of confidence, peer international statistics agencies have judged the ABS to be one of the world's best organizations in its business class [36, 38]. These accolades were also confirmed by the Australian Auditor General who found the work of the ABS to be high quality in terms of practice, process and systems [22]. Good software development has become great software development over the years at the ABS. Today executive management understands that ICT, particularly software, exists to serve the business and deliver the outputs and outcomes required by government. With a sound software development process, and requirements development approach to match, agency software is helping to shape and enable the ABS business of the future.

References

1. Australian Bureau of Statistics (1998) Balance of payments and international investment position, Australia: Concepts, sources and methods. Chapter 4. Detailed and supplementary tables. ISBN: 0 642 25670 5. Accessed on 6th December 2004. http://www.abs.gov.au/Ausstats/abs@.nsf/66f306f503e529a5ca25697e0017661f/50818 1cf2562d200ca25697e0018fdb1!OpenDocument

2. Australian Bureau of Statistics (2000) Annual report 1999-2000. Technology services division benchmarking. (ISSN 0314–0008. ISBN 0 642 25752 3) 52. Accessed 1st December 2004 http://www.abs.gov.au/Websitedbs/D3110126.NSF/0/7bc8d0774f3 9e898ca 2569040015e039/$FILE/10010_1999-00.pdf

3. Australian Bureau of Statistics (2000) Australian national accounts: Concepts, Sources and Methods. Appendix 3 - Seasonally adjusted and trend estimates, November 2000 ISBN 0 642 54212 0. Accessed 26th November 2004. http://www.abs.gov.au/Ausstats/abs@.nsf/66f306f503e529a5ca25697e0017661f/31377 8ba8bd656fcca2569a40006165c!OpenDocument

4. Australian Bureau of Statistics (2001) Annual report 2000-2001. Performance information, cost effective inputs. (ISSN 0314–0008, ISBN 0 642 47736 1), 80. Accessed 26th November 2004. http://www.ausstats.abs.gov.au/Ausstats/free.nsf/Lookup/ D9E50335A060BDDDCA256C540006B320/$File/10010_2000-01.pdf

5. Australian Bureau of Statistics (2001) Corporate plan, 1. Accessed on10th November 2004. http://www.abs.gov.au/websitedbs/d3310114.nsf/51c9a3d36edfd0dfca256acb001 18404/b1042c4ee5af9c71ca256a46008278d9!OpenDocument

6. Australian Bureau of Statistics (2001) Household Expenditure Survey (Cat. No. 6527.0), Australia: User Guide Chapter 3. Survey methodology. November 2001 (ISBN 0642542996). Accessed 10th November 2004 http://www.abs.gov.au /Ausstats/abs@.nsf/Lookup/D47FE4DF1A190335CA256B04007F53F5

7. Australian Bureau of Statistics (2002) Annual report 2001-2002. Information technology developments. (ISSN 0314–0008, ISBN 0 642 47834 1), 29. Accessed on 1st September 2004. http://www.ausstats.abs.gov.au/Ausstats/free.nsf/Lookup/8C2BB8FE7538 7EE4CA256C0E007FDCDD/$File/10010_ABS%20200102%20Annual%20Report.pdf

8. Australian Bureau of Statistics (2002) Enterprise architecture, software development process Version 1.0, June 2002. Internal agency document available from authors on request.

9. Australian Bureau of Statistics (2003) Annual report 2002-2003. Revenue raised from statistics, (ISSN 0314–0008), 23. Accessed on 5th December 2004 http://www.ausstats.abs.gov.au/Ausstats/free.nsf/Lookup/B1EE428F95070BD7CA256 DBB0003C7A1/$File/10010_2002-03.pdf

10. Australian Bureau of Statistics (2003) Annual report 2002-2003, ABS Outputs, (ISSN 0314–0008), 104 and 120. Accessed 5th December 2004 http://www.ausstats.abs. gov.au/Ausstats/free.nsf/Lookup/B1EE428F95070BD7CA256DBB0003C7A1/$File/10 010_2002-03.pdf.

11. Australian Bureau of Statistics (2003) Annual report 2002-2003. Financial statements, (ISSN 0314–0008), 178. Accessed 5th December 2004 http://www.ausstats.abs.gov.au /Ausstats/free.nsf/Lookup/B1EE428F95070BD7CA256DBB0003C7A1/$File/10010_2 002-03.pdf.

12. Australian Bureau of Statistics (2003) Annual report 2002-2003. Staffing overview, (ISSN 0314–0008), 187-189. Accessed 4th November 2004 http://www.ausstats.abs. gov.au/Ausstats/free.nsf/Lookup/B1EE428F95070BD7CA256DBB0003C7A1/$File/10 010_2002-03.pdf.

13. Australian Bureau of Statistics (2003) Enterprise architecture Version 2.0, March 2003. Available on http://www.agimo.gov.au/resources/events/2003/ent_arch.

14. Australian Bureau of Statistics (2003) Enterprise architecture. Business process taxonomy, Version 2.0, March: 4-10. Access 3rd December 2004 http://www.agimo.gov.au/ resources/events/2003/ent_arch.

15. Australian Bureau of Statistics (2003) Enterprise architecture. Information technology governance, Version 2.0, March 11. Access 3rd December 2004 http://www.agimo. gov.au/resources/events/2003/ent_arch.

16. Australian Bureau of Statistics (2003) Enterprise architecture, input data warehouse, Version 2.0, March: 26-29. http://www.agimo.gov.au/resources/events/2003/ent_arch.

17. Australian Bureau of Statistics (2003) Enterprise architecture, maintaining and using the ABS enterprise Architecture, Version 2.0, March: 13. Access 3rd November 2004. http://www.agimo.gov.au/resources/events/2003/ent_arch.

18. Australian Bureau of Statistics (2003) Enterprise architecture, technologies and toolsets, Version 2.0, March: 19. http://www.agimo.gov.au/resources/events/2003/ent_arch.

19. Australian Bureau of Statistics (2003) Time series analysis: seasonal adjustment methods, March 2003. Accessed 5th December 2004. http://www.abs.gov.au/Websitedbs/ D3310114.NSF/0/C890AA8E65957397CA256CE10018C9D8?Open

20. Australian Bureau of Statistics (2004) Forward work program 2004-2007, March: 6-7. Accessed 3rd November 2004 http://www.abs.gov.au/Websitedbs/D3310114.NSF /0/19fe4d5d3ab1189aca2567400012da51/$FILE/FWP-200405%202005-06.pdf

21. Australian Bureau of Statistics (2004) Introduction to the ABS and its IT environment, March 2004. Accessed 3rd September 2004 http://www.abs.gov.au/websitedbs /d3310114.nsf/51c9a3d36edfd0dfca256acb00118404/b9043642361d7a66ca256b59007 bdae7/$FILE/Vendor%20Information%20Pack%20Jan04_1.pdf.

22. Australian National Audit Office (1997) Performance audit of the 1996 census of population and housing, Audit Report No.35, 1996-97: 4-5. Accessed 1sr December 2004. http://www.anao.gov.au/WebSite.nsf/Publications/4A256AE90015F69B4A25690D002 430ED

23. Dawson LL, Swatman PA (1996) Investigating the efficacy of object-oriented methods for RE. In: Proceedings of the First Australian Workshop for Requirements Engineering, Melbourne, September, pp. 1–21

24. Hannan P (2003) Leading defense to enterprise architecture presentation, NOIE Seminar Program, Enterprise Architecture: Integrating Business and Technology across the APS, March 2003. Accessed 1st December 2004 http://www.agimo.gov.au/resources/events/2003/ent_arch.

25. Hofmann HF, Lehner F (2001) Requirements engineering as a success factor in software projects. IEEE Software, July-August, pp. 58–66

26. Institute of Electrical and Electronics Engineers (1998) IEEE 830:1998, IEEE Recommended Practice for Software Requirements Specification, June: 13-14 and 16

27. Institute of Electrical and Electronics Engineers/Electronic Industries Alliance (1998) IEEE/EIA 12207:1996, Software Life Cycle Processes, Software Requirements Analysis, March, pp. 17–18

28. Institute of Electrical and Electronics Engineers/Electronic Industries Alliance (1998) IEEE/EIA 12207:1996, Software Life Cycle Processes, Software Requirements, System Requirements, Software Design, Software Integration, March, pp. 19–20

29. Loucopoulos P, Karakostas V (1995) System requirements engineering. McGraw-Hill Book Company Europe

30. Mylopoulos J, Chung L, Liao S, Wang H, Yuy E (2001) Exploring alternatives during requirements engineering. IEEE Software, January-February, pp. 92–96

31. Paviour A (2003) ABS IT governance and project management. Lecture notes on Issues in IT Management, University of Canberra, August 2003. Notes available from authors on request

32. Reifer DJ (2000) Requirements management: The search for Nirvana. IEEE Software, May-June, pp.45–47

33. Sallis PJ, Tate G, MacDonell SG (1995) Software engineering: Practice, management and improvement. Addison Wesley Publishing Company Australia

34. Siddiqi J, Chandra Shekaran M (1996) Requirements engineering: The emerging wisdom. IEEE Software, March, pp.15–19

35. Paulk MC, Curtis B, Chrissis MB, Weber CV (1993) Capability maturity model for software. Version 1.1, Technical Report CMU/SEI-93-TR-24, Software Engineering In-stitute, Carnegie Mellon University, February 1993

36. The Economist (1991) The good statistics guide. July, 320, 7723: 88

37. The Economist (1993) The good statistics guide. November, 328, 7828: 65

38. Treadwell J (2003) Centrelink Capabilities and Connections Presentation, NOIE Seminar Program, Enterprise Architecture: Integrating Business and Technology across the APS, March 2003. Accessed on 13th December 2004. http://www.agimo.gov.au/resources/events/2003/ent_arch

39. Wensing F (1995) Update from Down Under: History, Plans and Functions we've (ABS) built for CAI and Blaise in Australia, 3rd International Blaise Users Conference, July 1995: 202-213. Accessed on 13th December 2004 http://www.blaiseusers.org/Ibucpdfs/1995-1998/wensin95.pdf

40. Zhang M, Sutcliffe A (2001) Use of ARIMA models for improving revisions of X-11 seasonal adjustment, ABS Staff Paper, November 2001. Accessed on 13th December 2004.   http://www.abs.gov.au/websitedbs/D3110122.NSF/0/10b42cd292e88668ca256 bbf000064f3/$FILE/Nov2001_2.pdf

41. Zowghi D, Offen R (1997) A logical framework for modeling and reasoning about the evolution of requirements. In: Proceedings of the 3rd IEEE International Symposium on Requirements Engineering (ISRE1997), Annapolis, USA, pp.247–257

Author Biography

Nigel Martin is a federal government manager and a doctoral candidate in information systems at the Australian National University. His principal research interests are in the areas of Enterprise Architecture, Requirements Engineering, Information Systems Governance and Electronic Government.

Professor Shirley Gregor heads the Electronic Commerce Research Centre and is Professor of Information Systems and Associate Dean Research for the Faculty of Economics and Commerce at the Australian National University. Professor Gregor has led several large projects in the electronic commerce area funded by the Meat Research Corporation, the Department of Communications, Information Technology and the Arts, and the Australian Research Council. Professor Gregor spent a number of years in the computing industry in Australia and the United Kingdom before beginning an academic career.

17 "Good Quality" Requirements in Unified Process

Nur Yilmaztürk

Abstract: As supported by many empirical evidences since early 1970s, "good quality" requirements are the leading factor for a successful software development project that delivers a "good quality" product with originally specified features and functionalities, on time, and within the originally estimated budget. The challenge gets tougher and more critical when the competition in the market is severe, the number of customers on the world is rather limited and static, and the customer demands are high. As functioning in such a market, with the main goal to maintain the leading position of the previous versions of its Stressometer®, ABB has adopted a RUP®[1]-based software development process in the new generation Stressometer systems development projects. Stressometer Unified Process (SUP) integrates the RUP essentials with some features of agile processes such as heavy involvement of various stakeholders, preparation of test cases before coding, and continuous testing during development. This chapter describes the essential quality characteristics of requirements –both individual and aggregates such as embodied in a use-case model or in a specification, analyses the relations among them, evaluates RUP regarding the means it provides or lacks for developing "good quality" requirements, and discusses how ABB Stressometer projects have tackled these shortcomings via SUP.

Keywords: Quality attributes of requirements, Requirements quality metrics, Requirements engineering and management via Rational Unified Process, Use-cases, Use-case model, Measuring quality of requirements.

17.1 Introduction

"Good quality" software requirements are prerequisite for "good quality" software products. Results of the research by Standish Group [23] verify our theory. The Standish Group's CHAOS report that covers the findings from study of 8380 IT projects illustrates that 31.1% of projects are cancelled before they are completed. The results indicate 52.7% of projects cost 189% of their original estimates, and still deliver fewer features and functionalities than originally specified. Only 16.2% of software projects are completed on time and on budget. Among the projects completed by the large companies, only 42% of them comprise the originally proposed features and functions. The top three factors on challenged projects are lack of user input (12.8%), incomplete requirements and specifications (12.3%), and changing requirements and specifications (11.8%). Finally, the major reason for projects cancellation is reported as incomplete requirements (13.1%).

---

[1] Rational Unified Process®

Cost of "bad quality" requirements have been studied since early 1970s. Boehm's study of 63 software projects from three companies, namely GTE, TRW, and IBM, illustrated that the cost of change grows exponentially as the project progresses [2]. [4] reiterates this result by stating that the relative cost of repair is two hundred times greater in the maintenance phase than if it is detected in the requirements phase. Further, it bases the escalation in cost on two factors: (i) the delay from when the defect was introduced until it was detected, (ii) the amount of rework needed to correct both the original defect as well as the consequent defects in the later stages. As referred to by [4], DeMarco states that 56% of the bugs detected during testing can be traced to the requirements errors.

Iterative nature of RUP assists in eliminating above mentioned risks by integrating a software product progressively throughout its development life cycle, by managing requirements change and "creep" in a controlled manner, by learning early and improving incrementally, and by detecting flaws early thus, building higher quality over several iterations. Yet, RUP is a generic process and it is inevitable to tailor it according to the needs of a particular project or the projects of a specific department for better efficiency and effectiveness. In an attempt to establish a balance between delivering good quality software products and delivering them on time, ABB's Stressometer product line adapted RUP in an agile fashion while adhering to the RUP essentials.

The main aim of this chapter is to evaluate a use-case driven, iterative software development process during which modeling is done via UML[2], within the context of requirements development and management, against the quality of the requirements established during such a process. To this end, Sect. 17.2 provides background information about ABB and the Stressometer product line. Section 17.3 presents the requirements management and engineering activities involved in ABB's RUP-based software development process, SUP. Section 17.4 describes the characteristics of "good quality" requirements, elaborates on the relations among the characteristics, and further discusses how ABB Stressometer projects managed to achieve "good quality" requirements, supplying the discussions with experiences from the three major projects at ABB. Finally, Sect. 17.5 concludes the chapter.

17.2 Background

ABB (Asea Brown Boveri Ltd.) began operations in 1988 following a merger of two parent companies namely, ASEA AB and BBC Brown Boveri Ltd, each of which has been in business for more than a century (*www.abb.com*). Today, with about 105000 employees in around 100 countries, the ABB Group of companies functions in two core business areas, automation and power technologies that enable utility and industry customers to improve performance while lowering environmental impact.

---

[2] Unified Modelling Language

ABB Power Technologies serves industrial and commercial customers, as well as electric, gas and water utilities, with a broad range of products, services and solutions for power transmission and distribution. The portfolio includes transformers, switchgear, breakers, capacitors and cables, as well as high- and medium-voltage applications, many of which are also sold through external channel partners like distributors, system integrators, contractors and original equipment manufacturers. ABB Automation Technologies serves the automotive, building, chemicals, consumer, electronics, life sciences, manufacturing, marine, metals, minerals, paper, petroleum, transportation, turbo-charging and utility industries. Key technologies include control, drives, enterprise software, instrumentation, low-voltage products, motors, robots and turbochargers. These offerings are supported by field maintenance and asset management services, and are sold both directly and through channel partners.

As a part of the ABB Automation Technologies, Force Measurement unit supplies products, systems, and services for measurement and control in a broad range of application from steel making to paper conversion. Stressometer is a Force Measurement product line that involves software intensive systems, which have been providing rolling mills with accurate online control of the flatness of cold rolled strips for more than 30 years. Stressometer system measures flatness, analyzes and stores flatness data, generates output for automatic flatness controls, and presents data in informative displays. Stressometer systems are designed for minimum maintenance and maximum uptime to ensure undisturbed continuous production and minimized scrap levels. Over the years, ABB has been continuously improving the Stressometer product line parallel to the technological progress in software engineering in an attempt to keep its number one position in the market [26].

17.3 Practice

New generation Stressometer systems are implemented by using SUP that is RUP tailored to fit the needs of the Stressometer department's development projects. The major issue considered during such tailoring is being agile by involving stakeholders with different profiles –external customers as well as the internal ones –actively and heavily throughout the development life cycle, preparing the test cases before coding, and having continuous testing during development. SUP facilitates agile, use-case driven, iterative development during which modeling is done via UML [26]. This section presents the requirements management and engineering activities that are involved in the SUP. For a comprehensive discussion on agile methods, and particularly, requirement engineering via agile methods readers should refer to Chap. 14 in this book.

The first step in the requirements engineering process via SUP is to elicit information from the stakeholders in order to understand their needs. SUP imposes the involvement of external customers with business knowledge and internal customers with technical domain knowledge, in this activity. It recommends interviews and requirements workshop as the techniques to elicit the needs. The findings are used as primary inputs to defining the features of the prospective product hence, the high-level requirements that are described in a Vision document. A Vision may include features that do not fit in the project scope or the existing business plans yet, should be kept for future references. Accordingly, the stakeholders prioritize the features based on pre-agreed attributes in order to identify the final set to be attended by the particular iteration of the project. Before moving to the lower level requirements identification, the complete Vision document and the prioritization results are reviewed and approved by all the stakeholders who took part in the elicitation. Eventually, approved Vision together with the prioritization matrix is checked into the configuration management database, and is labeled as "Approved–IterX". As the next activity, the same group of stakeholders gathers at a use-case workshop to define the functional requirements of the system. Initial group of actors and use-cases derived from appropriate features are compiled in a use-case model and illustrated in use-case diagram(s) during the meeting by using a tool. Brief descriptions for each actor and use-case are also entered. The results are further documented in a Use-Case Model Survey. A few review meetings with the same attendees follow in order to finalize an approved version. Features that could not be traced to functional requirements in use-cases, for example those that imply non-functional requirements such as performance requirements, are revisited in order to compile a Supplementary Specifications document. As any other formal artifact in the process, Supplementary Specifications document is also reviewed, approved by the stakeholders, and eventually, version controlled.

The identified use-cases are prioritized according to a set of pre-agreed attributes in a separate session by the same requirements team. Those use-cases assessed as high priority to attend are assigned to the requirements specifier for detailing.

The requirements specifier with assistance of the end-users from both external and internal customers describes the flows of each use-case under concern in detail in separate specification documents. She/he also writes the supplementary requirements to the level of detail needed to hand off to the next stages in the development. If required, she/he can prepare sub-supplementary specifications. For example, user-interface descriptions, control algorithms, digital and analogue signal descriptions are detailed in separate sub-supplementary specification documents. As soon as the first version of a specification is ready, it is passed to the test designer(s) for test case preparations. Each specification is reviewed by a group that includes the external customers with business knowledge, internal customers with technical domain knowledge, requirements specifier, end-users that assisted during detailing the requirements, software architect, designer, and test designer. Upon approval, each document is checked into the configuration management database and labeled as "Approved–IterX". Subsequently, the design team starts working on the architectural and detailed design of the requirements. The test cases are updated according to the final changes in the related requirements specifications, reviewed and approved by the requirements specifying team and the test team before they are version controlled and passed to the attention of the test team. Parallel to the above activities, the project team also continuously gathers terminology in a project Glossary.

17.4 Evaluation

Quality of requirements can be characterized by a number of attributes. We collect those that are commonly discussed by the academia and the industry, and merge them into a set of 26 quality attributes in Table 17.1. During our study of these attributes, we encountered the following inconsistencies: (i) Different references may use different terms for the same attribute. For example, the first attribute in the table is termed "Attainable" in [11], "Feasible" in [24], and "Achievable" in [11]. In such cases, we either include all different terms found in the literature, or refer to all of them by using the most common one; (ii) Content of an attribute may differ from reference to reference. For example, [12] and [5] define "Correct" as what is termed "Necessary" in [24], which also presents "Correct" as a separate requirements quality attribute but with a definition that differs from the one found in [12] and in [5]. In such cases, we keep both attributes and assume a positive relation between the two attributes; (iii) No clear distinction between quality attributes that are applicable only to individual requirements and quality attributes that are applicable only to the aggregate requirements. In most of the cases, the definition of an attribute presented as an attribute of an aggregate implies dependency on the individual requirements of the aggregate constituting the same quality. Moreover, one can hardly find a consensus between different references on whether an attribute is applicable to an individual requirement or to an aggregate. For example, "Complete"-ness is claimed to be an attribute of an aggregate by [4] and [5] whereas, it is suggested to be applicable to an individual requirement by [9], and to both an individual requirement and an aggregate by [24]. In our evaluation, we disregard such distinction and use the attribute to measure both individual requirements and aggregates, unless there is common consensus on the applicability of an attribute for example as in the case of "Achievable/Feasible/Attainable", "Clear/Precise/Meaningful" etc.

   These attributes are not independent: (i) It is not possible to achieve a certain quality unless another one exists. For example, if a requirement is not "Unambiguous" it cannot be "Verifiable". Naturally, there is no means to verify a requirement if multiple interpretations exist for it [4, 5, 24, 12]. (ii) An attribute may affect achievement of another attribute depending on the way the affecting attribute is achieved. For example, if we try to make a requirement more "Unambiguous", more "Verifiable", "Complete", and "Consistent" by using extremely formal notations, we definitely decrease the level of "Understandability" by especially the non-computer specialist stakeholders [4]. Whereas, on the other hand, by no means "Unambiguous", "Verifiable", "Complete", and "Consistent" requirements are un"Understandable". On the contrary, "Unambiguous"ness, "Complete"ness, and "Consisten(t)"cy enhance "Understandabl(e)"ity when achieved via less formal means such as by using Natural Language augmented with more formal models [5]. (iii) Existence of an attribute jeopardizes achievement of another attribute. For example, if all use-cases included in a use-case model were "Necessary" then why would we need to "Rank"ing one or more of them as *optional* "by relative importance"? We have summarized our findings from experiences with relations between various quality attributes in Tables 17.2(a) and 17.2(b).

Finally, most of the requirements attributes are subjective. In such cases, it can be difficult to measure a quality objectively via metrics; it may require performing expert reviews for the ultimate assessment. Still, it is possible to associate those characteristics with indicators that point at existence or absence of the quality under concern.

Our experiences at ABB have proven that the level of quality achieved in requirements produced during a software development project highly depends on the process adopted. A feature of a process can influence a specific quality by leading to an improvement in the quality, by detracting from the quality, or by doing both hence, a trade-off situation; as well as a process might not address the quality at all. An individual requirement or an aggregate of requirements created via RUP would score very well across most of the quality attributes, whereas fare rather insufficiently on others. Tailoring the standard RUP practices to fit a specific software development project's needs helps enhancing the poor quality but mainly those attributes that matter most to the project. In the following sub-sections, we describe those quality characteristics that were deemed important by the Stressometer projects at ABB, elaborate on their relations with other characteristics, discuss the indicators of strengths and weaknesses, evaluate how the projects attempted to achieve the quality, and specify the metrics for measuring the quality where applicable.

Table 17.1 Quality attributes of requirements

Quality Attributes	[4]	[5]	[9]	[11]	[12]	[14]	[19]	[24]	[25]
Achievable/Feasible/Attainable		I		I		I		I	
At the Right Level of Detail		I, A				I			
Clear/ Precise/Meaningful		I	I	I					
Complete	A	A	I		A	I, A	A	I, A	A
Concise	A	A		I		I			
Correct	I, A	I, A			I, A			I	A
Cross-Referenced		A							
Design Independent	I, A	I, A				I			
Electronically Stored		A							
Executable/Interpretable		A							
Externally Consistent	A	A						A	
Forward Traceable	I, A	I, A			I, A		I	I, A	I
Implementation Independent						I			
Internally Consistent	A	A			A	A		A	A
Modifiable	A	A			A			A	A
Necessary				I		I	I		
Not Redundant		I, A							
Organized	A	A							
Prioritized/Ranked/Annotated by Relative Importance	I	I, A			I, A			I	I, A
Prioritized/Ranked/Annotated by Relative Stability	I	I, A			I, A				I, A
Prioritized/Ranked/Annotated by Version		I, A							
Reusable		A							
Traced/Backward Traceable	I, A	I, A			I, A	I	I		I
Unambiguous	I, A	I, A	I	I	I, A	I	I	I	I
Understandable	A	I, A					A		
Verifiable	I, A	I, A		I	I, A	I		I	I, A

I= Applies to an individual requirement; A=Applies to aggregate requirements such as a complete SRS, a use-case model, a use-case specification etc.

Table 17.2(a) Relations between quality attributes of requirements

	Achievable/Feasible/Attainable	At the Right Level of Detail	Clear/Precise/Meaningful	Complete	Concise	Correct	Cross-Referenced	Design Independent	Electronically Stored	Executable/Interpretable	Externally Consistent	Forward Traceable	Implementation Independent	Internally Consistent
Achievable/Feasible/Attainable	▨													
At the Right Level of Detail		▨												
Clear/Precise/Meaningful			▨	+?						+				
Complete				▨						+				
Concise		+		-?	▨			+					+	
Correct						▨			+	+	+			+
Cross-Referenced							▨							
Design Independent								▨						
Electronically Stored									▨	+?				
Executable/Interpretable										▨		+		
Externally Consistent											▨			
Forward Traceable									+			▨		
Implementation Independent													▨	
Internally Consistent						+				+?				▨

Table 17.2(a) Relations between quality attributes of requirements (cont.)

	Achievable/Feasible/Attainable	At the Right Level of Detail	Clear/Precise/Meaningful	Complete	Concise	Correct	Cross-Referenced	Design Independent	Electronically Stored	Executable/Interpretable	Externally Consistent	Forward Trace-able	Implementation Independent	Internally Consistent
Modifiable							+		+			+		
Necessary														
Not Redundant														
Organized														
Prioritized/Ranked/Annotated by Relative Importance														
Prioritized/Ranked/Annotated by Relative Stability														
Prioritized/Ranked/Annotated by Version														
Reusable									+					
Traced/Backward Traceable														
Unambiguous									+?	+?				
Understandable			+							+				
Verifiable	+		+											

+ = Strengthens the related attribute; - = Weakens the related attribute; = No relation;
-? = May strengthen the related attribute; +? = May weaken the related attribute

Table 17.2(b) Relations between quality attributes of requirements

	Necessary	Not Redundant	Organized	Prioritized/Ranked/Annotated by Relative Importance	Prioritized/Ranked/Annotated by Relative Stability	Prioritized/Ranked/Annotated by Version	Reusable	Traced/Backward Traceable	Unambiguous	Understandable	Verifiable
Achievable/Feasible/Attainable											
At the Right Level of Detail											
Clear/Precise/Meaningful									+		
Complete	+		+					+			
Concise		+									
Correct	+							+			
Cross-Referenced		-									
Design Independent											
Electronically Stored											
Executable/Interpretable											
Externally Consistent								+			
Forward Traceable											
Implementation Independent											
Internally Consistent		+	+?								

	Necessary	Not Redundant	Organized	Prioritized/Ranked/Annotated by Relative Importance	Prioritized/Ranked/Annotated by Relative Stability	Prioritized/Ranked/Annotated by Version	Reusable	Traced/Backward Traceable	Unambiguous	Understandable	Verifiable
Modifiable			+	-?	-?	-?		+			
Necessary	▨			-?				+			
Not Redundant		▨									
Organized			▨	-							
Prioritized/Ranked/Annotated by Relative Importance			+?/ -?	▨	-?	-?					
Prioritized/Ranked/Annotated by Relative Stability			+?/ -?	-?	▨	-?					
Prioritized/Ranked/Annotated by Version			+?/ -?	-?	-?	▨					
Reusable							▨				
Traced/Backward Traceable								▨			
Unambiguous									▨		
Understandable		-?	+						+?/ -?	▨	
Verifiable									+		▨

+ = Strengthens the related attribute; - = Weakens the related attribute; = No relation;

-? = May weaken the related attribute; +? = May strengthen the related attribute

17.4.1 Achievable/Feasible/Attainable

A requirement or an aggregate is achievable/feasible/attainable if and only if there exists at least one system design and implementation that correctly implements the requirement or all the requirements stated in the aggregate [5] at a definable cost [14].

There are no particular means utilized or recommended by RUP to ensure or to measure the achievability of all kinds of requirements involved in a development project at an early stage of a software development project. Only standard RUP activity that have relevance to ensure feasibility is *constructing architectural-proof-of-concept*, which helps with determining whether there exists, or is likely to exist, a solution that satisfies the architecturally-significant requirements, i.e. the activity does not cover all the requirements.

Yet, for an industrial company that launches a software project with considerable amount of investment, tight time-to-market constraints, and severe competition, it is vital to know: (i) whether it is technically possible to achieve the identified requirements; (ii) whether it is possible to achieve the requirements within the limitations imposed by time and budget. At ABB, we ensure the first concern by including the developers in the reviews of the requirements artifacts. In the Vision document, which comprises the high-level requirements, feasibility is not a high priority quality to achieve; yet if a feature or a need is determined to be infeasible with today's technical knowledge, it is noted during the review meeting to be negotiated with the stakeholders. If the stakeholders insist keeping the requirement in the Vision, the requirement is annotated with "not to be included in an immediate release". Accordingly, infeasible requirements may stay in the Vision but they are not traced forward to any use-cases or any lower level supplementary requirements, at least not until the next iteration or until a new technological improvement in the area. It is higher importance to achieve feasibility nature in the lower level requirements, i.e. in the use-case model, in the supplementary specifications documents, and in the use-case specifications, because the actual work is defined based on these artifacts. The first concern, i.e. technical feasibility, is achieved via reviews and including not only the stakeholders but also the software architect(s), and designer(s) in the reviews. The second concern, i.e. financial feasibility, is ensured by preparing a number of scenarios, and computing the project length and cost in the case of each scenario (see Table 17.3). The calculations are performed to view the worst possible case, the best possible case and three optimal cases that demonstrate the probable, very probable, and most probable proceeding of the project. These states differ from each other based on the number of weeks per iteration, number of developers that can be involved throughout the development process, number of use cases identified for the whole system, number of weeks to be spent on the development of each use case, and the characteristics of each developer during the development process. Our method is adapted from "Use-Case Points" of Gustav Karner [15], [20]. We ignore the weight of actors in the calculations. We consider our "supplementary requirements" as the technical factors, and include their effect in the calculations indirectly via the complexity of use-cases. Finally, we decide on complexity of use-cases by ranking them on a 5-point scale, 5 illustrating the highest complexity.

Table 17.3 Financial feasibility scenarios

No. weeks /iteration (3..8)	L	8	7	6	5	5
No. of developers	N	2	3	4	4	4
No of use cases	K	15	15	15	15	15
No. weeks/use case	T	6	5	4	4	5
Efficiency per user (0..1)	U	0.5	0.6	0.5	0.5	0.7
		Worst	**Best**	**Optimal 1**	**Optimal 2**	**Optimal 3**
Developer effort (dev/iteration)	E	8	13	12	10	14
No of iterations	M	11.25	6	5	6	5
Project length (weeks)	S	90	42	30	30	27
Project costs (men* week)	P	90	75	60	60	75

The computations are done by using the following formulas:

$$E = U*L*N$$
$$M = T*K / (U*L*N) = T*K/E$$
$$S = T*K / (U*N) = M*L$$
$$P = S*N*U$$

Upon completion of computations, we compare the existing situation in the project with the results of different scenarios, and determine whether the project is too optimistic about the number and content of the requirements to be fulfilled by the final product. Measurement of requirements attainability is done at least once by the beginning of a project. Depending on the volatility of the requirements and changes in the environmental factors for the team, it may be repeated by the beginning of each iteration.

17.4.2 Clear/ Precise/Meaningful

A requirement or an aggregate is clear/precise/meaningful if and only if (a) numeric quantities are used whenever possible, and (b) the appropriate levels of precision are used for all numeric quantities [5]. Keeping a proper scope in the sense of providing a definite amount of information, avoiding "motherhood" statements like "shall provide a continuous service", "shall ensure the highest system security" is vital for clarity [9].

Executable requirements are Clear requirements. A requirement that is written in a formally defined computer executable, rather than a natural language, provides a more precise description. For example, the MATLAB simulation of the automatic mode of our cluster type control system operation provided more precise and validated requirements input into the design phase of the development. Moreover, Unambiguousness enhances Clarity of requirements. If we take an example to ambiguous requirements from one of our Stressometer projects at ABB, initially what the marketing department desired was "The system shall have a fast computation time". Such a requirement was rather vague and too general to work with for the development team. There were questions as "How fast is good enough?", "We can have various configurations of the system, which configuration are we talking about? The speed of computation time differs depending if it is a monolithic system or a distributed one; if it is a measurement only or a full control system; etc." Eventually, the requirement had to take a clearer format as "A full computation of the main functions, from the time the Base Measurement System TCP/IP signal is received until an output is issued (external communication not included), for a reversible mill single node flatness measurement system with 64 measurement zones, shall not be greater than 6.0 ms". The problem with this requirement was not only that it was ambiguously stated but also that there was quite a lot vital information missing. Accordingly, we can infer that incompleteness may lead to unclear requirements; or in other words, completeness may increase the possibility of having clear requirements.

RUP supplies templates and examples, which provide structure and guidance for content of different types of requirements thus assists in preparing clear/precise/meaningful requirements. Further, it recommends review of these artifacts against checkpoints, which include criteria for fulfilling the attribute. Some examples to the checkpoints for requirements clarity are "It is clear how and when the use case's flow of events starts and ends" "It is clear who wishes to perform a use case" "The purpose of the use case is also clear." "The actor interactions and exchanged information are clear." "The use case model clearly presents the behavior of the system." "The Introduction section of the use-case model provides a clear overview of the purpose and functionality of the system."

SUP did not add any new means to what is already suggested by the general RUP. In our Stressometer projects, we did not measure requirements clarity directly but rather ensured a common agreement on existence of it through reviews by the stakeholders that constituted the domain experts, representatives of the external customers who bought the system, and representatives of the internal customers who used the requirements in the subsequent steps of the development lifecycle.

17.4.3 Complete

A requirement is complete if it is capable of standing alone when separated from other requirements and does not need further amplification [14]. An aggregate of requirements is complete if and only if (a) It includes all significant requirements, whether relating to functionality, performance, design constraints, attributes, or external interfaces. In particular, any external requirements imposed by a system specification should be acknowledged and treated. (b) It involves all responses of the software to all realizable classes of input data in all realizable classes of situations –including responses to both valid and invalid input values. (c) All figures, tables, and diagrams in the aggregate are fully labeled and referenced; all terms are defined; units of measure are provided [12]. (d) No sections are marked "To Be Determined (TBD)" [4]. (e) It covers all allocations from higher level [14]. (f) It must not include situations that will not be encountered or unnecessary capability features [25].

Organizing the requirements in a logical way, for example by following a template recommended by a specific process or by a standard, helps readers understand the structure of a functionality described in a use-case or in a standard requirements specification document, and makes it easier for them to identify if something is missing; hence, complete requirements. In similar sense, executing requirements via prototyping or via simulation during requirements analysis gives the stakeholders opportunity to validate the requirements as well as reflect on the missing ones, leading to a more complete set of requirements and more complete definition of requirements. Further, considering the condition (f) in the above definition, we can conclude that for requirements to be complete they have to be necessary. In other words, preparing an immense use-case model with "golden plating" use-cases omitting the necessary functionalities does not make the use-case model more complete. In fact, if we refer to the condition (e) in our definition, we determine that it is essential to establish backward traceability from the use-case model to the higher-level requirements specification, for example in ABB's case, to the vision document that includes all the features and user needs of the prospective software system.

Focusing on user tasks instead of system functions during requirements elicitation avoids overlooking the requirements as well as including requirements that are not necessary [24]. To this end, using use-cases for capturing requirements are the ideal means. In addition, semi-formal nature of use-cases makes it easy for the stakeholders to read and understand a requirements document, and eventually, provide a feedback on the missing parts. Further, using a standard specification format, a template, can reveal omissions and prevent loss of requirements [10]. Moreover, iterative development of RUP brings about assessment of and maturing accordingly the quality of artifacts throughout the development life cycle. Every iteration results in an executable release, which facilitates identification of missing requirements that can be dealt with in the subsequent iterations.

During our projects at ABB, we considered completeness of requirements as one of the primary quality characteristics. SUP mainly utilized the strategies and tools provided by the RUP. Further, we ensured that the release produced by the end of an iteration was executed and continuously tested in an environment that simulated a typical final customer environment. Watching real life scenarios increased the interest level, the concentration, and the comprehension of the stakeholders thus opened new discussions, which led to identification of new, insufficiently described, or missing requirements. Even though, we highly depended on qualitative means as stakeholders' judgment, compliance with templates and guidelines, we also used the metrics listed in Table 17.4 in an attempt to quantify the maturity of completeness of different requirements artifacts by the end of each iteration:

Table 17.4 Completeness metrics

Metric	Related Requirement Artifact and Implications
Number of Use-Cases Traced Back to Features/Total Number of Use-Cases	Completeness of Use-Case Model. Low value indicates existence of use-cases without any origin.
Number of Supplementary Requirements Traced Back to Features/Total Number of Supplementary Requirements	Completeness of Supplementary Specifications. Low value indicates existence of non-functional requirements without any origin.
Number of Incompletes in a Use-Case Specification	Completeness of a Use-Case Specification. SUP recognizes incompletes such as TBD, TBS, Not defined, Not determined etc. as risk indicators for requirements completeness. SUP imposes minimizing the usage of incompletes, allows usage of such terms if and only if they are followed by information regarding when and by whom the incomplete portion will be attended, and considers it as high risk for the project if the number of incompletes were not decreased after two consequent iterations.
Number of Incompletes in a Supplementary Specification	Completeness of a Supplementary Specification document. Implications apply as in the case of use-case specifications.

17.4.4 Concise

A requirement or an aggregate is concise if it is as short as possible without adversely affecting any other quality [5].

Generally, conciseness is measured in terms of size. Going overboard with completeness may easily increase the size, and consequently, jeopardize the conciseness of the requirement or the aggregate. A requirement, no matter in which format it is, must only state what is required and not how it shall be met in terms of design or implementation. Obviously, including such unnecessary information will bring about unnecessary increase in size hence, less concise. Besides, requirements can be stated at different levels of abstraction highly depending on the preferences of different projects. For example, [3] has defined two different use-case specification formats, namely casual and fully dressed, both of which are valid but may differ in size and thus, in conciseness. Finally, in order to increase understandability, requirements specifiers often use redundancy, which is not an error itself [12, 4, 5], yet can easily lead to problems in achieving other qualities one of which is conciseness.

RUP does not provide any particular assistance for conciseness. During our projects at ABB, we were mainly concerned about the size of the use-case models increased with the number of use-cases, number of included use-cases, number of extending use-cases, and number of each type of relations. Besides, writing extensive use-cases by keeping a low level of abstraction was a topic discussed at almost every review meeting. Yet, the first two projects proved that conciseness of the use-case model or the conciseness of use-case specifications did not constitute a high risk for the project or for the quality of the final product. Accordingly, it was not addressed in the subsequent projects by the SUP.

17.4.5 Correct

A requirement is correct if it accurately describes a functionality to be delivered [24]. An aggregate is correct if and only if every requirement stated therein is one that the software shall meet [12].

As mentioned earlier in Sect. 17.4.3, executing requirements enables the stakeholders to validate the specified requirements, thus, to ensure the correctness of the requirements. Externally and/or internally inconsistent requirements hinder establishing correctness for it can be difficult to know which one of the conflicting requirements is correct if there is any. Further, regarding our definition of correctness it is explicit that a requirement or an aggregate of requirements is always correct if it is necessary. Finally, based on the relations both with external consistency and with necessity, we can infer that a requirement is correct if it can be traced back to its source at a higher-level –naturally, on the condition that the higher-level requirement itself is correct.

RUP suggests involvement of end users in the requirements review meetings only *if possible*. It provides guidelines for test case generation from the requirements, but leaves the preparation of the test cases until the implementation work is scheduled for them. It does not require review of test cases either. By recommending usage of UML, and tools that do not provide any facilities for internal or external consistency checks of requirements, RUP hinders achievement of correctness. Yet, the iterative nature of the process enables continuous learning and improving throughout the development life cycle, and accommodating corrective changes in requirements as a result of such learning, any time during the project. On the other hand, we believe it is only the end users who can determine the correctness of user requirements. Accordingly, SUP process imposes involvement of representatives of both external users that work at the customer site and the internal users that customize, install, and maintain the system, in the review of use-case model, use-case specifications, and supplementary specifications. Further, according to the SUP, test cases should be derived from the requirements and parallel to the specification of the requirements so that any errors in the requirements can be revealed and corrected before the design activities start. The test cases should be reviewed by the requirements reviewers. Finally, continuous execution and testing of incremental releases in an environment that simulated a typical final customer site provides continuous and realistic feedback to the development team about the requirements that conflict with customer expectations.

17.4.6 Design Independent

A requirement or an aggregate is design independent if and only if there exists more than one system design and implementation that correctly implements the individual requirement or the requirements in the aggregate [5].

RUP provides only assistance for design independence via brief information about how to distinguish "what" from "how" in the use-case model guidelines. Templates and examples provided are also useful but not sufficient. In order to ensure design independence of the requirements, SUP imposes including the software architect and designers in the review of requirements artifacts so that they can point out those details that may limit their ability to consider alternative design possibilities in order to synthesize the most optimal one.

17.4.7 Externally Consistent

An aggregate is externally consistent if and only if no requirement stated therein conflicts with any already baselined project documentation [5].

Traditionally, external consistency is defined in terms of compliance with the preceding documents [4] and in most of the cases, those that include higher-level requirements [24]. Yet, considering the importance of configuration and change management during the whole lifecycle of software development, especially when following an iterative and incremental approach, at ABB we preferred to adopt a definition that emphasizes the importance of promoted baselines. In this way, we aimed to: (i) handle inconsistencies as a part of our formal change management, (ii) extend the context of external inconsistency to include project artifacts other than the high-level requirements documents such as project plan, a baselined release from the previous iteration, etc. Traceability is the only characteristic that we have experienced to affect the external consistency. If there is a link from every low-level software requirement, for example a use-case in the use-case model, a supplementary requirement in a supplementary specifications document, to a higher-level requirement, for example a feature or a need in the vision document, i.e., backward traceable –then the aggregate including these requirements is externally consistent with the high-level requirements. In the same manner, if there is a link from each requirement to at least one lower-level requirement or to a further development artifact such as a sequence diagram, a class diagram, a test case, i.e. forward traceable –then the aggregate including these requirements is in agreement with the lower-level documentation thus externally consistent with the particular documentation.

RUP provides well-defined requirements management activities, which includes detailed guidance for establishing and maintaining implicit and explicit traceabilities to and from requirements at different levels, and for managing changing requirements, and change management activities. Further, it presents Requisite Pro to facilitate its requirements management practice. Yet, as being a UML-based software development process, both RUP and SUP suffer inter- and intra-model inconsistencies. For example, during our projects at ABB we experienced difficulties in keeping the use-case models of different sub-systems consistent with each other. Eventually, we decided to use one common use-case model, which was in the end too large to manage. Besides, without any support for automatic consistency checks from Rational Rose, it required considerable amount of manual effort to ensure consistency even among the elements of the same model. Similar situation applied in preserving the existing consistencies between different models during model transformations, for example while reflecting changes in the implementation model to the design model and eventually to the relevant use-case, actor, or portion of the specification of a use-case in the use-case model.

17.4.8 Forward Traceable

A requirement or an aggregate is forward traceable if and only if it is written in a manner that facilitates the referencing of the requirement or each individual requirement of the aggregate in future development or enhancement documentation [5, 12].

Common methods used for explicit traceability includes numbering every paragraph hierarchically, numbering every requirement with a unique number, using a convention to indicate a requirement and using a tool to extract and uniquely number all sentences that comply with the particular convention [4]. To this end, it will be much easier to achieve forward traceability if the requirements are electronically stored by using a tool that facilitates numbering and/or extracting sentences according to a defined convention. Besides explicit traceability, there is certain amount of traceability implicit in every development process [21]. For example in the case of projects that follow RUP, such traceabilities are achieved via: (i) Naming Conventions, (ii) The construction of mappings between the models, (iii) Relationships between the model items themselves, (iv) The creation of different perspectives illustrating how the elements of one model satisfy the demands implicit in the elements of another model. Some of these are easier to fulfill by electronically storing the requirements in a tool that has the UML meta-model defined in it, such as Rational Rose. A detailed discussion about forward traceability can also be found in Chap. 5.

One of the best practices with RUP is managing requirements [18]. As a major part of the requirements management, RUP puts specific emphasis on establishing traceabilities among different levels of requirements and from the requirements to the rest of the software development artifacts. It provides information about and guidance for various possible traceability strategies, most common of which are No Use-Case Model; Use-Case Model Only; Features Drive the Use Case Model; The Use-Case Model is an interpretation of the Software Requirements Specification; The Use Case Model reconciles multiple sets of traditional software requirements [21]. Further, RUP facilitates building and utilizing these strategies via tool support. For example, it recommends Rational RequisitePro as a tool for defining, capturing, and tracking the traceability links. Whereas, on the other hand, as being a UML-based software development process, RUP employs a "use-case driven approach", meaning use cases that can only describe the functional requirements are the basis for the entire development process [18]. It describes the activities to move from specifications of use-cases to the realization of use-cases subsequently to the implementation and testing of use-cases, in detail. It provides no similar assistance for the non-functional requirements, which must also be provided to the customer in the final product together with the functionality thus, must be designed and tested together with the functionality.

Table 17.5 Forward traceability metrics (1 of 2)

Metric	Related Requirement Artifact and Implications
(Number of Features Traced to Use-Cases) + (Number of Features Traced to Supplementary Specifications)/Total Number of Features	Forward Traceability of Vision. This metric is mainly used before lower level requirements specifications are prepared. Low value may suggest unsatisfactory quality in various areas. It directly illustrates poor forward traceability from the high-level requirements to the lower level ones. In addition, it may imply inconsistency between the high-level requirements and the lower level requirements. It may indicate incorrect requirements at the lower level. It may signal incompleteness unless the Vision includes requirements to be fulfilled in the long-term, as it was the case in our projects.
(Number of Features Traced to Use-Case Specification Sections) + (Number of Features Traced to Supplementary Requirements)/Total Number of Features	Forward Traceability of Vision. This metric can be used after starting to prepare the lower level requirements specifications. The implications are of the same nature as described regarding the previous metric; yet it provides results that are more accurate thus, facilitates identifying the root causes.
Number of Use-Case Specification Sections Traced to Sequence Diagrams / Total Number of Use-Case Specification Sections to be Traced to Sequence Diagrams (Previously: Number of Use-Case Specification Flows Traced to Sequence Diagrams/Total Number of Use-Case Specification Flows)	Forward Traceability of Use-Cases to the Design Model. Low value indicates low traceability to the sequence diagrams. All development cases prepared according to the SUP principles imposes one-to-one relation between the flows of a use-case specification and of a use-case realization specification. Yet, as it was observed in some projects, it might be easier, less redundant, more concise, and more understandable to describe the design of more than one flow in the same sequence diagram. Besides, due to the iterative nature of the projects, not all flows might be considered for a design in a particular iteration. Further, occasionally, we encountered the need to design use-case specification sections other than the flows via sequence diagrams. Accordingly, we adjusted our initial metric.

Table 17.5 *(cont.)* Forward traceability metrics (2 of 2)

Metric	Related Requirement Artifact and Implications
Number of Use-Case Specifications Traced to Class Diagrams/Total Number of Use-Case Specifications to be Traced to Class Diagrams (Previously: Number of Use-Case Specification Flows Traced to Class Diagrams/Total Number of Use-Case Specification Flows)	Forward Traceability of Use-Cases to the Design Model. Low value indicates low traceability to the class diagrams thus, eventually quality problems in the code. In the very first project, it was decided to illustrate each use-case flow with one class diagram in the design model. By doing so, we experienced difficulties in keeping the diagrams consistent, and the design model and the use-case realization documents concise. Accordingly, we adjusted the development case and our initial metric.
Number of Use-Case Scenarios Traced to Functional Test Cases/Total Number of Use-Case Scenarios to be Traced to Test Cases	Forward Traceability of Use-Cases to the Test Model. Low value indicates low traceability to the test cases thus, insufficient testing.

RUP does not recognize any explicit link between the use-cases and the supplementary, i.e. the non-functional, requirements, either. In brief, even though some of the traceability strategies include links from the Supplementary Specifications to the subsequent artifacts, there exists no particular RUP guidance for how to establish such traceabilities.

During our projects at ABB, we used "Features Drive the Use Case Model", which is the default strategy recommended by the Rational Unified Process. The Use-Case Model and Supplementary Specifications form a complete software requirements specification. Features are documented in the Vision Document and are traced to use cases. If they are not reflected in the Use Case Model then they are traced to supplementary requirements in the Supplementary Specifications [21]. Accordingly, we handled the tracing from features to the use-case sections and to the supplementary requirements, from use-case specifications to the use-case realizations, to the functional test cases and eventually to the test procedures whereas, we managed the linkage from the supplementary requirements to the use-case realizations and to the test procedures in an ad hoc manner. For example, we could easily point at which test case realized which part of which use-case in the test model; whereas, supplementary specifications were directly entered into the test procedures, and in most of the cases to a degree depending on the initiative of the test designer. Table 17.5 includes the forward traceability metrics we used in our projects run according to SUP:

17.4.9 Internally Consistent

An aggregate is internally consistent if and only if no subset of individual requirements stated in it conflict [12]. The same term is used for the same item in all requirements of the aggregate [14].

When an aggregate is not organized, it may be difficult to identify the inconsistencies [14]. Therefore, it should be preferred to organize the requirements according to a standard or by using a template recommended by the process used. In addition, we often use redundancies in documentation in order to increase the readability, while causing a risk for internal inconsistency. When altering one occurrence of a requirement we may forget to do so with other occurrences; hence, internal inconsistency; yet, we can decrease the risk by using cross-references. Finally, better consistency can be achieved with executable requirements depending on whether the tool used has a consistency check facility and how sophisticated the facility is. For example, [7] describes a consistency algorithm for the live sequence charts of the "play engine" [8] mentioned earlier. By adopting such an algorithm in the "play engine", it is aimed to automatically detect inconsistencies in a specification, enable a user to track the reason for inconsistencies via play out, suggest a consistent scenario with "good" order of events whenever there is one, and avoid abnormal abortion of play outs due to inconsistencies [8]. [4] identifies four types of inconsistencies: (i) Conflicting behavior; (ii) Conflicting terms; (iii) Conflicting characteristics; (iv) Temporal inconsistency.

RUP recommends developing a Glossary during the early phases of a project, in order to ensure consistent usage of the terms throughout the whole development life cycle hence, assistance to avoid conflicting terms. Even though, as our experiences showed, it might occasionally be difficult to keep the Glossary itself consistent, it is helpful to have one Glossary. On the other hand, both RUP and SUP rely highly on the reviews for detecting the conflicting behavior, conflicting characteristics, and temporal inconsistencies. Tracing such inconsistencies manually in a large, evolving use-case model or supplementary specifications can be hard and error prone.

17.4.10 Modifiable

An aggregate is modifiable if and only if its structure and style are such that any changes to the requirements can be made easily, completely, and consistently while retaining the structure and style [12].

Our experiences from software development projects at ABB have illustrated high importance of requirements modifiability for: (i) requirements change; (ii) concerns other than but affecting software requirements change; (iii) requirements evolve; (iv) requirements can be wrongly stated due to various inadvertent reasons. In such cases, it is easier to identify and subsequently, apply the modifications if (i) the requirements are organized in a coherent and easy-to-use way; (ii) redundancy is kept to minimum; (iii) cross-references are used where necessary; (iv) the requirements are uniquely labeled to ease both forward and backward traceabilities; and (iv) the requirements are electronically stored. On the other hand, ranking requirements by importance, stability, or version may inhibit modifiability if the aggregate is organized according to the ranking instead of according to some logical grouping recommended by a standard, or by a template provided by the process followed, or chosen by the project in order to keep the related concerns together and unrelated ones separate.

RUP iterative life cycle allows changes to the requirements at almost any point in the development. Besides, since development is done incrementally, it is easier to detect the effects, estimate the cost of, and eventually carry out a suggested modification. RUP distinguishes between different types of requirements, and provides templates for organizing each type of requirements. It recommends using Rational Rose to electronically store the use-case models and diagrams, and supplies specification templates ready to be used in Microsoft Word, Adobe Frame-Maker, and HTML formats. SUP inherits the advantages of the generic RUP as described above.

17.4.11 Necessary

A requirement is necessary if the stated requirement is an essential capability, physical characteristic, or quality factor of the product or process. If it is removed or deleted, a deficiency will exist, which cannot be fulfilled by other capabilities of the product or process [14].

One common way suggested by the literature to decide on the necessity of a requirement is to trace the requirement back to its origin, for example in the case of our projects, which use RUP as the software development process, to trace a use-case back to a feature or a need in the vision. If it cannot be traced it may not be necessary. All definitions of necessity introduce the characteristic as a primary condition for a requirement to qualify for being included in the final product [11], [14], and [24]. Yet, depending on the scheme we use, ranking a requirement for importance may conflict with the necessary nature of the requirement. For example, [12] suggests ranking requirements based on a degree of necessity that distinguishes classes of requirements as essential, conditional, and optional. According to the scheme, essential requirements are those that must be provided for the final product to be accepted, hence necessary requirements. Whereas, conditional requirements are those that would enhance the final product but would not make it unacceptable if they are absent, and optional requirements are those that may or may not be worthwhile, hence not necessary requirements.

Table 17.6 Necessity metrics

Metric	Related Requirement Artifact and Implications
Number of Use-Case Sections Traced Back to Features/Total Number of Use-Case Sections	Necessity of Use-Cases. A value other than 1 indicates existence of not required use-case flows, special requirements, post, or pre-conditions.
Number of Supplementary Requirements Traced Back to Features/Total Number of Supplementary Requirements	Necessity of Supplementary Requirements. A value other than 1 indicates existence of unnecessary non-functional requirements.

RUP describes specific and detailed activities for requirements elicitation. It suggests methods to follow for identifying what the stakeholders require. It enhances the assistance with guidelines where appropriate. It also provides related checkpoints to be adopted at the review meetings. As a part of its requirements management practice, RUP suggests various traceability strategies, which provide guidance on keeping links between requirements at different levels. Finally, the iterative nature of RUP allows continuous learning and improving the requirements throughout the development life cycle. SUP requires involvement of representatives of all types of stakeholders in the requirements elicitation and identification process. Besides, it uses well-defined traceability procedures between high level and lower level requirements. Accordingly, the risk with identifying requirements that do not contribute to the satisfaction of some customer needs is minimized. SUP also suggests collecting the metrics identified in Table 17.6 and discussing the results in the relevant review meetings.

17.4.12 Organized

An aggregate is organized if and only if its contents are arranged so that readers can easily locate information and logical relationships among adjacent sections are apparent [5].

RUP recommends organizing the functional requirements using use-cases. Instead of a traditional bulleted list of requirements, RUP suggests organizing them in a way that tells a story of how someone may use the final product [18]. Further, it provides templates complemented with guidelines and examples to assist in documenting the needs and features in Vision document, and lower level requirements in Use-Case Model survey, Use-Case Specifications, and Supplementary Specifications, in an organized manner. SUP adopts generic RUP means, with minor adaptations according to the ABB instructions. The "organized" nature of requirements is ensured via the checkpoints at the review meetings.

17.4.13 Prioritized/Ranked/ Annotated

A requirement is prioritized/ranked/annotated by relative importance if the requirement is assigned an implementation priority to indicate how essential it is to include it in a particular product [24]. An aggregate is prioritized/ranked/annotated by relative importance if each requirement in it has an identifier to indicate the importance of that particular requirement [12].

A requirement is prioritized/ranked/annotated by relative stability if the requirement is assigned an identifier to indicate the stability of the particular requirement [5]. An aggregate is prioritized/ranked/annotated by relative stability if each requirement in it has an identifier to indicate the stability of that particular requirement [12]. A requirement or an aggregate is prioritized/ranked/annotated by version if a reader can easily determine whether the particular requirement or which requirements of the aggregate will be satisfied in which version of the prospective product [5].

The characteristics that may hinder from achieving prioritized/ranked/annotated by relative importance are those that are related to the organization of requirements in the aggregates. If it is preferred by the project to organize the requirements to be modifiable, or to rank by relative stability, or to rank by version, then prioritization by relative importance cannot be performed in the structure of the aggregate. Yet, by extracting the requirements into another means such as a workbook or a database, the project can still rank the requirements by relative stability and by version without adversely affecting the ranking by relative importance nature of the original aggregate. Besides, if an aggregate is organized by following a standard or a template provided by the process adopted, it cannot be organized according to the ranking of its requirements by relative importance. Similar situations also apply to achieving prioritization of requirements by relative stability and by version. Finally, if a requirement is necessary, it represents functionality, a capability, a physical characteristic, or a quality factor essential for the final product; therefore, it cannot be ranked to a level that degrades its necessity.

Traditionally, it is suggested to establish ranking according to relative importance, stability, or version in the organization and the structure of an aggregate. Accordingly, an aggregate organized to be modifiable would have a negative impact on this characteristic. However, in SUP, it is suggested to extract the requirements from the aggregate into a workbook, execute the rankings based on the attributes chosen beforehand, and eventually, sort and save the matrix in separate datasheets per each ranking. In this way, the project could keep the original organizations of the use-case model, supplementary specifications, and the vision while at the same time it could refer to the rankings when needed, for example for (re-)planning by the beginning of an iteration. In this way, it was also possible to generate different combinations of rankings in summary tables depending on the aim of the planning. For example, if it was decided that we should plan the iteration to develop the use-cases with the critical benefits, and to stabilize the architecture, then it would be necessary to view the matrix sorted first by relative importance and then by stability on one worksheet. Table 17.7 illustrates a portion of a use-case matrix resulted from such combined ranking during one of our projects at ABB.

As a part of its Requirements Management activities, the generic RUP recommends defining the attributes to be tracked for each type of requirement. Examples to such attributes are Stability, Effort to implement, Risk to the development effort, etc. It provides detailed guidelines how to identify, store, and review the attributes. Further, it supplies a tool mentor to facilitate these activities via RequisitePro, which enables defining attributes for different types of requirements, storing the requirements together with the attribute values, and retrieving and organizing the requirements by attribute values via filtering or sorting in views. In conclusion, RUP excels the "prioritization" related quality attributes by delivering the means for sophisticated groupings of requirements.

Table 17.7 Example use-case attribute matrix

Use-Case No	Status	Benefit	Effort	Technical Risk	Architectural Impact	Stability	Priority	Scheduled for the Current Iteration	Responsible Party
UC-20	Proposed	Critical	High	Medium	Extends	High	High	Yes	Christer
UC-23	Proposed	Critical	High	Medium	None	Medium	High	Yes	Olle
UC-51	Proposed	Critical	Medium	Medium	None	Medium	High	Yes	Olle
UC-21	Proposed	Critical	Medium	Medium	None	High	Medium	Yes	Christer
UC-49	Proposed	Critical	Medium	Medium	None	High	Medium	Yes	Christer
UC-33	Proposed	Critical	Medium	Low	None	High	Low	Yes	LEM
UC-55	Proposed	Critical	Medium	Low	None	High	Low		

For a more detailed survey on requirements prioritization and requirements prioritization techniques, readers should also refer to Chap. 4 in this book.

Table 17.8 Backward traceability metrics

Metric	Related Requirement Artifact and Implications
Number of Use-Cases Traced Back to Features/Total Number of Use-Cases	Backward Traceability of Use-Case Model. A value other than 1 indicates poorly traced use-cases. It also suggests existence of use-cases without any origin.
Number of Use-Case Specification Traced Back to Features/Total Number of Use-Case Specification Sections	Backward Traceability of a Use-Case. A value other than 1 indicates poorly traced use-cases. It also suggests existence of use-case sections, such as pre or post conditions, or special requirements, without any origin.
Number of Supplementary Requirements Traced Back to Features/Total Number of Supplementary Requirements	Backward Traceability of Supplementary Specification. A value other than 1 indicates poorly traced supplementary specification and supplementary requirement. It also suggests existence of supplementary requirements without any origin.
Number of Sequence Diagrams Traced Back to Use-Case Specification Sections/Total Number of Sequence Diagrams	Backward Traceability of Design Model to the Use-Cases. A value other than 1 indicates poorly traced sequence diagrams. It signifies existence of design elements without any origin. It may also suggest inconsistencies between what the end customer expects and what is being developed.
Metric	Related Requirement Artifact and Implications
Number of Class Diagrams Traced Back to Use-Case Specification Sections/Total Number of Class Diagrams	Backward Traceability of Design Model to the Use-Cases. A value other than 1 indicates poorly traced class diagrams. It signifies existence of design elements without any origin. It may also suggest inconsistencies between what the end customer expects and what is being developed.
Number of Functional Test Cases Traced to Use-Case Scenarios/Total Number of Functional Test Cases	Backward Traceability of Test Model to the Use-Cases. A value other than 1 indicates poorly traced test cases. It suggests existence of test cases without origin. It also signifies that necessary functionalities were not tested and/or extra functionality was implemented without informing the requirements team first.

17.4.14 Traced/Backward Traceable

A requirement or an aggregate is traced/backward traceable if the origin of the requirement or of each requirement of the aggregate is clear [5].

The discussion about the explicit and implicit traceability and the influence of electronically stored characteristics on the forward traceability (see Sect. 17.4.8) also applies to the backward traceability. Further, the discussion about the support by the generic RUP and SUP for establishing traceability in the same section should also be considered here. Yet, what differs is the metrics we used in our projects in order to measure the degree of backward traceability achieved thus, detect possible risks and flaws in the projects:

17.4.15 Unambiguous

A requirement or an aggregate is unambiguous if different readers with similar backgrounds would be able to draw only one interpretation of the requirement [9, 24] or of each requirement in the aggregate [12]. As discussed in detail earlier in Chap. 11, natural language is inherently ambiguous. In order to decrease the ambiguity thus increase the unambiguousness, one can use more deterministic methods and languages with well-defined semantics, such as state machines, predicate calculus, prepositional calculus, petri nets. Most of these methods and languages are supported by software tools that can automatically detect lexical, syntactic, and semantic errors. Accordingly, electronically stored and/or executable requirements may constitute less ambiguity.

RUP is a UML-based software development process. UML has limited notation to express different types of requirements. In fact, it only helps visualizing the actors and the use-cases that constitute the lower level functional requirements. UML does not provide support for detailing the use-cases. Even though RUP suggests using sequence diagrams to show how an actor interacts with a use-case, or using activity diagrams or state charts to describe a single use-case in order to formalize use-cases, the common means to describe use-cases is Natural Language. In addition, use-cases are not the only requirements of a software product. RUP uses Vision documents for specifying the high-level requirements, and Supplementary Specifications to describe the non-functional requirements. Both Vision and Supplementary Specifications are created also by using Natural Language. Natural Language has inherent ambiguity. Yet, RUP defines a common vocabulary in order to decrease ambiguity among team members. It recommends checkpoints to be used during the review of requirements specification documents. Such checkpoints are too general and insufficient to ensure a satisfying level of unambiguousness in the requirements artifacts.

Active participation of all types of stakeholders in the elicitation and review of the requirements and preparation of test cases parallel to the preparation of the use-cases are the main means that SUP recommends in order to decrease the ambiguity in the requirements. It recognizes a list of weak phrases that may cause uncertainty and lead to multiple interpretations, such as flexible, fault tolerant, adequate, as appropriate, maximize, minimize, at a given time, up to etc., and options that give the developers freedom to satisfy the related requirement by following more than one way such as can, may, optionally etc. During review meetings, checks are done in order to detect usage of these words. In addition, the following metrics in Table 17.9 are used to measure the ambiguity level in a specification.

Table 17.9 Unambiguousness metrics

Metric	Related Requirement Artifact and Implications
Number of Weak Phrases + Number of Options in a Use-Case Specification	Unambiguousness of a Use-Case Specification. Values other than 0 indicate ambiguity in the specification.
Number of Weak Phrases + Number of Options in a Supplementary Specification	Unambiguousness of a Supplementary Specification. Values other than 0 indicate ambiguity in the specification.

17.4.16 Understandable

A requirement or an aggregate is understandable if all classes of readers can easily comprehend the meaning of the requirement or all requirements in the aggregate, with a minimum of explanation [5].

Naturally, an unambiguous requirement or aggregate is clearer/more precise and more meaningful thus more understandable. On the other hand, if the unambiguousness is achieved by using formal notations, understandability of the requirements by non-technical stakeholders will decrease. In addition, redundancy increases readability thus may increase understandability of requirements. Moreover, it is easier to comprehend behavior by seeing it in action than by reading about it in a document. Accordingly, executability/interpretability of requirements enhances the understandability of them. Further, organizing the requirements according to a standard or by using a template recommended by the process followed or according to another logical grouping accepted by the project will increase the understandability of the requirements. The iterative nature of the RUP process enables continuous learning and improving throughout the development life cycle. Every iteration results in an executable release, which improves effective understandability. Besides, our experiences have illustrated that organizing functional requirements by using use-cases leads to greater completeness and better understanding of the requirements hence, support by RUP for better understandability of requirements. In addition, RUP provides templates to organize the high-level requirements and non-functional requirements in logical groupings.

In the projects that follow SUP, since all types of stakeholders, i.e. representatives of end users, representatives of actual buyers of the system, architect, and designer of the system, those who do the installation and maintenance of the final product, and take part in the review of the requirements problems with understanding the requirements can easily be revealed and solved.

17.5 Conclusions

The Stressometer products have been providing rolling mills with accurate online control of the flatness of cold rolled strips for more than 30 years. As the early generation, PLC-based Stressometer systems have been migrated to a Java-based platform, ABB has faced a need for change in the way it works to continue providing value to its customers and ensuring customer satisfaction in a controlled manner. Accordingly, it adopted RUP in an agile fashion mainly by maintaining active and heavy involvement of stakeholders that include both external and internal customers, preparing the test cases before coding, and continuously testing during development. The resultant development process namely SUP has been applied in three projects and has presented satisfying results regarding the achievement of "good quality" requirements.

The Stressometer projects received major gains from the disciplined nature of RUP in *traceability*, *completeness*, and *necessity* attributes via well-defined traceability strategies that were provided as a part of thorough requirements management. Templates and examples together with the associated guidelines and checkpoints helped to achieve the *organized*, *modifiability*, and *clarity* qualities in the requirements. Further, iterative nature of RUP gave a considerable support in achieving *completeness*, *modifiability*, and *understandability*. On the other hand, standard RUP means was insufficient for ensuring *achievability*. Accordingly, in SUP we introduced financial feasibility scenarios and imposed active communication of the development team with the rest of the stakeholders including the external as well as the internal customers.

Tool support by RUP to "ease" achieving the *prioritization related attributes* was found not enough value providing to invest time and effort. Instead, in the SUP, simpler guidelines to follow were defined and usage of worksheets was suggested. Active involvement of the end users in the creation and review of the requirements artifacts, as imposed by SUP, proved to be an invaluable means to achieve *correctness*, and *unambiguousness*.

Completeness and *correctness* qualities were further excelled by producing an executable release by the end of every iteration, and allowing the external and the internal customers to interact with it in an environment, which simulates a typical final customer site, mainly as a part of continuous testing.

Including the architects and the designers in the review of requirements artifacts even though it is not required by the standard RUP procedures ensured *design independence* of the requirements. Preparing the test cases early in the development, parallel to the requirements specification, and having them reviewed by the stakeholders supported achievement of most of the quality attributes; however, the main benefits were perceived regarding the requirements *correctness*.

The projects had to put considerable amount of manual effort and had to maintain a close communication within the development team in order to ensure *internal* and *external consistency*. This was not a satisfactory practice and accordingly, was considered to be improved in the future.

References

1. Basili V, Weiss D (1981) Evaluation of a software requirements document by analysis of change data. In: Proceedings of 5th IEEE International Software Engineering Conference, March 9-12, 1981, San Diego, California, United States, pp.314–323

2. Boehm B (1981) Software engineering economics. Prentice Hall: Englewood Cliffs, New Jersey

3. Cockburn A (2001) Writing effective use cases. Addison-Wesley: Boston, Massachusetts

4. Davis AM (1993) Software requirements: Objects, functions, and states. Revision. PTR Prentice Hall: Englewood Cliffs, New Jersey

5. Davis A, Overmyer S, Jordan K, Caruso J, Dandashi F, Dinh A, Kincaid G, Ledeboer G, Reynolds P, Sitaram P, Ta A, Theofanos M (1993) Identifying and measuring quality in a software requirements specification. In: Proceedings of 1st International Software Metrics Symposium, Baltimore, Maryland, United States, pp.141–152

6. Grieskamp W, Lepper M (2000) Using use cases in executable Z. In: Proceedings of IEEE Conference on Formal Engineering Methods, September 4-7, York, England, pp.111–120

7. Harel D, Kugler H (2002) Synthesizing state-based object systems from LSC specifications. International Journal of Foundations of Computer Science (IJFCS), 13(1): 5–51

8. Harel D, Marelly R (2002) Specifying and executing behavioral requirements: The play-in/play-out approach. Technical Report MCS01-15, The Weizmann Institute of Science

9. Harwell R, Aslaksen E, Mengot R, Hooks I, Ptack K (1993) What is a requirement? In: Proceedings of 3rd International Symposium of the NCOSE, July 26-28, Arlington, Virginia, United States, 1: 17–22

10. Hooks I, Farry K (2000) Customer-centered products: Creating successful products through smart requirements management. American Management Association: New York, New York

11. Hooks I (1993) Writing good requirements. In: Proceedings of 3rd International Symposium of the INCOSE, July 26-28, Arlington, Virginia, United States, 2: 197–203

12. IEEE (1998) IEEE Recommended practice for software requirements specifications, IEEE Std. 830-1998

13. (2004) http://www.ilogix.com/fs prod.htm. Last accessed: 2004-09-09

14. Kar P, Bailey M (1996) Characteristics of good requirements. In: Proceedings of 6th International Symposium of the NCOSE, 7-11 July, Boston, Massachusetts, USA 2: 284–291

15. Karner G (1993) Metrics for objectory. Diploma thesis, University of Linköping, Sweden, No LiTHIDA-Ex-9344:21

16. Kruchten P (1999) The rational unified process. Addison-Wesley: Reading, Massachusetts

17. Oberg R, Probasco L, Ericsson M (2000) Applying requirements management with use-cases. Rational Software White Paper, Technical Paper TP505 (Version 1.3), http://www.pureproject.com/reqs_mgmt_usecases.htm

18. Rational Sofware Corporation (2002) Rational unified process software. Version 2002.05.00

19. Rosenberg L, Hyatt L, Hammer T, Huffman L, Wilson W (1998) Testing metrics for requirements quality. In: Proceedings of 2nd International Software Quality Week, 9-13 November, Brussels, Belgium. Access on 13th December 2004. http://satc.gsfc.nasa.gov/support/

20. Schneider G, Winters J P (1998) Applying use-cases - A practical guide. Addison-Wesley: Reading, Massachusetts

21. Spence I, Probasco L (2000) Traceability strategies for managing requirements with use cases. Rational Software White Paper, Access on 13th December 2004. http://www.isk.kth.se/proj/2003/6b3403/sa3/www/RationalUnifiedProcess/papers/traceability.htm

22. (2004) http://www.mathworks.com/. Last accessed: 2004-11-12

23. (2004) http://www.standishgroup.com/. Last accessed: 2004-11-10

24. Wiegers KE (1999) Writing quality requirements. Software Development Magazine, May, http://www.sdmagazine.com/

25. Wilson WM (1997): Writing effective requirements specifications. In: Proceedings of 9th Annual Software Technology Conference, 27 April–2 May, Salt Lake City, Utah, USA

26. Yilmaztürk N (2003) RE in flatness measurement and control systems development at ABB. In: Proceedings of 11th IEEE International Requirements Engineering Conference, 8-12 September, Monterey Bay, California, USA, pp. 293

Author Biography

Nur Yilmaztürk is a computer scientist in the Software Architecture and Processes (SWAP) Group of the Automation Technologies department at ABB Corporate Research. She worked in different roles including process and project management during development of new generation Stressometer systems at ABB. Her research interests involve software development processes mainly model-driven development, and iterative and incremental development, conceptual modeling, architectural visualization and analysis, and object oriented technologies. She received her bachelor's degree in mathematical engineering from Istanbul Technical University (ITU) in Turkey, and her MSc and PhD in computer science from the University of Manchester Institute of Science and Technology (UMIST) in UK.

18 Requirements Experience in Practice: Studies of Six Companies

Tony Gorschek and Mikael Svahnberg

Abstract: To understand how to apply different requirements engineering practices and where difficulties may arise when implementing a set of requirements engineering practices, it is often useful to consider how others have done and the troubles they have encountered. This chapter describes six industry cases of applied requirements engineering, with a focus on areas where further improvements are desired by or recommended to the companies. Many of these improvement areas are also identified by other, independent, requirements engineering state of practice surveys, and thus indicate areas that warrant special attention when constructing a requirements engineering process for an organization.

Keywords: Requirements engineering, Process assessment, Model-based assessment, Inductive assessment, Software process improvement, State of practice.

18.1 Introduction

In Parts 1 and 2 of this book, different aspects of requirements engineering are presented, ranging from requirements elicitation, specification, analysis, prioritization, negotiation and requirements management. One question that may arise is whether industry in fact uses everything presented. In this chapter we present studies of the requirements practices at six companies. The purpose of this presentation is to show a sample of what requirements practices industrial companies have implemented, and what practices the companies have hitherto not yet adapted.

Gaining insight into how companies in fact use different requirements engineering practices enables an understanding of how to balance different needs. Moreover, it gives an overview of areas within requirements engineering that are well understood and, more importantly, those areas that industry still finds too immature or lack sufficient training to implement. From this perspective, this chapter points towards areas within requirements engineering where further efforts are required to either develop the practices to suit industry needs or to focus requirements engineering training.

Please note that this chapter presents a series of case studies. As with all case studies, the findings may not be generalizable to a larger sample. However, this is not the intention of the presentation. The intention is, as mentioned earlier, to give an overview and some examples of which requirements engineering practices that are applied in industry and, more importantly, which practices that are not applied. Please also note that since the assessment efforts presented in this chapter are parts of software process improvement efforts, the assessments naturally tend to focus on areas that are in need of change and improvement. This does not imply that the requirements engineering processes of the companies are totally dominated by shortcomings.

The remainder of this chapter is organized as follows. In Sect. 18.2 a brief overview is given of the companies involved in this study. In Sect. 18.3 the methodology used to study (assess) the companies is described. Sect. 18.4 presents the findings of the assessments, i.e. the state of practice in the studied companies. In Sect. 18.5 a number of states of practice surveys are presented and how their results relate to the findings of our assessments. The chapter is discussed in Sect. 18.6 and concluded in Sect. 18.7.

18.2 Studied Companies

Understanding how requirements engineering practices are implemented to suit different companies' needs also entails having knowledge of the companies themselves (or, for some of the companies, the projects studied). In this section we describe the studied companies further. Because of confidentiality issues, we refer to the companies as company Alpha to company Zeta. The purpose of this brief presentation of the companies is to present the reader with an overview of the context for the study of requirements engineering practices detailed in Sect. 18.3. Company Alpha to Gamma were selected so that two larger companies (>150 employees) and two smaller companies were represented, and company Epsilon and Zeta were studied as a part of a larger research project in which they are partners. All contacted companies agreed to participate in the studies.

Company Alpha. In this company we studied a project scoping 11,000 person-hours, entailing a partially-finished standardized system solution for logistics and warehouse management. The company is highly specialized in the domain, as are the company's typical customers. Accordingly, the customer of the studied project has extensive system knowledge. They have used similar systems before, have considerable domain knowledge, and know what they want.

Company Beta. The project studied in this company developed a web based system for a government agency. The system assists companies that are FDA (Food and Drug Administration) regulated to capture data that will aid in the continued upkeep of their FDA status. The requirements engineering part of this project comprised 350 person-hours. The company's expertise includes the pharmaceutical domain and FDA approval and certification process. The company is primarily involved in bespoke development efforts aimed at large clients and government agencies.

Company Gamma. Studied in this company is a 1600 person-hours project developing a web based system designed to manage training activities for a specific medical device company, i.e. to keep track of courses available with regards to certification and education of medical practitioners and professionals. Bespoke projects dominate the development efforts.

Company Delta. The project studied in this company was an 18000 person-hour project. The project developed an application support system for a government agency. The system was based on a previous mainframe system. The project developed a downsized, modernized (e.g. updated functionality and implemented in an object-oriented programming language), and a graphical user interface was added. The company has considerable experience in the application domain of the studied project.

Company Epsilon. This company has over 30 years of experience developing hardware and software solutions within the domain of automated manufacturing support. The company has a mixture of large and small customers ranging from equipment manufacturers to end users worldwide. Approximately 200 persons work in the company developing products (both software and hardware) in a product line environment.

Company Zeta. This company is world leading within a specific area in the domain of guidance and navigation software. The company employs approximately 100 employees, of which 20–25 are software engineers. The company has a wide product portfolio in its niche of the overall domain, as they consider it important to be able to offer partners and customers a wide selection of general variants of hardware and supporting software. Tailoring and especially minor customer adaptation often follows the procurement and subsequent installation of one of their systems. This, in addition to development of new software and hardware, makes it necessary to plan, execute and manage a wide range of projects.

18.3 Methodology

The study of the companies consists of two parts. In the first part, we study all six companies using a lightweight model-based requirements engineering evaluation tool, the REPM (Requirements Engineering Process Maturity) model. This model is further described in Sect. 18.3.1. Two of the companies, i.e. companies Epsilon and Zeta, are studied in further detail using a more in-depth assessment method where e.g. data from different sources of the requirements engineering process are triangulated against each other. This approach is described further in Sect. 18.3.2. For a more thorough description of the investigation tools, please see [12, 14].

18.3.1 Model-Based Process Assessment

Model-based process improvement is a prescriptive approach which is based on a collection of best practices describing how, e.g., software should be developed. The prescriptive nature of such models lies in the fact that *one* set of practices is to be adhered to by all organizations. No special consideration is taken to an organization's situation or needs other than how the development process (at the organization subject to software process improvement) is in comparison to the one offered through the prescribed model [6, 35]. A general trait common for most model-based assessment methods is that the assessments are performed as a benchmarking against the set of practices advocated by the model in question.

This means that the techniques used, e.g. interviews, questionnaires, etc., are designed with a focus towards benchmarking rather than deeper root cause investigations. The Requirements Engineering Process Maturity Model (REPM model) is constructed to fill the need for a lightweight process assessment method focused towards requirements engineering. Although there exist several other methods for assessing software development processes, (e.g. CMM [26] and ISO9000 [3]), few models focus on requirements engineering, and those that do to some extent (e.g. Sommerville & Sawyer [31,33], CMMI [7] and SPICE [34]) are large and demand a fair amount of resources in order to be used. The use of the REPM model to benchmark the RE process, on the other hand, takes approximately 40 person-hours in total (including analysis of the data collected through structured interviews and documentation).

The content of the model was inspired mainly by the work done by Somerville et al. in the REAIMS project [28] but also other existing work, such as Sommerville and Sawyer [21, 31, 33] CMM [1,2], ISO9000 [18], and Jirotka and Goguen [19]. The REPM model was constructed by combining these sources with personal industrial experiences and was validated by additional experts from academia and industry in the model construction and validation process.

Overview of the REPM Model
The REPM is structured in a hierarchical manner. Three Main Process Areas (MPA) are at the top of the structure, i.e. *Elicitation*, *Analysis & Negotiation*, and *Management*. Under each of these MPAs several Sub-process Areas (SPA) resides covering best practice areas like e.g., quality assurance, verification & validation, and so on. The bottom and smallest constituents of the REPM model are called *Actions*. Actions are designed to establish if and how certain activities are performed during requirements engineering –directly indicating if and to what extent best practices are covered, i.e. offering a benchmarking of the same type found in other model-based assessment methods.

Another dimension of the REPM model is maturity. Every Action resides on a certain *Requirement Engineering Process Maturity level* (REPM level) spanning from 1 to 5, where level 1 represents a rudimentary requirements engineering process and level 5 represents a highly mature process. The Actions on each level ensure a consistent and coherent requirements engineering process for the particular maturity level, i.e., to obtain REPM level 1 you have to complete all Actions deemed to be on level 1 in the model. The maturity levels enable an evaluation of companies with respect to requirements engineering with a better accuracy. By "base-lining" the Actions into maturity levels it is possible to assess a particular company's potential for a certain maturity in its requirements engineering processes, and it shows what Actions should be focused on to achieve the particular maturity level, enabling smaller and step-wise improvements one maturity level at a time.

Based on the REPM model a checklist was constructed, which was used to guide structured interviews, i.e. the assessment tool. The checklist takes each Action and formulates it as a question which can be answered with one of the three ways: *completed*, *uncompleted* and *satisfied-explained*.

The purpose of the satisfied-explained category is to take model compatibility into consideration. Companies carrying out projects in special environments unlike the traditional customer-developer environment may deem certain Actions unnecessary and have compelling reasons for this opinion. An example can be a company where the developer and the customer both are specialists in a certain domain and hence "speak the same language". The need for extended clarification and validation of requirements may not be needed, e.g. the construction of proto-types can be omitted. Satisfied-explained thus denotes an Action that is not completed but the organization targeted by the evaluation in cooperation with the assessors deems the Action not applicable to their project and answers that it is to be considered satisfied-explained in regards to the assessment. It is important to notice that an Action should not be deemed satisfied-explained for reasons like lack of time, lack of money, lack of know-how or just "did not think of it", but rather when Actions (best practices) are inapplicable with the industry environment in which the company being assessed resides. The REPM model is prescriptive in nature (like all assessment methods based on a list of best practices) but it is however not static. It is possible to add both process areas and Actions to the model if needed to ensure that it fits the situation of e.g. a specific domain. Expansion of the REPM model should however be done with extreme caution as adding to the model without careful consideration may result in the model becoming a "jugger-naut" as size and complexity increases. In addition, by adding to the model in an attempt to establish one-size-fit-all will erode the lightweight nature of the REPM model and create another very large assessment model like e.g. CMMI, whose size and coverage is not purely a positive trait [29]. Further information about REPM structure and expansion etc will not be discussed here as it is not within the primary focus of this chapter. For further information please see [13].

The results of a project evaluation are presented as four tables, one for each MPA and one summarizing all of the results. An example of such a table is found in Table 18.1. This table is an example of a summary table for all three MPAs for one project evaluation. In Table 18.1 Actions for each REPM level are listed separately, and that e.g. REPM level 2 contains a total of 14 Actions, of which 9 are completed and 4 are satisfied-explained $(14 - (9+4) = 1$ is uncompleted).

Table 18.1 Example of project evaluation result

REPM level	Total Actions	Completed Actions	Satisfied-explained
1	10	8	2
2	14	9	4
3	19	11	4
4	11	4	2
5	6	1	4

To assist in the interpretation of the results graphs are also used, as the example in Fig. 18.1. In this graph, the solid gray line represents the total number of Actions, the solid black line represents a summary of all Actions that are completed and satisfied-explained. The dashed line represents the Actions that are actually completed. The area between the dashed line and the solid black line denotes to what extent the REPM model is inapplicable to the project being evaluated (called *model lag*), the area between the solid black line and the gray line represents the area of possible improvement of the RE process for the assessed project.

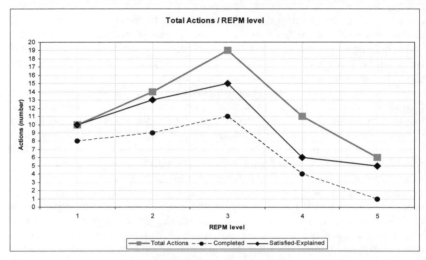

Fig. 18.1 Example of assessment result summary diagram

The tables and graphs are interpreted as follows. Starting with the first REPM level, if all Actions are completed or satisfied-explained, i.e., the solid black line overlays the solid gray line, this level of maturity is achieved. This would mean, if no more REPM levels are achieved, that the company has a consistent and complete requirements engineering process of a low maturity level. This is then repeated for each of the REPM levels. Note that all lower REPM levels must also be completed before a certain REPM level is achieved. In Table 18.1 and Fig. 18.1, for example, we see that REPM level one is achieved and only one Action more is required to achieve REPM level two, whereas four more are required to achieve level three. Strictly speaking, this project would be considered to be on REPM level 1, but as only one Action is necessary to get it up to level two this is the level that we think this company should aim for in a first step of improvement. This would ensure a consistent requirements engineering process that is fairly basic but may be sufficient for this company's needs.

The points distinguishing the REPM model from other model-based assessment methods can be summarized in three main points, which also were the basis for choosing the REPM model for the assessments presented in this chapter:

- Complete focus on requirements engineering –with contents taken from multiple sources and validated by experts both in academia and industry
- Lightweight and low cost

- Non-deterministic, i.e., allowing for inapplicability between best practices of the model and the reality of industry environments

Companies Alpha through Zeta (all six companies) were assessed using the REPM model. For each of the companies at least one project was assessed. The projects subject to the assessment were selected with regards to finding "typical" projects for each company, and in the case of company Epsilon and Zeta three projects were evaluated for each company (as one type of project could not be said to be typical).

The interview subjects that were directly involved in the structured interviews used in the assessment were chosen with regards to their roles in the projects assessed. Two roles were present, project managers and requirements engineers (or rather the role responsible for requirements engineering). In some instances this implied one physical person (e.g. if the project manager was also responsible for requirements engineering). The interviews were conducted as closed-ended interviews using the checklist described above. Each interview took approximately one hour.

18.3.2 Inductive Process Assessment

Whereas the REPM model (or other model-based assessments) can be used to get a quick overview of the requirements engineering process in a company and identify the need for improvements, it is not sufficient to exactly pinpoint the root causes of problems in the requirements engineering process, nor does it identify priorities among the improvement suggestions. To this end, a more in-depth assessment method is needed. As a consequence of this, an inductive process assessment was used for two of the cases. The idea with this assessment method is to use experiences from practices in currently executing projects to base improvements on, rather than a prescriptive checklist of (best) practices. An example of a well known inductive method is Basili's well-known QIP (Quality Improvement Paradigm) [4] which is based on a bottom-up approach that is inductive in nature, i.e. what is to be performed in terms of improvements is based on a thorough understanding of the current situation (processes) [10].

The Inductive Process Assessment method used for the in-depth assessment of company Epsilon and Zeta is inspired by other inductive methods like QIP, but in addition uses data point triangulation to identify potential improvement suggestions (issues that are lacking/need to be addressed in the process). Data point triangulation in the context of the assessment implies use of multiple data sources and methods (e.g. interviews and documentation) from multiple views (e.g. project and line organization) in order to identify and confirm (triangulate) improvement proposals.

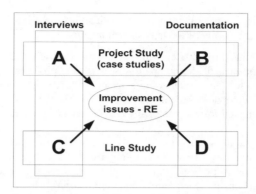

Fig. 18.2 Data point triangulation of improvement suggestions

Fig. 18.2 shows the four major data sources, (A) data from case study interviews, (B) data from project documentation, (C) data from line interviews, and (D) data gathered from line documentation. (A) and (B) together comprise the project study, i.e. interviews and project documentation from one or several projects. (C) and (D) are interviews and documentation from the line, i.e. the remaining organization supporting development projects. The idea is not to use all of the data sources solely for the purpose of getting more data, but rather to have a confirmation (validation) of the individual issues identified. This is achieved through triangulation. One issue is identified and specified, then checked against the other data sources for confirmation. An additional benefit is that this usage of different sources enables several perspectives, decreasing the possibility of missing crucial information.

In addition to the horizontal division of the data collected there is a vertical distinction to be made. Data gathered from the interviews, (A) and (C), are complemented and/or verified (occasionally contradicted) by the data gathered from the documentation, (B) and (D). The result of the assessment is an in-depth evaluation of the current state-of-practice regarding requirements engineering in an organization, as well as a list of tangible improvement proposals which can be used as input to an improvement activity. In addition, these proposals are not based solely on project assessments, since the line organization is also targeted. Using multiple sources, one need not rely on a single source, and thus a higher level of validity can be achieved [5].

Companies Epsilon and Zeta were assessed using the Inductive Process Assessment as described above. Three separate projects were assessed for each of the companies as parts of the line study (see data points (A) and (B) in Fig. 18.2), i.e. six projects in total for both companies. For every project a number of key roles were identified and interviews were conducted with representatives for these roles (see data point (A) in Fig. 18.2). In addition to this, interviews were conducted with line-personnel supporting the project organizations, e.g. representing roles like system testers and marketing (outside projects). All interviews for each company together with both project and line documentation served as input to the improvement proposal triangulation. The interviews were conducted as open-ended exploratory or confirmatory interviews.

18.3.3 Relation Between the Two Assessment Techniques

Because the REPM model is conducted in the form of a structured interview, there is a risk that vital information is not found if the REPM model's set of best practices is inappropriate. Although several tests and validations of the model were conducted before the REPM model was applied in industry, there may still be areas where the model does not completely cover the activities in the studied companies. This is a risk with all model-based assessments, and this is also the reason why the in-depth studies use a different inductive approach with open-ended interviews and multiple sources.

Conversely, a model-based approach can give information about practices not known to the company being assessed, thus being beneficial over inductive methods which base their results largely on the information and knowledge already present in the assessed company (see e.g. the Quality Improvement Paradigm [4]). However, there is a risk that using a model-based assessments imposes a *specific set* of practices that might not be perfectly suited for the organization in question [6, 35]. The risk is that rather than understanding the actual needs of the organization, a model-based approach prescribes a particular solution (based on a set of best practices). This is another reason why an inductive process assessment technique was used for the in-depth assessments for two of the companies, tuned to understanding the underlying needs of the companies rather than just prescribe a certain solution.

To come to terms with the liabilities of both the model-based and the inductive assessment method, and to utilize the benefits of the two, the assessments described in Sect. 18.4 use a combination of both methods.

18.4 Assessment Findings

In Sect. 18.4.1 a composite overview of the results from the model-based REPM assessments for company Alpha to Zeta is presented. Following this, Sect. 18.4.2 presents results from the inductive in-depth assessments of company Epsilon and Zeta. Section 18.5 offers a comparison with state of practice surveys. Combining and comparing the results and identifying similarities are done in Sect. 18.6, summarizing the state-of-practice in the six companies studied.

A detailed account of the results can be viewed in [12, 13] for the REPM assessments, and in [14, 15] for the inductive in-depth assessments.

18.4.1 Model-based Assessment Results

The results in this section are based on the extent the assessed companies have adopted and performed the recommended practices presented in the REPM model on the first three maturity levels. REPM level 3 represents a requirement engineering process that is fairly advanced and not just the bare basics, while still being streamlined and suitable for many software organizations. In essence, the assessments constitute a benchmarking against this level in the REPM model.

Practices on level 4 and 5 are not considered unless they positively distinguish the companies, i.e. give indications of instances where advanced practices are adopted in the RE process and performed during development.

Studying the model-based assessments of the six companies, identifying those areas where 50% or more of the companies leave room for improvement of the requirements engineering practices, the following areas can be discerned:

Requirements Specification and Description. Requirements were found to be heterogeneously specified in and across requirement specifications as no standardized template or minimum set of attributes for specifying requirements were used. Chapters 3 and 10 discuss some aspects of this topic in further detail.

Quantification of Requirements. Quality (non-functional) requirements were seldom expressed in a testable form, e.g. with a quantified fit-criterion. Chapters 3 and 10 discuss some aspects of this topic in further detail.

Requirements and Decision Rationale. The rationale behind requirements, providing answers to e.g. why a requirement is relevant, was seldom specified. In addition, decisions taken by e.g. engineers and management with regards to requirements were seldom documented and spread to all parties in the development group. An example of this is that the reason for e.g. rejecting a requirement was not documented. Chapter 12 discusses some aspects of this topic in further detail.

Traceability. Policies and structures for tracing requirements were often lacking, e.g. tracing requirements to e.g. design components, or design components to requirements. Moreover, versioning and version traceability was at best on document level (having versions of the requirements specification). Versioning of the requirements themselves was rare. Chapters 5 and 11 discuss some aspects of this topic in further detail.

Risk Assessment and Identification of Volatile Requirements. Risk assessment based on requirements was not premiered, as a result of this there was no active effort to identify and monitor volatile requirements (e.g. requirements prone to much change and/or requirements demanding implementation of new or unfamiliar technology). Chapter 12 discusses some aspects of this topic in further detail.

Requirements Review. After the initial specification requirement reviews were not common practice. This was true for all types of reviews, from informal reviews (e.g. walkthroughs) to formal reviews (e.g. inspections). Chapter 8 discusses some aspects of this topic in further detail.

Table 18.2 presents overview of the areas mentioned above, indicating which companies have room for improvement in specific areas (denoted with an "x" in the table).

Table 18.2 Overview of assessed companies' representation in the areas

	Alpha	Beta	Gamma	Delta	Epsilon	Zeta	Total
1.Requirements specification and description		x	x	x	x	x	5
2.Quantification of requirements	x	x	x		x	x	5
3.Requirements and decision rationale				x	x	x	3
4.Traceability	x		x		x	x	4
5.Risk assessment and identification of volatile requirements	x	x	x			x	4
6.Requirements review	x	x	x		x	x	5

In contrast to the areas described above, there were other areas in which the assessed companies were proficient in adopting and performing practices:

Domain Consideration. As requirements are elicited and specified, issues of the system's target domain are taken into account. This includes e.g. taking technical aspects into account regarding the future operating environment of the system, looking at interactions with other systems and personnel, as well as constraints put up by factors of e.g. environment and laws and regulations. Chapter 2 discusses some aspects of this topic in further detail.

Requirements Prioritization. All of the companies performed prioritizations of requirements. This is not to say that any formal prioritization method was adopted (e.g. AHP [30] or the 100-points method [23]), but rather that prioritization took place giving requirements some kind of attribute denoting its importance in development. The methods used, as well as the regularity of these prioritizations varied greatly, from having a formal control group (involving customers) performing prioritization, to ad-hoc practices where a manager took the final decisions. Chapter 4 discusses some aspects of this topic in further detail.

Requirements Validation through Models. The use of models to elicit and validate requirements was fairly common, although primarily from a technical perspective, e.g. using architectural models of to view the entire system, its subsystems, and links between them. Chapters 3 and 8 discuss some aspects of this topic in further detail.

18.4.2 Inductive Assessment Results

The results presented in this section are based on the inductive in-depth assessments performed at company Epsilon and Zeta. It should be noted that the inductive assessment's goal was to find improvement issues as input to a software process improvement initiative for each company. In this chapter we only present the findings relevant for establishing an indication of state-of-practice. For example, this means that findings only identified at one company are not discussed unless they are confirmed by the model-based assessment results presented in Sect. 18.4.1. In total, this amounts to eight findings, presented in further detail below:

Abstraction Level and Contents of Requirements. The level of abstraction/contents/detail of requirements varied between documents of the same type, and even inside the same document. Chapters 3 and 10 discuss some aspects of this topic in further detail.

Requirement Context, Benefit and Rationale. The specification of this attribute was felt to be logical step in asking "why" a requirement should be specified, something that was often missing. By stating information about the context of a certain requirement and why it was stated, as well as specifying non-obvious benefits to stakeholders a more complete understanding can be offered to all interested parties reading the requirements post specification. Chapters 2, 10 and 11 discuss some aspects of this topic in further detail.

Requirements Traceability. This was considered lacking in both company Epsilon and company Zeta. Several types of traceability can be identified in requirements engineering [13], although we only consider two types, i.e. Backward-from traceability denoting a link from requirement to their source in other documents or people, and Forward-from traceability denoting a link from requirements to the design and indirectly to the implemented components [13, 33]. Chapters 5 and 11 discuss some aspects of this topic in further detail.

Requirements Reviews and Review Support. It was realized by both companies that fixing defects early in the development process saves time and effort at later stages in the process (as supported by literature [33]); however routines and structure was lacking. It was identified that support and routines needed to be constructed and made available to enable review work to take place. Examples of support and routines include training of reviewers and moderators, formal checklists and methods for how and when different reviews should be conducted. Chapter 8 discusses some aspects of this topic in further detail.

Roles and Responsibilities in the Requirements Engineering Process. The need to explicitly identify roles and responsibilities (and making them a recognized part of the requirements engineering process) was identified, since a clear definition of these was lacking. Chapter 2 discusses some aspects of this topic in further detail.

Verification and Validation against Requirements. Testing (primarily functional testing [27]) was not always conducted based on the relevant requirements, but sometimes conducted ad-hoc, and sometimes based on functional specifications supplied by developers. It was identified as crucial that the system be tested against requirements, which in turn had to be kept up-to-date during development. In addition, it was deemed important that the requirements are made available to the system testers prior to entering the testing phase in order for test plans and test cases to be developed. Chapter 6 discusses some aspects of this topic in further detail.

Maintaining Requirements and Decision History. As many requirements were handled in multiple projects, spanning multiple products, the decisions taken in regards to these requirements were not systematically or regularly documented (or explicitly linked to the relevant requirement(s)). The implication of this was that some requirements were scrutinized several times, e.g. had to be dismissed more than once. Another implication was that information regarding analysis (decisions) about requirements was not easily accessible by e.g. developers. Chapter 10 discusses some aspects of this topic in further detail.

Requirements upkeep (During and Post Project). Frequently, as the actual requirements changed during the development life-cycle, the specifications of the requirements were not changed to reflect this. Changes in design did not lead to updates in the requirements specification, eventually causing the requirements specification to not reflect the current state of the system. Chapter 10 discusses some aspects of this topic in further detail.

Table 18.3 summarizes the findings described above. An "x" denotes that the issue was found in the company. An "x" in the REPM-column signifies that the issue was also found among some of the companies Alpha, Beta, Gamma or Delta in the model-based assessment presented in Sect. 18.4.1.

Table 18.3 Overview of in-depth assessment findings and relation to the model-based assessment results

	Epsilon	Zeta	REPM
Finding 1: Abstraction level & contents of requirements	x	x	x
Finding 2: Requirement context, benefit & rationale	x	x	x
Finding 3: Requirements traceability	x	x	x
Finding 4: Requirements reviews & review support		x	x
Finding 5: Roles and responsibilities RE process	x	x	
Finding 6: Verification and validation against requirements	x	x	
Finding 7: Maintaining requirements and decision history		x	x
Finding 8: Requirements upkeep (during & post project)	x	x	

As in the case of the model-based REPM assessment several areas were identified as strong points regarding requirements engineering during the inductive in-depth assessment of companies Epsilon and Zeta. The most notable are:

Domain Knowledge and Consideration. Companies Epsilon and Zeta had an advanced knowledge regarding the technical and organizational aspects of the customers. This implied that issues of the human domain area could be taken into account, realizing that political and organizational factors may influence the requirements. Chapters 2, 10 and 11 discuss some aspects of this topic in further detail.

Technical Domain Expertise. As both companies Epsilon and Zeta are experts at the systems (hardware and software) that they develop they also have been forced to gain a deep understanding of the customers' environment, i.e. the systems operational environment. Chapters 2, 10 and 11 discuss some aspects of this topic in further detail.

18.4.3 Inductive versus Model-based Assessment Results

Comparing the Inductive and the Model-based assessment findings there are both similarities (see Findings 1-4, and 7 in Table 18.3) but also differences, i.e. some findings were only identified during the Inductive assessments (see Findings 5,6,8 in Table 18.3). Two reasons for this may be found. First, the companies evaluated were different, i.e. issues found in companies Epsilon and Zeta may not have been present in companies Alpha through Delta. This would effectively explain the difference in findings between the Inductive and the Model-based assessments and list differences between the companies as the cause. Second, there are differences between the assessment methods themselves. As indicated in Sect. 18.3 the REPM model assessment is lightweight in nature and shallower than the Inductive assessment, i.e. there could be a risk that issues were missed by the REPM model as it is not as thorough. The thoroughness of the REPM model is also directly associated with the best practices covered by the model, i.e. if a part (Actions) is missing from the REPM model chances are that issues relating to the missing parts will not be caught. Nevertheless, as indicated above, there is considerable overlap between the findings of the two assessment methods.

18.5 Comparison with State of Practice Surveys

In this section we present surveys of state of practice in requirements engineering and compare the findings from these surveys with the findings from the case studies described in Sect. 18.4. It should be noted that the scope of the assessments performed to gather the data in Sect. 18.4 differs from the scope of the surveys discussed in this section. The assessments underlying Sect. 18.4 have all been created with the intention to present the results to the specific companies and instigate process improvement efforts, whereas the surveys discussed in this section focus on describing the state of practice for a wider audience of researchers and practitioners spanning multiple companies.

An early survey with focus on requirements engineering is Curtis et al. [8]. This study of 10 organizations is in fact a generic software engineering survey, but it focuses on "how requirements and design decisions were made, represented, communicated, and changed, as well as how these decisions impacted the subsequent development process". The survey is prescriptive in nature, identifying good or bad practices. The main findings from this study are that accurate knowledge of the application domain is crucial, that requirements fluctuate and conflict each other causing difficulties during development, and that communication and coordination frequently breaks down.

The companies in our assessments had extensive domain knowledge as this was actively recognized as a crucial competitive advantage. In many cases the knowledge of the developing companies surpassed the customers' knowledge. Unlike the few "super-designers" mentioned in Curtis et al., [8], the overall knowledge level of the studied companies in our case was high when compared to the customers. In other words, albeit still acknowledged as a crucial factor, the companies were not directly dependent on a few "heroes".

As indicated by the assessments' findings risk assessment and the explicit identification of volatile requirements was often neglected in the requirements engineering process. However the assessments do indicate a need for explicit risk analysis, thus confirming the findings from Curtis et al., [8]. The desire for explicit and well defined roles and responsibilities, as well as documented requirements and decision history and rationale can be seen as an effort to improve communication and the spreading of information regarding requirements over the entire development organization. In other words the assessments hint at communication breakdowns still being a problem.

Lubars et al., [24] studied requirements engineering ten US corporations. This study confirms the need for domain knowledge to avoid requirements misunderstandings. Identifying the customer (or stakeholders) is identified as an issue that many projects find difficult, as is requirements prioritization and requirements documentation (including specifying assumptions and requirements rationale). However, most companies in this survey seemed to have a requirements template, a DOD standard template, although many of the companies had difficulties knowing what to write in the different fields of the template. Moreover, most companies in the study have some organizational approach to requirements validation. Problems stemming from frequent requirements changes were identified in this survey too, influencing writing, interpretation, management, and design from requirements. The major conclusions from this study are that organizational solutions are preferred over technological solutions, and general-purpose tools are more common than special purpose requirements engineering tools.

This study [24] does not seem to confirm our assessments to a large extent. The only finding directly confirmed is the insufficiencies in documenting requirements, assumptions, and rationale. Contradicting the Lubars study, the companies in our assessments have a good grasp of their customers and their domain requirements, perform prioritization of requirements, do not consistently use any requirements template, and lack adequate routines and support for requirement reviews.

El Emam et al. [9] studies 60 cases and identifies seven key issues for successful requirements engineering. The issues are: Package Consideration (re-use of software and requirements), managing the level of detail of functional process models, examining the current system, user participation, managing uncertainty, benefits of CASE tools, and project management capability (necessary skills of project managers). These key issues are illustrated using statements from the case studies.

Some of these findings corroborate the findings of the assessments to some extent, although a detailed comparison is difficult due to the difference in abstraction level of the recommendations/findings, e.g. "examining the current system" could be construed as taking technical domain issues of the customer into account, which the assessments in Sect. 18.4.1 show as being done. "Managing uncertainty", on the other hand, is related to risk analysis, which, as mentioned before, could be improved.

Nikula et al., [25] describes a survey of 12 Finnish companies. The study investigates 35 issues in requirements engineering, of which 19 issues are related to documentation style, 4 are related to tool usage and 12 pertain to general requirements engineering practices. The findings include that few of the studied companies use requirements management tools, templates, checklists or metrics. The study concludes that the most pressing needs requested by the companies in the study are: development of own requirements engineering process adaptations, requirements engineering process improvement, and requirements engineering tool adoption. Moreover, a strong need for requirements completeness and support for requirements change management is expressed by the companies.

Using inductive assessment methods seem to be preferable over model-based prescriptive process improvement activities, as indicated by the willingness to improve, but preferring tailored solutions over prescriptive model-based practices. This is not directly related to requirements engineering state of practice in industry, however it does indicate the way in which companies prefer to improve their requirements engineering process, and their willingness to improve.

Other confirmed findings include the need for requirements completeness, requirements templates, and validation checklists (see Sect. 18.4).

Hofmann and Lehner [17] present a survey of 15 projects, identifying that an average of 6.2 persons are involved in requirements engineering per project, iterating the requirements engineering process three times for each project. Generally, the projects in this study follow an ad-hoc requirements engineering process, and have problems with rapidly changing requirements. Most projects verify and validate requirements with multiple stakeholders and are satisfied with their requirements specifications' consistency. However, the projects complain over a lack of traceability, and have problems with prioritizing the requirements. Based on this survey of requirements engineering practices a number of best practices are outlined in this article.

This survey [17] both confirms and confutes the findings in the assessments presented in Sect. 18.4. Rapidly changing, i.e. volatile, requirements and lack of traceability in the requirements engineering process are recognized in both studies. On the other hand, verification and validation efforts were not widespread in our assessments. Moreover, as mentioned earlier, prioritization of requirements was performed in our assessments, thus contradicting Hofmann and Lehner.

Juristo et al., [20] study the state of requirements engineering practice in Europe with a focus on tool usage, finding that most organizations use tools such as word processors for specifying requirements. For larger projects with more than 1000 requirements this causes problems, and organizations in the study that do use requirements tools in general work with larger applications. The companies also report general problems related to traceability, confirming earlier findings [17] and the assessments in Sect. 18.4.

18.6 Discussion

Looking at the assessments performed, several issues regarding state of practice in requirements engineering are identified in both the model-based and the inductive assessments (sometimes also found in the state of practice surveys discussed in Sect. 18.5):

Specification (Description) and Abstraction Level of Requirements. This consists of several aspects of how requirements are specified. For example, the attributes used (e.g. name, description, ID etc), and the level of detail of each of these attributes. Closely related is the level of abstraction, which conveys what abstraction level a requirement is specified on, e.g. "support for multiple languages in GUI" is more abstract than "support for European languages". The two are of course related as one puts demands on the other. A very abstract requirement would probably not have a detailed technical description, while a requirement on a lower level of abstraction could be described in further detail. The level of abstraction a requirement is specified on (and thus how it is specified regarding attributes and level of detail) depends on the needs of the users of the requirements and the intended use of the requirements, as well as the original description of the requirement when it was first posed. As is known among practitioners, requirements come in all "shapes and forms" depending on e.g., the source. The important thing is that requirements for a certain purpose, e.g., a specification that is to be used as a basis for design, are homogenous and on an appropriate abstraction level for the intended use. An example of this could be the practice of prioritizing requirements. If a specification consists of heterogeneous requirements, (for example requirements on multiple abstraction levels) it is difficult to compare the requirements and make a distinction that one is to be prioritized over the other.

Exactly what attributes to use and what level of detail to describe the requirements on is up to each organization, as long as the choices as explicit and the requirements specified accordingly. See Gorschek [11] for additional information about requirement abstraction.

The reality shown through the assessments was of a mix of very abstract and very detailed technical requirements in most specifications, regardless of the intended use of the requirements or the requirements specification. In addition, requirements were often specified incompletely, resulting in inadequate requirements. These findings were also supported by the findings of Juristo et al., [20].

Requirements Context and Rationale. Requirements rationale anchors a certain requirement to reality, i.e. contains information about why the requirement was specified in the first place and helps the user of the requirement to understand the underlying motivation of each requirement. This item is clearly related to Specification (Description) and Abstraction Level of Requirements as it denotes how a requirement should be specified, e.g. that there should be one or more attributes holding information about the context and rationale of the requirement. Several of the surveys mentioned in Sect. 18.5, e.g. Lubars et al., [24], Curtis et al., [8], Nikula et al., [25], indicate problems with communication breakdown during the requirements engineering process as well as incompletely specified requirements. By specifying the context of, and the rationale behind a requirement, the understanding of a requirement may be increased. This was the explicit view expressed during the assessments presented in Sect. 18.4.1, and especially during the assessments presented in Sect. 18.4.2. In so doing, the underlying understanding of the requirements, e.g. why a requirement was specified, could be provided throughout the specification. It may not be necessary to provide a rationale for all requirements, but it should be provided at least for those requirements that may give cause for misunderstandings or where the rationale may facilitate an increased understanding of the system being built.

Documenting Decision Rationale and Maintaining Decision History. By explicitly documenting decision information pertaining requirements and linking it to the relevant requirement(s), the finding of potentially important information is facilitated. This enables the rationale of a certain decision to survive indefinitely after the meeting where the decision was taken. The obvious benefits are that previous mistakes are not repeated, doing the same work all over again is avoided, and developers are able to see why a change was made to a requirement without the need to find people who can be hard to find and/or get access to. This issue relates to the previous two in terms of being a part (indirectly) of the specification of requirements.

Requirements Traceability. Traceability of requirements and its attributes (if e.g. "source of a requirement" is seen as an attribute) as well as putting requirements under configuration management with regards to version and change control [16]is an issue identified by both Nikula et al. [25]and Juristo et al., [20] in addition to the assessments in this chapter. During the assessments it was never proposed that any sort of "perfect" or "total" traceability was necessary or even wanted, rather that three main traceability areas should be satisfied. *Backward-from traceability*, denoting a link from requirement to their source in other documents or people, was considered important as this provides information of where a requirement comes from. For example, a requirement could originate from a pre-study document, and knowledge of this could be used by developers working with the requirement, e.g. by going back to the pre-study in its entirety rather than just working with the extracted requirement.

Forward-from traceability denoting a link from requirements to the design and indirectly to the implemented components was considered important primarily for the reasons of verification and validation, i.e. faults found when executing test-cases (based on requirements) could be traced to the area causing the fault faster than without this sort of traceability.

Version control of requirements (not only the requirement document) was considered greatly beneficial, and was primarily identified as an issue during the inductive assessments. Increased control over change, as well as version traceability were the main benefits voiced during the assessments.

Requirements Review and Review Support. As mentioned earlier (see Sects. 18.4.1 and 18.4.2) reviews of requirements were not common practice, mainly due to cost and time constraints during development. In addition to this there were insufficiencies in the "review-infrastructure" in terms of trained people to plan and perform reviews as well as availability of materials such as checklists, etc.

The overall most significant benefits of inspections is that between 50 and 90% of the defects can be caught [22] and, equally important, they can be caught in the early stages of development thus reducing the cost of rework. This is the main reason why there is a general consensus amongst most experience reports and research that requirements inspection is very beneficial [27, 32]. The recommendation given to organizations with limited resources for reviews and inspections is to prioritize requirements inspections over e.g. design and code inspections [22, 27], mainly due to the filtering-down effect of defects in requirements. In other words, the earlier problems like incompleteness, ambiguity, errors, conflicts, etc. can be caught, the less effort it costs to fix the problems and rework parts that have been influenced by the problems in question.

18.6.1 Other Issues

In addition to the aforementioned issues there are issues that are only found in one of the assessments (either model-based or inductive) which should be mentioned:

Risk Assessment and Volatile Requirements Identification. As requirements are prone to change and fluctuation during development, explicit risk analysis (including identifying volatile requirements) was considered important during the assessments, but seldom performed in practice. The importance of this issue was supported by Curtis et al., [8], El Emam et al. [9], and, Nikula et al. [25], who expressed concerns regarding the volatile nature of requirements, and that it was important to manage uncertainty.

Verification and Validation Against Requirements. Basing test-cases (essentially the entire process of functional testing) on either out-of-date requirements (see Requirements Upkeep During and Post project below), or on functional specifications supplied by developers (or often a combination of both), was commonly indicated during the assessments.

Roles and Responsibilities in the Requirements Engineering Process. In most of the assessments there were some descriptions of roles and even (in some cases) responsibilities pertaining to the requirements engineering process. These roles were, however, seldom used or known to the entire organization. Confusion about responsibilities and whom to elicit information from, as well as uncertainty regarding executive power over requirements, gave rise to confusion and loss of momentum during development. Curtis et al. [8] discuss that communication and coordination frequently breaks down. Having adequate roles and responsibilities may improve this situation.

Requirements upkeep During and Post Project. As earlier mentioned, requirements are prone to change. Making the requirements reflect these changes was considered crucial for several reasons. First and foremost, it is a prerequisite for being able to conduct tests based on the requirements. Furthermore, in order to achieve any reuse or re-prioritization of requirements, the issue of keeping requirements up-to-date has to be resolved. In the studied projects and companies, outdated requirements that poorly reflected the current state of the system was unfortunately frequent.

18.7 Conclusions

A description of state of practice serves several purposes. For a researcher, it outlines areas where further research may or may not be needed. For an educator, it may outline areas where training programs can be designed. For a practitioner, it outlines areas where care must be taken to obtain a working, consistent, and coherent set of practices. Moreover, it shares the experiences from other practitioners of what is working and what is not.

In this chapter we study the state of practice in six companies using two different study methods, i.e. a model-based process assessment method and an inductive process assessment. The assessments reveal several issues where the studied companies have room for improvement, as presented in Sects. 18.4.1 and 18.4.2. In Sect. 18.6 we then combine the findings of the two assessment methods and identify a set of improvement issues that are found using both methods in several of the six studied companies. It should be emphasized that since the assessments were performed as a part of a software process improvement effort at the companies, the assessments presented in Sect. 18.4 are intentionally focused on finding problems in the requirements engineering process. Nevertheless, some positive aspects regarding state of practice are also observed. The most prominent of these is the extensive domain knowledge present in the assessed companies, as well as the fact that the assessments found the companies going to great lengths to take domain issues of technical, application, political (human), and organizational type into consideration during the process of specifying and implementing requirements. This is despite the fact that other state of practice surveys [8, 9, 24] mention these issues as problematic for companies. One explanation for this could be that many of the companies in our assessments, especially companies Alpha, Epsilon, and Zeta, have specialized themselves within a specific and narrow domain, thus making it possible for them to be experts.

To conclude, the assessments reveals positive aspects of requirements engineering state of practice, i.e. areas that are mastered by the companies, as well as several negative aspects where further research and training is necessary and where the studied companies have room for improvement.

References

1. (2004) http://www.sei.cmu.edu/cmm/ipd-cmm.html. Last Accessed: 2004-04-11
2. (2004) http://www.sei.cmu.edu/cmm/cmm.html. Last Accessed: 2004-04-11
3. (2002) http://www.tickit.org/. Last Accessed: 2002-10-01
4. Basili VR (1985) Quantitative evaluation of software methodology. Technical report TR-1519, University of Maryland, College Park, Maryland, USA
5. Bratthall L, Joergensen M (2002) Can you trust a single data source exploratory software engineering case study? Empirical Software Engineering 7 (1): 9–26
6. Briand L, El Emam K, Melo WL (1995) An inductive method for software process improvement: concrete steps and guidelines. In: Proceedings of ESI-ISCN'95: Measurement and training based process improvement, ISCN. Vienna, pp.34–49

7. CMMI-PDT (2002) Capability maturity model integration (CMMI), Version 1.1. CMMI for systems engineering, software engineering, integrated product and process development, and supplier sourcing version 1.1 (CMMI-SE/SW/IPPD/SS, V1.1), Pittsburgh

8. Curtis B, Krasner H, Iscoe N (1998) A field study of the software design process for large systems. Communications of the ACM 31 (11): 1268–1287

9. El Emam K. Madhavji NH (1995) A field study of requirements engineering practices in information systems development. In: Proceedings of the 2nd IEEE international symposium on requirements engineering, IEEE Computer Society. Los Alamitos CA, pp.68–80

10. El Emam KE, Madhavji NHE (1999) Elements of software process assessment & improvement. Wiley-IEEE, Los Alamitos CA

11. Gorschek T (2004) Software process assessment & improvement in industrial requirements engineering. Licentiate thesis No. 2004:07, ISBN 91-7295-041-2. Blekinge Institute of Technology, Ronneby, Sweden

12. Gorschek T, Svahnberg M, Tejle K (2003) Introduction and application of a lightweight requirements engineering process evaluation method. In: Proceedings of the 9th international workshop on requirements engineering: foundation for software quality (REFSQ'03), Universität Duisburg-Essen. Essen, Germany, pp.101–112

13. Gorschek T, Tejle K (2002) A method for assessing requirements engineering process maturity in software projects. Master thesis in computer science. Thesis No: MCS-2002:2. Blekinge Institute of Technology, Ronneby, Download at http://www.bth.se/fou/cuppsats.nsf/

14. Gorschek T, Wohlin C (2003) Identification of improvement issues using a lightweight triangulation approach (Eurospi'03). In: Proceedings of European software process improvement conference (EuroSPI'2003), Verlag der Technischen Universität. Graz, Austria. Download at: http://www.bth.se/fou/Forskinfo.nsf/, pp.VI.1-VI.14

15. Gorschek T, Wohlin C (2004) Packaging software process improvement issues: A method and a case study. Software: practice & experience 34 (14): 1311–1344

16. Hass AMJ (2003) Configuration management principles and practice. Addison-Wesley, Reading MA

17. Hofmann HF, Lehner F (2001) Requirements engineering as a success factor in software projects, IEEE Software 18(4): 58–66

18. (1998) http://www.sei.cmu.edu/iso-15504/. Last Accessed: 2004-01-07

19. Jirotka M, Goguen JA (1994) Requirements engineering social and technical issues. Academic press, London

20. Juristo N, Moreno AM, Silva A (2002) Is the European industry moving toward solving requirements engineering problems? IEEE Software 19(6): 70–78

21. Kotonya G, Sommerville I (1998) Requirements engineering: processes and techniques. John Wiley, New York

22. Laitenberger O, Beil T, Schwinn T (2002) An industrial case study to examine a nontraditional inspection implementation for requirements specifications. In: Proceedings of the 8th IEEE symposium on software Metrics, IEEE Computer Society. Los Alamitos CA, pp.97–106

23. Leffingwell D, Widrig D (2000) Managing software requirements: a unified approach. Addison-Wesley, Reading MA

24. Lubars M, Potts C, Richter C (1992) A review of the state of the practice in requirements modeling. In: Proceedings of IEEE international symposium on requirements Engineering, IEEE. Los Alamitos CA, pp.2–14

25. Nikula U, Sajaniemi J, Kälviäinen H (2000) A state-of-the-practice survey on requirements engineering in small-and-medium-sized enterprises, Technical report (Http://www.Cs.Ucl.Ac.Uk/Research/Renoir/Tbrc_Rr01.Pdf). Lappeenranta University of Technology, Lappeenranta, Finland

26. Paulk MC (1995) The capability maturity model: guidelines for improving the software process. Addison-Wesley, Reading MA

27. Rakitin SR (2001) Software verification and validation for practitioners and managers. Artech House, Boston MA

28. (2003) http://www.comp.lancs.ac.uk/computing/research/cseg/projects/reaims/index.html. Last accessed: 2003-05-01

29. Reifer DJ (2000) The CMMI: It's formidable. Journal of Systems and Software 50(2): 97–98

30. Saaty TL, Vargas LG (2001) Models, methods, concepts & applications of the analytic hierarchy process. Kluwer Academic Publishers, Boston MA

31. Sawyer P, Sommerville I and Viller S (1999) Capturing the benefits of requirements engineering, IEEE Software 16 (2): 78–85

32. Shull F, Rus I, Basili V (2000) How perspective-based reading can improve requirements inspections. Computer 33 (7): 73–79

33. Sommerville I, Sawyer P (1999) Requirements engineering: a good practice guide. John Wiley & Sons, Chichester UK

34. (2003) http://www.sqi.gu.edu.au/spice/. Last accessed: 2003-09-11

35. Zahran S (1998) Software process improvement: practical guidelines for business success. Addison-Wesley, Reading MA

Author Biography

Tony Gorschek is a PhD Student in Software Engineering from Blekinge Institute of Technology, Sweden, at the Department of Systems and Software Engineering within the School of Engineering. His research areas include primarily Software Process Assessment and Improvement and Requirements Engineering. Tony Gorschek works and conducts research in close cooperation with industry.

Mikael Svahnberg received a PhD in Software Engineering from Blekinge Institute of Technology, Sweden. He is an assistant professor in software engineering in the Department of Systems and Software Engineering within the School of Engineering at Blekinge Institute of Technology in Sweden. His current research activities include software architectures, quality requirements and software engineering decision support methods.

19 An Analysis of Empirical Requirements Engineering Survey Data

Barbara Paech, Tom Koenig, Lars Borner and Aybüke Aurum

Abstract: The gap between research and practice in requirements engineering is immense. To understand practice and the reasons for this gap, empirical evidence about requirements engineering practice is needed. In the last ten years a number of empirical studies have been conducted to gather such data. This chapter gives an overview focusing on broad surveys. The aim of this overview is to understand the following three issues: (1) what kind of questions can and should we ask to understand practice, (2) what evidence do we have about practice, (3) what further evidence do we need about practice. To further illustrate the issues, we provide findings of new studies conducted by the authors in Germany and Australia. Altogether this chapter aims at establishing a basis for further empirical research on requirements engineering.

Keywords: Empirical software engineering, Requirements engineering practice, Survey.

19.1 Introduction

The gap between research and practice in requirements engineering (RE) is immense. Even base practices such as numbering requirements are not yet well established in industry. Many popular techniques in the research community such as formal modeling [23] or QFD [20] are almost unknown in industry. This gap has been investigated by leading researchers in [26]. They recommend in particular a two way transfer between industry and university emphasizing the knowledge transfer from industry to research. In the last 10 years more than 20 broad studies of RE practice have been conducted. Furthermore, the basics of empirical approaches to software engineering have been collected in books such as [57]. However, so far the results of the empirical RE studies have not been collected.

It is the purpose of this chapter to provide such a collection of broad studies on RE. The collection aims at giving an overview, i.e. it aims at describing the "landscape" of studies, the questions asked and the major results. This overview is used to understand: (1) what kind of questions can and should we ask to understand practice, (2) what evidence do we have about practice, (3) what further evidence do we need about practice. In addition, we sketch findings of new studies conducted by the authors in Germany and Australia. The main purpose of this presentation is to illustrate typical findings and issues in the interpretations of such findings. The results will be discussed in the light of previous studies. Altogether this chapter aims at establishing a basis for further broad studies on RE.

The chapter is structured as follows: In Sect. 19.2 we provide some basic terminology on empirical software engineering and motivate the need for empirical evidence in RE. Section 19.3 introduces the broad studies collected and analyses issue (1), namely what we can ask to understand practice. Thereby it provides a framework for questionnaires on RE. The outcomes of the studies are summarized in Sect. 19.4. This answers issue (2), namely what evidence we have so far about practices. Thus, it establishes the current state of large-scale empirical evidence on RE practice. Section 19.5 provides data from new RE practice studies conducted by the authors and thus illustrates typical findings of such studies. In Sect. 19.6 we briefly discuss the role of other types of empirical studies on RE, such as experiments. We conclude in Sect. 19.7 with an outlook on future empirical evidence needed in RE.

19.2 Empirical Research

This chapter provides some basic terminology on empirical research and motivates the need for empirical evidence on RE. We follow the terminology of Creswell [7]. Although some researchers e.g., Blake [1] may consider the following description relatively simplistic, Creswell is highly regarded and frequently cited in software engineering books. Creswell identifies three elements for empirical research design: the knowledge claim, the strategy of inquiry and the specific method for data collection and analysis.

The *knowledge claim* comprises the assumptions on how and what one will learn during the research. Creswell distinguishes the postpositive claims starting with a theory and continuously refining this theory through the research, the socially constructed knowledge claim looking for the complexity of views and developing a theory or pattern of meaning through the research, the advocacy/participatory claim extending the socially constructed approach by an action agenda for reform, and the pragmatic knowledge claim focusing on the problem and pluralistic approaches to derive knowledge.

There are seven basic *strategies for inquiry*: A *survey* gathers data (typically in retrospect) from a representative sample through interviews or questionnaires and tries to generalize this data to the whole population. An *experiment* is done in a laboratory environment where specific subjects are assigned to different treatments and their performance is measured. The objective is to manipulate specific variables and control all the other ones. A *case study* gathers data (typically monitoring projects) over a sustained period of time and tries to understand in more detail a specific factor and its relationship to other factors. In *grounded theory* multiple stages of data collection from different groups are employed in order to maximize the similarities and the differences and to compare the data with emergent categories. *Ethnography* focuses on observational data collected in a natural setting about an intact cultural group. *Narrative research* studies the lives of individuals and re-stories the information into a narrative chronology. *Phenomenol-*

ogical research studies the lived experiences of a small number of subjects to identify the essence of these experiences concerning a phenomenon.

There are also different strategies for *data collection and analysis*, varying in "their degree of predetermined nature, their use of closed-ended vs. open-ended questioning and their focus for numeric vs. non-numeric data analysis" [7]. One can distinguish three kinds of combination of these elements:

- *Quantitative studies* are typically based on post-positivist claims, use surveys and experiments and employ predetermined, close-ended questioning and numeric data analysis. However, they can involve open-ended and non-numeric analysis as well.
- *Qualitative studies* typically involve the constructivist and advocacy/participatory perspective, use the other five basic strategies of inquiry, and employ emergent, open-ended questioning and non-numeric analysis, but again can involve close-ended and numeric-analysis.
- *Mixed methods* are based on pragmatic knowledge claims and employ multiple strategies of inquiries and data collection and analysis methods. ,

In contrast to e.g. social science, so far, most research in software engineering does not involve empirical methods, but toy examples instead. Clearly, this does not demonstrate anything about applicability in practice. Endres and Rombach [16] argue that we need observations of the practice, which help to surface laws explained by theories. Only empirical research can produce valid observations, laws and theories. Unfortunately, the complexity of software engineering (SE) is often used as an excuse for omitting empirical research, as it is very difficult to identify general observations in SE. Nevertheless, there is successful empirical SE research. Endres and Rombach have collected the available SE laws and theories based on case studies and experiments. In particular, this gives evidence on the usefulness of specific techniques like e.g. patterns or prototypes. Juristo et al., [25] give a recent comprehensive overview on testing technique experiments.

In this chapter we focus on empirical research in RE and on the current state of the practice, not on the usefulness of specific techniques. The studies collected are presented in the next section.

19.3 Classification of Existing Broad RE Studies

In this subsection we first present the studies we have collected and then classify the kind of questions asked in these studies.

Table 19.1 to Table 19.3 list the studies we found in the literature on RE such as the international RE conferences, the RE journal, IEEE software or related conferences such as ECBS. We are aware that there are related studies in information and management sciences which are not covered. It is a topic of further research to include these studies too.

Table 19.1 Broad studies on the RE process in general

	Year	Mechanism	Sample	Topic
[8]	1986	Interviews	9 companies, 97 staff	Software design process for large systems
[30]	1992	Interviews	10 companies, 87 staff	State of the practice
[13]	1994	Interviews questionnaire	52 staff	Success criteria for RE
[12]	1994	Interviews documentation	17 staff	Problems and best practices
[15]	1996	Questionnaire	39 projects	User participation and RE success
[37]	1997	Workshop	26 staff	Industrial uptake of RE R&D
[14]	1998	Measurement questionnaire	70 assessments, 691 process in-stance	Relationships assessment score, project performance
[27]	1998	Workshop	10 companies	RE in SME
[19]	2000	Focus groups	12 companies, 200 staff	Problems
[21]	2000	Interviews questionnaires	15 companies, 76 staff	Impact of RE on project success
[40][41] [42]	2000	Interviews	12 companies, 15 staff	RE in SME
[24] [51][53]	2000	Questionnaire	11 companies, 150 staff	Progress in RE practice
[36][35]	2001	Interviews questionnaire	25 staff	RE for time to market pro-jects
[39]	2002	Questionnaire	194 staff	State of the practice

From this literature we collected surveys and grounded theory studies with a sample of at least around 10 individuals, but not experiments or the other quantitative studies focusing on specific individuals, cultures or phenomena. We call these studies *broad RE studies* in the following. They employ interviews, questionnaires or group discussions and different methods for data collection and analysis. We have divided the studies into three groups (as can be seen from the tables) depending on the focus of RE in general, SE in general or RE specifics. These distinctions will be explained in detail when we present the results in Sect. 19.4.

Table 19.2 Broad studies on SE in general

	Year	Mechanism	Sample	Topic
[22]	1995	Questionnaire	3805 per-sons	Problems and training needs
[11]	1995-1997	Questionnaire	397 staff	Adoption of best practices for SW management
[54]	Since 1994	Questionnaire	13522 IT projects	Status of IT project man-agement
[9]	2001/2002	Questionnaire	104 projects	Worldwide SW develop-ment

Table 19.3 Broad studies of specific RE phenomena

	Year	Mechanism	Sample	Topic
[28]	1991	Meeting minutes, videotape	3 companies, 41 meetings	Content of requirements document
[18]	1993	Focus groups, 2-stage questionnaire	100 staff	Requirements traceability
[46]	1994-1997	Interviews, focus groups, case study	26 companies, 138 staff	Requirements traceability
[20]	1994	Interviews	37 companies	Software quality function deployment
[60][61][62]	1995-2001	3 studies, interviews, question-naires	9 / 71 / 52 staff	Requirements volatility
[3][4]	1995	3 questionnaires	74 companies, 72/34/35 staff	Requirements capture and analysis
[56]	1997	Interviews	Roughly 20	Scenario usage
[29]	2002	2 pre-studies questionnaire	45 staff	Software documentation
[5]	2002	Questionnaire	226 staff	Software reviews

As can be seen from the tables, in the last ten years more than twenty broad studies have been conducted on RE practice. In the following we characterize the kind of information sought by them. We are not aware of any other such characterization besides [51]. In that report surveys are characterized according to purpose, mechanism of data capture and analysis method. We keep these categories, but go into much more detail on what kind of information is captured in these studies. We distinguish the following categories:

1. Set up of the study
   - Purpose
   - Sample population
   - Mechanism
   - Analysis
2. Information on the context and background of the sample
   - Personal context
   - Company context
   - Project context
3. General information on RE process
   - General facts
   - Problems with RE process
   - Success factors for RE
4. Information on specific parts of the process, e.g. tool, practice, activity X
   - Performance of X
   - Experience with X

These categories are explained in the following. Thereby we answer issue (1): what questions can and should we ask to understand practice. It is intended as a framework for questionnaires or interviews on RE.

19.3.1 Set up of the Study

The first category defines how the broad study is to be conducted. Of course, first the purpose of the study has to be determined. We adapt the distinction of [24]:

- *Descriptive study*: Tries to understand what is done in general or a specific practice, e.g., whether a RE tool is used, how requirements capture is carried out or what impact requirements volatility has on the overall project success.
- *Prescriptive study:* Tries to make a judgment. Thus it aims at identifying successful practices, or success factors and obstacles for a specific practice. In [57] this is called an explanatory study, as it tries to identify reasons for actions.
- *Prospective study:* Tries to identify future needs in industry.

Wohlin et al. [57] distinguishes in addition, *explorative* studies which are used as pre-studies to a more thorough investigation. We do not explicitly deal with such pre-studies here. The different RE *topics* investigated in the studies are mentioned in detail below in terms of the information sought from the participants. One can distinguish two general directions: on the one hand studies explore the state-of-the-practice (i.e. what practice is doing) on the other hand they explore more specifically the relationship between the state-of-the-art and the state-of-the-practice (i.e. what practice knows about research).

Depending on the *purpose* the sample population of the study has to be determined. The main facets are:

- *Number*: The typical number of participants ranges from 10 to 500 or more.
- *Heterogeneity*: For large studies participants are typically sought just by advertisement in the community (e.g. through the web). Sometimes specific address databases (e.g. university graduates) are used. For small studies, participants are filtered according to specific criteria, often participants are known to the study authors.

Clearly, a small sample is not suited for prescriptive studies in general, as only few data points cannot demonstrate the necessary generality. The same holds for low heterogeneity of participant backgrounds and contexts. On the other hand, it is very difficult, particularly in RE, to identify principles which apply to all kinds of environments. A possible mixture is to do a small study with the aim to be prescriptive (to give advise) for the involved population e.g. [27]. Several studies also use a multi-stage approach, starting with small descriptive study to understand the issue and later involving a large number of participants to establish general principles in a prescriptive study. In parallel with the sample population the *mechanism* for capturing data is determined. There are three typical choices:

- *Questionnaires*: a pre-determined list of open or closed questions. An example for the former is: what kind of RE tool do you use? Examples for the latter are yes/no-answers (e.g., do you use MS Word for requirement specification) or multiple-choice-answers (e.g., which of the following tools do you use) or prioritization-answers (e.g., prioritize the importance of budget, time and quality in your project). These questionnaires are typically distributed online or by mail to be filled in by the participants. Furthermore, they can be filled in jointly by an interviewer and the interviewee.
- *Direct interaction*: The list of questions is not fully pre-determined, instead the participants can influence the kind of information gathered. Examples are semi-structured interview or work observation. To involve more participants a workshop can be conducted.
- *Measurement data*: Data is not captured specifically for the study, but is available through a measurement program or an assessment.

Obviously, the choice depends on the sample and the amount of time available for data capture and analysis. Capturing measurement data needs the most effort, and thus, this data is very often not available. For a large sample, questionnaires are much easier to handle, but direct interaction gives more detail and more reliable information (as misunderstandings can be avoided). So the latter is often more suited for descriptive and prospective studies. In parallel with the mechanism the data *analysis* approach has to be determined. As mentioned in Sect. 19.2 the main alternatives are a numeric or non-numeric analysis. Clearly, a small sample does not allow valid numeric analysis and a large sample cannot be handled by non-numeric analysis.

19.3.2 Information on the Context and the Background of the Sample

To be able to analyze RE data it is important to understand the context and the background of the participants. Typically, RE practices depend very much on this context [4]. Unfortunately, there are no standards on how to capture which context factor. This makes the comparison between different studies very difficult. Here we distinguish three kinds of contexts: personal, company and project. The *personal context* determines the viewpoint of the participant. The following facets are typical:

- *Region*: This determines the cultural context. Several studies are only within one country. There has been no RE study so far which explicitly analyzes cultural differences. Cusumano et al. [9] discusses differences in the adoption of CMM practices between Europe, US/Canada, Japan and India.
- *Current role*: This determines the viewpoint and the involvement in the RE process. Typical roles are user, developer, quality expert, project manager, senior management, consultant and academic.
- *Past professional experience*: This determines whether the participant can only report preliminary insights or sustained experiences. Experience has so far only

rarely been captured. It can be measured by the number of years of professional experience or the number of projects involved.

Clearly, there are much more facets influencing the participants viewpoints, e.g. the education. It is, however, very difficult to define meaningful categories. The *company context* determines the setting for the SE processes. The typical facets are:

- *Size*: The number of employees involved in SE makes a big difference for the processes. The main distinction is between small and medium enterprises (SME) and large enterprises, where the boundary size of an SME typically is assumed to be 500, on sometimes 100 or 300. Also sometimes other indicators for size are used such as age of the company or annual budget.
- *Business*: Similarly, the business the software is aimed at makes a big difference. On the one hand one distinguishes primary industry, which has software as its main business, and secondary industry, where software is part of a product. On the other hand the product supports different business sectors such as finance, public, telecommunication, manufacturing, transportation, logistics and health. This also implies software types such as information systems or embedded systems. Unfortunately, there are no standard categories for business and software types. Thus, data of different existing studies cannot be compared.

To be able to ask specifics of the RE process also information on the typical *project context* is important. Often the interviewees are asked to choose one typical project to report on. The main facets are:

- *Customer/user*: The customer/supplier relationship has a big influence on RE practices. Therefore, it is important to distinguish whether the project produces bespoke software or commercial off the shell software. Orthogonal is the distinction whether the customer is internal or external. Furthermore the number of users is important and the sources of the requirements.
- *Size*: The size of the company does not fully determine the size of the project. The latter is measured by the number of staff involved, the number of person months and the duration of the project. Another important characteristic is the main project constraint in terms of budget, time or quality.
- *Software*: The size of the software not always agree with the size of the project. Thus, it is important to get information on the size of the code and the number of requirements. Also the price of the software is rarely captured. Of course, there are numerous other software characteristics of interest. So far studies have asked for specific properties such as the platform used, the number of variants involved or the reliability level required.

Clearly, many other facets of a project could be relevant, such as more detail on the project management or the standards in the companies. The process facts of the project are discussed in the following paragraph.

19.3.3 General Information on the RE Process

Many studies are concerned with the *process as the whole*: general facts, problems experienced with this process and benefits for success. Sometimes these general questions are only used as background information for more specific questions. Terminology specific to RE is an issue here (e.g. for documents and activities) as developers often use their own terminology. The *general facts* capture whether there is a defined RE process at all, how it was adopted, and how it is performed.

- *Defined RE process:* Besides asking for the existence of a process standard, studies ask for the adherence to certain development paradigms or lifecycles and for the existence of a role which is responsible for the RE activities in a project. Furthermore, the size of the process definition is important and the extent to which the defined process is adhered.
- The *extent of the requirements documentation* is an important indicator for the level of detail of the RE process.
- *Performance* is concerned with effort, tools, team characteristics and knowledge or use of established practices such as REAIMS or VOLERE. The effort can be measured for RE as a whole or for the individual activities. Besides asking for percentages one can also ask whether the activities are performed implicitly or explicitly.

Concerning the *problems*: Typically the studies ask for problems, categorize them and then compute the most common problems. The first example of such a study was [8] which was not confined to RE. Hall et al. [19] provide the only detailed study focusing solely on RE problems. Analyzing *success* is much more difficult. The first issue is how success can be measured at all. The next issue is how specific factors for success can be found.

Measuring success: Here we distinguish the overall project performance and the quality of the RE products and services. As discussed in El Emam and Birk [14] successful *project performance* can be measured through 6 variables: customer satisfaction, fulfillment of requirements, and cost within budget, duration within schedule, staff productivity and staff morale. The first variable can be measured through fitness for use and ease of use and the numbers of defects reported by the customer [8]. Because of the diversity of activities during RE it is even more difficult to measure the quality of the RE products and services. El Emam and Madhavji [13] present an empirical validated list of 34 criteria for the quality of RE products and services. These criteria can be used for two purposes: on the one hand they are an instrument for measuring success; on the other hand they can be used as a checklist of important characteristics of good RE processes.

19.3.4 Information on Specific Parts of the RE Process

Many studies are interested in a specific activity X performed or specific technique X used during RE. This comprises two issues: facts on the performance and experiences on performing X.

Facts on the performance: As for the whole process, facts capture effort and performance, e.g. the number of iterations during capture and analysis.

Experiences during performance: As for the whole RE process, problems and success factors for X are identified. This also includes the impact of X on the whole RE process or on the whole project. Furthermore, the impact of other factors on X is studied.

Summary

Not all studies ask for all information mentioned in categories 2–4. The detailed choice of course depends on the purpose and to some extent on the mechanism. However, in general we recommend cover all three categories. Information on the context is often difficult to evaluate, it is however, important to understand the plausibility of the answers. Sometimes it can be used to find patterns in the information on RE, e.g. a difference between RE processes of large or small companies. Similarly, information on the general RE process is helpful to understand the plausibility of the answers. It is interesting to try to exhibit patterns in the information on the RE specifics, e.g. differences between technique usage between companies with a defined process or without a defined process.

To allow the combination of data from different studies it is necessary to have standard questions. Such standard questions have not yet been established. They seem feasible for the context and the general RE process information, however, as illustrated in Sect. 19.5. It is very difficult to identify all context factors relevant to RE practice. Thus, this is an issue for further research.

19.4 Broad Studies Outcomes

The collected studies are very heterogeneous with respect to the study set up and the information captured on the sample, so it is not possible to aggregate their data. We summarize the important findings according to the above categories and indicate when studies have similar results. This answers issue (2): What evidence do we have about practice? So, what do we know about the RE process in general and about the specific activities?

19.4.1 Set up and Context of the Studies

The set up and context of the studies is quite diverse. Tables 19.1–19.3 list the year they were conducted, the sample size, the mechanism and the main topic. Due to the lacking standard of context description, it is not possible to summarize the context in the tables. Most studies are confined to US, Canada and UK, but some also span several countries in Europe. Most samples also cover several roles of the participants, several kinds of business and system types, as well as different project types, sizes of the companies and their software.

19.4.1.1 General Information on the RE Process
Here we summarize the findings of the studies of Table 19.1 and Table 19.2.

General Facts
- *Defined RE process standard:* The percentage of companies with a defined standard evolved from only few [30], through 50% [21] and roughly 30% for SMEs [40] to 60% in general [39]. Interestingly, 70% of companies without process are happy with RE product quality [39]. More information on the process, e.g., the size of the documentation, has only been captured in the studies discussed in Sect. 19.5.
- *Explicit requirements document:* The existence of documents is an issue. It varied widely between the SMEs in [27]. Recently, 85.6% worldwide reported about explicit RE documents [9]. However, the sample of the last study consists mainly of large companies with explicit contact to academia. The studies discussed in Sect. 19.5 capture detailed data on the kind of RE documents.
- *Performance:* The *effort spent on RE* was only noted twice. 14% of overall project effort was the mean in [15] and 15.7% in [21]. 38.6% of project duration was found in [21]. They also found that the ideal effort for RE in their context is estimated at 15–30%. 25% is the estimate for the ideal effort in [36]. Furthermore, one can distinguish the effort spent on individual activities. Successful teams allocate 11% of project effort on elicitation, 10% of project effort on modeling and 7% on validation and verification [21]. This distribution of the RE effort has been roughly confirmed in [32], which is discussed in Sect. 19.5. In these studies activities are also characterized as being performed explicitly or implicitly.

The information on overall cost and time adherence indicates heavier time overrun: little cost but significant time overrun [21], 35% cost and 44% time overrun [39]. The well known CHAOS report indicated for 2003 43% projects with cost overruns and 82% with time overruns [54].

Average RE team size is 6.2 [21] and 7 [15]. Team skill is an issue. Curtis et al. [8] found thin spread of application domain knowledge, [30] confirmed particularly for market-driven projects. In contrast, Hoffmann and Lehner [21] found that team knowledge is rated "good".

RE-Tool usage is not widespread: Typically general purpose tools prevail [30]. Even for SMEs only 30% use standard word processor and commercial RE-tools are not used at all [40]. Another study found 30% using only word processors, but for large projects mostly RE tools (inhouse, commercial) [24]. Most recently, 29% tracing tool usage was found in [11].

Little is known about the *Adoption of new RE process:* For SMEs reasons for process improvements are schedule overruns due to high effort for testing/rework and ISO 9001 certification [27]. Juristo et al. [24] found that more than half of the participants had recently improved RE. It was noted very early that organizational RE problem solutions are preferred over technology [30].

Still, the *importance of RE for project success* is recognized: The CHAOS studies give a good overview on IT project success in general [54]. According to the

2003 summary, IT project success evolved from 16% successful projects in 1994 to over 26% in 1998 to 34% in 2003. RE is very often identified as major contributor to problems: requirements specification and managing customer requirements exhibit the most problems in SW development in [21]. Similarly, RE problems had the highest share (48%) of development problems mentioned in [19]. This fact is confirmed in [54], however, to have downward trend. In 1994 requirements problems scored high in the top ten. In 1998 user involvement got again the highest mark, but firm basic requirements scored only in the lower half after being third in 1994. Still, 80% of the SMEs found RE of strategic importance in [40]. Seventy percent indicated that not enough time is spent on RE in [36], and this number was reconfirmed in [39].

Expectations on academia are training and technology transfer, particularly templates [40].

Problems with the RE Process: The three problems identified in the very first study [8] have been confirmed over and over.

- *Thin spread of application domain knowledge*: This has been confirmed in [30], particularly for market-driven projects. Inappropriate skills are a problem in [19].
- *Fluctuating and conflicting requirements:* Managing uncertainty was raised in [12], vague initial requirements, requirements growth and complexity of application was mentioned in [19], completeness, change management, and traceability were the main problems in [40].
- *Communication and coordination breakdown:* User participation and project management capabilities were raised in [12]. Organizational process problems are two thirds of the RE related problems [19]. Particularly, developer communication, inadequate resources, staff retention and user communication was mentioned, as well as the undefinedness of the RE process [19]. Identification of requirements sources was a problem in [24] and the main problem in [36] was communication.

The two other typical problems are tools and documentation:

- Tools are a problem because benefits are not clear [12], and because of tool integration, tool selection [24] and tool adaptation [40].
- Documentation often does not exist [24, 27]. If it exists, management is a problem [30], the detail of the functional process model [12] and prioritization [21], or missing template [40].

Other important problems noted are the increasing importance of the market-driven segment [30], COTS usage [12], the detail of the examination of the current system [12], own RE adaptations [40] and quantitatively establishing dependability [24]. Problems for industrial uptake of RE R&D are training, inherent complexity, integration into internal business, and business culture [37].

Success Factors for RE: El Emam and Madhavji [13] have exhibited the most refined list of success criteria. It can be structured into the following five areas. Some of them have been confirmed several times.

- *Fitness of recommended solution* (change culture, strategic adequacy, management support for change, fitness to business and technology).
- *User satisfaction and commitment* (user buy in, user consensus, fitness to user work, adequacy of first release). User involvement and team relationships were confirmed [20].
- *Quality of requirements architecture* (clear business processes, correct requirements, links from objectives to models, valid business cases). Related factors were identified in [21]: coverage of requirements sources, usage of templates, prioritization, combination of prototypes and models, traceability matrix, user peer reviews, scenarios, and walk-throughs. Similarly, unambiguous specification, prioritization for projects with short time to market (TTM), and change management of non-TTM were identified in [36].
- *Quality of cost/benefit analysis* (management support, high business priority, accurate benefits and cost estimates for intangible benefits).
- *Cost-effectiveness of RE process* (compared to similar projects and to overall project effort, little change, usefulness of deliverables).

This list shows that as for the problems many factors are organizational. Adequate team skills were identified as a further success factor in [21]. El Emam et al. [15] also investigated the relationship between user participation, uncertainty and RE success. They found that in presence of uncertainty user participation enhances the first two categories (called RE service success) and vice versa that user participation has less impact on RE service success if uncertainty is low. The relationship to the other three categories (dealing with RE product quality) could not be established. It also has been established several times that *RE makes a difference for project success*: Adoption of SPICE RE practices has positive impact on project productivity for large companies (impact on team morale, budget and schedule, customer satisfaction and fitness to requirements could not be shown) [14]. RE problems are reduced for higher CMM maturity levels [19]. Main impact of RE are common goals and scope according to [36]. A more complete functional specification increases productivity (in terms of code produced per day) [9]. However, the latter also found that the incompleteness of the specification can be compensated through techniques to generate early feedback on product performance such as prototypes or testing.

19.4.1.2 Specific Parts of the RE Process

Some broad studies of Table 19.1 and Table 19.2 have also captured data on the usage of established best practices. For SMEs, only 33% have standard document structure, even less use a modeling language as standard, formal methods are never used, scenarios are rarely used, requirements are numbered only in 15% of the companies, only a quarter had more than marginal use of the top 10 REAIMS practices [40].

In general, the following has been found: tool and method is not distinguished and elicitation techniques are not known [24]. Scenarios/use case are the best known practice in [36]. Also according to [39], 50% apply scenarios or use cases, but better known techniques are prototyping (60%) and inspections (59%). Less well known techniques are OOA (30%), focus groups (30%), informal modeling (30%) and, even in large companies only, 7% use formal models [39]. This might often still be related to missing knowledge as known techniques are more likely to be perceived as useful [36]. The adherence to very traditional processes is also confirmed by the fact that 35% of the companies still use waterfall [39].

However, it is important to note that large studies found that best practice adoption in general varies greatly: In Hoffmann and Lehner [21] the estimated use of practices varied by 30% depending on the role of the interviewee. In Dutta et al., [11] a variation of management practices from 65% to 32% between countries and similarly from 60% to 36% between business sectors was found. This phenomenon was observed in three consecutive studies from 1995 to 1997. The variation in [9] for a specific development practice was up to 70% between the countries. In that study the relative importance of the different practices did not vary much. So, for example, the creation of a functional specification was one of the most adopted practices in all countries.

McPhee and Eberlein [36] asked for the main features a new RE technique should have: easy to use, facilitates good communication, complete requirements, and traceability. Other broad studies have investigated specific activities. They are listed in Table 19.3. In addition the broad study on general RE [30] gives some insight on specific phenomena. Each specific phenomenon besides traceability has only been studied once in depth. Here we just list the main results:

- *Requirements documents* should focus on what and how as this is what designers want to know. Typically they want to know how a user will realize this task with the system functionality. This importance remained stable in very different company settings [28].
- *Traceability* is a problem because of lack of common definition and inadequate pre-traceability. The latter is due to problems for the providers (e.g., extra amount of work) and users of traceability information (e.g., reliance on personal communication) [18]. Sixty percent are high-end traceability users with more than 10,000 requirements and elaborate traceability schemes in [46].
- *Quality Function Deployment* is a front-end requirements elicitation technique. It improves user involvement, management support and involvement, team involvement and shortens the development lifecycle [20].
- *Requirements volatility* consists of instability, missing analyzability and diversity. It is related to the size of the requirements, project cost and most significantly project delay. Furthermore, developer capability has negative impact on volatility; volatility has no relationship with code quality and project management quality. High volatility is related to missing customer satisfaction. A defined methodology, frequent user communication and inspections induce volatility, while user representatives reduce volatility. Traceability could not be shown to account for the latter [60, 61, 62].

- *Requirements capture and analysis* is an iterative process, where more than half of the projects have 3 or more iterations. The number of iterations depends on the project characteristics, the methodology and the tools. In half of the projects original plans had to be changed due to lack of information, need for validation and verification, changes in requirements and inexperienced project managers. Some recommendations can be given based on the project characteristics [3, 4].
- *Scenarios/use cases* can be used in many different ways. They are particularly useful in combination with prototyping and glossaries. They help to complement abstract dynamic models and static models, to reduce complexity and to reach partial agreement and consistency. Issues are partial views, managing distributed scenario development, reviews, test case derivation, traceability and evolution [56].
- *Software documentation* is mainly needed to learn about software (61%), to test software (58%), work with new software (54%), to answer questions in case of problems (50%). Maintenance was only important for 35%. High-level documentation is also useful when out-of-date. Requirements are updated less frequently than all other documentation, while testing documentation is updated most frequently [29].
- *Requirements reviews* are slightly more common (42%) than design reviews (49%) for those companies who have documentation. Often (60%) reviewers do not have time for review preparation. When there is time, checklists (50%) are more common than ad-hoc (35%). Only 25% collect data during review and use this for improvement [5].

Summary

The studies collected show a quite interesting picture of RE practice. They confirm the evidence from CMM measurements of general SE [55] that process performance and practice adoption vary extremely between different companies. This is also obvious from Chap. 18 which shows differences between companies and some agreement and some disagreement of their findings with the findings of the general studies collected here. Thus, in particular, it seems not valid to generalize quantitative results (percentages) found in one study to all companies. This can only be done based on a careful analysis of all context factors. Taking into account the context factors the data of large studies can be used to find patterns of practice usage as in [11, 21].

The qualitative results, however, indicate some trends. For instance, an explicit RE process standard was more often found today than in earlier studies. Many broad studies establish the importance of RE. On the one hand RE scores high in the general SE problems and on the other hand positive impact of RE on project productivity has been established. It would be very beneficial to study more such relationships between RE in general or specific RE practices and overall project success or problems. The identified problems within RE seem to be quite stable, namely thin spread of application domain knowledge, fluctuating and conflicting requirements and communication and coordination breakdown. As discussed in Chap. 18 the first is less of an issue as companies specialize in certain domains.

The other two problems were confirmed in the studies of Chap. 18. Similarly, some success factors for RE have been established several times, namely user satisfaction and commitment (in particular in the presence of uncertainty) and quality of the requirements process. Thus, there is sustained evidence on the general RE needs of companies. It seems worthwhile to focus future studies on the details of these needs. The studies on requirements volatility exemplify such detailed investigations into the problem of requirements fluctuation.

19.5 Requirements Engineering Practice: A New Study

In this subsection we present new data on RE practice collected in Germany and Australia. This serves to further illustrate findings and issues in the interpretation of such studies and their aggregation. In addition, it shows some type of questions not found in the other studies. It is, however, not a complete presentation of the studies. Full presentations are referenced.

The work started 1999 with a pre-study in Germany. A small group in the RE special interest group of German computer science society (GI) collected nine two hour interviews on general RE process characteristics and experiences. The main purpose was to test whether the RE process questions are meaningful and to collect best practices. The latter did not work as the interview time was already consumed through the RE process questions. The former however was confirmed, as the questions were found very useful to characterize the RE process.

Based on this pre-study, the work commenced into two directions: In 2002 at the Fraunhofer Institute Experimental Software Engineering (Fh IESE) a questionnaire was created where participants get feedback on their RE process (in terms of recommendation of specific practices) based on the data submitted on the RE process. For that purpose the questionnaire has been extended with questions on perceived problems. The main difference to the prior investigation of problems is that the problems are related to different roles, e.g., problems of the tester or the project manager with the requirements documents, or problems of the person responsible for RE with the RE process. This questionnaire answered by 33 German companies by the end of 2003. It is still available under http://www.iese.fhg.de/re-checkup/. Participants were mainly project managers and people responsible for RE as these people actively sought advice in the area of RE. The main outcome has so far only has been published in Germany [43].

In Australia, at the University of New South Wales, the original questionnaire was used for four in-depth-studies [32, 34, 44, 58]. The data is collected from 11 multi-national companies including the banking industry, pharmaceutical and the healthcare industry, telecommunications industry and food industry included 23 projects. People who participated in the interviews were project managers, business and systems analysts. The objectives of these studies were (a) to investigate the state of the art RE practice in these industries which included identifying the state of RE process in project life cycle, the degree of awareness about this process and whether there is a structured approach towards RE in each project, and identifying responsible role for RE as well as roles assigned to different RE activities, (b) to examine the RE activities, (c) to explore the amount of effort used in each RE activity and identify implicit and explicit activities in each project, and (d) to construct high-level process models that describe RE process models on the projects. Some of the results are published in [33, 45].

In the following we report on the general RE process data of all three studies (combined and individually) and on the problems found in the Fh IESE study. As will be seen there is some difference between the data. This can be attributed to the small sample sizes and to cultural differences. In addition, it is important to note that by chance the study participants had very different company context: In the pre-study two third of the participants came from companies with more than 10,000 employees. At UNSW mainly companies with more than 100 employees have been interviewed, with more than 50% over 1000. At Fh IESE two third had less than 100 employees and 18% between 100 and 1000. Furthermore, the sample of Fh IESE consists of participants actively looking for feedback to their RE process. All the three together provide a very good variety with 20% each for less than 20, less than 100, less than 1000, less than 10,000 and more than 10,000 employees.

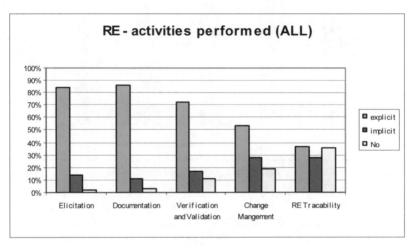

Fig. 19.1 RE activities

General Facts:
The three studies confirm the trend (noted in the summary of 19.4.) to an *RE process standard*: Of the combined data 72% had a standard. These standards have quite considerable length. In the UNSW study all were over 6 pages, and were two thirds over 25 pages. In the IESE study, one-third was below 6 pages and half between 6 and 25 pages. Altogether, more than two third were over 6 pages. Almost all companies confirm that the real processes adhere to this standard.

The studies did not investigate the effort for different RE activities, but instead investigated whether RE activities are performed explicitly, implicitly or not at all (see Fig. 19.1). This is easier to estimate for the participants than the effort. Figure 19.2 shows that elicitation, documentation and V&V are almost equally important. However, looking at the explicit activities in each study separately, one can see a high variation (Fig. 19.2). The SMEs in the IESE study do not perform so many activities explicitly, while in the GI pre-study many perform all activities explicitly. In all studies all company have at least one explicit activity.

More than half of the combined data have an explicit *RE responsible role*. Interestingly, for Fh IESE data this is even more than 70%, although these are mainly small companies. This does not seem to be due to cultural reasons, as in both the UNSW study and the German pre-study only 30% have such a role.

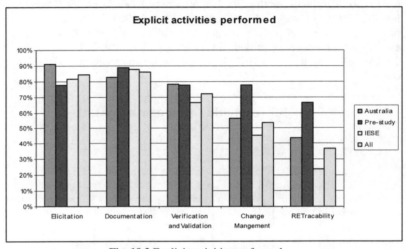

Fig. 19.2 Explicit activities performed

As shown in Fig. 19.3 the companies use different kinds of *RE documents*: Customer and developer requirements are most popular, and, if one is created, then the other is also created. However, as for general practice adoption (see the summary of 19.4.), the level of adoption varies by more than 30% between the samples.

To get a better understanding of this variety, we also investigated the relationship between the context factors (like company size, business sector) and the RE process characteristics (such as the existence of a process standard or the kind of RE documents created). The only significant relationship we found is between project size and the number of RE activities pursued explicitly and the number of different roles involved in RE. This relationship is quite obvious. So the context factors listed in Sect. 19.3 are not sufficient to explain the variety of processes. In the Fh IESE study we also investigated the main RE problems. In particular we asked whether the different roles (customer, RE responsible person, developer, tester, project manager) have problems with the RE process or its outcomes. The results confirm the findings on problems discussed in the last section. Problems are mainly related to project management and change management. It is stated that cost estimation is a problem (48%), that requirements are not stable (45%) and the need for change is detected too late (42%). The communication between RE and design is a problem for only 33%.

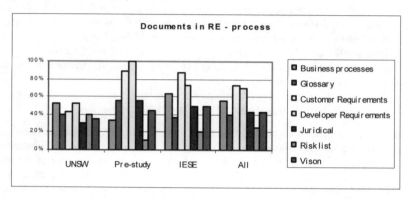

Fig. 19.3 Documents created

We tried to establish relationships between context, general RE process and problems. Only a few relationships could be established: Creation of business processes reduces the number of problems with the finished system. It also improves communication between the tester and designer. Also, the existence of customer requirements reduces problems for tester, and the existence of developer requirements reduces the problems of the designers and the RE engineers. These relationships are not really surprising, but they support the plausibility of the data and give more detail to the fact also observed in [9] that creation of requirements documents is of benefit for the overall project.

Altogether the studies confirm the general findings on problems and success factors. Again, they show the great variation between different projects. They also give examples for more detailed questions on the RE process such as the different documents or the problems for the different roles. Unfortunately, they also show that it is difficult to find patterns relating project context and general process or problems. At least the context data captured in these studies is not sufficient to explain the differences.

19.6 Remarks on Empirical RE Research

During our literature survey we have made some observations on the broad studies which might be helpful for further studies:

• Several studies indicate that facts about RE practice depend heavily on the context. Thus, we recommend capturing the context factors carefully and to investigating thoroughly the relationship between the context, the general RE process and the observed RE phenomenon (see the summary of 19.4. and last section). This investigation would be alleviated through a more careful selection of the study sample. An example of a very careful quantitative analysis of the relationship between different process factors is [31].

- It is difficult to assess practice progress over time as the different studies have used quite different questions. It would be helpful when, at least partly, a framework such as the one proposed here is used in all studies. Also, recently benchmarks for SE have been proposed [52]. It is, however, an open questions whether the benchmarking paradigm can be applied to RE because of the high involvement of humans [1].
- There is a high risk of misunderstandings in standardized questionnaires. At least a glossary of terms should be provided in questionnaires.

The broad studies discussed so far can inform research on general constraints and urgent problems in practice. A thorough understanding of specific phenomena or situations can be better achieved through in-depth studies. It is out of the scope of the paper and a topic of further research to provide an overview of these in-depth studies on RE, such as case studies in one company or experiments. Chapter 16 is an example of an in-depth study of one company. Chapter 18 provides further examples based on what is called inductive process assessment. In the following we just give some examples of existing literature with no claim of completeness whatsoever.

Experiments have so far mainly studied requirements inspection and, much less frequently, modeling techniques. Cox et al., [6] replicate an experiment on use case guidelines, while Regnell et al. [47] and Sandahl et al. [49] replicate experiments on different reading techniques for requirements inspection. Moynihan [38] has compared object-oriented and functional decomposition as paradigms for communicating system functionality to users [37]. Similar comparisons can be found at the EMMSAD workshops during the annual CAISE conferences. The most established results of SE in-depth studies have been collected in [16]. They are mainly based on case studies. One example for a recent case study has investigated RE in multi-site development projects. This case study has confirmed the problems reported in Sect. 19.4 [59]. Another recent case study has investigated the benefits of RE process improvement [10]. These in-depth studies give very valuable insights in the RE process. So far, replications of these studies typically have not completely confirmed previous results. This indicates that not all variables (very often related to the individuals) are completely understood. Thus, we are far from a standard process for empirical RE research.

19.7 Conclusion

Neither the state of the practice nor the state of the knowledge about the practice is satisfying. Sects. 19.4 and 19.5 have collected the results of different studies. As summarized in 19.4, it is so far not possible to come up with numbers characterizing RE practice adoption uniformly. But there are repeated findings on problems and success factors. So what does this tell about future empirical research questions, and what should we find out about practice?

Given the broad consensus about the problems encountered in practice, it seems to be time to study these particular problems in more detail. As there is less evidence of success factors, studies should be conducted to confirm the success factor list provided in [13]. In particular, it seems important to find out why a specific technique such as, e.g., scenarios has been quite widely adopted, while another such as e.g. QFD is not adopted in spite of positive evidence. Another important point is to integrate studies from the information systems community which focus on strategic requirements and success in terms of strategic change in contrast to SE studies, which focus on more operational requirements (for a detailed discussion of these levels see also Chap. 1). An example for such a study is [50].

As argued before, understanding of the context and the general RE setting is important, but hindered by the diversity of terminology and the great variety of factors. Thus, we should do interdisciplinary research to get a better understanding of context factors relevant for SE projects and also to provide standard terminology for capturing this context. Standard RE terminology could be achieved through certification schemes, such as, e.g., the certified tester programs offered by ISTQB. This would greatly alleviate more standardized RE education, which seems essential to widespread adoption of RE practices.

The standardization would also help replication of studies. Replication is important for insights on practice progress over time. We also believe that it is important to combine the practice analysis with improvement actions. Reifer [48] has collected critical success factors for industrial uptake of a specific technique: It must have been proven feasible in a number of projects, the related body of knowledge must have been codified and the related rules must have been documented, tools and training must be available, and hard data has been collected. Furthermore, people other than the inventors are promoting its use and the organization is prepared for the change. From this it follows that clearly there is a hen and egg problem, if industry is only willing to use a practice which is already proven. However, a set of several studies would come close to this model. First a broad study is conducted. Thereby, some companies and improvement actions are identified that are likely to be successfully adopted according to the scheme above. The execution of these actions would be the subject of empirical studies on their progress problems and success factors. The evidence of these studies can be used to find participants for in-depths studies of specific factors, such as experiments, or to find further participants for empirical studies. In-depth studies of RE improvement in specific companies can be found in the ESSI trials [17]. However, they have not been accompanied by broad studies and the findings have not been carried over to other companies.

Overall, it is good to see the increasing number of empirical studies in RE. However, we see the need for a more sustained approach for empirical research in RE.

Acknowledgements

We thank the authors of many studies for providing more detail on their data. We also thank the anonymous referees for many valuable comments.

References

1. Blaike N (2000) Designing social research: The logic of anticipation. Blackwell Publishers, Oxford, UK
2. CERE, Workshop Comparative Evaluation in Requirements Engineering, http://www.di.unipi.it/CERE03/
3. Chatzoglou P, Macaulay L (1996) Requirements capture and analysis: A survey of current practice. Requirements Engineering Journal (1): 75–87
4. Chatzoglou P (1997) Factors affecting completion of the requirements capture stage of projects with different characteristics. Information and Software Technology 39(9): 627–640
5. Ciolkowski M, Laitenberger O, Biffl S (2003) Software reviews: the state of the practice. IEEE Software 20(6): 46–51
6. Cox K, Phalp K (2000) Replicating the CREWS use case authoring guidelines experiment. Empirical Software Engineering 5(3): 245–267
7. Creswell JW (2003) Research design: Qualitative, quantitative and mixed methods approaches. Sage Publications, Thousand Oaks California
8. Curtis B, Krasner H, Iscoe N (1988) A field study of the software design process for large systems. Communications of the ACM 31(11): 1268–1287
9. Cusumano M, MacCormack A, Kemerer Ch, Crandall B (2003) Software development worldwide: The state of the practice. IEEE Software 20(6): 28–34
10. Damian D, Zowghi D, Vaidyanathasamy L, Pal Y (2004) An industrial case study of immediate benefits of requirements engineering process improvement at the Australian center for Unisys software. Empirical Software Engineering (9): 45–74
11. Dutta S, Lee M, Wassenhove L (1999) Software engineering in Europe: A study of best practices. IEEE Software 16(3): 82–-89
12. El Emam K, Madhavji NH (1995) A field study of requirements engineering practices in information systems development. In: Proceedings of the 2nd International Symposium on Requirements Engineering. York, England, pp.68–80
13. El Emam K, Madhavji NH (1995) Measuring the success of requirements engineering processes. In: Proceedings of the 2nd International Symposium on Requirements Engineering. York, England, pp.204–211
14. El Emam K, Birk A (1999) Validating the ISO/IEC 15504 measure of software requirements analysis process capability. In: IESE Report 003.99/E
15. El Emam K, Quintin S, Madhavji NH (1996) User participation in the requirements engineering process: an empirical study. Requirements Engineering Journal (1): 4–26
16. Endres A, Rombach D (2003) A Handbook of Software and Systems Engineering – Empirical Observations, Laws and Theories. Pearson Education Limited
17. ESSI, http://www.cordis.lu (Last access 9th January 2005)

18. Gotel OCZ, Finkelstein ACW (1994) An analysis of the requirements traceability problem. In: Proceedings of IEEE International Conference on Requirements Engineering. Colorado Springs, CO, USA, pp.94–101

19. Hall T, Beecham S, Rainer A (2002) Requirements problems in twelve companies: an empirical analysis. IEE Proceedings Software 149(5): 153–160

20. Haag S, Raja M., Schkade LL (1996) Quality function deployment usage in software development. Communications of the ACM 39(1): 41–49

21. Hoffmann HF, Lehner F (2001) Requirements engineering as a success factor in software projects. IEEE Software 18(4): 58–66

22. Ibanez M, Rempp H (1996) European user survey analysis, ESPITI, ESI TR 95104, http://www.esi.es/VASIE/Reports/All/11000/Download.html

23. Jones S, Till D, Wrightson AM (1998) Formal Methods and Requirements Engineering: Challenges and Synergies. Journal of Systems and Software (40): 263–273

24. Juristo N, Moreno A, Silva A (2003) Is the European industry moving toward solving requirements problems? IEEE Software 19(6): 71–77

25. Juristo N, Moreno AM, Vegas S (2004) Reviewing 25 years of testing technique experiments. Empirical Software Engineering, (9):7–44

26. Kaindl et al. (2002) Requirements engineering and technology transfer: obstacles, incentives and improvement agenda. Requirements Engineering Journal (7): 113–123

27. Kamsties E, Hörmann K, Schlich M (1998) Requirements engineering in small and medium enterprises. Requirements Engineering Journal (3): 84–90

28. Kuwana E, Herbsleb JD (1993) Representing knowledge in requirements engineering: an empirical study of what software engineers need to know. In: Proceedings of IEEE International Symposium on Requirements Engineering. San Diego, CA, USA, pp.273–276

29. Lethbridge TC, Singer J, Forward A (2003) How software engineers use documentation: the state of the practice. IEEE Software 20(6): 35–37

30. Lubars M, Potts C, Richter Ch (1992) A review of the state of the practice in requirements modeling. In: Proceedings of IEEE International Symposium on Requirements Engineering. San Diego, CA, pp.2–14

31. MacCormack A, Kemerer ChF, Cusumano M, Crandall B (2003) Trade-Offs between productivity and quality in selecting software development practices. IEEE Software 20(5): 78–85

32. Martin S (2002) Requirements Engineering Processes in Australian Practice. Honours thesis, School of Information Systems, Technology and Management, University of South Wales, Sydney, Australia

33. Martin S, Aurum A, Jeffery R, Paech B (2002) Requirements engineering process models in practice. In: Proceedings of the 7th Australian Workshop on Requirements Engineering. Deakin University, Melbourne, Australia, pp.41–47

34. Masya KK (2003). Requirements Engineering in Australia's Banking Industry. Honours Thesis, School of Computer Science and Engineering, University of New South Wales, Sydney, Australia

35. McPhee Ch (2001) Requirements Engineering for Projects with Critical Time to Market. Master thesis, University of Calgary, Canada

36. McPhee C, Eberlein A (2002) Requirements engineering for time-to-market projects. In: Proceedings of 9th Annual IEEE International Conference on the Engineering of Com-puter Based Systems (ECBS 2002), Lund, Sweden, pp.17–26

37. Morris Ph, Masera M, Wilikens M (1998) Requirements engineering and industrial up-take. In: Proceedings of the 3rd Third International Conference on Requirements Engi-neering. Colorado Springs, CO, USA, pp.130–137

38. Moynihan T (1996) An experimental comparison of object-orientation and functional decomposition as paradigms for communicating system functionality to users. Journal of Systems Software (33): 163–169

39. Neill CJ, Laplante PhA (2003) Requirements engineering: the state of the practice. IEEE Software 20(6): 40–45

40. Nikula U, Sajeniemi J, Kalviane, H (2000) A State-of-the-Practice survey on require-ments engineering in Small-and-medium-Sized-Enterprises. Technical report, Telecom Business Research Ctr., Lappeenrata University of Technology

41. Nikula U, Sajeniemi J, Kalvianen H (2000) Management view on current requirements engineering practices in small and medium enterprises. In: 5th Australian Workshop on Requirements Engineering (AWRE 2000). Queensland University of Technology, Brisbane, Australia, pp.81–89

42. Nikula U, Sajeniemi J, Kalvianen H (2000) A State-of-the-Practice Survey on Require-ments Engineering: Industry education and technology transfer. In: Fifth International Conference on Software Process Improvement Research, Education and Training (INSPIRE). The University of North London, London, Great Britain, pp.13–24

43. Paech B, Koenig T (2004). Charakterisierung und Probleme von Anforderungsprozes-sen deutscher Unternehmen – Auswertung einer Erhebung. In: Proceedings of 3rd HOOD Requirements Engineering Conference (www.reconf.de). Munich, Germany, pp.86–90

44. Prakash S (2003) Analysing Requirements Engineering Practices for Mission and Safety Critical Systems in the Pharmaceutical and Healthcare Industry. Honours thesis, University of South Wales, Sydney, Australia

45. Prakash S, Aurum A, Cox K (2004) Benchmarking a Best Practice Requirements Engi-neering Process for Pharmaceutical and Healthcare Manufacturing. In: Proceedings of 11th Asian-Pacific Conference on Software Engineering, 30 Nov -3 Dec, Busan, Korea

46. Ramesh B (1998) Factors influencing requirements traceability practice. Communica-tions of the ACM 41(12): 37–44

47. Regnell B, Runeson P, Thelin Th (2000) Are the perspectives really different? – Further experimentation on scenario-based reading of requirements. Empirical Software Engi-neering 5(4): 331–356

48. Reifer D (2003) Is the software engineering state of the practices getting closer to the state of the art? IEEE Software 20(6): 78–83

49. Sandahl K, Blomkvist O. Karlsson J, Krysander Ch, Lindvall M, Ohlsson N, (1998) An extended replication of an experiment for assessing methods for software requirements. Empirical software engineering 3(4): 327–354.

50. Seddon PB, Staples DS, Patnayakuni R, Bowtell M (1999) Dimensions of IS Success. Communications of the AIS. 2(20). http://www.dis.unimelb.edu.au/staff/peter/publica-tions.htm

51. Silva A, Morris Ph (1998) Analysis of recent surveys and survey methods. Deliverable D1.1, RESUME project

52. Sim S, Easterbrook S, Holt R (2003) Using benchmarks to advance research: a challenge to software engineering. In: Proceedings of 25th International Conference on Software Engineering. Portland, Oregon, pp.74–83
53. Silva A, Morris Ph (1999) Final report, Deliverable D6.1., RESUME project.
54. Standish group international inc. (2000) Extreme CHAOS, www.standishgroup.com
55. Thomas M, McGarry F (1994) Top-Down vs. Bottom-Up Process Improvement. IEEE Software, 11(4): 12–13
56. Weidenhaupt K, Pohl, K, Jarke, M, Haumer P (1998) Scenario usage in system development: a report on current practice. IEEE Software 15(2): 34–45
57. Wohlin C, Runeson P, Höst M, Ohlsson MC, Regnell B, Wesslen A (2002) Experimentation in software engineering: An Introduction. Kluwer Academic Publishers, Boston, Dordrecht, London
58. Yu J (2003) Requirements engineering in mission critical systems. Honours Thesis, School of Computer Science and Engineering, University of New South Wales, Sydney, Australia
59. Zowghi D, Damian D, Offen R (2001) Field studies of requirements engineering in a multi-site software development organization: research in progress. In: Proceedings of 6th Australian Workshop on Requirements Engineering, Sydney Australia, pp. 14–21
60. Zowghi D, Nurmuliani X (2002) A study of impact of requirements volatility on software project performance. In: Proceedings of the 9th Asia Pacific Software Engineering Conference. Gold Coast, Australia, pp.38–48
61. Zowghi D, Offen R, Nurmuliani X (2000) The impact of requirements volatility on the software development lifecycle. In: Proceedings of the International Conference on Software Theory and Practice, Beijing, China, pp.19–27
62. Zowghi D, Nurmuliani X (1998) Investigating requirements volatility during software development: research in progress. In: Proceedings of the 3rd Australian Conference on Requirements Engineering. Geelong, Victoria, pp.14–21

Author Biography

Barbara Paech holds the chair "Software Engineering" at the University of Heidelberg. Untill October 2003 she was department head at the Fraunhofer Institute Experimental Software Engineering. Her teaching and research focuses on methods and processes to ensure quality of software with adequate effort. For many years she has been particularly active in the area of requirements and usability engineering. She has headed several industrial, national and international research and transfer projects. She is spokeswoman of the special interest group "Requirements Engineering" in the German computer science society.

Tom Koenig received his MSc in computer sciences from the University of Kaiserslautern, Germany. He has been working as a scientist at the Fraunhofer Institute Experimental Software Engineering (IESE) since 2003, in the department of Requirements and Usability Engineering. His work areas include e-government and requirements engineering, more specifically elicitation and specification of requirements, as well as business process modeling. He is currently involved in several research and transfer projects in these areas.

Lars Borner has studied computer science at the University of Dresden from October 1998 till October 2003. Since December 2003 he has been a staff member of the "Software Engineering" chair at the University of Heidelberg.

Aybüke Aurum is a senior lecturer at the School of Information Systems, Technology and Management, University of New South Wales. She received her BSc and MSc in geological engineering, and MEngSc and PhD in computer science. She is the founder and group leader of the requirements engineering Research Group (ReqEng) at the University of New South Wales. She also works as a visiting researcher in National ICT, Australia (NICTA). She is on the editorial board of *Journal of Requirements Engineering* published by Springer. She edited three books, including *"Managing Software Engineering Knowledge"* and *"Value-Based Software Engineering"*, and published over 70 articles. Her research interests include management of software development process, software inspection, requirements engineering, decision making and knowledge management in software development. She is on the editorial boards of Requirements Engineering Journal and Asian Academy Journal of Management.

20 Requirements Engineering: Solutions and Trends

Christof Ebert and Roel J. Wieringa

Abstract: This last chapter of the book describes solutions and trends in the discipline of RE. Starting from a wrap-up of what was presented throughout this book, it suggests a framework of requirements engineering and indicates what current solutions are available in this framework. Beyond providing a short overview of the state of the practice, this chapter also summarizes current trends in RE. Four trends are evaluated, namely the growing usage of commercial off-the-shelf components and systems and how RE activities need to be adjusted; the evolving focus on product lifecycle management and the need to collaborate amongst very heterogeneous communities; the wish to learn and to share experiences on effective ways to implement RE in an organization and the growing interest in requirements engineers' skill sets. We finally provide an outlook into where requirements engineering is heading for.

Keywords: Systems engineering, Implementing requirements engineering, Product life cycle management, COTS

20.1 Introduction

Requirements engineering (RE) is the branch of systems engineering concerned with the desired properties and constraints of software-intensive systems, the goals to be achieved in the software's environment, and assumptions about the environment. It deals with these aspects of systems engineering from the problem analysis stage to the system implementation and maintenance stages. RE is both a problem-oriented and a solution-oriented discipline. As a problem-oriented discipline, RE interfaces with systems engineering in that it analyzes the software problems that exist in the socio-technical system in which the software is to play a role. Problem-oriented RE borrows from product management and psychology; it deals with goals to be achieved, the stakeholders who have these goals, and the problems to be solved within given business constraints. As a solution-oriented discipline, RE interfaces with software engineering in that it specifies the desired functions, quality attributes, and other properties of the software that is to be built or assembled. Because both views of RE are valid, RE is a discipline that maps needs to solutions (see also Chap. 1).

In this last chapter of the book we take a solution-oriented view of RE. Thus, we describe solutions and trends in the discipline of RE. This chapter is not so much backwards looking or trying to provide a tutorial summary, but rather indicating what's next and what's relevant in the discipline of RE.

We first describe a common framework of solution-oriented RE. This framework covers the activities of collecting, analyzing, allocating, specifying, verifying and managing requirements. Within this framework we embed a description of currently successfully used processes and methodologies. A short summary of the mainstream tools and their usage is included to provide concrete guidance.

Beyond providing a short overview of the state of the practice, this chapter also summarizes current trends in RE. These trends indicate close collaboration between industrial needs and research at both universities and enterprises. We look into the growing usage of commercial off-the-shelf components and systems and how RE activities need to be adjusted. The second major trend is the evolving focus on product lifecycle management (PLCM) and the need to collaborate amongst very heterogeneous communities. PLCM with respective engineering workflow support facilitates collaboration across the boundaries of companies (e.g., suppliers of components amongst each other and with integrators) and across countries and regions (e.g., offshoring). We discuss the needs and what solutions are practically available. Another trend we observed is the wish to learn and to share experiences on effective ways to implement RE in an organization. We discuss the needs and what solutions are practically available. Another trend we observed is the wish to learn and to share experiences on effective ways to implement RE in an organization. We describe current best practices to introduce RE, both the processes and the underlying tools. A fourth trend is the growing interest in requirements engineers' skill sets. In the context of large systems, a requirements engineer must be able to identify and understand problems related to policy planning and business strategy, marketing and finance, systems integration, and product development. Academic programs alone cannot create and shape these skills. They must be acquired through years of practice and reflection on effective practices in various contexts. Different answers are available starting from guided skill evolution up to certification trials.

A last section provides an outlook into how we portray the evolution of the RE discipline. It rounds off this book insofar as it summarizes many of the described open issues and needs that we still face to better integrate RE into the successful inception, definition, creation, marketing and sales of innovative software-driven products and solutions.

20.2 A Requirements Engineering Framework: Available Solutions

To fit risks and solutions to a comprehensive understanding of requirements engineering, let us briefly summarize key terminology and from there derive a framework of existing solutions.

A requirement is a "condition or capability needed by a user to solve a problem or achieve an objective" [18]. Requirements are typically broken down into different types that are implemented and traced with different techniques (Fig. 20.1). We distinguish process versus product requirements. Amongst the product requirements we classify functional requirements and nonfunctional requirements (also called quality attributes). For the product-related requirements we can see a second dimension, namely internal (or development-oriented) versus external (or user-oriented) requirements. The on-line dictionary of computing is more to the point, claiming "a common feature of nearly all software is that the requirements change during its lifetime" [13].

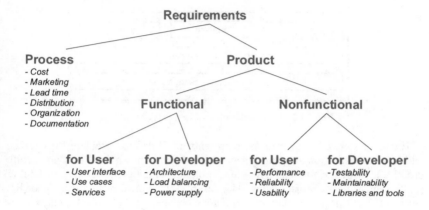

Fig. 20.1 A classification of different types of requirements

Requirements engineering is the systematic approach to collecting, specifying, analyzing, verifying, allocating, tracing and managing the requirements (functional, non-functional, process) of the system, and establishing and maintaining an agreement between the customer/user and the project team on the changing requirements of the system (Fig. 20.2).

A problem to be dealt with by RE is that requirements are uncertain. That's almost by definition, which is captured by an old requirements analyst slogan, "I know it when I see it". These uncertainties are increasing in fast changing markets, as we observe in various industries. Requirements uncertainties originate from various causes, such as cognitive limitations (i.e., users find it hard to imagine the product and state their requirements and their opinions about their own requirements evolve by the very exercise of requirements elicitation) or changing circumstances so that requirements change (e.g., introducing the system changes the situation too, and therefore changes requirements!), but yield similar results. Projects are delayed and do not fulfill the original expectations.

The discipline of RE is heavily impacted by this uncertainty. It explains why RE is not as "precise" and "well-bounded", as for instance, software testing or project management.

A clear relationship between requirements management and project success has been reported since the 1970s from various empirical research and surveys, typically putting insufficient requirements management (covering both development and change management of requirements) on top of the list of factors contributing to project failures [19, 36, 6, 32, 27] (see also Chaps. 18 and 19).

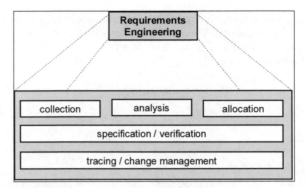

Fig. 20.2 The activities of requirements engineering

Handling software requirements represents an ill-defined problem [5] because within a software system, requirements are not fully known until it is practically used [27]. However, not managing this problem results in requirements instability [5, 7], which means project delays [19, 36, 6, 32]. Typical results from poor RE are insufficient project planning, continuous changes in the project, delays, configuration problems, defects, and overall customer dissatisfaction due to not keeping commitments or not getting the product they expect (see also Chaps. 2 and 11).

As a recent example, the 2003 Chaos report of IT project failure shows that, based on data from over 13,000 cases, only 34% of IT projects were considered successful [36]. 15% of projects were complete failures and the balance of 51% was what is referred to as challenged. Challenged in this context means, a project overruns on time and/or cost. Data from the evaluated projects showed that only 52% of the originally allocated requirements appear in the final released version.

We can identify several risks that characterize RE [23]:

- Overlooking a crucial requirement
- Inadequate customer representation
- Modeling only functional requirements
- Not inspecting requirements
- Attempting to perfect requirements before beginning construction
- Representing requirements in the form of designs

Following the above described framework of RE (Fig. 20.2; see also Chaps. 2, 4, 5 and 6), and based on our experiences in systems engineering projects, these risks are most effectively addressed during collection, analysis and specification by:

- Categorizing requirements (i.e., grouping requirements, permitting a higher-level understanding of relationships and dependencies, consistently applying a specification template).

- Organizing requirements (i.e., using automated tools to assist in understanding and tracing of requirements from inception to allocation to delivery, applying strict change management)
- Prioritizing requirements (i.e., determining the order of consideration based on criticality of need and level of associated risk, implementing in increments following the priorities, de-scoping those requirements with lowest priority).

Many standards have been set up over the last two decades to facilitate a sound RE. Life cycle processes are currently driving the underlying specific standards. ISO 15288 summarizes the system life cycle processes, while ISO 12207 is the standard for software life cycle processes. Both ISO and IEEE currently work heavily to aligning underlying process standards with these life cycle standards. From an overall process viewpoint formal approaches to guarantee quality products have lead to international guidelines (e.g. ISO 9001-2000) and currently established methods to assess the product/solution engineering processes of suppliers (e.g. SEI CMM and CMMI). The systems engineering process is described in IEEE 1220. Distinct standards for requirements management, such as IEEE 1233 and IEEE 830, focus on generic techniques to ensure that customer needs are recorded and traced throughout the development life cycle. The key standard covering nonfunctional requirements and classifying generic quality attributes is ISO 9126.

RE research has focused on two major questions, namely how to extract the "right" requirements and how to deal with changing requirements (see also Chap. 8). We find several approaches how to extract the right requirements, such as:

- Elicitation and analysis techniques (e.g., creating scenarios and use cases, interviewing different stakeholders, extracting requirements from an existing system, synthesizing requirements from user needs and behaviors, uncovering requirements by experiments or prototypes, determining problem frames) [6, 14, 26, 16, 17]
- Psychological techniques for identifying weaknesses (e.g., context-free questioning, workshops, analyzing different viewpoints and interaction schemes, interaction theory, protocol analysis) [16, 35]

For dealing with continuous requirements changes, the key techniques are:

- Evolutionary life cycles and prototyping (e.g., JAD, incremental development, various agile methods) [30]
- Sensitivity analysis (i.e., determining the localization, scope and impacts of changes, portfolio management) [10, 5, 33]
- Practical risk management (e.g., traceability, impact analysis, improved maintainability, modularity, isolating features that are subject to changes) [3, 22, 32, 8, 27].

These solutions are, however, not widely used in industry. In fact, we realized in our own projects but also in discussions during previous RE conferences that except of iterative development, none of above-mentioned techniques really made it to mainstream usage. Using a specific elicitation technique from the broad range described before is insufficient due to the inherent weaknesses of each single technique [14, 17]. In fact, experienced analysts use them rather mixed, but without specific rules one could pass on to practitioners [17].

Table 20.1 A selection of tools for RE [25, 39, 41], sorted alphabetically

Tool	Supplier	Key features	Entry-level cost
Caliber-RM	Borland (www.borland.com)	Lifecycle-oriented, large systems, traceability, TestDirector, Borland Star Team, MS Project	High
C.A.R.E.	Sophist Technologies (www.sophist.de)	Database-like view, requirements-centric, UML-Tools, MS Office, Lotus Notes	Low
DOORS	Telelogic (www.telelogic.com)	Integrated management, large projects, PLM, UML-Tools, XML support, MS Project, API available. Imports requirements in a big variety of formats. Strong interfaces into third-party change management tools	High
IRqA (Integral Requisite Analyzer)	TCP Sistemas & Ingeniería (www.tcpsi.es/irqa/ingles/irqa.htm)	Requirements classification, OO analysis and ER, traceability, test support, XML support, MS Office	Medium
Reqtify	TNI-Valiosys (www.tni-valiosys.com)	Traceability and impact analysis, text processing, office tools, Simulink	Low
Requisite Pro	IBM Rational (www.rational.com)	Change management, traceability, MS Word, XML support, Rational Rose, TeamTest, MS Project, Internet.	High
RM Trak	RM Trak (www.rmtrak.com)	Entry-level requirements management, MS Office, SQL interface	Low
RTM Workshop	Integrated Chipware (www.chipware.com)	Multiuser distributed projects, modeling, UML-Tools, test tools, SQL, API available, information modeling, interfaces to third-party reporting tools. Stands out with support of multiple distributed repositories.	High
Truereq	Truereq (www.truereq.com)	Lifecycle-oriented, team-centric, entry level, XML support, Web browser forms	Low
Vital Link	Compliance Automation (www.complianceautomation.com)	Database-centric, large projects, SQL, API available, Adobe Framemaker	Medium

Evolutionary techniques combined with repetitive risk management, specifically prototyping, which was always claimed as the best way to deal with requirements uncertainty, are rarely used in practice [36]. Changes are addressed primarily ex post facto [5]. This is increasingly done with good tools support to visualize and manage requirements changes [8, 16, 17].

In line with [14, 26] we claim that poor usage of available solutions in RE is often a problem of technology transfer. A single technique as it is mostly described in above references will not help because it remains unclear for the practitioner how to introduce it and what (other) environmental characteristics she needs to observe. We will come back to this problem when discussing the requirements engineer's skill set. This book tries to support effective technology transfer towards better project results with improved RE.

Numerous tools are available to support RE. They fall into three main areas:

1. Requirements databases (i.e., requirements should be managed in a secure, managed data store)
2. Change management tools (i.e., assuring the process of change management is a workflow process whose stages can be defined and information flow between these stages partially automated)
3. Traceability management tools (i.e., automated retrieval of the links between requirements and from requirements to other product or project artifacts)

Table 20.1 lists some selected tools. It provides the current supplier (supplier names change sometimes, but tool names typically remain), a URL, some key distinguishing features as the authors sees it, and an entry-level cost (based upon [39]). This is a non-exhaustive and subjective selection and description, which the authors compiled with own experiences. The difference between low and high cost is at least one order of magnitude. Some low-cost tools offer free licenses for restricted purposes. A more complete reference to such tools can be found in the Internet resources at the end of the chapter. The market at the high end is equally split between Telelogic and IBM-Rational [15]. Together with Borland these three vendors represent the majority of the market with around 75% of the installed base [25]. We are beginning to see an evolution of these RE tools towards integrating with other development tools (i.e., so-called IDEs) and moving towards product life-cycle management (PLM) from a systems engineering perspective.

At a minimum, these RE tools must support:

- Capturing of individual requirements and identification
- Classifying requirements and sorting
- Associating requirements with further information, such as different type of requirements (customer, system, software) or with test cases
- Baselining and configuration management (e.g., to preserve time-stamped status summary)
- Open application interfaces to connect to other tools

At the high-end one expects also traceability support, not only between different types of requirements in the same database (see above), but also with various other artifacts (e.g., design documents, test cases, project plans).

Most companies start their own RE tool support on the basis of word processing tools or spreadsheets. The evolution then often goes towards a "small database" in a second step. When demands are still growing companies realize that any home-made tool will ultimately mean lots of recurring effort, and they start looking to commercial tools. Changing that late in the usage life-cycle often means that their own users (i.e., system analysts, product managers, software engineers) ask to preserve all this nice home-made functionality. Though vendors of commercial tools normally like such tailoring, as it generates recurring income for them, we recommend being careful and selecting a commercial tool that is close to the typical usage needs and then not to change it, except for report layout and routing or status parameters. This keeps lifecycle cost of such tool manageable.

20.3 Trends in Requirements Engineering

This section explores four current trends in RE, namely:

1. The growing usage of commercial off-the-shelf components and systems and how RE activities need to be adjusted.
2. The evolving focus on product life cycle management and the need to collaborate amongst very heterogeneous communities.
3. Effectively introducing RE into an organization, both the processes and the underlying tools.
4. The growing interest in requirements engineers' skill sets.

20.3.1 Commercial Off-the-Shelf Components and Systems

A commercial off-the-shelf (COTS) product is a commercially available piece of software that a software project can reuse and integrate into their own products [37]. It includes (packaged) open source software (OSS), which gains increasing relevance in the COTS domain [31]. COTS products are developed for a market, and users of COTS products are engineers, who want to incorporate the COTS product as a component into their own system. A system containing COTS components is called a *COTS-based system,* and a development project of a COTS-based product is called *COTS-based development.* A COTS-based system may itself be a product to be brought to the market, or it may be a system developed and used by one particular customer. Today, most development is COTS-based, and an increasing number of development projects consist *only* of combining COTS products.

The motivation for doing COTS-based development, i.e. for using products developed elsewhere in your own product, is that this speeds up development of the COTS-based product and therefore reduces the time to market. Also, COTS-based products are easier to develop, because some or even all of the components come ready-made.

However, software engineering principles for COTS-based systems differ from those of custom-made systems. Experience shows that there are frequent changes in COTS products, over which the COTS user has little control, because they are driven by the market, not by any particular user. An average COTS product goes through a new release every 8 to 9 months, with support provided only for the latest three releases [1]. The changes in each release may cause the functionality of the COTS product to evolve to what you don't need, and this in turn may force you to write costly wrappers around the COTS source code. Maintaining this code is three times as expensive per line of code than maintaining custom code [29]. Some reasons for this are that the maintainer has to deal with fixes and patches for the COTS product and with glue that connects it to other systems, and with assumptions made by the COTS product that are not satisfied by the COTS-based system in which it is incorporated [31].

We distinguish such vendor, or supplier-driven changes fully from modifications as part of the product development, inside the project. Unfortunately, and especially with availability of source code (e.g., with GNU and other license schemes), some big customers have a nasty habit of taking a COTS product and asking for so many modifications that the risk is driven up immeasurably. We suggest that practitioners who use COTS software need to be acutely aware that making modifications increases the risks to levels that may approach new software developments. This has to do with reducing maintainability, portability or efficiency. In this type of environment, requirements and risks need to be managed with high levels of discipline. Recently, research in COTS-based software engineering has picked up steam. The Software Engineering Institute has started a research program on COTS-based systems [4].[1] In 2002, the International Conference on COTS-Based Software Systems was started[2] and in 2003, the International Workshop on Requirements Engineering and COTS Components was started.[3] This research has yielded first insights in the peculiarities of RE for COTS-based systems, which are summarized here.

The basic insight is that it makes no sense to first collect all requirements for COTS products, and then search for a product that satisfies these requirements [2, 4, 24]. No product is going to satisfy all these requirements, because they are all developed for a market and will not satisfy requirements that are specific to the COTS-based system your are developing. And they certainly will not be adapted to specific requirements, if they are not already built in. Open source software might be exceptional here, as it allows building specific functions, since the source code is openly available (however, see above our warnings not to do so —despite the possibility). Given the general kind of system you need, such as a middleware system or a database management system, all COTS products on the market will more or less provide the same functionality with more or less the same quality. These products compete with each other and products in the same market niche and will have similar properties.

The way to approach requirements is to first determine them on a general level, specific enough to determine the market in which you will search for the product, but without specifying detailed functions and quality attributes. Once you know in

---

[1] http://www.sei.cmu.edu/cbs/overview.html

[2] http://www.iccbss.org/

[3] http://www.lsi.upc.es/events/recots/04/general.html

which part of the market to search, you compare the available products on the properties that discriminate them, not on the properties that they all share. Therefore, you need to specify only the detailed requirements that differentiate the products from each other.

Once you have specified the general requirements of a COTS product, three processes are performed in parallel [4]:

- Requirements engineering
- Market research
- Architecture design

These three processes will mutually influence each other. Requirements determine the direction in which we look for products, but conversely, a requirement that is not satisfied by any of the products on the market will be dropped. The architecture of the COTS-based system constrains which COTS products we can use, but conversely, an architecture that is incompatible with any of the products on the market, will be changed. Continuous trade-offs occur between these three processes. Maiden, Ncube and Moore [24] recommend sorting products on discriminating requirements. Each requirement will determine an ordering of COTS products. Different requirements may determine different orderings, but standard multi-attribute decision theory should help to select a COTS product that best fits the requirements. However, Torchiani and Morisio [37] observed in several projects that in practice, developers seldom use requirements to select COTS products: Familiarity with the product or with its generic architecture was the overriding factor in the selection. Furthermore, the architecture of the COTS-based system was often decided upon based on the COTS products to be incorporated, and this then placed constraints on the detailed requirements of the COTS-product. These findings may be explained by the type of COTS-based system development projects studied by Torchiani and Morisio: large infrastructural systems such as integrated phone and Internet voice services, workflow management systems and a web-based search service with a public as well as private interface. More research is needed on the different kinds of COTS-based systems and interplay between requirements, architecture and market in COTS-product selection for these systems.

An initial classification is given by Lauesen [20], which we slightly enhance for completeness:

- Standard COTS applications, software components or frameworks that are used without any change. They are typically embedded into a broader system and the value-add stems from specific tailoring, adaptations, parameterizations or wrapping the system into a more complex functionality. Examples include using standard-middleware with enhancements (e.g., MySQL), using specific components of a standard middleware to build a new system (e.g., with Dot-GNU, J2EE, .NET or CORBA) or embedding a standard operating system into an embedded system (e.g., Linux). In this category one has to accept what is delivered by the supplier and ensure that new releases are carefully checked before accepting as a baseline for the product built on top of them. It is helpful not to expect for such mainstream components or middleware specific evolution streams, or there will be uncontrollable dependencies on specific vendors.

- In-house COTS-based systems are developed for and used by one organization. The developers of this system look around for COTS products to use in this system. Examples are the infrastructural systems studied by Torchiani and Morisio. Community source components (i.e., proprietary software for a closed community developed and maintained following the OSS principles) fall into that category.

- Complex COTS-based products are software products to be brought on the market. The COTS-based product will itself contain a number of COTS products obtained from other software vendors. An example is a requirement management tool that incorporates a database management system.

- COTS-based application systems are COTS applications obtained from software vendors, customized for a single company and integrated with other applications used by the company. Examples are ERP systems and banking systems.

- Tendered COTS-based systems for public organizations are large systems obtained through a tender process. In the EU, public acquisitions above a certain amount (roughly 150,000 Euro) have to be selected through a public tender process. Although these may fall under one of the categories above (COTS-based systems or COTS-based application systems), their size places them in a different category as far as requirements engineering is concerned.

A useful requirements acquisition and product selection technique for COTS-based application systems is the task and support method [21,22]. In this style, one does not support product requirements at all: One specifies the tasks to be supported by the products and, possibly, specific problems to be solved by the product. These descriptions are then sent to COTS product suppliers, who then indicate how they would support the tasks and solve the problems. This nicely focuses the selection process on the product properties that discriminate the products, and in particular on those differentiating properties that are relevant for the customer, because they solve his problems. It also directs the attention of the supplier to his customer's needs and it may surface ways of using the product not immediately apparent to the customer but known to the supplier from other customers of the product.

Tendered COTS-based systems for public acquisition have special problems due to their size. They are too large to ask for a trial version, because installing them may take weeks and learning how to use them may take additional weeks. Discovering experiences of other users does not help either, because different installations have too many differences. Lauesen [20] proposes to let the customer state soft requirements in the form of the goal to be achieved by the system, rather than the precise functionality required of the system. The vendor is then asked to explain how his system would achieve this goal. This is a generalization of the task and support method and has the same advantages. Another property of COTS product selection is that they have fuzzy boundaries [20, 24]. A COTS product may require additional products to be able to run, and it may require changes in interfaces of other systems already used by the customer. In addition, required COTS product functionality, even at a general level, may have fuzzy boundaries. Should it use the middleware owned by the client or should it include its own middleware? Should we implement different functionalities by means of different COTS product, each the best of its breed, or should we implement all required functionality using one big COTS product? In the first case we may have serious interfacing problems and we must deal with evolution of different COTS products with a different release frequency. In the second case we may get a suboptimal solution for each business goal, and are tied to one supplier. The choice where to put the COTS product boundary is not made in advance of a market search, and the customer cannot therefore give clear-cut requirements to the vendor. The solution proposed by Lauesen [20] is, again, to state business goals only and let the vendor suggest possible solutions to these goals.

A final property of COTS–based system development that we discuss here is that the vendor of the COTS product vendor finally incorporated in the COTS–based system, obtains a monopoly on part of the COTS-based system [38]. Even if a vendor claims to comply with open standards, it can keep the details of API interfaces secret so that the customer is hooked to this supplier [20]. Two solutions were observed in practice by Torchiani and Morisio [37]:

- The customer can buy shares in the COTS product supplier, to the extent of completely taking over the supplier.
- If there is a single large customer in a niche market, then this customer can exert considerable influence on suppliers who would otherwise behave monopolistically.

20.3.2 Product Life Cycle Management

RE is a process throughout the product life cycle. No wonder that product life cycle management (PLM) is increasingly linked with RE. The major drivers for embedding RE into PLM are:

- Mastering requirements uncertainty and requirements changes
- Managing configurations and product lines
- Bringing multiple disciplines together for effective collaboration

Requirements change heavily during the product life cycle. The traditional rule of thumb indicates a change rate 1–3% per month in terms of effort related to the allocated requirements [10, 19, 30]. This translates into more than 30% overall requirements change rate in terms of total project effort for a project duration of two years. With product managers, analysts and engineers becoming paranoid about these ever-lasting requirements changes, we observed an increasing duration of the analysis (or elaboration) phase of a project that is, before the actual project start. This syndrome of trying to resolve all uncertainties and fixing all requirements (which of course is hardly possible and a waste of lead time), often called "paralysis by analysis" contributed to project duration and cost, but did not really improve much on the side of reducing or coping with requirements changes. We observed the following root causes:

- Requirements management and specifically formal elicitation and analysis techniques are perceived as overly "technical". Stakeholders, especially outside the engineering domain, have little understanding for the process steps and intermediate results.
- Uncertainties tend to "disappear" at the interface of marketing, product management and engineering. This is typically caused by the need to achieve consensus over well-defined and accessible contents. Often the prevailing attitude is to start and fix it later, resulting in delays as we will see.
- Customers have not much time and resources to actively contribute to projects beyond what is necessary for contracting and monitoring. Agile and evolutionary techniques thus have their limits in getting sufficient customer support.
- Due to not getting all requirements specified in sufficient detail, engineers and project managers tend to guess actual needs and thus give wrong answers to uncertainties.
- Product managers and project managers focus on those risks that are meaningful to them. Certain types of risks (e.g. marketing) are not dealt with as they cannot be approached with product or project management "language".
- Prototyping and evolutionary development is considered theoretical and thus rarely practiced −except the domains of user interfaces and hardware innovations. It is considered difficult to plan (i.e. when will the prototyping cycles be closed?) and it creates configuration risks. What we increasingly see is plain iterative development as a form to mitigate risks of delays.

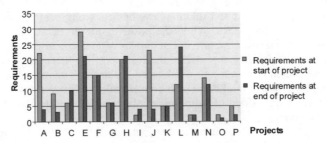

Fig. 20.3 A project survey of 15 projects with respective requirements evolution during project duration

As a practical example let us look into a concrete snapshot of 15 projects in a single product line that were developed in 2002 (Fig. 20.3). We found that 73% of a project's requirements are changing in average (median: 50%). Typically one third of the changes are of technical background (e.g. a specification was infeasible for design), while two thirds are of commercial background (covering the majority of requirements uncertainties). The perceived flexibility of software-driven products often results in an amount of variants and local evolutions which make it impossible to synchronize development activities, be it corrective or additive. The absence of clear linkages to business value invites over-engineering that is, implementing functions that may only rarely be used or adding excessive functions that are not necessary to attain the desired business results.

Such over-engineering not only wastes resources, but more importantly, it produces a proliferation of variants and complexity, as each further enhancement has undesired side effects with other features. We faced this evolution in a product that was customized for a multitude of markets, but not synchronized in the way it was customized. As each customization reused big portions of software in a white box approach (i.e. minor internal changes to the reused components which are embedded), any major change to the architecture would foster generic evolution of the product creating huge overheads, specifically for retesting existing functionality. No customer is willing to pay these costs. The only resolution to this problem is to stubbornly stick to the principle that engineering change requests must be based on allocated requirements. To support management of variants we recommend product line scenarios where some of the tools we recommend later on can help with managing the baseline of reused and reusable requirements as well as those that are market-specific. Linking those requirements to test cases reduces the overheads in managing the evolution of variants.

Software development involves profound technological knowledge, teamwork, processes, methods and tools. To reduce complexity, it looks just as rational to put all engineers at one place, share the objectives, agree on one process and technology to apply, and let the project run. Reality is different, especially in times of global development of solutions with lots of different players, components, interfaces, and anything else that could possibly increase complexity.

Today's global software engineering, with short project cycles, interacting product lines, and product and solution development from many sources, has advantages but also drawbacks. While the positive side accounts for faster cycle time, time-zone effectiveness or reduced cost in various countries, we should not close our eyes in front of the severe disadvantages. For instance, working in a globally distributed project means overheads for planning and managing people. It means language and cultural barriers. It creates jealousy between the more expensive engineers being afraid of losing their jobs, while forced to train their much cheaper counterparts.

As an example, let's look into the development of web-based information systems (see also Chap. 15). Especially requirements elicitation of web-based systems shows differences to more conventional approaches as described earlier in this chapter. Often requirements for web-based information systems are "created from scratch" by developers themselves rather than being discovered through the normal process of identifying system stakeholders and gathering their requirements. Such ad hoc elicitation along the way of development necessarily has life-cycle impacts. Evolutionary life-cycles dominate, often used in an explorative approach. The development cycle for a web-enabled application is short, i.e. only few months and highly iterative [9], which leaves very little time for any formal requirements gathering and their consolidation. In such compressed timeframe, adaptations of web applications to different geographical locations, cultures or varying knowledge and background (i.e., skill level) of prospective users, is done by explorative development. Based on such explorative product life-cycle, web-based information systems first prototypes a running solution which serves as simplified executable for exploring more requirements or constraints. Unfortunately, such iterative approach without a full view on architectural impacts and business rules to govern future usage often yields inadequate quality, ultimately [9].

Of growing importance in such ever-changing environments is effective collaboration across the entire product life cycle. To benefit from improved business processes, the different functions of the enterprise plus potential external partners (e.g., outsource manufacturing) need to agree on processes, tools and practices. They need to apply common access to knowledge, performance metrics and decision-making protocols. They need to share information, communication, and underlying resources. The barriers to such harmonization and cooperation are not to be underestimated. They range from language barriers to time zone barriers to incompatible technology infrastructures to clash-in product line cultures and not-invented here syndromes. An obvious barrier is the individual profit and loss responsibility that in tough times means primarily to focus on current quarter results and not to invest in future infrastructures. Incumbents perceive providing visibility a risk, because they become accountable and more subject to internal competition.

Practitioners do not look for heavy process documentation, but rather for process support, that exactly describes what they have to do at the moment they have to do it. Modular process elements must be combined according to a specific role or work product to be delivered. Still the need for an organizational process, as described by CMM L3 is strongly emphasized and reinforced.

The need for workflow management stems from the heterogeneity of underlying engineering tools and detailed processes that overlap considerably, such as logon procedures, document management and product data management. Given current focus on PLM and collaborative product commerce (CPC), specifically from an end-to-end perspective, software engineering processes must integrate with interfacing business processes. For instance, configuration management for software artifacts belonging to a single product line and reused in a variety of products must relate to the overall product data management (PDM). Or software defect corrections must relate to overall service request management as part of the customer relationship management (CRM) solution.

While PLM tools interwork with many HW design and manufacturing tools, they only recently started to look into specific software engineering environments. Examples include MatrixOne[4], Agile[5] or PTC[6], which try to interwork with specific software engineering tools, such as Telelogic's Synergy[7] or IBM Rational's Clear-DDTS[8]. More generic enterprise resource management (ERM) would not

---

[4] http://www.matrixone.com/

[5] http://www.agile.com

[6] http:// www.ptc.com

[7] http://www.telelogic.com/products/synergy

[8] http://www.rational.com/products/clear_ddts

sufficiently support software engineering on the more specific workflows. CRM environments have recently integrated with defect tracking tools, but more is needed to also support requirements engineering end to end (e.g., a defect often results in a new requirement). Their scope is limited to various front-end processes. However, all mentioned tools could be extended to facilitate interworking, as they are event-driven.

Interworking with legacy and proprietary tools can be achieved by deploying an object request broker to give to such tools an open interface. However, the transactional interface between such tools often does not adequately support the fine-grained integration of data thus avoiding as much as possible replication of data. For example, the product life cycle view must include data from the PDM system, software documentation system, the defect tracking system, the personnel database (for the actors), the process assets library, and the authorized tools list, all in one view. For that reason Eclipse[9] is increasingly used as reference platform to integrate existing (legacy or proprietary) tools with COTS tools.

The availability and empowerment of key stakeholders must be ensured throughout the product life cycle for effective RE. Three roles must be present in this core team, namely a product manager, a marketing manager and a technical project manager. They represent not only the major internal stakeholders in product or solution development, but also sufficiently represent the sales and customer perspective. This core team must have a clear mandate to "own" the project. We found that if such core team is available but underlying commitments are not baselined, it is of no value. Life cycle management based on RE protects and guides both the supplier and the customer. The supplier should:

- Express disagreement and unrealistic conditions openly
- Offer compromise approaches, once needs are understood
- Have a signed contract with requirements: Agree on clear and reasonable acceptance criteria
- Include a software key that will operate after the date of contracted software acceptance
- State in the contract that the supplier owns the software until final payment
- Clearly agree on liabilities and support after handover

For the client or customer it is relevant to:

- Clearly state that payment will be provided only for systems that meet the agreed upon functionality
- Require milestone presentations of progress for continued funding
- provide a realistic and precise expectation of functional and nonfunctional requirements (e.g. reliability)

The product life cycle must be mandatory for all projects. This implies that it is sufficiently agile to handle different types of projects. Standardized tailoring of the life cycle to different project types with predefined templates or intranet web

---

[9] http://www.eclipse.org

pages simplifies usage and reduces overheads. Its mandatory elements must be explicit and auditable. Some online workflow support facilitates ease of implementation and correctness of information. Gate reviews (decision reviews) must be well prepared. They must not result in lengthy meetings, but are rather prepared with online checklists so all attendees are prepared and can decide in short time the go/no go for next phase. Project information should generally be available online.

A useful product life-cycle has to acknowledge that requirements may never be complete and may indeed be in a "continuum" state. Sometimes requirements being purposefully incomplete (see Chap. 16) and RE must deal with such situation. The product life-cycle should guide with defining stopping criteria, i.e., determining what is good enough or stable enough.

Requirements must be evaluated by the entire core team to ensure that different perspectives are considered. While each single requirement must be justified to support the business case and to allow managing changes and priorities, a Pareto-based evaluation is recommended to focus on where it makes sense. For instance, the heaviest requirements in terms of cost or impact or business value are selected and analyzed more specifically on the value proposition. Often a business case is done and impact analysis is done for a group of requirements. If those start changing later on, it is very difficult to assess what is really necessary and what was a lower priority or maybe only an enhancement to existing features.

Underlying financial figures must be correct. This holds for both sides of the equation, cost and value. Often business cases are flawed on the value side and never followed through to see if a single requirement actually contributed as much to value creation as was expected by those who asked for it.

Impact analysis is based on requirements, as well as priority setting and portfolio management. What are the requirements? How do they relate between markets and correlate with each other? What is their impact? What markets have asked for it and for what reason? Are they necessary for a solution or just inherited from an incumbent approach perhaps becoming obsolete in meantime? To address these questions requirements must be documented in a structured and disciplined way. They must be expressed allowing both technical as well as business judgment. Any incoming requirement should be reviewed with the product catalog and global product evolution in mind to also evaluate marginal value versus marginal costs.

By definition all requirements must be accessible online together with other relevant product and project information. Different tools can be used, starting with simple spreadsheets. We have seen agile project using one spreadsheet to manage the entire project. Such a spreadsheet has all requirements, their status, effort, responsible and mapping to increments, test cases and work products. Reporting can be generated directly from such spreadsheet. For bigger projects we recommend online accessible vaulting systems to trace requirements to work products. A requirements database helps with this effort. Contents include requirements, implementation status of each requirement, priorities, estimated cost, value assessment, mapping to releases (especially future releases to communicate the roadmap) relationships between requirements, and links to related implementation and test details.

Having a project plan that is directly linked with requirements is mandatory for all projects. If there is a change to plan or contents, both must be synchronized and approved by the entire core team.

Data quality of project information and requirements lists is key. A minimum quality assurance is necessary to check for completeness and consistency of requirements and the traceability to work products. Inconsistencies and errors in requirements are often found best by testers because they think in terms of testability. If there are inconsistent or vague requirements, they should be corrected on the spot. If detected during the project, it is a requirements change, which has to be approved by the core team. Project information builds an online accessible history database to base further impact analysis and project planning upon.

Properly expressed requirements form a high-level abstraction of the functional and nonfunctional behavior of the product. Formalizing such a description helps in identifying reusable aspects of systems at a level independent of any particular solution or component structure.

In product-line scenarios with many variants, requirements must be explicit per release and still linked with each other across the entire family of domain and application projects. To provide access to what solutions already exist for a given need, it is mandatory to keep all requirements and their variants in one database. For managing requirements, features and portfolio, we use interacting tools. A tailored commercial tool should be used in such scenario for the feature catalogue, traceability and release mapping.

20.3.3 Introducing Requirements Engineering into an Organization

A persistent issue for requirements practitioners is about introducing RE in their organization. This problem has not yet been studied in academia nor been systematically reported about, so our remarks here can only be based upon anecdotal evidence and our own experience.

One open issue is how we can classify organizations with respect to their RE maturity. A large aerospace corporation developing a new satellite system for telecom applications has a different level of maturity with respect to requirements engineering than a small company looking to buy a customer relationship management system. Our remarks below are independent from the type of organization, but we here note that an empirical study of maturity levels in different kinds of organizations is indispensable to overcome with the problem of introducing RE into any individual organization.

The standard ingredients of any business case have been neatly summarized by different sources, such as Firesmith [12] or Ebert et al. [10]:

- Different empirical studies performed in variety of organizations time and again show that the percentage of defects in a final product that originated during RE is estimated around 50%, with low estimates around 40% and high estimates around 60%.

- Defects introduced in RE have an impact on almost all other development and deployment activities, including scoping the system, system architecture, design and implementation, testing, and nonfunctional properties such as security and safety, reuse and training.
- Repairing defects introduced during RE cost at least 10 times as much to repair once the system is fielded than they cost to repair during RE itself. Some estimates go up to 100 or 200 times as much
- Reworking requirements defects in a development project may take 40% of the total project cost, with some estimates going up to 80% of the project cost.

Despite these estimates, RE is often viewed as a foreign activity outside the interests of engineers, and as a waste of time by managers. If requirements are specified at all, then requirements management often goes the same way as documentation: An activity to be done later, when the "real work" is finished. Managers often view RE as an unproductive activity distinct from development.

Strangely enough, the same perspective is shared by sales, marketing or product management. RE clearly is an interdisciplinary engineering activity, and this often adds to, rather than reduces, the difficulties with introducing a standard process across a company. Often engineers and organizations familiar with the CMM will approach RE as a process that is part of standard technical project management. the difficulties arise latest when looking into the intergroup coordination aspects, which are very heavy for RE. If not agreed with the sales function, there will always be tensions because engineers try to analyze before commitment, while sales emphasizes flexibility and speed. Clearly shorted lead-time in industry is achieved with very rigid RE processes, immature sales and product management organizations feel a defined and managed RE process as overhead. Training across the different organizational functions is key. Often only a dedicated orchestrated improvement project will help to overcome legacy perceptions on what RE is or should be.

These and other observations motivate the claim that in order to introduce RE in an organization, requirements engineers with their own skills set must be included in a project, and that the practice of RE should have explicit and permanent management support. Obtaining management support starts with awareness of the arguments given above, but a real business case should also consist of a success story in the form of a successful pilot project in the organization.

20.3.4 The Requirements Engineer's Skill Sets

Recently, attention has grown for the skill set of requirements engineers. Stoewer [34] places requirements engineering in the context of systems engineering and identifies system engineering skills relevant for requirements engineers. Young [40] summarizes the roles and skills of requirements engineering based on his experience in directing a large number of engineering processes. Both these proposals are based on practice, and there is room for a more systematic study of roles and skills of successful requirements engineers. Here, we give an initial list based on these two sources and our own experience.

We distinguish technical skills, which are skills that can be learned and applied in a reproducible way across different persons, from personal skills, which are unique to each person. Both kinds of skills can be developed, but the development of personal skills requires a reflection by the requirements engineer about one's own person that is not needed for the development of technical skills.

Technical skills::

- RE skills: The standard division of RE tasks in elicitation, specification and validation is a useful frame to classify technical skills. To do elicitation, the requirements engineer must master interview techniques, observation techniques, etc. Specification requires skills in modeling, and validation requires skills in empirical validation as well as formal validation. This list of skills is obviously incomplete, but it gives an impression of what needs to be taught in any RE curriculum.
- Systems engineering skills: RE takes place in the context of a larger systems engineering process, in which hardware and other software are developed and in which business processes and organization structures may be changed or developed. Systems engineering skills include managing traceability, determining priorities and performing trade-offs, product innovation, and system integration skills.
- Management skills: Requirements engineers must at least be knowledgeable of a number of management skills, including policy planning, product strategy, product marketing, financing, and project management.

Personal skills:.

- Communication skills: Characteristic of every practicing engineer is the need to communicate with engineers and domain specialists from other disciplines. Communication across disciplinary boundaries may take up to 70% of an engineer's time. For requirements engineers, this activity arguably takes up 100% of their time. Skills needed to do this successfully include listening, questioning, presentation skills and technical writing skills.
- Cognitive skills: Requirements engineers are bridge builders, because they must connect the world of the user with that of the system developer. This means that they must be able to learn the outlines of a new knowledge domain quickly. They must be able to handle large volumes of documentation and abstract the essence from a mass of details. They need to build a holistic view of the system and its context, and know when to omit details.
- Social skills: Like all practicing engineers, requirements engineers work in teams. But even more than other engineers, requirements engineers must close differences and bring people with different backgrounds together. The requirements engineer must be a team player. At the same time, the requirements engineer must be able to handle and smooth out conflicts, and be able to negotiate

requirements and their priorities with stakeholders that may have conflicting interests.

20.4 Conclusions and Outlook: Where is Requirements Engineering Heading?

This final section provides an outlook into how we portray the evolution of the RE discipline. It rounds off this book insofar as it summarizes many of the described open issues and needs that we still face to better integrate RE into the successful inception, definition, creation, marketing and sales of innovative software-driven products and solutions. The followings highlight several issues.

- Better to predict changes to requirements on an individual level. Which requirements are most volatile and at same time exposing the project to highest risk? How can they be addressed by sufficiently flexible solution architecture?
- Focus on value-oriented requirements engineering, i.e. improving the evaluation of requirements within a business case from a portfolio management perspective. What is the business case behind the collected requirements? Is the business case valid? What is the contribution of requirements to this business case?
- Reduce the time to project start (e.g., what is good enough for requirements analysis? Which level of change is feasible to cope with in given scenarios/markets?).
- Introduce knowledge management techniques for simulative collection, evaluation, modeling and retrieval of requirements and underlying decisions.
- Further develop a systems engineering perspective in RE, covering for instance the usage of commercial components, including a variety of partners or suppliers, managing the quality delivered by such external partners, adapting systems quality requirements as our business needs change.

To conclude this chapter, we briefly summarize the major focus points. First we gave a framework on what is RE in the context of an evolving discipline. We looked into some specific project risks as they materialize and frequently point towards RE as being inadequate for professional software and system engineering. Requirements elicitation was described as a major area that needs further improvement to better manage uncertainties and thus mitigate project risks. The example of web solutions was discussed briefly to underline the need to deal with uncertainties both in the dimension of product or solution usage and also in not knowing stakeholders or potential users. To show where the discipline is heading, we summarized and explained four current trends in RE, namely the growing usage of commercial off-the-shelf components and systems and how RE activities need to be adjusted; the evolving focus on product life cycle management and the need to collaborate amongst very heterogeneous communities; effectively introducing RE into an organization, both the processes and the underlying tools; the growing interest in requirements engineers' skill sets.

References

1. Basili VR, Boehm BW (2001) COTS-based systems top 10 list. Computer, 34(5): 91–93
2. Boehm BW, Abts C (1999) COTS integration: plus and pray? Computer, 32(1): 135–138
3. Boehm BW (1988) A Spiral model of software development and enhancement. IEEE Computer, 21(5): 61–72
4. Brownsword L, Oberndorf T, Sledge CA (2000) Developing new processes for COTS-based systems. IEEE Software, 17(4): 48–55
5. Bush D, Finkelstein A (2003) Requirements stability assessments using scenarios. In: Proceedings of 11th international conference on requirements engineering RE03, IEEE Computer Society Press, Los Alamitos, USA, pp.23–32
6. Davis GB (1982) Strategies for information requirements determination. IBM Systems Journal, 21(1): 3–30
7. DeMichelis G, Dubois E, Jarke M, Matthes F, Mylopoulos J, Papazoglou M, Pohl K, Schmidt J, Woo C, Yu E (1997) Cooperative information systems: a manifesto. In: Cooperative Information Systems: Trends and Directions, M. P. Papazoglou and G. Schlageter (Eds), Academic Press, pp.315–363
8. Doernemann H.(2002) Tool-based risk management made practical. In: Proceedings of International Conference on requirements engineering, RE02, IEEE Computer Society Press, Los Alamitos, USA
9. Earl M, Khan B (2001) E-commerce is changing the face of IT. MIT Sloan management Review 43(1): 64–72
10. Ebert C, Dumke R, Bundschuh M, Schmietendorf A (2004) Best practices in software measurement. Springer, New York, Heidelberg
11. Ebert C (1997) Dealing with nonfunctional requirements in large software systems. Annals of Software Engineering, 3: 367–395
12. Firesmith, D (2003) The business case for requirements engineering. In: Proceedings of 11th IEEE International requirements engineering conference, September 2003, Monterey Bay, California, USA. http://www.sei.cmu.edu/programs/acquisition-support/presentations/firesmith/business-case/business-case.pdf
13. Free On-Line Dictionary of Computing. Accessed on 07 July 2004. http://foldoc.doc.ic.ac.uk/foldoc/foldoc.cgi?query=requirement&action= Search.
14. Galetta DF, El Loudadi M (1995) L'effet de l'incertidue et des strategies de determination des besoins de l'utilisateur sur les projets d'informatisation. Canadian Journal of Administrative Systems 12(1): 56–76
15. Gartner Dataquest: Market Share: Requirements Management, Worldwide, 2003. Available through www.gartner.com. Accessed 23 June 2004
16. Giesen J, Voelker A (2002) Requirements interdependencies and stakeholder preferences. In: Proceedings of international conference on requirements engineering, RE02, IEEE Computer Society Press, Los Alamitos, USA
17. Hickey AM, Davis AM (2003) Elicitation technique selection: How do experts do it? In: Proceedings of 11th International conference on requirements engineering RE03, IEEE Computer Society Press, Los Alamitos, USA, pp.169–178
18. IEEE Standard 610.12-1990. IEEE Standard glossary of software engineering terminology. IEEE, New York, NY, USA. ISBN 1-55937-067-X (1990).
19. Jones C (2001) Software assessments, benchmarks, and best practice. Addison Wesley, Reading

20. Lauesen S (2004) COTS tenders and integration requirements. In Proceedings of 12th IEEE International requirements engineering conference, 6-10 September 2004, Kyoto, Japan

21. Lauesen S (2002) Software requirements: styles and techniques. Addison-Wesley, UK

22. Lauesen S (2003) Task descriptions as functional requirements. IEEE Software, 19(2): 58–65

23. Lawrence B, Wiegers K, Ebert C (2001) The top risks of requirements engineering. IEEE Software, 18(6): 62–63

24. Maiden NAM, Ncube C, Moore A (1997) Lessons learned during requirements acquisition for COTS systems. Communications of the ACM, 40(12): 21–25

25. Meta Practice: Mastering the requirements of requirements management. Practice report 2020. Available through www.metagroup.com. Accessed 16 April 2003

26. Naumann JD, Jenkins AM, Wetherbe JC (1983) The information requirements determination contingency model: An empirical investigation. University of Minnesota, Minneapolis, MIS Research Center, Report pp.83–15

27. Parnas DL (1979) Designing software for ease of extension and contraction. IEEE transaction on software engineering, 5(2): 128–137

28. Ramesh B, Jarke M (2001) Toward reference models for requirements traceability. IEEE transactions on software engineering, 27(1): 58–93

29. Reifer DJ, Basili VR, Boehm BW, Clark B (2003) Eight lessons learned during COTS-based system maintenance. IEEE Software, 19(5): 94–96

30. Royce W (1999) Software Project Management, Addison Wesley, Reading

31. Ruffin M, Ebert C (2004) Using open source software in product development: A primer. IEEE Software, special issue on developing with open source software. 21(1): 82–86

32. Saarinen T, Vepsalainen A (1993) Managing the risks of information systems implementation. European Journal of Information Systems. 2(4): 283–295

33. Schmid K (2002) A comprehensive product line scoping approach and its validation. In: Proceedings of 24th International conference on software engineering ICSE'02, IEEE Computer Society Press, Los Alamitos, USA, pp.593–603

34. Stoewer, H (2003) Modern systems engineering-A driving force for industrial productivity. Keynote delivered at the 11th IEEE International Requirements Engineering Conference (RE 2003), 8-12 September 2003, Monterey Bay, California USA

35. Strens MR, Sugden RC (1996) Change analysis: A step towards meeting the challenge of changing requirements. In: Proceedings of the IEEE Symposium and Workshop on Engineering of Computer Based Systems (ECBS'96), IEEE Computer Society Press, pp.278–283

36. The Standish Group International Inc.: CHAOS Chronicles v3.0. http://www.standish-group .com/chaos/toc.php. West Yarmouth, USA, 2003

37. Torchiani M, Morisio M (2004) Overlooked aspects of COTS-based development. IEEE Software, 21(2): 88-93

38. Voas J (1998) COTS software: the economical choice? IEEE Software, 15(2): 16–19

39. Wieringa R, Ebert C (2004) Practical requirements engineering solutions. Guest editor Introduction for special issue. IEEE Software, 21(2): 16–18

40. Young RR (2004) The requirements engineering handbook. Artech house publishers, UK

41. Yphise: Software Assessment Report: Requirements management tools. Executive Volume. Available through www.yphise.com. October 2002

Internet Resources

Requirements Engineering summary sites:
    http://www.shu.ac.uk/tfre/web.links.html
    http://www.cc.gatech.edu/computing/SW_Eng/hotlist.html#requirements
IEEE Task Force on Requirements Engineering
    http://www.shu.ac.uk/tfre/welcome.html
RENOIR (Requirements Engineering Network Of Int. cooperating Research groups):
    http://www.cs.ucl.ac.uk/research/renoir/
Requirements Engineering Journal: http://rej.co.umist.ac.uk/
Intern. Council on Systems Engineering – Requirements Working Group:
    http://www.incose.org/rwg/
Guidance to select a requirements management tool:
    http://www.incose.org/toc.html, www.volere.co.uk/tools.htm
Self ranking of the tools suppliers versus a rich set of requirements:
    http://www.incose.org/tools/tooltax.html
Practical examples for requirements documents, inspection checklists, requirements prioritization:
    http://www.processimpact.com
Estimation tools (and more):
    http://www.methods-tools.com
COTS-based systems overview:
    http://www.sei.cmu.edu/cbs/overview.html
International Conference on COTS-Based Systems:
    http://www.iccbss.org/
International Workshop on Requirements and COTS Components:
    http://www.lsi.upc.es/events/recots/04/general.html

Author Biography

Christof Ebert is Alcatel's director of R&D Processes and Tools, where he drives world-wide R&D innovation and improvement programs. He also lectures at the University of Stuttgart, Germany, on real-time systems. He is a senior member of the IEEE and IEEE Software's associate editor in chief for requirements.

Roel Wieringa is full professor of information systems at the University of Twente, The Netherlands. He also chairs the Steering Committee of the IEEE International Requirements Engineering Conference.

Index